D0890097

THE WORKS OF

SIR THOMAS URQUHART.

AMS PRESS INC.
NEW YORK, N.Y. 10003

JOHNSON REPRINT CORP.
NEW YORK, N.Y. 10003

~~828~~

~~#79~~

PR 3736
.M6 A6
1971

THE WORKS OF
SIR THOMAS URQUHART
OF CROMARTY, KNIGHT.

REPRINTED FROM THE ORIGINAL EDITIONS.

EDINBURGH : M.DCCG.XXXIV.

AUG 2 8 1972

Reprinted from the edition of 1834, Edinburgh
First reprint edition published 1971
Manufactured in the United States of America

International Standard Book Number:
Complete Set :0-404-52920-8
Volume 30   :0-404-52989-5
Library of Congress Number :76-165339

AMS PRESS INC.   JOHNSON REPRINT CORP.
NEW YORK, N.Y. 10003   NEW YORK, N.Y. 10003

THE MAITLAND CLUB.

M.DCCC.XXXIV.

THE EARL OF GLASGOW,

PRESIDENT.

ROBERT ADAM, ESQ.

ROBERT AIRD, ESQ.

JOHN BAIN, ESQ.

ROBERT BELL, ESQ.

SIR DAVID HUNTER BLAIR, BART.

WALTER BUCHANAN, ESQ.

THE MARQUIS OF BUTE.

ALEXANDER CAMPBELL, ESQ.

LORD JOHN CAMPBELL.

JOHN DONALD CARRICK, ESQ.

HENRY COCKBURN, ESQ.

JAMES DENNISTOUN, ESQ.

JAMES DOBIE, ESQ.

RICHARD DUNCAN, ESQ.

WILLIAM JAMES DUNCAN, ESQ.

JAMES DUNLOP, ESQ.

JAMES EWING, ESQ. LL. D.

KIRKMAN FINLAY, ESQ.

REV. WILLIAM FLEMING, D. D.

THE MAITLAND CLUB.

WILLIAM MALCOLM FLEMING, ESQ.

JOHN FULLARTON, ESQ.

RIGHT HON. THOMAS GRENVILLE.

JAMES HILL, ESQ.

LAURENCE HILL, ESQ.

GEORGE HOUSTOUN, ESQ.

JOHN KERR, ESQ.

ROBERT ALEXANDER KIDSTON, ESQ.

GEORGE RITCHIE KINLOCH, ESQ.

JOHN GIBSON LOCKHART, ESQ. LL.B.

ALEXANDER MACDONALD, ESQ.

WILLIAM MACDOWALL, ESQ.

THE VERY REV. PRINCIPAL MACFARLAN, D.D.

ANDREW MACGEORGE, ESQ.

ALEXANDER MACGRIGOR, ESQ.

DONALD MACINTYRE, ESQ.

JOHN WHITEFOORD MACKENZIE, ESQ.

GEORGE MACINTOSH, ESQ.

ALEXANDER MACNEILL, ESQ.

JAMES MAIDMENT, ESQ.

THOMAS MAITLAND, ESQ.

WILLIAM MEIKLEHAM, ESQ.

WILLIAM HENRY MILLER, ESQ.

WILLIAM MOTHERWELL, ESQ.

WILLIAM MURE, ESQ.

ALEXANDER OSWALD, ESQ.

JOHN MACMICHAN PAGAN, ESQ. M.D.

WILLIAM PATRICK, ESQ.

EDWARD PIPER, ESQ.

ROBERT PITCAIRN, ESQ.

JAMES CORBET PORTERFIELD, ESQ.

THE MAITLAND CLUB.

HAMILTON PYPER, ESQ.
PHILIP A. RAMSAY, ESQ.
JOHN RICHARDSON, ESQ.
WILLIAM ROBERTSON, ESQ.
ANDREW SKENE, ESQ.
JAMES SMITH, ESQ.
JOHN SMITH, ESQ.
JOHN SMITH, YGST., ESQ.
WILLIAM SMITH, ESQ.
GEORGE SMYTHE, ESQ.
MOSES STEVEN, ESQ.
DUNCAN STEWART, ESQ.
SYLVESTER DOUGLAS STIRLING, ESQ.
JOHN STRANG, ESQ.
HIS ROYAL HIGHNESS THE DUKE OF SUSSEX.
THOMAS THOMSON, ESQ.
PATRICK FRASER TYTLER, ESQ.
ADAM URQUHART, ESQ.
SIR PATRICK WALKER.
WILSON DOBIE WILSON, ESQ.

INTRODUCTION.

I N the varied and eventful life of SIR THOMAS URQUHART OF CROMARTY, certainly one of the most remarkable men of his age and country, much must have occurred worthy of being recorded; yet the scanty materials for his biography exist only in occasional notices in his different publications.

Probably with some credulity, and certainly with no want of vanity, Urquhart has seriously attempted, in his *Promptuary of Time*, to carry back "the true pedigree and lineal descent" of the House of Cromarty to the creation of the world. But while many of his genealogical details are manifestly fabulous, it is unquestionable that his family was of great antiquity, and high consideration in the north of Scotland. Nisbet states, that " they enjoyed not only the honourable office of hereditary Sheriff-principal of the Shire of Cromarty, but the far greater part, if not the whole, of the said shire did belong to them, either in property or superiority, and they possessed a considerable estate besides in the Shire of Aberdeen."[1] The family of Cromarty also enjoyed the patronage of various churches, and the admiralty of the seas from Caithness to Inverness. These great possessions and privileges descended unimpaired through a long line of ancestors to Urquhart's father, Thomas Urquhart of Cromarty, who was born in 1582. He succeeded his father, Henry Urquhart, on the 13th of April 1603, and his grandfather, Walter Urquhart, on the 11th of May 1607 ; and it is recorded that he received his estate from his guardian, " without any burthen of debt, how little soever, or provision of brother, sister, or any other of his kindred or allyance wherewith to affect it."[2]

A short time before Thomas Urquhart attained majority, he married Christian Elphinston, daughter of Alexander, fourth Lord Elphinston. We are informed that, at the time of the marriage, this nobleman was High Treasurer of Scotland ;[3] and as he held that office only from the 24th of June 1599, till the 5th of September 1601, the alliance must have taken place during the intermediate period—probably in 1600. Lord Elphinston, fully aware of the prosperous state of his son-in-law's affairs, required him to leave his estate to the heir of the marriage, " in the same freedome and entirenesse every way, that it was left unto himself, which, before many noble men and others, he solemnly promised to doe to the utmost of his

---

[1] System of Heraldry, Vol. II. p. 274.   [2] Logopandecteision, Ed. 1652, p. 42.   [3] P. 42.

power."[4] The anticipations which this pledge was calculated to raise were never realized. Thomas Urquhart was knighted at Edinburgh in 1617, by James the Sixth, but from this period till his death in 1642, his course of life was not prosperous. His affairs ultimately got into great disorder, and during his latter years he was oppressed by pecuniary embarrassment, while his domestic happiness was disturbed by family dissension. It appears from the following entry in an *Inventory of the old Writs of the family of Urquhart of Cromarty,* preserved in the library of the Faculty of Advocates, that he was obliged to resort to royal protection from his creditors. " Letter of Protection granted by King Charles the First, under his great seal, to Sir Thomas Urquhart of Cromarty, from all dilligence at the instance of his creditors, for the space of one year, thereby giving him a *persona standi in judicio,* notwithstanding he may be at the horn, and taking him under his royal protection during the time. Dated at St James's, 20th March 1637."[5]

He was also at this time a sufferer from domestic oppression. It appears, from the records of the Court of Justiciary, that on the 19th of July 1637, our author and his younger brother Alexander, were indicted at the instance of their father, and of Sir Thomas Hope, his Majesty's Advocate, on a charge of " putting violent hands on the persone of the said Sir Thomas Urquhart of Cromartie, Knycht, their father, taking him captive and prissoner, and detening him in sure firmance within ane upper chalmer, callit the Inner Dortour, within his place of Cromertie, *tanquam in privato carcere,* fra the Mononday to the Fryday in the efter none therefter, committit in the mo-

---

[4] Logopan. *ut sup.*

[5] M'Farlane's Genealogical Collections, Vol. II. p. 283. MS..Adv. Lib. Jac. V. 4. 16.

neth of December last, 1636." When the case first came on for trial, it was adjourned till the 26th of July, when it was finally abandoned, in consequence of John M'Rannald producing " for the saidis Thomas and Alexander Urquhartis ane Act of the Lordis of Secreit Counsall, commanding his Maiesteis Justices, and thair deputtis to desert the dyet above writtin, for the reasonis quhilk wer specifeit thairintill." The part of the record in which this Act is engrossed, is greatly mutilated; but it appears to have proceeded upon the award of certain noblemen, who had been appointed by the Lords of Council to adjust all differences betwixt Thomas Urquhart and his sons; and upon considering it, the Court " desertis the dyet above writtin, and criminall letteris raiset aganis the saidis Thomas and Alexander Urquhartis, for the crymes thairin contenit, and discharges the outgeving of ony letteris aganis thame, for the crymes foirsaidis in tyme cuming." If the sons were guilty of violence in the transaction of which these judicial proceedings were the result, it is probable they survived to deplore their misconduct to a parent, whose estimable character, and blameless life were, long afterwards, acknowledged by our author in the most affectionate terms, and at a time when his testimony was above all suspicion.

After what has been stated, it will not be thought remarkable that the father should have failed in fulfilling the solemn obligation undertaken by him, to leave an unincumbered inheritance to his heir. This was probably the result partly of imprudence, and partly of misfortune; for at the distance of many years, his son, the great sufferer by his embarrassments, described his parent as " of all men living the justest, equallest, and most honest in his dealings: his humor was, rather than to break his word, to lose all he had, and stand to his most undeliberate promises, whatever they might cost, which too strict adherence to the austerest principles of veracity, proved oftentimes dammageable to him in his negotiations with many cunning sharks, who knew with what profitable odds they could scrue themselves in upon the windings of so good a nature."[6] Taking this to be an accurate account of Thomas Urquhart's character, it fully explains the fact, that although he succeeded to his estates free from all incumbrances, and possessed them for six and thirty years in such "halcyonian dayes," that there was no call on him to bestow his means otherways than might best please himself, all he bequeathed to "his eldest son, in matter of worldly means, was twelve or thirteen thousand pounds sterling of debt, five brethren, all men, and two sisters, almost marriageable, to provide for, and less to defray all this burden with, by six hundred pounds sterling a-year, then what, for the maintaining of himself alone in a peaceable age, he inherited for nothing."[7]

So sensible was Thomas Urquhart of his breach of faith to Lord Elphinston, and of the injustice he had done to his heir by the extent to which he had incumbered the family estates, that two days before his death he assembled his younger children, and bound them before "famous witnesses," and "under pain of his everlasting curse and execration," to take certain measures for the relief of their eldest brother, which he has thus described:—
" To assist, concur with, follow, and serve me, to the utmost of their power, industry, and means, and to spare neither charge nor travel, though it should cost them all they had, to release me from the undeserved bondage of the domineering creditor, and extricate my lands from the impestrements wherein they were involved; yea, to bestow nothing of their owne upon

[6] Logopan. The Designe of the Third Book.   [7] Ib. p. 42, 43.

no other use till that should be done, and all this under their owne handwriting, secured with the clause of registration, to make the opprobrie the more notorious, in case of failing, as the paper itself, which I have *in retentis*, together with another signed to the same sense by my mother, and also by my brothers and sisters, *Dunbugar* only excepted, will more evidently testifie."[8] The " domineering creditor" referred to in this singular deed, was probably Robert Leslie of Findrassie, who had acquired heritable securities over the estate of Cromarty, and although deeply indebted to the proprietor for many important acts of friendship, had been the first to attach the lands, and had induced others to adopt the same rigorous course.

Previous to the time of Thomas Urquhart, the family of Cromarty had been Roman Catholics. He was the first of the race who adopted the Protestant faith, but notwithstanding this change of his religion, he remained a staunch friend to Episcopacy, and was one of the very few gentlemen in the north of Scotland, who refused to subscribe the solemn league and covenant, when it was imposed on the whole country by the General Assembly in 1638. He died in August 1642, after an illness brought on by anxiety, and hastened to its fatal termination by the relentless persecution of his creditors.[9]

It is difficult to fix precisely the period of our author's birth. He was the eldest son of the family, and born in the fifth year of the marriage of his parents.[10] If they were united, as has already been conjectured, in 1600, Urquhart must have been born in 1605. He has said nothing of his early education, beyond remarking that his father had not expended more than the rent of his estate for two years and a half in portioning his daughters,

[8] Logopan. p. 44. [9] Ib. p. 57. Rothes's Relation, p. 105. [10] Logopan. p. 42.

and on the " education of his whole children."[11]   Slender as this expenditure may appear, it is impossible to doubt that the education of the Knight of Cromarty must have been liberal; and indeed this is sufficiently attested by the varied productions of his fertile pen.   That his youth was devoted rather to study than amusement, may be gathered from the following detail of his avocations in the dead of winter, while his friends were enjoying the sports of the field.   " I was employed in a diversion of another nature, such as optical secrets, mysteries of natural philosophie, reasons for the variety of colours, the finding out of the longitude, the squaring of a circle, and wayes to accomplish all Trigonometrical calculations by signes without tangents, with the same compendiousness of computation; which, in the estimation of learned men, would be accounted worth six hundred thousand partridges, and as many moor fowles."[12] It is not, however, to be supposed from this that he was deficient in personal activity, or incapable of joining in manly exercises.   On the contrary, we find that he occasionally disported himself in the breaking of a wild horse, and such other hardy pursuits as might in any way conduce to the accomplishment of his body.

Urquhart tells us that, in his younger years, and " before his brains were ripened for eminent undertakings," he repaired to foreign parts.   The most striking feature of his early character was an ardent and enthusiastic love for the land of his birth.   This led him to adventure, when abroad, " thrice to enter the lists against men of three several nations, to vindicate his native country from the calumnies wherewith they had aspersed it, wherein it pleased God so to conduct his fortune,"[13] that he succeeded in disarming his adversaries; and having generously

---

[11] Logopan. p. 43.   [12] Ib. p. 36.   [13] Ib. p. 10.

c

spared their lives, which, by the laws of arms, he might have taken, they acknowledged their error, and became ever after his constant and steady friends. We are not informed where these chivalrous rencounters took place, but it appears that, at different periods, Urquhart visited France, Spain, Italy, and Sicily.[14]

He inherited his father's religious and political principles, as an Episcopalian and a Royalist. On returning from his travels, he was present on the side of the Barons, who were then in arms against the Covenanters, at the *Trott of Turreff*, in 1639. A few weeks afterwards he embarked at Aberdeen for England, along with several other gentlemen of the same principles, and entered the service of Charles the First, by whom he was knighted in Whitehall Gallery, on the 7th of April 1641. At this period he commenced his career as an author, by publishing the first edition of his Epigrams; and he remained in England till August 1642, when he " repaired homewards" on his father's decease.[15] The disordered state of the family affairs required immediate attention; and upon arriving in Scotland, he took the decided step of setting apart the whole rents of his estates, with the exception of his mother's jointure, for the payment of debt. Having committed the entire management of his affairs to some of his friends as trustees, he again left his native country with the view of sojourning for a considerable time on the continent, and in the hope of ultimately returning to enjoy unencumbered the inheritance of his ancestors.

But matters fell out far otherwise than he had anticipated. After residing for some years abroad, and when he was indulging the reasonable expectation that no inconsiderable part of his

---

[14] Logopan. p. 74.   [15] Ib. p. 51. Spalding's History, Vol. I. p. 133, 138.

father's debts must have been paid, he learned with infinite disappointment, that beyond the mere transference of the securities over his estates to new creditors, his trustees had been unable to make any progress towards his ultimate relief from the hereditary incumbrances by which he was oppressed. Finding his " Egyptian bondage by such means remaining still the same, under task-masters different only in name," he resolved to return to Scotland, assume the management of his own affairs, and "take that solid and deliberate course with the crazed estate left unto him, as might make the subsistance of his House compatible with the satisfaction of his father's creditors." [16]

It was with these discouraging feelings that Urquhart revisited Scotland about the year 1645, and took up his residence in the ancient Mansion of Cromarty. He describes " the stance thereof as stately, and the house itselfe of a notable good fabrick and contrivance."[17] The building was of great antiquity. In the Inventory of Writs already referred to, there is a royal grant by James the Third to William Urquhart of Cromarty, dated 6th April 1470, of the *Mote-hill* or *Mount* of Cromarty, with the privilege of erecting a Tower or Fortalice thereon, *et ejusdem apparatibus bellicis et defensivis præparandi, et omnia alia singula faciendi et perficiendi, quæ ad confirmationem et ædificationem dicti Turris sive Fortalicii necessaria fuerunt.* Under this warrant the Mansion of Cromarty assumed the form of a fortress, and it was still a place of considerable strength in Urquhart's time. No trace of the ancient building now remains, it having been converted into a quarry for the purpose of erecting a modern residence soon after the year 1767, when the estate passed, by sale, from the family of Urquhart to Sir William Pulteney.

[16] Logopan. p. 52, 53.   [17] Ib. p. 11.

It is more than probable that the curious and fantastic taste of Urquhart was occasionally exercised in improving and adorning his paternal residence.[18] He collected a considerable library, of which he writes, although in a different style, with the liveli-

---

[18] A curious specimen of the interior decoration of the Mansion is still extant in a carved stone about five feet long and three broad, which formed the *lintel* of the fire-place in the great Hall, and is supposed to have been executed under the immediate directions of Urquhart. It bears his initials T. V. and the date 1651. The wood cut upon the title page of the present volume exhibits a reduced fac-simile of this fanciful and characteristic relic of the Knight of Cromarty. The equestrian figure on the left of the cut represents Astioremon, the husband of Bonita, who, according to Urquhart's family tree, flourished 361 years before Christ. In the history of the Urquharts, this hero is chiefly remarkable as the conqueror of Ethus, the first king of the Picts, in single combat, and as the author of certain important changes in the armorial bearings of his family. He adopted the motto,—Εὐνοεῖτω, εὐλογε, κὴ ευπράτ[ε,—*Meane weil, speak weil, and doe weil,* and substituted a palm for a myrtle branch in the left hand of the female figure forming the crest. The warrior, again, on the right of the wood cut, represents Vocompos, the husband of Androlema, to whom Urquhart assigns the year 775 of the Christian Era, as the period of his birth. It is recorded of this distinguished member of the Cromarty family, that, besides many other heroic exploits, on one occasion he slew three bears in the Caledonian Forest in presence of king Solvatius. To commemorate this remarkable feat, the monarch suggested that Vocompos should substitute three bears' heads on his shield for the lions, which he had previously borne, and at the same time the supporters were changed into two greyhounds. The armorial bearings, as thus altered by Astioremon and Vocompos, were subsequently carried by the Urquharts, and they are so represented in the centre of the wood cut. With an altered crest, the arms of Urquhart of Meldrum, the representative of the ancient family of Cromarty, remain the same to the present day. Most of the old papers and title-deeds of the House of Cromarty, which are still extant, are in the possession of Urquhart of Craigston, and the charter chest there has been examined with a view to discover any relic of the author of the *Jewel,* but none has been found, except two unimportant private deeds which are subscribed by him. From one of these, the following fac-simile of his signature has been taken.

ness of Montaigne.[19] " There were not three books therein,"
says he, " which were not of mine owne purchase, and all of them
together, in the order wherein I had ranked them, compiled like
to a compleat nosegay of flowers, which, in my travels, I had
gathered out of the gardens of above sixteen several kingdoms." [20]
No misfortune ever affected Urquhart so deeply as the "sequestration" and removal of his books from Cromarty by his creditors.
All his efforts to recover or repurchase them were unavailing, and
he mentions that none were ever restored to him, except a few
volumes which had been accidentally dispersed through the neighbouring country.

A considerable part of our author's works is occupied with a
detail of the various difficulties and hardships which he encountered in his unwearied efforts to relieve his paternal estates.
He complains that his tenants were slain and plundered—that
a garrison was placed in his house to his utter undoing—that
troops of horse were quartered on his lands without any allowance—that his library was rifled—that old stipends were un-
reasonably augmented, and new stipends unnecessarily created
by the disuniting of parishes—that the *Kirk* had denuded him
of his heritable right to the patronage of the whole churches in
the shire of Cromarty—and that his creditors had been " iron-
handed" in the use of " hornings and apprisings." In all this
there may be some exaggeration, but there is no reason to doubt
that Urquhart was harshly dealt with by his father's creditors.
They oppressed him by legal proceedings ; they interrupted and
disappointed all his splendid plans for the improvement of agriculture, trade, manufactures, and education in his native shire ;
and above all, if we are to believe his own story, they pre-

[19] Essais, B. III. ch. 3.   [20] Logopan. B. VI. p. 43.

vented him from " emitting" to public view above five hundred several treatises on inventions never hitherto thought upon by any. In short, says the Knight of Cromarty, " I should have been a Mecænas to the scholar, a pattern to the souldier, a favorer of the merchant, a protector of the tradesman, and upholder of the yeoman, had not the impetuosity of the usurer overthrown my resolutions, and blasted my aims in the bud."[21]

So extravagant was the estimate formed by Urquhart of his literary and inventive powers, that he demanded from the State the benefit of the 36th statute of the 5th Parliament of James the Third, as of itself a sufficient protection against the oppression of his creditors, " in so far as it provideth that the debtor's moveable goods be first valued and discussed before his lands be apprised, much less possessed. And if, conform to the aforesaid act, this be granted, I doe promise shortly to display before the world wares of greater value then ever from the East Indias were brought in ships to Europe."[22] The " wares" here referred to, were to have been the offspring of his own brain, which he confidently believed to be " of farre greater value then any peece of money due to his father's creditors."[23] There is a melancholy earnestness, almost approaching to insanity, in Urquhart's wild speculations on what he might have done for himself and his country, but for the weight of worldly incumbrances. " Even so may it be said of my self, that when I was most seriously imbusied about the raising of my own and countrie's reputation to the supremest reach of my endeavours, then did my father's creditors, like so many milstones hanging at my heels, pull down the vigour of my fancie, and violently hold it under, what other wayes

[21] Logopan. B. VI. p. 36.   [22] Ib. p. 26.   [23] Ib. p. 33.

would have ascended above the sublimest regions of vulgar conception." [24]

Urquhart was still in Scotland when Charles the First perished
on the scaffold. Shortly after this event he joined the M'Ken-
zies of Pluscarden, Monros of Lumlair, and others, who rose
in arms, placed themselves at the head of their respective
followers, possessed themselves of the garrison of Inverness,
and planted the standard of Charles the Second in that town.
For this, Urquhart was proclaimed a rebel and a traitor by the
Estates of Parliament at Edinburgh, on the 2d of March
1649. [25] It does not appear whether any proceedings were ever
adopted against him, but this denunciation certainly had no effect
in restraining his zeal for the royal cause. We find him in
arms at the battle of Worcester, on the 3d of September 1651,
where, after losing all his papers, he was taken prisoner, and
carried to London. He was at first placed in strict confinement, under Marshal-General Captain Alsop, of whose kindness he makes honourable mention; but afterwards, in consequence of the personal interposition of Cromwell, the Council of State liberated him on his parole. He was also indebted
at this period to Captain Goodwin, an officer of Colonel Pride's
regiment, for the recovery of the greater part of his manuscripts;
which enabled him to prepare for the press and publish his *Most
Exquisite Jewel* and *Logopandecteision*, certainly his two most
curious and valuable works. The former appeared in 1652, and
the latter in 1653, and the " scope and chief end" of both is
avowed to have been, to induce the State " to vouchsafe unto the
aforesaid Sir Thomas Urquhart, knight, a grant of the releasement of his person from any imprisonment, whereunto at the

[24] Logopan. p. 30, 31.   [25] Acts of the Parliament of Scotland, vol. 6. p. 392.

discretion of those that took his parole he is engaged"—to relieve him of all debts not of his own contracting—and to restore to him the estates, privileges, and immunities, due by inheritance to the House of Cromarty. [26]

The repeated and earnest appeals of Urquhart appear at length to have made some impression on the Council of State. In addition to the ordinary privileges of his parole, they allowed him five months to visit Scotland, with a view to an adjustment of his private affairs.[27] These were now in greater disorder than ever, and upon arriving in Scotland, he found himself absolutely at the mercy of his creditors. In the belief that he had perished on the field of Worcester, they had possessed themselves of all his property; and even when assured by letters under his own hand that he was still in life, they insisted for payment of bond debts which had been long before extinguished, in the hope that the discharges must have been lost with his other papers. They had been missing for a time, but having been fortunately recovered by him, and " produced before his creditors, they then, looking as if their noses had been a-bleeding, could not any longer, for shame, retard his cancelling of the aforesaid bonds."[28] Disappointed in these fraudulent schemes, the creditors, headed by Leslie of Findrassie, the ancient enemy of his House, continued to persecute him. This man, at the head of a body of horse and foot, invaded and pillaged the farm of Ardoch belonging to Urquhart, who, nevertheless, generously interfered to prevent some of the "hot-spirited gentlemen" of his name from avenging this insult to the House of Cromarty, by seizing Findrassie and his three sons, and leaving them, bound hand and foot, to perish within flood-mark in the *Yares of Udoll.*

[26] Jewel, Ed. 1652. p. 284.   [27] Logopan. B. V. p. 9.   [28] Ib. B. V. p. 10.

Findrassie's next attempt was to procure the arrest of Urquhart's person as a prisoner of war " till he were contented in all his demands."[29] To effect this, he spared no effort to instigate the deputy-governor, and other officers of the English garrison, quartered at Cromarty, to place him in confinement. From all these machinations, however, Urquhart ultimately escaped; and after travelling in safety through many of the principal towns of Scotland, made good his retreat to London, where he again surrendered himself to the Council of State, by whom it is generally believed he was committed a prisoner to the Tower. Urquhart closes the account of this, his last, visit to Scotland, by a panegyric upon William Robertson of Kindeasse, or rather *Kindnesse*, as he designs him, " for his going contrary to that stream of wickednes, which carried headlong his fellow creditors to the black sea of unchristian-like dealing." On this ground our author enjoins all his clan ever to hold Kindeasse in the highest esteem and honour, and " to do all manner of good offices to each one that bears the name of Robertson." [30]

The duration of Urquhart's imprisonment is uncertain; but it has been generally said, that having effected his escape from the Tower, he retired to the Continent, where he died suddenly, in a fit of excessive laughter, on being informed by his servant, that Charles the Second had been restored to the throne. This must have been in 1660, when Urquhart was about fifty-five years of age. He was succeeded by his brother, Sir Alexander Urquhart of Dunlugas, who had married an Elphinston, and died without male issue in 1661. The representation of the family of Cromarty has now devolved upon the Urquharts of Meldrum, the lineal descendants of John Urquhart of Craigfintry, second son of Alex-

[29] Logopan. B. V. p. 16. [30] Ib. B. V. p. 19.

d

ander Urquhart of Cromarty, who lived in the time of James the Fifth.

THE volume now presented to the Club, contains, in as far as has been ascertained, a complete collection of the *original* works of Urquhart, arranged according to the dates of their publication. The Epigrams, with which the volume commences, were first published at London in 1641, and a second edition appeared in 1645, both in quarto. This work scarcely entitles the author to the appellation of a poet. His verses are not absolutely deficient in smoothness of versification, and occasional point of expression, but they are certainly wanting in all the essential requisites of good epigrammatic poetry.

Although much devoted to science, *The Trissotetras* is the only one of Urquhart's publications purely scientific. It issued from the press at London in 1645, in quarto; and as some apology may appear necessary, even to an Antiquarian Club, for reprinting a work apparently so unintelligible and useless, it shall be made in the words of the present learned Professor of Mathematics in the University of Edinburgh. " I have looked at Sir Thomas Urquhart's *Trissotetras,*" says Mr Wallace, in a letter to a friend, who had requested his opinion of that work, " but I hardly know what to think of it. The book is not absolute nonsense, but is written in a most unintelligible way, and so as never book was written before nor since. On this account it is truly a literary curiosity. There appears to have been a perverted ingenuity exercised in writing it, and I imagine that, with some patience, the author's plan might be understood, but I doubt if any man would take the trouble; for after he had overcome the difficulty, there is nothing to reward his labour. I presume the object of the author was to fix the rules of Trigonometry in the memory, but no writer since his time has adopted his invention. Indeed, I do not observe the least mention of his book in the history of mathematical science. Yet, for his time, he seems not to have been a bad mathematician. Urquhart speaks in terms of great praise of Napier, yet not greater than he deserved. I infer from this, that he was well acquainted with the subject as then known. The book in question is certainly a *curious*, if not a valuable relic of Scottish genius in the olden time, and it is a good specimen of the pedantry and fantastic taste of the Author. If, therefore, by reprinting his works, it be intended to give a true portraiture of him, *The Trissotetras* should, on that account, and I see no better reason, again pass through the press." On the strength of this opinion, a place has been given to the work in the following collection.

Urquhart's first publication, after the disastrous battle of Worcester, was ΠΑΝΤΟΧΡΟΝΟΧΑΝΟΝ, or *The Promptuary of Time*, the manuscript of which was found among the spoil, and restored to him by Captain Goodwin. The object of this work is to deduce the genealogy of the Urquharts from the " red earth" in the hands of the Creator, of which Adam was framed, to the year 1652, when the book was printed. Although full of fabulous details, and consequently of little value even as a piece of family history, it exhibits a curious picture of the author's mind, from whose pen it flowed with apparently as sincere a belief in its historical accuracy, as if he had been describing persons living in his own time, and events passing under his own eye. The work is tinctured throughout with that overweening vanity so remarkable in Urquhart's character, and which never disclosed itself more strongly than in his attempts to exaggerate the antiquity, and illustrate the ancient glories, of his line. In a question of law between the Earl of Sutherland and the Earls of Crawfurd, Errol, and Mareshal, touching precedency in the rolls of Parliament, decided on the 7th of February 1705, and reported by Lord Fountainhall,[31] it was stated as a serious objection to the retour of a party in 1630, as " heir of blood to the ancient Earls of Sutherland," that Urquhart had been Chancellor of the Inquest ; and that he might "as well have retoured the claimant up to Noah, as he had deduced his own genealogy from Adam." The advocate who used this argument, however, must evidently have made a mistake in point of fact; as it is clear from the preceding narrative, that Sir Thomas Urquhart, who was Chancellor of the Inquest which, in 1630, retoured the Earl of Sutherland as heir to his ancestor, must have been the *first* Sir Thomas, and not his more celebrated son.

In the same year, 1652, EΚΣΚΥΒΑΛΑΥΡΟΝ, or *The Discovery of a most Exquisite Jewel,* issued from the press at London, in small octavo, and it was reprinted with some of the author's other tracts, at Edinburgh, in 1774. He gives a somewhat marvellous account of the rapidity with which it was originally written and printed. Speaking of himself and the compositor, he says, " We, in the space of fourteen working days, compleated this whole book, such as it is, from the first notion of the brain, till the last motion of the press." The title page describes the work as " more precious than diamonds enchassed in gold, the like whereof was never seen in any age," and bears that it had been " found in the Kennel of Worcester-streets the day after the fight." It had been carried off, with all his other manuscripts, from the author's lodging, in an upper chamber " of Master Spilsbury's house, who is a very honest man, and hath an exceeding good

[31] Decisions, Vol. II. p. 265 & 315.

woman to his wife." The *Jewel* is certainly the most interesting of Urquhart's works. It was written professedly as a vindication of the honour of Scotland, against the slanders of the Presbyterian party in that nation; and amidst all its extravagance and exaggeration, it abounds in curious notices of men, eminent in war and in literature, whose fame has not been chronicled elsewhere. The book is written under an assumed character, apparently for the purpose of enabling the author more easily to indulge in his egotistical propensities; and it has been justly observed, that " his own praise is one of the topics on which he is apt to expatiate in extravagant terms." [32] Feeling that he had laid himself open to such remarks, Urquhart justifies the prodigality of his self commendation by many ingenious and elaborate illustrations. [33] The style of the *Jewel* is prolix and " Euphuestic," but withal lively and eloquent, and the work abounds with exquisite humour, and luxuriant description. The curious and picturesque account of the Admirable Crichton has been often quoted, and the accuracy of its leading details has been in a great measure confirmed by the researches of Mr Tytler, who graphically describes the author as a sort of Ancient Pistol in his diction.

Logopandecteision, or an *Introduction to the Universal Language,* from which the greater part of the preceding details has been taken, was published in quarto in 1653. The author describes the work as " now lately *contrived* and published, both for his own utilitie, and that of all pregnant and ingenious spirits." But it appears that the design of forming an universal language did not originate with Urquhart. So early as 1633, Bishop Bedell had suggested the composition of a *universal character,* that might be equally well understood by all nations, as a

---

[32] Irving's Lives of the Scottish Poets, Vol. I. p. 123.   [33] Logopan. p. 34—37.

fit subject to exercise the ingenuity of one Johnston, a clergyman of his diocese of "mercurial wit" and great capacity. Burnet mentions that Johnston undertook the task, and that Bedell prepared a scheme of the work for him, which he brought to considerable perfection, when its progress was interrupted by the rebellion.[34] Urquhart's plan of an universal language is rather indicated than fully developed in the first book of his work, entitled *Neaudethaumata*, or *Wonders of the New Speech*; and the reader will scarcely regret that the subject is, in a great measure, abandoned in the remaining books, which are chiefly occupied with domestic details, exhibiting a lively picture of the times, drawn by the pencil of no unskilful limner. The subject of the different books is disclosed by their titles,—*Chrestasebeia*, or the *Impious Dealing of Creditors*—*Cleronomaporia*, or the *Intricacy of a Distressed Successor or Apparent Heir*—*Chryscomystes*, or the *Covetous Preacher*—*Neleodicastes*, or the *Pitiless Judge*—and *Philoponauxesis*, or *Furtherance of Industry*. These topics are illustrated by a great variety of personal anecdotes and local notices; and the work, which may be truly described as instructive and entertaining, concludes with a fanciful summary of the author's just demands, or " proquiritations" upon the State.

Urquhart is perhaps still more celebrated as a translator, than an original author. His version of Rabelais, of which two books were published in his life-time, and the third, with a fragment of the fourth, after his death, is of the highest merit. Motteux, who finished the translation, represents Urquhart to have been a complete master of the French language, and to have possessed both learning and fancy equal to the task he undertook. It has been justly remarked, that " his extravagance, his drollery, his

[34] Burnet's Life of Bishop Bedell, p. 79.

imagination, his burlesque and endless epithets, are, in the task of translating Rabelais, transplanted into their true field of action, and revel through his pages with a license and buoyancy which is quite unbridled, yet quite allowable."[35] Urquhart's Rabelais has not now been reprinted, partly because it is less rare, and more easily accessible to general readers than his other works, and partly because it would have extended the volume beyond the reasonable limits of a private contribution.

If we may judge from engraved portraits, Urquhart's appearance was prepossessing, although with a considerable air of foppery. His portrait was twice engraved by George Glover. One of these prints, a small whole length, in a rich habit, occasionally occurs as a frontispiece to the *Epigrams* and *The Trissotetras.* The other, which represents Urquhart seated on Parnassus, and surrounded by the Muses, is not mentioned by Walpole in his list of Glover's works, and is of extreme rarity. It was probably a private plate, as the only impression of it known to exist, is in a copy of *Logopandecteision,* preserved in the library at Craigston. Very accurate fac-similes of both portraits have been engraved for this publication by Mr Lizars.

The unguarded candour with which Urquhart never fails to open his heart in his writings, affords ample means of forming a just estimate of his personal character. His failings—and he had many—lean to the side of virtue. His vanity is amiable, and altogether free from selfishness—his egotism is intimately connected with a love of his country, and a desire to raise her in the scale of nations—his wildest aspirations after fame, though hopeless, are pure and noble—his devotion to the Royal cause is after the fashion of a *cavalier* of the best order—his

[35] Tytler's Life of the Admirable Crichton, p. 184.

quickness in resenting injury or oppression is not more remarkable, than his readiness to acknowledge the obligations of friendship and generosity—and the general tone of his feelings and
sentiments, betokens a man of a lofty and heroic spirit. Although
perhaps not pre-eminently distinguished in any single depart-
ment, it must be admitted, looking to the variety of his attain-
ments in science and literature, in arts and arms, that the Knight
of Cromarty, like his favourite hero, the Admirable Crichton, had
considerable pretensions to the character of a *Universal Genius*.

EDINBURGH : M.DCCC.XXXIV.

EPIGRAMS:
DIVINE
AND
MORAL·

BY
Sir Thomas Vrchard, *Knight.*

LONDON:

Printed by Barnard Alsop. and Thomas Favvcet, in the
Yeare, 1641.

TO

THE RIGHT HONOURABLE,

JAMES, LORD MARQVIS OF HAMILTON,

EARLE OF ARREN, AND CAMBRIDGE, LORD BARON OF
EVEN, AND INNERDALE, LORD MASTER OF HIS MA-
JESTIES HORSES, KNIGHT OF THE MOST NOBLE
ORDER OF THE GARTER, AND ONE OF HIS
MAJESTIES MOST HONOURABLE PRIVIE
COUNSELL IN BOTH KINGDOMES, &c.

MY LORD,

BEING confident, that your gracious disposition will hold in
greater account the ingenuous meaning of who gives, then the
sufficiency of the present, I here tender to the favour of your
Honours acceptance a bundle of Epigrams; which though they be
but flashes of wit, and such as may with advantage receive point
from your ordinary conceptions, yet for that nothing doth better

recommend them then vivacitie of conceit, I cannot figure to my fancie a fitter Patron to protect the sublimest Poems of this nature, then your owne noble selfe; of whose valour, and prudence, even from your infancie, both this, and forraine nations will afford an approbation so authentick, that by the universal consent of all that ever knew your Lordship, the depth of experience since the memory of man was never seene wedded to fewer yeares; nor the splendor of heroicke vertue to the astonishment of whole armies, and princes' palaces, more evidently apparent, then in the magnanimity of your generous carriage.

What formerly, by the most virtuous, and pregnant wits, could not bee acquired without a long continuance of time: and was esteemed to be incompatible with youth, and much more extraordinary in young gallants, then gray haires, or the gout, hath beene still in your Lordship, a quality concomitant to the source of all your actions: cœval with the gentile powers of your mind: and no lesse naturall, then to speake, or thinke.

And what others, not being able to reach into, have therefore admired in the Legend of the Worthies, hath, since the yeeres of discretion, bin the constant object of your dailie exercise, and complyed with your very most neglected cogitations: which glorious and rare endowments, out-reaching the extent of vulgar goodnesse, and seeming the more wonderfull, that it is not long since by your birth, you did grace the world with the honour of your presence, doe possesse the faculties of my soul with a stedfast resolution, so unfainedly to acknowledge the absolute right, your Lordship hath over me, and the inclinations of my mind; that, as I cannot impart that portion of the fruits thereof to any, which by a prior disposition is not already yours, so may not I, though the matter be but small, without breach of duty, devote this Dedication to another.

Therefore, my Lord, you may be pleased, according to your accustomed manner, to vouchsafe a courteous entertainment to this testimony of my regard; till fortune be so favourable, as to blesse me with the opportunity one day to make knowne my designments more effectually yours; for the best of my affections, being touched with the magnetick vertue of your good parts, are fixed on you, as on their pole-star which serveth to direct the course of my life in a continual progresse of embracing all the occasions, whereby I may testifie how earnest I am, and always shall be, deservingly to obtain the title

Of Yours,

My Lord,

In all humilitie of sincere respect, to
serve your Lordship,

THOMAS VRCHARD.

EPIGRAMS.

THE FIRST BOOKE.

TO THE KING.

GREAT Monarch fince the worlds nativity,
No mind, nor body had fo divine parts
To grace the State of Sov'rain Majefty,
As hath your Royall perfon ; whofe deferts
    Soare higher 'bove the reach of other Kings,
    Then the bright fun tranfcends terreftriall things.

THAT THOSE OF A SOLID WIT, CANNOT BE PUFFED VP WITH APPLAUSE ; NOR INCENSED BY CONTUMELIE.

WHAT vulgar people fpeake, if we be wife,
Will neither joy nor mifcontentment breed us ;
For we ought mens opinions fo to prife,
As that they may attend us, and not lead us,
    It not being fit their praife fhould rule our actions,
    Or that we fhun what's good for their detractions.

A BRAVE SPIRIT DISDAINETH THE THREATS OF FORTUNE.

No man of refolution, will endure
His liberty in Fortune's hands to thrall;
For he's not free, o'er whom fhe hath leaft pow'r,
But over whom fhe hath no pow'r at all;
   Nor hath fhe any chaine, wherewith to bind,
   The inclination of a noble mind.

HOW TO BECOME WISE.

Who would be truly wife, muft in all hafte
His mind of perturbations difpoffeffe;
For wifedome is a large, and fpatious guheft,
And can not dwell, but in an empty place;
   Therefore to harbour her, we muft not grudge,
   To make both vice, and paffion to diflodge.

THE WISE, AND NOBLE RESOLUTION OF A TRULY CURAGIOUS, AND DEVOUT SPIRIT, TOWARDS THE ABSOLUTE DANTING OF THOSE IRREGULAR AFFECTIONS, AND INWARD PERTURBATIONS, WHICH READILY MIGHT HAPPEN TO IMPEDE THE CURRENT OF HIS SANCTIFIED DESIGNES, AND OPPOSE HIS ALREADY INITIATED PROGRESSE, IN THE DIVINELY PROPOSED COURSE OF A VERTUOUS, AND HOLY LIFE.

My foule fhall rule my body, raigne o'r it,
And curb the Pentarchie of fenfuall charmes;
For though they live togither, 'tis not fit,
They be compagnons upon equall termes;
But in my mind I'l harbour fuch a reafon,
As ftrongly may o'rmafter each temptation
Can be fuggefted to't, and choake the treafon
Of all, and ev'ry will-betraying paffion.
In this judicious order the realme,
Or little world of mine owne felfe to guide,
It is my whole intent, till I make calme
Rebellious motions, and fuppreffe the pride
   Of flefh; then, while I breath, maintaine that right,
   In fpight of Satan, and all worldly might.

THAT THE FELLOWSHIP OF VERTUOUS, OR VICIOUS PEOPLE, CONTRIBUTES MUCH TO THE BETTERING, OR DEPRAVING OF THE MIND.

THAT he muſt needs be bad, there is ſome likeneſſe,
Who to lewd company is much affected ;
For it is the beginning of a ſickneſſe
T' aſſociat with him, that is infected :
    Would you be good then, haunt the converſation
    Of them, whoſe actions merit eſtimation.

RICHES WITHOUT FURTHER, CAN MAKE NO MAN HAPPY.

As he, whoſe body is not well in health,
To ſearch for eaſe, from bed to bed will riſe,
So to a mind, that is diſeaſed, wealth
Is not the end, but change of miſeries ;
    And that, which made his poverty to vexe him,
    Will make his riches likewiſe to perplexe him.

WHAT MAN IT IS, THAT IS TRULY WEALTHIE.

WHO meaſures poverty by Nature's rules,
And frames his mind to what he hath, is rich ;
For we can never doe, but vexe our ſoules,
So long's we ſtraine them to a higher pitch :
    And hee, whoſe heart is diſcontented, is
    But a poore wretch, though all the world were his.

HOW A VALIANT MAN OUGHT TO BEHAVE HIMSELFE TOWARDS THOSE, THAT BASELY OFFER TO OFFEND HIM.

HE is beyond the reach of common men,
Who can deſpiſe an injury ; for, as
The billowes of the ſea inſult in vaine
Againſt a rocke, a ſtout breaſt finds no cauſe

B

Of being commov'd at wrongs, whereof the dart,
Resiles from him, as from a brasen wall,
On the offender, while his mighty heart,
And noble mind, far more sublime then all
   The regions of the ayre, most bravely scorne
   Th' inferiour dangers of a boystrous storme.

WHY THE WORLD IS AT VARIANCE.

EACH man hath his owne sense, and apprehension,
And faith wherein he lives ; but from this ill,
That each hath his owne will, springs all dissension ;
For that all men agree, their lackes but will ;
   Warres never raging in so shrewd a cace,
   But that, if men were pleas'd, would turne to peace.

HOW TO BE ALWAYES IN REPOSE.

So that desire, and feare may never jarre
Within your soule ; no losse of meanes, nor ryot
Of cruell foes, no sicknesse, harme by warre,
Nor chance whats'ever will disturbe your quiet ;
   For in a setled, and well temper'd mind,
   None can the meanest perturbation find.

A WISE MAN ONELY MAY PROPERLY BE SAID TO ENJOY LIFE.

His life is short, who present times neglects,
Feares times to come, and hath past-times forgot ;
Or rather, while he breaths his age, hee makes
A base abode in time, but liveth not ;
   For onely he leades, in judicious eyes,
   The longest life, who lives, till he be wise.

WHO IS NOT SATISFIED WITH HIS OWNE FORTUNE, HOW GREAT
SOEVER IT BE, IS MISERABLE.

THOUGH the Septemvirat of Dutch Electors
Jnaugurat him Cæsar ; and each one
Extoll his valour above that of Hectors ;
In wit, and wealth furpaffing Salomon ;
   Yet if he proudly foare a higher pitch,
   He's neither mighty, valiant, wife, nor rich.

A CERTAIN OLD MAN'S EXPRESSION BEFORE HIS DEATH
TO HIS SON.

THAT I am at the period of mine age,
Nor you, nor I, have any caufe to mourne,
For life is nothing, but a pilgrimage ;
When we have travel'd long, we muft returne :
   Let us be glad then, that my fpirit goes,
   After fo many toiles, to his repofe.

TO ONE OF A GREAT MEMORY, BUT DEPRAVED LIFE.

THOUGH many things your memory containe,
If by your mind, to matters it be led,
Which are leffe profitable to retaine,
Then to commit t' oblivion, it is bad :
And whatfoever arts it comprehend,
If it remember not on piety,
Repentance for enormous fins, the end
Of life, God's judgments, and his clemencie ;
   Thofe neceffary precepts while you lake,
   You but forget your felfe, and it is weake.

HOW A MAN SHOULD OPPOSE ADVERSITIE.

GAINST mifadventure being refolv'd to fight,
My mind fhall be the bow, whence I'l apace
Shoot back the arrows, Fortune out of fpight,
Affaults me with ; and breake them in her face ;
   For all her foverain'ties I abjure,
   Her harmes I dread not, and defye her pow'r.

THE EXPRESSION OF A CONTENTED MIND IN POVERTIE.

THAT I'm not covetous, is all my land,
From whence my thoughts new treafours dayly bring ;
And the beft moveable, which I command
Is, I buy no unneceffary thing :
   By thefe, I of true wealth poffeffe fuch ftore,
   That all the Kings on earth can have no more.

NOT TIME, BUT OUR ACTIONS, ARE THE TRUE MEASURE OF OUR LIFE.

THAT life is fhort, which meafur'd by the fpan
Of time hath been of vertuous actions fcant ;
And one day's longer in a learned man,
Then twenty lufters of an ignorant ;
   For life is good, and 'tis the quality
   Of goodneffe, that extends its quantity.

INGRATITUDE IS SUCH A COMMON VICE, THAT EVEN THOSE WHO EXCLAME MOST AGAINST IT, ARE NOT FREEST OF IT.

IT would not be an univerfall cace,
Nor could each man have fo true caufe to fall
In rayling 'gainft ingratitude, unleffe
There were fome reafon to complaine of all :

Thus, who have with unthankfulneffe beene met,
May from fuch dealing this inftruction draw,
That if themfelves did ever prove ingrate,
They get but juftice from the Talion-Law,
  To th' end they may from thofe their faults refraine,
  Which they fo ugly fee in other men.

OF NEGATIVE, AND POSITIVE GOOD.

Not onely are they good, who vertuoufly
Employ their time, now vertue being fo rare,
But likewife thofe, whom no neceffity,
Nor force can in the meaneft vice infnare;
  For fin's fo mainly further'd by the Devill,
  That 'tis a fort of good, to doe no evill.

TO ONE BEWAILING THE DEATH OF ANOTHER.

You have no caufe to thinke it ftrange, that he
Hath yeelded up his laft, and fatall breath;
For 'tis no wonder for a man to dye,
Whofe life is but a journey into Death:
  Nor is there any man of life deprived
  For age, or fickneffe, but becaufe he lived.

WHY COVETOUS, AND TOO AMBITIOUS MEN PROVE NOT SO THANKFULL AS OTHERS FOR RECEIVED FAVOURS.

Whose mind with pride, and avarice doth flow,
Remember feldome of a courtefie,
So well, as humbler fpirits doe; for who
Lean's moft on hope, yeelds leaft to memory;
  Their thoughts fo farre on future aimes being fet,
  That by-paft things they purpofely forget.

A COUNSELL NOT TO VSE SEVERITY, WHERE GENTLE DEALING MAY PREVAILE.

STRIVE, never by conftraint to croffe his will,
Whofe beft affection fairely may be had ;
The noble mind of man being fuch, as ftill
Follow's more heartily, then it is led :
   For there was never power, charme, nor Art,
   That could without confent, obtaine the heart.

THAT THEY MAY BE ALIKE RICH, WHO ARE NOT ALIKE ABUN-DANTLY STORED WITH WORLDLY COMMODITIES.

I HAVE of lands, nor moneyes no large portion :
   Yet, if I be content to thinke, that I
     Am not as rich as any, were great dulneffe ;
For wealth not being in plenty, but proportion,
   Though veffels have not like capacity,
     They may be all of them alike in fulneffe.

VERTUE AND GOODNESSE ARE VERY MUCH OPPOSED BY THE SELFE-CONCEIT, THAT MANY MEN HAVE OF THEIR OWNE SUFFICIENCIE.

THER's nothing hinders vertue more, then the
Opinion of our owne perfection ;
For none endeavours to doe that, which hee
Imagineth he hath already done :
   And fome by thinking t'have what they have not,
   Neglect the wifedome, which they might have got.

HOW TO SUPPORT THE CONTUMELIE OF DEFAMATORIE SPEECHES.

IF men defervedly fpeake ill of you,
Be angry not at them, but at the caufe,
Which you to them did furnifh fo to doe :
But if they ftill continue 'gainft the Lawes

Of truth, and modefty their bad report,
While with a valiant heart, and teftimony
Of a good confcience, you your felfe comfort,
Contemne thofe rafcals, that infult upon ye ;
   For a reproach, by honeft meanes obtain'd,
   Doth full of glory to the heav'ns afcend.

OF LUST, AND ANGER.

Lust taking pleafure in its owne delite,
Communicats it felfe to two togither ;
But far more bafe is anger, whofe defpite
Rejoyceth at the forrow of another ;
   For th' one is kindly, th' other fows debate ;
   Luft hath a fmack of love, but wrath of hate.

AN ENCOURAGEMENT TO AN IMPATIENT MAN IN AN AGUE.

Why fhould you in your fickneffe thus enrage,
Seeing patience doth a gen'rous mind befit ?
You may be fure, it will not laft an age ;
For if it leave not you, you muft leave it :
   Take courage then, faint not, but bravel' endure
   Whats'êr to kill the foule hath not the pow'r.

THE FIRME, AND DETERMINATE RESOLUTION OF A COURAGIOUS SPIRIT, IN THE DEEPEST CALAMITIES, INFLICTED BY SINISTER FATE.

Seeing croffes cannot be evited, I'l
   Expofe my felfe to Fortune, as a rock
      Within the midft of a tempeftuous ocean,
         So to gainftand the batt'ry of her fpight,
That though jaile, fickneffe, poverty, exile
   Affault me all, with each a grievous ftroak
      Of fev'rall mifery, at the devotion
         Of mifadventure, ev'ry day, and night,

Yet with a mind, undanted all the while,
  I will refift her blows, till they be broke
    In the rebounding, and without commotion,
      Till all her rage be fpent, fuftaine the fight :
So that fhe fhall not b' able to fubdue
One thought of mine, with all that fhe can doe ;
For when fh' hath try'd her worft, I will not yeeld,
Nor let her thinke, that fhe hath gain'd the field.

THAT WISE MEN, TO SPEAK PROPERLY, ARE THE MOST POWERFULL MEN IN THE WORLD.

THE greateft power is to wife men due :
The pow'r of all men elfe to theirs being nought ;
For wife men onely, what they will, can doe ;
Becaufe they will not doe, but what they ought :
  Such being their cariage, that their reafon ftill
  Directs their power, and informes their will.

TO A RICH MAN BECOME POOR.

YOUR poverty fhould be the more efteemed,
That by the meanes thereof you are exeemed
From ftubborne fervants, lying fycophants,
And faigned friends : in lieu whereof, it grants
Thefe three of a more vertuous company,
Eafe, humble cariage, and fobriety.

THAT IF WE STROVE NOT MORE FOR SUPERFLUITIES, THEN FOR WHAT IS NEEDFUL, WE WOULD NOT BE SO MUCH TROUBLED, AS WE ARE.

IF by the neceffary ufe of things,
  The ornaments wee meafure of our honour,
    And not by that, which fancy doth fuggeft us ;
Wee will not need thofe wares, the marchant brings
  From forraine countries ; and withall exoner
    Our minds of what might otherwife moleft us.

THE ONELY TRUE PROGRESSE TO A BLESSED LIFE.

Who hath of confcience a profound remorfe
For fins committed, and to keepe his fenfes
From all finifter practice, doth divorce
His thoughts from their accuftomed offences,
　Is in the way of vertue, which will tend,
　It being continu'd, to a happy end.

THAT WEE OUGHT NOT TO BE EXCESSIVELY GRIEVED AT THE LOSSE OF ANY THING THAT IS IN THE POWER OF FORTUNE.

All thofe externall ornaments of health,
Strength, honour, children, beauty, friends, and wealth,
Are for a while concredited to men,
To deck the Theater, whereon the fcene
Of their fraile life is to be acted : fome
Of which muft, without further, be brought home
To day, and fome to morrow ; th'ufe of them
Being onely theirs, till new occafions claime
A reftitution of them all againe,
As time thinkes fit, to whom they appertaine.
Though fuch like things therefore be taken from us,
Wee fhould not fuffer griefe to overcome us ;
But rather render thankes, they have beene lent us
So long a fpace, and never difcontent us.

WHEREIN TRUE WEALTH CONSISTS.

Who's truly rich, we ought not to efteeme
By lands, nor goods, but by the mind ; the title
Of a poore man, being farre more due to him,
That covets much, then that poffeffeth little ;
　For he is richer, doth the world neglect,
　Then who poffeffing all, complaines for lack.

c

HOW DIFFICULT A THING IT IS TO TREAD IN THE PATHES OF VERTUE.

THE way to vertue's hard, uneafie, bends
Aloft, being full of fteep, and rugged alleys;
For never one to a high place afcends,
That always keepes the plaine, and pleafant valleyes:
     And reafon in each humane breaft ordaines,
     That precious things be purchafed with paines.

A COUNSELL TO ONE OPPRESSED WITH BONDAGE AND CRUELL DISASTERS.

WHATS'EVER be your fortune, let your deeds
With your affection always jump; for by
Defiring to do that, which you muft needs,
You'll blunt the fharpneffe of neceffity:
     And making of conftraint a willingneffe,
     Be glad in fpight of croffes, and diftreffe.

HOW FORTUNE OFTENTIMES MOST PRÆPOSTEROUSLY POND'RING THE ACTIONS OF MEN, WITH A GREAT DEALE OF INJUSTICE BESTOWETH HER FAVOURS.

FORTUNE, with wealth and honour at her feet,
And holding in her hand a ballance, fits
Weighing human defert, as fhe thinks fit:
One of the fcales whereof the learn'deft wits,
Moft vertuous, and of choifeft parts containes;
The other being appointed for fuch, as
Are vicious, light, and deftitute of braines.
The light are mounted up into the place,
Where riches, and preferment lye expofed
To thofe, can reach them; while the other fcale,
By th'only weight of worth, therein inclofed,
Is more fubmiffively depreft, then all
That hangs on Fortune's ballance. And the higher,
That hair-brain'd heads b'advanc'd above the ftates
Of others in this world; fo much the nigher
To want and bondage are the wifer pates.

Of fuch things then, as to the difpofition
Of Fortune doe pertaine, let no man wonder,
While the moft wicked gaine the acquifition,
That by their meanes, the good be brought at under ;
  For wherefoever vice is moft refpected,
  The greateft vertues are the more rejected.

WHEN A TRUE FRIEND MAY BE BEST KNOWNE.

As the glow-worme fhines brighteft in the darke,
And frankincenfe fmells fweeteft in the fire ;
So croffe adventures make us beft remarke
A fincere friend from a diffembled lyer ;
  For fome, being friends to our profperity,
  And not to us, when it failes, they decay.

THE DUTY OF A HUSBAND TO HIS WIFE.

Though he be head, he muft not tyrannize
Over his mate in facred bonds of marriage ;
For in the head the wit, and judgement is :
And therefore he, with a judicious cariage,
  Should towards her behave himfelfe, refpect her,
  Inftruct her, love her, and from harme protect her.

CONCERNING THOSE WHO MARRY FOR BEAUTY AND WEALTH, WITHOUT REGARD OF VERTUE.

How can fuch wedded people lead their lives,
With a refpect unfainedly entire,
Where hufbands are not married to their wives,
But money to the covetous defire :
Where men in little eftimation hold
Womens difcretion, wit, and chaftitie ;
But merely aime at handfomneffe, and gold,
To ferve their avarice, and leacherie :
  Which fafhion lately is become fo common,
  That firft w'efpoufe the money, then the woman.

THE SPEECH OF A NOBLE SPIRIT TO HIS ADVERSARY, WHOM
AFTER HE HAD DEFEATED, HE ACKNOWLEDGETH TO BE NO-
THING INFERIOR TO HIMSELFE IN WORTH, WIT, OR VALOUR,
THEREBY INSINUATING THAT A WISE MAN CANNOT PROPERLY
BE SUBDUED, THOUGH HE BE O'RTHROWN IN BODY AND
WORLDLY COMMODITIES.

I WILL not of this victorie be glorious ;
Nor ought you for being vanquish'd to repine,
You not being overcome, nor I victorious ;
Your fortune onely is o'ercome by mine ;
  For by the force of judgment, grace, and will,
  You have a mind, that is invincible.

IN HOW FARRE MEN ARE INFERIOR TO MANY OTHER LIVING
CREATURES, IN THE FACULTIES OF THE EXTERIOR SENSES.

IN touching, Spiders are the fubtilleft ;
The Bores, in hearing ; vulturs, in the fmell ;
In feeing, Eagles, and the Apes in tafte :
Thus beafts in all the fenfes men excell ;
  So that, if men were not judicious creatures,
  Some brutes would be of more accomplifh'd natures.

TO ONE WHO WAS HEAVILY CAST DOWNE IN SPIRIT, BY REASON
OF SOME SCANDALOUS SPEECHES, BLASED FORTH TO HIS
DISADVANTAGE.

BE not difcouraged at calumnies,
Which are not, at the worft, but loads of wind ;
And therefore, with a ftrong and patient mind
Moft eafie to fupport, if you be wife ;
  For nat'rally fuch burthens are but light :
  Unleffe the bearer's weakneffe give them weight.

THUS ENDETH THE FIRST BOOKE OF SIR THOMAS VRCHARDS EPIGRAMS.

EPIGRAMS.

THE SECOND BOOKE.

NO CROSSE ADVENTURE SHOULD HINDER US FROM BEING GOOD,
THOUGH WE BE FRUSTRATE OF THE REWARD THEREOF.

By any meanes, with all your might endeavour
For honesty, whats'ever be th'event :
Although sinister fortune should dissever
Vertue from honour, be not discontent ;
   For if you be deprived of your due,
    The fault is in the time, and not in you.

THOSE THAT HAVE GREATEST ESTATES ARE NOT ALWAYES
THE WEALTHIEST MEN.

They're richer, who diminish their desires,
Though their possessions be not amplified,
Then Monarchs, who in owning large Empires,
Have minds, that never will be satisfied ;
   For he is poore, that wants what he would have,
    And rich, who having nought, doth nothing crave.

THE COURAGIOUS RESOLUTION OF A VALIANT MAN.

SEEING Nature entred me on this condition
Into the world, that I muſt leav't, I vow,
A noble death ſhall be my chiefe ambition ;
To dye being th'end of all I ought to doe,
   And rather gaine, by a prime vertue, death,
   Then to protraƈt with common ones my breath.

HOW ABJECT A THING IT IS FOR A MAN TO HAVE BIN LONG IN THE WORLD WITHOUT GIVING ANY PROOFE, EITHER BY VERTUE OR LEARNING, THAT HE HATH BEENE AT ALL.

THAT aged man, we ſhould, without all doubt,
Of all men elſe the moſt diſgracefull hold,
Who can produce no teſtimonie, but
The number of his yeares, that he is old ;
   For of ſuch men what can bee teſtifyed,
   But that being borne, they lived long, then dyed.

THAT A VERTUOUS MIND IN A DEFORMED BODY MAKETH ONE MORE BEAUTIFULL, THEN A HANDSOME BODY CAN DOE, ENDOWED WITH A VICIOUS MIND.

EXTERNAL comelineſſe few have obtain'd
Without their hurt ; it never made one chaſt,
But many adulterers ; and is ſuſtain'd
By qualities, which age, and ſickneſſe waſte :
But that, whoſe luſtre doth the mind adorne,
Surpaſſeth farre the beauty of the bodie ;
For that, we make our ſelves, to this, we're borne ;
This onely comes by chance, but that by ſtudy ;
It is by vertue then, that wee enjoy
Deſervedly the ſtile of beautifull,
Which neither time, nor Fortune can deſtroy ;
And the deformed body, a faire ſoule
   From duſt to glory everlaſting caries,
   While vicious ſoules in handſome bodies periſh.

TO ONE WHOM POVERTY WAS TO BE WISHED FOR, IN SO FARRE
AS HE COULD HARDLY OTHERWISE BE RESTRAINED FROM
EXCESSIVE RYOT AND FEASTING.

You ſhould not be a whit the more dejećted,
  That, as in former times, not being ſuſtain'd,
   Your fare, and dyet daily doe decreaſe ;
For want doing what your modeſtie neglećted,
  It is a happy thing to be conſtrain'd
   To that, which willingly you ought t'embrace.

THAT MEN ARE NOT DESTITUTE OF REMEDIES WITHIN THEMSELVES
AGAINST THE SHREWDEST ACCIDENTS THAT CAN BEFALL THEM.

IF you expećt to be of toyle, and care
Sometime exeem'd, hope may your griefe diminiſh,
And patience comfort you, ere you deſpaire ;
Though both thoſe faile, death will your troubles finiſh :
  Thus are you fitly ſerved with reliefes,
  'Gainſt Fortune's moſt elaboured miſchiefes.

WHAT SORT OF BENEFITS ONE OUGHT TO BESTOW.

WOULD you oblige to you a friend, by giving
Moſt cheerfully your favours to acquite,
Give that, which gives content in the receiving,
And when it is received yeelds delight ;
  For if it faile in either of thoſe two,
  It will impaire his thankfulneſſe to you.

TO ONE WHO DID GLORY TOO MUCH IN THE FAIRE AND DUR-
ABLE FABRIC OF A GORGIOUS PALACE WHICH HE HAD
CAUSED LATELY TO BE BUILT.

BOAST never of the permanence of that,
Which neither can prolong your dayes, nor houres ;
For that your houſe is ſtately, ſtrong, and great,
The praiſe is the artificers, not yours.

Death cares not for your Palace, who can climb,
Without a ladder to the tops of towers ;
And fhortly, with a vifage pale and grim,
Will come, and turn you naked out of doores :
  But make your body, like a Church of Marbre,
  A Caftle fit, a vertuous mind to harbour.

THAT A CONTENTED MAN IS RICH, HOW LITTLE WEALTH SOEVER HE HAVE.

He's rich who craving nothing elfe, doth find
Content in the poffeffion of his owne ;
For in fo much as doth concerne the mind,
Not to defire, and have, is all but one ;
  For if the thoughts thereof be rich, we're fure
  Fortune hath not the fkill to make us poore.

HOW DANGEROUS IT IS TO WRITE OR SPEAKE OF MODERNE TIMES.

Though all fome errors doe commit, yet few
Having committed them, would have them told :
That talke then being difpleafing which is true,
Who cannot flatter, he his peace muft hold ;
  So hard a thing it is, to fay or pen,
  Without offence, the truth of living men.

THAT THE MOST SOLID GAINE OF ANY, IS IN THE ACTION OF VERTUE, ALL OTHER EMOLUMENTS, HOW LUCRATIVE THEY SO EVER APPEARE TO THE COVETOUS MIND, BEING THE CHIEFEST PRECIPITATING PUSHES OF HUMAN FRAILTY TO AN INEVITABLE LOSSE.

Such is the thin, and ragged mafke of vice,
That whofoe'r to peevifh thoughts are proneft,
Will know fome time b'experience, that there is
No profitable thing, which is not honeft :
  Nor can there be to God a man more odious,
  Then he who leaves the good, for what's commodious.

WHAT THE SUBJECT OF YOUR CONFERENCE OUGHT TO BE WITH MEN
OF JUDGMENT AND ACCOUNT.

LET the difcourfe be ferious you impart
To the grave audience of judicious eares;
Being either of the common-wealth, fome art
Or fcience, on your owne, or friendes affaires;
 For if it can to none of thofe pertaine,
 It muft be idle, frivolous, and vaine.

THAT A TRULY GENEROUS MIND HAD RATHER GIVE A CURTESIE
THEN BE RESTING ONE, AFTER THE PRESENTED
OPPORTUNITY TO REPAY IT.

As ftill a greater care doth men poffeffe,
To keepe things well, then freely to beftowe them;
So to a noble fpirit it is leffe
Laborious to giue benefites then owe them;
 In whom brave actions are more naturall,
 Then to the flame to mount, or earth to fall.

TO A CERTAIN LADY OF A MOST EXQUISIT FEATURE AND COMELY
PRESENTATION, BUT WHO GLORIED TOO MUCH IN THE DECEITFUL
EXCELLENCIE OF THESE FADING AND PERISHABLE QUALITIES.

THOUGH you be very handfome, doe but ftay
A little while, and you will fee a change;
For beautie flieth with the tyme away,
Wherwith it comes : nor muft you think it ftrange,
That hardly being fkin deepe in the moft faire,
And but a feparable accident
Of bodys, which but living fhadowes are,
And therfore frayle, it is not permanent;
 Be then not proud of that, which at the beft
 Decrepit age will fpoyle, or fickneffe waft.

D

WHO IS TRULY RICH, AND WHO POOR.

By the contempt, not value of the matter
Of worldly goods, true riches are poſſeſſ'd ;
For our deſire by ſeeking groweth greater,
And by deſiring, povertie's increaſs'd ;
   So that on earth there can be none ſo poore,
   As he whoſe mind in plentie longs for more.

HOW GENEROUS A THING IT IS NOT TO SUCCUMBE TO PLEASURE AND SENSUALITIE.

No great exploit can be expected from
That man, who being profoundly plung'd in his
Owne ſenſe, permits himſelfe to be o'rcome
B' a foe 's effeminat, as pleaſure is ;
   For mightie minds moſt pleaſures doe conceive,
   When pleaſures over them no power have.

THAT WE OUGHT NOT TO BE SORIE AT THE LOSSE OF WORLDLY GOODS.

Those things which are to us by fortune lent,
We ſhould ſequeſtrat ; and to ſuch a place
From whence ſhe may without our diſcontent,
Fetch them away againe before our face ;
   For if we grudge thereat by any meanes,
   We doe but vexe our ſelves, and loſe our paines.

WHAT IS NOT VERTUOUSLY ACQUIRED, IF ACQUIRED BY US, IS NOT PROPERLY OURS.

Whos'ever by ſiniſter meanes is come
   To places of preferment, and to walke
     Within the bounds of vertue takes no pleaſure,
Provideth onely titles for his tombe,

And for the baſer people pratling talke,
    But nothing for himſelfe in any meaſure ;
For fortune doth with all things us befit,
Save the ſole mind of ours, and vice kills it.

RICHES AFFOORD TO VERTUE MORE MATTER TO WORKE UPON, THEN POVERTIE CAN DOE.

For temperance, and other qualities
Of greater moment, men have beene reſpected
In riches ; but in poverty there is
This onely goodneſſe, not to be dejected ;
    Whence ſhunning want, we means embrace which yeeld
    To vertue a more large and ſpacious field.

DEATH MAKETH US ALL ALIKE IN SO FARRE AS HER POWER CAN REACH.

'Mongst all the rites that Nature can pretend
In juſtice, this is chiefeſt, and a ſequell
Which doth on mortall principles depend,
That drawing neare to death we are all equall ;
    Therefore we otherwiſe then by the ſenſe,
    Should betwixt man and man make difference.

A VERY READY WAY TO GOODNESSE AND TRUE WISEDOME.

Who vertuouſly would ſettle his endeavours
To mortifie his paſſions and be wiſe,
Muſt ſtill remember on received favours,
Forgetting alwaies by-paſt injuries :
    For that a friend ſhould prove ingrate, is ſtrange,
    And mercy is more noble then revenge.

WE OUGHT NOT TO REGARD THE CONTUMELIES AND CALUMNIES OF LYARS AND PROFANE MEN.

ASPERSIONS, which bafe people vicioufly
Inflict upon mens credits, I contemne ;
That fentence having fmall authoritie,
Where he that is condemned doth condemne ;
   And to be hated by a wicked fpirit,
    Doth argue oftentimes the greater merit.

NO MAN SHOULD GLORY TOO MUCH IN THE FLOURISHING VERDURE OF HIS YOUTH.

LET none be proud of life ; nor thinke that longer
He then another will, becaufe he's younger,
Enjoy his pleafures ; for though old age ftand
A great way off, death alwaies is at hand ;
   Who, without taking heed to time or yeares,
    No living creature fpares when fhe appeares.

THAT VERTUE IS OF GREATER WORTH THEN KNOWLEDGE TO A SPECULATIVE PHILOSOPHER.

WHY doe you ftudy morals, if you take
No paines t'abate your avarice and luft ?
For how can vertue's definition make
You valiant, prudent, temperate, or juft,
   If you induftrioufly purge not your mind
    Of any vice to which you are inclin'd ?

CONSOLATION TO A POORE MAN.

THAT you are poore, it fhould not much difheart you ;
For povertie fecurely keeps your houfe
From theeves and robbers, and makes roome to vertue,
By banifhing of pride, and the abufe

Of riches; the loſſe thereof, and feare of loſſe,
Surfets, and vices that prejudge the health;
Which being ſhut out of doores, ſtrive to compoſe
Your mind to quietneſſe, more worth then wealth;
   For without wealth you may have happineſſe,
   But not without tranquillitie and eaſe.

THE BAD RETURNES OF INGRATE MEN SHOULD NOT DETERRE US FROM BEING LIBERALL.

THOUGH you ingrate receivers dayly find,
Let not their faults make you leſſe noble prove;
It not being th' action of a gen'rous mind
To give and loſe ſo, as to loſe, and give;
   For that, a churle may doe, in hope of gaine,
   But this partakes of a heroick ſtraine.

THAT RICHES IS A SICKNESSE TO THOSE THAT DOE NOT POSSESSE THE GOOD THEREOF, SO MUCH AS THEY ARE POSSEST THEREBY.

SOME peoples ſenſes wealth doth ſo bereave,
That they to nothing elſe their minds can frame;
So have they wealth, as men are ſaid to have
The ague, when 'tis th' ague that hath them;
   For it afflicts them with the maladies
   Of covetous deſire and avarice.

A TRUELY LIBERALL MAN NEVER BESTOWETH HIS GIFTS IN HOPE OF RECOMPENCE.

A HEARTY giver, will conceive ſuch pleaſure
In th' onely action of his good intent,
That though he be not met in the like meaſure,
It never breeds him any diſcontent;
For when he doth beſtow a benefit,
He meerely lookes to the receiver's profit;

And in the inftant that he guideth it,
Reapes all the vfe that he exfpected of it ;
   Vertue no other recompence allowing,
   The price of honeft deeds being in the doing.

THAT THE SETLED QUIET OF OUR MIND OUGHT NOT TO BE MOVED AT SINISTER ACCIDENTS.

Man fhould for no infortunate event
Deprive himfelfe of that, which fortune is
Vnable to reftore him ; the content
Of mind, eafe, and tranquillity of his
   Repofed fpirit ; for who lacketh thofe,
   Can nothing elfe poffeffe that's worth to lofe.

AS IT WAS A PRECEPT OF ANTIQUITY, TO LEANE MORE TO VERTUE THEN PARENTAGE ; SO IS IT A TENET OF CHRISTIANITY, TO REPOSE MORE TRUST ON THE BLOOD OF CHRIST THEN OUR OWNE MERITS.

Vertue, not blood, was thought of anciently ;
Yet blood more then our vertue ought to pleafe us,
For we on blood, not vertue, fhould rely ;
Not on our vertue but the blood of Jefus ;
   His blood being able to make Heavenly Kings
   Of men, plagu'd here for lacke of earthly things.

OUR INCLINATION IS SO DEPRAVED, THAT IT IS APT ENOUGH OF IT SELFE TO RUN TO SIN, WITHOUT ANY INSTIGATION WHEREBY TO DRIVE IT FORWARD.

Our mind's fo prone to vice, it needs a bridle
   To hold it, rather then a fpurre to prick it ;
      For left unto it felfe, it hardly ftands,
But if perverfe enticements find it idle,
   And pufh it, it then, running on a wicked
      And headlong courfe, no reafon underftands,
   While at the windows of the eares and eyes
   Temptations enter, which the foule furprife.

THAT THERE IS NO TRUE RICHES BUT OF NECESSARY THINGS.

THE ufe of money is, to have the meanes
  Whereby all needfull things may be poffefs'd,
    Which are but few and fmall, and got with eafe ;
What we have more then that, 's not wealth, but chains
  Or fetters of the mind ; and at the beft
    But heapes of labour, feare, and carefulneffe.

THE MISERY OF SUCH AS ARE DOUBTFULL AND SUSPICIOUS
OF THEIR WIVES CHASTITIE.

CLOSE jealous men make not fo evident
In any thing the madneffe of their braines,
As that, the more that they are diligent,
They have the greater hope to lofe their paines ;
  For their whole care to fearch that, is imployed,
  Which not to find, they would be overjoyed.

HOW DEPLORABLE THE CONDITION OF MOST MEN IS, WHO, THOUGH
THEY ATTAINE TO THE FRUITION OF THEIR PRÆTERIT PROJECTS,
BY COVETING NEVERTHELESSE THE POSSESSION OF FUTURE PLEA-
SURES, HONOURS, AND COMMODITIES, NEVER RECEIVE CONTENT-
MENT, AS THEY OUGHT, IN THE PRESENT TIME.

IN things to fortune fubject, when we get
What we did long for, we anew defire
To have wherewith t' uphold the former ftate ;
Which likewife, we obtaining, more require ;
For bufineffe engendreth bufineffe,
And hope, being th' ufher of another hope,
Our enjoy'd wifhes ferve but to make place
To after aimes, whofe purchafe to the top
Of our ambition never reacheth ; thus
By ftill afpiring higher we can find

No end in miſeries that trouble us,
Turmoyle the body, and perplex our mind;
  Although we change, with great varietie,
  The matter which procures our miſerie.

THE DIFFERENT FRUITS OF IDLENESSE AND VERTUE IN YOUNG MEN.

As ſinging graſhoppers, a fond Youth revels
In ſummer blinks, and ſtarves when tempeſts rage;
But wiſe men, Piſmire like, enjoy the travels
Of their young yeares in th' winter of their age:
  Theſe by their providence have wealth in treaſure,
  While thoſe are pained for their by-gone pleaſure.

TO A GENEROUSLY DISPOSED GENTLEMAN, WHO WAS MAINE SORRIE THAT HE HAD NOT WHEREWITH TO REMUNERAT THE FAVOURS BY THE WHICH HE WAS OBLIGED TO THE CURTESIE OF A FRIEND.

You have reſtor'd his kindneſſe, if you owe
It willingly, and doth not prove forgetfull;
For with all mankind it would hardly goe,
If no man could with empty hands be gratefull;
  And in what may concerne a benefit,
  'Tis th' onely mind refounds and maketh it.

THE TRUEST WEALTH, MAN HATH IT FROM HIMSELFE.

If you from diſcontents have a deſire
To live exeem'd, the way is ne'r t' importune
Your friends with ſuits, but alwaies to require
Your riches from your ſelfe, and not from fortune:
  For your diſlike, affection, and opinion,
  Are things ſtill ſubject to your owne dominion.

THAT THE IMPUDICITY OF A LASCIVIOUS WOMAN STAINES
BUT HER OWNE, AND NOT HER HUSBANDS HONOUR.

THOUGH of her ſacred matrimoniall oath
Your wife make no account, if what be due
To a wiſe huſband you performe ; ſhe doth
Bring to her ſelfe diſcredit, not to you ;
For others' faults can no diſgrace impart you,
Though to your loſſe they tend, and make you ſorrie,
No more then you can by another's vertue,
Though it breed joy and gaine, reape any glorie :
　'Tis our owne vertu' and vice muſt praiſe or blame us,
　And either make us glorious or infamous.

WHO ARE REALLY RICH, AND WHO POORE.

HE that agreeth with his povertie
Is truly rich ; while, on the other part,
He's poore, who 'midſt the ſuperfluitie
Of wealth, in new deſires conſumes his heart :
　For 'tis an empty mind inflicts the curſe
　Of poverty, and not an empty purſe.

HOW TO OPPOSE SINISTER FATE.

IF of misfortune you ſuppoſe t'exoner,
By any other meanes then thoſe of vertue,
Your troubled ſpirit, you beſtow upon her
Both your own ſkill, and weapons to ſubvert you ;
For that, wherewith you 'magine to reſiſt
Her furie, is already in her hand ;
And which ſhe holds extended to your breaſt,
To make you plyable to her command.
It is not then great friends, nobilitie,
E

Health, beauty, ſtrength, nor ſtore of worldly treaſure,
That can preſerve you from her blowes, for ſhe
Of all thoſe things diſpoſeth at her pleaſure :
But you, your ſelfe muſt furniſh with ſuch armes
As may defend you againſt vice and ſin,
And ſo you ſhall not need to feare her harmes ;
For being ſo warded, you are happy in
   The tumults of the world ; and ſhe unable,
   With all her might, to make you miſerable.

THE DESERVED MUTABILITY IN THE CONDITION OF TOO AMBITIOUS MEN.

As is the tortoiſe uſed by the eagle,
So fortune doth vaine-glorious men inveagle ;
Who carries them upon the wings of honour,
The higher up, that they may breake the ſooner.

THAT INCONVENIENCES OUGHT TO BE REGARDED TO BEFOREHAND.

To wait for croſſes that may happen, is
The meane, whereby to beare them eaſily ;
They not being much unlike the cockatrice,
Which, if fore-ſeene by us, dyes inſtantly ;
   While unexpected miſadventures kill
   Joy in the breed, and tyrannize the will.

CONCERNING THOSE WHO DISDAINE TO WALKE ON THEIR OWNE FEET, WHEN, AT ANY RATE, THEY MAY HAVE THE CONVENIENCE TO BE CARRIED.

WE will not ſee with others' eyes, nor heare
With borrow'd eares ; yet hath fond cuſtome ſo
Prevailed, that we take eſpeciall care,
Upon the feet of others ſtill to goe,

Although our owne be nere fo ftrong, to beare
The burthen of our bodies : I am fure
That no man came into this world in chaire,
On horfeback, or in coach ; our birth was poore,
And we muft dye in no leffe poore eftate ;
But 'twixt thofe abject ends fuch pride there is,
And in fo fhort a courfe of life fo great
Forgetfulneffe of both extremities,
    As if enjoying an immortall breath,
    We could not have been borne, nor taft of death.

THUS ENDETH THE SECOND BOOKE OF SIR THOMAS
VRCHARDS EPIGRAMS.

EPIGRAMS.

THE THIRD BOOKE.

HOW TO BEHAVE ONES SELFE IN ALL OCCASIONS.

No kind of trouble to your felfe procure,
And fhun as many croffes as you can ;
Stoutly fupport what you muft needs endure,
And with the refolution of a man,
   Whofe fpirit is affliction-proofe, poffeffe
   A joyfull heart in all occurrences.

THAT NO MAN, TO SPEAKE PROPERLY, LIVETH, BUT HE THAT IS WISE AND VERTUOUS.

If wee lacke vertue and good deeds to hold
Our life into, what ferves it us ? Our breath
True life affords not, though it make us old ;
Nor lived he that lives not after death,
   For in good minds the lives of men confift,
   And they alone mortalitie refift.

WE OUGHT ALWAYS TO THINKE UPON WHAT WE ARE TO SAY
BEFORE WE UTTER ANY THING; THE SPEECHES AND TALK
OF SOLID WITS BEING STILL PREMEDITATED, AND NEVER
USING TO FORERUNNE THE MIND.

Our tongu's the heart's interpreter, and ftill
In wife difcourfe hath but the fecond place :
The heart fhould end ere th' tongue begin ; for while
The legate fpeakes, the truch-man holdes his peace :
  Which order being inverted, we abufe
  The hearer's patience, and our felves confufe.

THAT LUST AND DRUNKENNESSE ARE ODIOUS VICES.

Wrath makes a man to fin couragioufly,
And pride doth fwell with faire appearances ;
But drunkeneffe, and too much leacherie
Are floven, filthie, villanous, and bafe ;
  For by the one God's image being exil'd,
  His temple by the other is defil'd.

A CERTAINE ANCIENT PHILOSOPHER DID HEREBY INSINUATE
HOW NECESSARY A THING THE ADMINISTRATION OF JUSTICE
WAS, AND TO BE ALWAIES VIGILANT IN THE JUDICIOUS
DISTRIBUTION OF PUNISHMENT AND RECOMPENCE.

Seeing by the multitude of thofe offend,
The fhame of fin's diminifh'd now in fuch
A meafure, that a common crime in end
Will ceafe to be accounted a reproach ;
I am affray'd that, if iniquitie
Be fuffer'd thus to propagate, it will,
With bad example, fafer be to ftray,
Then to prove fingular in doing well :
Nor is this grievous inconvenience, though
Pernicious to the ftate, to be withftood,

If any the leaſt care be wanting to
Chaſtiſe the wicked, and reward the good:
   Which law each Prince ſhould in his boſome nouriſh,
   That vice may be ſuppreſt, and vertue flouriſh.

THAT OVERWEENING IMPEDETH OFTENTIMES THE PERFECTIONING OF THE VERY SAME QUALITIE WEE ARE PROUDEST OF.

FOND ſelfe-conceit likes never to permit
One's mind to ſee it ſelfe with upright eyes;
Whence many men might have attain'd to wit,
Had they not thought themſelves already wiſe:
   To boaſt of wiſedome then is fooliſhneſſe,
   For while we thinke we're wiſe, we're nothing leſſe.

TO ONE WHO SEEMED TO BE GRIEVOUSLY DISCONTENTED WITH HIS POVERTY.

LET never want of money vexe your braine,
Seeing all contentment is in th'only mind;
To the which mony doth no more pertaine,
Then to the hierarchies of angel-kind:
   Thus gold being earthly, and the mind ſublime,
   T'abaſe your ſpirit is a ſort of crime.

THE RESOLUTION OF A PROFICIENT IN VERTUE.

I HOPE ſo little to tranſgreſſe the law
My conſcience will endite me, or be proud
Of wealth and pomp as not to care a ſtraw
For fortune's frownes; ſo that my deeds be good,
   Which eternize my bliſſe, while ſhe makes kings
   T'enjoy at beſt but tranſitory things.

THAT A COURTESIE OUGHT TO BE CONFERRED SOONE, AND WITH A GOOD WILL.

No man will from his heart owe that which was
Extorted by meere importunity,
Without regard of true defert, becaufe
It feems to have beene giv'n unwillingly :
Who diftributes his benefits that way,
Needs not then wait for a gratification
From him whom he hath dulled with delay,
And tortured with grievous expectation ;
   For we acknowledge gifts according to
   Th'intent of him who doth the fame beftow.

THE BEST WITS, ONCE DEPRAVED, BECOME THE MOST IMPIOUS.

THE whiteft lawne receives the deepeft moale,
The pureft chryfolit is fooneft ftained ;
So without grace the moft ingenious foule
Is with the greateft wickedneffe profaned ;
   And the more edge it have, apply'd to fin,
   Where it fhould fpare, it cuts the deeper in.

THAT THOSE EMPLOY NOT THEIR OCCASIONS WELL WHO SPEND THE MOST PART OF THEIR LIFE IN PROVIDING FOR THE INSTRUMENTS OF LIVING.

SOME wafting all their life with paine and forrow,
To feeke the meanes of life no leafure give
Their thoughts, from ayming alwaies at to morrow ;
Whereby they live not, but are ftill to live ;
   In their whole age the fruits that iffue from
   Their labours, being but hopes of times to come.

AN VPRIGHTLY ZEALOUS AND TRULY DEVOUT MAN IS
STRONG ENOUGH AGAINST ALL TEMPTATIONS.

THAT man in whom the grace of God begins
His foule with divine comfort to refrefh,
May the whole heptarchie of deadly fins,
In fpite of all the devill, the world, the flefh
　　Are able to fuggeft, enforce to yeeld ;
　　Chrift being his guide, and Chriftian faith his fhield.

THAT TO EMPLOY OUR THOUGHTS ON THE STUDY OF MORTA-
LITY AND FRAILTY OF OUR NATURE IS A VERY NECESSARY
AND PROFITABLE SPECULATION.

BE not from death, by any meanes, a ftranger,
But make her your familiar friend ; that if
The caufe require it, vilipending danger,
You may ftep forth t'embrace her without griefe ;
　　For the more boldly you intend to meet her,
　　The relifh of your life will prove the fweeter.

THE GENEROUS SPEECH OF A NOBLE CAVALLIER AFTER HE
HAD DISARMED HIS ADVERSARY AT THE SINGLE COMBAT.

THOUGH with my raper, for the guerdon
Your fault deferveth, I may pierce ye,
Your penitence in craving pardon,
Tranfpaffions my revenge in mercy ;
　　And wills me both to end this prefent ftrife,
　　And give you leave in peace t'enjoy your life.

TO ONE WHO WAS EXCESSIVELY CHEERFULL FOR BEING RE-
COVERED OF A FEVER, WHEREWITH HE HAD BEENE FOR
A TIME EXTREAME SORELY SHAKEN.

THAT to your health you are reftored, you
May in fome fort be joyfull ; and yet pleafed

To know your dying day is nearer now,
Then when you were most heavily diseafed ;
For to its journeye's end your life ftill goes,
Which cannot ftay ; nor flow its pace, nor hath
It any Inne to reft in ; toyle, repofe,
Sickneffe and health being alike fteps to death :
　　Let this thought then your gladneffe mortifie,
　　That once againe you muft fall ficke and dye.

THAT THE MOST OF OUR CONTENTMENT WHILE WE ARE UPON THE
　　EARTH, CONSISTETH RATHER IN NEGATIVES, AS NOT TO BE PER-
　　PLEXED WITH MENTALL PERTURBATIONS, OUTWARD DISEASES,
　　AND OTHER SUCH LIKE LIFE-TORMENTING CROSSES, THEN IN THE
　　REALL FRUITION OF ANY POSITIVE DELIGHT THAT CAN BEFALL US.

THERE being no poffibility that men
Can here enjoy a greater delectation,
Then to poffeffe a body without paine,
And mind untroubled by the meaneft paffion ;
　　Without defire of further pleafure, health
　　And a good confcience fhould be our chiefe wealth.

WHY WE MUST ALL DYE.

IT being the law of nations to reftore
What we have borrow'd, ther's no remedy ;
But being engaged to a creditor
Who will not lofe his debt, we muft needs dye ;
　　Nor can we plead one halfe a terme's delay,
　　For when Death craves it, we are forc'd to pay.

OF THE COVETOUS AND PERVERSE INCLINATION OF THE GREATEST
PART OF MANKIND.

WHEN profit goes with vertue, we refpect her,
So that her very foot-fteps we adore ;
F

But if fhe walke alone, then we neglect her,
And will not wait upon her any more :
  So bafely 'gainft their confciences, moft men
  Defcend from honour to attend on gaine.

THE PARALLEL OF NATURE AND FORTUNE.

A FLY, which is a defpicable creature,
Obtaines, befide her wings, fix feet from Nature ;
Yet foure feet onely fhe is pleaf'd to grant
To the huge body of an elephant ;
So Fortune doth withdraw her gifts from fome,
Whofe real worth furpaffeth theirs on whom
She hath beftowed them, as forcibly
As elephants in ftrenth exceed a fly.

HOW WE SHOULD ENJOY THE DELIGHTS WE HAVE, AND CON-
TEMNE SUCH AS WE HAVE NOT.

Let not the want of pleafures be unpleafant
To your remembrance ; and with moderation
Make ufe of thofe contentments which are prefent,
If you would ne'r be griev'd with expectation ;
  For to our owne, things abfent to preferre,
  Fruftrates our hope when it hath bred us feare.

TO ONE WHO DID CONFIDE TOO MUCH IN THE SOUND TEMPERAM ENT
AND GOODLY CONSTITUTION OF HIS BODILY COMPLEXION.

BOAST not of outward health, but have a care
Your foule be not diftemper'd ; for we find
The cafe of them moft dangerous, who are,
In wholfome bodies, of a fickly mind ;
  Vice tyrannizing over flefh and blood,
  In thofe whofe will and judgment are not good.

A COUNSELL TO BE PROVIDENT AND CIRCUMSPECT IN ALL OUR
ACTIONS, WITHOUT EITHER COWARDISE OR TEMERITIE.

Doe nothing tim'roufly, and yet b'aware
You be not rafh ; let prudence therefore guard
Your words and deeds ; for he needs not to feare
What's to be fhun'd, that fhuns what's to be fear'd ;
   Nor in the prefent time be vex't, who, from
   Things paft, difcerne of what is like to come.

OF FOURE THINGS IN AN EPALLELED WAY VANQUISHED
EACH BY OTHER.

As death o'rthroweth man, and cuts his breath,
And fame moft glorioufly fubdueth death ;
So gourmandizing time doth fame o'rcome,
And to eternity time muft fuccumbe.

A CONSOLATION TO THOSE THAT ARE OF A LITTLE STATURE,
NOT TO BE SORRY THEREAT.

None of a little burthen fhould complaine ;
You're cloth'd with flefh and bones, and not fupprefft ;
A little houfe a gyant may containe,
And little bulks great fpirits oft inveft ;
   For vertue hath not fuch defire to find
   The ftature of the body, as the mind.

THAT TOO MUCH BEWAILING AND GRIEFE IS TO BE AVOIDED AT
FUNERALS, TO ONE LAMENTING THE DECEASE OF A FRIEND.

It were more fit that you relinquifhed forrow,
Then that you fhould be left by it ; that may,
What ever may be done, be done to-morrow,
And what to-morrow may be done to-day ;
   We fhould therefore, as foon's we can, defift
   From that wherein we cannot long infift.

THE VERTUOUS SPEECH OF A DISEASED MAN, MOST PATIENT IN HIS SICKNESSE.

My flefh ftill having beene an enemy
Unto my fpirit, it fhould glad my heart
That paines, which feize now on my body, may
Be profitable to my better part;
For though difeafes feeme at firft unpleafant,
They point us out the way we ought to goe;
Admonifh us exactly of our prefent
Eftate; and t' us at laft this favour fhew,
    That they enlarge us from that ruinous,
    Clofe, and darke prifon, which confined us.

WE SHOULD NOT BE SORRY TO BE DESTITUTE OF ANY THING, SO LONG AS WE HAVE JUDGMENTS TO PERSWADE VS THAT WE MAY MINISTER TO OURSELVES WHAT WE HAVE NOT, BY NOT LONGING FOR IT.

To want what I fhould have, fhould never make
My heart leffe cheerfull; reafon ftill requiring
That I be pleaf'd whatf'ever things I lacke,
To furnifh to my felfe, by not defiring;
    For not to wifh for things, againft the griefe
    Of feare and fruftrate hopes, provides reliefe.

THAT VERTUE IS BETTER AND MORE POWERFULL THAN FORTUNE.

Vertue denyeth nought, but what to grant
Hurts the receiver, and is good to want;
Nor takes fhe ought away, which would not croffe
The owner, and is lucrative to loffe;
She no man can deceive; fhe lookes not ftrange;
Nor is fhe fubject to the meaneft change:
Embrace her then, for fhe can give that which
Will, without gold or filver, make you rich.

HOW MAGNANIMOUS A THING IT IS IN ADVERSITY PATIENTLY
TO ENDURE WHAT CANNOT BEE EVITED.

WHAT grievous weight fo ever be allowed
By mifadvent'rous fate wherewith to load ye,
Shrinke not thereat, but yeeld your fhoulder to it,
And with a ftedfaft mind fupport your body ;
    For valiant fpirits can not be o'rcome,
    Though Fortune force their bodies to fuccumbe.

THAT NOTHING MORE OPPOSETH THE TRANQUILLITY OF LIFE, WHICH
IS PROPER AND PECULIAR TO WISE MEN, THEN TO BE TYED TO A
GENERALITY OF PUBLICKE EXAMPLE IN ALL OUR ACTIONS.

AMONGST the caufes of our evils, this
Is one of the moft ordinary, that
We live b' example ; things which are amiffe
Supplying oftentimes the place of what
    'Is righteft and moft vertuous ; for there's no man
    Scarce holds that error which is done in common.

A TEMPERATE DYET IS THE BEST PHYSICKE.

To keepe a moderation in our dyet,
Is the chiefe meane to be of health affured ;
For nothing fickens fo as too much ryot,
And feafts kill more then Galen ever cured ;
    Nor is ther phyficke fhould fo fully pleafe us,
    Others expell, but this preveens difeafes.

THAT ALL OUR LIFE IS BUT A CONTINUALL COURSE AND VICISSI-
TUDE OF SINNING, AND BEING SORRY FOR SINNE.

WE finne with joy ; and having fin'd, we mourn ;
Then kindle, after teares, new finfull fires ;
There being a turne perpetuall, and returne
'Twixt our repentance and profane defires ;
    For fenfes to delights are wedded wholly,
    Which purchaf'd, reafon doth bewaile their folly.

WHY OUR THOUGHTS, ALL THE WHILE WE ARE IN THIS TRAN-
SITORY WORLD, FROM THE HOURE OF OUR NATIVITY TO THE
LAYING DOWNE OF OUR BODIES IN THE GRAVE, SHOULD NOT
AT ANY TIME EXSPACIAT THEMSELVES IN THE BROAD WAY
OF DESTRUCTION.

SEEING the ſtrait lodging of your mother's wombe
Brought you to life, from whence you muſt depart
To the darke entry of a little tombe,
Betwixt your birth and buriall let your heart
Tread vertue's narrow path, till you contract
To ſo ſtrict bounds the pleaſures of this wide
And ſpacious world, as that you may draw backe
The reines of covetous deſire, hate, luſt, and pride ;
    For by ſo doing, you will make your death
    A bleſſed paſſage to eternall breath.

IT IS THE SAFEST COURSE TO ENTERTAINE POVERTY IN OUR
GREATEST RICHES.

YOUR thoughts in greateſt plentie moderate,
Leſt with ſuperfluous things you be inſnared ;
Let poverty be your familiar mate,
That fortune may not find you unprepared ;
    For ſo it will not lye into her pow'r,
    T' inflict that croſſe which you cannot endure.

TO A GENTLEMAN WHO WAS EXTREAMLY OFFENDED AT THE
DEFAMATORY SPEECHES OF A BASE DETRACTOR.

AT his reproachfull words doe not conceive
The meaneſt grudge, for curs will ſtill be barking ;
Nor take you notice of him, ſeeing a knave
Is like a ſcabbed ſheepe, not worth the marking ;
    And this your ſetting him at nought will make him
    Swell, as a toad, till his owne poyſon breake him.

OF DEATH AND SIN.

Bodies, which lack the foules did them inform,
Turn'd to corruption, lofe their former grace,
And out of hearts corrupted breeds a worme,
Still gnawing upon guilty confciences.
As from deceafed bodies, death withdrawes
The living foules, another life t' enjoy,
So fince, contrary to the divine lawes,
In living bodies doth the foule deftroy.
Death is not vanquifh'd till the refurrection
Of bodies teftifie the foule's conjunction;
And by regeneration fin's infection
Is buri'd in a mortifi'd compunction;
   Leffe then is death then finne, the tomb then hell,
   The more that foules the bodies doe excell.

THE ADVANTAGES OF POVERTIE.

If you have povertie, you have no fumptuous,
But a moft eafie ghueft, fecure and quiet,
Who will preferve your mind from being prefumptuous,
From prodigality, exceffive ryot;
   From vicious pleafures, robbers, and the ftealth
   Of theeves, which ills befall to thofe have wealth.

HOW TO MAKE ALL THE WORLD PEACEABLE.

If fo in ev'ry man the flefh would dwell
At concord with the fpirit, that it ceafe
Againft its foverainty to rebell,
The univerfall world would be at peace;
   For if there were no avarice, no hate,
   No pride, nor luft, there could be no debate.

ONE WHO DID EXTREAMLY REGRET HIS BESTOWING OF A GREAT
BENEFIT UPON AN INGRATE MAN.

By giving moneyes to a thankleſſe man,
You loſt the matter of your benefit;
But the beſt part thereof doth ſtill remaine,
Which was your willingneſſe in giving it;
For his repaying of your gratefull action,
Had made you gaine all that you had received,
And getting nought, you lacke not ſatiſfaction,
It onely being to give it that you gave it;
   Elſe in your gifts a bargaine we ſhould find,
   And not the noble acts of a free mind.

OF WISEDOME IN SPEECH, IN ACTION, IN REALITY, AND REPUTATION.

WISELY to talke deſerveth much reſpect;
   Yet to live wiſely, without doubt, is better;
   To be accounted wiſe is a great matter,
   But it is moſt to be it in effect;
   Such as would follow wiſedome then, let them
   Strive more for deeds then words, for life then fame.

TO ONE WHO WAS GRIEVED WITHIN HIMSELFE THAT HE WAS
NOT ENDEWED WITH SUCH FORCE AND VIGOUR OF BODY
AS MANY OTHERS WERE.

THOUGH you be not ſo ſtrong as other men,
If you have health, the matter is but ſmall,
You being reſerv'd for taſks more noble then
The labours of the body; therefore all
You can complaine of, is not of defect,
But of imparitie. Nature did grant
Milo great ſtrength, in whoſe regard you're weake;
So was he weaker then an elephant;
His ſtrength decay'd, but Solon's laſted longer,
And wiſe men love not what's not durable;

Care not for ftrength, feeing fickneffe will be ftronger ;
But with your foule, as with a fword of fteele,
Within a fheath of wooll, fubdue temptations ;
For the true ftrength of man being in the mind,
He is much ftronger, overcomes his paffions,
Then who can with main force a lyon bind ;
    And who himfelfe thus in fubjection brings,
    Surmounts the power of all earthly kings.

AN ENCOURAGEMENT TO THOSE OF MEANE PARENTAGE, NOT TO BE
HINDERED BY THE OBSCURITY OF THEIR EXTRACTION, FROM
THE UNDERTAKING OF GLORIOUS ENTERPRISES.

THE bafer that your parents are, the greater
    Renowne and honour will to you redound,
        If all your actions be on vertue grounded ;
To give being more then to receive, and better
    To have a noble life then birth, to found
        A new nobility then find it founded.

WE SHOULD NOT BE TROUBLED AT THE ACCIDENTS OF FORTUNE,
NOR THOSE THINGS WHICH CANNOT BE ESCHEWED.

LET's take in patience, fickneffe, banifhments,
Paine, loffe of goods, death, and enforced ftrife ;
For none of thofe are fo much punifhments,
As tributes which we pay unto this life ;
    From the whole tract whereof we cannot borrow
    One dram of joy, that is not mix'd with forrow.

AGE MEERLY DEPENDING ON THE CONTINUALL FLUX OF TIME, WE
HAVE VERY SMALL REASON TO BOAST OF A LONG LIFE ALREADY
OBTAINED, OR BE PROUD OF THE HOPE HEREAFTER TO ATTAINE
UNTO IT.

THE prefent time doth fly away fo faft,
That one can hardly follow't with his mind ;

The præterit's a time already paſt,
And ſeeing the futur's ſtill to come, we find,
Both thoſe being abſent, that they are not ours;
Although they breed to us no mean vexation,
Th' one with the ſlip'ry thought of ill-ſpent houres,
And th' other with a carefull expeƈtation.
Thus life is almoſt nothing in effeƈt,
Whereof two parcels never are our owne,
The third being ſuch, as e'r we can refleƈt
Upon th' enjoying of it, is quite gone;
　　The longeſt time not having bounds to meaſure
　　A reall, permanent, and ſolid pleaſure.

HERE END THE FIRST THREE BOOKES OF SIR THOMAS
VRCHARD'S EPIGRAMS.

LAUD TO THE FATHER, WITH THE SON
    AND GHOST, TRIUN, AS FORE
AND STILL HATH BEENE SINCE TIMES BEGUN,
    BE NOW, AND EVERMORE.

THE
TRISSOTETRAS:
OR,
A MOST EXQUISITE TABLE
FOR

Refolving all manner of Triangles, whether
Plain or Sphericall, Rectangular or Obliquangular, with greater facility, then ever
hitherto hath been practifed:

Moft neceffary for all fuch as would attaine to the exact
knowledge of Fortification, Dyaling, Navigation, Surveying, Architecture, the Art of Shadowing, taking of
Heights, and Diftances, the ufe of both the Globes,
Perfpective, the skill of making Maps, the
Theory of the Planets, the calculating of their
motions, and of all other Astronomicall computations whatfoever.

Now lately invented, and perfected, explained, commented on,
and, with all poffible brevity, and perfpicuity, in the hid-
dest, and most re-searched mysteries, from the very
first grounds of the Science it felfe, proved,
and convincingly demonstrated.

By Sir THOMAS URQUHART of *Cromartie*, Knight.

Published for the benefit of those that are Mathematically affected.

LONDON,
Printed by *Iames Young.* 1645.

TO THE

RIGHT HONOURABLE AND MOST NOBLE LADY,

MY DEARE AND LOVING MOTHER,

THE LADY DOWAGER OF CROMARTIE.

MADAM,

FILIALL duty being the more binding in me, that I doe owe it to the beſt
of Mothers; if in the diſcharge thereof I obſerve not the uſuall manner of
other ſonnes, I am the leſſe to blame, that their obligation is not ſo great
as mine. Therefore in that I doe preſume to imprint your Ladiſhips name
in the frontiſpiece of this book, and proffer unto you a Dedication of that
which is beyond the capacity of other Ladies, my boldneſſe therein is the
more excuſable, that in your perſon the moſt vertuous woman in the world
is intreated to patronize that, which by the learnedeſt men may happily be
peruſed.

I am confident, Madam, that your gracious acceptance of this prefent is the more eafily obtainable, in that it is a grand-child of your own whom I thus make tender of to be fheltered under the favour of your protection; and that unto your Ladifhip it will not be the more unwelcome for proceeding from the braines of him, whofe body is not more yours by generation, then by a moft equitable purchafe are the faculties of his mind; the dominion which over my better halfe you by your goodneffe have acquired, being, in regard of my obedience, no leffe voluntary then that of the other is for procreation naturall.

Thus, Madam, unto you doe I totally belong; but fo as that thofe exteriour parts of mine, which by birth are from your Ladifhip derived, cannot be more fortunate in this their fubjection, notwithftanding the egregious advantages of bloud and confanguinity thereby to them accruing, then my felfe am happy, as from my heart I doe acknowledge it, in the juft right your Ladifhip hath to the eternall poffeffion of the never-dying powers of my foule. For though, Soveraignty excepted, there be none in this ifland more honourably defcended then is your Ladifhip, nor whofe progenitors thefe many ages paft, have been, on either fide, of a more noble extraction; yet, laying apart nobility, beauty, wealth, parentage, and friends, which, together with many other gifts of fortune, have hitherto ferved to adorn your Ladifhip beyond others of your fex, who for all thefe have been defervedly renowned; and in fome meafure not efteeming that properly to be yours, the receiving whereof did not altogether depend upon your owne election; it is the treafure of thofe excellent graces wherewith inwardly you are enriched, that in praifing of your Ladifhip is moft to be pitch'd upon, and for the which you are moft highly to be commended, feeing by the means of them, you, from your tendereft yeeres upwards untill this time, in the ftate of both virginity and matrimony, have fo conftantly and indefatigably proceeded in the courfe of vertue, with fuch alacrity fixed your gallant thoughts on the fweetneffe thereof, and thereunto fo firmly and cheerefully devoted all your words and actions, as if righteoufneffe in your Ladifhip had been an inbred quality, and that in your will there had beene no aptitude of declining from the way of reafon.

This much is fufficiently well known to thofe that have at any time enjoyed the honour of your Ladifhip's converfation, by whofe moft unpartiall reports the fplendour of your reputation is both in this and foraine nations accounted precious, in the minds even of thofe that have never feen you. But in fo much more efpecially doe the moft judicious of either fex admire the rare and fublime endowments wherewith your Ladifhip is qualified, that as a patterne of perfection worthy to be univerfally followed, other Ladies, of what dignity foever, are truly by them efteemed of the choifer merit the nearer they draw to the paragon propofed, and refemble your Ladifhip ; for that, by vertue of your beloved fociety, your neighbouring Counteffes, and other great dames of your kindred and acquaintance, become the more illuftrious in your imitation ; amidft whom, as Cynthia amongft the obfcurer planets, your Ladifhip fhines, and darteth the angelick rayes of your matchleffe example on the fpirits of thofe who by their good Genius have been brought into your favourable prefence, to be enlightened by them.

Now, Madam, left by infifting any longer upon this ftraine, I fhould feeme to offend that modefty and humility which, without derogating from your heroick vertues, are feated in a confiderable place of your foule, I will here, in all fubmiffion, moft humbly take my leave of your Ladifhip ; and befeech Almighty God, that it may pleafe his Divine Majefty fo to bleffe your Ladifhip with continuance of dayes, that the fonnes of thofe whom I have not as yet begot may attaine to the happineffe of prefenting unto your Ladifhip a brain-babe of more fufficiencie and confequence ; and that your Ladifhip may live with as much health and profperity to accept thereof, and cherifh it then, as I hope you doe now at your vouchfafing to receive this, which, though difproportionable both to your Ladifhip's high deferts, and to that fervencie of willingneffe in me fometime to make offer

H

of what is of better worth, and more futable to the grandour of your acceptance, in all fincerity of heart, confiding in that candour and ingenuity
wherby your Ladifhip is accuftomed to value gifts according to the intention of the giver, and in all duty and lowlineffe of mind, together with my
felfe in whole, and all my beft endeavours, I tender unto your Ladifhip,
as becometh,

MADAM,

Your Ladifhip's moft affectionate Sonne
and humble Servant,

THOMAS URQUHART.

TO THE READER.

To write of Trigonometry, and not make mention of the illustrious Lord Neper of Marchiston, the inventer of Logarithms, were to be unmindfull of him that is our daily benefactor; these artificiall numbers by him first excogitated and perfected, being of such incomparable use, that by them we may operate more in one day, and with lesse danger of errour, then can be done without them in the space of a whole week. A secret which would have beene so precious to antiquity, that Pythagoras, all the seven wise men of Greece, Archimedes, Socrates, Plato, Euclid, and Aristotle, had, if coævals, joyntly adored him, and unanimously concurred to the deifying of the revealer of so great a mystery; and truly, besides them, a great many other learned men, who for the laboriousnesse of long and various Multiplications, Divisions, and Radicall extractions of severall sorts, were deterred from the prosecuting and divulging of their knowledge in the chiefest and most noble parts of the Mathematicks, would have left behind them diverse exquisite volumes, of an incomprehensible value, if the Arithmetical equality of difference, agreeable to every continued Geometricall proportion, had been made known unto them.

Wherefore, I am infallibly perswaded, that in the estimation of scientifically disposed spirits, the philosophers stone is but trash to this invention, which will alwayes, in their judicious opinions, be accounted of more worth to the Mathematicall world, then was the finding out of America to the King of Spaine, or the discovery of the nearest way to the East Indies would be to the Northerly Occidentall merchants.

What the merit then of the Author is, let the most envious judge; for my owne part, I doe not praise him so much for that he is my compatriot, as I must extoll the happinesse of my countrey for having produced so brave a spark, in whom alone, I may with confidence averre, it is more glorious then if it had beene the conquering kingdome of five hundred potent nations; for, by how much the gifts of the mind are more excellent then those of either body or fortune, by so much the divine effects of the faculties thereof are of greater consequence then what is performed by meer force of armes or chance of warre.

I might say more in commendation of this gallant man, but that my discourse being directed to the Reader, he will possibly expect to be entertained with some other purpose then encomiasticks; and therefore, to undeceive him of those hopes, if any such there be, I will assure him, that to no other end I did require his observance here, but to be informed by me of the laudable endowments of that honourable Baron, whose eminencie above others, wher-ever he be spoke of, deserveth such an ample elogie by it selfe, that the paper, graced with the receiving of his name and character, should not be blurred with the course impression of any other stuffe.

However, the Reader ought not to conceive amisse for his being detained so long upon this eulogistick subject, without the variety of any peculiar instruction bestowed on him, seeing I am certaine there is nothing more advantagious to him, or that more efficaciously can tend to his improvement, then the imitation of that admirable Gentleman, whose immortall fame, in spite of time, will out-last all ages, and look eternity in the face.

The Reader's well-wisher,

T. U.

AN EPÆNETICK AND DOXOLOGETICK EXPRESSE, IN COMMENDATION OF THIS BOOK AND THE AUTHOR THEREOF.

TO ALL PHILOMATHETS.

SEEING Trigonometry, which handsomely unlocketh the choycest and most intime mysteries of the Mathematicks, hath beene hitherto exposed to the world in a method whose intricacy deterreth many from adventuring on it, we are all, and every one of us, by duty bound to acknowledge our selves beholding to the Author of this Treatise ; who, by reducing all the secrets of that noble science into a most exquisite order, hath so facilitated the way to the learner, that in seven weeks, at most, he may attaine to more knowledge therein, then otherwise he could doe for his heart in the space of a twelve-moneth ; and who, for the better encouragement of the studious, hath so gentilely expatiated his spirits upon all its actions, principles, analogies, precepts, and whole subjected matter, that this Mathematicall tractate doth no lesse bespeak him a good Poet and Orator, then by his elaboured poems he hath showne himselfe already a good Philosopher and Mathematician.

Thus doth the various mixture of most excellent qualities in him give such evidence of the transcendent faculties of his mind, that, as the Muses never yet inspired sublimer conceptions in a more refined stile then is to be found in the accurate strain of his most ingenious Epigrams ; so, on the other part, are the abstrusest difficulties of this science by him so neatly unfolded, and with such exactnesse hath he resolved the hardest and most intangled doubts thereof, that I may justly say, what praise in his epistle, or rather preface to the Reader, he hath beene pleased out of his ingenuity to confer on the learned and honourable Neper, doth, without any diminution, in every jot as duly belong unto himselfe.

For I am certainly perswaded, he that useth Logarithms shall not gaine so much time on the worker by the naturall sines and tangents, as by vertue of the succinct manner of calculation shall be got on him that knoweth it not, how compendiously so-ever else, with addition and substraction, or addition alone, he frame his computations. However, he who, together with that of the Logarithms, maketh use of this invention, is in a way which will bring him so straight and readily to the perfect practice of Trigonometry, that, compared with the old beaten path trod upon by Regiomontanus, Ptolomy, and other ancient Mathematicians, it is like the sea voyage, in regard of that by land, betwixt the two Pillars of Hercules, commonly called the Straits of Gibraltar, whereof the one is but of six houres sailing at most, and the other a journey of seven thousand long miles.

If we then consider how a great many, despairing ever to get out, if once entred, of the confused obscurity wherein the doctrine of Triangles hath beene from time to time involved, have rather contented themselves barely with scale and compasse, and other mechanick tooles and instruments, to prosecute their operations, and in any reasonable measure to glance somewhat neare the truth, then thorough so many pesterments and harsh incumbrances, to touch it to a point in its most indivisible and infallible reality ; and how others, for all their being more industrious in proving their conclusions by the mediums from which they are necessarily inferr'd, are neverthelesse, even when they have bestowed half an age in the trigonometricall practice, oftentimes so farre to seek, that without a great deale of premeditation, advisement, and recollecting of themselves, they know not how to discusse some queries, corollaries, problems, consectaries, proportions, wayes of perpendicular falling, and other such like occurring debatable matters, incident to the scientifick measuring of Triangles ; we cannot choose, these things being maturely prepended, but be much taken with the pregnancy of this device, whereby we shall sooner hit to a minute upon the verity of an angle or side demanded, and trace it to the very source and originall from whence it flowes, then another mechanically shall be able to come within three degrees thereof, although he cannot, for the same little he doth, afford any reason at all ; and so suddenly resolve any Trigonometricall question, without paines or labour, how perplexed soever it be, with all the dependances thereto belonging, as if it were a knowledge meerly infused from above, and revealed by the peculiar inspiration of some favourable angel.

Besides these advantages, administred unto us by the meanes of this exquisite book, this maine commodity accreweth to the diligent perusers of it, that, instead of three quarters of a yeere, usually by professors allowed to their schollers for the right conceiving of this science, which notwithstanding, through any little discontinuance, is by them so apt to be forgotten, that the expence of a week or two will hardly suffice to reseat it in their memories, they shall not need by this method to bestow above a moneth, and with such ease and facility for retention when they have learned and acquired it, that, if multiplicity of businesses or serious plodding upon other studies happen to blot it out of their minds, they may as firmly recover in one quarter of an hour the whole knowledge and remembrance thereof, as when they had it best, and were most punctually versed in it.

A secret in my opinion so precious, that, as the Author spoke of Marchiston, I may with the like pertinencie avouch of him, that his countrey and kindred would not have been more honoured by him had he purchased millions of gold, and severall rich territories of a great and vast extent, then for this subtile and divine invention, which will out-last the continuance of any inheritance, and remaine fresh in the understandings of men of profound literature, when houses and possessions will change their owners, the wealthy become poor, and the children of the needy enjoy the treasures of those whose heires are impoverished.

Therefore, seeing for the many-fold uses thereof in divers arts and sciences, in speculation and practice, peace and war, sport and earnest, with the admirable furtherances we reape by it in the knowledge of sea and land, and heaven and earth, it cannot be otherwise then permanent, together with the Author's fame, so long as any of those endure; I will, God willing, in the ruines of all these, and when time it selfe is expired, in testimony of my thankfulnesse in particular for so great a benefit, if after the resurrection there be any complementall affability, expresse my selfe then as I doe now,

The Author's most affectionate, and most

humbly devoted servant,

J. A.

IN ERUDITUM D. THOMÆ VRQUHARTI EQUITIS TRISSOTETRADOS LIBRUM.

SI CUPIS ÆTHERIOS TUTÒ PERAGRARE MEATUS,
    ET SULCARE AUDES SI VADA SALSA MARIS;
VEL TIBI SI CORDI EST TERRÆ SPATIA AMPLA METIRI,
    HUC ADES, HUNC DOCTUM PERCIPE MENTE LIBRUM.
HOC, SINE DÆDALEIS PENNIS VOLITARE PER AURAS,
    ET SINE NEPTUNO NARE PER ALTA VALES;
HOC DUCE, JAM LYBICOS POTERIS SUPERARE CALORES,
    ATQUE PATI SCYTHICI FRIGORA SÆVA POLI.
PERGE THOMA; TALI TANDEM GAUDEBIT ALUMNO
    SCOTIA, QUAM SCRIPTIS TOLLIS IN ASTRA TUIS.

AL. ROSS.

The plane Triangles have 13. Moods. Planorectangulars 7.

Upalem   Ubeman.   Uphener.   Ekarul.   Egalem.   Echemun.   Etenar.

Planobliquangulars 6.

Danarele.   Therelabmo.   Zelemabne.   Xemenoro.   Shenerolem.   Pferelema.

The Sphericals have 28. Moods.

Orthogonosphericals 16.

1 Upalam. 2. Ubamen. 3. Uphanep.
4. Ukelamb. 5. Ugemon. 6. Uchener
7. Etalum. 8. Edamon. 9. Ethaner.
10 Ezolum. 11. Exoman. 12. Epfoner
13. Alamun. 14. Amaner.
15 Enerul. 16. Erelam.

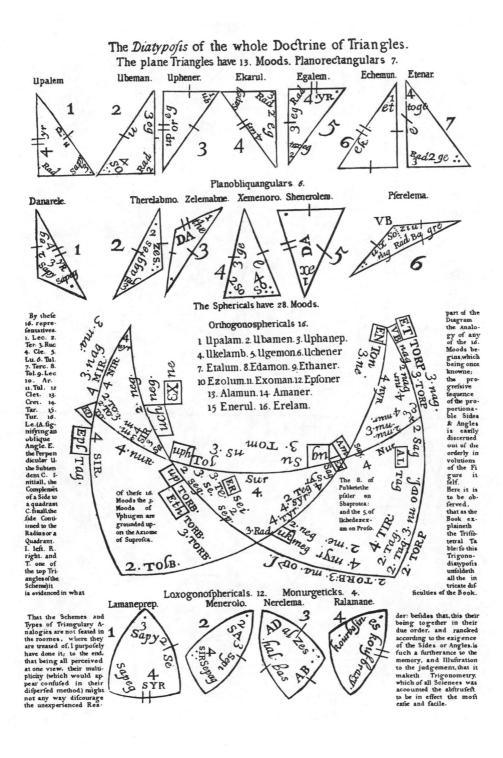

By these 16. representatives. 1. Lec. 2. Ter. 3. Ruc 4. Cle. 5. Lu. 6. Tul. 7. Terc. 8. Tol. 9. Lec 10. Ar. 11. Tul. 12 Clet. 13. Cret. 14. Tar. 15. Tur. 16. Le. (A. fignifying an oblique Angle. E. the Perpendicular U. the Subtendent C. Initiall, the Complement of a Side to a quadrant C. finall, the fide Continued to the Radius or a Quadrant. I. left. R. right. and T. one of the top Triangles of the Scheme) it is evidenced in what

Of these 16. Moods the 3. Moods of Vphugen are grounded upon the Axiome of Suprofca.

The 8. of Pubketethe pfaler on Sbaprotca: and the 5. of Uchedezexam on Profo.

part of the Diagram the Analogy of any of the 16. Moods begins, which being once knowne; the progrefsive fequence of the proportionable Sides & Angles is eafily difcerned out of the orderly involutions of the Figure it felf. Here it is to be obferved, that as the Book explaineth the Triffotetral Table: fo this Trigonodiatyposis unfoldeth all the intricate difficulties of the Book.

Loxogonofphericals. 12.   Monurgeticks. 4.

Lamaneprep.   Menerolo.   Nerclema.   Ralamane.

That the Schemes and Types of Triangulary Analogies are not feated in the roomes, where they are treated of, I purpofely have done it; to the end, that being all perceived at one view, their multiplicity (which would appear confufed in their difperfed method) might not any way difcourage the unexperienced Rea-

der: befides that, this their being together in their due order, and rancked according to the exigence of the Sides or Angles, is fuch a furtherance to the memory, and Illufiration to the judgement, that it maketh Trigonometry, which of all Sciences was accounted the abftrufeft, to be in effect the moft eafie and facile.

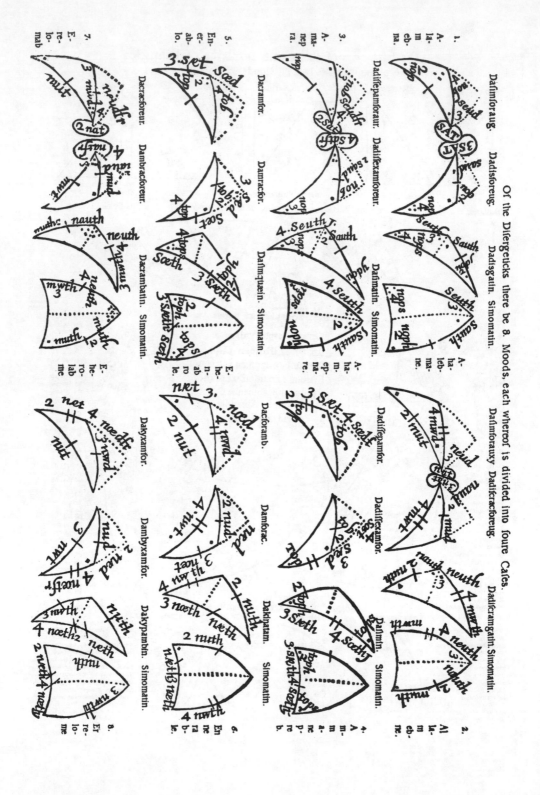

Dafimforaug. Dadisforeug; Dadisgauin. Simomatin. Dafimforauxy Dadifcracforeug.

1.
A- la-
m eb-
na.

2.
Al la-
m eb-
ne.

Dadiffepamforaur. Dadiffexamforeur.

3.
nep ma-
na.
ra.

4.
A- m-
eb-
ne.

Dacramfor. Damracfor.

Dadiffepamfor. Dadiffexamfor.

5.
En- er-
ab-
lo.

Dacracforeur. Dambracfioreur.

Dafimquein. Simomatin. Dafimln. Simomatin.

A- ha-
eb-
re.

A- ha-
ma-
re.

Dacrambatin. Simomatin. Dadifcramgatin.Simomatin.

Dacforamb. Dadifcexamfor. Damforac.

6.
E- n-
ab-
le.

7.
E- re-
lo-
mab

Dakyxamfor. Dambyxamfor. Dakipatam. Simomatin.

8.
Ei re-
lo-
me

Dakypambin. Simomatin.

THE

TRISSOTETRAS.

POSITIONS.

EVERY circle is divided into three hundred and sixty parts, called degrees, whereof each one is sexagesimated, subsexagesimated, resubsexagesimated, and biresubsexagesimated, in minutes, seconds, thirds, fourths, and so far forth as any computist is pleased to proceed, for the exactnesse of a research, in the calculation of any orbiculary dimension.

2. As degrees are the measure of arches, so are they of angles; but that those are called circumferentiall, these angulary degrees, each whereof is the three hundred and sixtieth part of four right angles, which are nothing else but the surface of a plain to any point circumjacent, for any space whatsoever about a point, is divided in 360 parts; and the better to conceive the analogie that is betwixt these two sorts of graduall measures, we must know, that there is the same proportion of any angle to 4 right angles, as of an arch of so many circumferential degrees to the whole circumference.

3. Hence it is that the same number serves the angle and the arch that vaults it, and that divers quantities are measured, as it were, with the same graduall measure. Angles and arches then are analogicall, and the same reason is of both.

4. Seeing any given proportion may be found in numbers, and that any two quantities have the same proportion that the two numbers have, according to the which they are measured; if for the measuring of triangles, there must be certain proportions, of all the parts of a triangle to one another, known, and those proportions explained in numbers, it is most certain, all magnitudes being figures, at least in power, and all figures either triangles or triangled, that the arithmeticall solution of any geometricall question, dependeth on the doctrine of triangles.

I

5. And though the proportion betwixt the parts of a triangle cannot be without some errour, because of crooked lines to right lines, and of crooked lines amongst themselves, the reason is inscrutable, no man being able to finde out the exact proportion of the diameter to the circumference; yet both in plain triangles, where the measure of the angles is of a different species from the sides, and in sphericalls, wherein both the angles and sides are of a circular nature, crooked lines are in some measure reduced to right lines by the definition of quantity, which right lines, viz. sines, tangents, and secants, applyed to a circle, have in respect of the radius, or half-diameter.

6. And therefore, though the circle's quadrature be not found out, it being in our power to make the diameter, or the semi-diameter, which is the radius of as many parts as we please, and being sure so much the more that the radius be taken, the error will be the lesser; for albeit the sines, tangents and secants, be irrationall thereto for the most part, and their proportion inexplicable by any number whatsoever, whither whole or broken, yet if they be rightly made, they will be such as that in them all no number will be different from the truth by an integer, or unity of those parts whereof the radius is taken; which is so exactly done by some, especially by Petiscus, who assumed a radius of twenty-six places, that according to his supputation, the diameter of the earth being known, and the globe thereof supposed to be perfectly round, one should not fail in the dimension of its whole circuit, the nine hundreth thousand scantling of the million part of an inch, and yet not be able, for all that, to measure it without amisse; for so indivisible the truth of a thing is, that come you never so near it, unlesse you hit upon it just to a point, there is an errour still.

DEFINITIONS.

A cord, or subtense, is a right line drawn from one extremity to the other of an arch.

2. A right sine is the half cord of the double arch proposed, and from one extremity of the arch falleth perpendicularly on the radius, passing by the other end thereof.

3. A tangent is a right line, drawn from the secant by one end of the arch, perpendicularly on the extremity of the diameter, passing by the other end of the said arch.

4. A secant is the prolonged radius, which passeth by the upper extremity of the arch, till it meet with the sine tangent of the said arch.

5. Complement is the difference betwixt the lesser arch and a quadrant, or betwixt a right angle and an acute.

6. The complement to a semi-circle, is the difference betwixt the half-circumference and any arch lesser, or betwixt two right angles and an oblique angle, whither blunt or sharp.

7. The versed sine is the remainder of the radius, the sine complement being sub-

tracted from it; and though great use may be made of the versed sines, for finding out of the angles by the sides, and sides by the angles, yet in logarithmicall calculations they are altogether uselesse, and therefore in my Trissotetras there is no mention made of them.

8. In amblygonosphericalls, which admit both of an extrinsecall and intrinsecall demission of the perpendicular, nineteen severall parts are to be considered; viz. the perpendicular, the subtendentall, the subtendentine, two cosubtendents, the basall, the basidion, the chief segment of the base, two cobases, the double verticall, the verticall, the verticaline, two coverticalls, the next cathetopposite, the prime cathetopposite, and the two cocathetopposites; fourteen wherof, to wit, the subtendentall, the subtendentine, the cosubtendents, the basall, the basidion, the cobases, the verticall, the verticaline, the coverticalls, and cocathetopposites, are called the first, either subtendent, base, topangle, or cocathetopposite, whither in the great triangle or the little, or in the correctangle, if they be ingredients of that rectangular whereof most parts are known, which parts are alwayes a subtendent and a cathetopposite; but if they be in the other triangle, they are called the second subtendents, bases, and so forth.

9. The externall double verticall is included by the perpendicular and subtendentall, and divided by the subtendentine; the internall is included by cosubtendents, and divided by the perpendicular.

APODICTICKS.

The angles made by a right line falling on another right line, are equall to two right angles; because every angle being measured by an arch, or part of a circumference, and a right angle by ninety degrees, if upon the middle of the ground line, as center, be described a semi-circle, it will be the measure of the angles, comprehended betwixt the falling and sustaining lines.

2. Hence it is that the four opposite angles made by one line crossing another, are always each to its own opposite equall; for if upon the point of intersection, as center, be described a circle, every two of those angles will fill up the semi-circle; therefore the first and second will be equall to the second and third, and consequently the second, which is the common angle to both these couples, being removed, the first will remain equall to the third, and by the same reason, the second to the fourth, which was to be demonstrated.

3. If a right line falling upon two other right lines make the alternat angles equall, these lines must needs be paralell; for if they did meet, the alternat angles would not be equall, because in all plain triangles, the outward angle is greater then any of the remote inward angles, which is proved by the first.

4. If one of the sides of a triangle be produced, the outward angle is equall to both

the inner and opposite angles together; because according to the acclining or declining of the conterminall side, is left an angulary space for the receiving of a paralell to the opposite, in the point of whose occourse at the base, the exterior angle is divided into two, which for their like and alternat situation with the two interior angles, are equall each to its own, conform to the nature of angles made by a right line crossing divers paralells.

5. From hence we gather, that the three angles of a plain triangle are equall to two rights; for the two inward being equall to the externall one, and there remaining of the three but one, which was proved in the first Apodictick to be the externall angle's complement to two rights, it must needs fall forth, what are equall to a third being equall amongst themselves, that the three angles of a plain triangle are equall to two right angles, the which we undertook to prove.

6. By the same reason, the two acute of a rectangled plain triangle are equall to one right angle, and any one of them, the others complement thereto.

7. In every circle, an angle from the centre is two in the limb, both of them having one part of the circumference for base; for being an externall angle, and consequently equall to both the intrinsecall angles, and therefore equall to one another; because of their being subtended by equall bases, viz. the semi-diameter, it must needs be the double of the foresaid angle in the limb.

8. Triangles standing between two paralells, upon one and the same base, are equall; for the identity of the base whereon they are seated, together with the equidistance of the lines, within the which they are confined, maketh them of such a nature, that how long so ever the line paralell to the base be protracted, the diagonall cutting of in one of the triangles, as much of breadth as it gains of length, the one's losse accruing to the profit of the other, quantifies them both to an equality, the thing we did intend to prove.

9. Hence do we inferre, that triangles betwixt two paralells are in the same proportion with their bases.

10. Therefore, if, in a triangle, be drawn a paralell to any of the sides, it divideth the other sides, through which it passeth, proportionally; for, besides that it maketh the four segments to be four bases, it becomes, if two diagonall lines be extended from the ends thereof to the ends of its paralell, a common base to two equall triangles, to which two, the triangle of the first two segments having reference, according to the difference of their bases, and these two being equall, as it is to the one, so must it be to the other, and therefore the first base must be to the second, which are the segments of one side of the triangle, as the third to the fourth, which are the segments of the second, all which was to be demonstrated.

11. From hence do we collect, that equiangled triangles have their sides about the equall angles proportionall to one another. " This," says Petiscus, " is the golden foundation, and chief ground of Trigonometry."

12. An angle in a semi-circle is right, because it is equall to both the angles at the base, which, by cutting the diameter in two, is perceivable to any.

13. Of four proportionall lines, the rectangled figure, made of the two extreames, is equall to the rectangular composed of the means; for, as four and one are equall to two and three by an arithmetical proportion, and the fourth term geometrically exceeding, or being lesse then the third, as the second is more or lesse then the first; what the fourth hath, or wanteth, from and above the third, is supplyed, or impaired by the surplusage or deficiency of the first from and above the second. These analogies being still taken in a geometricall way, make the oblong of the two middle equall to that of the extreams, which was to be proved.

14. In all plain rectangled triangles, the ambients are equall in power to the subtendent; for, by demitting from the right angle a perpendicular, there will arise two correctangles, from whose equiangularity with the great rectangle will proceed such a proportion amongst the homologall sides of all the three, that if you can set them right in the rule, beginning your analogy at the main subtendent, seeing the including sides of the totall rectangle prove subtendents in the partiall correctangles, and the bases of those rectanglets the segments of the great subtendent, it will fall out, that as the main subtendent is to his base, on either side, for either of the legs of a rectangled triangle, in reference to one another, is both base and perpendicular, so the same bases, which are subtendents in the lesser rectangles, are to their bases the segment of the prime subtendent. Then by the golden rule we find, that the multiplying of the middle termes, which is nothing else but the squaring of the comprehending sides of the prime rectangular, affords two products equall to the oblongs made of the great subtendent, and his respective segments, the aggregat whereof, by equation, is the same with the square of the chief subtendent, or hypotenusa, which was to be demonstrated.

15. In every totall square, the supplements about the partiall and interior squares are equall the one to the other; for, by drawing a diagonall line, the great square being divided into two equall triangles, because of their standing on equall bases betwixt two paralells, by the ninth Apodectick, it is evident that, in either of these great triangles, there being two partiall ones equall to the two of the other, each to his own, by the same reason of the ninth. If, from equall things, viz. the totall triangles, be taken equall things, to wit, the two pairs of partiall triangles, equall things must needs remain, which are the foresaid supplements, whose equality I undertook to prove.

16. If a right line, cut into two equall parts, be increased, the square made of the additional line, and one of the bisegments, joyned in one, lesse by the square of the half of the line bisected, is equall to the oblong contained under the prolonged line, and the line of continuation; for, if annexedly to the longest side of the proposed oblong, be described the foresaid square, there will jet out beyond the quadrat figure a space or rectangle, which, for being powered by the bisegment and additionall line, will be equall to the neerest supplement, and consequently to the other, the equality

of supplements being proved by the last Apodectick, by vertue whereof, a gnomon in the great square, lacking nothing of its whole area but the space of the square of the bisected line, is apparent to equalize the parallelogram proposed, which was to be demonstrated.

17. From hence proceedeth this sequell, that, if from any point without a circle, two lines cutting it be protracted to the other extremity thereof, making two cords, the oblongs contained under the totall lines, and the excesse of the subtenses, are equall one to another; for, whether any of the lines passe through the center, or not, if the subtenses be bisected, seeing all lines from the center fall perpendicularly upon the chordall point of bisection, because the two semi-diameters, and bisegments sub-sterned under equall angles, in two triangles, evince the equality of the third angle, to the third, by the fift Apodictick, which two angles being made by the falling of one right line upon another, must needs be right by the tenth definition of the first of Euchilde. The Bucarnon of Pythagoras, demonstrated in my fourteenth Apodictick, will, by quadrosubductions of ambients from one another, and their quadrobiquadre-quations, with the hypotenusa, together with other analogies of equation with the powers of like rectangular triangles, comprehended within the same circle, manifest the equality of long squares, or oblongs radically meeting in an exterior point, and made of the prolonged subtenses, and the lines of interception betwixt the limb of the circle, and the point of concourse, *quod probandum fuit*.

18. Now, to look back on the eleaventh Apodictick, where, according to Petiscus, I said, that upon the mutuall proportion of the sides of equiangled triangles, is founded the whole science of Trigonometry, I do here respeak it, and with confidence maintain the truth thereof; because, besides many others, it is the ground of these subsequent theorems: 1. The right sine of an arch is to its co-sine, as the radius to the co-tangent of the said arch. 2. The co-sine of an arch is to its sine, as the radius to the tangent of the said arch. 3. The sines and co-secants, the secants and co-sines, and the tangents and co-tangents, are reciprocally proportionall. 4. The radius is a mean proportionall, betwixt the sine and co-secant, the secant and co-sine, and the tangent and co-tangent. The verity of all these, if a quadrant be described, and upon the two radiuses two tangents, and two or three sines be erected, which in respect of other arches will be co-sines and co-tangents, and two secants drawn, which are likewise co-secants, from the center to the top of the tangents, will appear by the foresaid reasons out of my eleaventh Apodictick.

THE TRISSOTETRAS.

Plain.   Sphericall.

Plain Trissotetras.

Axiomes four.

1. Rulerst,   .   { Vradesso :   Directory :   Enodandas.
               Eradetul :   Vpechet :   3. Orth. 1. Obl.
               Directorie :   Enodandas   } 3. Ax. Grediftal : Dir. θ.

2. Eproso,   .   { Pubkegdaxesh :   4. Orth.
                          3. Obl.   } 4. Ax. Bagrediffiu : Dir. ψ.

THE PLANORECTANGULAR TABLE :

Figures four.

1. Va*le,   .   { Datus Quæsitas.   *Resolvers.*
               Vp* Al§em.   Rad—V—Sapy(☞ Yr.
               Vb*em§an.   V—Rad—Eg(☞ So.

2. Ve*mane,   *Præsubserv.*   *Possubserv.*
               Vph*en§er   Vb*em§an.   Vp*al§em, or, Eg*al§em.

3. Ena*ve,   .   { Ek*ar§ul.   Sapeg—Eg—Rad(☞ Vr.
               Eg*al§em.   Rad—Taxeg—Eg(☞ Yr.
                          Præsubserv.   *Possubserv.*

4. Ere*va,   .   { Ech*em§un.   Et*en§ar.   Ek*ar§ul.
               Et*en§ar.   E—Ge—Rad(☞ Toge.

THE PLANOBLIQUANGULAR TABLE :

Figures four.

1. Alahe*me, | Da*na*re§le.   Sapeg—Eg—Sapyr(☞ Yr.
              { The*re*lab§mo.   Aggres—Zes—Talfagros(☞ Talzos.

2. Emena*role,   *Præsubserv.*   *Possubserv.*
              { Ze*le*mah§ne.   The*re*lab§mo.   Da*na*re§le.
              { Xe*me*no§ro.   E—So—Ge(☞ So.

3. Enero*lome,   *Præsubserv.*   *Possubserv.*
              { She*ne*ro§lem.   Xe*ne*no§ro.   Da*na*re§le.
                        Præsubserv.   *Possubserv.*

4. Erele*a,   . | Pse*re*le§ma.   Bagreziu.   Vb*em§an.
     Finall Resolver.   Vxiuo—Rad— uα(☞ Sor.

THE SPHERICALL TRISSOTETRAS.

Axiomes three.

1. Suprosca.
   Dir. uphugen.

2. Sbaprotca.
   pubkutethepsaler.

3. Seproso.
   uchedezexam.

THE ORTHOGONOSPHERICAL TABLE.

Figures 6.   Datoquæres 16.

	Dat. Quæs.	*Resolvers.*
1. Valam*menep,	Vp*al§am.	Torb—Tag—Nu☞Mir.
	Vb*am§en.	Nag—Mu—Torp☞Myr. *or,*
		Torp—Mu—Lag☞Myr.
	Vph*an§ep.	Tol—Sag—Su☞Syr.
2. Veman*nore,	Vk*el§amb.	Meg—Torp—Mu☞Nir. *or,*
		Torp—Teg—Mu☞Nir.
	Ug*em§on.	Su—Seg—Tom☞Sir. *or,*
		Tom—Seg—Ru☞Sir,
	Uch*en§er.	Neg—To—Nu☞Nyr. *or,*
		To—Le—Nu☞Nyr.
3. Enar*rulome,	Et*al§um.	Torp—Me—Nag☞Mur.
	Ed*am§on.	To—Neg—Sa☞Nir.
	Eth*an§er.	Torb—Tag—Se☞Tyr.
4. Erol*lumane,	Ez*ol§um.	Sag—Sep—Rad☞Sur. *or,*
		Rad—Seg—Rag☞Sur.
	Ex*om§an.	Ne—To—Nag☞Sir. *or,*
		To—Le—Nag☞Sir.
	Eps*on§er.	Tag—Tolb—Te☞Syr. *or,*
		Tolb—Mag—Te☞Syr.
5. Acha*ve,	Al*am§un.	Tag—Torb—Ma☞Nur. *or,*
		Torb—Mag—Ma☞Nur.
	Am*an§er.	Say—Nag—Tw☞Nyr. *or,*
		Tw—Noy—Ray☞Nyr.
6. Eshe*va,	En*er§ul.	Ton—Neg—Ne☞Nur.
	Er*el§am.	Sei—Teg—Torb☞Tir. *or,*
		Torb—Tepi—Rexi☞Tir.

THE LOXOGONOSPHERICAL TRISSOTETRAS.

Monurgetick   Disergetick.

THE MONURGETICK LOXOGONOSPHERICAL TABLE.

Axiomes two.

1. Seproso. Dir. Lame.   2. Parses. Dir. Nera.

Figures two.   ### Moods two.

Figures.	*Datas. Quæs.*	*Resolvers.*
1. Datamista,	{ Lam*an*ep§rep. Me*ne*ro§lo.	Sapeg—Se—Sapy☞Syr. Sepag—Se—Sapi☞Sir. ad
2. Datapura,	{ Ne*re*le§ma. Ra*la*ma§ne.	Hal Basaldileg Sad Sab Re Regals Bis*ir. ab Parses—Powto—Parsadsah☞Powsalverti R. Kour Bfasines (ereled) Kouf Br*axypopyx.

THE LOXOGONOSPHERICAL DISERGETICKS

Axiomes four.

1. Na Badprosver.   2. Naverpror Tes.   3. Siubpror Tab.   4. Niubprodnesver.
   Dir Alama.   Allera.   Ammena.   Errenna.

Figures 4.   ### Moods 8.

Fig.	M.	Sub.	Res.	Dat. Præn.	Cathetothesis.	Final Resolvers.
Ab } A	A				Cafregpiq.	
	La	Vp	Tag	ut *Op §At	Dasimforaug	Sat-nop-Seud †nob. Kir.
A	Meb	Al	Nu	ud *Ob §Aud	Dadisforeug	Saud-nob-Sat †nop. Ir.
	Na	Am	Mir	uth*Oph§Auth	Dadisgatin	Sauth-noph-Seuth †nops Ir.
1. { Leb } 2.		*Sub.*	*Res.*	*Dat. Præn.*	*Cathetothesis.*	*Final Resolvers.*
	Al				Cafyxigeq.	
Ma	La	Vp	Tag	ut *op §at	dasimforauxy	nat -mut -neud † mwd
	Meb	Al	Nu	ud *ob §aud	dadiscracforeug	naud -mud -nat † mwt
Ne }	Ne	Am	Mir	uth*oph§auth	dadiscramgatin	nauth-muth-neuth † mwth

K

Fig.	M.					Cathetothesis.		Plus minus.	

A	A	Sub.	Re.	Dat.Pr.		Cafriq.		Final Resolvers.	Sindifora.
									At
Ha	Ma	up	Tag	ut *Op§At		Dadissepamforaur	Nop-Sat-Nob🖘Seudfr	Autir.	
	Nep	al	Nu	ud *Ob§Aud		Dadissexamforeur	Nop-Saud-Nop🖘Satfr	Eutir.	
	Ra	Am	Mir	uth*Oph§Auth		Dasimatin	Noph-Sauth-Nops🖘Seuthj	Authir.	
Mep	4.								Aud
						Cathetothesis.		Plus minus.	
	Am	Sub.	Re.	Dat. Pr.		Cafregpagiq.		Final Resolvers.	Sindiforiu.
									Æt
Na	Ma	ub	Mu	ut *Op§Æt		Dadissepamfor	Tob-Top-Sæt 🖘Sœdfr	Dyr.	
	Nep	Am	Lag	ud *Ob§Æd		Dadissexamfor	Top-Tob-Sæd 🖘Sœtfr	Dyr.	
Re	Reb	En	Myr	uth*Oph§æth		Dasimin	Tops-Toph-SÆth🖘Sœthj æth	Syr.	Æd

Fig.	M.					Cathetothesis.	

Eh	En	Sub.	Re.	Dat. Pr.		Cafregpigeq.		Final Resolvers.
	Er	ub	Mu	ut *Op §æt		Dacramfor	Sœd-Top-Sæt🖘 Tob. Kir.	
En	Ab	Am	Lag	ud *Ob §æd		Damracfor	Sœt-Tob-Sæd🖘 Top. Ir.	
	Lo	En	Myr	uth*Oph§æth		Dasimquæin	Sœth-Toph-Sæth🖘 Tops. Ir.	
Ab	6.					Cathetothesis.	
	En	Sub.	Re.	Dat. Q. Pr.		Cafregpiq.		Final Resolvers.
Ro	Ne	ub	Mu	ut *Op §æt		Dacforamb	Næt-Nut-Nœd🖘 Nwd. Yr.	
	Rah	Am	Lag	ud *Ob §æd		Damforac	Næd-Nut-Nœt🖘 Nwt. Yr.	
Le	Le	En	Myr	uth*Oph§æth		Dakinatam	Næth-Nuth-Nœth🖘 Nwth. Yr.	

Fig.	M.					Cathetothesis.		Plus minus.	

Eh	E	Sub.	Re.	Dat. Pr.		Cafriq.		Final Resolvers.	Sindifora.
									At
Er	Re	Up	Tag	ut *Op§at		Dacracforaur	Mut-Nat-Mwd🖘Neudfr	Autir.	
	Lo	Al	Nu	ud *Ob§aud		Dambracforeur	Mud-Naud-Mwt🖘Natfr	Eutir.	
	Mab	Am	Mir	uth*Oph§auth		Dacrambatin	Muth-Nauth-Mwth🖘Neuthj	Authir	Aud
Om	8.					Cathetothesis.		Plus Minus.	
	Er	Sub.	Re.	Dat. Pr.		Cacurgyq.		Final Resolvers.	Sindiforiu.
									Æt
Ab	Re	ub	Mu	ut *Op§æt		Dakyxamfor	Nut-Næt-Nwd🖘 Nœdf	Dyr.	
	Lo	Am	Lag	ud *Ob§æd		Dambyxamfor	Nud-Næd-Mwt🖘 Nœtfr	Dyr.	
Me	Me	En	Myr	uth*Oph§æth		Dakypambin	Nuth-Næth-Nwth🖘Nœthj ÆthSyr.		Æd

The novelty of these words I know will seeme strange to some, and to the eares of illiterate hearers sound like termes of conjuration ; yet seeing that since the very infancie of learning, such inventions have beene made use of, and new words coyned, that the knowledge of severall things representatively confined within a narrow compasse, might the more easily be retained in a memory susceptible of their impression, (as is apparent by the names of Barbara, Celarent, Darii, Ferio, and fifteen more syllogistick moods, and by those likewise of Gammuth, A-re, B-mi, C-fa-uth, and seventeen other steps of Guido's Scale, which are universally received by men of understanding, and that have their spirits tuned to the harmony of reason,) I know not why Logick and Musick should be rather fitted with such helps then Trigonometrie, which, for certitude of demonstration, hath been held inferior to no science, and for sublimity and variety of object, is the primest of the Mathematicks. This is the cause why I framed the Trissotetras, wherein the termes by me invented, without regard of the initiall letters of the words by them expressed, are composed of such as, joyned together, are of most easie pronunciation ; as the tangent complement of a subtendent is sooner uttered by *Mu* then by T C S ; and the secant complement of the side required, by *Ry*, then in the usuall apocopating way, by the first syllables or letters of secant complement, side, and required ; and considering that without opening of the mouth no word can be spoken, which overture is performed by the vowel, to all the sides and angles I designed vowels, that in the coalescencie of syllables, sines, tangents, and secants might the better consound therewith.

THE EXPLANATION OF THE TRISSOTETRAS.

A. signifieth an angle ; *Ab.* in the resolvers signifieth *abstraction,* but in the figures and datoquæres the *angle between.* *Ac.* or *Ak.* the *acute angle.* *Ad.* addition. *Æ.* the first base. *Amb.* or *Am.* an obtuse angle. *As.* angles in the plurall number. *At.* the double verticall, *whether externall or internall.* *Au.* the first verticall angle. *Ay,* the angle adjoyning to the side required.

B. or *Ba.* the true base. *Bis,* the double of a thing.

Ca. the perpendicular. *Cra.* the concurse of a given and required side. *Cur.* the concurse of two given sides.

D. the partiall or little rectangle or rectanglet. *Da.* the datas. *Di.* or *Dif.* the difference. *Dir.* the directories. *D. q.* Datoquæres. *Diss.* of unlike natures.

E. a side. *Eb.* the side between. *Enod.* enodandas. *Ereled.* turned into sides. *Es,* sides in the plurall number. *Ei,* the side conterminall with the angle required. *Eu,* the second verticall angle.

F. the new base, or angularie base, it being an angle converted into a side. *Fig.* figures. *Fin. Res.* finall resolvers. *For,* or *Fo,* outwardly, often made use of in the Cathetothesis. *Fr.* a subducting of a lesser from a greater, whether it be side or angle.

G. An angle or side given. *Gre,* or *aggre,* the summe or aggregat.

Hal, or *al,* the halfe.

I. Vowel, an angle required. *J. Consonant,* the addition of one thing to another used in the clausuls of some of the finall resolvers. *In,* intus or inwardly, and sometimes turned into *Iu,* the segments of the base, or the segmented base.

K. The complement of an angle to a semicircle.

L. The secant. *Leg,* one of the comprehending sides of an angle. This representative is once only mentioned.

M. A tangent complement.

N. A sine complement.

O. An opposite angle, or rather cathetopposite. *Ob.* the next cathetopposite angle, by some called the first opposite. *Op.* the prime cathetopposite angle, by some called the second opposite. *Oph.* the first of the coopposite angles. *Orth.* an acute angle. *Ops.* the second of the coopposits. *Os.* opposite angles in the plurall number. *Oe.* the second base. *Ou.* the angle opposite to the base.

P. Opposite, whether angle or side. *Par.* a parallelogram or oblong. *Præs.* præsubservient. *Possub.* possubservient. *Pro.* proportionall. *Prod.* directly proportionall. *Pror.* reciprocally proportionall. *Pow.* the square of a line. *Præn.* prænoscendas.

Q. Continued if need be. *Quæs.* quæsitas. *Quæ.* quære or required.

R. The secant complement, and sometimes in the middle of the Cathetothesis signifies required, as alwayes in the latter end of a finall resolver it doth by way of emphasis, when it followes *I.* or *Y.* *R.* likewise in the axiom of Rulerst, stands for radius. *Ra.* the radius, and in the scheme, the middle angularie radius.

S. The sine, and in the close of some resolvers, the summe. *Sim.* of like affection or nature. *Subs.* subservient.

T. The tangent. *To.* the radius or total sine, but in the diagram it is taken for the left angularie radius. *Tw.* the right angularie radius in the scheme proposed. *Tol.* the first hypotenusal radius thereof. *Tom.* the second hyp. radius. *Ton.* the third hyp. rad. *Tor.* the fourth hyp. rad. *Tolb.* the basiradius on the left hand. *Torb.* the basiradius on the right. *Tolp.* the cathetorabdos, or radius on the left. *Torp.* the cathetoradius on the right. *Th.* the correctangle.

U. The subtendent side. *V.* consonant, to avoid vastnesse of gaping, expresseth the same in severall figures. *Ur.* the subtendent required.

W. The second subtendent.

X. Adjacent or conterminal.

Y. The side required.

Z. The difference of segments, and is the same with *di,* or *dif.*

Neverthelesse the reader may be pleased to observe, that no consonants in the figures or moods are representative save P. and B., and that only in a few ; both these two, and all the other consonants, merely serving to expresse the order and series of the moods and figures respectively amongst themselves, and of their constitutive parts in regard of one another.

ANIMADVERSIONS.

In the letter *T.* I have been something large in the enumeration of severall radiuses ; for there being eleven made use of in the grand scheme, whereof eight are circumferentiall and three angularie, that they might be the better distinguished from one another, when falling in proportion we should have occasion to expresse them, I thought good to allot to every one of them its owne peculiar character : all which I have done with the more exactnesse, that by the variety of the radiuses amongst themselves, when any one of them in particular is pitched upon, we may the sooner know what part of the diagram, by meanes thereof, is fittest for the resolving of any orthogonosphericall problem ; though indeed, I must confesse, when sometimes to a question propounded I adapt a figure apart, I doe indifferently, excluding all other characters, make use of *To,* or *Rad,* or *R.* onely, for the totall sine, which, without any obscurity or confusion at all, I have practised for brevities sake.

Likewise, it being my maine designe in the framing of this table, to make all capable trigonometrically-affected students with much facility and little labour attaine to the whole knowledge of the noble science of the doctrine of triangles, I deemed it expedient, the more firmly and readily to imprint the severall datoquæres or præscinded problems thereof in their memories, to accommodate them accordingly with letters proper for the purpose ; which, if the ingenious reader will be pleased to consider, he will find, by the very letters themselves, the place and number of each datoquære. This is the reason why my Trissotetras, conforme to the etymologie of its name, is in so many divers ternaries and quæternaries divided ; and that the sharp, meane, blunt, double, and liquid consonants of the Greek alphabet, are so orderly bestowed in their severall roomes, being all and every one of them seated according to the nature of the moods and figures whose characteristicks they are.

Thirdly, The moods of the planotriangular table, being in all thirteene, whereof there be seven rectangular, and six obliquangular, are fitly comprehended by the three blunt, three meane, three sharp, and foure double consonants, the Hebrew *Shin* being accounted for one of them.

Fourthly, The sixteen moods of the orthogonosphericall Trissotetras, are contained under three sharp, three mean, three blunt, three double, and foure liquids, which foure doe orderly particularise the binaries of the last two figures.

Fifthly, The foure monurgetick loxogonosphericals are deciphred by each its owne liquid in front, according to their literall order.

Sixthly, The eight loxogonosphericall disergeticks are also distinguished by the foure liquids, but with this difference from the monurgeticks, that the vowels of A and E precede them in the first syllable, importing thereby the datas of an angle or a side. Now, because these disergeticks are eight in all, there being a binary allotted to every liquid that characteriseth the figures, the better to diversifie the first and second datas of each respective binarie from one another, in so farre as they have reference to each its own quæsitum, the figurative liquid is doubled when a side is required, and remaineth single when an angle.

Furthermore, In the oblique sphericodisergeticks, so farre as the sense of the resolvers could beare it, I did trinifie them with letters convenient for the purpose, according to the severall cases of their datoquæres, whose diversity reacheth not above the extent of π. ς. φ. and τ. δ. θ.

I had almost omitted to tell you, that, for the more variety in the last two figures of the orthogonosphericals, are set downe the two letters of *Ch.* and *Shin*, the first a Spanish, and the second an Hebrew letter. Now, if to those helps for the memorie which in this table I have afforded the reader, both by the alphabetical order of some consonants, and homogeneity of others in their affections of sharpnesse, meannesse, obtusity, and duplicity, he joyne that artificiall aid in having every part of the schemes locally in his mind, of all wayes, both for facility in remembring, and stedfastnesse of retention, without doubt the most expedite, or otherwise place the representatives of words, according to the method of the art of memory in the severall corners of a house, which, in regard of their paucity, are containable within a parlour and dining roome at most, he may, with ease, get them all by heart in lesse then the space of an houre, which is no great expence of time, though bestowed on matters of meaner consequence.

THE COMMENTARY.

The axioms of plain triangles are four, viz. Rulerst, Eproso, Grediftal, and Bagrediffiu.

Rulerst, that is to say, the subtendent in plain triangles may be either radius or secant, and the ambients either radius, sines, or tangents ; for it is a maxime in planangular triangles, that any side may be put for radius, grounded on this, that from any point at any distance a circle may be described ; therefore, if any of the sides of a plain triangle be given together with the angles, each of the other two sides is given by a threefold proportion, that is, whether you put that, or this, or the third side for the radius ; which difference occasioneth both in plaine and sphericall triangles great variety in their calculations.

The branches of this axiom are Vradesso and Eradetul.

Vradesso, that is, when the hypotenusa is radius, the sides are sines of their oppo-sit angles, so that there be two arches described with that hypotenusal identity of distance, whose centres are in the two extremities of the subtendent; for so the case will be made plaine in both the legs, which otherwise would not appeare but in one.

Eradetul, when any of the sides is radius, the other of them is a tangent, and the subtendent a secant. The reason of this is found in the very definitions of the sines, tangents, and secants, to the which, if the reader please, he may have recourse; for I have set them downe amongst my definitions. Hence it is, according to Mr Speidel's observation in his book of sphericals, that the sine of any arch being radius, that which was the totall sine becomes the secant complement of the said arch, and that the tangent of any arch being radius, what was radius becomes tangent complement of that arch.

The directory of this axiome is Vphechet, which sheweth us that there be three planorectangular enodandas belonging thereto, viz. Vphener, Echemun, and Etenar; as for Pserelema, which is the Loxogonian one pointed at in my Trissotetras, because it is but a partiall enodandum, I have purposely omitted to mention it in the directory of Eradetul.

The second axiome is Eproso, that is, the sides are proportionall to one another as the sines of their opposite angles; for, seeing about any triangle a circle may be cir-cumscribed, in which case each side is a cord or subtense, the halfe whereof is the sine of its opposite angle; and there being alwayes the same reason of the whole to the whole, as of the halfe to the halfe, the sides must needs be proportionall to one another as the sines of their opposite angles, *quod probandum erat.*

The directory of this second axiome is Pubkegdaxesh, which declareth that there are seven enodandas grounded on it, to wit, four rectangular, Upalem, Ubeman, Ekarul, Egalem, and three obliquangular, Danarele, Xemenoro, and Shenerolem.

The third axiom is Grediftal, that is, in all plain triangles, as the summe of the two sides is to their difference, so is the tangent of the halfe sum of the opposite angles to the tangent of halfe their difference; for, if a line be drawne equall to the summe of the two sides, and if, on the point of extension with the distance of the shorter side, a semicircle be described, and that from the extremity of the protracted line a diameter be drawne thorough the circle where it toucheth the top of the triangle in question, till it occurre with a parallel to the third side, there will arise two equicrurall triangles, one whereof having one angle common with the triangle proposed, and the three of the one being equall to the three of the other, any one of the equall angles in the fore-said Isosceles must needs be the one halfe of the two unknowne angles. This is the first step to the obtaining of what we demand. Then do we find that the third side cutteth the sides of the greatest triangle according to the analogie required, which is perceivable enough, if, with the distance of the outmost parallel from the lower end thereof as centre, be described a new circle; for then will the tangents be perspicuous, and so much the more for their rectangularity, the one with the radius, and the other with its parallel, which, being touched at an angle described in a semicircle, confirmeth the rectangularity of both. By the parallels likewise is inferred the equality of the alternate angles, whose addition and subduction to and from halfe the sum of the two unknown angles make up both the greater and lesser angle. Hereby it is evident how the sum of the two sides, &c. which was to be proved.

The directory of this third axiom is θ. onely; for it hath no enodandum but Therelabmo.

The fourth axiom is Bagrediffiu, that is, as the base or greatest side is to the summe of the other sides, so the difference of the other sides to the difference of the segments of the base; for, if upon the center of the verticall angle, with the distance of the shortest side, be described a circle, it will so cut the two greater sides of the given triangle, that, finding thereby two oblongs of the nature of those whose equality is demonstrated in my Apodicticks, we may inferre the oblong made of the summe of the sides, and difference of the sides being equall to the oblong made of the base, and the difference of its segments, that their sides are reciprocally proportionall; that is, as the greatest side is to the sum of the other sides, so the difference of the other sides to the difference of the segments of the base or greater side.

The directory of this axiom is ψ. and its onely enodandum, though but a partiall one, Pserelema.

THE PLANORECTANGULAR TABLE HATH FOURE FIGURES.

It is to be observed, that figure here is not taken geometrically, but in the sense that it is used in the logicks, when a syllogism is said to be in the first, second, or third figure; for, as there, by the various application of the medium or mean terme, the figures are constituted diverse, so doth the difference of the datas in a triangle distin-guish these Trissotetrall figures from one another, and, to continue yet further in the syllogisticall analogy, are according to the severall demands, when the datas are the same, subdivided into moods.

The first two vowels give notice of the datas, and the third of what is demanded, so that Uale, and euphonetically pronounced Vale, which is the first figure, shewes that the subtendent, and one angle are given, and that one of the containing sides is required.

Vemane is the second figure, which pointeth out all those problems wherein the hypotenusa, and one leg are given, and an angle or the other leg is required.

The third figure is Enave, which comprehendeth all the problems wherein one of the ambients is given with an oblique angle, and the subtendent or other ambient required.

The fourth and last of the rectangular figures is Ereva, which standeth for those datoquæres, wherein the including sides are given, and the subtendent or an angle demanded.

Now let us come to the Moods of those Figures.

The first figure, Vale, hath but one mood, and therefore of as great extent as it selfe, which is Upalem ; whose nature is to let us know, when a plane right angled triangle is given us to resolve, whose subtendent and one of the obliques is proposed, and one of the ambients required, that we must have recourse unto its resolver, which being Rad—U—Sapy☞Yr sheweth, that if we joyne the artificiall sine of the angle opposite to the side demanded with the Logarithm of the subtendent, the summe searched in the canon of absolute numbers will afford us the Logarithm of the side required. The reason hereof is found in the second axiom, the first consonant of whose directory evidenceth that Upalem is Eprosos Enodandum; for it is, As the totall sine to the hypotenusa, so the sine of the angle opposite to the side required, is to the said required side, according to the nature of the foresaid axiom, whereupon it is grounded.

The second figure, Vemane, hath two Moods, Ubeman and Uphener; the first whereof comprehendeth all those questions, wherein the subtendent and an ambient being given, an oblique is required, and by its resolver, V—Rad—Eg☞So, thus satisfieth our demand, that if we subtract the logarithm of the subtendent from the summe of the logarithms of the middle termes, we have the logarithm of the sine of the opposite angle we seek for; for it is, As the subtendent to the totall sine, so the containing side given to the sine of the opposite angle required. The reason likewise of this analogy is found in the second axiom, Eproso, upon the which this mood is grounded, as the second consonant of its directory giveth us to understand.

The second mood or datoquære of this figure is Uphener, which sheweth that those questions in plaine triangles wherein the hypotenusa and a leg being given the other leg is demanded, are to be calculated by its resolver, which, because the canon of logarithms cannot performe it at one operation, there being a necessity to find one of the oblique angles before the fourth terme can be brought into an analogie, alloweth two subservients for the atchievement thereof, viz. Vbeman, the first mood of the second figure, for the finding out of the angle, and here, because anterior in the work, called præsubservient: then Vpalem, the first mood of all, for finding out of the leg inquired, and here called possubservient, because of its posteriority in the operation ; yet were it not for the facility which addition and subtraction only afford us in this manner of calculation, we might doe it with one work alone by the Bucarnon, or Pythagorase's Diodot, which plainly sheweth us, that by subducing the square of the leg given from

L

the square of the subtendent, we have for the remainder another square, whose root is the side required. The reason of this is in my Apodicticks; but that of the former resolver by two operations is in the first axiom, as by the first syllable of its directory is manifest.

The third figure is Enave, which hath two moods, Ekarul and Egalem. The first comprehendeth all those problems, wherein one of the including sides, and an angle being given, the subtendent is required, and by its resolver Sapeg—Eg—Rad☞Ur, sheweth, that if we subtract the sine of the angle opposite to the given side from the summe of the middle termes, I meane the logarithms of the one and the other, which are the totall sine, and the leg proposed, we shall have the hypotenusa required; for it is as the sine of the angle opposite to the side given, to the foresaid given side, so the totall sine to the subtendent required. The reason of this proportion is grounded on the second axiom Eproso; for K. the third consonant of its directory, giveth us to understand that it is one of the enodandas thereof.

The second mood of Enave is Egalem, which comprehendeth all those problems, wherein one of the ambients, and an oblique angle being given, the other ambient is required; and by its resolver Rad—Taxeg—Eg☞Yr sheweth, that if we adde the logarithm of the side given to the logarithm of the tangent of the angle conterminall with that side, and from the summe, if we cut off the first digit on the left hand, which is equivalent to the subtracting of the radius, whether double or single, the remainder will afford us a logarithm, so neare as the irrationality of the termes will admit, in the table of equall parts, expressive of the side required; for it is as the whole sine to the tangent of an angle insident on the given side, so the side proposed to the side required. The reason hereof is grounded on the second axiom, for the fourth consonant of its directory sheweth that Egalem is Eprosos enodandum.

The fourth figure is Ereva, whose moods are Echemun and Etenar.

The first, viz. Echemun, comprehendeth all those problems, wherein the two ambients being given, the subtendent is required, and, not being logarithmically resolvable in lesse then two operations, hath for its præ and possubservients the moods of Etenar and Ekarul; for an oblique angle by this method is to be searched before the subtendent can be found out, and by reason of these severall works, this mood is grounded on the two first axioms, and is an enodandum partially depending on Eradetul and Eproso. Yet, if you will be pleased to be at the paines of extracting the square root, you may have the subtendent at one work by a quadrobiquadræquation as the Bucarnon doth instruct us, whose demonstration you have plainly set downe in the fourteenth of my Apodicticks.

The second mood of this figure is Etenar, which includeth all those questions wherein the two containing sides being given, one of the obliques is required, and by its resolver E—Ge—Rad☞Toge manifesteth, that, if from the summe of the radius and logarithm of the side given, we subtract the logarithm of the other proposed side, the remainder will afford the tangent of the angle opposite to one of the given sides, the complement of which angle to a right one is alwayes the measure of the other angle, by the fifth of my Apodicticks; for it is, as the one ambient is to the other ambient, so the totall sine to the tangent of an angle; which found out, is either the angle required, or the complement thereof to a right angle. The reason of this analogie is grounded on the second branch of the first axiom, as by the characteristick of the directory is perceivable enough to any industrious reader.

OF THE PLANOBLIQUANGULAR TRIANGLES THERE BE FOURE FIGURES:

Alaheme, Emenarole, Enerolome, and Erelea.

The first and last of these foure are Monotropall figures, and have but each one mood; but the other two have a couple a piece, so that for the planobliquangulars all the foure together afford us six datoquæres.

The mood of Alaheme is Danarele, which comprehendeth all those problems, wherein two angles being given and a side, another side is demanded, and by its resolver Sapeg—Eg—Sapyr☞Yr sheweth, that, if to the summe of the logarithm of the side given, and of the sine of the angle opposite to the side required, we adde the difference of the secant complement from the radius, by some called the arithmeticall complement of the sine, and in Master Speidel's logarithmicall canon of sines, tangents, and secants, with good reason, termed the secant; for, though it doe not cut any arch, thereby more etymologically to deserve the name of secant, yet worketh it the same effect that the prolonged radius doth, the operation will proceed so nearly, that, if from these three logarithms thus summed up, we onely cut off a digit at the left hand, we will find as much by addition alone performed in this case, as if from the proposed summe the sine of the angle had beene abstracted; for the totall summe thus unradiused is the logarithm of the side required. But such as are not acquainted with this compendious manner of calculating, or peradventure are not accommodated with a convenient canon for the purpose, may, in God's name, use their own way, the resolver being of such amplitude, that it extends it selfe to all sorts of operations, whereby the truth of the fourth ternary in this mood may be attained unto; for it is analogised thus, as the sine of the angle opposite to the side given is to the same given side, so the sine of the angle opposite to the side required to the required side. The reason of this proportion is grounded on the second axiom, the first determinator of whose directory sheweth that Danarele is one of Eprosos enodandas.

The second figure of the planobliquangulars is Emenarole, whose moods are Therelabmo and Zelemabne.

The first comprehendeth all those planobliquangular problems, wherein two sides being given with an interjacent angle, an opposite angle is demanded, and by its resolver Aggres—Zes—Talfagros⟨☞Talzos, sheweth, that, if from the summe of the logarithm of the difference of the sides, and tangent of halfe the summe of the opposite angles, be subduced the aggregat or summe of the logarithms of the two proposed sides, the remainder thereof will prove the logarithm of the tangent of halfe the difference of the opposite angles; the which joyned to the one, and abstracted from the other, affords us the measure of the angle we require; for the theoreme is, as the aggregate of the given sides to the difference of these sides, so the tangent of halfe the summe of the opposite angles to the tangent of halfe the difference of those angles; which, without any more adoe, by simple addition and subtraction, affordeth the angle we demand.   The third axiom and the theorem of the resolver of this mood being but one and the same thing, I must make bold to remit you to my Apodicticks for the reason of the analogie thereof, the onely determiner of whose directory being θ. pointeth out the mood of Therelabmo for the sole enodandum appropriated thereunto.

The second mood of this figure is Zelemabne, which involveth all the planobliquangulary problemes, wherein two sides being given with the angle between, the third side is demanded; and not being calculable by the logarithmicall canon in lesse then two operations, because it requireth the finding out of another angle before it can fix upon the side, Therelabmo is allowed it for a præsubservient, by vertue whereof an opposite, angle is obtained, and Danarele for its possubservient and final resolver, by whose meanes we get the side required.   The reason of the first operation is grounded on the third axiom, and of the second operation on the second; but because this mood is meerly a partiall enodandum, neither of the foresaid axioms affordeth any directory concerning it otherwise then in the two subservients thereof.

The third figure is Enerolome, whose two moods are Xemenoro and Shenerolem.

The first mood of this figure includeth all those planobliquangularie problems, wherein two sides being given, with an opposite angle, another opposite angle is demanded, and by its resolver E—Sog—Ge⟨☞So, sheweth that, if from the aggregat of the logarithm of one of the given sides, and that of the sine of the opposite angle proposed, we subtract the logarithm of the other given side, the residue will afford us the logarithm of the sine of the opposite angle required; for it is analogised thus, as one of the sides to the sine of the opposite angle given, so the other side proposed to the sine of the opposite angle required.   The reason of this proportion is from the second axiom, the sixth characteristick of whose directory importeth that Xemenoro is one of Eprosos enodandas.

The second mood of this figure is Shenerolem, which containeth all those planobliquangularie problems, wherein two sides being given, with an opposite angle, the third side is demanded; which, not being findable by the logarithmicall table upon the foresaid datas in lesse then two operations, because an angle must be obtained first before the side can be had, Xemenoro præsubserves it for an angle, and Danarele becomes its possubservient for the side required. The reason of both these operations is founded on the second axiom, the last characteristick of whose directory inrolleth Shenerolem for one of Eprosos enodandas.

The fourth figure is Erelea, which, being Monotropall, hath no mood but Pserelema.

This Pserelema encompasseth all those planobliquangulary problems, wherein the three sides being proposed, an angle is required. This datoquære not being resolvable by the logarithms in lesse then two operations, because the segments of the base, or sustaining side must needs be found out, that, by demitting of a perpendicular from the top angle, we may hit upon the angle demanded; the resolver for the segments is Ba—Gres—Zes☞Zius, whereby we learne, that, if from the logarithm of the summe of the sides, joyned to the logarithm of the difference of the sides, we subtract the logarithm of the base, the remainder is the logarithm of the difference of the segments, which difference being taken from the whole base, halfe the difference proves to be the lesser segment. This theorem being thus the præsubservient of this mood, its possubservient is Vbeman, whose generall resolver V—Rad—Eg☞Sor, is particularised for this case Uxiug—Rad—Iug☞Sor, which sheweth, that, if from the summe of the logarithms of the totall sine, and of one of the segments given, we subduce the logarithm of the hypotenusa conterminall with the segment proposed, the remainder will be the logarithm of the sine of the opposite angle required; for the demitting of the perpendicular opens a way to have the theorem to be first in generall propounded thus, as the subtendent to the totall sine, so the containing side given to the sine of the angle required; or, in particular, thus, as the cosubtendent adjoyning the segment given is to the radius, so is the said segment proposed to the sine of the angle required.

THUS FARRE FOR THE CALCULATING OF PLAINE TRIANGLES, BOTH RIGHT AND OBLIQUE: NOW FOLLOW THE SPHERICALS.

There be three principall axioms, upon which dependeth the resolving of sphericall triangles, to wit, Suprosca, Sbaprotca, and Seproso.

The first maxime or axiom, Suprosca, sheweth, that, of severall rectangled sphericals, which have one and the same acute angle at the base, the sines of the hypotenusas are proportionall to the sines of their perpendiculars; for, from the same inclination every where of the one plaine to the other, there ariseth an equiangularity in the two rectangles, out of which we may confidently inferre the homologall sides, which are the sines of the subtendents, and of the perpendiculars of the one and the other, to be amongst themselves proportionall.   Its directory is Uphugen, by the which we learn, that Uphanep, Ugemon, and Enarul, are its three enodandas.

The second axiom is Sbaprotca, whereby we learne, that in all rectangled sphericals that have one and the same acute angle at the base, the sines of the bases are proportionall to the tangents of their perpendiculars; which analogie proceedeth from the equiangularity of such rectangled sphericals by the semblable inclining of the plaine towards them both.   This proportion neverthelesse will never hold betwixt the sines of the bases, and the sines of their perpendiculars; because, if the sines of the bases were proportionall to the sines of the perpendiculars, the sines of the perpendiculars being already demonstrated proportionall to the sines of the subtendents, either the sine of the perpendicular, or the sine of the base, would be the cord of the same arch, whereof it is a sine; which is impossible, by reason that nothing can be both a whole and a part, in regard of one and the same thing ; and therefore doe we only say, that the sines of the bases, and tangents of the perpendiculars, and contrarily, are proportionall. Its directory is Pubkutethepsaler, which sheweth, that Upalam, Ubamen, Vkelamb, Etalum, Ethaner, Epsoner, Alamun, and Erelam, are the eight enodandas thereupon depending.

The third axiom is, that the sines of the sides are proportionall to the sines of their opposite angles, the truth whereof holds in all sphericall triangles whatsoever, which is proved partly out of the proportion betwixt the sines of the perpendiculars substerned under equall angles, and the sines of the hypotenusas, and partly by the analogy that is betwixt the sines of the angles sustained by severall perpendiculars, demitted from one point, and the sines of the perpendiculars themselves.   The directory of this axiom is Vchedezexam, whereby we know that Uchener, Edamon, Ezolum, Exoman, and Amaner, are the five enodandas thereof.

THE ORTHOGONOSPHERICALL TABLE CONSISTETH OF THESE SIX FIGURES:

Valamenep, Vemanore, Enarulome, Erolumane, Achave, and Esheva.

The first figure, Valamenep, comprehendeth all those questions wherein the subtendent and an angle being given, either another angle or one of the ambients is demanded.

Of this figure there be three moods, viz. Upalam, Ubamen, and Uphanep.   The first, to wit, Upalam, containeth all those orthogonosphericall problems wherein the subtendent and one oblique angle being given, another oblique angle is required; and by its resolver, Torb—Tag—Nu☞Mir, sheweth, that the summe of the sine complement of the subtendent side and tangent of the angle given, the logarithms of these are alwayes to be understood, a digit being prescinded from the left, is equall to the tangent complement of the angle required; for the proposition goeth thus, As the radius to the tangent of the angle given, so the sine complement of the subtendent side to the tangent complement of the angle required; and because tangents and tangent complements are reciprocally proportionall, instead of To—Tag—Nu☞Mir, or, To —Lu—Mag☞Tir, which, for that the radius is a meane proportionall betwixt the L. and N., the T. and M., is all one for inferring of the same fourth proportionall, or foresaid quæsitum, we may say, Mag—Nu—To☞Mir, that is, As the tangent complement of the given angle to the cosine of the subtendent, so the totall sine to the antitangent of the angle demanded; for the totall sine being, as I have told you, a meane proportionall betwixt the tangents and cotangents, the subtracting of the cotangent or tangent complement from the summe of the radius and antisine, residuats a logarithm equall to that of the remainder, by abstracting the radius from the sum of the cosine of the subtendent and tangent of the angle given, either of which will fall out to be the antitangent of the required angle.

Notandum.

[Here alwayes is to be observed, that the subtracting of logarithms may be avoyded, by substituting the arithmeticall complement thereof to be added to the logarithms of the two middle proportionals; which arithmetical complement, according to Gellibrand, is nothing else but the difference between the logarithm to be subtracted and another consisting of an unit, or binarie with the addition of cyphers, that is, the single or double radius, for so the sum of the three logarithms, cutting off an unit or binarie towards the left hand, will still be the logarithm of the fourth proportionall required.

For the greater ease therefore in trigonometricall computations, such a logarithmicall canon is to be wished for, wherein the radius is left out of all the secants, and all the tangents of major arches, according to the method prescribed by Mr Speidel, who is willing to take the paines to make such a new canon, better then any that ever hitherto hath been made use of, so that the publike, whom it most concerneth, or some potent man well minded towards the mathematicks, would be so generous as to releeve him of the charge it must needs cost him; which, considering his great affection to, and ability in those sciences, will certainly be as small a summe as possibly he can bring it to.]

This parenthesis, though somewhat with the longest, will not, I hope, be displeasing to the studious reader.

The second mood of the first figure is Ubamen, which comprehendeth all those problems wherein the subtendent and one oblique angle being given, the ambient adjoyning the angle given is required, and by its resolver, Nag—Mu—Torp☞Myr, sheweth that, if to the summe of the logarithms of the two middle proportionals we adde the arithmeticall complement of the first, the cutting off the index from the aggregat of the three, will residuat the tangent complement of the side required ; and therefore, with the totall sine in the first place, it may be thus propounded, Torp—Mu—Lag ☞Myr ; for the first theorem being, As the sine complement of the angle given to the tangent complement of the subtendent side, so the totall sine to the tangent complement of the side required : just so the second theorem, which is that refined, is, As the totall sine to the tangent complement of the subtendent, so the secant of the given angle to the tangent complement of the demanded side.   Here you must consider, as I have told you already, that of the whole secant I take but its excesse above the radius, as I doe of all tangents above 45 degrees ; because the cutting off the first digit on the left, supplieth the subtraction requisite for the finding out of the fourth proportionall ; so that by addition onely the whole operation may be performed, of all wayes the most succinct and ready.   Otherwise, because of the totall sines meane proportionality betwixt the sine complement and the secant, and betwixt the tangent and tangent complement, it may be regulated thus, To—Tu—Nag☞Tyr, that is, As the radius to the tangent of the subtendent, so the sine complement of the angle given to the tangent of the side required.   The reason of the resolution both of this and of the former datoquære, is grounded on the second axiom, and the proportion that, in severall rect-angled sphericals which have the same acute angle at the base, is found betwixt the sines of their perpendiculars and tangents of their base, as is shewne you by the two first consonants of the directory of Sbaprotca.

The third and last mood of the first figure is Uphaner, which comprehendeth all those problems wherein the hypotenusa and one of the obliques being given, the oppo-site ambient is required ; and by its resolver, Tol—Sag—Su☞Syr, sheweth, that if we adde the logarithms of the sine of the angle and sine of the subtendent, cutting off the left supernumerarie digit from the summe, it gives us the logarithm of the sine of the side demanded ; for it is, As the totall sine to the sine of the angle given, so the sine of the subtendent side to the sine of the side required ; and because by the axiom of Rulerst it was proved, that when the sine of any arch is made radius, what was then the totall sine becomes a secant, and therefore secant complement of that arch ; instead of Tol—Sag—Su☞Syr, we may say, To—Ru—Rag☞Ryr, that is, As the totall sine is to the secant complement of the subtendent, so the secant com-plement of the angle given to the secant complement of the side demanded.   The re-solution of this datoquære by sines, is grounded on the first axiom of Sphericals, which elucidates the proportion betwixt the sines of the hypotenusas and perpendiculars, as it is declared to us by the first syllable of Suprosca's directory.

The second figure is Vemanore, which containeth all those orthogonosphericall questions wherein the subtendent and an ambient being proposed, either of the obliques or the other ambient is required, and hath three moods, viz. Ukelamb, Ugemon, and Uchener.

The first mood, Ukelam, comprehendeth all those orthogonosphericall problems, wherein the subtendent, and one including side being given, the interjacent angle is demanded, and by its resolver Meg—Torp—Mu☞Nir, or because of the totall sines mean proportion betwixt the tangent, and tangent complement, Torp—Teg—Mu☞ Nir, which is the same in effect, sheweth, that, if from the summe of the logarithms of the middle termes, which in the first analogy is the radius and tangent complement of the subtendent, we subtract the tangent complement of the given ambient, or, in the second order of proportionals, joyne the tangent of the side given to the tangent complement of the subtendent, and from the sum cut off the index, if need be, both will tend to the same end, and produce, for the fourth proportionall, the sine complement of the angle required; for to subtract a tangent complement from the radius, and another number joyned together, whether that tangent complement be more or lesse then the radius, it is all one as if you should subtract the radius from the said tangent complement and that other number; because the tangent, or rather logarithm of the tangent, (for so it must be alwayes understood, and not onely in tangents, but in sines, secants, sides, and angles, though for brevity sake the word logarithm be oftentimes omitted,) because, I say, the logarithms of the tangent and tangent complement together being the double of the radius, if first the tangent complement surpasse the radius, and be to be subtracted from it, and another number, it is all one as if from the said number you would abstract the radius and the tangent complement's excesse above it, so that the radius being in both, there will remaine a tangent with the other number.   Likewise, if a tangent complement lesse then the radius be to be subtracted from the summe of the radius and another logarithm, it is yet all one as if you had subtracted the radius from the same summe; because, though that tangent complement be lesse then the radius, yet that parcell of the radius which was abstracted more then enough, is recompensed in the logarithm of the tangent to be joyned with the other number; for, from which soever of the tangents the radius be subduced, its antitangent is remainder; both which cases may be thus illustrated in numbers; and first, where the tangent complement is greater then the radius, as in these numbers, 6, 4, 3, 1, and 4, 2, 3, 1, where let 6 be the tangent complement, 4 the radius, 3 the number to be joyned with the radius or either of the tangents, and 1 the remainer; for 4 and 3 making 7, if you abstract 6 there will remaine 1.   Likewise 2 and 3 making 5, if you subtract 4 there will remaine 1.   Next, if the tangent complement be lesse then the radius, as in 2, 4, 3, 5, and 4, 6, 3, and 5, where let 2 be the tangent complement; for if from 4 and 3 joyned together you abstract 2, there will remaine 5, which will also be the remainder when you substract 4 from 6 and 3 added together.   Now, to make the same resolver, the variety whereof I have been so large in explaining, to runne altogether upon tangents, instead of Meg—To—Mu☞Nir, that is, As the tangent complement of the side given is to the totall sine, so the tangent complement of the subtendent side to the sine complement of the angle required, we may say, Tu—Teg—To☞Nir; that is, As the tangent of the subtendent is to

M

the tangent of the given side, so the totall sine to the sine complement of the angle required. All this is grounded on the second axiom, Sbaprotca, and upon the reciprocall proportion of the tangents and antitangents, as is evident by the third characteristick of its directory.

The second mood of Vemanore is Ugemon, which comprehendeth all those orthogonosphericall problems wherein the subtendent with an ambient being given, an opposite oblique is required; and by its resolver, Su—Seg—Tom☞Sir, or, by putting the radius in the first place, according to Uradesso, the first branch of the first axiom of the planorectangulars, To—Seg—Ru☞Sir, sheweth, that the summe of the side given and secant of the subtendent, the supernumerarie digit being cut off, is the sine of the angle required; for the theorem is, As the sine of the subtendent to the sine of the side given, so the radius to the sine of the angle required; or, As the totall sine to the sine of the side given, so the secant complement of the subtendent to the sine of the angle required; or, changing the sines into secant complements, and the secant complements into sines, we may say, To—Su—Reg☞Rir; because, betwixt the sine and secant complement, the radius is a middle proportion. Other varieties of calculation, in this as well as other problems, may be used; for, besides that every proportion of the radius to the sine, tangent, or secant, and contrarily, may be varied three manner of wayes, by the first axiom of plaine triangles, the alteration of the middle termes may breed some diversity, by a permutat or perturbed proportion, which I thought good to admonish the reader of here, once for all, because there is no problem, whether in plaine or sphericall triangles, wherein the analogie admitteth not of so much change. The reasons of this mood of Ugemon depend on the axiom of Suprosca, as the second characteristick of Uphugen seemeth to insinuate.

The last mood of the second figure is Uchener, which comprehendeth all those problems wherein the subtendent and one ambient being given, the other ambient is required, and by its resolver, Neg—To—Nu☞Nyr, or, To—Le—Nu☞Nyr, sheweth, that the summe of the sine complement of the subtendent and the secant of the given side, which is the arithmeticall complement of its antisine, giveth us the sine complement of the side desired, the index being removed; for the theorem is, As the sine complement of the given side to the totall sine, so the sine complement of the subtendent to the sine complement of the side required; or more refinedly, As the radius to the sine complement of the subtendent, so the secant of the leg given to the sine complement of the side required; and besides other varieties of analogie, according to the axiom of Rulerst, by making use of the reciprocall proportion of the sine complements with the secants, we may say, To—Ne—Lu☞Lyr, that is, As the totall sine is to the sine complement of the given side, so the secant of the subtendent to the secant of the side required. The reason of this datoquære's resolution is in Seproso, the third axiom of the sphericals, as is manifest by the first figure of its directorie, Uchedezexam.

The third figure is Enarrulome, whose three moods are Etalum, Edamon, and Ethaner.

This figure comprehendeth all those orthogonosphericall questions wherein one of the ambients with an adjacent angle is given, and the subtendent, an opposite angle, or the other containing side is required.

Its first mood, Etalum, involveth all those orthogonosphericall problems wherein a containing side with an insident angle thereon is proposed, and the hypotenusa demanded ; and by its resolver, Torp—Me—Nag☞Mur, or, by inverting the demand upon the scheme, Tolp—Me—Nag☞Mur sheweth, that the cutting off the first left digit from the summe of the tangent complement of the ambient proposed and the sine complement of the given angle, affords us the tangent complement of the subtendent required ; for the theorem goes thus, As the totall sine to the tangent complement of the given side, so the sine complement of the angle given to the tangent complement of the hypotenusa required.   And because the totall sine hath the same proportion to the tangent complement which the sine hath to the sine complement, we may as well say, To—Meg—Sag☞Nur, that is, As the radius to the tangent complement of the ambient side, so the sine of the angle given to the sine complement of the subtendent required.   The progresse of this mood dependeth on the axiom of Sbaprotca, as you may perceive by the fourth consonant of its directorie, Pubkutethepsaler.

The second mood of the third figure is Edamon, which comprehendeth all those orthogonosphericall problems wherein an ambient and an adjacent angle being given, the opposite oblique, viz. the angle under which the ambient is subtended, is required ; and by its resolver, To—Neg—Sag☞Nir, sheweth, that the addition of the cosine of the ambient and of the sine of the angle proposed, affordeth us, if we omit not the usuall presection, the cosine of the angle we seek for ; for it is, As the radius to the cosine or sine complement of the given side, so the sine of the angle proposed to the antisine or sine complement of the angle demanded ; now, the radius being alwayes a meane proportionall betwixt the sine complement and the secant, we may for To—Neg—Sag☞Nir say, To—Leg—Rag☞Lir, or To—Rag—Leg☞Lir ; that is, As the totall sine to the secant, or cutter of the side given, or to the cosecant or secant complement of the given angle, so is the secant complement of the angle, or secant of the side, to the secant or cutter of the angle required.   The reason of all this is grounded on Seproso, because it runneth upon the proportion betwixt the sines of the sides and the sines of their opposite angles, as is perspicuous to any by the second syllable of the directory of that axiome.

The last mood of the third figure is Ethaner, which comprehendeth all those orthogonosphericall problems wherein an ambient with an oblique annexed thereto is given, and the other arch about the right angle is required ; and by its resolver, Torb—Tag—Seg☞Tyr, sheweth, that if we joyne the logarithms of the two middle proportionals, which are the tangent of the given angle, and the sine of the side, the usual presection being observed, we shall thereby have the tangent or toucher of the ambient side desired; for it is, As the radius to the tangent of the angle given, so the sine of the containing side proposed to the side required; and because the tangent complement and tangent are reciprocally proportionall, the sine likewise and secant complement, for To—Tag—Se☞Tyr, we may say, keeping the same proportion, To—Reg—Ma☞Myr, that is, As the radius to the secant complement of the given side, so the tangent complement of the angle proposed to the tangent complement of the side required. The truth of all these operations dependeth on Sbaprotca, the second axiome of the sphericals, as is evidenced by θ. the fifth characteristick of its directory, Pubkutethepsaler.

The fourth figure is Erollumane, which includeth all orthogonosphericall questions wherein an ambient and an opposite oblique being given, the subtendent, the other oblique, or the other ambient is demanded: It hath likewise, conforme to the three former figures, three moods belonging to it; the first whereof is Ezolum.

This Ezolum comprehendeth all those orthogonosphericall problems wherein one of the legs with an opposite angle being given, the subtendent is required; and by its resolver, Sag—Sep—Rad☞Sur, or by putting the radius in the first place, To—Se—Reg☞Sur, sheweth, that the abstracting of the radius from the sum of the sine of the side and secant complement of the angle given, residuats the sine of the hypotenusa required; for it is, As the sine of the angle given to the sine of the opposite side, so the radius to the sine of the subtendent; or more refinedly, As the totall sine to the sine of the side, so the secant complement of the angle given to the sine of the subtendent side; and because of the sine's and antisecant's, or secant complement's reciprocall proportionality, To—Sag—Re☞Ru, that is, As the radius to the sine of the angle given, so the secant complement of the proposed side to the secant complement of the subtendent required. The reason of all this is grounded on the third axiom, Seproso, as is made manifest by the third syllable of its directory.

The second mood of this figure is Exoman, which comprehendeth all those problems wherein a containing side and an opposite oblique being given, the adjacent oblique is required; and by its resolver, Ne—To—Nag☞Sir, or more refinedly, To—Le—Nag☞Sir, sheweth that the summe of the sine of the angle, together with the arithmeticall complement of the antisine of the leg, which in the table I have so much recommended unto the reader, is set downe for a secant, the usuall presection being observed, affordeth us the sine of the angle required; and because of the reciprocall proportion betwixt the sine complement and secant, and betwixt the sine and secant complement, the theorem may be composed thus, To—Neg—La☞Rir; that is, As the radius to the sine complement of the given side, so the secant of the angle proposed to the secant complement of the angle demanded. The reason of this is likewise grounded on Seproso, as you may perceive by the fourth characteristick of its directory.

The last mood of this figure is Epsoner, which containeth all those orthogonosphericall problems wherein an ambient and an opposite oblique being given, the other ambient is demanded; and by its resolver, Tag—Tolb—Te₢☞Syr, or more elabouredly, Tolb—Mag—Te₢☞Syr, sheweth that the præscinding of the radius from the summe of the tangent of the side and antitangent of the given angle, residuats the sine of the side required; for it is, As the tangent of the angle proposed to the totall sine, so the tangent of the given side to the sine of the side demanded; or, As the radius to the tangent complement of the angle given, so the tangent of the given side to the sine of the side required; and because of the reciprocall analogy betwixt the tangents and cotangents, and betwixt the sines and cosecants, we may with the same confidence as formerly set it thus in the rule, To—Meg—Ta₢☞Ryr, and it will find out the same quæsitum. The reason of the operations of this mood, because of the ingrediencie of tangents, dependeth on Sbaprotca, as is perceivable by the sixth determiner of its directory Pubkutethepsaler.

The fifth figure of the orthogonosphericals is Achave, which containeth all those problems wherein the angles being given, the subtendent or an ambient is desired, and hath two moods, Alamun and Amaner.

Alamun comprehendeth all those problems wherein the angles being proposed, the hypotenusa is required; and by its resolver, Tag—Torb—Ma₢☞Nur, or more compendiously, Torb—Mag—Ma₢☞Nur, sheweth that the summe of the cotangents not exceeding the places of the radius, is the sine complement of the subtendent required; for it is, As the tangent of one of the angles to the radius, so the tangent complement of the other angle to the sine complement of the hypotenusa demanded; or, As the totall sine to the tangent complement of one of the angles, so the tangent complement of the other angle to the sine complement of the subtendent we seek for. The running of this mood upon tangents notifieth its dependance on Sbaprotca, as is evident by the seventh determiner of the directory thereof.

The second mood of this figure is Amaner, which comprehendeth all those orthogonosphericall problems wherein the angles being given, an ambient is demanded; and by its resolver, Say—Nag—Tω₢☞Nyr, or more perspicuously, Tω—Noy—Ray₢☞ Nyr, sheweth that the summe of the logarithms of the antisine of the angle opposite to the side required, and the arithmeticall complement of the sine of the angle adjoyning the said side, which we call its secant complement, with the usual presection, is equall to the sine complement of the same side demanded; for it is, As the sine of the angle adjoyning the side required to the antisine of the other angle, so the totall sine to the antisine of the side demanded; or, As the radius to the antisine of the angle opposite to the demanded side, so the antisecant of the angle conterminat with that side to the antisine of the side required: and because of the analogy betwixt the antisines and secants: and likewise betwixt the antisecants and sines, we may expresse it, To—Say—La₢☞Lyr; that is, As the radius to the sine of the angle insident on the required side, so the secant of the other given angle to the secant of the side that is demanded. Here the angulary intermixture of proportions giveth us to understand that this mood dependeth on Seproso, as is manifested by the last characteristick of Uchedezexam the directory of this axiom.

The sixth and last figure is Escheva, which comprehendeth all those problems wherein the two containing sides being given, either the subtendent or an angle is demanded; it hath two moods, Enerul and Erelam.

The first mood thereof Enerul, containeth all such problems as having the ambients given, require the subtendent; and by its resolver, Ton—Neg—Ne☞Nur, sheweth that the summe of the Logarithms of the cosines of the two legs unradiated, is the logarithm of the cosine of the subtendent; for it is, As the totall sine to the cosine of one of the ambients, so the cosine of the other including leg given to the cosine of the required subtendent; and because of the cosinal and secantine proportion, we may safely say, To—Leg—Le☞Lur. That is, As the radius to the secant of one shanke or leg, so the secant of the other shanke or leg to the secant of the hypotenusa demanded. The coursing thus upon sines and their proportionals evidenceth that this mood dependeth on Suprosca, the first of the sphericall Axioms, which is pointed at by the third and last characteristick of Uphugen the directorie thereof.

The second mood of the last figure, and consequently the last mood of all the orthogonosphericals, is Erelam, which comprehendeth all those orthogonosphericall problems wherin the two containing sides being proposed, an angle is demanded; and by its resolver, Sei—Teg—Torb☞Tir, or by primifying the radius, Torb—Tepi—Rexi ☞Tir, giveth us to understand that the cutting off the radius from the summe of the tangent of the side opposite to the angle demanded, and the cosecant of the side conterminat with the said angle, residuats the touch-line of the angle in question; for it is, As the sine of the side adjoyning the angle required to the tangent of the other given side, so the radius to the tangent of the angle demanded; or, As the totall sine to the tangent of the ambient opposite to the angle sought, so the antisecant of the leg adjacent to the said asked angle to the tangent or toucher thereof; and because sines have the same proportion to cosecants which tangents have to cotangents, we may say, To—Sei—me☞mir, that is, As the radius to the sine of the side conterminat with the angle required, so the cotangent of the other leg to the cotangent of the angle searched after; or yet more profoundly by an alternat proportion changing the relation of the fourth proportionall, although the same formerly required angle, thus, To—Rei—me☞mor, that is, As the radius to the antisecant of the side adjacent to the angle sought for, so the antitangent of the other side to the antitangent of that side's opposit angle, which is the angle demanded. The reason hereof is grounded on Sbaprotca; for the tangentine proportion of the terms of this mood specifieth its dependance on the second axiom, which is showen unto us by the eight and last characteristick of its directorie Pubkutethepsaler.

Here endeth the doctrine of the right-angled sphericalls, the whole diatyposis wherof is in the Equisolea or hippocrepidian diagram, whose most intricate amfractuosities, renvoys, various mixture of analogies, and perturbat situation of proportionall termes, cannot choose but be pervious to the understanding of any judicious reader that hath perused this comment aright. And therefore let him give me leave (if he think fit) for his memorie sake, to remit him to it, before he proceed any further.

THE LOXOGONOSPHERICALL TRIANGLES, WHETHER AM-BLYGONOSPHERICALL OR OXYGONOSPHERICALL, ARE EITHER MONURGETICK OR DISERGETICK.

The Monurgetick have two figures, Datamista and Datapura.

Datamista is of all those loxogonospherical monurgetick problems wherein the angles and sides being intermixedly given, and therefore one of them being alwaies of another kind from the other two, either an angle or a side is demanded; it hath two moods, Lamaneprep and Menerolo.

The first mood Lamaneprep, comprehendeth all those loxogonosphericall problems wherein two angles being given and an opposit side, another opposit side is demanded; and by its resolver, Sapeg—Se—Sapy—☞ Syr, sheweth that if to the logarithms of the sine of the side given, and sine of the angle opposit to the side required, we joyne the arithmeticall complement of the sine of the angle opposit to the proposed side, which is the refined antisecant, we will thereby attain to the knowledge of the sine of the side demanded. The reason of this is grounded on the third axiom, Seproso, as you may perceive by the first syllable of the obliquangularie directory, Lame.

The second mood of this figure is Menerolo, which comprehendeth all those ambly-gonosphericall problems, wherein two sides being given with an opposit angle, another opposit angle is demanded; and by its resolver Sepag—Sa—Sepi☞ Sir, sheweth that if to the summe of the Logarithms of the sine of the given angle, and sine of the side opposit to the angle required, we joyne the arithmeticall complement of the sine of the side opposit to the given angle, which is the refined cosecant of the said angle, it will afford us the sine of the angle required. The reason of this operation is grounded on the third axiom of sphericalls, a progresse in sines shewing clearly how that both this and the former doe totally depend on the axiom of Seprosa, as is evident by the second syllable of its directorie Lame.

The second figure of the monurgetick loxogonosphericalls treateth of all those questions wherein the datas being either sides alone or angles alone, an angle or a side is demanded. This figure of Datapura is divided into two moods, viz. Nerelema and

Ralamane, which are of such affinity, that upon one and the same theorem dependeth the analogy that resolveth both.

The first mood thereof Nerelema, comprehendeth all those problems wherein the three sides being given, an angle is demanded, and is the third of the monurgeticks, as by its characteristick the third liquid is perceivable.

The curteous reader may be pleased to take notice, that in both the moods of the datapurall figure, I am in some measure necessitated, for the better order sake, to couch two precepts or documents for the faciendas thereof, and to premise that one concerning the three legs given, before I make any mention of the maine resolver, whereupon both the foresaid moods are founded; to which resolver, because of both their dependencies on it, I have allowed here in the glosse, the same middle place which it possesseth in the table of my Trissotetras.

The precept of Nerelema is Halbasalzes *Ad*Ab* Sadsabreregalsbis Ir; that is to say, for the finding out of an angle when the three legs are given, as soone as we have constituted the sustentative leg of that angle a base, the halfe thereof must be taken, and to that halfe we must adde halfe the difference of the other two legs, and likewise from that halfe subtract the half difference of the foresaid two legs; then the summe and the residue being two arches, we must to the logarithms of the sine of the summe, and sine of the remainer, joyne the logarithms of the arithmeticall complements of the sines of the sides, which are the refined antisecants of the said legs, and halfe that summe will afford us the logarithm of the sine of an arch, which doubled, is the verticall angle we demand; for out of its resolver, Parses—Powto—Parsadsab☞Powsalvertir, is the analogy of the former work made cleare, the theorem being, As the oblong or parallelogram contained under the sines of the legs to the square, power or quadrat of the totall sine, so the rectangle or oblong made of the right sines of the sum and difference of the halfe base and difference of the legs to the square of the right sine of halfe the verticall angle.

The reason hereof will be manifest enough to the industrious reader, if when by a peculiar diagram, of whose equiangular triangles the foresaid sines and differences are made the constitutive sides, he hath evinced their analogy to one another, he be then pleased to perpend how, in two rowes of proportionall numbers, the products arising of the homologall roots are in the same proportion amongst themselves that the said roots towards one another are; wherewithall if he doe consider how the halfs must needs keep the same proportion that their wholes; and then in the work it selfe of collationing severall orders of proportionall termes, both single and compound, be carefull to dash out a divider against a multiplyer, and afterwards proceed in all the rest according to the ordinary rules of Æquation and Analogy, he cannot choose but extricat himselfe with ease forth of all the windings of this elaboured proposition.

Upon this theorem, as I have told you, dependeth likewise the document for the faciendum of Ralamane, which is the second mood of Datapura, and the last of the monurgetick loxogonosphericals, as is pointed at by Nera the directory thereof. This mood Ralamane, comprehendeth all those loxogonosphericall problems, wherein the three angles being given, a side is demanded; and by its resolver, Parses—Powto—Parsadsab☞Powsalvertir, according to the peculiar precept of this mood, Kourbfasines (Ereled) Koufbraxypopyx, sheweth, that if we take the complement to a semicircle of the angle opposite to the side required, which, for distinction sake, we doe here call the base, and frame, of the foresaid complement to a semicircle, a second base for the fabrick of a new triangle, whose other two sides have the graduall measure of the former triangle's other two angles; and so the three angles being converted into sides, the complement to a semicircle of the new verticall, or angle opposite to the new base, will be the measure of the true base or leg required, and the angle insident on the right end of the new base in the second triangle falleth to be the side conterminall with the left end of the true base in the first triangle, and the angle adjoyning the left end of the false base in the second triangle becomes the side adjacent to the right end of the old base in the first triangle: so that thus, by the angles, all and each of the sides are found out, all which works are to be performed by the preceding mood, upon the theorem whereof the reason of all these operations doth depend.

THE DISERGETICK LOXOGONOSPHERICALS ARE GROUNDED ON FOURE AXIOMS, VIZ.

1. *Nabadprosver.* 2. *Naverprortes, Siubprortab*, and *Niubprodnesver;* the foure directories whereof, each in order to its own axiome, are *Alama, Allera, Ammena,* and *Ennerra.*

The first axiome is Nabadprosver, that is, in obliquangular sphericals, if a perpendicular be demitted from the verticall angle to the opposite side, continued if need be, the sines complements of the angles at the base will be directly proportionall to the sines of the verticall angles, and contrary; the reason hereof is inferred out of the proportion, which the sines of angles, substerned by perpendiculars, have to the sines of the said perpendiculars, so that they belong to the arches of great circles, concurring in the same point, and that from some point of the one they be let fall on the other arches; which proportion of the sines of the said perpendiculars to the sines of the angles subtended by them, floweth immediately from the proportion, which, in severall orthogonosphericals, having the same acute angle at the base, is betwixt the sines of the hypotenusas, and the sines of the perpendiculars; the demonstration whereof is plainly set downe in my Glosse on Suprosca, the first generall axiome of the sphericals of which this axiome of Nabadprosver is a consectary.

The directory of this axiome is Alama, which sheweth that the moods of Alamebna and Amanepra are grounded on it.

The second disergetick axiome is Naverprortes, that is to say, the sine's complements of the verticall angles, in obliquangular triangles, a perpendicular being let fall from the double verticall on the opposite side, are reciprocally proportionall to the tangents of the sides; the reason hereof proceedeth from Sbaprotca, the second general axiome of the sphericals; according to which, if we doe but regulate, after the customary analogicall manner, two quaternaries of proportionals of the former sine's complements, and tangents proposed, we will find by the extremes alone, excluding all the intermediate termes, that the sine's complements of the verticall angles, both forwardly and inversedly, are reciprocally proportioned to the tangents of the sides, and contrariwise from the tangents to the sines. The directory of this axiome is Allera, which evidenceth that the moods of Allamebne and Erelomab depend upon it.

The third disergetick axiome is Siubprortab, that is to say, that, in obliquangular sphericals, if a perpendicular be drawne from the verticall angle unto the opposite side, continued if need be, the sines of the segments of the base are reciprocally proportionall to the tangents of the angles conterminate at the base, and contrary; the proofe of this, as well as that of the former consectary, dependeth on Sbaprotca, the second generall axiome of the sphericals: according to which, if we so diagrammatise an amblygonosphericall triangle, by quadranting the perpendicular, and all the sides, and describing from the basangulary points two quadrantall arches, till we hit upon two rowes of proportionall sines of bases to tangents of perpendiculars, then shall we be sure, if we exclude the intermediate termes, to fall upon a reciprocall analogy of sines and tangents, which, alternately changed, will afford the reciprocall proportion of the sines of the segments of the base, to the tangents of the angles conterminat thereat, the thing required.

The directory of this axiome is Ammena, which certifieth that Ammanepreb and Enerablo are founded thereon.

The fourth and last disergetick axiome is Niubprodnesver, that is to say, that, in all loxogonosphericalls, where the cathetus is regularly demitted, the sine's complements of the segments of the base are directly proportionall to the sine's complements of the sides of the verticall angles, and contrary. The reason hereof is made manifest, by the proportion that is betwixt the sines of angles, subtended by perpendiculars and the sines of these perpendiculars; out of which we collation severall proportions, till, both forwardly and inversedly, we pitch at last upon the direct proportion required.

The directory of this axiome is Ennerra, which declareth that Ennerable and Errelome are its dependents.

OF THE DISERGETICK LOXOGONOSPHERICALS THERE BE IN ALL FOURE FIGURES: TWO ANGULARY AND TWO LATERALL.

The two angulary are Ahalebmane and Ahamepnare; the two laterall are Ehenabrole and Eheromabne.

The first angulary disergetick loxogonosphericall figure, Ahalebmane, comprehendeth all those problems, wherein two angles being given with a side betweene, either the third angle, or an opposite side is demanded, and accordingly hath two moods, the first whereof is Alamebna, and the second Allamebne.

Alamebna concerneth all those loxogonosphericall disergetick problems, wherein two angles being proposed, with an interjacent side, the third angle is required; which angle, according to the severall cases of this mood, is always one of the angles at the base, that is to say, in the termes of my Trissotetras, a prime, or next opposite, or at least one of the co-opposites to the perpendicular to be demitted. And therefore, conforme to the nature of the case of the datoquære in hand, and that it may the more conveniently fall within the compasse of the axiome of Nabadprosver, an angle by the first operation of this disergetick is to be found out, which must either be a double verticall, a verticall in the little rectangle, or a verticall, or co-verticall, as sometimes I call it, in one of the correctangles.

Thus much I have thought fit to premise of the prænoscendum of this mood, before I come to its Cathetothesis; because, in my Trissotetrall table, to avoid the confusion of homogeneall termes, though the order of doctrine would seeme to require another method, the first and prime orthogonosphericall work is totally unfolded before I speak any thing of the variety of the perpendicular's demission, to which, owing its rectangularity, it thereby obtaineth an infallible progresse to the quæsitum; but, seeing in the glosse I am not to astrict my selfe to so little bounds as in my table, I will observe the order that is most expedient; and, before the resolution of any operation in this mood, deduce the diversity of the perpendicular's prosiliencie in the severall cases thereof.

Let the reader then be pleased to consider, that the generall maxim for the Cathetothesis of this mood is Cafregpiq, the meaning whereof is, that, whether the side whereon the perpendicular is demitted be increased or not, that is to say, whether the perpendicular fall outwardly or inwardly, it must fall from the extremity of the given side, and opposite to the angle required; however, it is to be remarked, that, in this mood, whatever be the affection of the angles, unlesse they be all three alike, the perpendicular may fall outwardly.

The generall maxim for the Cathetothesis of this mood, as well as for that of all the rest, is divided into foure tenets, according to the number of the cases of every mood.

Here must I admonish the reader, that he startle not at the mentioning of foure especiall cathetothetick tenets, and foure severall cases belonging to each disergetick mood, seeing, to the most observant eye, there be but three of either perceptible in my Trissotetras; for, the fourth, both tenet and case, being the same by way of expression in all the moods, and being fully resolved by the third case of every mood, it shall suffice to speak thereof here once for all; the tenet of this common case is Simmomatin, that is to say, when all the three angles in any of those disergeticks are of the same affection, either all acute, or all oblique, the perpendicular falleth inwardly, whether the double verticall be an angle given, an angle demanded, or neither. Yet here it is to be considered, that, seeing triangles may be either calculated by their reall and naturall, or by their circular parts, or by both together, and that for the more facility, we oftentimes, instead of the proposed triangle, resolve its opposite; it is not the reall and given triangle that, in this case, we so much take notice of, as of its resolvable and equivalent, the opposite triangle; as, for example, if a sphericall triangle, with two obtuse angles, and one acute, be given you to resolve, it will fall within the compasse of Simomatin, because its opposite sphericall is simply acute angled; and also, if you be desired to calculate a sphericall triangle, with two acute angles, and one obtuse, it will likewise fall within the reach of the same case, because its opposite sphericall is simply obtusangled. The reason of both the premises is from the equality of the opposite angles of concurring quadrants, which, that they are equall, no man needs to doubt, that will take the paines to let fall a perpendicular from the middle of the one quadrant upon the other; for so there will be two triangles made equilaterall; and seeing it is an universally received truth, that equall sides sustaine equall angles, the identitie of the perpendicular in both the foresaid triangles must needs manifest the equality of the two opposite angles.

I have been the ampler in the elucidating of this case, that, it over-running all the moods of the disergetick loxogonosphericals, the reader, in what mood or datoquære soever he please to resolve this foresaid case, may, for that purpose, to this place have recourse; to the which, without any further intended reiteration of this tenet, I doe heartily remit him.

The first especiall tenet of the generall maxim of the cathetothesis of this mood is Dasimforaug, that is, when the given angles are of the same nature, but different from the required, the perpendicular falleth outwardly, and the first verticall is a given angle; the second tenet belonging to the second case of this mood is Dadisforeug, that is, when the proposed angles are of different affections, the perpendicular is externally demitted, and one of the given angles is a second verticall; yet this discrepance is to be observed betweene the externall prosiliencie of the perpendicular arch in this case, and that other of the former; that in the former, it is no matter from which of the ends of the proposed side the perpendicular be let fall upon one of the comprehending legs of the angle required, which leg must be increased, for it is a generall notandum that the sustentative leg of a perpendicular's exterior demission must alwayes be continued; but, in this case, the outward falling of the perpendicular is onely from one extremity of the given side; for, if it be demitted likewise from the other end, it falleth then inwardly, and so produceth the third tenet of this mood, which is Dadisgatin, that is, if the given angles be of a different quality, and that the perpendicular be internally demitted, the double verticall is one of the proposed angles.

The nature of the perpendicular's demission in all the cases of this mood being thus to the full explained, we may, without impediment, proceed to the performance of all the orthogonosphericall operations, each in its own order thereto belonging.

To begin therefore at the first, whose quæsitum, as I have told you already, is a verticall angle, we must know, seeing the work is orthogonospherically to be performed, that the forementioned prænoscendum cannot be obtained without the helpe of one of the sixteen datoquæres; and therefore, in my Trissotetras, considering the nature of what is given, and asked in the cases of this mood, I have appointed Upalam to be the subservient of its prænoscendum; for by the resolver thereof, To—Tag—Nuꞔ Mir, the subtendent and an angle being given; for one of the given sides of every loxogonosphericall, if the perpendicular be rightly demitted, becomes a subtendent, and sometimes two given sides are subtendents both, we frame these three peculiar problems for the three prænoscendas; to wit, Utopat, for the double verticall, by the meanes of the great subtendent side, and the prime opposite angle; secondly, Udobaud, for obtaining of the first verticall in the little rectangle, by vertue of the lesser subtendent in the same rectangle, and the next opposite angle; lastly, Uthophauth, for the first co-verticall, by meanes of the first co-subtendent, and first co-opposite angle, all which is at large set downe in the first partition of Alamebna in my table.

The first and chiefe operation being thus perfected, the verticall angles so found out must concurre with each its correspondent opposite, for the obtaining of the perpendicular necessary for the accomplishment of the second operation in every one of the cases of the foresaid mood; to which effect, Amaner is made the subservient, by whose resolver, Say—Nag—TⱳꞔNyr, these three datoquæres, Opatca, Obautca, and Ophauthca come to light, and is manifestly shown how, by any paire of three severall couples of different angles, the perpendicular is acquirable.

Now, though of this work, as it is a single one, no more then of the other succeeding it in the same mood, nor of the last two in any of the disergeticks in their full analogy, I doe not make any mention at all in my table; but, after the couching of the first operation for the prænoscendas, supply the roomes of the other two, with an equivalent row of proportionals out of them specified, for attaining to the knowledge of the maine quæsitum; yet in this comment upon that table, for the more perspicuities sake, and that the reader may as well know what way the rule is made, as how thereby a demand is to be found out, I have thought fit to expatiat my selfe for his satisfaction on each operation apart, and analytically to display in the glosse what is compounded in the Trissotetras.

And therefore, according to that prescribed method, to proceed in this mood, the perpendicular by the second operation being already obtained, it is requisite for the promoving of a third work, that the said perpendicular be made to joyne with the second verticaline, the double verticall, and second co-verticall, conforme to the quality of the three cases, thereby to obtaine the angles at the base, for the which all these operations have been set on foot; to wit, the next cathetopposite, whose complement to a semicircle is alwayes the angle required, the prime cathetopposite and the second cocathetopposite. For the prosecuting of this last work, Edoman is the subservient, by whose resolver, To—Neg—Sa☞Nir, we are instructed how to regulate the Problemets of Catheudob, Cathatop, and Catheuthops.

Now, these two last operations being thus made patent in their several structures, it is not amisse that we ponder how appositely they may be conflated into one, to the end that the verity of all the finall resolvers of the disergeticks in my Trissotetras, which are all and each of them composed of the ingredient termes of two different works, may be the more evidently knowne, and obvious to the reach of any ordinary capacity; for the performance hereof, the resolvers of these two operations are to be laid before us, Sa—Nag—Tw☞Nyr, and To—Neg—Sa☞Nir: and, seeing out of both these orders of proportionals there must result but one, it is to be considered which be the foure ejectitious termes, and which those foure we should reserve for the analogy required; all which, that it may be the better understood by the industrious reader, I will interpret the resolvers so farre forth as is requisite; and therefore, Say—Nag—To☞Nyr, being, As the sine of one of the angles at the base or cathetopposite is to the sine complement of a verticall, so the radius to the sine complement of the perpendicular; and the other, To—Neg—Sa☞Nir, being, As the radius to the sine complement of the perpendicular, so the sine of a verticall to the sine complement of a cathetopposite or angle at the base; it is perceivable enough how both the radius and the perpendicular are in both the rows; nor can it well escape the knowledge of one never so little versed in the elements of arithmetick, that the perpendiculars being the fourth terme in the first order of proportionals, is nothing else but that it is the quotient of the product of the middle termes, divided by the first, or logarithmically the remainder of the first terme's abstraction from the summe of the middle two, so that the whole power thereof is inclosed in these three termes; whereby it is most evident, that with what terme soever the foresaid perpendicular be employed to concurre in operation, the same effect will be produced by the concurrence of its ingredients with the said terme, and therefore in the second row of proportionals, where it is made use of for a fellow multiplyer with the third terme to produce a *factus*, which divided may quote the maine *quæsitum*, or logarithmically to joyne with the third terme for the summing of an aggregat, from which the first terme being abstracted, may residuat the terme demanded; it is all one whether the work be performed by it selfe or by its equivalent, viz. the three first termes of the first order of proportionals, in whose potentia it is; whereupon the fourth terme in the second row being that for the obtaining whereof both the analogies are made, we need not waste any labour about the finding out of the perpendicular, though a subservient to the chiefe quæsitum, but leaving roome for it in both the rows, that the equipollencie of its conflaters may the better appeare, go on in the work without it, and by the meanes of its constructive parts with as much certainty effectuat the same designe.

Thus may you see, then, how the eight termes of the forementioned resolvers are reduced into six; but there remaining yet two more to be ejected, that both the orders may be brought unto a compound row of foure proportionals, let us consider the radius, which being in both the rows, as I have once told you already, may peradventure, without any prejudice to the work, be spared out of both. Thus much thereof to any is perceivable, that in the first resolver it is the third proportionall, and in the second the first, and consequently a multiplyer in the one, and in the other a divider; or, logarithmically, in the second a subtracter, and in the first an adder. Now, it being well known that division overthrowes the structure of multiplication, and that what is made up by addition is by subtraction cast down, we need not undergoe the laboriousnesse of such a Penelopæan task, and by the division and abstraction of what we did adde and multiply, weave and unweave, build up and throw downe, the self same thing, but choose rather, seeing the radius undoeth in the one what it doth in the other, which in effect is to doe nothing at all, to dash the one against the other, and race it out of both, then idely to expend time, and have the proportion pestred with unnecessarie termes. Thus, from those two resolvers foure termes being with reason ejected, we must, for the finding out of the last in the second resolver, effectuat as much by three as formerly was on seven incumbent; which three being the first and second termes in the first row of proportionalls, and the third in the second, the two resolvers, Say—Nag—To(☞Nyr, and To—Neg—Sa(☞Nir, are comprehended by this one, Say—Nag—Sa(☞Nir, that is, As the sine of one verticall to the antisine of an opposite, so the sine of another verticall to the antisine of another opposite; and though the second resolver doth import that this other opposite is to be found out by the antisine of the perpendicular and sine of a secondarie verticall, yet doth it in nothing evince the coincidence of the two operations in one, because the first two termes of the resultative analogie doe adæquatly stand for the perpendicular, which I have proved already, and therefore these two in their proper places, co-working with the third terme according to the rule of proportion, have the selfe same influence that the perpendicular so seconded hath upon the operatum.

Now, to contract the generality of this finall resolver, Say—Nag—Sa(☞Nir, to all the particular cases of this mood, we must say, When the given angles are of the same affection, and the required diverse, as in Dasimforaug, the first case, Sat—

Nop—Seud☞Nob*Kir, that is, As the sine of the double verticall to the antisine of the prime cathetopposite, so the sine of the second verticaline, or verticall in the lesser rectangle, to the antisine of the next cathetopposite, whose complement to a semicircle is the angle required.

But when, the affection of the given angles being different, the perpendicular is made to fall without, as in Dadisforeug, the second case of this mood, the resolver thereof is particularised thus, Saud—Nob—Sat☞Nop*Ir, that is, As the sine of the first verticaline, or verticall in the rectanglet, to the sine complement of the nearest cathetopposite, so the sine of the double verticall to the sine complement of the prime cathetopposite, which is the angle required.

And, lastly, if with the different qualities of the given and demanded angles the perpendicular be let fall within, as in Dadisgatin, the third case of this mood, then is the finall resolver to be determined thus, Sauth—Noph—Seuth☞Nops*Ir, that is, As the sine of the first co-verticall to the co-sine of the first co-opposite, so is the sine of the second co-verticall to the co-sine of the second co-opposite, which is the angle required.

The originall reason of all these operations is grounded on the axiome of Nabad-prosver, as the first syllable of its directory, Alama, giveth us to understand, which we may easily perceive by the analogy, that is onely amongst the angles without any intermixture of sides in the termes of the proportion.

The second mood of the first angulary figure, that is to say, the first two termes of whose datas are angles, is Allamebne, which comprehendeth all those disergetick questions, wherein two angles being given and a side betweene, one of the other sides is demanded; which side, the perpendicular being let fall, is alwayes one of the second subtendents, viz. in the first case a second subtendent of the lesser triangle, in the second a second subtendent in the great rectangle, and in the last a second co-sub-tendent.

To the knowledge of all these, that we may the more easily attaine, we must consider the generall maxim of the cathetothesis of this mood, which is Cafyxe-geq, that is to say, that in all the cases of Allamebne the perpendicular falleth from the side required, and from that point thereof where it conterminats with the given side upon the third side, continued if need be; and according to the variety of the second subtendent, which is the side demanded, there be these three especiall tenets of this generall maxim, to wit, Dasimforauxy, Dadiscracforeug, and Dadiscramgatin.

Dasimforauxy, the first especiall tenet of the generall maxim of the cathetothesis of this mood, sheweth, that when the proposed angles are of the same quality and ho-mogeneall, the perpendicular falleth externally, and the first verticall is one of the given angles, and annexed to the required side.

The second tenet, Dadiscracforeug, which pertaineth to the second case of this mood, sheweth, that when the given angles are of a discrepant nature and heterogeneall, and that the concurse of the proposed and required sides is at an acute angle, that then the perpendicular must be demitted outwardly, and one of the proposed angles becomes a second verticall.

The third tenet is Dadiscramgatin, whereby we learne, that if with the various affection of the angles given, the concurse, mentioned in the preceding tenet, be at an obtuse angle, the perpendicular falleth inwardly, and that one of the foresaid angles is a double verticall. This is the onely case of Allamebne, wherein the perpendicular is demitted inwardly, save when the three angles are qualified all alike, of which case, because it falleth in all the moods of the loxogonosphericall disergeticks, and that in Alamebna I have spoke at large thereof, I shall not need, I hope, to make any more mention hereafter.

Having thus unfolded the mysteries of the perpendicular's demission in all the cases of this mood, as I must doe in all those of every one of the other loxogonosphericall disergeticks, because such obliquangulars, till they be reduced to a rectangularity, which, without the perpendicular, is not performable, can never logarithmically be resolved, I may safely go on, without any let to the reader, to the three severall orthogonosphericall operations thereof, as they stand in order.

The quæsitas of the first operation, which are alwayes the prænoscendas of the mood, are in this mood the same that they were in the last, to wit, the double verticall, the first verticaline, and the first covertical, and are likewise to be found out by the same datas, both of side and angle here, that they were in the former mood ; that is, for the side by the first and great subtendent, the first but little subtendent, and the first co-subtendent; and for the angle, by the prime cathetopposite, the nearest cathetopposite, and the first co-cathetopposite : so that the datoquære sounding thus, the subtendent and an oblique angle being given to find the other oblique, the subservient of this computation must needs be Upalam, and its resolver To—Tag—Nut☞Mir, which sheweth that the subducing of the logarithm of the radius from the summe of the logarithms of the sine complement of one of the first subtendents, and tangent of one of the angles at the base, residuats the logarithm of the tangent complement of one of the verticals required, and consequently involveth within so much generality the particular resolutions of the sub-problems of Upalam, viz. Utopat, Vdobaud, and Vthophauth, diversified thus according to the variety of their prænoscendas, whereon, to speak ingenuously, I intend to insist no longer ; for, besides that the peculiar enodation of all the three apart is clearly set downe in my glosse on the last mood, they are in both the first partitions of the moods of Ahalebmane to the full expressed in the table of my Trissotetras.

The verticall angles, according to the diversity of the three cases, being by the foresaid datas thus obtained, must concurre with each its correspondent first subtendent, notified by the characteristicks of τ. δ. θ. for finding out of the perpendicular requisite for the performance of the second work in every one of the cases of this mood.

o

And to this effect, Ubamen is made the subservient, by whose resolver, Nag—Mu—☞Torp☞Myr, these three problems, Utatatca, Udaudca, and Uthauthca, are made manifest, and the same quæsitum attained unto by the datas of three severall subtendents and verticals.

The perpendicular being thus found out, must, for the furtherance of the third operation, joyne with the second verticaline, the double verticall, and second co-verticall, according to the nature of the case in question, the datas being the same with those of the third work of the last mood, thereby to attaine unto the knowledge of the second little subtendent, the second great subtendent, and the second co-subtendent, the which are all the maine quæsitas of this mood. To the performance of this last operation, Etalum is the subservient, whose resolver, Torp—Me—Nag☞Mur, teacheth us how to deale with the under datoquæres of Catheudwd, Cathetwt, and Catheuthwth.

Now, the coalescencie of these two last operations in one, proceeding from the casting out of the radius in both the orders of proportionals, and leaving roome for the perpendicular, without taking the paines to know its value, as hath beene shewne already in the first mood of the same figure, it cannot be much amisse, in this place, to give a further illustration thereof, and make the reader, by an arithmeticall demonstration, feele, as it were, how palpable the truth is of compacting eight proportionals into foure; let there be then these two orders of numbers, 4—6—8☞12, and 8—12—14☞21, where we may suppose eight to be the radius, and twelve the perpendicular, for such like suppositions can inferre no great absurdity, and then let us consider how those termes doe beare to one another, especially the 12 and 8, which, by possessing foure places, make up halfe the number of the proportionals. First, we see that twelve in the first row is nothing else but the result of the product of 6 in 8 divided by 4. And secondly, that 8 in the second row casteth downe, by its division, whatsoever, by its multiplication, it builded up in the first; upon which observations, we may ground these sequels, that 12 may be safely left out, both in the fourth and sixth place, taking, instead of it, the number of 4. 6. and 8. in whose potentia it is; and next, 8 undoing in one place what it doth in another, may, with greater ease, void them both. So that, by this abbreviated way of analogising 4 and 6 alone in their due order before 14, which is the third terme of the second row, conduce as much to the obtaining of the fourth, or if you will eighth proportional 21, as if the other foure termes of the two eighths and twelves were concurrent with it. How plaine all this is, no question needs to be made; and, therefore, to returne to our resolvers, for the explicating whereof we thought good to make this digression, we must understand that the finall resolver, in its generall expression, made out of them, they being, as they are, materially displayed, Nag—Mu—Torp☞Myr, and Torp—Me—Nag☞Mur, is no other then Nag—Mu—Na☞Mur, that is, As the sine complement of one verticall is to the tangent complement of a subtendent, so the sine complement of another verticall to the tangent complement of another subtendent; and analytically to trace the running of this operation, even to the source from whence it flowes, by foysting in the perpendicular and radius, we may bring it to the consistence of the former two subordinate resolvers, whereof the first is, As the sine complement of a first, or a double verticall, to the tangent complement of a first subtendent, so the radius to the tangent complement of the perpendicular; and the second, As the radius to the tangent complement of the perpendicular, so the sine complement of a second, or a double verticall, to the tangent complement of a second subtendent, which is the side required, and the fourth proportionall of Nag—Mu—Nat☞Mur, whose generality is to be contracted to every one of the three cases of this mood thus : If both the angles given be of the same nature, they being the first verticals, from which the cathetus fals on either side, increased according to the demand of the side, as in the first case, Dasimforauxy, we must particularise the common resolver in this manner, Nat—Mut—Neud☞Nwd*Yr, that is, As the antisine of the double verticall is to the antitangent of the first and great subtendent, so the antisine of the second verticall in the lesser rectangle to the antitangent of the second subtendent in the same little rectangle, which subtendent is the side required. For the second case of this mood, viz. Dadiscracforeug, we must say, Naud —Mud—Nat☞Mwt*Yr, that is, As the sine complement of the first and little verticall to the tangent complement of the first and little subtendent, so the sine complement of the double verticall to the tangent complement of the second and great subtendent. And lastly, for the third case, Dadiscramgatin, the finall resolver, is determined thus, Nauth—Muth—Neuth☞Mwth*Yr, that is, As the co-sine of the first co-verticall is to the co-tangent of the first co-subtendent, so the co-sine of the second co-verticall to the co-tangent of the second co-subtendent, which is the side in this third case required.

The truth of all these operations is grounded on the axiome of Naverprortes, as we are certified by the first syllable of its directory Allera, which we may perceive by the direct analogy that is betweene the sine's complements of the verticall angles, and the tangent's complements, and consequently reciprocall 'twixt them and the tangents, of the verticall sides, which, in this mood, are always second subtendents.

The second disergetick and angulary figure, is Ahamepnare, which embraceth all those obliquangularie sphericals, wherein two angles being given, with an opposite side, another angle, or the side interjacent, is demanded. This figure, conforme to the two severall quæsitas, hath two moods, viz. Amanepra, and Ammanepreb.

The first mood hereof, which is Amanepra, belongeth to all those loxogonosphericall questions, wherein, two angles with an opposite side being proposed, the third angle is required, which is alwayes a first verticall, a second verticall, or a first co-verticall ; to the notice of all which, that we may with ease attaine, the generall maxim of the cathetothesis of this mood is to be considered, which is Cafriq, that is to say, that in all the cases of Amanepra, the perpendicular falleth from the angle required upon the side opposite to that angle, and terminated by the other two angles, which side is to be increased if need be.

Now, in regard, that besides the cathetothesis of this mood, and some three more, to wit, all those loxogonosphericals wherein the quæsitum is either a partiall verticall, or segment at the base, there is a peculiar mensurator pertaining to every one of the foure, called, in my Trissotetras, the *plus minus*, because it sheweth by the species thereof to the moods appropriated, whether the summe, or difference of the verticall angles, and segments at the base, be the angle or side required, and so clearly leadeth us thorough all the cases of each of the moods, that either by abstracting the fourth proportionall from an angle or a segment, or by abstracting an angle or a segment from it, or lastly, by joyning it to an angle or a segment, with an incredible facility we attaine to the knowledge of the maine quæsitum, whether angulary or laterall. Let the reader then be pleased to know, that the mensurator, or plus minus of this mood, is Sindifora, which evidently declareth, as by its representatives in the explanation of the table is apparent, that, if the demission of the perpendicular be internall, the summe; if exterior, the difference of the verticall angles is the angle required.

Seeing thus the notice of the manner of the perpendiculars falling is so necessary, it is expedient, for our better information therein, that we severally perpend the three especiall tenets of the generall maxim of the cathetothesis of this mood, which are Dadissepamforaur, Dadissexamforeur, and Dasimatin.

Dadissepamforaur, which is the tenet of the first case, sheweth, that when the angles given are of a different nature, and that the proposed side is opposite to an obtuse angle, the perpendicular falleth outwardly, and the first verticall is the angle required.

The second tenet belonging to the second case of this mood, viz. Dadissexamforeur, sheweth, that if the proposed angles be of discrepant affections, and that the side given be conterminat with an obtuse angle, the perpendicular is demitted externally, and the demanded angle is a second verticall.

The third tenet pertaining to the last case of this mood, to wit, Dasimatin, evidenceth, that if the angles proposed be of the same quality, the perpendicular falleth interiourly, and the double verticall is the angle required.

Having thus, as I suppose, hereby evinced every difficulty of the perpendicular's demission in all the cases of this mood, I may the more boldly, in the interim, proceed to the three rectangular works thereto belonging. Now, it being manifest that the prænoscendas of this mood, or the quæsitas of the first operation thereof, are the same with those of the two moods of the first disergetick figure, to wit, the double verticall, the first verticaline, and the first co-verticall; and that, without any alteration at all, they are to be obtained by the same datas, both of side and angle, in this mood of Amanepra, that they were in the former moods of Alamebna and Allamebne, without any further specifying what these given sides and angles are, which are to the full expressed in the last two forementioned moods, I must make bold thither to direct you, where you shall be sure also to learne all that is necessary to know of the subservient and resolver of the first operation of this mood, both which, to wit, Upalam and To—Tag—Nu☞Mir, are inseparable dependents on all the angularie prænoscendas of the loxogonosphericall disergeticks; and though, within the generality of this subservient, be comprehended the peculiar problemets of Utopat, Udobaud, and Uthophauth, which are all three at large couched in the Trissotetras of this mood; yet, because what hath beene already said thereof in the foresaid figure, may very well suffice for this place, the reader's diligence, I hope, in the turning of a leaf, will save me the labour of any further recapitulation.

The prænoscendas, or the verticall angles, according to the nature of the case, being by the foresaid datas thus found out, must needs joyne with each its correspondent opposite, specified by the characteristicks of π. ϛ. φ. for the obtaining of the perpendicular, which, in all the rest of the disergetick moods, as well as this, is alwayes the quæsitum of the second operation thorough all the cases thereof. Of this work, Amaner is the subservient, by whose resolver, Say—Nag—To☞Nyr, the three subproblems, Opatca, Obaudca, and Ophauthca, are made known, and the same quæsitum attained unto by the datas of three several both cathetopposites and verticals, it being the only mood which, with Alamebna, hath a cathetopposite and verticall catheteuretick identity. The perpendicular being thus obtained, is, for the effecting of the third and last operation, to concurre with the next cathetopposite, the prime cathetopposite, and the second co-cathetopposite, as the case requires it, thereby to find out the main quæsitum, which, in the first case, by abstracting the fourth proportionall, in the second, by abstracting from the fourth proportionall, and in the third, by adding the fourth proportionall to another verticall, is easily obtained by those that have the skill to discerne which be the greater or lesser of two verticals proposed. To the perfecting of this third word, Exoman is the subservient, whose resolver, Ne—To—Nag☞ Sir, instructeth us how to unfold the peculiar problems of Cathobeud, Cathopat, and Cathopseuth.

Now, the nature of proportion requiring that of two rowes of proportionals, when the fourth in the first order is first in the second, that then the multiplyers become dividers, and the dividers multiplyers, as by these numbers following you may perceive, viz. 2—4—6☞12, for the first row, and 12—4—15☞5, for the second; of which proportionals, because of the fourth terme in the first rowes being first in the second, if you turne as many multiplyers into dividers, as you can, and where the identity of a figure requires it, dash out a multiplyer against a divider, you will find the two foures by this reason being raced out, and the two twelve, because of their being in the power of the three first proportionals of the first row, likewise left out, that this analogy of 6—2—15, doth the same effect, that the former seven proportionals, for obtaining of the quæsitum, viz. 5; the reason whereof is altogether grounded upon the inversion of a permutat proportion, or the retrograd analogy of the alternat termes, whereby the consequents are compared to consequents, and antecedents to antecedents, in the preposterous method of beginning at the second of both the consequents and antecedents, and ending at the first; therefore, as I was telling you, the nature of proportion requiring that in such a case the multiplyers and dividers be bound to interchange their places, the resolvers of the last two operations, viz. Say—Nag—To☞Nyr, and Ne—To—Nag☞Sir, the first whereof being, As the sine of a verticall angle to the sine complement of an angle at the base, or one of the Cathetopposites, so the radius to the sine complement of the perpendicular; and the second, As the sine complement of the perpendicular to the radius, so the sine compliment of one of the Cathetopposite angles, to one of the verticals, may both of them, according to the former rule, be handsomely compacted in this one analogy, Na—Say—Nag☞ Sir, that is, As the sine complement of an opposite is to the sine of a verticall, so the sine complement of another opposite to the sine of another verticall.

This foresaid generall resolver, according to the three severall cases of this mood, is to be specialised into so many finall resolvers; the first whereof for Dadissepamforaur, Nop—Sat—Nob☞Seudfr*At*Aut*ir, that is, As the sine complement of the prime cathetopposite to the sine of the double verticall, so the sine complement of the nearest cathetopposite to the sine of the second verticalin; the which subtracted from the double verticall, leaveth the first and great verticall, which is the angle required.

Next, for the second case of this mood, Dadissexamforeur, we must make use of Nob—Saud—Nop☞Satfr, *Aud*Eut*ir, that is, As the sine complement of the next opposite to the sine of the first verticallet, so the sine complement of the prime opposite, to the sine of the double verticall, from which, if you deduce the first verticalin, there will remaine the second and great verticall for the angle demanded.

Lastly, for the third case, Dasimatin, we must say Noph—Sauth—Nops☞Seuth* jauth*ir, that is, As the sine complement of the first co-opposite to the sine of the first co-verticall, so the sine complement of the second co-opposite, to the sine of the second co-verticall, which added to the first co-verticall, maketh up the angle we desire.

The veritie of all these operations is grounded on the axiome Nabadprosver, as the second syllable of its directorie Alama giveth us to understand, and as we may discerne more easily by the samenesse in species amongst the proportionall termes; for they are all angles, the first and third being angles at the base, for these are alwaies of the opposits, and the second and fourth termes of the verticall angles, which verticall angles in the finall resolvers of this mood, are, according to the foresaid axiome, to the angles of the base directly proportionall and contrarily.

The second mood of the second angularie figure of the loxogonosphericall disergeticks, named Ahamepnare is Ammanepreb, which is said of all those obliquangularie problems, wherein two angles and an opposite side being given, the side between is required, and is alwaies one of the basal segments; to the knowledge whereof, that

we may the more easily attaine, we must consider the generall maxime of the cathetothesis of this mood, which is Cafregpagyq; that is, that the perpendicular falleth
still from the given side, opposite to both the angles given, and upon the side required, continued, if need be, in all and every one of the cases of Amanepreb.

The Plusminus of this mood is Sindiforiu, that is to say, the summe of the segments
of the base, if the perpendicular fall inwardly, and the difference of the bases, if exte-
riorly, is the side demanded.

The perpendicular's demission being a *sine quo non* in all disergetick operations, it
will not be amisse, that we ponder what the three severall tenets are of the cathetothesis of this mood, and what is meaned by Dadissepamfor, Dadissexamfor, and
Dasimin.

Dadissepamfor, the tenet of the first case of this mood, sheweth that if the given
angles be of severall natures, and that the proposed side be opposite to an obtuse
angle, the perpendicular falleth externally.

The second tenet, Dadissexamfor, expresseth that if the proposed angles be different, and that the side given be conterminat with the obtuse angle, it falleth likewise
outwardly.

But Dasimin, which is the third tenet, signifieth that if the given angles be of the
same affection, the falling of the perpendicular is internall.

This much being premised of the perpendicular, we may securely goe on to the
orthogonosphericall works of the mood; and so beginning with the first operation,
consider what the prænoscendas are, which are alwaies the quæsitas by the first operation obtainable, and in this mood the bases of the triangle; but more particularly to
descend to the illustration of the cases of Amanepreb, the prænoscendum of the first
case, is the first and great base of the second, the first but little base, and of the third,
the first co-base. Now, though these three prænoscendas be totally different from
those of the three former moods, yet are they to be acquired by the same, and no
other datas; because none of the angularie figures must differ from one another in the
datas of their prænoscendas, as out of the definition of an angularie figure in the entrie
of the second mood set downe, is easie to be collected; these datas being tendred to
us of intermixed circularie parts, that is to say, of both sides and angles, the side
being the first subtendentall, or great subtendent, the first subtendentine, or little subtendent, and the first co-subtendent; and the angles the prime cathetopposite, the
next cathetopposite, and the first co-cathetopposite; so that, considering what is demanded, and that the datoquære thereof must be expressed thus, the hypotenusa and
an oblique being given, to finde the ambient conterminat with the proposed angle, we
are for the calculation of this work necessitated to have recourse to Ubamen, which
in the table of my Trissotetras obtaineth the roome of its subservient, to the end that
by its resolver, Torp—Mu—Lag☞Myr, being instructed how by cutting off the
logarithm of the radius from the summe of the logarithms of the M. of one of the first

subtendents, and secant complement of one of the cathetopposits, or angles at the base, residuats the logarithm of the tangent complement of the base required, we may deliveredly extract, out of the generality of that proposition, the peculiar subordinate resolutions of these three problems of Ubamen, viz. Utopæt, Udobæd, and Uthophæth, varied, as you see, according to the diversity of the prænoscendas, which being, as you were told already, the first basal or great base, the first baset or little base, and the first co-base, I will not detain you any longer upon this matter, but the rather hasten my transition to the other work, that in the prænoscendall partition of Ammanepreb, there is enough thereof set downe in the table of my Trissotetras.

The prænoscendas of Ammanepreb, or the three severall first bases, conforme to the various nature of the cases thereof, being by the foresaid datas happily obtained, must concurre with each its correspondent cathetopposite, discernable, in their severall qualities, by the characteristicks of π. 6. φ. for finding out of the perpendicular, which is the perpetuall quæsitum of the operation. The subservient of this work is Ethaner, by whose resolver, To—Tag—Se℘☞Tyr, we come to the knowledge of Ethaners three subdatoquæres, viz. Ætopca, Ædobca, and Æthophca, whereby we may perceive that the same quæsitum, to wit, the perpendicular is obtained by the datas of the three severall, both bases and cathetopposite angles.

This so often mentioned perpendicular being thus made known, must, for the performance of the last and third work, joyne with the nixt cathetopposite, the prime cathetopposite, and the second co-cathetopposite, as the case will beare it, the datas being the same in every point here, that in the last operation of the foregoing mood, as by the subservients Exoman and Epsoner, is obvious to any judicious reader, thereby to obtaine the maine quæsitum, which in the first case, by abstracting the fourth proportionall from the first great base, in the second by abstracting from the fourth proportionall the first little base, and in the third by adding the fourth proportionall to another segment of the base, is findable by any that will undergoe the labour of adding and substracting. For the accomplishment of this last operation Epsoner is the subservient, by whose resolver Tag—Tolb—Te℘☞Syr, we are taught how to deale with its three subproblems, Cathobœd, Cathopœt, and Cathopsœth.

These last two operations being thus to the full extended, it remaineth now to treat how they ought to be in one compacted, or rather, for brevitie of computation, we should compact them both in one before we take the paines to extend them ; yet, because practice requireth one method, and the order of doctrine another, we will, that we may be the lesse troublesome to the readers memory, goe on, by ejecting some, and reserving other proportional termes, in our usuall course of conflating two resolvers together. These resolvers are in this mood, To—Tag—Se℘☞Tyr, and Tag—To—Te℘☞Syr, the first thereof sounding, As the radius to the tangent of one of the cathetopposite angles, or angles at the base, so the sine of one of the first bases to the tangent of the perpendicular ; and the second, As the tangent of one of the other cathetopposite angles to the radius, so the tangent of the perpendicular to the sine of the side required.

Here may the reader be pleased to consider, that in all the glosse upon the posterior operations of my disergeticks, I have beene contented to set downe, as he may see in the last two propositions, the bare theorems of the resolvers, conforme to the nature of their analogy, without troubling my selfe or any body else, with repeating or reiterating the way how the logarithms of the middle and initiall termes are to be handled for the obtaining of a fourth logarithm ; all that can be desired therein, being to the full expressed already in my ample comments upon the orthogonosphericall problems ; to the which the industrious reader, in case of doubting, may, if he please, have recourse, without any great losse of time or labour; however, for his better encouragement, I give another hint thereof in the closure of this treatise.

But, to returne where we left, seeing out of these two resolvers, To—Tag—Se ☞Tyr, and Tag—To—Te☞Syr, according to the rules of coalescency, mentioned in both the moods of Ahalebmane, both the perpendicular and radius may be ejected without any danger of losing our aime of the maine quæsitum, it is evident that the proportion of the remanent termes, is Ta—Tag—Se☞Syr, which comprehendeth both the last two resolvers, and the three foresaid problemets thereto belonging ; and being interpreted, As the tangent of one cathetopposite angle to the tangent of another cathetopposite, so the sine of one of the first bases to the sine of a side, which ushers in the side required.

This generall resolver, according to the three severall cases of this mood, is to be particularised into so many finall resolvers ; the first whereof, for Dadissepamfor, is Tob—Top—Sæt☞Sædfr*Æt*Dyr, that is, As the tangent of the next opposite to the tangent of the prime opposite, so the sine of the first great base to the sine of the second little base ; which, subducted from the foresaid first great base, will, for the remainder, afford us that segment of the base, which is the side in the first case required.

Then, for the second case, Dadissexamfor, the finall resolver, is Top—Tob—Sæd ☞Sœtfr*Æd*Dyr, that is, As the tangent of the prime cathetopposite to the tangent of the next opposite, so the sine of the first baset, or little base, to the sine of the second and great base ; from which, if we abstract the foresaid first little base, the difference or remainder will be that segment of the base, which is the side demanded.

Lastly, for the case Dasimin, the finall resolver is Tops—Toph—Sæth☞Sœthj* Æth*Syr, that is, As the tangent of the second co-opposite to the tangent of the first co-opposite, so the sine of the first co-base to the sine of the second co-base ; the summe of which two co-bases is the totall base or side in the third case required.

The reason of all this is proved by the third disergetick axiome, which is Siubprortab, as is pointed at by the first syllable of its directory, Ammena, and manifested to us in all the analogies of this mood, every one whereof runneth upon tangents of angles, and sines of segments, both to the base belonging ; nor can any doubt, that heares the resolution of the cases of Ammanepreb, but that the habitude, which all the termes thereof have to one another, proceedeth meerly from the reciprocall proportion which the tangents of the opposite angles have to the basal segments, and contrariwise.

The third loxogonosphericall disergetick figure, and first of the later, that is, the first two termes of whose datas are sides, what ere the quæsitum be, is Ehenabrole, which comprehendeth all those problems, wherein two sides being given, and an angle betweene, either a cathetopposite angle, or the third side is demanded. This figure, conforme to the two severall quæsitas, hath two moods, to wit, Enerablo and Ennerable.

The first mood hereof, Enerablo, containeth all those obliquangularie questions, wherein two sides, with the angle comprehended with them, being proposed, another angle is required, which angle is alwayes one of the cathetopposites or angles at the base, that is, either the complement to a semicircle of the next cathetopposite, the prime cathetopposite, or the second co-cathetopposite ; to the knowledge of all which, that we may with facility attaine, let us consider the generall maxim of the cathetothesis of this mood, which is Cafregpigeq, that is to say, that the perpendicular in all the cases of Enerablo falleth from that given side, which is opposite to the angle required, upon the other given side, continued if need be ; and according to the variety of the angle at the base, which is the angle sought for, there be these three especiall tenets of the generall maxim of this mood, viz. Dacramfor, Damracfor, and Dasimquæin.

Dacramfor, which is the tenet of the first case, sheweth, that if the proposed angle be sharp, and the required flat, the perpendicular must fall outwardly.

Damracfor, the tenet of the second case, signifieth, that if a blunt or obtuse angle be given, and an acute or sharp demanded, the demission of the perpendicular must, as in the last, be externall.

Lastly, Dasimquæin, the tenet of the third case, sheweth, that if the given and required angles be of the same nature, the perpendicular must fall inwardly.

Having thus unfolded all the intricacies in my Trissotetras of the cathetothetick partition of this mood, I may, without breaking order, step back, to explicate what is contained in the preceding partition ; and for the accomplishing of the first orthogonosphericall work of this mood, consider what its prænoscendas are, and by what datas they are to be obtained ; but, seeing both the prænoscendas and the datas, together with the subservient and its resolver, with all the three subdatoquæres, and, in a word, the whole contents of the first partition of this mood of Enerablo is the same in all and every jot with the prænoscendas, datas, subservient, resolver, and problemets, contained in the first partition of the last mood Ammanepreb ; I will not need to tell you any more, then that the Trissotetras it selfe, though otherwise short enough, shewing that Ubamen is the subservient to the prænoscendas, Torp—Mu—Lag☞Myr, its resolver ; and Utopæt, Udobæd, and Uthophæth, the three subproblems, both of this and the next preceding mood, you be pleased to have recourse to the glosse upon the last mood, where this matter is treated of at large ; to the which, for avoyding of repetition, I doe heartily recommend you.

The first work being thus expedited, we are to find out the perpendicular by the second ; but so as that my direction to the reader for the performance thereof shall detaine me no longer here then the time I am willing to bestow in telling him, that the whole progresse of this operation, as well as of the preceding, is amply expressed in my comment on the last mood, from which, what ere is written of the subservient, Ethaner, its resolver, To—Tag—Se☞Tyr, or the under-problems, Ætopca, Ædobca, and Æthophca, thereby resolved, may conveniently be transplaced hither, and reseated there againe, without any prejudice to either ; Ammanepreb being the onely mood, which, with this of Enerablo, hath a basal and opposite catheteuretick identity.

The perpendicular, by these meanes being found out, must be employed in the last work of this mood, to concurre with the second basidion, or little base, the second great base, and the second co-base, for obtaining of such cathetopposites as are, or usher the maine quæsitas, which, in the first case, is the complement of the fourth proportionall, viz. the next cathetopposite, to a semicircle ; in the second case the prime cathetopposite, and in the third the second co-cathetopposite. For the perfecting of this operation, Erelam is the subservient, by whose resolver, Sei—Teg—To☞Tir, we are instructed how to unfold its peculiar problemets, Œdcathob, Œtcathop, and Œthcathops.

All the three operations being thus singly accomplished, according to our wonted manner, the last two must be inchaced into one, and therefore their resolvers, To—Tag—Se☞Tyr, and Sei—Teg—To☞Tir, must be untermed of some of their proportionals ; the which, that we may performe the more judiciously, let us consider what they signifie apart ; the first importeth, as in the last mood I told you, that, As the radius is to the tangent of one of the opposite angles, so the sine of one of the first bases to the tangent of the perpendicular ; the second soundeth, As the sine of one of the second bases to the tangent of the perpendicular, so the radius to the tangent of an angle, which either ushers, or is the angle required.

Hereby it is evident how the radius is a multiplyer in the one, and a divider in the other, and that the perpendicular, which, with the radius, is a multiplyer in the second row, is in the power of the three first termes of the first row, whereof the radius is one, by vertue of all which we must proceed just so with these last two operations here, as we have already done with the two last of the moods of Alamebna, Allamebne, and Ammanepreb ; and ejecting the radius and perpendicular out of both, instead of To—Tag—Se☞Tyr, and Sei—Teg—To☞Tir, set downe Sei—Tag—Se☞Tir, that is, As the sine of one of the second bases to the tangent of one of the cathetopposites, so is the sine of one of the first bases to the tangent of one of the other cathetopposites ; which proposition comprehendeth to the full the last two operations, and according to the three severall cases of this mood, is to be individuated into so many finall resolvers.

The first thereof, for Dacramfor, is Sœd—Top—Sæt☞Tob*Kir, that is, As the sine of the second basidion, or little base, is to the tangent of the prime cathetopposite, so the sine of the first and great base to the tangent of the next cathetopposite, whose complement to a semicircle is the angle required.

The second finall resolver, is for Damracfor, the tenet of the second case, and is Sœt—Tob—Sæd☞Top*Ir, that is to say, As the sine of the second and great base to the tangent of the next cathetopposite, so the sine of the first basidion to the tangent of the prime opposite, which is the angle required.

The third and last finall resolver, is for the third case Dasimquæin, and is couched thus, Sœth—Toph—Sæth☞Tops*Ir, that is, As the sine of the second co-base is to the tangent of the first co-cathetopposite, so is the sine of the first co-base to the tangent of the second co-cathetopposite, which is the angle required.

The fundamentall reason of all this, is from the third disergetick axiome Siubprortab, the second determinater of whose directory, Ammena, sheweth that the mood of Enerablo, in all the finall resolvers thereof, oweth the truth of its analogy to the maxim of Siubprortab, because of the reciprocall proportion that is amongst its termes to be found betwixt the sines of the basall segments, and the tangents of the cathetopposite angles.

The second mood of Ehenabrole is Ennerable, which comprehendeth all those obliquangulary problems, wherein two sides being given, with an angle intercepted therein, the third side is demanded, which side is alwayes one of the second subtendents, that is, either the second subtendentine, the second subtendentall, or the second co-subtendent; to the notice of all which, that we may the more easily attaine, let us perpend the generall maxim of the cathetothesis of this mood, Cafregpaq; the meaning whereof is, that in this mood, whatever the case be, the perpendicular may fall from the extremity of either of the given sides, but must fall from one of them opposite to the angle proposed, and upon the other given side, continued if need be.

Here may the reader be pleased to observe, that the clause of the perpendiculars falling opposite to the proposed angle, though it be onely mentioned in this place, might have as well beene spoke of in any one of the rest of the cathetothetick comments; because it is a generalltie incumbent on the demission of perpendiculars in all loxogonosphericall disergetick figures, whether amblygonian or oxygonian, that it fall alwayes opposite to a knowne angle, and from the extremity of a knowne side.

Of this generall maxim, Cafregpaq, according to the variety of the second subtendent, which is the side required, there be these three especiall tenets, Dacforamb, Damforac, and Dakinatam.

Dacforamb, the tenet of the first case, giveth us to understand, that if the given angle be acute, and that one onely of the other two be an obtuse angle, the perpendicular falleth outwardly.

Damforac, the tenet of the second case, signifieth, that if the given angle be obtuse, and the other two acute, that the demission of the perpendicular is externall, as in the first.

Thirdly, Dakinatam, the tenet of the third case, and variator of the first, sheweth, that if the proposed angle be of the same affection with one of the other angles of the triangle, as in the first case, the perpendicular may fall inwardly.

The cathetology of this mood being thus expeded, the prænoscendas come next in hand to be discussed, which are the first bases, whose subservient is Vbamen, and its resolver, Torp—Mu—Lag☞Myr, upon which depend the three subdatoquæres of Vtopæt, Vdobæd, and Vthophæth.

Thus much I beleeve is expressed in the very table of my Trissotetras; and though a large explication might be with reason expected in this place, of what is but summarily mentioned there, yet because what concerneth this matter hath beene already treated of in the last two moods of Enerablo and Ammanepreb, the whole discourse whereof may be as conveniently perused as if it were couched here, I will not dull the reader with tedious rehearsals of one and the same thing, but, letting passe the progresse of this first work, with the manner of which, by my former instructions, I suppose him sufficiently well acquainted, will proceed to the catheteuretick operation of this mood, and perpend by what datas the perpendicular is to be found out.

To this effect, the prænoscendas of Ennerable, to wit, the first basal, the first basidion, and the first co-base, being, by the last work, already obtained, must concurre with each its correspondent first subtendent, viz. the first subtendentall, the first subtendentine, and the first co-subtendent, discernable in their severall natures by the figuratives of τ. δ. θ. for the perfecting of this second operation. The subservient of this work, is Uchener, by whose resolver, Neg—To—Nu☞Nyr, the three subproblems, Utæta, Utædca, and Uthæthca, are made manifest; by vertue whereof, it is perceivable how the same quæsitum is attained unto by the datas of three severall, both first subtendents and first bases.

The perpendicular being thus obtained, must assist some other terme in the third operation, for the finding out of the maine quæsitum; which quæsitum, though it be different from the finall one of the last mood, yet is the knowledge of them both attained unto by meanes of the same datas; the perpendicular and the three second bases being ingredients in both.

It being certaine then, that the perpendicular must concurre in the last work of this mood with the second basidion, the second basal, and second co-base, for obtaining the second subtendentine, the second subtendentall, and second co-subtendent; Enerul is made use of for their subservient, by whose resolver, To—Neg—Ne☞Nur, we are taught how to deale with its subordinat problems, Cathœdwd, Cathœtwt, and Cathœthwth.

All the three works being thus specified apart, according to our accustomed method, we will declare what way the last two are to be joyned into one; for the better effectuating whereof, their resolvers, Neg—To—Nu☞Nyr, and To—Neg—Ne☞Nur, must be interpreted; the first being, As the sine complement of a first base to the radius, so the sine complement of a first subtendent to the sine complement of the perpendicular. And the second, As the radius to the sine complement of a second base, so the sine complement of the perpendicular to the sine complement of a second subtendent, which is the side required.

Now, seeing a multiplier must be dashed against a divider, being both quantified alike, and that all unnecessary pestring of a work with superfluous ingredients is to be avoided, we are to deale with the radius and perpendicular in this place, as formerly we have done in the moods of Alamebna, Allamebne, Ammanepreb, and Enerablo, where we did eject them forth of both the orders of proportionalls; and when we have done the like here, instead of Neg—To—Nu☞Nyr, and To—Neg—Ne☞Nur, we may with the same efficacie say, Neg—Nu—Ne☞Nur, that is, As the sine complement of one side is to the sine complement of a subtendent, so the sine complement of another side to the sine complement of another subtendent; or more determinatly, As the sine complement of a first base to the sine complement of a first subtendent, so the sine complement of a second base to the sine complement of a second subtendent.

This theorem comprehendeth to the full both the last operations, and according to the number of the cases of this mood, is particularized into three finall resolvers, the first whereof for the first case, Dacforamb, is Næt—Nut—Nœd☞Nwd*yr, that is, As the sine complement of the first basal, or great base, to the sine complement of the first subtendentall, or great subtendent, so the sine complement of the second basidion, or little base, to the sine complement of the second subtendentine, or little subtendent, which is the side required.

The second finall resolver, is for Damforac, the second case, and is set downe thus, Næd—Nud—Nœt☞Nwt*yr, that is, As the sine complement of the first basidion to the sine complement of the first subtendentine, so the sine complement of the second basal to the sine complement of the second subtendentall, which is the side in this case required.

The third and last finall resolver is for Dakinatamb, and is expressed thus, Næth—Nuth—Nœth☞Nwth*yr, that is to say, As the sine complement of the first co-base to the sine complement of the first co-subtendent, so the sine complement of the second co-base to the sine complement of the second co-subtendent, which in the third case is always the side required.

The reason of all this is proved out of the fourth and last disergetick axiom, Niubprodnesver, whose directer Ennerra, sheweth by its determinater, the syllable Enn, that the datoquære of Ennerable is bound for the veritie of its proportion, in all the finall resolvers thereof, to the maxime of Niubprodnesver, because of the direct analogie that, amongst its termes, is to be seen betwixt the sines complements of the segments of the base, and the sines complements of the sides of the verticall angles, which in all this treatise, both for plainesse and brevity sake, I have thought fit to call by the names of first and second subtendents.

The fourth and last loxogonosphericall disergetick figure, and second of the lateralls, is Eherolabme, which is of all those obliquangularie problems, wherin two sides being given, and an opposite angle, the interjacent angle, or one of the other sides is demanded, and conforme to its two severall quæsitas, hath two moods, viz. Erelomab and Errelome.

The first mood hereof, Erelomab, comprehendeth all those loxogonosphericall problems, wherein two sides with an opposite angle being proposed, the angle between is demanded, which angle is still one of the verticals, that is, the first verticall, the second verticall, or the double vertical; to the notice of all which, that we may the more easily attain, we must consider the generall maxim of the cathetothesis of this mood, which is Cafriq, the very same in name with the generall cathetothetick maxim of Amanepra, and thus far agreeing with it, that the perpendicular in both must fal from the angle required, and upon the side opposite to that angle, increased if need be; but in this point different, that in Amanepra, the perpendicular's demission is from the angle required upon the opposite side, conterminat with the two proposed angles, and in Erelomab, it falleth from the required angle, upon the opposite side conterminat with the two proposed sides; and according to the variety of the fourth proportionall, which, in the analogies to this mood belonging, ushers in the verticall required, there be those three especiall tenets of the generall maxim of this mood, viz. Dacracforaur, Damracforeur, and Dacrambatin.

Dacracforaur, which is the tenet of the first case, sheweth that if the given and demanded angles be acute, and the third an obtuse angle, the perpendicular falleth outwardly upon the third side, and the required angle is a first verticall.

Dambracforeur, the tenet of the second case, importeth, that if the proposed angle be obtuse, and an acute angle required, the third angle being acute, the perpendicular must likewise in this case fall outwardly upon the third side, and the angle demanded be a second verticall.

Dacrambatin, the tenet of the third case, signifieth that if the proposed angle be acute, and an obtuse angle required, the perpendicular falleth inwardly, and the demanded angle is a double verticall.

I had almost forgot to tell you that Sindifora is the plus-minus of this mood, whereby we are given to understand, that the summe of the top angles, if the perpendicular fall within, and their difference, if it fall without, is the angle required; and seeing it varieth neither in name nor interpretation from the mensurator of Amanepra, the diversity betwixt them being onely in this, that the verticals there are invested with sines, and here with sine complements, I must make bold to desire the reader to look back to that place, if he know not why it is that some moods are plus-minused, and not others; for there he will find that Sindiforation is meerly proper to those cases, in the analogies whereof the fourth proportionall is not the maine quæsitum it selfe, but the illaticious terme that brings it in.

The prænoscendas of the mood, or quæsitas of the first operation, falling next in order to be treated of, it is fitting we perpend of what nature they be in this mood of Erelomab, that if they be different from those of other moods, we may, according to our accustomed diligence, formerly observed in the like occasions, appropriate in this parcell of the comment to their explication, for the reader's instruction, the greater share of discourse, the lesse that before in any part of this tractat they have beene mentioned: But if it be so farre otherwise, that for their coincidence with other pro-turgetick quæsitas, there can no materiall document concerning them be delivered here, which hath not beene spoke of already in some one or other of our foregoing datoquæres, it were but an unnecessary wasting of both time and paper to make repetition of that which in other places we have handled to the full; and therefore seeing the prænoscendas of this mood, to wit, the double top angle or verticall, the first top anglet or verticalin, and the first co-top-angle, or co-verticall, together with the datas whereby these are obtained, viz. for the side, the first subtendentall, the first subtendentine, and the first co-subtendent, and for the angle, the prime cathetopposite, the next cathetopposite, and the first co-cathetopposite, and consequently the subservient Upalam, its resolver, To—Tag—Nu☞Mir, and their three peculiar problemets, Utopat, Udobaud, and Uthophauth, are all and every one of them the same in this mood of Erelomab, that they were in the three preceding moods of Alamebna, Allamebne, and Amanepra, for these are the foure moods which have an angulary prænoscendall identity, we will not need, I hope, to talk any more thereof in this place, seeing what hath beene already said concerning that purpose, will undoubtedly satisfie the desire of any industrious civill reader.

The prænoscendas of the mood, or the verticall angle, according to the nature of the case, being by the foresaid datas thus obtained, must needs concurre with each its correspondent first subtendent, determined by the figuratives of τ. ծ. ɵ. for finding out of the perpendicular, of which work Ubamen being the subservient; by whose resolver, Nag—Mu—Torp☞Myr, the sub-problems of Utatca, Udaudca, and Uthauthca, are made known; if I utter any more of this purpose, I must intrench upon what I spoke before in the second operation of Allamebne, it being the onely mood which, with this of Erelomab, hath a verticall and subtendentine catheteuretick identity.

The second operation being thus accomplished, the perpendicular, which is alwayes an ingredient in the third work, must joyne with one of the rere subtendents for obtaining of the illatitious terme of the maine quæsitum; or, more particularly, by the concurrence of the perpendicular with the second subtendentine, the second subtendentall, and second co-subtendent, according to the variety of the case, we are to find out three verticals, which, by abstracting the first from another verticall, then by abstracting another verticall from the second, and lastly by adding the third verticall to another, afford the summe and differences which are the required verticals.

All this being fully set downe in my comment upon the resolutory partition of Amanepra, in which mood the maine quæsitum is the same as here, though otherwise endowed, I need not any longer insist thereon.

For the performance of this work, Ukelamb is the subservient, by whose resolver, Meg—To—Mu☞Nir, we are taught how to unfold the peculiar problemets of Wdcathaud, Wtcathat, and Wthcatheuth.

All the three works being in this manner perfected, according to our accustomed method, we will shew unto you what way the last two are to be compacted in one; for the better expediting whereof, their resolvers, Nag—Mu—To☞Myr, and Meg —To—Mu☞Nir, must be explained, the first being, As the sine complement of an angle to the tangent complement of a subtendent, so the radius to the tangent complement of the side required; or, more particularly, As the sine complement of a verticall to the tangent complement of a first subtendent, so the radius to the tangent complement of the perpendicular: And the second resolver being, As the tangent complement of a given side to the radius, so the tangent complement of a subtendent to the sine complement of a required angle; or, more particularly, As the tangent complement of the perpendicular to the radius, so the tangent complement of a first subtendent to the sine complement of a verticall which ushers the quæsitum.

Now, seeing it falleth forth that the perpendicular, which is the fourth terme in the first order of proportionals, becometh first in the second row; and that in such an exigent, as I proved already for illustration of the same point in the mood of Amanepra, the multiplyers and dividers of the first row must interchange their roomes, and consequently make the radius ejectable, without any prejudice or hindrance to the progresse of the analogy; and a place being left for the perpendicular in both the rowes, without taking the paines to find out its value, because it is but a subordinate quæsitum for obtaining of the maine, and lieth hid in the power of the three first proportionals, instead of Nag—Mu—To☞Myr, and Meg—To—Mu☞Nir, we may with as much truth and energy say, Mu—Nag—Mu☞Nir, that is, As the tangent complement of a subtendent to the sine complement of an angle, so the tangent complement of another subtendent to the sine complement of another angle; or, more particularly, As the tangent complement of a first subtendent to the sine complement of a verticall, so the tangent complement of a second subtendent to the sine complement of a verticall illative to the quæsitum.

This proposition to the full containeth all that is in both the last operations, and according to the number of the cases of this mood, is specialized into so many finall resolvers; the first whereof, for the first case, Dacracforaur, is Mutnat—Mwd☞ Neudfr*At*Aut*ir, that is, As the tangent complement of the first subtendentall to the sine complement of the double verticall, so the tangent complement of the second subtendentine to the sine complement of the second verticalin, which subtracted from the double verticall, leaves the first verticall for the angle required.

The second finall resolver is for Damracforeur, the second case, and is expressed thus, Mud—Naud—Mwt☞Natfr*Aud*Eut*ir, that is, As the tangent complement of the first subtendentine to the sine complement of the first verticalin, so the tangent complement of the second subtendentall to the sine complement of the double verticall, from which if you deduce the first verticalin, there will remaine the second verticall for the angle required.

The last finall resolver is for the third case, Dacrambatin, and is couched thus, Muth—Nauth—Mwth☞Neuth*jauth*ir, that is, As the tangent complement of the first co-subtendent to the sine complement of the first co-verticall, so the tangent complement of the second co-subtendent to the sine complement of the second co-verticall, which joyned to the first co-verticall, affordeth the angle required.

The proofe of the veritie of all these analogies is taken out of the second disergetick amblygonosphericall axiome, Naverprortes, the second determiner of whose directorie sheweth that this mood is one of its dependents; and with reason, because of the reciprocall analogie that amongst its termes is perceivable betwixt the tangents of the verticall sides, which in this mood are always first subtendents, and the sine complements of the verticall angles; that is to say, according to the literal meaning of my finall resolvers of this mood, the direct proportion that is betwixt the tangent complements of the verticall sides, or rere subtendents, and the sine complements of the vertical angles; for the proportion is the same with that whereof I have told you somewhat already in the mood of Allamebne, the fellow dependent of Erelomab.

The second mood of Eherolabme, fourth of the laterals, eighth of the sphericobliquangularie disergeticks, twelfth of the loxogonosphericalls, eight and twentieth of the sphericals, and one and fourtieth or last of the triangulars, is Errelome, which comprehendeth all those obliquangularie problems, wherein two sides being given with an opposite angle, the third side is required, which side is always either one of the segments of the base, or the base it selfe; to the knowledge of all which that we may reach with ease, we must perpend the generall maxim of the cathetothesis of this mood, which is Cacurgyq, that is to say, the perpendicular's demission, in all the cases of Errelome, must be from the concurse of the given sides upon the side required, continued if need be.

The plus-minus of this mood is Sindiforiu, which importeth that if the perpendicular fall internally, the summe of the segments of the base, or the totall base, is the side demanded; and if it fall without, the difference of the bases, the little base being always but a segment of the greater, is the maine quæsitum.

The mood of Ammanepreb is sindiforated in the same manner as this is, because the maine quæsitas and fourth proportionals of both doe in nothing differ, but that those are sinused, and these run upon sine complements.

The prosiliencie of the perpendicular in all sphericall disergeticks, being so necessary to be knowne, as I have often told you, because of the facility thereby to reduce them to rectangulary operations, it falleth out most conveniently here, according to the method proposed to my selfe, to speak somewhat of the three severall tenets of the cathetothesis of this mood, and what is understood by Dakyxamfor, Dabyxamfor, and Dakypambin.

Dakyxamfor, which is the tenet of the first case, declareth that if the proposed angle be acute, and the side required conterminate with an obtuse angle, the demission of the perpendicular is extrinsecall.

Dabyxamfor, the tenet of the second case, importeth that if the given angle be obtuse, and that the side required be annexed thereto, the perpendicular must, as in the last, fall outwardly.

Thirdly, Dakypambin, the tenet of the last case, signifieth, that if the angle proposed be sharp, and that the demanded side be subjacent to an obtuse or blunt angle, the perpendicular falleth inwardly.

Having thus proceeded in the enumeration of the cathetothetick tenets of this mood, according to the manner by me observed in those of all the former disergeticks, save the first, I am confident the reader, if he hath perused all the tractat untill this place, will not think strange why Dakypambin being but the third, I should call it the tenet of the last case of this mood; for though in Alamebna I spoke somewhat of every amblygonosphericall disergetick moods generall cathetothetick maximes division into foure especiall tenets, appropriable to so many severall cases; yet the fourth case, viz. that wherein all the angles are homogeneall, whether blunt or sharp, not being limited to any one mood, but adequately extended to all the eight, it seemed to me more expedient to let its generality be known by mentioning it once or twice, then, by doing no more in effect, to make superfluous repetitions; and as in the first disergetick case, for the reader's instruction, I did under the name of Simomatin, explicate the nature thereof, so, for his better remembrance, have I choosed rather to shut up my cathetothetick comment with the same discourse wherewith I did begin it, then unnecessarily to weary him with frequent reiterations, and a tedious rehearsall of one and the same thing in all the six severall intermediat moods.

It is not amisse, now that the perpendicularity of this mood is discussed, to consider what the prænoscendas thereof are, or the quæsitas of the first operation; but, as I said in the last mood, that there is no need to insist so long upon the explication of those prænoscendas, whereof ample relation hath beene already made in some of my proturgetick comments, as upon those others which, for being altogether different from such as have beene formerly mentioned, claim, by the law of parity, in their imparity, right to a large discourse apart, I will confine my pen upon this subject within those prescribed bounds, and seeing the first basal, the first basidion, and first co-base, together with the datas whereby they are found out, viz. for the side, the first subtendentall, the first subtendentine, and the first co-subtendent, and for the angle the prime cathetopposite, the next cathetopposite, and the first co-cathetopposite, the datas being both for side and angle the same here that they were in the former mood, then the subservient Ubamen, and its resolver Torp—Mu—Lag☾☞Myr, with the three peculiar problemets thereto belonging, Utopæt, Udobæd, and Vthophæth, are all and every one of them the same in this mood of Errelome, that they were in the three foregoing moods of Ammanepreb, Enerablo, and Ennerable, these being the onely foure moods which have a laterall prænoscendal identity, the reader will not, in my opinion, be so prodigall of his owne labour, nor covetous of mine, that either he would put himselfe or me to any further paines, then have beene already bestowed upon this matter by my selfe for his instruction ; and therefore, leaving it for a supposed certainty that the prænoscendas or first bases, according to the nature of the case, cannot escape the reader's knowledge, by what hath beene by me delivered of them, I purpose here to give him notice that these foresaid first bases must concurre with each its correspondent first subtendent, to wit, the first subtendentall, the first subtendentine, and first co-subtendent, dignoscible by the characteristicks of $\tau.\ \delta.\ \theta.$ for obtaining of the perpendicular, of which operation, Vchener being the subservient, by whose resolver, Neg—To—Nu☾☞Nyr, the problemets of Utætca, Udædca, and Uthæthca are made manifest, as to the same effect it remaines couched in my comment upon Ennerable, which is the onely mood that, with this of Errelome, hath a subtendentine and basal catheteuretick identity.

The second work being thus perfected, the perpendicular thereby found out, is to assist one of the rere subtendents in obtaining the illatitious terme of the maine quæsitum correspondent thereto, discernable by the characteristicks or figuratives of $\delta.\ \tau.\ \theta.$ or, more plainly to expresse it, the perpendicular must concurre, according as the case requires it, with the second subtendentine, the second subtendentall, and second co-subtendent, as you may see in the last mood, the datas of the resolutory partition whereof are the same as here, to find out three bases which, by abstracting the first from another base, then by abstracting another base from the second, and lastly, by adding the third base to another, afford the summe and differences, which are the required bases.

For the performance of this operation, the same subservient and resolver suffice, which served for the last ; so that Uchener subserveth it, by whose resolver, Neg—To—Nu☾☞Nyr, we are instructed how to explicate the subdatoquæres of Wdcathœd, Wtcathœt, and Wthcathœeth, or more orderly, Cathwdœd, Cathwtœet, and Cathwthœeth.

All the three works being thus accomplished, the manner of conflating the last two

in one rests to be treated of; for the better perfecting of which designe, the two resolvers, or the same in its greatest generality doubled, viz. Neg—To—Nu☞Nyr,
and Neg—To—Nu☞Nyr, must be interpreted; the truth is, both of them, as they
sound in their vastest extent of signification, expresse the same analogy, without any
difference, which is, As the sine complement of a given side to the radius, so the sine
complement of a subtendent to the sine complement of another side; but when more
contractedly, according to the specification of the side, they doe suppone severally,
they should be thus expounded; the first, As the sine complement of a first base to
the totall sine, so the sine complement of a first subtendent to the sine complement of
the perpendicular; and the second, As the sine complement of the perpendicular to
the totall sine, so the sine complement of a second subtendent to the sine complement
of a second base, which ushers the main quæsitum.

Now, the perpendicular and radius being both to be expelled these two foresaid
orders of proportionall termes, for the reasons which, in the last preceding mood, and
some others before it, I have already mentioned, and which to repeat, further then
that the sympathy of this place with that may be manifested in the trans-seating of
multiplyers and dividers, occasioned by the fourth terme in the first rowes, being first
in the second, is altogether unnecessary; in lieu of Neg—To—Nu☞Nyr, and Neg
—To—Nu☞Nyr, we may say with as much truth, power, and efficacie, and farre
more compendiously, Nu—Ne—Nu☞Nyr, that is, As the sine complement of a
subtendent to the sine complement of a side, so the sine complement of another subtendent to the sine complement of another side; or, more particularly and appli-
ably to the present analogy, As the sine complement of a first subtendent to the sine
complement of a first base, so the sine complement of a second subtendent to the sine
complement of a second base illative to the quæsitum.

This theorem or proposition comprehendeth in every point all that is in the two last
operations, and, not transcending the number of the cases of this mood, is divided into
so many finall resolvers; the first whereof for the first case, Dakyxamfor, is Nut—
Næt—Nwd☞Nœdfr*Æt*Dyr, that is, As the sine complement of the first subtendentall to the sine complement of the first basall, so the sine complement of the second
subtendentine to the sine complement of the second basidion, which subducted from
the first basal, residuats the segment that is the side required.

The second finall resolver of this mood, and that which is for the second case thereof, Dambyxamfor, is Nud—Næd—Nwt☞Nœtfr*Æd*Dyr, that is, As the sine
complement of the first subtendentine to the sine complement of the first basidion, so
the sine complement of the second subtendentall to the sine complement of the second
basall; which, the first basidion being subtracted from it, leaves for remainder or difference that segment of the base which is the side demanded.

The last finall resolver of this mood, belonging to the third case, Dakypambin, as
also to the fourth, Simomatin, if what we have already spoke of that matter will per-

mit us to call it the fourth, for Simomatin, together with the third case of every mood, is still resolved by the last finall resolver thereof, is Nuth—Næth—Nwth⟨☞Nœthj* Æth*Syr, that is, As the sine complement of the first co-subtendent to the sine complement of the first co-base, so the sine complement of the second co-subtendent, or alterne subtendent, to the sine complement of the second co-base, or alterne base, which added to the first co-base, summes an aggregat of subjacent sides, which is the totall base, or side required.

The fundamentall ground of the truth of these analogies is in the fourth and last amblygonosphericall axiome, Niubprodnesver, as we are made to understand by the second determinater of its directory Ennerra, for by the direct proportion that amongst the terms thereof is visible, viz. betwixt the sines complements of the subtendents or sides of the verticall angles and the segments of the bases, and inversedly, it is apparent that this mood doth no lesse firmely depend upon it, then that of Ennerable formerly explained.

Now, with reason doe I conjecture, that without disappointing the reader of his expectation, I may here securely make an end of this Trigonometricall Treatise, because of that Trissotetrall table which comprehendeth all the mysteries, axiomes, principles, analogies, and precepts of the science of triangular calculations, I have omitted no materiall point unexplained; yet seeing, for avoyding of prolixity, I was pleased in my comment upon the eighth loxogonospherical disergeticks, barely to expresse in their finall resolvers the analogie of the termes, without putting my selfe to the paines I took in my sphericorectangulars, how to order the logarithms and antilogarithms of the proportionals for obtaining of the maine quæsitas; and that by having to the full explicated the variety of the proportions of the foresaid moods, and upon what severall axiomes they doe depend, thereby making the way more pervious thorough logarithmicall difficulties for the reader's understanding, I deliberately proposed to my selfe this method at first, and chose, rather then dispersedly to treat of those things in the glosse, where, by reason of the disturbed order, the correspondencie or reference to one another of these sphericobliquangulary datoquæres, could not by any meanes have beene so conceivable, to summon their appearance to the catastrophe of this tractat, that, having them all in a front before us, we may the more easily judge of the semblance or dissimilitude of their proportionalities, and what affinity or relation, whether of parity or imparity, is amongst their respective proportionall terms; all which, both for intelligibility and memory, are quicklier apprehended and longer retained, by being accumulatively reserved to this place, then if they had beene each in its proper cell, though never so amply discoursed upon apart.

Here, therefore, that the reader may take a generall view at once of all the disergetick amblygonosphericall analogised ingredients, ready for logarithmication, I have thought fit to set downe a list of all the eight forenamed moods, together with the finall resolvers, in their amplest extent thereto belonging, in the manner as followeth.

Alamebna.	Say–Nag–Sa☞Nir.	Enerablo.	Sei–Tag–Se☞Tir.
Allamebne.	Nag–Mu–Na☞Mur.	Ennerable.	Neg–Nu–Ne☞Nur.
Amanepra.	Na–Say–Nag☞Sir.	Erelomab.	Mu–Nag–Mu☞Nir.
Ammanepreb.	Ta–Tag–Se☞Syr.	Errelome.	Nu–Ne–Nu☞Nyr.

These being the eight disergeticks, attended by their adæquat finall resolvers, it is not amisse that we examine them all one after another, and shew the reader how, with the help of a convenient logarithmicall canon, he may easily out of the analogie of the three first termes of each of them frame a computation apt for the finding out of a fourth proportionall, to every severall ternarie correspondent; and so in order, beginning at the first, we will deale with Say—Nag—Sa☞Nir, which is the adæquat finall resolver of Alamebna, and composed, as it is appropriated to the first mood of the disergeticks, of the sines of verticals and the antisines of cathetopposites, and so proceed therein, that by adding to the summe of the sine of a verticall and cosine of a cathetopposite, the arithmetical complement of the sine of another verticall, we will be sure, cutting off the supernumerary digit or digits towards the left, to obtaine the cosine of the cathetopposite required, which cathetopposites and verticals are particularised according to the cases of the mood.

The second is Nag—Mu—Na☞Mur, which, running upon the antisines of verticals and the co-tangents of subtendent sides, sheweth, that if to the aggregat of a first hypotenusall co-tangent and verticall antisine, we joyne the arithmeticall complement of the antisine of another verticall, observing the usuall presection, we cannot misse of the cotangent of the second subtendent side required, which, both second and first subtendents, have their peculiar denominations, according to the cases of the mood.

The third resolver is Na—Say—Nag☞Sir, which, being nothing else but the first inverted, runneth the same very way upon the antisines of cathetopposites and sines of verticals; and therefore doth the unradiused summe of the antisine of a cathetopposite, the sine of a verticall, and the arithmeticall complement of the antisine of another cathetopposite, afford the sine of the verticall, illatitious to the angle required; which verticals and cathetopposites are particularised according to the variety of the cases of this Sindiforating mood.

The fourth generall resolver is Tu—Tag—Se☞Syr, which, coursing on the tangents of the cathetopposites and sines of the bases, evidenceth that the summe of the tangent of a cathetopposite and sine of a first base, added to the arithmeticall complement of the tangent of another cathetopposite, unradiated, is the sine of the second base, illative to the segment required; which bases, both first and second, and cathetopposites, are specialised conform to the cases of this Sindiforiuting mood.

The fifth resolver is Sei—Tag—Se☞Tir, which, composed of the sines of the second and first bases and the tangents of cathetopposites, giveth us to know, that if to the summe of the sine of a first base and the tangent of a verticall, we adde the arithmeticall complement of the sine of a second base, not omitting the usuall presection, we cannot faile of the tangent of the cathetopposite required, which cathetopposites and bases, both first and second, are particularised according to the cases of the mood.

The sixth generall resolver is Neg—Nu—Ne✲☞Nur, which, running along the cosines of all the bases and subtendents, sheweth, that by the summe of the cosines of a second base and first subtendent, joyned with the arithmeticall complement of the cosine of a first base, if we observe the customary presection, we find the second subtendent required ; which, both first and second subtendents, together with the first and second bases, are all of them particularised conforme to the cases of the mood.

The seventh resolver is Mu—Nag—Mu✲☞Nir, which, coursing along the antitangents of first and second subtendents and the antisines of verticals, sheweth, that the summe of the antitangent of a second subtendent and antisine of a verticall, together with the arithmeticall complement of the antitangent of a first subtendent, the usuall presection being observed, is the antitangent of that verticall which ushers in the verticall required ; all which, both verticals and subtendents, both first and second, have their peculiar denominations conforme to the cases of this Sindiforating mood.

The eighth and last generall resolver is Nu—Ne—Nu☞Nyr, which running altogether upon co-sines of subtendents and bases, both first and second of either, and is nothing else but the sixth inverted, sheweth, that the summe of the co-sines of a second subtendent and first base, with the arithmeticall complement of the co-sine of a first subtendent, observing the usuall presection, affords the co-sine of the second base, illatitious to the segment required ; which bases and subtendents, both first and second, are peculiarly denominated according to the severall cases of this Sindiforiuting mood.

Thus have I finished the logarithmication of the generall resolvers of the loxogonosphericall disergeticks, so farre as is requisite, wherein I often times mentioned the arithmeticall complement of sines, co-sines, tangents, and co-tangents; and though I spoke of that purpose sufficiently in my sphericorectangular comments, yet, for the reader's better remembrance thereof, I will once more define them here.

The arithmeticall complements of sines are co-secants ; of co-sines, secants ; of tangents, co-tangents ; and of co-tangents, tangents ; each being the other's complement to the double radius; but if such a canon were framed, wherein the single radius is left out of all secants and tangents of major arches, then would each be the other's complement to the single radius, and all logarithmicall operations in questions of Trigonometry, so easily performable by addition onely, that seldome would the presectional digit exceed an unit.

Having already said so much of these eight disergeticks, I will conclude my discourse of them with a summary delineation of the eight severall concordances which I observed amongst them ; for either they resemble one another in the datas of their moods, or in their proturgetick operations, or in their dependance upon the same axiome, or in the work of perpendicular finding, or in their datas for the main demand, or in their materiall quæsitas, though diversely endowed, or in their inversion, or, lastly, in their sindiforation, which affinity is onely betwixt two paires of them, as the first two amongst two quaternaries apeece, and the next five between foure couples each one, the brief hypotyposis of all which is here exposed to the view of the reader.

CONCORDANCES.
DATALL.

Datangulary.
1. Alamebna. 3. Amanepra.
2. Allamebne. 4. Ammanepreb.

Datolaterall.
1. Enerablo. 3. Erelomab.
2. Ennerable. 4. Errelome.

PRÆNOSCENDALL.

Verticall.
1. Alamebna. 3. Amanepra.
2. Allamebne. 4. Erelomab.

Basall.
1. Ammanepreb. 3. Ennerable.
2. Enerablo. 4. Errelome.

THEOREMATICK.

Nabadprosver
1. Alamebna.
2. Amanepra.

Naverprortes.
1. Allamebne.
2. Erelomab.

Siubprortab
1. Ammanepreb.
2. Enerablo.

Niubprodnesver.
1. Ennerable.
2. Errelome.

CATHETEURETICK.

Oppoverticall
1. Alamebna.
2. Amanepra.

Hypoverticall.
1. Allamebne.
2. Erelomab.

Oppobasall
1. Ammanepreb.
2. Enerablo.

Hypobasall.
1. Ennerable.
2. Errelome.

DATYSTERURGETICK.

Cathetoverticall
1. Alamebna.
2. Allamebne.

Oppocatheticall.
1. Amanepra.
2. Ammanepreb.

Cathetobasall
1. Enerablo.
2. Ennerable.

Hypocathetal.
1. Erelomab.
2. Errelome.

ZETETICK.

Cathetopposite
1. Alamebna*S.
2. Enerablo*T.

Hypotenusall.
1. Allamebne*M.
2. Ennerable*N.

Verticall
1. Amanepra*S.
2. Erelomab*N.

Basall.
1. Ammanepreb*S.
2. Errelome*N.

INVERSIONALL.

Sinocosinall
1. Alamebna.
2. Amanepra.

Sinocotangentall.
1. Allamebne.
2. Erelomab.

Tangentosinall.
1. Ammanepreb.
2. Enerablo.

Cosinocosinall.
1. Ennerable.
2. Errelome.

SINDIFORALL.

Sindiforatall
1. Amanepra. 2. Erelomab.

Sindiforiutall.
1. Amanepreb. 2. Errelome.

R

THE EPILOGUE.

WHAT concerneth the resolving of all manner of triangles, whether plain or spherical, rectangular or obliquangular, being now, conform to my promise in the title, to the ful explained, commented on, perfected, and with all possible brevity and perspicuity in all its abstrusest and most difficult secrets, from the very first principles of the science it selfe, made manifest, proved, and convincingly demonstrated, I will here shut up my discourse and bring this tractat to a period, which I may do with the more alacrity, in that I am confident there is no precept belonging to that faculty which is not herein included, or reducible thereto; and therefore, I believe, the judicious reader will not be frustrate of his expectation, though, by cutting the threed of my Glosse, I doe not illustrate what I have written with variety of examples, seeing practically to treat of triangulary calculations, in applying their doctrine to use, were to digresse from the purpose in hand, and incroach upon the subject of other sciences, a privilege which I must decline, as repugnant to the scope proposed to my selfe, in keeping this book within the speculative bounds of Trigonometry; for, as *Logica Utens* is the science to the which it is applyed, and not logick, so doth not the matter of Trigonometry exceed the theory of a triangle; and as arithmeticall, geometricall, astronomicall, physicall, and metaphysicall definitions, divisions, and argumentations, are no part of the art that instructeth how to define, divide, and argue, nor matter incumbent to him that teacheth it; even so, by divulging this treatise, doe I present the reader with a key, by meanes whereof he may enter into the chiefest treasures of the mathematicall sciences; for the which, in some measure, I deserve thanks, although I helpe him not to unshut the coffers wherein they lie inclosed; for, if the Lord Chamberlain of the King's household should give me a key, made to open all the doores of the Court, I could not but graciously accept of it, though he did not goe along with me to try how it might fit every lock. The application is so palpable, that, not minding to insist therein, I will here stop the current of my pen, and by a circulary conclusion, ending where I begun, certifie the reader, that if he intend to approve himselfe an artist in matters of pleusiotechnie, poliechyrologie, cosmography, geography, astronomy, geodesie, gnomonicks, sciography, catoptricks, dioptricks, and many other most exquisite arts and sciences, practical and theoretick, his surest course for attaining to so much knowledge, is to be well versed in Trigonometry; to understand this treatise aright, resolve all the passages thereof, ruminate on the table, and peruse the Trissotetras.

A LEXICIDION OF SOME OF THE HARDEST WORDS THAT OCCURRE IN THE DISCOURSE OF THIS INSTITUTION TRIGONOMETRICALL.

BEING certainly perswaded that a great many good spirits ply Trigonometry that are not versed in the learned tongues, I thought fit for their encouragement to subjoyne here the explication of the most important of those Greek and Latin termes, which for the more efficacy of expression I have made use of in this Treatise; in doing whereof, that I might both instruct the Reader and not weary him, I have endeavoured perspicuity with shortnesse; though, I speak it ingenuously, to have been more prolixe therein could have cost but very little labor to me, who have already been pretty well versed in the like, as may appear by my Etymologicall dictionary of above twenty-seven thousand proper names, mentioned in the Lemmas of my several volums of Epigrams, the words whereof are for the most part abstruser, derived from moe languages, and more liable to large and ample interpretations. However, *cæteris paribus*, brevity is to be preferred; therefore let us proceed to the Vocabulary in hand.

THE LEXICIDION.

A.

Acute, comes from *acuo, acuere*, to sharpen ; and is said of an angle whose including sides, the more that its measure is lesse then a quadrant, have their concursive and angulary point the more penetrative, sharp, keen and pierceing.   Whence an acut-angled triangle.

Adæquat, is that which comprehendeth to the full whatever is in the thing to the which it is compared ; and, for the most part, in my Trissotetras is said of the general finall resolvers, in relation to the moods resolved by them.   It is compound-ed of *ad* and *æquo, æquare, parem facere*, to make one thing altogether like, or equall to another.

Adjacent, signifieth to lie neare and close, and is applyed both to sides and angles ; in which sense, likewise, I make use of the words, adjoyning the, conterminat, or con-terminall with, annexed to, intercepted in, and other such like, for the more va-riety, as adherent, bounding, bordering, and so forth.   It comes from *adjaceo, adjacere*, to lie neere unto, as the words *ad* and *jaceo*, which are the parts whereof it is compounded, most perspicuously declare.

Additionall, is said of the line, which in my comment is indifferently called the line of addition, the line of continuation, the extrinsecall line, the excesse of the secant above the radius, the residuum, or the new secant.   It comes from *addo, addere*, which is compounded of *ad* and *do*, to put to and augment.

Affection, is the nature, passion, and quality of an angle, and consisteth either in the obtusity, acutenesse, or rectitude thereof.   It is a verball from *afficio, affeci, affec-tum*, compounded of *ad* and *facio*.

Aggregat, is the summe, totall, or result of an addition ; and is compounded of *ad* and *grex* ; for as the shepheard gathers his sheep into a flock, so doth the arithme-tician compact his numbers to be added into a summe.

Alternat, is said of angles made by a line cutting two or more parallels, which angles may be properly called so, because they differ in nothing else but their situation ; for if the sectionary line, to the which I suppose the parallels to be fixed, have the highest and lowest points thereof to interchange their sites, by a motion progressive towards the roome of the under alternat, and terminating in that of the upper one, we will find that both the inclination of the lines towards one another and the quality of the angles, will, notwithstanding that alteration, be the same as before ; hence it is that they are called alternat, because there is no other difference betwixt them ; or if alternat be taken, as arithmetically it is, for that proportion wherein the antecedent is compared to the antecedent, and the consequent to the consequent, the sense will likewise hold in the foresaid angles ; for if by the parallelisme of two right lines, cut with a third, two blunt and two keen angles be produced, as must needs, unlesse the secant line be to the parallels a perpendicular, the keen or acute angle will be to its complement, or successively following obtuse angle, as the other acute unto its following obtuse ; therefore, alternly, as the antecedents are to one another, viz. the acute to the acute, so the consequents, the obtuse to the obtuse. And if the angles be right, the direct and alternat proportion is one and the same, the third and fourth terms of the analogy being in nothing different from the first and second.

Ambient, is taken for any of the legs of a rectangle, or the including, containing, or comprehending sides of the right angle. It comes from *ambio, ambire,* which is compounded of *am* and *eo,* i. e. *circumeo,* and more properly applied to both then to any one of them, though usually it be usurped for one alone. Vide *Leg.*

Amblygonian, is said of obtuse-angled triangles ; and *Amblygonosphericall,* of obtuse sphericals. It is composed of Αμβλὺs and γωνία, *angulus.*

Amfractuosities, are taken here for the cranklings, windings, turnings, and involutions belonging to the equisoleary scheme ; of *am* and *frango, quod sit quasi via crebris mœandris undequaque interrupta.*

Analogy, signifieth an equality of proportion, a likenesse of reasons, a conveniencie or habitude betwixt termes : It is compounded of ἀνὰ, *æqualiter,* and λόγος, *ratio.*

Analytick, resolutory, and is said of those things that are resolved into their first principles, of ἀνὰ, *re,* and λύω, *solvo.*

Antilogarithm, is the logarithm of the complement ; as for example, the anti-logarithm of a sine is the logarithm of the sine complement, *vide* Logarithm.

Anti-secant, anti-sine, and anti-tangent, are the complements of the secant, sine, and tangent, and are called sometimes co-secant, co-sine, and co-tangent ; they have *anti* prefixed, because they are not in the same colume, and *co,* because they are in the next to it.

Apodictick, is that which is demonstrative, and giveth evident proofs of the truth of a conclusion ; of ὡπὸ, and δείνυμι, *monstro, ostendo, unde* ἀπόδειξις, *demonstratio.*

Area, is the capacity of a figure, and whole content thereof.

Arch, or *ark,* is the segment of a circumference lesse then a semicircle ; major arch is above 45 degrees, a minor arch lesse then 45, vide *Circle.*

Arithmeticall complement, is the difference betweene the logarithm to be substracted, and that of the double or single radius.

Artificiall numbers, are the logarithms, and artificiall sine the logarithm of the sine.

Axiome, is a maxim, tenet, or necessary principle, whereupon the science of a thing is grounded. It cometh from ἄξιος, dignus ; because such things are worthy our knowledge.

B.

Basall, adjectively, is that which belongeth to the base, or the subjacent side, but substantively the great base.

Basangulary, is said of the angle at the base.

Basidion, or baset, is the little base, all which come from the Greek word ϛαίνω, βέϛηκα.

Basiradius, is the totall sine of that arch, a segment whereof is the base of the proposed sphericall triangle.

Bisected, and *Bisegment,* are said of lines cut into two equall parts : it comes from *biseco, bisecare, bisectum, bisegmen.*

Bluntnesse, or *flatnesse,* is the obtuse affection of angles.

Bucarnon, by this name is entitled the seven and fortieth proposition of the first of the elements of Euclid ; because of the oxe, or, as some say, the hecatomb which Pythagoras, for gladnesse of the invention, sacrificed unto the gods ; of ῥὺς, bos, and ἄρνυμαι, *vicissim aliquid capio* ; they being, as it is supposed, well pleased with that acknowledgement of his thankfulnesse for so great a favour, as that was which he received from them. You may see the proposition in the seventeenth of my Apodicticks.

C.

Canon, is taken here for the table of sines and tangents, or of their logarithms : it properly signifieth the needle or tongue of a balance, and metaphorically a rule whereby things are examined.

Cases, are the parts wherein a mood is divided from *cado.*

Cathetos, is a perpendicular line, from καθίημι, demitto, of κατὰ, and ἵημι.

Catheteuretick, is concerning the finding out of the perpendicular of Κάθετος, and ἐυρίσκω, ἐυρήσω, invenio.

Cathetobasall, is said of the concordances of loxogonosphericall moods, in the datas of the perpendicular and the base, for finding out of the maine quæsitum.

Cathetopposite, is the angle opposite to the perpendicular; it is a hybrid or mungrell word, composed of the Greek κάθετος, and Latin *oppositus.*

Cathetorabdos, or *Cathetoradius,* is the totall sine of that arch, a segment whereof is the cathetos, or perpendicular of the proposed orthogonosphericall.

Cathetothesis, and *Cathetothetick,* are said of the determinat position of the perpendicular, which is sometimes expressed by cathetology, instructing us how it should be demitted; of κάθετος and θέσις, from τίθημι, *pono, colloco.*

Cathetoverticall, is said of the concordances of loxogonosphericall moods in the datas of the perpendicular, and the verticall angle in the last operation.

Catoptrick, the science of perspective; from κατόπ]ομαι, *perspicio, cerno.*

Characteristick, is said of the letters, which are the notes and marks of distinction, called sometimes figuratives, or determinaters; from Χαγάκτω, *sculpo, imprimo.*

Circles, great circles are those which bisect the sphere, lesser circles those which not.

Circular parts, are in opposition to the reall and naturall parts of a triangle.

Circumjacent, things which lie about, of *circum* and *jaceo.*

Coalescencie, a growing together, a compacting of two things in one; it is said of the last two operations of the loxogonosphericals conflated into one; from *coalesco* or *coaleo,* of *con* and *alo.*

Cobase, a fellow base, or that which with another base hath a common perpendicular, of *con* and *basis.*

Cocathetopposite, is said of two angles at the base, opposite to one and the same Cathetos.

Coincidence, a falling together upon the same thing; from *coincido,* of *con* and *incido,* ex *in* and *cado.*

Comment, is an interpretation, or exposition of a thing, and comes from *comminiscor, comminisci, mentionem facere.*

Compacted, joyned and knit together, put in one; from *compingo, compegi, compactum,* vide *Coalescencie.*

Complement, signifieth the perfecting that which a thing wanteth, and usually is that which an angle or a side wanteth of a quadrant or 90 degrees; and of a semicircle, or 180, from *compleo, complere,* to fill up.

Concurse, is the meeting of lines, or the sides of a triangle; from *concurro, concursum.*

Conflated, compacted, joyned together; from *conflo, conflatum, conflare,* to blow together, vide *Inchased.*

Consectary, is taken here for a corollary, or rather a secondary axiome, which dependeth on a prime one, and being deduced from it, doth necessarily follow; from *consector, consectaris,* the frequentative of *consequor.*

Consound, to sound with another thing; it is said of consonants which have no vocality without the help of the vowell.

Constitutive, is said of those things which help to frame, make, and build up; from *constituo*, of *con* and *statuo*.

Constitutive sides, the ingredient sides of a triangle.

Constructive parts, are those whereof a thing is built and framed; from *construo*, *constructum*, to heap together, and build up, of *con* and *strues*.

Conterminall, is that which bordereth with, and joyneth to a thing; of *con* and *terminus*, vide *Adjacent* or *Insident*.

Cordes, and cordall, are said of subtenses metaphorically, because the arches and subtenses are as the bow and string; *chorda* comes of the Greek word χορδὴ, *intestinum, ilia, quia ex illis chordæ conficiuntur.*

Correctangle, that is one which, with another rectangle, hath a common perpendicular.

Correspondent, that which answereth with, and hath a reference to another thing; of *con* and *respondeo.*

Cosinocosinall, is said of the concordances of loxogonosphericall moods agreeing, in that the termes of their finall resolvers run upon co-sines.

Cosmography, is taken here for the science whereby is described the celestial globe; of κόσμος and γράφω.

Co-subtendent, is the subtendent of a correctangle, or that which, with another, is substerned to two right angles, made by the demission of one and the same perpendicular.

Co-verticall, is the fellow top angle, from whence the perpendicular falleth.

D.

Data, is said of the parts of a triangle which are given us, whether they be sides or angles, or both; of *do, datum, dare.*

Datimista, are those datas which are neither angles onely, nor sides onely, but angles, and sides intermixedly; of *data* and *mista*, from *misceo.*

Datangulary, is said of the concordances of those moods, for the obtaining of whose prænoscendas we have no other datas but angles, unto the foresaid moods common.

Datapurall, comes from *datapura*, which be those datas that are either meerly angles, or meerly sides.

Datolaterall, is said of the concordances of those moods, for the obtaining of whose prænoscendas the same sides serve for datas.

Datoquære, is the very problem it selfe, wherein two or three things are given, and a third or fourth required, as by the composition of the word appears.

Datisterurgetick, is said of those moods which agree in the datas of the last work; of *data*, ὕσερον, *postremum*, and ἔργον, *opus.*

Demission, is a letting fall of the perpendicular; from *demitto, demissum.*

Determinater, is the characteristick or figurative letter of a directory; from *determinare*, to prescribe and limit.

Diagonall, taken substantively, or *diagonie,* is a line drawn from one angle to another; of ὁιὰ and γωνία, what the *diagonie* is in the surfaces, the axle is in solids.

Diagrammatise, to make a scheme or diagram; from διαγράφω, *delineo.*

Diatyposis, is a briefe summary description and delineation of a thing, or the couching of a great deale of matter, for the instruction of the reader, in very little bounds, and in a most neat and convenient order; from διατυπόω, *instituo, item melius dispono,* vide Υποτύπωσις.

Diodot, is Pythagorase's Bucarnon, or the gift bestowed on him by the gods; of διὸς, the genitive of ζεὺς and δοτὸς, *datus,* from δίδωμι, *do,* vide *Bucarnon.*

Dioptrick, the art of taking heights and distances; from διόπΊομαι, *pervidendo, altitudinem dimensionemque turrium et murorum exploro.*

Directly, is said of two rowes of proportionals, where the first terme of the first row is to the first of the second as the last of the first is to the last of the second.

Directory, is that which pointeth out the moods dependent on an axiome.

Discrepant, different, dissonant, *id est, diverso modo crepare.*

Disergeticks, of two operations; of δὶς and ἔργον.

Document, instruction; from *doceo.*

E.

Elucidation, a clearing, explaining, resolving of a doubt, and commenting on some obscure passage; from *elucido, elucidare.*

Energie, efficacie, power, force; from ἐνεργὸς, *qui in opere est,* of ἐν and ἔργον, *opus.*

Enodandum, that which is to be resolved and explicated, declared, and made manifest; from *enodo, enodare,* to unknit, or cut away the knot.

Equation, or rather æquation, a making equall; from *æquo, æquare.*

Equiangularity, is that affection of triangles whereby their angles are equall.

Equicrurall, is said of triangles whose legs or shanks are equall; of *æquale,* and *crus, cruris;* leg being taken here for the thigh and leg.

Equilaterall, is said of triangles which have all their sides, shanks, or legs equall; of *æquale,* and *latus, lateris.*

Equipollencie, is a samenesse, or at least an equality of efficacie, power, vertue, and enetgie; of *æquus* and *polleo.*

Equisolea, and *Equisolearie,* are said of the grand orthogonosphericall scheme, because of the resemblance it hath with a horse shooe, and may in that sense be to this purpose applied with the same metaphoricall congruencie, whereby it is said that the royall army at Edge-hill was imbattled in a half moon.

Equivalent, of as much worth and vertue; of *æquus* and *valeo.*

Erected, is said of perpendiculars which are set or raised upright upon a base; from *erigere,* to raise up or set aloft.

Externall, extrinsecall, exteriour, outward or outer, are said oftest of angles, which, being without the area of a triangle, are comprehended by two of its shanks meeting or cutting one another accordingly, as one or both of them are protracted beyond the extent of the figure.

F.

Faciendas, are the things which are to be done; *faciendum* is the gerund of *facio.*

Figurative, is the same thing as characteristick, and is applied to those letters which doe figure and point us out a resemblance and distinction in the moods.

Figures, are taken here for those partitions of Trigonometry which are divided into moods.

Flat, is said of obtuse or blunt angles.

Forwardly, is said of analogies progressive from the first terme to the last.

Fundamentall, is said of reasons taken from the first grounds and principles of a science.

G.

Geodesie, the art of surveying; of γῆ, or γαῖα, *terra,* and δαίω, *divido, partior.*

Geography, the science of the terrestriall globe; of γῆ, *terra,* and γράφω, *describo.*

Glosse, signifieth a commentary or explication; it cometh from γλῶσσα.

Gnomon, is a figure lesse then the totall square, by the square of a segment; or, according to Ramus, a figure composed of the two supplements, and one of the diagonall squares of a quadrat.

Gnomonick, the art of dyalling; from γνώμων, the cock of a dyall.

Great Circles, vide *Circles.*

H.

Homogeneall and *Homogeneity,* are said of angles of the same kind, nature, quality, or affection; from ὁμογένεια, *communio generis.*

Homologall, is said of sides congruall, correspondent, and agreeable, viz. such as have the same reason or proportion; from ὁμολογια, *similis ratio.*

Hypobasall, is said of the concordances of those loxogonosphericall moods which, when the perpendicular is demitted, have for the datas of their second operation the same subtendent and base.

Hypocathetall, is said of those which, for the datas of their third operation, have the same subtendent and perpendicular.

Hypotenusall, is said of subtendent sides; from ὑπὸ and τείνω.

Hypotyposis, a laying downe of severall things before our eyes at one time; from ὑποτυπόω, *oculis subjicio, delineo, et repræsento,* vide Δαιτύπωσις.

Hypoverticall, is said of moods agreeing in the same catheteuretick datas of subtendent and verticall, as the analysis of the word doth shew.

I.

Identity, a samenesse; from *idem*, the same.

Illatitious, or *Illative*, is said of the terme which bringeth in the *quæsitum*; from *infero, illatum*.

Inchased, coagulated, fixed in, compacted, or conflated, is said of the last two loxogonosphericall operations put into one, vide *Compacted, Conflated*, and *Coalescencie*.

Including sides, are the containing sides of an angle of what affection soever it be, vide *Ambients, Legs, &c.*

Individuated, brought to the lowest division, vide *Specialised* and *Specification*.

Indowed, is said of the termes of an analogie, whether sides or angles, as they stand affected with sines, tangents, secants, or their complements, vide *Invested*.

Ingredient, is that which entreth into the composition of a triangle, or the progresse of an operation, from *ingredior*, of *in* and *gradior*.

Initiall, that which belongeth to the beginning, from *initium, ab ineo, significante incipio*.

Insident, is said of angles, from *insideo*, vide *Adjacent* or *Conterminall*.

Interjacent, lying betwixt, of *inter* and *jaceo*; it is said of the side or angle betweene.

Intermediat, is said of the middle termes of a proportion.

Inversionall, is said of the concordances of those moods which agree in the manner of their inversion; that is, in placing the second and fourth termes of the analogy, together with their indowments, in the roomes of the first and third, and contrariwise.

Invested, is the same as indowed, from *investio, investire*.

Irrationall, are those which are commonly called surd numbers, and are inexplicable by any number whatsoever, whether whole or broken.

Isosceles, is the Greek word of *equicrurall*, of ἴσος, ἴσον, and σκέλος, *crus*.

L.

Laterall, belonging to the sides of a triangle, from *latus, lateris*.

Leg, is one of the including sides of an angle, two sides of every triangle being called the legs, and the third the base; the legs therefore, or shankes of an angle, are the bounds insisting or standing upon the base of the angle.

Line of interception, is the difference betwixt the secant and the radius, and is commonly called the residuum.

Logarithms, are those artificiall numbers, by which, with addition and subtraction onely, we work the same effects, as by other numbers, with multiplication and division; of λόγος, *ratio, proportio,* and ἀριθμος, *numerus.*

Logarithmication, is the working of an analogy by logarithms, without having regard to the old laborious way of the naturall sines, and tangents; we say likewise logarithmicall and logarithmically, for logarithmeticall and logarithmetically; for by the syncopising of *et,* the pronunciation of those words is made to the eare more pleasant; a priviledge warranted by all the dialects of the Greek, and other the most refined languages in the world.

Loxogonosphericall, is said of oblique sphericals, of λόξος, *obliquus,* and σφαιρικὸς, *ad sphæram pertinens,* from σφαῖρα, *globus.*

M.

Major and *Minor* arches, vide *Arch.*

Maxim, an axiome or principle, called so, from *maximus,* because it is of greatest account in an art or science, and the principall thing we ought to know.

Meane, or middle proportion, is that the square whereof is equall to the plane of the extremes; and called so because of its situation in the analogy.

Mensurator, is that whereby the illatitious terme is compared, or measured with the maine *quæsitum.*

Monotropall, is said of figures which have one onely mood, of μόνος, and τρόπος, from τρέπω.

Monurgeticks, are said of those moods, the maine *quæsitas* whereof are obtained by one operation, of μόνος and ἔργον.

Moods, determine unto us the severall manners of triangles, from *modus,* a way or manner.

N.

Naturall, the naturall parts of a triangle are those of which it is compounded, and the circular those whereby the maine *quæsitum* is found out.

Nearest or *next,* is said of that cathetopposite angle, which is immediatly opposite to the perpendicular.

Notandum, is set downe for an admonition to the reader of some remarkable thing to follow, and is the gerund of *noto, notare.*

O.

Oblique, and *obliquangulary,* are said of all angles that are not right.

Oblong, is a parallelogram or square more long than large; from *oblongus,* very long.

Obtuse, and *obtuse-angled,* are said of flat and blunt angles.

Occurse, is a meeting together, from *occurro, occursum.*

Oppobasall, is said of those moods which have a catheteuretick concordance in their datas of the same cathetopposite angles, and the same bases.

Oppecathetall, is said of those loxogonosphericals which have a datisterurgetick concordance in their datas, of the same angles at the base and the perpendicular.

Oppoverticall, is said of those moods which have a catheteuretick concordance in their datas of the same cathetopposites and verticall angles.

Orthogonosphericall, is said of right-angled sphericals, of ὀρθὸς, *rectus,* γωνία, *angulus,* and σφαῖρα, *globus.*

Oxygonosphericall, is said of acute-angled sphericals, of ὀξὺς, γονία, and σφαῖρα.

P.

Parallelisme, is a parallel, equality of right lines, cut with a right line, or of sphericals with a sphericall, from παράλληλος, *equidistans,* of παρὰ and ἄλληλος.

Parallelogram, is an oblong, long square, rectangle, or figure made of parallel lines; of παράλληλος, and γράμμη, *linea.*

Partiall, is said of enodandas depending on severall axioms.

Particularise, specialise, by some especiall difference to contract the generality of a thing.

Partition, is said of the severall operations of every loxogonosphericall mood, and is divided in prænoscendall, catheteuretick, and hystcrurgetick.

Permutat proportion, or proportion by permutation, or alternat proportion, is when the antecedent is compared to the antecedent, and the consequent to the consequent, vide *Perturbat.*

Perpendicularity, is the affection of the perpendicular, or plumb-line; which comes from *perpendendo, id est, explorando altitudinem.*

Perturbat, is the same as *permutat,* and called so because the order of the analogie is perturbed.

Planobliquangular, is said of plaine triangles, wherein there is no right angle at all.

Planorectangular, is said of plaine right-angled triangles.

Planotriangular, is said of plaine triangles, that is, such as are not sphericall.

Pleuseotechnie, the art of navigation; of πλεύσις, πλεύσεως, *navigatio,* and τέχνη, *ars.*

Plusminused, is said of moods which admit of mensurators, or whose illatitious termes are never the same, but either more or lesse then the maine *quæsitas.*

Poliechyrologie, the art of fortifying townes and cities; of πόλις, *urbs, civitas,* ἐχυρόω, *munio, firmo,* and λόγος, *ratio.*

Possubservient, is that which after another serveth for the resolving of a question; of *post,* and *subserviens;* of *sub* and *servio.*

Potentia, is that wherein the force and whole result of another thing lies.

Power, is the square, quadrat, or product of a line extended upon it selfe, or of a number in it selfe multiplied.

Powered, squared, quadrified.

Precept, document, from *præcipio, præceptum.*

Prænoscenda, are the termes which must be knowne before we can attaine to the knowledge of the maine quæsitas ; of *præ* and *nosco.*

Prænoscendall, is said of the concordances of those moods, which agree in the same prænoscendas.

Præsection, præsectionall, is concerning the digit towards the left, whose cutting off saveth the labour of subtracting the double or single radius.

Præscinded problems, are those speculative datoquæres which are not applied to any matter by way of practice.

Præsubservient, is said of those moods which in the first place we must make use of for the explanation of others ; of *præ* and *subservio.*

Prime, is said of the furthest cathetopposite, or angle at the base contained within the triangle to be resolved.

Primifie the radius, is to put the radius in the first place ; *primumque inter terminos collocare proportionales.*

Problem, Problemet, a question or datoquære ; from προϐάλλομαι, *unde* προβλημα, *prospoitum objectaculum.*

Product, is the result, *factus*, or *operatum* of a multiplication ; from *produco, productum.*

Proportion, Proportionality, are the same as analogy and analogisme ; the first being a likenesse of termes, the other of proportions.

Proposition, a proposed sentence, whether theorem or problem.

Prosiliencie, is a demission or falling of the perpendicular ; from *prosilio,* ex *pro* and *salio.*

Proturgetick, is said of the first operation of every disergetick mood ; of πρῶτον and ἔργον, the οϵ being Attically contracted into ȣ.

Q.

Quadrant, the fourth part of a circle.

Quadranting, the protracting of a sphericall side unto a quadrant.

Quadrat, a square, a *forma quadræ*, the power or possibility of a line. Vide *Power.*

Quadrobiquadræquation, concerneth the square of the subtendent side, which is equall to the biquadrat, or two squares of the ambients.

Quadrosubduction, is concerning the subtracting of the square of one of the ambients from the square of the subtendent.

Quæsitas, the things demanded ; from *quæro, quæsitum.*

Quotient, is the result of a division ; from *quoties*, how many times.

R.

Radically meeting, is said of those oblongs or squares whose sides doe meet together.

Radius, ray or beame, is the semi-diameter; called so metaphorically from the spoake of a wheel, which is to the limb thereof as the semi-diameter to the circumference of a circle.

Reciprocall, is said of proportionalities, or two rowes of proportionals, wherein the first of the first is to the first of the second as the last of the second is to the last of the first, and contrarily.

Rectangular, is said of those figures which have right angles.

Refinedly, is said when we go the shortest way to work, by primifying the radius.

Renvoy, a remitting from one place to another. It comes from the French word *renvoyer.*

Representative, is said of the letters which stand for whole words; as, E. for side, L. for secant, U. for subtendent.

Residuat, is to leave a remainder; *nempe id quod residet et superest.*

Resolver, is that which looseth and untieth the knot of a difficulty; of *re* and *solvo.*

Resolutory, is said of the last partition of the loxogonosphericall operations.

Result, is the last effect of a work.

Root, is the side of a square, cube, or any cossick figure.

S.

Scheme, signifieth here the delineation of a geometricall figure, with all parts necessary for the illustrating of a demonstration; from ἔχω, *habeo.*

Sciography, the art of shadowing; of σκία, *umbra,* γραφω, *scribo.*

Segment, the portion of a thing cut off; *quasi secamentum, quod a re aliqua secatur.*

Sexagesimat, Subsexagesimat, Resubsexagesimat, and *Biresubsexagesimat,* are said of the division, subdivision, resubdivision, and reer-resubdivision of degrees into minuts, seconds, thirds, and fourths, in 60 of each other; the divisor of the fore-goer being successively the following dividend, and the quotient alwayes sixty.

Sharp, is said of acute angles.

Sindiforall, is said of those moods the fourth terme of whose analogie is onely illatitious to the maine quæsitum.

Sindiforation, is the affection of those foresaid moods whereby the value of the mensurator is knowne.

Sindiforatall, is concerning those moods whose illatitious terme is an angle.

Sindiforiutall, is of those moods whose illatitious terme is a side. All these foure words are composed of representatives, and, if I remember well, mentioned in my explanation.

Sinocosinall, is said of the concordances of those moods which agree in this, that their analogies run upon sines and sine-complements.

Sinocotangentall, is said of those moods which agree in that the termes of their analogie run upon sines and tangent-complements.

Sines, is so called, I believe, because it is alwayes in the very bosom of a circle.

Sinused, is said of termes endowed or invested with sines.

Specialized, contracted to more particular termes. Vide *Individuated.*

Specifying, determinating, particularising.

Specification, a making more especiall, by contracting the generality of a thing. Vide *Specialized.*

Sphericodisergeticks, are the sphericall triangles of two operations.

Structure of an operation, is the whole frame thereof; from *struo, structum.*

Subdatoquære, is a particular datoquære, and is applied to the problems of the cases of every sphericodisergetick mood. Vide *Subproblems.*

Subjacent, is the substerned side or the base; of *sub* and *jaceo,* vide *Sustentative, Sustaining side* and *Substerned.*

Subordinate problems, is the same with subdatoquære.

Subproblems, is the same with subordinate problems, or problemets.

Subservient, is said of moods which serve in the operation of other moods.

Substerned, is the subjacent side or base, or, more generally, any side opposite to an ˙angle; of *sub* and *sterno, sternere,* vide *Subjacent.*

Subtendent, is˙ the side opposite to the right angle; of *sub* and *tendo,* as if you would say, Under-stretched.

Subtendentine, is the subtendent of a little rectangled triangle, comprehended within the area of a great one, and is sometimes called the little subtendent, and reere subtendent.

Subtendentall, is the subtendent of a great rectangled triangle, within whose capacity is included a little one; it is likewise called the great subtendent, and maine subtendent.

Supernumerary, is said of the digit, by the which the proposed number exceeds in places the number of the places of the radius.

Supplements, are the oblongs made of the segments of the root of a square; and so called, because they supply all that the diagonals or squares of the segments, joyned together, want of the whole lines square.

Suppone severally, is to signifie severall things.

Sustaining side, is the substerned or subjacent side.

Sustentative, is the same with sustaining, substerned, subjacent, and base.

Sympathie of angles, is a similitude in their affection; of σὺν and πάθος, *passio,* vide *Homogeneall.*

T.

Table, is an index sometimes, and sometimes it is taken for a briefe and summary way of expressing many things.

Tangentine, is that which concerneth tangents or touch-lines.

Tangentosinall, is said of the concordance of those loxogonosphericals, the termes of whose analogie runne upon tangents and sines.

Tenet, is a secondary maxim, and is onely said here of cathetothetick principles.

Theorematick, speculative ; from θεώρημα, a speculation, which cometh from θεωρεῖν or θεορᾶν, *speculare* or *contemplare*.

Topanglet, and verticaline, are the same.

Trigonometry, is the art of calculating and measuring triangles ; of τρίγωνος, *triangulus*, and μετρέω, *metior*.

Trissotetras, is that which runneth all along upon threes and foures ; of τρίοσος, and *in plurali* τρίσοι, *tertius, trinus, triplex, tres*, and τετράς, *numerus, quaternarius*, from τέοσαρες, *quatuor*.

U.

Variator, is from *vario, variare*, to diversifie, and is said of cases, which, upon the same datas, are onely diverse in the manner of resolving the quæsitum.

Verticaline, Verticall, Verticalet, are the top angles and top anglets ; from *vertex, verticis*.

Under-problem, Problemet, Subordinate Problem, Sub-problem, Under-datoquære, and *Sub-datoquære*, are all the same thing.

Unradiated, or *Unradiused*, is said of a summe of logarithms from which the radius is abstracted.

Z.

Zetetick, is said of loxogonospherical moods which agree in the same quæsitas ; from ζητέω, *quæro, inquiro*.

THE FINALL CONCLUSION.

I<small>F</small> the novelty of this my invention be acceptable, as I doubt not but it will, to the most learned and judicious Mathematicians, I have already reaped all the benefit I expected by it, and shall hereafter, God willing, without hope of any further recompence, cheerfully undergoe more laborious employments of the like nature, to doe them service. But as for such, who, either understanding it not, or vain-gloriously being accustomed to criticise on the works of others, will presume to carp therein at what they cannot amend, I pray God to illuminate their judgments and rectifie their wits, that they may know more and censure lesse: for so by forbearing detraction, the venom whereof must needs reflect upon themselves, they will come to approve better of the endeavours of those that wish them no harme.

SIT DEO GLORIA.

THE DIORTHOSIS.

T<small>HE</small> mistakes of the presse can breed but little obstruction to the progresse of the Ingenius Reader, if with his pen, before he enter upon the perusal of this Treatise, he be pleased thus to correct, as I hope he will, these ensuing Erratas—

[The list of Errata is omitted, as they have been corrected in the Text.]

What errors else, if any, have slipt animadversion, besides their not being very materiall, are so intelligible, that being by the easiest judgement with as much facility eschewable as I can observe them, not to mention the commission of such faults is no great omission; and therefore will I heartily, without further ceremony, conduct the Student, (who, making this the beginning of the book, as it is most fit he doe, seeing a ruler should be made streight before any thing be ruled by it,) is willing to go along with me from hence circularly through the title to the end of the Treatise in the proposed way, as followes.

AND SO GOD BLESSE US BOTH.

ΠΑΝΤΟΧΡΟΝΟΧΑΝΟΝ :

OR,

A peculiar

PROMPTUARY

Of

TIME ;

Wherein (not one inſtant being omitted ſince the beginning
of motion) is diſplayed

A most exact DIRECTORY

for all particular *Chronologies,*
in what Family ſoever :

And that by deducing the true

Pedigree and Lineal descent of the
most ancient and honorable name of the

V R Q V H A R T S,

in the houſe of CROMARTIE,

ſince the Creation of the world,
until this preſent yeer of God. 1652.

London, Printed for *Richard Baddeley,*
and are to be ſold at his Shop, within
the *Middle-Temple*-gate, 1652.

TO THE READER.

SOME few months after that, amongst other papers of the Author's of very great concernment and knowledge, which were totally lost in the pillage ensuing the fatal blowe given to the Royal party at Worcester, this ancient Pedigree, from amongst the regardless fingers of the promiscuous souldiery, was, by a surpaſsing honest and civil officer of Colonel Pride's regiment, most opportunely rescued from the inexorable rage of Vulcan, to whom by a file of musquettiers it was consecrated, to afford smoak to their pipes of tobacco; it falling by meer chance into my hands, and after perusal perceiving it to be exceeding useful and ingenious, I thought my self in duty to the Publike, obliged, lest at any time hereafter it should incur the like hazard of imbezelling, faithfully to commit it to the preſs. Which designe I the rather undertook, that the Author, whose Genealogie it is, hath already been highly esteemed of for his literature and other qualifications; whereof by treatises long ago evulged, and actions of more then ordinary vertue, he hath at several occasions given many ample testimonies. And albeit the condition wherein for the present he stands with the State, in matters of his charge and deportment in the Regal Army, appear not, in the judgements of those have taken his examination, to be, as I am informed, so desperate as that he thereby will be much endangered; yet, leaving these mysteries to whom they are competent, and medling with no more then what by a common obligation to learning, and excellent endowments of the interior faculties, where ever they be found, I am tyed unto; I will onely make bold to speak a word or two in behalf of the Author, and in all humility submit the censure thereof to the judicious construction of the State, whose prisoner he is.

It being here every way perceptible by the Chronologie of his House, in this little tractate so punctually deduced, that Providence hath been so favourable to that his family, as to preserve it amidst the many various revolutions, and almost innumerable changes of monarchies and estates, wherein it was in several nations very often interefsed ; it is humbly desired, and, as I believe, from the hearts of all that are acquainted with him, that the greatest State in the world stain not their glory by being the Atropos to cut the thred of that which Saturne's sithe hath not been able to mow in the progrefs of all former ages, especially in the person of him whose inward abilities are like to produce effects conducible to the State of as long continuance for the future. And although, as Christians, we be not obliged to assert the truth of that philosophical position, whereby the future is always maintained to be for duration equal with what is past ; yet would his minde, by all probability, if cherished with encouragements, emit for utility, pleasure, and honesty, such fruits of goodness, as might reach the one, *ad post*, with no lefs extent of space, then, *ab ante*, fortune hath conveyed the other. So that, to make use of Aristotle's other division fo good, taken from its threefold variety of subject, to which it oweth its existence, the Author's minde and fortune will conjunctly, by appearance, be able to dilate themselves over the whole course of time, provided his body, now in the custody of the State, may of their grace receive that inlargement, together with other favours thereunto concomitant, the want whereof would quite dash and utterly overthrow the other two aforesaid branches of that Trichotomie in his person, to the great prejudice of this Commonwealth ; which truly, considering how formerly he hath been a Mecænas to the scholar, a patron to the souldier, a favourer of the marchant, a protecter of the artificer, and upholder of the yeoman, it were a thousand pities that by the austerity of a State, which dependeth in both its *esse* and *bene esse* upon the flourishing of these worthy professions, effects so advantagious thereto, should, by not conferring deserved courtesies on him, be extinguished in the very brood. This, out of my duty to the State and affection to the Author, I have thought fit to premise, as it becomes the Reader's well-wisher   G. P.

PRÆNOSCENDUM.

THE figures in the rows above the proper names, are to be understood thus : the first denotes the yeer of the world wherein such a one was born, to which effect, at the top of the page, just above that figure, are set down the letters A. M. designing *Anno Mundi*. The second shews their number or series, in order from their first fore father, and to this effect the word *Series* is placed above it, at the upper end of the page. The third signifies the difference of yeers betwixt any two predecessors as they follow one another, for which cause the words *Common Difference* is posited above it, at the beginning of the page ; it being termed Common Difference for no other reason, but that by adding and abstracting it from the epochs of the world and incarnation, in the nativities of any one of the list, it will afford the true foresaid epochs in the birth of his successor. Lastly, the fourth number expresseth the epoch of Christ, either before or after the incarnation, and to this purpose are supraposited the words *Ante Chr. Anno Christi*. As for example, Esormon was born in the yeer of the world 1810, was the sixteenth from Adam, he was 32 yeers younger then his father Pasiteles, and lived 2139 yeers before the incarnation, &c.

THE TRUE PEDIGREE, AND LINEAL DESCENT OF THE MOST ANCIENT AND HONORABLE FAMILY OF THE VRQUHARTS IN THE HOUSE OF CROMARTIE, SINCE THE CREATION OF THE WORLD UNTIL THIS PRESENT YEER OF GOD, 1652.

GOD the FATHER, SON, and HOLY GHOST, who were from all eternity, did in time of nothing create red earth; of red earth framed Adam, and of a rib out of the side of Adam fashioned Eve. After which creation, plasmation, and formation, succeed the generations, as followeth :—

AN. MUN.	SERIES.	COM. DIFFER.	ANTE CHR.
1	1		3948

ADAM maried EVE.
He was surnamed the Protoplast; and on his wife Eve begot
SETH.

AN. MUN.	SERIES.	COM. DIFFER.	ANTE CHR.
130	2	129	3819

SETH maried SHIFKAH.
He was father of the Righteous, and such as called upon the name of God; and his wife Shifkah was his own coenixed sister; on whom he begot
ENOS.

AN. MUN.	SERIES.	COM. DIFFER.	ANTE CHR.
235	3	105	3714

ENOS maried MAHLA;
And on her begot
CAINAN.

AN. MUN.	SERIES.	COM. DIFFER.	ANTE CHR.
325	4	90	3624

CAINAN maried BILHAH;
and on her begot
MAHALALEEL.

AN. MUN.	SERIES.	COM. DIFFER.	ANTE CHR.
396	5	71	3553

MAHALALEEL maried TIMNAH;
And on her begot
JARED.

AN. MUN.	SERIES.	COM. DIFFER.	ANTE CHR.
460	6	64	3481

JARED maried AHOLIMAH;
And on her begot
ENOCH.

AN. MUN.	SERIES.	COM. DIFFER.	ANTE CHR.
622	7	162	3327

ENOCH maried ZILPAH.
This Enoch was translated alive unto the

AN. MUN.	SERIES.	COM. DIFFER.	ANTE CHR.

heavens, and was the first that gave occasion to the Apotheosis of the Greeks. On Zilpah he begot

METHUSALAH.

687	8	65	3262

METHUSALAH maried NOEMA.

He lived till he was full 960 yeers of age; and on Noema begot

LAMECH.

874	9	187	3075

LAMECH maried ADA;
And on her begot

NOAH.

1056	10	182	2893

NOAH maried TITEA.

In the six hundreth yeer compleat of Noah's age occurred the universal Deluge. His wife Titea was the daughter of Tubal-Cain, the son of Jubal. On her he begot

JAPHET.

1557	11	501	2392

JAPHET maried DEBORA.

To Japhet's inheritance befel all the regions of Europe. On Debora he begot

JAVAN.

1700	12	143	2259

JAVAN maried NEGINOTHI.

For his portion, being Japhet's eldest son, he had all the territories of Greece. His wife Neginothi was the daughter of Arphaxad the son of Sem, Japhet's second brother, and elder then Cham. After him, for many hundreds of yeers together, the Grecians were called Javanites. On Neginothi he begot

PENUEL.

1730	13	30	2219

PENUEL maried HOTTIR.

This Penuel was a most intimate friend of Nimrod the mighty hunter, and builder of Babel. On his wife Hottir he begot

TYCHEROS.

1751	14	21	2198

TYCHEROS maried ORPAH.

Of this Tycheros, Orpah the daughter of Sabatius Saga, Prince of the Armenians, made choice to be her husband, because of his gallantry and good success in the wars. On Orpah he begot

PASITELES.

1778	15	27	2171

PASITELES maried AXA.

This Axa was the daughter of Samothee King of the Gauls, on whom he begot

ESORMON.

1810	16	32	2139

ESORMON maried NARFESIA.

He was soveraign Prince of Achaia. For his fortune in the wars, and affability in conversation, his subjects and familiars surnamed him ἐξοχάϱτ☿, that is say, fortunate and well beloved. After which time, his posterity ever since hath acknowledged him the father of all that carry the name of Vrquhart. He had for his arms, three banners, three ships, and three ladies, in a field dor, with the picture of a young lady above the waste, holding in her right hand a brandished sword, and a branch of myrtle in the left, for crest; and for supporters, two Javanites after the souldier-habit of Achaia, with this motto in the scroll of his coat-armour, Ταύτα ἡ τρία ἀξιοθιάτα; that is, These three are worthy to behold. Upon his wife Narfesia, who was soveraign of the Amazons, he begot

CRATYNTER.

| 1837 | 17 | 27 | 2112 |

CRATYNTER.

He was likewise surnamed ἱροχάρτ☉, as ever since have been all the male race of Esormon. He was a victorious prince, yet all his issue male dying before himself, there succeeded to him in his inheritance his brother German

THRASYMEDES.

| 1841 | 18 | 4 | 2108 |

THRASYMEDES maried GOSHENNI.
On Goshenni he begot
EVIPPOS.

| 1873 | 19 | 32 | 2076 |

EVIPPOS maried BRIAGETA.
On Briageta he begot
CLEOTINUS.

| 1899 | 20 | 26 | 2053 |

CLEOTINUS maried ANDRONIA.
This Andronia was the daughter of Egialeus ruler of the Sicyonians. On her he begot
LITOBOROS.

| 1930 | 21 | 31 | 2019 |

LITOBOROS maried two wives,
PUSENA and EMPHANEOLA.

Yet he had, besides these two ladies, several other both wives and concubines, as the fashion was over the whole world even then, and for the space of above a thousand yeers thereafter; yet, in matter of the genealogie of this house, no other women are collaterally placed but such as have been mothers of the chiefs thereof, or if there be any mentioned, it is onely here and there the most especial, without having regard to any of the rest. Litoboros on Pusena begot
APODEMOS.

| 1961 | 22 | 31 | 1988 |

APODEMOS.

Athough Apodemos was begot on Pusena the daughter of Æmathius Prince of Macedonia, yet to him succeeded his half brother Bathybulos, begotten on Emphaneola the daughter of Tyrus ruler of Thracia.

| 1962 | 23 | 1 | 1987 |

BATHYBULOS maried BONARIA;
And on her begot
PHRENEDON.

| 1991 | 24 | 29 | 1958 |

PHRENEDON maried PENINAH.
This Phrenedon was in the house of the Patriarch Abraham at the time of the destruction of Sodom and Gomorrha. On Penina he begot
ZAMELES.

| 2023 | 25 | 32 | 1926 |

ZAMELES maried ASYMBLETA;
And on her begot
CHORONOMOS.

AN. MUN.	SERIES.	COM. DIFFER.	ANTE CHR.
2055	26	32	1894

Choronomos maried Carissa.

He on Carissa, who was sister-in-law to Istavon king of the Germans, begot
Leptologon.

AN. MUN.	SERIES.	COM. DIFFER.	ANTE CHR.
2083	27	28	1866

Leptologon maried Calaglais;
And on her begot
Aglæstos.

2114	28	31	1835

Aglæstos maried Theoglena;
And on her begot
Megalonus.

2143	29	23	1806

Megalonus.

He having no children by his wife Primilla, there succeeded to him his uncle
Evemeros.

2120	30	6	1829

Evemeros maried Pammerissa.

Here is to be remarked, that we are not to regard the difference betwixt the ages of Megalonus and Aglæstos, which is 29; nor yet that betwixt Megalonus and Evemeros, which is 23; but the difference onely 'twixt Evemeros and Aglæstos, because it retrogrades not the time, but continues in an even outright course upon the track thereof. This Evemeros was six yeers younger then his brother Aglæstos; and on his wife Pammerissa begot
Callophron.

2150	31	30	1799

Callophron maried Floridula;

And on her begot
Arthmios.

AN. MUN.	SERIES.	COM. DIFFER.	ANTE CHR.
2183	32	33	1766

Arthmios maried Chrysocomis;
And on her begot
Hypsegoras.

2207	33	24	1742

Hypsegoras maried Arrenopas.

On Arrenopas, who was the daughter of Hercules Lybius, he begot
Autarces.

2234	34	27	1715

Autarces maried Tharsalia.

On Tharsalia, who was the sister of Spartus that built Lacedemon, he begot
Evages.

2266	35	32	1683

Evages maried Maia;
And on her begot
Atarbes.

2295	36	29	1654

Atarbes maried Roma;
And on her begot
Pamprosodos.

2326	37	31	1623

Pamprosodos maried Termuth.

On this Termuth, who was that daughter of Pharaoh Amenophis which found Moses amongst the bulrushes, and brought him up as if he had been her own childe, he begot
Gethon.

AN. MUN.	SERIES.	COM. DIFFER.	ANTE CHR.
2355	38	29	1594

GETHON maried VEGETA;
And on her begot
HOLOCLEROS.

AN. MUN.	SERIES.	COM. DIFFER.	ANTE CHR.
2384	39	29	1565

HOLOCLEROS maried CALLIMERIS.

On this Callimeris, who was the daughter of Siceleus the soveraign of those countries in Spain which now are called Galicia, Andaluzia, Murcia, and Granada, he begot

MOLIN.

AN. MUN.	SERIES.	COM. DIFFER.	ANTE CHR.
2415	40	31	1534

MOLIN maried PANTHEA.

This is he that came with Gathelus from Egypt into Portugal, and of whom are descended the Clanmolinespick in Ireland. His wife Panthea was the daughter of Deucalion and Pirra, of whom Ovid maketh mention in the first of his Metamorphosis. In that part of Africk which, after his name, is till this hour called Molinea, by cunning and valour together he killed in one morning three lions; the heads whereof, when in a basket presented to his lady Panthea, so terrified her, that, being quick with childe, for putting her right hand to her left side, with this sudden exclamation, O Hercules, what is this! the impression of three lions heads was found upon the left side of the childe as soon as he was born. How Portugal was so called after Gathelus, the Scots after Scota, and that the Scotobrigants were the race of Molin in Spain, is clearly set down in the ample story of the House. Molin on Panthea begot

EPITIMON.

AN. MUN.	SERIES.	COM. DIFFER.	ANTE CHR.
2446	41	31	1503

EPITIMON maried GONIMA.

This Gonima was the sister of Hiber, after whom Ireland was called Hibernia, and daughter of Gathelus, begotten on Scota; in honour of whom Epitimon, she being his mother-in-law, after her name called his second son Scotus; of whose progenie, shortly after, the surname of Scot took its beginning, together with the arms which Molin ἐραχάρτⓌ by his valour had acquired on the coast of Africk, and which upon the left side of Epitimon by nature were imprinted from his mother's womb, as hath already been sufficiently enough glanced at in the description of Molin. Then began the old Arms of Vrquhart in the house of Esormon, viz. three banners, three ships, and three ladies, to be exchanged into three lions heads. Epitimon on Gonima begot

HYPOTYPHOS.

AN. MUN.	SERIES.	COM. DIFFER.	ANTE CHR.
2474	42	28	1475

HYPOTYPHOS maried GANYMENA;
And on her begot
MELOBOLON.

AN. MUN.	SERIES.	COM. DIFFER.	ANTE CHR.
2503	43	29	1446

MELOBOLON.

His wife Actosa was the daughter of Chusan Raschataim, whose male-issue Melabolon surviving, there succeeded to him his cousin-germane Propetes, who was begotten by Nepenthes, the brother of Hypotyphos, on the lady Thespesia.

AN. MUN.	SERIES.	COM. DIFFER.	ANTE CHR.
2509	44	6	1440

PROPETES maried HYPERMNESTRA.

This Hypermnestra was the choicest of

Danaus' fifty daughters; and on her Propetes begot

EUPLOCAMOS.

| 2539 | 45 | 30 | 1410 |

EUPLOCAMOS maried HORATIA;
And on her begot
PHILOPHRON.

| 2567 | 46 | 28 | 1382 |

PHILOPHRON maried PHILUMENA;
And on her begot
SYNGENES.

| 2598 | 47 | 31 | 1351 |

SYNGENES.

His wife Accorta bearing him no children, there succeeded to him his uncle
POLYPHRADES.

| 2581 | 48 | | 1368 |

POLYPHRADES maried NEOPIS.

This Neopis was the sister of Amphion ruler of Thebes, on whom Polyphrades begot

CAINOTOMOS.

| 2627 | 49 | 29 | 1322 |

CAINOTOMOS maried THYMELICA.

Here is onely set down the difference between the ages of Syngenes and Cainotomos, which is 29, and not that of Polyphrades, to either of them, as hath been formerly observed in Aglæstos, Magalonus, and Evemeros; because Polyphrades, though posterior in succession, is elder in yeers, and therefore to regard his difference, would but intangle the progress of our chronological Genealogie. This Cainotomos took to wife Thy-

melica the daughter of Bacchus, in recompence of his having accompanyed him in the conquest of the Indies. Cainotomos in his return from thence into Greece, passed through the territories of Israel, where being acquainted with Debora the Judge and Prophetess, he received from her a very rich jewel, which afterwards by one of his succession was presented to Pentasilea, that Queen of the Amozons that assisted the Trojans against Agamemnon. On his wife Thymelica he begot

RODRIGO.

| 2656 | 50 | 29 | 1295 |

RODRIGO maried EPHAMILLA.

This Rodrigo being invited by his kindred the Clanmolinespick into Ireland, bore rule in that country all the days of his life, with so much applause and good success, that of him is descended the Clanrurie, of which name there were 26 rulers and kings of Ireland before the days of Ferguse the first, King of Scots in Scotland. On Ephamilla he begot

DICARCHES.

| 2685 | 51 | 29 | 1264 |

DICARCHES maried PORRIMA.

His mariage with Porrima the sister of Carmenta, Evander's mother, was made in his younger yeers, when he travelled from Ireland into Italy; and on her begot
EXAGASTOS.

| 2713 | 52 | 28 | 1236 |

EXAGASTOS maried LAMPEDO;
And on her begot
DENAPON.

AN. MUN.	SERIES.	COM. DIFFER.	ANTE CHR.
2750	53	37	1199

DENAPON maried TELECLYTA ;
And on her begot
ARTISTES.

AN. MUN.	SERIES.	COM. DIFFER.	ANTE CHR.
2775	54	25	1174

ARTISTES maried CLARABELLA ;
And on her begot
THYMOLEON.

2806	55	31	1143

THYMOLEON maried EROMENA ;
And on her begot
EUSTOCHOS.

2834	56	28	1115

EUSTOCHOS maried ZOCALLIS ;
And on her begot
BIANOR.

2864	57	30	1085

BIANOR maried LEPIDA ;
And on her begot
THRYLLUMENOS.

2893	58	29	1056

THRYLLUMENOS.
His wife Metaceras was the daughter of Calcedo the Tyrian that founded Carthage ; but he having no sons by her, there succeeded to him his own brother-german
MELLESSEN.

2900	59	7	1049

MELLESSEN maried NICOLIA.
This Nicolia, before she was maried to him, travelled from the remote eastern countries to have experience of the wisdom of Solomon, and by many is supposed to have been the Queen of Sheba. Mellessen nevertheless sent some of his children to Ireland and Britain, to be brought up with the best of his own father and mother's kindred ; the name of the eldest son Mellessen begot on Nicolia, was
ALYPOS.

2930	60	30	1019

ALYPOS maried PROTEUSA.
Proteusa was the sister of Eborak, who founded the city of York. In the time of this Alypos was Scotland named Olbion, afterwards by an Æolick dialect termed Albion ; the castle of Edinburgh built, for that Ethus king of the Picts did build it is fabulous, and the promontories at Cromartie, called the σωλῆρες, vulgarly, Soters. Alypos Proteusa begot
ANOCHLOS.

2951	61	21	998

ANOCHLOS maried GOZOSA ;
And on her begot
HOMOGNIOS.

2981	62	30	968

HOMOGNIOS maried VENUSTA ;
And on her begot
EPSEPHICOS.

3012	63	31	937

EPSEPHICOS.
He begot on his wife Oncumena several sons and daughters; but the sons not living, there succeeded to him his nephew EUTROPOS, begotten of his brother Phenricos on Prosectica.

3045	64	33	904

EUTROPOS maried DELOTERA.

x

AN. MUN.	SERIES.	COM. DIFFER.	ANTE CHR.

On Delotera, who was the daughter of Agesilaus, he begot
CORYPHÆUS.

| 3075 | 65 | 30 | 874 |

CORYPHÆUS maried TRACARA;
And on her begot
ETOIMOS.

| 3104 | 66 | 29 | 845 |

ETOIMOS maried POTHINA.
On this Pothina, who was neece to Lycurgus, and sister to Cabrilaus, he begot
SPUDÆOS.

| 3132 | 67 | 28 | 817 |

SPUDÆOS maried CORDATA;
And on her begot
EUMESTOR.

| 3163 | 68 | 31 | 786 |

EUMESTOR maried ARETIAS;
And on her begot
GRIPHON.

| 3190 | 69 | 27 | 759 |

GRIPHON maried MUSURGA;
And on her begot
EMMENES.

| 3219 | 70 | 29 | 730 |

EMMENES maried ROMALIA;
And on her begot
PATHOMACHON.

| 3248 | 71 | 27 | 701 |

PATHOMACHON maried ORTHOIUSA.
On Orthoiusa he begot
ANEPSIOS.

AN. MUN.	SERIES.	COM. DIFFER.	ANTE CHR.
3279	72	31	670

ANEPSIOS maried RECATADA.
This Recatada was the daughter of Simon Brek, who was the first crowned king of the Scots in Ireland; and on her Anepsios begot
AULOPREPES.

| 3308 | 73 | 29 | 641 |

AULOPREPES maried CHARIESTERA;
And on her begot
COROSYLOS.

| 3337 | 74 | 29 | 612 |

COROSYLOS maried REXENORA;
And on her begot
DÆTALON.

| 3365 | 75 | 28 | 584 |

DÆTALON maried PHILERGA.
This Dætalon was agnamed Char, the reason whereof is set down in the voluminous history of the house, as likewise of the agnames of many of Dætalon's predecessors; which, for compendiousness sake, must needs be here omitted. Upon Philerga he begot
BELTISTOS.

| 3395 | 76 | 30 | 554 |

BELTISTOS maried THOMYRIS.
This Beltistos was agnamed Chonchar, for which cause a certain progeny descended of him is till this hour called the generation of the Ochonchars; a race truly of great antiquity and renown in the dominion of Ireland. Beltistos founded the castle of Vrquhart above Innernasse, which being afterwards compleated by his posterity, hath ever since been called the castle Vickichonchar. On Thomyris he begot HORÆOS.

AN. MUN.	SERIES.	COM. DIFFER.	ANTE CHR.
3426	77	31	523

HORÆOS maried VARONILLA ;
And on her begot
ORTHOPHRON.

AN. MUN.	SERIES.	COM. DIFFER.	ANTE CHR.
3449	78	23	500

ORTHOPHRON maried STRANELLA ;
And on Stranella begot
APSICOROS.

AN. MUN.	SERIES.	COM. DIFFER.	ANTE CHR.
3480	79	31	469

APSICOROS maried ÆQUANIMA.
On this Equanima, which was the sister of Marcus Coriolanus, and daughter of Volumina, he begot
PHILAPLUS.

AN. MUN.	SERIES.	COM. DIFFER.	ANTE CHR.
3510	80	30	439

PHILAPLUS maried BAROSA ;
And on her begot
MEGALETOR.

AN. MUN.	SERIES.	COM. DIFFER.	ANTE CHR.
3531	81	21	418

MEGALETOR maried EPIMONA ;
And on her begot
NOMOSTOR.

AN. MUN.	SERIES.	COM. DIFFER.	ANTE CHR.
3560	82	29	389

NOMOSTOR maried DIOSA.
This Diosa was the daughter of Alcibiades and Hipparete. Nomostor, after the lamentable decease of his father-in-law, whom his native country had so ungratefully used, took his farewel of Greece ; and after many dangerous voyages both by sea and land, arrived at last at the harbour of Ochonchar, now called Cromartie, or *Portus Salutis*, first found out by his predecessors Alypos and Beltistos, agnamed Conchar, inhabited by many of his kindred at the time of his landing there, and thereafter all the days of his life honoured with his presence, as prince of the race. On Diosa he begot
ASTIOREMON.

AN. MUN.	SERIES.	COM. DIFFER.	ANTE CHR.
3588	83	28	361

ASTIOREMON maried BONITA,
And on her begot Phronematias. He maried afterward Aretusa, and on her begot Lutork. This Astioremon, by killing the outlandish king Ethus the first, and first king of the Picts, in duel, before the face of both armies, gained the great battel of Farnua, fought within a mile of Cromartie; the reliques of that stranger king's trenches, head-quarters, and castramentation of his whole army, being till this day conspicuous to any that passeth that way. He likewise for his valour, honesty, and eloquence, made proof of at that time, was induced to change his old motto and embrace this : Εὐνοεῖτω, εὐλόγει, κ̔ εὐπράτ[ε, that is to say, *Mean, speak, and do well;* which device till this hour is kept in the scroll of the coat-armor of the house of Cromartie. The lady likewise made use of for a crest, instead of a mirtle branch which before that time she in her left hand carried, from thence forth bore a palm, which, in the Vrquhart's arms of the foresaid house, is as yet observed. To Astioremon succeeded his son
PHRONEMATIAS.

AN. MUN.	SERIES.	COM. DIFFER.	ANTE CHR.
3607	84	19	342

PHRONEMATIAS.
This Phronematias, agnamed Chonchardou, had to wife one Panagia ; of whom, nevertheless, having no male issue that lived

to any perfection, there succeeded to him his brother Lutork, begot on Aretusa.

| 3614 | 85 | 7 | 335 |

LUTORK maried BENDITA.

Ferguse the first, at his coming into Olbion, after he had in honour of his predecessor Gathelus given unto his landing-place the name of Argile, and called the whole country he was to possess, Scotland, after the Scotobrigants, (by Seneca in his Satyrs called Scutobrigantes, by a Dorick dialect, for Scotobrigantes, from Brigansa, a town in Galicia, now called Compostella, which the Scots of old both built and inhabited; he likewise giveth them the epithet of Cærulei, because, in my opinion, the most of the inhabitants there were accustomed, even then, to the wearing of blew caps,) after the Scotogalli, of whom our Scots-Irish language is termed Galick, as they from Galicia, and lastly, after those that had the surname of Scot, without any other designation. He gave in marriage to Lutork ἐροχάρτ⊙, the captain general of all his forces, because of his dexterity both in the Macedonian and Romish discipline of war, his own sister Bendita; for which cause, the river upon whose bank the promise was made, hath ever since been called Vrquhart; and the valley, or glen as they term it there, where the marriage was consummated, Glen-Vrquhart, or Glenurchi, and that in honour of the Odocharties, Ochonchars, Clanrurie, Scotobrigants, Clanmolinespick, and Esormon, who were all of them Lutork's predecessors, and surnamed Vrquharts. This Lutork, besides his own ancient inheritance from Cromartie to castle Vrquhart inclusive,

and several other lands successively derived to him from Nomostor, took possession then of the Thanedom of Lochaber, with many other territories of a large extent. On Bendita he begot

MACHEMOS.

| 3637 | 86 | 23 | 312 |

MACHEMOS maried REGALETTA.

This Machemos was agnamed Chonchar Roy, and on Regaletta, who was the daughter of Dæphron Gramus, the first of the name of Grame, father of the honourable family of Montrose, and founder of the old town of that title, now corruptly called Monross, begot

STICHOPÆO.

| 3668 | 87 | 31 | 281 |

STICHOPÆO maried ISUMENA;
And on her begot
EPALOMENOS.

| 3697 | 88 | 29 | 252 |

EPALOMENOS maried ANTARIA;
And on her begot
TYCHEROS the second.

| 3726 | 89 | 29 | 223 |

TYCHEROS maried BERGOLA.

He was called Tycheros the second, but first that was chief of the name of Vrquhart; was agnamed Titus, and on Bergola, who was the daughter of Getus king of the Picts, begot

APECHON.

| 3755 | 90 | 29 | 194 |

APECHON maried VIRACIA;

AN. MUN.	SERIES.	COM. DIFFER.	ANTE CHR.

And on her begot
ENACMES.

AN. MUN.	SERIES.	COM. DIFFER.	ANTE CHR.
3784	91	29	165

ENACMES maried DYNASTIS ;
And on her begot
JAVAN the second.

3825	92	41	124

JAVAN maried DALGA.

He was named Javan the second, but first nevertheless so called amongst the heads of the family of Vrquhart. On his wife Dalga, the daughter of Conan captain of the Brigants, and after whom ever since the river running along by Cromartie hath been called Conon, he begot
LEMATIAS.

3853	93	28	96

LEMATIAS maried EUTOCUSA ;
And on her begot
PROSENES.

3883	94	30	66

PROSENES maried CORRIBA ;
And on her begot
SOSOMENOS.

3914	95	31	35

SOSOMENOS maried PRÆCELSA ;
And on Præcelsa begot
PHILALETHES.

3945	96	31	4

PHILALETHES maried PLAUSIDICA ;
And on Plausidica begot
THALEROS.

AN. MUN.	SERIES.	COM. DIFFER.	ANNO CHR.
3976	97	31	27

THALEROS maried DONOSA ;
And on her begot
POLYÆNOS.

3995	98	19	46

POLYÆNOS maried SOLICÆLIA ;
And on her begot
CRATESIMACHOS.

4025	99	30	76

CRATESIMACHOS maried BONTADOSA ;
And on her begot
EUNOEMON.

4056	100	31	107

EUNOEMON maried CALLIPARIA.

This Calliparia was the daughter of Rodrigo captain of the Morrays, and first Morray that ever came into Scotland ; on whom Eunoemon begot
DIASEMOS.

4084	101	28	135

DIASEMOS maried CRELEUCA.

On this Creleuca, who was the daughter of Ardgudus captain of Argyle, he begot
SAPHENUS.

4114	102	30	165

SAPHENUS maried PANCALA ;
And on her begot
BRAMOSO.

4142	103	28	193

BRAMOSO maried DOMINELLA.

This Bramoso, agnamed Timothy, on Dominella begot
CELANAS.

AN. MUN.	SERIES.	COM. DIFFER.	ANNO CHR.
4173	104	31	226

CELANAS maried MUNDULA ;
And on her begot
VISTOSO.

AN. MUN.	SERIES.	COM. DIFFER.	ANNO CHR.
4212	105	39	265

VISTOSO maried PAMPHAIS.
This Vistoso, agnamed Gabriel, on Pamphais begot
POLIDO.

AN. MUN.	SERIES.	COM. DIFFER.	ANNO CHR.
4242	106	30	295

POLIDO maried PHILTRUSA.
This Philtrusa was the daughter of Clarence, brother to Findok king of Scotland ; on her Polido begot
LUSTROSO.

AN. MUN.	SERIES.	COM. DIFFER.	ANNO CHR.
4274	107	32	327

LUSTROSO.
This Lustroso maried Glycerina the daughter of Fincormacus king of Scotland ; of whom, nevertheless, he having no children at all, there succeeded to him his own brother
CHRESTANDER.

AN. MUN.	SERIES.	COM. DIFFER.	ANNO CHR.
4276	108	2	329

CHRESTANDER maried MELIGLENA ;
And on this Meliglena begot
SPECTABUNDO.

AN. MUN.	SERIES.	COM. DIFFER.	ANNO CHR.
4305	109	29	358

SPECTABUNDO maried PHILETIUM.
On this Philetium, who was the daughter of Nectanus king of the Picts, he begot
PHILODULOS.

AN. MUN.	SERIES.	COM. DIFFER.	ANNO CHR.
4337	110	32	390

PHILODULOS maried TERSA ;

And on her begot
PALADINO.

AN. MUN.	SERIES.	COM. DIFFER.	ANNO CHR.
4368	111	31	421

PALADINO maried DULCICORA.
This Paladino, agnamed Nicolas, upon Dulcicora begot
COMICELLO.

AN. MUN.	SERIES.	COM. DIFFER.	ANNO CHR.
4399	112	31	452

COMICELLO maried GETHOSYNA ;
And on Gethosyna begot
REGISATO.

AN. MUN.	SERIES.	COM. DIFFER.	ANNO CHR.
4427	113	28	480

REGISATO maried COLLABELLA ;
And on her begot
ARGUTO.

AN. MUN.	SERIES.	COM. DIFFER.	ANNO CHR.
4456	114	29	509

ARGUTO maried EUCNEMA ;
And on her begot
NICARCHOS.

AN. MUN.	SERIES.	COM. DIFFER.	ANNO CHR.
4487	115	31	540

NICARCHOS maried TORTOLINA.
On this Tortolina, who was the daughter of Arthur of Britain, he begot
MARSIDALIO.

AN. MUN.	SERIES.	COM. DIFFER.	ANNO CHR.
4518	116	31	571

MARSIDALIO maried REPULITA ;
And on this Repulita begot
HEDOMENOS.

AN. MUN.	SERIES.	COM. DIFFER.	ANNO CHR.
4546	117	28	599

HEDOMENOS maried URBANA ;
And on her begot
AGENOR.

AN. MUN.	SERIES.	COM. DIFFER.	ANNO CHR.
4575	118	29	628

AGENOR maried LAMPUSA.

This Agenor, agnamed Ibraim, on Lampusa begot

DIAPREPON.

AN. MUN.	SERIES.	COM. DIFFER.	ANNO CHR.
4607	119	32	660

DIAPREPON maried VISTOSA ;
And on her begot

STRAGAYO.

AN. MUN.	SERIES.	COM. DIFFER.	ANNO CHR.
4634	120	27	687

STRAGAYO maried HERMOSINA ;
And on this Hermosina, who was the daughter of Natasil Thane of Athol, begot

ZERON.

AN. MUN.	SERIES.	COM. DIFFER.	ANNO CHR.
4661	121	27	714

ZERON maried BRAMATA.

This Zeron was agnamed Bacchus, and is he in whose old age, for his supposed hospitality to Donald of the Isles, his ancient and most stately castle of Vrquhart was demolished, and himself forfeited of his whole inheritance, by Eugenius Octavus, king of Scotland. Zeron, nevertheless, on the aforesaid Bramata begot

POLYTELES.

AN. MUN.	SERIES.	COM. DIFFER.	ANNO CHR.
4690	122	29	743

POLYTELES maried ZAGLOPIS.

On this Zaglopis, who was the daughter of Cutbert, ruler of the Westsaxons, he begot

VOCOMPOS.

AN. MUN.	SERIES.	COM. DIFFER.	ANNO CHR.
4720	123	30	775

VOCOMPOS maried ANDROLEMA.

This Vocompos, for his valour and gallantry in the field, was by king Solvatius restored to that part of his land which is called the shire of Cromartie, together with other parcels of his old inheritance in the counties of Buchan and Ross, and invested him with more privileges and immunities, to be derived to his posterity, then he had done to any other subject in that dominion; in compensation, as it were, of thrice as many moe lands, which Eugenius Octavus, father to the said Solvatius, had taken from his grandfather Zeron, and which the said Solvatius was unwilling to cause restore to Vocompos. He had to his second brother one named Phorbas Vrquhart, and Hugh to the third; of whom, some few hundreds of yeers after that, the names of Forbes and Macky had their beginning. What Holinshed, out of Hector Boece, relates of the origine of the name of Forbes, is spoken at random, without other ground then the meer ambition of the said Boece for the honour of his own name. That Forbes, by true orthographie Φόρβας, of which name there was a king of Athens, and several second brothers of the predecessors of this family, of whom some mention is made in the chronological legend thereof, it being a name in Greece as commonly made use of as Φιλίππ☉, Αλεξάνδηρ, Διόγενης, or such like, should of a name, which then it was, become afterwards a surname to the successors of Phorbas, the second brother of Vocompos, occurred meerly by reason of the aphæretical and apocopal curtailing of the syllables Mack, Ap, and Son, for the quicker and more expedite deliverie in the expression of those that, without regard of surnames, were pleased to design men by their

patronymical titles. By means of which
scurvy custom, too much cherished as yet
in many parts of both Scotland and Wales,
the Forbeses, since they began to have two
several Lords of that name, besides many
other very especial knights and gentlemen
of good estates and fortunes, becoming
almost forgetful of the stock from whence
they descended, would set up a genarchie
by themselves, although, by the ordinary
rules of heraldry, their very arms do sufficiently declare their cadency. Nor need
we think strange why they are called Forbas
or Forbes, and not Mack Phorbas, Ap-
Phorbas, or Phorbasson, because for the
reason before deduced, not onely it, but
likewise very many other more vulgar
names, such as George, Henry, Alexander, Andrew, Wat, Som, Gib, Dick, Peter,
James, &c. pass for surnames over the
whole Isle of Britain, in the mouths of
all; of whom not any, for the proper and
peculiar designation of several thousands of
its inhabitants, is able to afford any other
cognominal denomination. Vocompos was
the first in the world that had the bears'
heads to his arms, being induced to exchange, by the instigation of king Solvatius, his arms of three lyons heads for the
three bears' heads razed, because of the
great exploit, in presence of the king, done
by him and his two foresaid brothers, in
killing one morning three wild bears in the
Caledonian forrest; the supporters were
also changed into two grey-hounds, the crest
and impress remaining still the same as it
was since the days of Astioremon. Vocompos upon Androlema, the daughter of Sciolto
Douglas, who was the first of that most

noble family, begot
    CAROLO, the godson of Charlemain.

4749   124   29   802
    CAROLO maried TRASTEVOLE.
This Trastevole was an Italian lady, and
daughter to William, brother to Achaio
king of the Scots.   On her Carolo begot
    ENDYMION.

4780   125   31   833
    ENDYMION maried SUAVILOQUA;
        And on her begot
        SEBASTIAN.

4810   126   30   863
    SEBASTIAN maried FRANCOLINA;
        And on her begot
        LAWRENCE.

4839   127   29   892
    LAWRENCE maried MATILDA;
        And on her begot
        OLIPHER.

4868   128   29   921
    OLIPHER maried ALLEGRA;
        And on her begot
        QUINTIN.

4897   129   29   950
    QUINTIN maried WINNIFRED;
        And on her begot
        GOODWIN.

4925   130   28   978
    GOODWIN maried DOROTHY.
This Goodwin, agnamed Cordæto, on Do-
rothy begot   FREDERICK.

AN. MUN.	SERIES.	COM. DIFFER.	ANTE CHR.
4960	131	35	1013

FREDERICK maried LAWRETTA.

He had to his first wife Castisa, the daughter of Banco Thane of Lochaber, but she had no sons to him. To his second wife he took Lauretta, the daughter of Patrick Dumbar Thane and Earl of March, and on her begot

SIR JASPER.

AN. MUN.	SERIES.	COM. DIFFER.	ANTE CHR.
4989	132	29	1042

SIR JASPER maried GENEVIEVE.

This Jasper, agnamed Soldurio, was the seventh son begot betwixt Frederick and Lauretta without the intermixture of a female, and was said to have had the dexterity, by a single touch of his hand, to cure the disease lately called the king's-evil. He was for his valour dubbed knight by Malcolm Kiænmore, at Forfar, in the yeer of our Lord 1058; in whose reign began the surnames, even of those Scots that were originally Albionites, by an express command from the king, to be more heedfully regarded then formerly they had been; and that by disinvolving the preposited names of the respective owners, from that patronimical confusion which till this hour is observed in the Highlands of that nation, under the designation of Mack before the father's name, as the Welsh men use their Ap, in saying Macdonald, Mackie, Mackain, and so forth through all other names, which, either at christenings or lustrations, have accordingly been given to their ancestors of the male kind; for which, translatitiously, both in England and the low-countries of Scotland, we, by an inveterate custom derived from thence, do say as yet, Donaldson, Hugh-

son, Johnson, &c., vicecognomentally distinguishing such persons, by an especial sillable in the rear of the word, that represents the sire or progenitor; not much unlike to the manner of the Greeks, whose fashion was to denominate the successors of Æacus, Philippus, Hercules, &c. by those patronymicals, Æacedes, Philippides, Herculides, and so forth. He on his wife Genevieve begot

SIR ADAM.

AN. MUN.	SERIES.	COM. DIFFER.	ANTE CHR.
5018	133	29	1071

SIR ADAM maried MARJORIE.

This Sir Adam, agnamed Ardito, was first of the name of Adam that was chief of the family of Vrquhart. He was knighted by king Edgar at his coronation at Scone, anno 1101. On his wife Marjorie, who was the daughter of Griffin Prince of Wales, he begot

EDWARD.

AN. MUN.	SERIES.	COM. DIFFER.	ANTE CHR.
5047	134	29	1100

EDWARD maried JANE.

This Edward, agnamed Philotimos, begot on Jane, the sister of Sir Alexander Caron, who was the first that ever was called Scrimjour, a son named

RICHARD.

AN. MUN.	SERIES.	COM. DIFFER.	ANTE CHR.
5075	135	28	1128

RICHARD maried ANNE.

This Richard, agnamed Dichoso, on Anne begot

SIR PHILIP.

AN. MUN.	SERIES.	COM. DIFFER.	ANTE CHR.
5105	136	30	1158

SIR PHILIP maried MAGDALENE.

This Sir Philip, agnamed Periergos, was

AN. MUN.   SERIES.   COM. DIFFER.   ANTE CHR.

knighted by king William, agnamed for his animosity The Lion, in the yeer 1186. On his wife Magdalene, who was the daughter of Gilcrist earl of Angus, he begot

ROBERT.

| 5134 | 137 | 29 | 1187 |

ROBERT maried GIRSEL.

This Robert, agnamed *De Nova Sede*, upon Girsel, the daughter of Keith Marshall, begot

GEORGE.

| 5162 | 138 | 28 | 1215 |

GEORGE maried MARIE.

This George, agnamed Organder, had on Mary the daughter of Crawford Lindsay, a son named

JAMES.

| 5191 | 139 | 29 | 1244 |

JAMES maried SOPHIA.

This James, agnamed Acolastanas, begot on his wife Sophia, the daughter of Macduff earl of Fife,

DAVID.

| 5219 | 140 | 28 | 1272 |

DAVID maried ELEONORE.

This David, agnamed Polydorus, on Eleonore, a daughter of the house of Seaton, begot

FRANCIS.

| 5246 | 141 | 27 | 1299 |

FRANCIS maried ROSALIND.

This Francis, agnamed Philogynes, begot on Rosalind, the daughter of Gilbert Hay of Arrol, a son named WILLIAM.

AN. MUN.   SERIES.   COM. DIFFER.   ANTE CHR.

| 5261 | 142 | 15 | 1314 |

WILLIAM maried LILLIAS.

His first wife was Lillias, the daughter of Hugh Earl of Rosse; to his second wife he took Violet Cumming, the daughter of John Cumming earl of Buchan, and lord of Straboghie; at which mariage Hugh earl of Ross was so incensed, that he begged of king Robert the Bruce the gift of his forfeiture, because the Cumming had been disloyal to him. Whatever the king's facility was, this William Vrquhart caried himself so lovingly towards king Robert, that when almost all Scotland was possest by king Edward's faction, and his lands at Cromartie altogether overrun by them, and his house garrisoned and victualed with three yeers provision of all necessaries for one hundred men, he by a stratagem gained the castle, and with the matter of fourty men, keept it out against the forces of Edward for the space of seven yeers and a half, during which time all his lands there were totally wasted, and his woods burnt; so that, having nothing then he could properly call his own but the mote-hill onely of Cromartie, which he fiercely maintained against the enemies, he was agnamed *Gulielmus de Monte Alto*. At last William Wallace came to his relief, but, as I conceive, it was the brother's son of the renowned William, who in a little den within two miles of Cromartie, till this hour called Wallace Den, killed six hundred of king Edward's unfortunate forces. Afterwards, raising the siege from about the mote-hill of Cromartie by the assistance of his namesake the other William, the shire of Cromartie was totally purged of the enemy; and shortly after, by king David,

AN. MUN.	SERIES.	COM. DIFFER.	ANTE CHR.

son to the said king Robert, confirmed upon Adam, son to the aforesaid William, with all priviledges, royalties, and immunities, that to the said William formerly did belong, which the Earl of Ross consented unto, upon whose daughter, Lillias by name, the said William begot

ADAM.

5288	143	27	1341

ADAM maried BRIGID.

This Adam, who was Adam the third, but second amongst the chiefs of the house of Vrquhart, was agnamed Philalbianax, because of his love to the king of Scots. On Brigida, the daughter of Robert Fleeming of Cummernald, he begot

JOHN.

5312	144	24	1365

JOHN maried AGNES.

This John, agnamed Aroimon, on Agnes, the daughter of Sir Alexander Ramsey of Dahousie, begot

SIR WILLIAM.

5341	145	29	1394

SIR WILLIAM maried SUSANNA.

This Sir William, being the second of that name, was knighted by king Robert the second, who before his coronation was named John, in the yeer of Christ 1416. On his wife Susanna the daughter of Forbes of that ilk, he begot

WILLIAM.

5386	146	45	1439

WILLIAM.

This William, the third of that name,

took to wife one Elze, the daughter of Pitsligo, but having no issue-male of her, there succeeded to him his own brother-german

ALEXANDER.

5392	147	6	1445

ALEXANDER maried CATHERINE.

This Alexander, the first of that name, was agnamed *Ab Imo Clivo,* before he attained to be chief of the family of the Vrquharts. From this Alexander's second son, is descended lineally that learned and valourous gentleman, collonel John Vrquhart, now in Germany, who for many yeers together, most faithfully discharged the duty of lievtenant-collonel to the queen regnant of Swedeland. Upon his wife Catharine, who was a daughter of the house of Finlatour, he begot

THOMAS.

5423	148	31	1476

THOMAS maried HELEN.

He was agnamed Paterhemon, because he had of his wife Helen Abernethie, a daughter of my lord Salton, five and twenty sons, all men, and eleven daughters, all married women. Seven of those sons were killed at the battel of Pinckie, and of some of those others of them that travelled with great gallantry to forrain countries is descended, as I am informed, that worthy knight in Devonshire, called Sir John Vrquhart, who, both for his considerable fortune and far greater merit, is highly renowned in the south parts of England, as likewise several families neer Carlile, designed by the name of Vrquhart, of such estimation there, that, as I was told, some of them not long ago have been Majors of the city and Sheriffs of the county. To this Thomas succeeded his son

ALEXANDER.

5445   249   22   1498
ALEXANDER maried BEATRICE.

This Alexander, the second of that name, was called Obrimos. The fourth son of this Alexander and the foresaid Beatrice, named Iohn, who afterwards was better known by the title of Tutor of Cromartie, was over all Britain renowned for his deep reach of natural wit, and great dexterity in acquiring of many lands and great possessions, with all men's applause. Upon this Beatrice Innes, daughter of Achintoule, he begot

WALTER.

5482   150   37   1535
WALTER maried ELIZABETH.

This Walter, who was agnamed *Exaftallocrinus*, because he judged of other men by himself, upon Elizabeth Mackenzie, daughter to Seaforte, then designed Mackenzie of that ilk, begot

HENRY.

5502   151   20   1555
HENRY maried ELIZABETH.

This Henry, agnamed Acompos, on Elizabeth Ogilvy, daughter of Bamf, begot

SIR THOMAS.

5532   152   30   1585
SIR THOMAS maried CHRISTIAN.

This Sir Thomas, the second of that name, was knighted by king James at Edinburgh in the yeer 1617. And upon his wife Christian Elphinstoun, who as yet liveth, and is the daughter of Alexander lord Elphinstoun, he begot

SIR THOMAS,
agnamed Parresiastes.

This Sir Thomas, who now liveth, and is the third of that name, chief of the honourable house of the Vrquharts, was knighted by king Charles in White-hall gallery, in the yeer 1641, the 7 of April; and is in line, and by succession to his most remarkable predecessors, the same in number orderly as is set down in the subsequent Table, the first figure denoteth the line, the second the succession.

THE SAID SIR THOMAS, IS			THIS GENEALOGIE WAS DEDUCED	
	By Line	By suc-cession.		
From ADAM the	143	153	Anno Mundi	5598
From NOAH the	134	144	Anno Esormonis	3789
From ESORMON the	128	138	Anno Molini	3184
From MOLIN the	108	114	Anno Rodrici	2943
From RODRIGO the	100	104	Anno Alypou	2669
From ALYPOS the	91	94	Anno Chari	2202
From CHAR the	76	79	Anno Astioremonis	2011
From ASTIOREMON the	68	71	Anno Lutorci	1986
From LUTORK the	67	69	Anno Christi	1651
From ZERON the	32	33	Anno Zeronis	937
From VOCOMPOS the	30	31	Anno Vocompotis	878

SUBDICTIS.

By the chief of the family, Sir Thomas Urquhart by name, the history of the lives of all these his predecefsors is already broached, he making account to finish it how soon the amicable influence of the State, in dependance whereupon his fortune is involved, will, by acquitting him of his parole, wherein to them he stands ingaged, be pleased to release him, and in giving him full enjoyment of his own, allow him the leisure to go about it and other things of greater importance.

The history being continued from the creation of the world till this present time, will contain many specious synchronisms worthy of remark, and as it comprehendeth all the time that is past, so shall few actions of moment, or persons of either sexe, that have been illustrious for any commendable quality, escape the tract of that his pen which treats of their contemporaneans.

POSTILLA.

In the great chronicle of the house of Urquhart, the aforesaid Sir Thomas purposeth, by God's afsistance, to make mention of the illustrious families from thence descended, which as yet are in esteem in the countries of Germany, Bohemia, Italy, France, Spain, England, Scotland, Ireland, and several other nations of a warmer climate, adjacent to that famous territory of Greece, the lovely mother of this most ancient and honourable stem.

How, by the iniquity of time and confusion of languages, their names have been varied, their coat armour altered, and as new sions transplanted unto another soil, without any reference almost to the stock from whence they sprung.

And how many towns, castles, churches, fountains, rivers, nafses, bays, harbours, and such like, have from the name of Urquhart received their denomination.

He likewise intendeth to omit the nominating of no family wherewith at any time the foresaid house hath contracted alliance, which, for more compendiousnefs, hath in the contexture of this epitome been of set purpose left out.

As also to set down the branches of the foresaid name in order as they sprung from the root, together with their alliances, exploits, and other notorie things, delectable even to those that have no interest in the family.

Why the shire of Cromartie alone, of all the places of the Ile of Britain, hath the names of its towns, villages, hamlets, dwellings, promontories, hillocks, temples, dens, groves, fountains, rivers, pools, lakes, stone heaps, akers, and so forth, of pure and perfect Greek.

And finally, for confirmation of the truth in deriving of his extraction from the Ionian race of the Princes of Achaia, and in the deduction of all the considerable particulars of the whole story, is resolved to produce testimonies of Arabick, Greek, Latin, and other writers of such authentick approbation, that we may boldly from thence infer consequences of no lefs infallible verity then any that is not grounded on faith by means of a Divine illumination, as is the story of the Bible, or on reason, by vertue of the unavoidable inference of a necessary concluding demonstration, as that of the Elements of Euclid; which being the greatest evidence that in any narration of that kinde is to be expected, the judicious reader is bid farewel, from whom the Author for the time most humbly takes his leave.

FINIS.

ΕΚΣΚΥΒΑΛΑΥΡΟΝ:

OR,

The Discovery of

A moſt exquiſite JEWEL,

more precious then Diamonds
inchaſed in Gold, the like whereof
was never ſeen in any age ; found in the
kennel of *Worcester*-ſtreets, the day
after the Fight, and ſix before the Au-
tumnal Equinox, *anno* 1651.
Serving in this place,

To frontal a VINDICATION

of the honour of *SCOTLAND*,
from that Infamy, whereinto the Rigid
Presbyterian party of that Nation,
out of their Covetouſneſs and
ambition, moſt diſſembled-
ly hath involved it.

Diſtichon ad Librum ſequitur, quo tres ter adæquant
Muſarum numerum, caſus, & articuli.

voc.　　　*nom.*　　　*1 abl.*　　　*2 abl.*　　　*dat.*
O thou'rt a Book in truth with love to many,
3 abl.　　*4 abl.　acc.*　　　　　　　　　　　　*gen.*
Done by and for the freeſ't ſpoke *Scot* of any.

Efficiens & finis ſunt sibi invicem cauſæ.

LONDON, Printed by *Ja: Cottrel*; and are to
be ſold by *Rich. Baddeley*, at the Middle-
Temple-gate. 1652.

THE EPISTLE LIMINARY.

THE scope of this Treatise is, for the weal of the publick in the propagation of learning and vertue throughout the whole Isle of Great Britain, in all humility to intreat the honorable Parliament of this Commonwealth, with consent of the Councel of State thereof, to grant to Sir Thomas Vrquhart of Cromarty his former liberty, and the enjoyment of his own inheritance, with all the immunities and priviledges thereto belonging. The reasons of this demand in an unusual, though compositive way, are so methodically deduced, that their recapitulation here, how curt soever I could make it, would afford but little more compendiousneſs to the Reader; unleſs all were to be summed up in this, that seeing the obtaining of his desires would be conducible to the whole land, and prejudicial to no good member in it, he should therefore be favoured with the benefit of the grant thereof, and refusal of nothing appertaining to it.

By reason of his being a Scotish man, a great deal therein is spoken in favor of that country, and many pregnant arguments inferred for the incorporating of both nations into one, with an indiſsolubility of union for the future, in an identity of priviledges, laws, and customs. As by the praising of many the coetaneans and compatriots of his no-leſs-deserving predeceſsors, Scotland is much honored; so, to vindicate the reputation thereof from any late scandal, it is fitly represented how the miscariage of a few should not occasion an universal imputation. The unjust usurpation of the clergy, the judaical practices of some merchants, and abused simplicity of the gentry, have in the mindes of forraigners engraven a discredible opinion of that nation, which will never be wiped off under a Presbyterial government; for where ever it bears sway, &c. Here I must stop, for should I give way to my pen to decipher the enormities of that rule, I would, by outbulking the book with this Epistle, make the porch greater then the lodging, enter into a digreſsion longer then the purpose, and outstrip the period with the parenthesis. Therefore out of that inclination which prompts me to conceal the faults of those, in whom there may be any hope of a cordial penitency for having committed them, I will not at this time lanch forth into the prodigious depth of Presbyterian plots, nor rip up the sores of their ecclesiastical tyranny, till their implacable obduredness, and unreclaimability of nature, give open testimonies of their standing to their first erroneous principles, and not acknowledging a subordination to a secular authority.

For the present, then, it shall suffice that I bestow upon them a gentle admonition to refrain from that ambitious designe of spiritual soveraignty; or, to use the phrase of their patron Knox, that I warn them with the first sound of the trumpet, to give the civil magistrate his due : but if after this Diansounding, they, instead of apparelling their consciences with the garment of righteousness, come forth to the field of publick affaires, with their rusty armour of iniquity, then let them not blame me, if for the love of my country, whose honour they have defaced, and the best inhabitants whereof they have born down with oppreſsion, I refuse not the employment of taking up banner against them, and giving them a home charge with clareens, under the conduct of reason and common sense, their old and inveterate enemies. Now, seeing that in this introitory discourse, to avoid the excursive pomp of a too large ranging at random, I am limited to some few pages, should I employ them all to attend the Presbyter's greatneſs, it would argue in me great inconsideracy, in preferring him to his betters; therefore till I have the leisure to bestow a whole sheet by it self upon honest Sir John, who in that kind of liberality towards the fornicator and malignant, was the nonpareil of the world, that therein, as in a habit of repentance, he may be exposed to the publike view of the honest men of Scotland, whom he hath so much injured, I must confine my self now to so much bounds, without more, as barely may suffice to excuse the superficial erratas both of pen and preſs.

This Treatise, like the words of maſs, dinner, supper, and such like, which besides the things by them signified, do connotate the times of morning, noon, night, or any other tide or season, importing beyond what is primarly expreſsed in it, a certain space of time, within which unto the world should be made obvious its final promulgation; and that being but a fortnight, lest a longer delay, by not giving timely information to the State, might prove very prejudicial, if not totally destructive, to the aforesaid Sir Thomas Vrquhart, in whose house, as he is informed by letters from thence, there is at this present an English garison; and whose lands are so over-run and exhausted by these publike preſsures, that since he hath been a prisoner of war, which is now half a yeer, he hath not received the value of one farthing of his own means, and having designed for the preſs at first but five sheets, viz. the three first, and some two about the latter end, I deemed the aforesaid time of two weeks, of extent sufficient for encompaſsing a work of so short a breath. But by chance two diurnals having been brought to me, in one whereof was contained the relation of the irrational prooceedings of the Presbytery of Aberdeen, against Sir Alexander Iruin of Drum, together with his just appeal from their tyrannical jurisdiction to Colonel Overton, the then only competent judge that was there; and in the other a petition or grievance of the commons of Scotland, against the merciless and cruel task-masters that the Presbyterian zeal had set above them these many yeers past; wherein, whether that petition was supposititious or no, there was not any thing the truth whereof might not be testified by thousands of honest people in Scotland, and ten times more of their roguery, then in it is specified. And besides all that, there being nothing in the mouthes almost of all this country more common then the words of the perfidious Scot, the treacherous Scot, the false brother, the covetous Scot, and knot of knaves, and other ſuchlike indignities fixed upon the whole nation for the baseness of some; I resolved on a sudden, for the undeceiving of honest men, and the imbuing of their minds with a better opinion of Scotish spirits, to insert the martial and literary endowments of some natives of that soyle, though much eclipsed by their coclimatary wasps of a Presbyterian crue.

Thus my task increasing, and not being able to enlarge my time, for the cause aforesaid, I was necessitated to husband it the better, to over-triple my diligence, and do the work, by proportion of above three dayes in the space of one; wherefore, laying aside all other busineſses, and cooping my self up daily for some hours together, betwixt the case and the printing preſs, I usually afforded the setter copy at the rate of above a whole printed sheet in the day; which, although by reason of the smallneſs of a pica letter, and close couching thereof, it did amount to three full sheets of my writing; the aforesaid setter, neverthelefs, so nimble a workman he was, would in the space of 24 hours make dispatch of the whole, and be ready for another sheet.   He and I striving thus who should compose fastest, he with his hand, and I with my brain; and his uncasing of the letters, and placing them in the composing instrument, standing for my conception; and his plenishing of the gally, and imposing of the form, encountering with the supposed equi-value of my writing, we would almost every foot so jump together in this joynt expedition, and so neerly overtake other in our intended course, that I was oftentimes, to keep him doing, glad to tear off parcels of ten or twelve lines apeece, and give him them, till more were ready; unto which he would so suddenly put an order, that almost still before the ink of the written letters was dry, their representatives were, out of their respective boxes, ranked in the composing-stick; by means of which great haste, I writing but upon the loose sheets of cording-quires, which, as I minced and tore them, looking like pieces of waste paper, troublesome to get rallyed, after such dispersive scattrednefs, I had not the leisure to read what I had written, till it came to a proof, and sometimes to a full revise.   So that by vertue of this unanimous contest, and joint emulation betwixt the theoretick and practical part, which of us should overhye other in celerity, we in the space of fourteen working daies, compleated this whole book, such as it is, from the first notion of the brain to the last motion of the prefs; and that without any other help on my side, either of quick or dead, for books I had none, nor possibly would I have made use of any, although I could have commanded them, then what, by the favour of God, my own judgment and fancy did suggest unto me; save so much as, by way of information, a servant of mine would now and then bring to me, from some reduced officer of the primitive parliament, touching the proper names of some Scotish warriors abroad, which I was very apt to forget.

I speak not this to excuse grofs faults, if there be any, nor yet to praise my owne acutenefs, though there were none, but to shew that extemporaneannefs, in some kinde of subjects, may very probably be more succefseful then premeditation; and that a too punctually digested method, and over-nicely selected phrase, savouring of affectation, diminish oftentimes very much of the grace that otherwayes would attend a natural ingenuity. If the State of England be pleased with this book, I care neither for Zoil nor Momus ; but if otherwaies, then shall it displease me, whose resolution from its first contrivance was willingly to submit it to their judicious censure.

It is intituled ΕΚΣΚΥΒΑΛΑΥΡΟΝ, because of those few sheets of Sir Thomas Vrquhart's papers, which were found in the kennel of Worcester streets ; they being the cream, the marrow, and the most especial part of the book ; and albeit they extend not in bulk to above two sheets and a quarter of that small letter as it lieth in an octavo size, yet that synecdochically the whole be designed by it, lacketh not its precedent ; for logick sometimes is called dialectica, although it be but a part of logick ; and that discipline which treats of the dimensions of continuate quantity, named geometry, albeit how to mesure the earth be fully instructed by geodesie, one of the smallest parts of that Divine Science. That which is properly France, is not the hundredth part of the kingdom of that name. Moscovy, Fez, and Morocco, though empires, have their denominations from cities of the same name ; so have the kingdoms of Leon, Toledo, Murcia, Granada, Valencia, and Naples, with the Isles of Mayorca, Minorca, Sardinia, Malta, and Rhodes, and so forth through other territories.

It mentioneth Sir Thomas Vrquhart in the third person, which seldom is done by any author in a Treatise of his own penning ; although Virgil said, *Ille ego qui quondam ;* and Scaliger the younger, *Ego sum magnus ille Josephus ;* neverthelefs, to satisfie the reader's curiosity, and all honest men of the Isle of Britain, rather then to write Anonymos, I will subscribe my self,

CHRISTIANUS PRESBYTEROMASTIX.

THE NAMES OF THE CHIEFS OF THE NAME OF VRQUHART, AND OF THEIR PRIMITIVE FATHERS;

As by Authentick Records and Tradition they were from time to time, through the various Generations of that Family, sucessively conveyed, till the present yeer 1652.

1 Adam. 1	25 Zameles.	49 Cainotomos.	73 Auloprepes.
2 Seth.	26 Choronomos.	50 Rodrigo.	74 Corosylos.
3 Enos.	27 Leptologon.	51 Dicarches.	75 Detalon.
4 Cainan.	28 Aglætos.	52 Exagastos.	76 Beltistos.
5 Mahalaleel.	29 Megalonus.	53 Denapon.	77 Horæos.
6 Jared.	30 Evemeros.	54 Artistes.	78 Orthophron.
7 Enoch.	31 Callophron.	55 Thymoleon.	79 Apsicoros.
8 Methusalah.	32 Arthmios.	56 Eustochos.	80 Philaplus.
9 Lamech.	33 Hypsegoras.	57 Bianor.	81 Megaletor.
10 Noah.	34 Autarces.	58 Thryllumenos.	82 Nomostor.
11 Japhet.	35 Evages.	59 Mellessen.	83 Astioremon.
12 Javan. 1	36 Atarbes.	60 Alypos.	84 Phronematias.
13 Penuel.	37 Pamprosodos.	61 Anochlos.	85 Lutork.
14 Tycheros. 1	38 Gethon.	62 Homognios.	86 Machemos.
15 Pasiteles.	39 Holocleros.	63 Epsephicos.	87 Stichopæo.
16 ESORMON.	40 Molin.	64 Eutropos.	88 Epalomenos.
17 Cratynter.	41 Epitomon.	65 Coryphæus.	89 Tycheros. 2
18 Thrasymedes.	42 Hypotyphos.	66 Etoimos.	90 Apechon.
19 Evippos.	43 Melobolon.	67 Spudæos.	91 Enacmes.
20 Cleotinus.	44 Propetes.	68 Eumestor.	92 Javan. 2
21 Litoboros.	45 Euplocamos.	69 Griphon.	93 Lematias.
22 Apodemos.	46 Philophon.	70 Emmenes.	94 Prosenes.
23 Bathybulos.	47 Syngenes.	71 Pathomachon.	95 Sosomenos.
24 Phrenedon.	48 Polyphrades.	72 Anepsios.	96 Philalethes.

96 Philalethes.	111 Paladino.	126 Sebastian.	141 Francis.
97 Thaleros.	112 Comicello.	127 Lawrence.	142 William.
98 Polyænos.	113 Regisato.	128 Olipher.	143 Adam.
99 Cratesimachos.	114 Arguto.	129 Quintin.	144 John.
100 Eunæmon.	115 Nicarchos.	130 Goodwin.	145 Sir William.
101 Diasemos.	116 Marsidalio.	131 Frederick.	146 William.
102 Saphenus.	117 Hedumenos.	132 Sir Jaspar.	147 Alexander.
103 Bramoso.	118 Agenor.	133 Sir Adam.	148 Thomas.
104 Celanas.	119 Diaprepon.	134 Edward.	149 Alexander.
105 Vistoso.	120 Stragayo.	135 Richard.	150 Walter.
106 Polido.	121 Zeron.	136 Sir Philip.	151 Henry.
107 Lustroso.	122 Polyteles.	137 Robert.	152 Sir Thomas.
108 Chrestander.	123 Vocompos.	138 George.	153 Sir Thomas.
109 Spectabundo.	124 Carolo.	139 James.	
110 Philodulos.	125 Endymion.	140 David	

THE NAMES OF THE MOTHERS OF THE CHIEFS OF THE NAME OF VRQUHART, AS ALSO OF THE MOTHERS OF THEIR PRIMITIVE FATHERS.

The authority for the truth thereof being derived from the same Authentick Records and Tradition on which is grounded the above-written Genealogie of their male collaterals.

1 Eva.	23 Peninah.	45 Neopis.	67 Orthoiusa.
2 Shifka.	24 Asymbleta.	46 Thymelica.	68 Recatada.
3 Mahla.	25 Carissa.	47 Ephamilla.	69 Chariestera.
4 Bilha.	26 Calaglais	48 Porrima.	70 Rexenora.
5 Timnah.	27 Theoglena.	49 Lampedo.	71 Philerga.
6 Aholima.	28 Pammerisla.	50 Teleclyta.	72 Thomyris.
7 Zilpa.	29 Floridula.	51 Clarabella.	73 Varonilla.
8 Noema.	30 Chrysocomis.	52 Eromena.	74 Stranella.
9 Ada.	31 Arrenopas.	53 Zocallis.	75 Æquanima.
10 Titea.	32 Tharsalia.	54 Lepida.	76 Barosa.
11 Debora.	33 Maia.	55 Nicolia.	77 Epimona.
12 Neginothi.	34 Roma.	56 Proteusa.	78 Diosa.
13 Hottir.	35 Termuth.	57 Gozosa.	79 Bonita.
14 Orpah.	36 Vegeta.	58 Venusta.	80 Aretusa.
15 Axa.	37 Callimeris.	59 Prosectica.	81 Bendita.
16 Narfesia.	38 Panthea.	60 Delotera.	82 Regalletta.
17 Goshenni.	39 Gonima.	61 Tracara.	83 Isumena.
18 Briageta.	40 Ganymena.	62 Pothina.	84 Antaxia.
19 Andronia.	41 Thespesia.	63 Cordata.	85 Bergola.
20 Pusena.	42 Hypermnestra.	64 Aretias.	86 Viracia.
21 Emphaneola.	43 Horatia.	65 Musurga.	87 Dynastis.
22 Bonaria.	44 Philumena.	66 Romalia.	88 Dalga.

89 Eutocusa.	104 Philetium.	119 Trastevole.	134 Sophia.
90 Corriba.	105 Tersa.	120 Suaviloqua.	135 Eleonore.
91 Præcelsa.	106 Dulcicora.	121 Francoline.	136 Rosalind.
92 Plausidica.	107 Gethosyna.	122 Matilda.	137 Lillias.
93 Donosa.	108 Collabella.	123 Allegra.	138 Brigid.
94 Solicælia.	109 Eucnema.	124 Winnifred.	139 Agnes.
95 Bontadosa.	110 Tortolina.	125 Dorothy.	140 Susanna.
96 Calliparia.	111 Ripulita.	126 Lawretta.	141 Catherine.
97 Creleuca.	112 Urbana.	127 Genivieve.	142 Helen.
98 Pancala.	113 Lampusa.	128 Marjory.	143 Beatrice.
99 Dominella.	114 Vistosa.	129 Jane.	144 Elizabeth.
100 Mundala.	115 Hermosina.	130 Anne.	145 Elizabeth.
101 Pamphais.	116 Bramata.	131 Magdalen.	146 Christian.
102 Philtrusa.	117 Zaglopis.	132 Girsel.	
103 Meliglena.	118 Androlema.	133 Mary.	

Let such as would know more hereof, be pleased to have recourse to the book treating of the Genealogy of that Family, intitled Παντοχρονοχανον, which together with this is to be sold by one and the same stationer.

HE SHOULD OBTAIN ALL HIS DESIRES,

WHO OFFERS MORE THEN HE REQUIRES.

No sooner had the total rout of the regal party at Worcester given way to the taking of that city, and surrendring up of all the prisoners to the custody of the marshal-general and his deputies, but the liberty, customary at such occasions to be connived at in favours of a victorious army, imboldened some of the new-levied forces of the adjacent counties, to confirm their conquest by the spoil of the captives. For the better atchievement of which designe, not reckoning those great many others that in all the other corners of the town were ferreting every room for plunder, a string or two of exquisite snaps and clean shavers, if ever there were any, rushing into Master Spilsbury's house, who is a very honest man, and hath an exceeding good woman to his wife, broke into an upper chamber, where finding, besides scarlet cloaks, buff suits, arms of all sorts, and other such rich chaffer, at such an exigent escheatable to the prevalent soldier, seven large portmantles ful of precious commodity; in three whereof, after a most exact search for gold, silver, apparel, linen, or any whatever adornments of the body, or pocket-implements, as was seized upon in the other four, not hitting on any things but manuscripts in folio, to the quantity of sixscore and eight quires and a half, divided into six hundred fourty and two quinternions and upwards, the quinternion consisting of five sheets, and the quire of five and twenty; besides some writings of suits in law, and bonds, in both worth above three thousand pounds English, they in a trice carried all whatever els was in the room away save those papers, which they then threw down on the floor as unfit for their use; yet immediately thereafter, when upon carts the aforesaid baggage was put to be transported to the country, and that by the example of many hundreds of both horse and foot, whom they had loaded with spoil, they were assaulted with the temptation of a new booty, they apprehending how useful the paper might be unto them, went back for it, and bore it straight away; which done, to every one of those their camarads whom they met with in the streets, they gave as much thereof, for packeting up of raisins, figs, dates, almonds, caraway, and other such like dry confections and other ware, as was requisite; who, doing the same themselves, did together with others kindle pipes of tobacco with a great part thereof, and threw out all the remainder upon the streets, save so much as they deemed necessary for inferiour employments and posteriour uses.

Of those dispersedly-rejected bundles of paper, some were gathered up by grocers, druggists, chandlers, pie-makers, or such as stood in need of any cartapaciatory utensil, and put in present service, to the utter undoing of all the writing thereof, both in its matter and order. One quinternion, nevertheless, two days after the fight on the Friday morning, together with two other loose sheets more, by vertue of a drizelling rain, which had made it stick fast to the ground, where there was a heap of seven and twenty dead men lying upon one another, was by the command of one Master Braughton taken up by a servant of his; who, after he had in the best manner he could cleansed it from the mire and mud of the kennel, did forthwith present it to the perusal of his master; in whose hands it no sooner came, but instantly perceiving by the periodical couching of the discourse, marginal figures, aud breaks here and there, according to the variety of the subject, that the whole purpose was destinated for the press, and by the author put into a garb befitting either the stationer or printer's acceptance; yet because it seemed imperfect, and to have relation to subsequent tractates, he made all the enquiry he could for trial whether there were any more such quinternions or no; by means whereof, he got full information that above three thousand sheets of the like paper, written after that fashion, and with the same hand, were utterly lost and imbezzeled, after the manner aforesaid; and was so fully assured of the misfortune, that to gather up spilt water, comprehend the windes within his fist, and recover those papers again, he thought would be a work of one and the same labour and facility. Therefore, because he despaired of attaining to any more, he the more carefully endeavoured to preserve what he had made purchase of; and this he did very heedfully in the country for three months together, and afterwards in the city of London; where at last, I getting notice thereof, thought good, in regard of the great moan made for the loss of Sir Thomas Vrquhart's manuscripts, to try at the said Sir Thomas whether these seven sheets were any of his papers or no. Whereupon, after communication with him, it was found that they were but a parcel of the preface he intended to premise before the grammar and lexicon of an Universal Language, the whole preface consisting of two quires of paper, the grammar of three, and the lexicon of seven; the other five score and sixteen quires and a half, treating of metaphysical, mathematicall, moral, mythological, epigrammatical, dialectical, and chronological matters, in a way never hitherto trod upon by any; being brought by the said Sir Thomas into England for two reasons—first, lest they should have been altogether lost at Sterlin; and next, to have them printed at London, with the best conveniencie that might stand with indemnity of the Author; whom, when I had asked if his fancie could serve him to make up these papers again, especially in so far as concerned the

New Language; his answer was, that if he wanted not encouragament, with the favour of a little time, he could do much therein; but unless he were sure to possess his own with freedom, it would be impossible for him to accomplish a task of so great moment and laboriousness. This modest reply, grounded upon so much reason, hath emboldened me to subjoyn hereto what was couched in those papers which were found by Master Braughton, to the end the reader may perceive whether the performance of so great a work as is mentioned there be not worth the enjoyment of his predecessors' inheritance, although he had not had a lawful title thereunto by his birthright and lineal succession, which he hath.

The Title of those found Papers was thus ;

An Introduction to the Universal Language ; wherein, whatever is uttred in other Languages, hath signification in it, whilst it affordeth expressions, both for copiousness, variety, and conciseness in all manner of subjects, which no Language else is able to reach unto : most fit for such as would with ease attaine to a most expedite facility of expressing themselves in all the learned sciences, faculties, arts, disciplines, mechanick trades, and all other discourses whatsoever, whether serious or recreative.

THE MATTER OF THE PREFACE BEGUN AFTER THIS MANNER, AS IT WAS DIVIDED INTO SEVERAL ARTICLES.

1. WORDS are the signes of things; it being to signifie that they were instituted at first, nor can they be, as such, directed to any other end, whether they be articulate or inarticulate.

2. All things are either real or rational; and the real, either natural or artificial.

3. There ought to be a proportion betwixt the signe and thing signified; therefore should all things, whether real or rational, have their proper words assigned unto them.

4. Man is called a Microcosme, because he may by his conceptions and words containe within him the representatives of what in the whole world is comprehended.

5. Seeing there is in nature such affinity 'twixt words and things, as there ought to be in whatever is ordained for one another; that language is to be accounted most conform to nature, which with greatest variety expresseth all manner of things.

6. As all things of a single compleat being by Aristotle into ten classes were divided, so may the words whereby those things are to be signified be set apart in their several store-houses.

7. Arts, sciences, mechanick trades, notional faculties, and whatever is excogitable by man, have their own method, by vertue whereof the learned of these latter times have orderly digested them; yet hath none hitherto considered of a mark whereby words of the same faculty, art, trade, or science should be dignosced from those of another by the very sound of the word at the first hearing.

8. A tree will be known by its leaves, a stone by its grit, a flower by the smel, meats by the taste, musick by the ear, colours by the eye, the several natures of things, with their properties and essential qualities, by the intellect; and accordingly as the things are in themselves diversified, the judicious and learned man, after he hath conceived them aright, sequestreth them in the several cels of his understanding, each in their definite and respective places.

9. But in matter of the words whereby those things are expressed, no language ever hitherto framed hath observed any order relating to the thing signified by them ; for if the words be ranked in their alphabetical series, the things represented by them will fall to be in several predicaments ; and if the things themselves be categorically classed, the word whereby they are made known will not be tyed to any alphabetical rule.

10. This is an imperfection incident to all the languages that ever yet have been known ; by reason whereof, foraign tongues are said to be hard to learn, and when obtained, easily forgot.

11. The effigies of Jupiter in the likeness of a bull, should be liker to that of Io metamorphosed into a cow, then to the statue of Bucephalus, which was a horse ; and the picture of Alcibiades ought to have more resemblance with that of Coriolanus, being both handsome men, then with the image of Thersites, who was of a deformed feature ; just so should things semblable in nature be represented by words of a like composure ; and as the true intelligible species do present unto our minds the similitude of things as they are in the object, even so ought the word expressive of our conceptions so to agree or vary in their contexture, as the things themselves which are conceived by them do in their natures.

12. Besides this imperfection in all languages, there is yet another, that no language upon the face of the earth hath a perfect alphabet, one lacking those letters which another hath, none having all, and all of them *in cumulo* lacking some. But that which makes the defect so much the greater, is, that these same few consonants and vowels commonly made use of are never by two nations pronounced after the same fashion ; the French A with the English being the Greek Ητα, and the Italian B with the Spanish, the Hebrew *vau*.

13. This is that which maketh those of one dominion so unskilful in the idiome of another, and after many yeers abode in a strange land, despaire from attaining at any time to the perfect accent of the language thereof, because, as the waters of that stream cannot be wholesome whose source is corrupted, nor the superstructure sure whereof the ground-work is ruinous, so doth the various manner of pronouncing one and the same alphabet in several nations, produce this great and most lamentable obstruction in the discipline of Languages.

14. The *g* of the Latin word *legit*, is after four several manners pronounced by the English, French, Spanish, and Dutch. The *ch* likewise is differently pronounced by divers nations ; some uttering it after the fashion of the Hebrew *shin*, as the French do in the words *chasteau, chascun, chastier, chatel* ; or like the Greek *kappa*, as in the Italian words, *chiedere, chiazzare, chinatura* ; or as in Italy are sounded the words *ciascheduno, ciarlatano* ; for so do the Spanish and English pronounce it, as in the words *achaque, leche, chamber, chance* : other nations of a guttural flexibility, pronounce it after the fashion of the Greek χ. Nor need we to labor for examples in

2 B

other letters, for there is scarce any hitherto received, either consonant or vowel, which in some one and other, taking in all nations, is not pronounced after three or four several fashions.

15. As the alphabets are imperfect, some having but 19 letters, others 22, and some 24, few exceeding that number, so do the words composed of those letters in the several languages come far short of the number of things, which, to have the reputation of a perfect tongue, ought to be expressed by them.

16. For supply of this deficiencie, each language borrows from another ; nor is the perfectest amongst them, without being beholden to another, in all things enuncible, bastant to afford instruction. Many astronomical and medicinal terms have the Greeks borrowed from the Arabians, for which they by exchange have from the Grecians received payment of many words naturalized in their physical, logical, and metaphysical treatises. As for the Latin, it oweth all its scientifick dictions to the Greek and Arabick, yet did the Roman Conquest give adoption to many Latin words in both these languages, especially in matters of military discipline and prudential law.

17. And as for all other languages as yet spoke, though to some of them be ascribed the title of original tongues, I may safely avouch there is none of them which, of it self alone, is able to afford the smattring of an elocution fit for indoctrinating of us in the precepts and maximes of moral and intellectual vertues.

18. But, which is more, and that which most of all evinceth the sterility of all the languages that since the deluge have been spoke, though all of them were quintescenced in one capable of the perfections of each, yet that one so befitted and accommodated for compendiousness and variety of phrase, should not be able, amidst so great wealth, to afford without circumlocution the proper and convenient representation of a thing, yea of many thousands of things, whereof each should be expressed with one single word alone.

19. Some languages have copiousness of discourse, which are barren in composition ; such is the Latine. Others are compendious in expression, which hardly have any flection at all ; of this kinde are the Dutch, the English, and Irish.

20. Greek hath the agglutinative faculty of incorporating words, yet runneth not so glib in poesie as doth the Latine, though far more abundant. The Hebrew likewise, with its auxiliary dialects of Arabick, Caldean, Syriack, Æthiopian, and Samaritan, compoundeth prettily, and hath some store of words, yet falleth short by many stages of the Greek.

21. The French, Spanish, and Italians, are but the dialects of the Latine, as the English is of the Saxon tongue, though with this difference, that the mixture of Latine with the Gaulish, Moresco, and Gotish tongues, make up the three first languages, but the meer qualification of the Saxon with the old British frameth not the English to the full, for that, by its promiscuous and ubiquitary borrowing, it consisteth almost of all languages ; which I speak not in dispraise thereof, although I

may with confidence aver, that were all the four aforesaid languages stript of what is not originally their own, we should not be able with them all, in any part of the world, to purchase so much as our breakfast in a market.

22. Now, to return from these to the learned languages, we must acknowledge it to be very strange, why, after thousands of yeers continual practice in the polishing of them by men of approved faculties, there is neither in them, nor any other tongue hitherto found out, one single word expressive of the vice opposite either to temperance or chastity in the defect, though many rigid monks, even now-a-days, be guilty of the one, as Diogenes of old was of the other.

23. But that which makes this disease the more incurable, is, that when an exuberant spirit would to any high researched conceit adapt a peculiar word of his own coyning, he is branded with incivility, if he apologize not for his boldness with a *Quod ita dixerim parcant Ciceronianæ manes, ignoscat Demosthenis genius*, and other such phrases, acknowledging his fault of making use of words never uttered by others, or at least by such as were most renowned for eloquence.

24. Though learning sustain great prejudice by this restraint of liberty to endenizon new citizens in the commonwealth of languages, yet do I conceive the reason thereof to proceed from this, that it is thought a less incongruity to express a thing by circumlocution, then by appropriating a single word thereto to transgress the bounds of the language; as in architecture it is esteemed an errour of less consequence to make a circuitory passage from one room to another, then by the extravagancie of an irregular sallie, to frame projectures disproportionable to the found of the house.

25. Thus is it, that, as according to the largeness of the plat of a building, and compactedness of its walls, the work-master contriveth his roofs, platforms, outjettings, and other such like parts and portions of the whole, just so, conform to the extent and reach which a language in its flexions and compositions hath obtained at first, have the sprucest linguists hitherto bin pleased to make use of the words thereto belonging.

26. The bonification and virtuification of Lully Scotus's hexeity, and albedineity of Suarez, are words exploded by those that affect the purity of the Latine diction; yet if such were demanded, what other no less concise expression would comport with the neatness of that language, their answer would be, *altum silentium*; so easie a matter it is for many to finde fault with what they are not able to amend.

27. Nevertheless, why for representing to our understandings the essence of accidents, the fluency of the form as it is *in fieri*, the faculty of the agent and habit that facilitates it, with many thousands of other such expressions, the tearms are not so genuine as of the members of a man's body, or utensils of his house; the reason is, because the first inventers of languages, who contrived them for necessity, were not so profoundly versed in philosophical quiddities as those that succeeded after them; whose literature increasing, procured their excursion beyond the representatives of the common objects imagined by their forefathers.

28. I have known some to have built houses for necessity, having no other aime before their eyes but barely to dwell in them, who nevertheless in a very short space were so enriched, that after they had taken pleasure to polish and adorn what formerly they had but rudely squared, their moveables so multiplyed upon them, that they would have wished they had made them of a larger extent.

29. Even so, though these languages may be refined by some quaint derivatives and witty compositions, like the striking forth of new lights and doors, outjetting of kernels, erecting of prickets, barbicans, and such like various structures upon one and the same foundation, yet being limited to a certain basis, beyond which the versed in them must not pass, they cannot roam at such random as otherwise they might, had their language been of a larger scope at first.

30. Thus, albeit Latine be far better polished now then it was in the days of Ennius and Livius Andronicus, yet had the Latinists at first been such philosophers as afterwards they were, it would have attained to a great deale of more perfection then it is at for the present.

31. What I have delivered in freedome of the learned languages, I would not have wrested to a sinister sense, as if I meant any thing to their disparagement, for truly I think the time well bestowed which boyes in their tender yeers employ towards the learning of them, in a subordination to the excellent things that in them are couched.

32. But ingenuously I must acknowledge my averseness of opinion from those who are so superstitiously addicted to these languages, that they account it learning enough to speak them, although they knew nothing else; which is an error worthy rebuke, seeing *Philosophia sunt res, non verba;* and that whatever the signes be, the things by them signified ought still to be of greater worth.

33. For it boots not so much by what kind of tokens any matter be brought into our minde, as that the things made known unto us by such representatives be of some considerable value; not much unlike the Innes-a-court-gentlemen at London, who usually repairing to their commons at the blowing of a horne, are better pleased with such a signe, so the fare be good, then if they were warned to courser cates, by the sound of a bell or trumpet.

34. Another reason prompteth me thereto, which is this, that in this frozen climate of ours, there is hardly any that is not possessed with the opinion, that not only the three fore-named languages, but a great many other, whom they call original— whereof they reckon ten or eleven in Europe, and some fifty-eight more, or thereabouts, in other nations—were at the confusion of Babel, immediately from God by a miracle infused into men; being induced to believe this, not so much for that they had not perused the interpretation of the Rabbies on that text, declaring the misunderstanding whereunto the builders were involved by diversity of speech, to have proceeded from nothing else but their various and discrepant pronunciation of one and the

same language, as that they deemed languages to be of an invention so sublime, that naturally the wit of man was not able to reach their composure.

35. Some believe this so pertinaciously, that they esteem all men infidels that are of another faith; whilst in the mean while I may confidently assever, that the assertors of such a tenet do thereby extreamly dishonour God, who doing whatever is done by nature, as the actions of an ambassador, as an ambassador, are reputed to be those of the soveraign that sent him, would not have the power he hath given to nature to be disclaimed by any, or any thing said by us in derogation thereof.

36. Should we deny our obedience to the just decree of an inferior Judge, because he from whom his authority is derived, did not pronounce the sentence? Subordinate magistrates have their power, even in great matters, which to decline, by saying they have no authority, should make the averrer fall within the compass of a breach of the statute called *scandalum magnatum.*

37. There are of those with us, that wear gowns and beards longer then ever did Aristotle and Æsculapius; who, when they see an eclipse of the sun or moon, or a comet in the aire, straight would delude the commons with an opinion that those things are immediately from God, for the sins of the people, as if no natural cause could be produced for such like apparitions.

[Here is the number of twelve articles wanting.]

50. For which cause they are much to blame, that think it impossible for any man naturally to frame a language of greater perfection then Greek, Hebrew, or Latine.

51. For who, instead of affording the true cause of a thing, unnecessarily runs to miracles, tacitely acknowledgeth that God naturally cannot do it; wherein he committeth blasphemie, as that souldier may be accounted guilty of contumacie and disobedience, who, rejecting the orders wherewith an inferiour officer is authorized to command him, absolutely refuseth compearance, unless the General himself come in person to require it of him.

52. As there is a possibility such a language may be, so doe I think it very requisite such a language were, both for affording of conciseness and abundance of expression.

53. Such as extol those languages most, are enforced sometimes to say, that *Laborant penuria verborum ;* and thereunto immediately subjoyn this reason, *Quia plures sunt res quam verba.*

54. That is soon said, and, *ad pauca respicientes facile enuntiant.* But here I ask them how they come to know that there are more things then words, taking things, as in this sense they ought to be taken, for things universal; because there is no word spoken, which to the conceit of man is not able to represent more individuals then one, be it sun, moon, Phœnix, or what you will, even amongst verbs, and syncategorematical signes, which do onely suppone for the modalities of things; therefore is each

word the sign of an universal thing, Peter signifying either this Peter, or that Peter, and any whatever name, surname, or title, being communicable to one and many.

55. Thus though both words and thoughts, as they are signs, be universal, yet do I believe that those who did attribute less universality to words then things, knew not definitely the full number of words, taking words for any articulate pronunciation.

56. Nay, I will go further: there is no alphabet in the world, be the calculator never so well skilled in arithmetick, by vertue whereof the exact number of words may be known, because that number must comprehend all the combinations that letters can have with one another, and this cannot be done if any letter be wanting; and consequently, by no alphabet as yet framed, wherein, as I have already said in the twelfth article, there is a deficiency of many letters.

57. The universal alphabet therefore must be first conceived, before the exactness of that computation can be attained unto.

58. Then is it, when, having couched an alphabet materiative of all the words the mouth of man, with its whole implements, is able to pronounce, and bringing all these words within the systeme of a language, which, by reason of its logopandocie, may deservedly be intituled The Universal Tongue, that nothing will better merit the labour of a grammatical arithmetician then, after due enumeration, *hinc inde*, to appariate the words of the universal language with the things of the universe.

59. The analogie therein 'twixt the signe and thing signified holding the more exactly, that as, according to Aristotle, there can be no more worlds but one, because all the matter whereof worlds can be composed is in this; so can there be no universal language but this I am about to divulge unto the world, because all the words enunciable are in it contained.

60. If any officious critick will run to the omnipotency of God for framing more worlds, according to the common saying, Nothing is impossible to God, that implies not a contradiction, so must he have recourse to the same omnipotent power for furnishing of man with other speech-tools then his tongue, throat, roof of the mouth, lips, and teeth, before the contexture of another universal language can be warped.

61. That I should hit upon the invention of that, for the furtherance of philosophy, and other disciplines and arts, which never hitherto hath been so much as thought upon by any, and that in a matter of so great extent, as the expressing of all the things in the world, both in themselves, actions, ways of doing, situation, pendicles, relations, connexions, pathetick interpositions, and all other appurtenances to a perfect elocution, without being beholden to any language in the world; insomuch as one word will hardly be believed by our fidimplicitary gown-men, who, satisfied with their predecessors' contrivances, and taking all things litterally, without examination, blaterate, to the nauseating even of vulgar ears, those exotick proverbs, There is no new thing under the sun, *Nihil dictum quod non dictum prius*, and, Beware of philosophers; authoridating this on Paul, the first on Solomon, and the other on Terence.

62. But, poor souls, they understand not that in the passage of Solomon is meant, that there is no innovation in the essence of natural things; all transmutations on the same matter, being into formes, which, as they differ from some, so have an essential uniformity with others pre-existent in the same kind.

63. And when it was said by Paul, Beware of philosophers, he meant such sophisters as themselves, who, under the vizzard of I know not what, corrupt the chanels of the truth, and pervert all philosophy and learning.

64. As for the sayings of Terence, whether Scipio couched them or himself, they ought to be inferred rather as testimonies of neat Latine, then for asserting of infallible verities.

65. If there hath been no new thing under the sun, according to the adulterate sense of those pristinary lobcocks, how comes the invention of syllogisms to be attributed to Aristotle, that of the sphere to Archimedes, and logarithms to Neper? It was not Swart, then, and Gertudenburg, that found out gunpowder and the art of printing, for these two men lived after the decease of Solomon.

66. Had there been canon in Solomon's dayes, Rehoboam, by all appearances, would have made use of them for the recovery of his inheritance; nor had some mention of artillery been omitted in the books of the Macchabees.

67. Pancerola's Treatise *De novis adimpertis*, although Polydor Virgil were totally forgot, would be, had there been no new thing since Solomon penn'd Ecclesiastes, but as a discourse of platonick reminiscences, and calling to minde some formerly lost fancies.

68. Truly, I am so far from being of the opinion of those archæomanetick coxcombs, that I really think there will alwayes be new inventions where there are excellent spirits.

69. For, as I ascribe unto my self the invention of the trissotetrail trigonometry, for facility of calculation by representatives of letters and syllables, the proving of the equipollencie and opposition both of plaine and modal enunciations by rules of geometry, the unfolding of the chiefest part of philosophy by a continued geographical allegory, and above a hundred other severall books on different subjects, the conceit of so much as one whereof never entered into the braines of any before my selfe, although many of them have been lost at Worcester fight, so am I confident that others after me may fall upon some straine of another kind, never, before that, dreamed upon by those of foregoing ages.

70. Now to the end the reader may be more enamored of the language, wherein I am to publish a grammer and lexicon, I will here set down some few qualities and advantages peculiar to it self, and which no language else, although all other concurred with it, is able to reach unto.

71. First, There is not a word utterable by the mouth of man, which, in this lan-

guage, hath not a peculiar signification by it self, so that the allegation of Bliteri by the Summulists will be of small validity.

72. Secondly, Such as will harken to my instructions, if some strange word be proposed to them, whereof there are many thousands of millions, deviseable by the wit of man, which never hitherto by any breathing have been uttered, shall be able, although he know not the ultimate signification thereof, to declare what part of speech it is; or if a noune, into what predicament or class it is to be reduced, whether it be the signe of a real or notional thing, or somewhat concerning mechanick trades in their tooles or tearmes; or if real, whether natural or artificial, complete or incomplete; for words here do suppone for the things which they signifie, as when we see my Lord General's picture, we say, there is my Lord General.

73. Thirdly, This world of words hath but two hundred and fifty prime radices, upon which all the rest are branched; for better understanding whereof, with all its dependant boughs, sprigs, and ramelets, I have before my lexicon set down the division thereof, making use of another allegory, into so many cities, which are subdivided into streets, they againe into lanes, those into houses, these into stories, whereof each room standeth for a word; and all these so methodically, that who observeth my precepts thereanent, shall, at the first hearing of a word, know to what city it belongeth, and consequently not be ignorant of some general signification thereof, till, after a most exact prying into all its letters, finding the street, lane, house, story, and room thereby denotated, he punctually hit upon the very proper thing it represents in its most specifical signification.

74. Fourthly, By vertue of adjectitious syllabicals annexible to nouns and verbs, there will arise of several words, what compound, what derivative, belonging in this language to one noune or to one verb alone, a greater number then doth pertaine to all the parts of speech in the most copious language in the world besides.

75. Fifthly, So great energy to every meanest constitutive part of a word in this language is appropriated, that one word thereof, though but of seven syllables at most, shall comprehend that which no language else in the world is able to express in fewer then fourscore and fifteen several words; and that not only a word here and there for masteries sake, but several millions of such, which, to any initiated in the rudiments of my grammar, shall be easie to frame.

76. Sixthly, In the cases of all the declinable parts of speech, it surpasseth all other languages whatsoever, for whilst others have but five or six at most, it hath ten, besides the nominative.

77. Seventhly, There is none of the learned languages but hath store of nouns defective of some case or other; but in this language there is no heteroclite in any declinable word, nor redundancie or deficiency of cases.

78. Eighthly, Every word capable of number, is better provided therewith in this

language then by any other; for in stead of two or three numbers, which others have, this affordeth you four; to wit, the singular, dual, plural, and redual.

79. Ninthly, It is not in this as other languages, wherein some words lack one number, and some another, for here each casitive or personal part of speech is endued with all the numbers.

80. Tenthly, In this tongue there are eleven genders; wherein likewise it exceedeth all other languages.

81. Eleventhly, Verbs, mongrels, participles, and hybrids, have all of them ten tenses besides the present; which number no language else is able to attaine to.

82. Twelfthly, Though there be many conjugable words in other languages defective of tenses, yet doth this tongue allow of no such anomaly, but granteth all to each.

83. Thirteenthly, In lieu of six moods which other languages have at most, this one enjoyeth seven in its conjugable words.

84. Fourteenthly, Verbs here, or other conjugable parts of speech, admit of no want of moodes, as doe other languages.

85. Fifteenthly, In this language the verbs and participles have four voices, although it was never heard that ever any other language had above three.

86. Sixteenthly, No other tongue hath above eight or nine parts of speech, but this hath twelve.

87. Seventeenthly, For variety of diction in each part of speech, it surmounteth all the languages in the world.

88. Eighteenthly, Each noun thereof, or verb, may begin or end with a vowel or consonant, as to the peruser shall seem most expedient.

89. Nineteenthly, Every word of this language, declinable or indeclinable, hath at least ten several synomymas.

90. Twentiethly, Each of these synomymas, in some circumstance of the signification, differeth from the rest.

91. One and twentiethly, Every faculty, science, art, trade, or discipline, requiring many words for expression of the knowledge thereof, hath each its respective root from whence all the words thereto belonging are derived.

92. Two and twentiethly, In this language the opposite members of a division have usually the same letters in the words which signifie them; the initial and final letter being all one, with a transmutation only in the middle ones.

93. Three and twentiethly, Every word in this language signifieth as well backward as forward, and how ever you invert the letter, still shall you fall upon significant words, whereby a wonderful facility is obtained in making of anagrams.

94. Four and twentiethly, There is no language in the world, but for every word thereof it will afford you another of the same signification, of equall syllables with it, and beginning or ending, or both, with vowels or consonants as it doth.

95. Five and twentiethly, By vertue hereof there is no hexameter, elegiack, saphick,

2 c

asclcpaid, iambick, or any other kind of Latin or Greek verse, but I will afford you another in this language of the same sort, without a syllable more or less in the one then the other, spondæ answering to spondæ, dactil to dactil, cæsure to cæsure, and each foot to other, with all uniformity imaginable.

96. Six and twentiethly, As it trotteth easily with metrical feet, so at the end of the career of each line hath it the dexterity, after the manner of our English and other vernaculary tongues, to stop with the closure of a rime; in the framing whereof, the well-versed in that language shall have so little labour, that for every word therein he shall be able to furnish at least five hundred several monosyllables of the same termination with it.

97. Seven and twentiethly, In translating verses of any vernaculary tongue, such as Italian, French, Spanish, Slavonian, Dutch, Irish, English, or whatever it be, it affords you words of the same signification, syllable for syllable, and in the closure of each line a ryme, as in the original.

98. Eight and twentiethly, By this language, and the letters thereof, we may do such admirable feats in numbers, that no cyfering can reach its compendiousness; for whereas the ordinary way of numbring by thousands of thousands of thousands of thousands, doth but confuse the hearer's understanding, to remedy which I devised, even by cyfering it self, a far more exact maner of numeration, as in the treatise of arithmetick which I have ready for the press is evidently apparent. This language affordeth so concise words for numbering, that the number for setting down, whereof would require in vulgar arithmetick more figures in a row then there might be grains of sand containable from the center of the earth to the highest heavens, is in it expressed by two letters.

99. Nine and twentiethly, What rational logarithms do by writing, this language doth by heart, and by adding of letters, shall multiply numbers, which is a most exquisite secret.

100. Thirtiethly, The digits are expressed by vowels, and the consonants stand for all the results of the Cephalisme, from ten to eighty-one inclusively, whereby many pretty arithmetical tricks are performed.

101. One and thirtiethly, In the denomination of the fixed stars, it affordeth the most significant way imaginary; for by the single word alone which represents the star, you shall know the magnitude, together with the longitude and latitude, both in degrees and minutes, of the star that is expressed by it.

102. Two and thirtiethly, By one word in this language we shall understand what degree, or what minute of the degree of a signe of the zodiake, the sun, or moon, or any other planet is in.

103. Three and thirtiethly, As for the yeer of God, the moneth of that yeer, week of the moneth, day of that week, partition of the day, hour of that partition, quarter

and half-quarter of the hour, a word of one syllable in this language will express it all to the full.

104. Four and thirtiethly, In this language also, words expressive of herbs represent unto us with what degree of cold, moisture, heat, or driness they are qualified, together with some other property distinguishing them from other herbs.

105. Five and thirtiethly, In matter of colours, we shall learn by words in this language the proportion of light, shadow, or darkness, commixed in them.

106. Six and thirtiethly, In the composition of syllables by vowels and consonants, it affordeth the aptest words that can be imagined for expressing how many vowels and consonants any syllable is compounded of, and how placed in priority and situation to one another. Which secret in this language is exceeding necessary for understanding the vigour of derivates in their variety of signification.

107. Seven and thirtiethly, For attaining to that dexterity which Mithridates, king of Pontus, was said to have, in calling all his souldiers, of an army of threescore thousand men, by their names and surnames, this language will be so convenient, that if a general, according to the rules thereof, will give new names to his soldiers, whether horse, foot, or dragoons, as the French use to do to their infantry by their *noms de guerre*, he shall be able, at the first hearing of the word that represents the name of a souldier, to know of what brigade, regiment, troop, company, squadron, or division he is, and whether he be of the cavalry or of the foot, a single souldier or an officer, or belonging to the artillery or baggage. Which device, in my opinion, is not unuseful for those great captains that would endear themselves in the favour of the souldiery.

108. Eight and thirtiethly, In the contexture of nouns, pronouns, and prepositai articles, united together, it administereth many wonderful varieties of laconick expressions, as in the grammar thereof shall more at large be made known unto you.

109. Nine and thirtiethly, Every word in this language is significative of a number, because, as words may be increased by addition of letters and syllables, so of numbers is there a progress *in infinitum*.

110. Fourtiethly, In this language every number, how great soever, may be expressed by one single word.

111. One and fourtiethly, As every number essentially differeth from another, so shall the words expressive of several numbers be from one another distinguished.

112. Two and fourtiethly, No language but this hath in its words the whole number of letters, that is, ten vowels, and five and twenty consonants, by which means there is no word escapes the latitude thereof.

113. Three and fourtiethly, As its interjections are more numerous, so are they more emphatical in their respective expression of passions, then that part of speech is in any other language whatsoever.

114. Four and fourtiethly, The more syllables there be in any one word of this lan-

guage, the manyer several significations it hath ; with which propriety no other language is endowed.

115. Five and fourtiethly, All the several genders in this language are as well competent to verbs as nouns ; by vertue whereof, at the first uttering of a verb in the active voice, you shall know whether it be a god, a goddess, a man, a woman, a beast, or any thing inanimate, and so thorow the other five genders, that doth the action, which excellencie is altogether peculiar unto this language.

116. Six and fourtiethly, In this language there is an art, out of every word, of what kinde of speech soever it be, to frame a verb ; whereby, for expressing all manner of actions, a great facility is attained unto.

117. Seven and fourtiethly, To all manner of verbs, and many syncategorematical words, is allowed in this language a flexion by cases, unknown to other tongues, thereby to represent unto our understandings more compendious expressions then is possible to afford by any other means.

118. Eight and fourtiethly, Of all languages, this is the most compendious in complement, and consequently fittest for courtiers and ladies.

119. Nine and fourtiethly, For writing of missives, letters of state, and all other manner of epistles, whether serious or otherways, it affordeth the compactest stile of any language in the world ; and therefore, of all other, the most requisite to be learned by statesmen and merchants.

120. Fiftiethly, No language in matter of prayer and ejaculations to Almighty God is able, for conciseness of expression, to compare with it ; and therefore, of all other, the most fit for the use of church-men, and spirits inclined to devotion.

121. One and fiftiethly, This language hath a modification of the tense, whether present, preterite, or future, of so curious invention for couching much matter in few words, that no other language ever had the like.

122. Two and fiftiethly, There is not a proper name in any country of the world, for which this language affords not a peculiar word, without being beholding to any other.

123. Three and fiftiethly, In many thousands of words belonging to this language, there is not a letter which hath not a peculiar signification by it self.

124. Four and fiftiethly, The polysyllables of this language do all of them signifie by their monosyllables, which no word in any other language doth, *ex instituto*, but the compound ones ; for, though the syllabical parts of *ex lex* separately signifie as in the compound, yet those of *homo* do it not, nor yet those of *dote* or *domus*, as in the whole ; and so it is in all other languages, except the same ; for there are in the Italian and Latine tongues words of ten, eleven, or twelve syllables, whereof not one syllable by it self doth signifie any thing at all in that language, of what it doth in the whole ; as *adolescenturiatissimamente*, *honorificicabilitudinitatibus*, &c.

125. Five and fiftiethly, All the languages in the world will be beholding to this, and this to none.

126. Six and fiftiethly, There is yet another wonder in this language, which, although a little touched by the by in the fifty eighth article of this preface, I will mention yet once more; and it is this, That though this language have advantage of all other, it is impossible any other in time coming surpass it, because, as I have already said, it comprehendeth, first, all words expressible; and then, in matter of the obliquity of cases and tenses, the contrivance of indeclinable parts, and right disposure of vowels and consonants, for distinguishing of various significations within the latitude of letters, cannot be afforded a way so expedient.

127. Seven and fiftiethly, The greatest wonder of all is, that of all the languages in the world, it is the easiest to learn; a boy of ten yeers old, being able to attaine to the knowledge thereof, in three moneths space; because there are in it many facilitations for the memory, which no other language hath but it self.

128. Eight and fiftiethly, Sooner shall one reach the understanding of things to be signified by the words of this language, then by those of any other, for that as logarithms in comparison of absolute numbers, so do the words thereof in their initials respectively vary according to the nature of the things which they signifie.

129. Nine and fiftiethly, For pithiness of proverbs, oracles, and sentences, no language can parallel with it.

130. Sixtiethly, In axioms, maximes, and aphorisms, it is excellent above all other languages.

131. One and sixtiethly, For definitions, divisions, and distinctions, no language is so apt.

132. Two and sixtiethly, For the affirmation, negation, and infinitation of propositions, it hath properties unknown to any other language, most necessary for knowledge.

133. Three and sixtiethly, in matter of Enthymems, Syllogisms, and all manner of illative ratiocination, it is the most compendious in the world.

134. Besides these sixty and three advantages above all other languages, I might have couched thrice as many more, of no less consideration then the aforesaid, but that these same will suffice to sharpen the longing of the generous reader, after the intrinsecal and most researched secrets of the new grammer and lexicon which I am to evulge.

TO contrive a language of this perfection, will be thought by the primest wits of this age a work of a great undertaking, and that the promover of so excellent an invention should not lack for any encouragement tending to the accomplishment of a task of such maine concernment. If any say there are too many languages already, and that, by their multiplicity and confusion, the knowledge of things having been much retarded, this fabrick of a new one may be well forborn, because it would but intangle the minde with more impestrements, where there was too much difficulty before, I answer that this maketh not one more, but in a manner comprehendeth all in it, whereby it facilitates, and doth not obstruct; for by making Greek, Latin, and all the other languages the more expressive, it furthers the progress of all arts and sciences, to the attaining whereof the uttering of our conceptions in due and significant tearms hath, by some of the most literate men in former ages, been esteemed so exceeding requisite, that, for attributing a kind of necessity thereunto, they are till this houre called by the name of Nominal Philosophers; it being thus very apparent to any well affected to literature, that the performance of such a designe would be of a great expediency for scholars: equity it self seemeth to plead, that unto him by whom a benefit redounds to many, is competent by many a proportionable retribution; yet, seeing nothing ought to be charged on the publick, but upon considerations of great weight, I will premise some few infallible principles, that upon them the world may see how demonstratively are grounded the author's most reasonable demands.

1. Each good thing is desirable, because goodnesse is the object of the will.

2. Every thing that ought to be desired is really good, because a well-directed will is not deceived with appearances.

3. The better a thing be the more it is to be desired, because there is a proportion betwixt the object and the faculty.

4. The mind is better then the body, because by it we are the image of God.

5. The goods of the minde are better then those of the body, because they give embellishment to the nobler part.

6. The goods of either minde or body are better then wealth, because wealth is but subservient to either, and the end is more able then the means which are ordained for it.

7. Learning is the good of the minde, because it beautifieth it.

8. This new language is an invention full of learning, because the knowledge of all arts and disciplines is much advanced by it.

9. A discovery is the revealment of some good thing which formerly was either concealed, or not at all known; for, in a discovery, two things are requisite; first, that it be good; secondly, that it be revealed.

10. Who discovereth a secret of money, should have the fifth or third part, because there is an Act of Parliament for it.

11. If there be any discovery in learning, the act ought to extend to it, because the state is endowed with a soul as well as a body.

12. This new found out invention is a discovery of learning, because the two requisitas of a discovery, together with the description of learning, are competent thereto.

13. Who discovereth most of the best good, deserveth the best recompense, because merit and reward are analogical in a proportion of the greater reward to the greater merit.

14. Though money be not proportionable to learning, yet seeing the learned man may have need of money, he should not lack it ; if not as a full recompence, at least as a donative or largess, should it be given unto him in testimony of his worth, and the respect of others toward him, and withal to encourage him the more to eminent undertakings; for, were it otherwise, the more deserving a man were, the worse he would be used, there being nothing so unreasonable as to refuse a little to any that stands in need thereof, because a great deal more is due unto him; as if, in time of famine, there being no more but one penny-loaf to give unto a prince, he should be made starve for the want of it, because of his deserving better fare ; for, that which comprehends the more, comprehends the less.

15. In matter of recompence for good things proceeding from the minde, which, in the midst of flames, cannot be conquered, and by vertue whereof a gallant man is alwayes free, and invincible in his better part, we ought altogether to prescind and abstract from the conditions of the native country, and person of the deserver, whether that be fertil or barren, or this at liberty or indurance ; for these being things, *quæ non fecimus ipsi*, we ought to say, *Vix ea nostra voco* ; and therefore, seeing punishment and reward should attend the performance of nothing else but what did lye in our power to do or not to do, and that the specifying of good or bad actions dependeth upon the qualification of the attention, no man should be either punished or rewarded for being either Scottishman or a prisoner, or both, if no other reason concur therewith, because the country of our birth, and state of our person, as being oftentimes the effects of a good or bad fortune, are not alwayes in our power to command.

16. If by means of the aforesaid discovery may be effectuated the saving of great charges to the subjects of the land, a pecunial or prædial recompense will, in so far, be very answerable to the nature of that service, because, in matter of merit, and the reward proportionable thereunto, money is with money, and things vendible, no less homogeneal then honor with vertue.

17. The State no doubt will deal proportionably with their prisoners of war, without prosopolepsie, or any respect to one more then another, and that by a geometrical equity, because it is just.

18. The State assuredly will grant the same freedom to one prisoner, *cæteris paribus*, which they do to another, and upon the same terms, those of a like condition not being unequally faulty, because they will not be unjust.

19. If any one prisoner of a like condition and quality, at the least, *in cæteris*, with another that hath obtained his liberty, represent to the publick somewhat conducible thereunto, which the other is not versed in, common equity requireth, that he have a compensation suitable to that additional endowment ; for, *si ab inæqualibus æqualia*

demas, quæ restant sunt æqualia, and the Act for discoveries maintaines the truth thereof.

20. Though it be commonly maintained amongst the Protestants, that we cannot supererogate towards Almighty God, albeit those of the Romish faith be of another opinion, for that God cannot be unjust, how severely soever he inflict his afflictions, and that all the favours he conferreth on mankind are of his meer grace, not our deserving ; yet, that a subject may be capable of supererogation towards any sublunary state or sovereignty, is not only agreeable with all the religions of the world, but also a maine principle of humane society, and ground unalterable of politick government ; for who transgresse not the limits of those good subjects, whose actions, thoughts, and words, shew at all times faithfulness, loyalty, and obedience to the sovereign power under which they live, are universally esteemed by so doing, to discharge their duty so to the full, that in reason no more can be required of them. If, therefore, it happen, besides this general bond of fidelity, whereunto all the natives and inhabitants of a country are by their birth and protection inviolably ingaged, that any one more obliging then others performe some singular good office, unto which he was not formerly tyed by the strictness of his allegiance, there is no doubt but that the publick, whom nature exempteth not from thankfulness more then private persons, should and will acknowledge such an action, exceeding the reach of his fellow-patriots and co-habitants, to be meritorious, and therefore worthy of recompense ; upon which consideration, according to the people's diversity of carriage in the well or ill demeaning of themselves, are built the two maine pillars of reward and punishment, without which the strongest commonwealth on earth is not able to subsist long from falling to pieces. That is to say, I appeal to Scipio, who, with the approbation of all that lived since his dayes, exclaimed against Rome, in these words, *O ingratam patriam !* as likewise to those many great statesmen and philosophers, who, from age to age, twitted the Athenians with ingratitude for the ostracizing of Astrides ; for, if humane frailties were not incident to princes, states, and incorporations, as well as unto individuals in their single and private callings and particular deportments, there would never be any need of protestations, declarations, or decisive war against the tyranny, usurpations, and oppressions of misrule. Hence do I think, that in a well pollished state, reward will not be wanting to him that merits it for his good service, because punishment by the law attends the offender, and *contrariorum eadem est ratio.*

21. It is acknowledged by the laws and customs of this island, that the subjects thereof have a right of propriety to their goods, notwithstanding the titles of dominion and supremacy remaining in the persons of others above them ; and that if for erecting a castle, fort, church, hospital, colledge, hall, magazine, or any other kind of edifice tending to publike use, the state should be pleased to incroach upon the land of any private person, who doubteth but that such a man, of how mean soever a condition he be, will in justice be heard to give up, and require the full value of his land, that a

compensation suitable to the worth thereof may be allowed to him ? founding the equity of so just a retribution upon Ahab's case in Naboth's vineyard. Now the soul and body of man being more a man's own, they being the constitutive parts whereof physically he is composed, then are the goods of fortune, which totally are accidental to him, it follows clearly that a man hath a full right of propriety to the goods of his own mind, and consequently such goods being better, as hath been evidenced by the sixth axiome, then any external means, what can be more manifest, than that he who is endowed with them, so careful a course being taken for the satisfaction of any in matter of outward wealth, may at the best rate he can, capitulate for their disposal with what persons he thinks most concerned in the benefits and utility by them accrescing ; because it is an argument *a minore ad majus,* and therefore *a fortiori.*

22. If such a one nevertheless voluntarily accept of a lesser recompence, then by his deserving he may claim right unto, he is not unjustly dealt with ; *quia volenti non fit injuria,* and *pactum hominis tollit conditionem legis.*

THESE specious axiomes, definitions, and uncontroulable maximes thus premised, I must make bold, in behalf of the author, to deduce from thence the equity of his desires, in demanding that the same inheritance, which for these several hundreds of yeers, through a great many progenitors, hath by his ancestors, without the interruption of any other, been possest, be now fully devolved on him, with the same priviledges and immunities in all things, as they enjoyed it. But the better to make appear his ingenuity in this his suit, and modestie in requiring no more, it is expedient to declare what it is he offereth unto the State, for obliging them to vouchsafe him the grant of no less. May the reader therefore be pleased to understand, that it is the discovery of a secret in learning, which, besides the great contentment it cannot chuse but yield to ingenious spirits, will afford a huge benefit to students of all sorts, by the abridgement of their studies, in making them learn more in three yeers, with the help thereof, then, without it, in the space of five. This saving of two yeers charges to scholars, in such a vast dominion as this is, although I speak nothing of the sparing of so much time, which, to a methodical wit of any pregnancie, is a menage of an inestimable value, cannot be appreciated, how parsimonious soever they be in their diet and apparel, at less then ten thousand pounds English a yeer.

That this is a secret, it is clear by this, That never any, since the laying of the foundation of the earth, did so much as divulge a syllable thereof; which undoubtedly, they would have done, had they had any knowledge therein. And that none now living, be it spoken without disparagement of any, either knoweth it, or knoweth how to go about it, save the aforesaid author alone, who is willing to forfeit all he demands, although by birth-right it be his own already, and worth neer upon a thousand pounds sterlin a yeer, if without his help, any breathing, notwithstanding the instructions may possibly be had by his lost papers, and by what in the preceding articles hath been in this little tractate promulgated, shall, within half a yeer after the date hereof, give any apparent testimony to the world that he hath any insight in this invention.

Which, that it is good and desirable, is evident by the first and second axiomes; and that it is a discovery, and a discovery of learning, by the ninth and twelfth; that the discovery of a matter of less moment then it, deserveth great sums of money, is manifest by the tenth and thirteenth; and that a retribution of great value should attend the disclosure of so prime a secret, by the eleventh and fourteenth; that the knowledge of this invention is of more worth then either strength or wealth, is proved by the fifth and sixth; and that it is more to be desired then any thing that is at the disposure of fortune, by the third and fourth; that it doth promote reason, illuminate the judgement, further and improve literature, by polishing and imbellishing the inward abilities of man, and faculties of his minde, is clear by the seventh and eighth.

Thus much of the invention, or thing invented; which, as the fruit is to be accounted of less worth then the tree, which yeerly produceth the like; cistern-water, that daily diminisheth, then that of a fountain, which is inexhaustible; and a haymow, then the meadow on which it grew, being, as in reason it ought, to be estimated at a rate much inferior to the inventer, from whose brains have already issued offsprings every whit as considerable, with parturiencie for greater births, if a malevolent time disobstetricate not their enixibility, it followeth of necessity that he should reap the benefit that is due for the invention, with hopes of a higher remuneration for what of the like nature remaineth as yet unsatisfied. And although his being a Scot, and a prisoner of war, may perhaps, in the opinion of some, eclipse the splendor of so great an expectation, yet that it should not, is most perspicuously evinced by the fifteenth axiome.

That he is a Scot, he denieth not; but that he thereby meriteth to be either praised or dispraised, is utterly to be disavowed, because it lay not in his power to appoint localities for his mother's residence at the time of his nativitie, or to enact any thing before he had a being himself.

True it is, that nothing is more usual in speech, then to blame all for the fault of the greater part; and to twit a whole country with that vice to which most of its inhabitants are inclined. Hence have we these sayings; The Spaniards are proud; The French inconstant; The Italians lecherous; The Cretians lyers; The Sicilians false; The Asiaticks effeminate; The Crovats cruel; The Dutch temuleucious; The Polonians quarrelsome; The Saxons mutinous; and so forth thorow other territories, nurseries of enormities of another kinde; although nothing be more certain, then that there are some Spaniards as humble, French as constant, Italians chaste, Cretians true, Sicilians ingenuous, Asiaticks warlike, Crovates merciful, Dutch sober, Polonians peaceable, and some Saxons as loyal, as any in the world besides. By which account, all foreigners, for such are all the inhabitants on the earth in relation to those that are not their compatriots, yeelding to the *most* and *some* of each stranger-land, in its respective vice and vertue; it may safely be avouched, that there is under the sun no national fault, nor national deserving, whereby all merit to be punished, or all rewarded; because the badness of most in each destroys the universality of vertue; and the good inclination of some in all, cuts off the generality of vice.

But to come neerer home: seeing Scotland was never loaded with so much disreputation, for covetousness and hypocrisie, as it is at this present; and that the Knight for whom this treatise is intended, hath, as a patriot, some interest in the good name thereof; it is not amiss that, for the love of him and all honest Scots, I glance a little at the occasion, if not the cause, of so heavie an imputation; especially that country having been aspersed therewith, long before it had sustained the loss of any battel, wherein the several miscarriages looked rather like the effect of what formerly had procured the said reproach, then any way as the causes thereof; for where covetousness is predominant, fidelity, fortitude, and vigilancie, must needs discamp, if Mammona give the word; the concomitancie of vices, seeing *contrariorum eadem est ratio*, being a sequele from that infallible tenet in the morals, the concatenation of vertues.

How this covetousness, under the mask of religion, took such deep root in that land, was one way occasioned by some ministers, who, to augment their stipends and cram their bags full of money, thought fit to possess the mindes of the people with a strong opinion of their sanctity, and implicite obedience to their injunctions; to which effect, most rigidly Israelitizing it in their Synagogical Sanhedrins, and officiously bragging in their pulpits, even when Scotland, by divers notorious calamities of both sword, plague, and famine, was brought very lowe, that no nation, for being likest to the Jews of any other, was so glorious as it; they, with a Pharisaical superciliosity, would always rebuke the Non-Covenanters and sectaries as publicans and sinners, unfit for the purity of their conversation, unless, by the malignancie or over-mastering power of a cross winde, they should be forced to cale the hypocritical bunt, let fall the top-gallant of their counterfeit devotion, and tackling about, to sail a quite contrary course, as many of them have already done, the better at last to cast anchor in the harbour of Profit, which is the butt they aimed at, and sole period of all their dissimulations.

For I have known some, even of the most rigid zealots, who, rather then to forgo their present emoluments, by continual receiving and never erogating; by never sowing, and always reaping; and by making the sterility of all men prove fruitful to them, and their fertility barren to all, would wish presbytery were of as empty a sound, as its homæoteleft, Blitery; and the covenant, which asserts it no less exploded from all ecclesiastical societies, then Plautus exolet phrases have been from the eloquent orations of Ciceron.

But this affecting only a part of the Tribe of Levi, how the remainder of new Palestine, as the kirkomanetick Philarchaists would have it called, comes to be upbraided with the opprobry of covetousness, is that which I am so heartily sorry for, that to wipe off its obloquy, I would undertake a pilgrimage to old Judea, visit the ruínes of Jerusalem, and trace the foot-steps of Zedekiah's fellow captives to the gates of Babylon.

Yet did this so great an inconvenience proceed meerly from an incogitancy, in not taking heed to what is prescribed by prudence, the directress of all vertues, and consequently of that which moderates the actions of giving and receiving, although it be *nobilius dare quam accipere*, the non-vitiosity whereof, by her injunctions, dependeth on the judicious observing of all the circumstances mentioned in this mnemoneutick hexameter, *quis, quid, ubi, quibus auxiliis, cur, quomodo, quando*, whose last particle, by the untimely taking of a just debt, and unseasonable receiving of what at another time might have been lawfully required, being too carelessly regarded by the state and milice of that country, gave occasion to that contumely, the staine whereof remaineth still, notwithstanding the loss in money, besides other prejudices, sustained since of ten times more then they got.

I heard once a Maronite Jew, to vindicate the reputation of the family and village of the Iscariots, in which he pretended to have some interest, very seriously relate, that according to the opinion of Rabbi Ezra, the thirty pieces of silver delivered to Judas was but the sum which, long before that, when Christ went up from Galilee to celebrate the feast of tabernacles at Jerusalem, Malchus the servant of Caiaphas had borrowed from him, whilst he had the charge of his Master's bag, with assurance punctually to repay it him again at the subsequent term of the passover, as the fashion was then amongst the inhabitants of Judea. But although it were so, which we are not bound to give ear to, because it is plainly set down in the fifth verse of the two and twentieth chapter of the Evangile according to Saint Luke, that the high priests made a covenant with Judas, yet should he not have received the money in the very nick of time that his master was to be apprehended.

This I the rather believe, for that I likewise heard a minister say, that he offends God who stretcheth forth his hand to take in the payment of any debt, how just soever it be, upon a Sunday; and that though a purse full of gold were offered unto himself whilst he is a preaching in the pulpit, he would refuse it.

These collateral instances I introduce, not for application but illustration sake; not for comparison, but explication of the congruent adapting of necessary puntilios for the framing of a vertuous action.

Another thing there is that fixeth a grievous scandal upon that nation in matter of philargyrie, or love of money, and it is this: There hath been in London, and repairing to it, for these many years together, a knot of Scotish bankers, collybists, or coine-coursers, of traffickers in merchandise to and againe, and of men of other professions, who by hook and crook, *fas et nefas*, slight and might, all being as fish their net could catch, having feathered their nests to some purpose, look so idolatrously upon their Dagon of wealth, and so closely, like the earth's dull center, hug all unto themselves, that for no respect of vertue, honor, kinred, patriotism, or whatever else, be it never so recommendable, will they depart from so much as one single peny, whose emission doth not, without any hazard of loss, in a very short time superlucrate beyond all conscience an additionall increase to the heap of that stock which they so much adore; which churlish and tenacious humor hath made many that were not acquainted with any else of that country, to imagine all their compatriots infected with the same leprosie of a wretched peevishness, whereof those *quomodocunquizing* cluster-fists and rapacious varlets have given of late such cannibal-like proofs, by their in-humanity and obdurate carriage towards some, whose shoes-strings they are not wor-thy to unty, that were it not that a more able pen then mine will assuredly not faile to jerk them on all sides, in case, by their better demeanor for the future, they endea-vour not to wipe off the blot wherewith their native country, by their sordid avarice and miserable baseness, hath been so foully stained, I would at this very instant blaze them out in their names and surnames, notwithstanding the vizard of Presbyterian zeal wherewith they maske themselves, that like so many wolves, foxes, or Athenian Timons, they might in all times coming, be debarred the benefit of any honest con-versation.

Thus is it perceptible how usual it is, from the irregularity of a few, to conclude an universal defection, and that the whole is faulty because a part is not right; there being in it a fallacy of induction, as if because this, that and the other are both greedy and dissembling, and therefore all other their country-men are such; which will no wayes follow, if any one of these others be free from those vices, for that one particu-lar negative, by the rules of contradictory opposites, will destroy an universal affirma-tive; and of such there are many thousands in that nation, who are neither greedy nor dissemblers.

And so would all the rest, if a joint and unanimous course were taken to have their noblemen free from baseness, their church-men from avarice, their merchants from deceit, their gentlemen from pusillanimity, their lawyers from prevarication, their tradesmen from idleness, their farmers from lying, their young men from pride, their old men from morosity, their rich from hard heartednes, their poor from theeving, their great ones from faction, their meaner sort from implicit sectatorship, the magis-trates from injustice, the clients from litigiousness, and all of them from dishonesty and disrespect of learning; which, though but negatives of vertue, and at best but the *ultimum non esse* of vice, would nevertheless go near to restore the good fame of that country to its pristine integrity; the report whereof was raised to so high a pitch of old, that in a book in the last edition of a pretty bulk, written in the Latine tongue by one Dempster, there is mention made, what for armes and arts, of at least five thousand illustrious men of Scotland, the last liver whereof dyed above fifty yeers ago.

Nor did their succession so far degenerate from the race of so worthy progenitors, but that even of late, although before the intestine garboyles of this Island, several of them have for their fidelity, valor and gallantry, been exceedingly renowned over all France, Spain, the Venetian territories, Pole, Moscovy, the Low-countryes, Swedland, Hungary, Germany, Denmark, and other states and kingdoms; as may appear by general Rudderford; my lord General Sir James Spence of Wormiston, afterwards by the Swedish king created earl of Orcholm; Sir Patrick Ruven, governor of Vlme, general of an army of High-Germans, and afterwards earl of Forth and Branford; Sir Alexander Leslie, governor of the cities along the Baltick coast, field-marshal over the army in Westphalia, and afterwards intituled *Scoticani fœderis supremus dux;* General James King, afterwards made lord Ythen; Colonel David Leslie, commander of a regiment of horse over the Dutch, and afterwards in these our domestick wars advanced to be lieutenant-general of both horse and foot; Major General Thomas Kar; Sir David Drummond, general major and governor of Statin in Pomer; Sir George Douglas, Colonel, and afterwards employed in embassies betwixt the soveraigns of Britain and Swedland; Colonel George Lindsay, Earl of Craford; Colonel lord Forbas; Colonel lord Sancomb; Colonel Lodowick Leslie, and in the late troubles at home, governor of Berwick and Tinmouth-sheels; Colonel Sir James Ramsey, governor of Hanaw; Colonel Alexander Ramsay, governor of Crafzenach, and quartermaster-general to the duke of Wymar; Colonel William Bailif, afterwards in these our intestin broyls promoved to the charge of lieutenant-general; another Colonel Ramsey besides any of the former two, whose name I cannot hit upon; Sir James Lumsden, colonel in Germany, and afterwards governor of Newcastle, and general major in the Scotish wars; Sir George Cunningham, Sir John Ruven, Sir John Hamilton, Sir John Meldrum, Sir Arthur Forbas, Sir Frederick Hamilton, Sir James Hamilton, Sir Francis Ruven, Sir John Jnnes, Sir William Balantine, and several other knights, all colonels of horse or foot in the Swedish wars.

As likewise by Colonel Alexander Hamilton, agnamed dear Sandy, who afterwards in Scotland was made general of the artillery, for that in some measure he had exercised the same charge in Dutchland, under the command of Marquis James Hamilton, whose generalship over six thousand English in the Swedish service I had almost forgot; by Colonel Robert Cunningham; Colonel Robert Monro of Fowls; Colonel Obstol Monro; Colonel Hector Monro; Colonel Robert Monro, lately general major in Ireland, who wrote a book in folio, intituled Monroe's Expedition; Colonel Assen Monro; Colonel James Seaton, and Colonel James Seaton; Colonel John Kinindmond; Colonel John Vrquhart, who is a valiant souldier, expert commander, and learned scholar; Colonel James Spence; Colonel Hugh Hamilton; Colonel Francis Sinclair; Colonel John Leslie of Wardes; Colonel John Leslie, agnamed the omnipotent, afterwards made major-general; Colonel Robert Lumsden; Colonel Robert Leslie; Colonel William Gun, who afterwards, in the yeer 1639, was knighted by King CHARLES, for his service done at the bridge of Dee, neer Aberdeen, against the earl of Montross, by whom he was beaten; Colonel George Colen, Colonel Crichtoun, Colonel Liddel, Colonel Armestrong, Colonel John Gordon, Colonel James Cockburne, Colonel Thomas Thomson, Colonel Thomas Kinindmond, Colonel James Johnston, Colonel Edward Johnston, Colonel William Kinindmond, Colonel George Leslie, Colonel Robert Stuart, Colonel Alexander Forbas, agnamed the *Bauld,* Colonel William Cunningham, another Colonel Alexander Forbas, Colonel Alexander Leslie, Colonel Alexander Cunningham, Colonel Finess Forbas, Colonel David Edintoun, Colonel Sandilands, Colonel Walter Leckie, and divers other Scotish colonels, what of horse and foot, many whereof within a short space thereafter attained to be general persons, under the command of Gustavus the Cæsaromastix, who confided so much in the valour, loyalty, and discretion of the Scotish nation, and they reciprocally in the gallantry, affection, and magnanimity of him, that immediately after the battel at Leipsich, in one place and at one time, he had six and thirty Scotish colonels about him; whereof some did command a whole brigad of horse, some a brigad composed of two regiments, half horse half foot, and others a brigade made up of foot only, without horse ; some againe had the command of a regiment of horse only, without foot ; some of a regiment of horse alone, without more, and others of a regiment of dragoons; the half of the names of which colonels are not here inserted, though they were men of notable prowesse, and in martial atchievements of most exquisite dexterity ; whose regiments were commonly distinguished by the diversity of nations of which they were severally composed, many regiments of English, Scots, Danes, Sweds, Fins, Liflanders, Laplanders, High Dutch, and other nations, serving in that confederate war of Germany under the command of Scotish colonels.

And besides these above-mentioned colonels, when any of the foresaid number either dyed of himself, was killed in the fields, required a pass for other countryes, or otherwise disposing of himself, did voluntarily demit his charge, another usually of the same nation succeeding in his place, other as many moe Scotish colonels, for any thing I know, as I have here set down, did serve in the same Swedish wars, under the conduct of the Duke of Wymar, Gustavus Horne, Baneer, and Torsisson, without reckoning amongst them, or any of the above-recited officers, the number of more then threescore of the Scotish nation, that were governors of cities, townes, citadels, forts, and castles in the respective conquered provinces of the Dutch empire.

Denmark, in my opinion, cannot goodly forget the magnanimous exploits of Sir Donald Mackie Lord Reay, first colonel there, and afterwards commander of a brigade under the Swedish standard; nor yet of the colonels of the name of Monro and Henderson, in the service of that king ; as likewise of the Colonel Lord Spynay, and others ; besides ten governors at least, all Scots, intrusted with the charge of the most especial strengths and holds of importance, that were within the confines of the Danish authority ; although no mention were made of exempt Mouat living in Birren, in whose judgment and fidelity, such trust is reposed, that he is as it were vice-king of Norway ; what obligation the State of France doth owe to the old Lord Colvil, colonel

of horse; the two Colonel Hepburnes, Sir John Hepburn by name, and Colonel
Heburn of Wachton, and Colonel Lord James Douglas, the last three whereof were
Mareschaux de camp, and, had they survived the respective day wherein they successively dyed in the bed of honor, would undoubtedly very shortly after have been all
of them made Mareschals of France, one of the highest preferments belonging to the
Milice of that nation, is not unknown to those that are acquainted with the French
affaires; and truly as for Sir John Heburn, albeit no mention was made of him in the
list of Scots officers in the Swedish service, he had under Gustavus the charge of a
Brigad of Foot; and so gallantly behaved himself at the battel of Leipsich, that unto
him, in so far as praise is due to man, was attributed the honour of the day.

Sir Andrew Gray, Sir John Seatoun, Sir John Fulerton the Earl of Irwin, Sir
Patrick Morray, Colonel Erskin, Colonel Andrew Lindsay, Colonel Mouat, Colonel
Morison, Colonel Thomas Hume, Colonel John Forbas, Colonel Liviston, Colonel
John Leslie, besides a great many other Scots of their charge, condition, and quality,
were all colonels under the pay of Lewis the thirteenth of France. Some of those
also, though not listed in the former roll, had, before they engaged themselves in the
French employment, standing regiments under the command of the Swedish King.

The interest of France, Swedland, and Denmark, not being able to bound the valour of the Scotish nation within the limits of their territories; the several expeditions
into Hungary, Dalmatia, and Croatia, against the Turks; into Transylvania against
Bethleem Gabor; to Italy, against the Venetians; and in Germany, against Count
Mansfield and the confederate princes, can testifie the many martial exploits of Colonel
Sir John Henderson, Colonel William Johnston, who shortly thereafter did excellent
service to this king of Portugal, and is a man of an upright mind, and a most undaunted courage, Colonel Lithco, Colonel Wedderburne, Colonel Bruce, and of many
other colonels of that country, whose names I know not; but above all, the two eminent ones, Colonel Leslie and Colonel Gordon; the first whereof is made an hereditary marquess of the empire, and colonel-general of the whole infantry of all the imperial forces; and the other gratified with the priviledge of the golden key, as a cognizance of his being raised to the dignity of high chamberlain of the Emperour's court;
which splendid and illustrious places of so sublime honour and pre-eminence, were deservedly conferred on them, for such extraordinary great services done by them for the
weal and grandeur of the Cæsarean majesty, as did by far surpass the performance of
any, to the Austrian family, now living in this age.

But lest the emperour should brag too much of the gallantry of those Scots, above
others of that nation, his cousin the king of Spaine is able to outvie him in the person
of the ever-renowned Earl of Bodwel, whose unparallel'd valour, so frequently tried
in Scotland, France, Germany, the Low-Countries, Spain, Italy, and other parts,
in a very short time began to be so redoubtable, that at last he became a terrour to
all the most desperate duellists and bravos of Europe, and a queller of the fury of the

proudest champions of his age; for all the innumerable combats which he fought against both Turks and Christians, both on horse and foot, closed always with the death or subjection of the adversary, of what degree or condition soever he might be, that was so bold as to cope with and encounter him in that kinde of hostility; the Gasconads of France, Rodomontads of Spain, Fanfaronads of Italy, and Bragadochio brags of all other countries, could no more astonish his invincible heart, then would the cheeping of a mouse a bear robbed of her whelps. That warlike and strong Mahometan, who dared, like another Goliah, and appealled the stoutest and most valiant of the Christian faith to enter the lists with him, and fight in the defence of their reli_ gion, was, after many hundreds of galliant Christians had been foyled by him, thrown dead to the ground by the vigour and dexterity of his hand. He would very often, in the presence of ladies, whose intimate favourite he was, to give some proof of the undantedness of his courage, by the meer activity of his body, with the help of a single sword, set upon a lyon in his greatest fierceness, and kill him dead upon the place. For running, vaulting, jumping, throwing of the barr, and other such-like feats of nimbleness, strength, and agility, he was the only paragon of the world, and unmatched by any.

Whilst in Madrid, Genua, Milan, Venice, Florence, Naples, Paris, Bruxelles, Vienna, and other great and magnificent cities, for the defence of the honour and reputation of the ladies whom he affected, he had in such measure incurred the hatred and indignation of some great and potent princes, that, to affront him, they had sent numbers of Spadassins, and Acuchilladores to surprise him at their best advantage; he would often times, all alone, buckle with ten or twelve of them, and lay such load, and so thick and threefold upon them, that he would quickly make them for their safeties betake themselves to their heels, with a vengeance at their back; by which meanes he gave such evidence of his greatness of resolution, strenuitie of person, excellency in conduct, and incomparable magnanimity of spirit, that being comfortable to his friends, formidable to his foes, and admirable to all; such as formerly had been his cruellest enemies, and most deeply had plotted and projected his ruine, were at last content, out of a remorse of conscience, to acknowledge the ascendent of his worth above theirs, and to sue, in all humility, to be reconciled to him. To this demand of theirs, out of his wonted generosity, which was never wanting, when either goodness or mercie required the making use thereof, having fully condescended, he past the whole remainder of his dayes in great security, and with all ease desirable, in the city of Naples; where, in a vigorous old age, environed with his friends, and enjoying the benefit of all his senses till the last hour, he dyed in full peace and quietness; and there I leave him. For should I undertake condignly to set down all the martial atchievements and acts of prowess performed by him, in turnaments, duels, battels, skirmishes, and fortuite encounters, against Scots, French, Dutch, Polonians, Hungarians, Spaniards, Italians, and others, were it not that there are above ten thousand

2 E

as yet living, who, as eye-witnesses, can verifie the truth of what I have related of him, the history thereof to succeeding ages would seem so incredible, that they would but look upon it, at best, but as on a romance, stuft with deeds of chivalrie; like those of Amades de Gaule, Esplandian, and Don Sylves de la Selve.

Next to the renowned Count Bodwel, in the service of that great Don Philippe, Tetrarch of the world, upon whose subjects the sun never sets, are to be recorded, besides a great many other colonels of Scotland, those valorous and worthy Scots, Colonel William Sempil, Colonel Boyd, and Colonel Lodowick Lindsay, Earl of Crawford. There is yet another Scotish Colonel that served this king of Spain, whose name is upon my tongue's end, and yet I cannot hit upon it; he was not a souldier bred, yet for many yeers together bore charge in Flanders under the command of Spinola. In his youth-hood, he was so strong and stiff a Presbyterian, that he was the onely man in Scotland made choice of, and relied upon for the establishment and upholding of that government, as the arch-prop and main pillar thereof; but as his judgment increased, and that he ripened in knowledge, declining from that Neoterick faith, and waining in his love to Presbytery, as he waxed in experience of the world, of a strict Puritan that he was at first, he became afterwards the most obstinate and rigid Papist that ever was upon the earth. It is strange my memory should so faile me, that I cannot remember his title; he was a lord I know, nay more, he was an earle, I that he was, and one of the first of them. Ho now! pescods on it, Crauford Lodi Lindsay puts me in minde of him; it was the old Earl of Argile, this Marquis of Argile's father; that was he, that was the man.

Now, as steel is best resisted and overcome by steel, and that the Scots, like Ismael, whose hand was against every man, and every man's hand against him, have been of late so ingaged in all the wars of Christendome, espousing, in a manner, the interest of all the princes thereof; that, what battel soever, at any time these forty yeers past hath been struck within the continent of Europe, all the Scots that fought in that field, were never overthrown and totally routed; for if some of them were captives and taken prisoners, others of that nation were victorious, and givers of quarter; valour and mercy on the one side, with misfortune and subjection upon the other side, meeting one another in the persons of compatriots on both sides; so the gold and treasure of the Indias not being able to purchase all the affections of Scotland to the furtherance of Castilian designes, there have been of late several Scotish colonels under the command of the Prince of Orange, in opposition of the Spagniard; viz. Colonel Edmond, who took the valiant Count de Buccoy twice prisoner in the field; Sir Henry Balfour, Sir David Balfour, Colonel Brog, who took a Spanish general in the field upon the head of his army; Sir Francis Henderson, Colonel Scot, Earl of Bucliugh, Colonel Sir James Livistoun, now Earl of Calander, and lately in these our tourmoyles at home lieutenant-general of both horse and foot, besides a great many other worthy colonels, amongst which I will only commemorate one, named Colonel Dowglas, who to the States of Holland was often times serviceable, in discharging the office and duty of general engineer; whereof they are now so sensible, that, to have him alive againe, and of that vigour and freshness in body and spirit, wherewith he was endowed in the day he was killed on, they would give thrice his weight in gold; and well they might; for some few weeks before the fight wherein he was slaine, he presented to them twelve articles and heads of such wonderful feats for the use of the wars both by sea and land, to be performed by him, flowing from the remotest springs of mathematical secrets, and those of natural philosophy, that none of this age saw, nor any of our fore-fathers ever heard the like, save what out of Cicero, Livy, Plutarch, and other old Greek and Latin writers we have couched, of the admirable inventions made use of by Archimedes in defence of the city of Syracusa, against the continual assaults of the Romane forces both by sea and land, under the conduct of Marcellus.   To speak really, I think there hath not been any in this age of the Scotish nation, save Neper and Crichtoun, who, for abilities of the minde in matter of practical inventions useful for men of industry, merit to be compared with him; and yet of these two, notwithstanding their excellency in learning, I would be altogether silent, because I made account to mention no other Scotish men here, but such as have been famous for souldiery, and brought up at the schoole of Mars, were it not that, besides their profoundness in literature, they were inriched with military qualifications beyond expression.   As for Neper, otherwayes designed Lord Marchiston, he is for his logarithmical device so compleatly praised in that preface of the author's, which ushers a trigonometrical book of his, intituled *The Trissotetras*, that to add any more thereunto, would but obscure with an empty sound, the clearness of what is already said; therefore I will allow him no share in this discourse, but in so far as concerneth an almost incomprehensible device, which being in the mouths of the most of Scotland, and yet unknown to any that ever was in the world but himself, deserveth very well to be taken notice of in this place; and it is this: he had the skill, as is commonly reported, to frame an engine, for invention not much unlike that of Architas Dove, which, by vertue of some secret springs, inward resorts, with other implements and materials fit for the purpose, inclosed within the bowels thereof, had the power, if proportionable in bulk to the action required of it, for he could have made it of all sizes, to clear a field of four miles circumference, of all the living creatures exceeding a foot of hight, that should be found thereon, how neer soever they might be to one another; by which means he made it appear that he was able, with the help of this machine alone, to kill thirty thousand Turkes, without the hazard of one Christian.   Of this it is said, that, upon a wager, he gave proof upon a large plaine in Scotland, to the destruction of a great many herds of cattel, and flocks of sheep, whereof some were distant from other half a mile on all sides, and some a whole mile. To continue the thred of the story, as I have it, I must not forget, that, when he was most earnestly desired by an old acquaintance and professed friend of his, even about the time of his contracting that disease whereof he dyed, he would be pleased, for the honour of his family, and his own everlasting memory to posterity, to reveal unto him the manner of the contrivance of so ingenious a mystery; subjoining thereto, for the better perswading of him, that it were a thousand pities that so excellent an invention should be buryed with him in the grave, and that after his decease nothing should be known thereof; his answer was, That for the ruine and overthrow of man, there were too many devices already framed, which, if he could make to be fewer, he would with all his might endeavour to do; and that therefore seeing the malice and rancor rooted in the heart of mankind will not suffer them to diminish, by any new conceit of his, the number of them should never be increased. Divinely spoken, truly.

To speak a little now of his compatriot Crichtoun, I hope will not offend the ingenuous reader; who may know, by what is already displayed, that it cannot be heterogeneal from the proposed purpose, to make report of that magnanimous act atchieved by him at the Duke of Mantua's court, to the honour not only of his own, but to the eternal renown also of the whole Isle of Britain; the manner whereof was thus.

A certaine Italian gentleman, of a mighty, able, strong, nimble, and vigorous body, by nature fierce, cruell, warlike, and audacious, and in the gladiatory art so superlatively expert and dextrous, that all the most skilful teachers of Escrime, and fencing-masters of Italy, which in matter of choice professors in that faculty, needed never as yet to yeild to any nation in the world, were by him beaten to their good behaviour, and by blows and thrusts given in, which they could not avoid, enforced to acknowledge him their over comer; bethinking himself, how, after so great a conquest of reputation, he might by such means be very suddenly enriched, he projected a course of exchanging the blunt to sharp, and the foiles into tucks. And in this resolution providing a purse full of gold, worth neer upon four hundred pounds English money, traveled alongst the most especial and considerable parts of Spaine, France, the Low-Countryes, Germany, Pole, Hungary, Greece, Italy, and other places, where ever there was greatest probability of encountring with the eagerest and most atrocious duellists. And immediately after his arrival to any city or town that gave apparent likelihood of some one or other champion that would enter the lists and cope with him, he boldly challenged them with sound of trumpet, in the chief market-place, to adventure an equal sum of money against that of his, to be disputed at the sword's point who should have both. There failed not several brave men, almost of all nations, who accepting of his cartels, were not afraid to hazard both their person and coine against him; but, till he midled with this Crichtoun, so maine was the ascendent he had above all his antagonists, and so unlucky the fate of such as offered to scuffle with him, that all his opposing combatants, of what state or dominion soever they were, who had not lost both their life and gold, were glad, for the preservation of their person, though sometimes with a great expence of blood, to leave both their reputation and mony behind them. At last, returning homewards to his own country, loaded with honor and wealth, or rather the spoile of the reputation of those forraginers, whom the Italians call Tramontani, he, by the way, after his accustomed manner of abording other places, repaired to the city of Mantua, where the Duke, according to the courtesie usually bestowed on him by other princes, vouchsafed him a protection and savegard for his person: he, as formerly he was wont to do, by beat of drum, sound of trumpet, and several printed papers, disclosing his designe, battered on all the chief gates, posts, and pillars of the town, gave all men to understand, that his purpose was to challenge, at the single rapier, any whosoever of that city or country that durst be so bold as to fight with him, provided he would deposite a bag of five hundred Spanish pistols over against another of the same value, which himself should lay down, upon this condition, that the enjoyment of both should be the conqueror's due. His challenge was not long unanswered, for it happened, at the same time, that three of the most notable cutters in the world, and so highly cryed up for valour, that all the bravos of the land were content to give way to their domineering, how insolent soever they should prove, because of their former constantly obtained victories in the field, were all three together at the court of Mantua, who, hearing of such a harvest of five hundred pistols to be reaped, as they expected, very soon, and with ease, had almost contested amongst themselves for the priority of the first encounterer, but that one of my Lord Duke's courtiers moved them to cast lots for who should be first, second, and third, in case none of the former two should prove victorious. Without more adoe, he whose chance it was to answer the cartel with the first defiance, presented himself within the barriers, or place appointed for the fight, where, his adversary attending him, as soon as the trumpet sounded a charge, they jointly fel to work; and, because I am not now to amplifie the particulars of a combat, although the dispute was very hot for a while, yet, whose fortune it was to be the first of the three in the field, had the disaster to be the first of the three that was foyled; for, at last, with a thrust in the throat, he was killed dead upon the ground. This, nevertheless, not a whit dismayed the other two, for the nixt day he that was second in the roll, gave his appearance after the same manner as the first had done, but with no better success; for he likewise was laid flat dead upon the place, by means of a thrust he received in the heart. The last of the three, finding that he was as sure of being engaged in the fight as if he had been the first in order, pluckt up his heart, knit his spirits together, and, on the day after the death of the second, most couragiously entering the lists, demeaned himself for a while with great activity and skill; but at last, his luck being the same with those that preceded him, by a thrust in the belly, he within four and twenty hours after gave up the ghost. These, you may imagine, were lamentable spectacles to the Duke and citie of Mantua, who, casting down their faces for shame, knew not what course to take for reparation of their honour. The conquering duellist, proud of a victory so highly tending to both his honour and profit, for the space of a whole fortnight, or two weeks together, marched daily along the streets of Mantua, without any opposition or controulment, like another Romulus, or

Marcellus in triumph; which, the never too much to be admired Crichtoun perceiving, to wipe off the imputation of cowardise lying upon the court of Mantua, to which he had but even then arrived, although formerly he had been a domestick thereof, he could neither eat nor drink till he had first sent a challenge to the conqueror, appelling him to repair with his best sword in his hand, by nine of the clock in the morning of the next day, in presence of the whole court, and in the same place where he had killed the other three, to fight with him upon this quarrel, that in the court of Mantua there were as valiant men as he; and, for his better encouragement to the desired undertaking, he assured him, that, to the aforesaid five hundred pistols, he would adjoyn a thousand more, wishing him to do the like, that the victor, upon the point of his sword, might carry away the richer booty. The challenge, with all its conditions, is no sooner accepted of, the time and place mutually condescended upon kept accordingly, and the fifteen hundred pistols *hinc inde* deposited, but of the two rapiers of equal weight, length, and goodness, each taking one, in presence of the Duke, Duchess, with all the noblemen, ladies, magnificos, and all the choicest of men, women, and maids of that citie, as soon as the signal for the duel was given, by the shot of a great piece of ordnance of threescore and four pound ball, the combatants, with a lion like animosity, made their approach to one another, and, being within distance, the valiant Crichtoun, to make his adversary spend his fury the sooner, betook himself to the defensive part; wherein, for a long time, he shewed such excellent dexterity in warding the other's blows, slighting his falsifyings, in breaking measure, and often, by the agility of his body, avoiding his thrust, that he seemed but to play, while the other was in earnest. The sweetness of Crichtoun's countenance, in the hotest of the assault, like a glance of lightning on the hearts of the spectators, brought all the Italian ladies on a sudden to be enamoured of him; whilst the sternness of the other's aspect, he looking like an enraged bear, would have struck terrour into wolves, and affrighted an English mastiff. Though they were both in their linens, to wit, shirts and drawers, without any other apparel, and in all outward conveniences equally adjusted, the Italian, with redoubling his stroaks, foamed at the mouth with a cholerick heart, and fetched a pantling breath; the Scot, in sustaining his charge, kept himself in a pleasant temper, without passion, and made void his designes; he alters his wards from tierce to quart; he primes and seconds it, now high, now lowe, and casts his body, like another Prothee, into all the shapes he can, to spie an open on his adversary, and lay hold of an advantage, but all in vain; for the invincible Crichtoun, whom no cunning was able to surprise, contrepostures his respective wards, and, with an incredible nimbleness of both hand and foot, evades the intent and frustrates the invasion. Now is it, that the never before conquered Italian, finding himself a little faint, enters into a consideration that he may be over matched; whereupon a sad apprehension of danger seizing upon all his spirits, he would gladly have his life bestowed on him as a gift, but that, having never been accustomed to yeeld, he knows not how to beg it. Matchless Crichtoun, seeing it now high time to put a gallant catastrophe to that so long dubious combat, animated with a divinely inspired servencie to fulfil the expectation of the ladies, and crown the Duke's illustrious hopes, changeth his garb, falls to act another part, and, from defender, turn assailant; never did art so grace nature, nor nature second the precepts of art with so much liveliness, and such observancie of time, as when, after he had struck fire out of the steel of his enemie's sword, and gained the feeble thereof with the fort of his own, by angles of the strongest position, he did, by geometrical flourishes of straight and oblique lines, so practically execute the speculative part, that, as if there had been Remoras and secret charms in the variety of his motion, the fierceness of his foe was in a trice transqualified into the numbness of a pageant.   Then was it that, to vindicate the reputation of the Duke's family, and expiate the blood of the three vanquished gentlemen, he alonged a stoccade *de pied ferme;* then recoyling, he advanced another thrust, and lodged it home; after which, retiring again, his right foot did beat the cadence of the blow that pierced the belly of this Italian, whose heart and throat being hit with the two former stroaks, these three franch bouts given in upon the back of the other; besides that, if lines were imagined drawn from the hand that livered them, to the places which were marked by them, they would represent a perfect isosceles triangle, with a perpendicular from the top angle cutting the basis in the middle; they likewise give us to understand, that by them he was to be made a sacrifice of atonement for the slaughter of the three aforesaid gentlemen, who were wounded in the very same parts of their bodies by other such three venees as these, each whereof being mortal; and his vital spirits exhaling as his blood gushed out, all he spoke was this, That seeing he could not live, his comfort in dying was, that he could not dye by the hand of a braver man; after the uttering of which words, he expiring, with the shril clareens of trumpets, bouncing thunder of artillery, bethwacked beating of drums, universal clapping of hands, and loud acclamations of joy for so glorious a victory, the aire above them was so rarified by the extremity of the noise and vehement sound, dispelling the thickest and most condensed parts thereof, that, as Plutarch speakes of the Grecians, when they raised their shouts of allegress up to the very heavens at the hearing of the gracious proclamations of Paulus Æmilius in favour of their liberty, the very sparrows and other flying fowls were said to fall to the ground for want of aire enough to uphold them in their flight.

When this sudden rapture was over, and all husht into its former tranquility, the noble gallantry and generosity, beyond expression, of the inimitable Crichtoun, did transport them all againe into a new extasie of ravishment, when they saw him like an angel in the shape of a man, or as another Mars, with the conquered enemies sword in one hand, and the fifteen hundred pistols he had gained in the other, present the sword to the Duke as his due, and the gold to his high treasurer, to be disponed equally to the three widowes of the three unfortunate gentlemen lately slaine, reserving only to himself the inward satisfaction he conceived, for having so opportunely discharged his duty to the House of Mantua.

The reader perhaps will think this wonderful; and so would I too, were it not that I know, as Sir Philip Sydney sayes, that a wonder is no wonder in a wonderful subject, and consequently not in him, who for his learning, judgement, valour, eloquence, beauty, and good-fellowship, was the perfectest result of the joynt labour of the perfect number of those six deities, Pallas, Apollo, Mars, Mercury, Venus, and Bacchus, that hath been seen since the dayes of Alcibiades; for he was reported to have been inriched with a memory so prodigious, that any sermon, speech, harangue, or other manner of discourse of an hour's continuance, he was able to recite without hesitation, after the same manner of gesture and pronuntiation, in all points, wherewith it was delivered at first; and of so stupendious a judgment and conception, that almost naturally he understood quiddities of philosophy; and as for the abstrusest and most researched mysteries of other disciplines, arts, and faculties, the intentional species of them were as readily obvious to the interiour view and perspicacity of his mind, as those of the common visible colours to the external sight of him that will open his eyes to look upon them; of which accomplishment and Encyclopedia of knowledge, he gave on a time so marvelous a testimony at Paris, that the words of *Admirabilis Scotus*, the Wonderful Scot, in all the several tongues and idiomes of Europ, were, for a great while together, by the most of the echos resounded to the peircing of the very clouds. To so great a hight and vast extent of praise, did the never too much to be extolled reputation of the seraphick wit of that eximious man attaine, for his commanding to be affixed programs, on all the gates of the schooles, halls, and colledges of that famous university, as also on all the chief pillars and posts standing before the houses of the most renowned men for literature, resident within the precinct of the walls and suburbs of that most populous and magnificent city, inviting them all, or any whoever else versed in any kinde of scholastick faculty, to repaire at nine of the clock in the morning of such a day, moneth, and yeer, as by computation came to be just six weeks after the date of the affixes, to the common schoole of the colledge of Navarre, where, at the prefixed time, he should, God willing, be ready to answer to what should be propounded to him concerning any science, liberal art, discipline, or faculty, practical or theoretick, not excluding the theological nor jurisprudential habits, though grounded but upon the testimonies of God and man, and that in any of these twelve languages, Hebrew, Syriack, Arabick, Greek, Latin, Spanish, French, Italian, English, Dutch, Flemish, and Sclavonian, in either verse or prose, at the discretion of the disputant; which high enterprise and hardy undertaking, by way of challenge to the learndst men in the world, damped the wits of many able scholars to consider whether it was the attempt of a fanatick spirit, or lofty designe of a well-poised judgment; yet after a few days enquiry concerning him, when information was got of his incomparable endowments, all the choicest and most profound philosophers, mathematicians, naturalists, mediciners, alchymists, apothecaries, surgeons, doctors of both civil and canon law, and divines both for controversies and positive doctrine, together with the primest grammarians, rhetoricians, logicians and others, professors of other arts and disciplines at Paris, plyed their studys in their private cels for the space of a moneth, exceeding hard, and with huge paines and labor set all their braines awork how to contrive the knurriest arguments, and most difficult questions could be devised, thereby to puzzle him in the resolving of them, meander him in his answers, put him out of his medium, and drive him to a *non plus ;* nor did they forget to premonish the ablest there of forraign nations not to be unprepared to dispute with him in their own maternal dialects, and that sometimes metrically, sometimes otherwayes, *pro libitu.* All this while, the Admirable Scot, for so from thenceforth he was called, minding more his hawking, hunting, tilting, vaulting, riding of well managed horses, tossing of the pike, handling of the musket, flourishing of colours, dancing, fencing, swimming, jumping, throwing of the bar, playing at the tennis, baloon, or long catch ; and sometimes at the house games of dice, cards, playing at the chess, billiards, trou-madam, and other such like chamber sports, singing, playing on the lute, and other musical instruments, masking, balling, reveling ; and, which did most of all divert, or rather distract him from his speculations and serious employments, being more addicted to, and plying closer the courting of handsome ladyes, and a jovial cup in the company of bacchanalian blades, then the forecasting how to avoid, shun, and escape the snares, grins, and nets of the hard, obscure, and hidden arguments, ridles, and demands, to be made, framed, and woven by the professors, doctors, and others of that thrice-renowned university. There arose upon him an aspersion of too great proness to such like debordings and youthful emancipations, which occasioned one less acquainted with himself then his reputation, to subjoyn, some two weeks before the great day appointed, to that program of his, which was fixed on the Sorbone gate, these words : " If you would meet with this monster of perfection, to make search for him, either in the taverne or bawdy-house, is the readyest way to finde him." By reason of which expression, though truly as I think, both scandalous and false, the eminent sparks of the university, imagining that those papers of provocation had been set up to no other end, but to scoff and delude them, in making them waste their spirits upon quirks and quiddities, more then was fitting, did resent a little of their former toyle, and slack their studyes, becoming almost regardless thereof, till the several peals of bells ringing an hour or two before the time assigned, gave warning that the party was not to flee the barriers, nor decline the hardship of academical assaults ; but, on the contrary, so confident in his former resolution, that he would not shrink to sustaine the shock of all their disceptations. This sudden alarm so awaked them out of their last fortnight's lethargy, that calling to minde the best way they might, the fruits of the foregoing moneth's labour, they hyed to the fore-named schoole with all diligence ; where, after all of them had, according to their several degrees and qualities, seated

themselves, and that by reason of the noise occasioned through the great confluence of
people, which so strange a novelty brought thither out of curiosity, an universal silence
was commanded, the Orator of the university, in most fluent Latine, addressing his
speech to Crichtoun, extolled him for his literature and other good parts, and for that
confident opinion he had of his own sufficiency, in thinking himself able to justle in
matters of learning with the whole university of Paris. Crichtoun answering him in
no less eloquent terms of Latine, after he had most heartily thanked him for his elogies, so undeservedly bestowed, and darted some high encomiums upon the university
and the professors therein; he very ingeniously protested that he did not emit his programs out of any ambition to be esteemed able to enter in competition with the university, but meerly to be honoured with the favour of a publick conference with the
learned men thereof.   In complements after this manner, *ultro citroque habitis*, tossed
to and again, retorted, contrerisposted, backreverted, and now and then graced with a
quip or a clinch for the better relish of the ear, being unwilling in this kind of strain-
ing curtesie to yeeld to other, they spent a full half hour and more; for he being the
centre to which the innumerable diameters of the discourses of that circulary convention did tend, although none was to answer but he, any of them all, according to the
order of their prescribed series, were permitted to reply, or commence new motions on
any subject in what language soever, and howsoever expressed; to all which, he being
bound to tender himself a respondent, in matter and form suitable to the impugners
propounding, he did first so transcendently acquit himself of that circumstantial kinde
of oratory, that, by well-couched periods, and neatly running syllables, in all the
twelve languages, both in verse and prose, he expressed to the life his courtship and
civility; and afterwards, when the Rector of the university, unwilling to have any more
time bestowed on superficial rhetorick, or to have that wasted on the fondness of quaint
phrases, which might be better employed in a reciprocacy of discussing scientifically
the nature of substantial things, gave direction to the professors to fall on, each according to the dignity or precedency of his faculty, and that conform to the order given.
Some metaphysical notions were set abroach, then mathematical, and of those arithmetical, geometrical, astronomical, musical, optical, cosmographical, trigonometrical,
statical, and so forth through all the other branches of the prime and mother sciences
thereof; the next bout was through all natural philosophy, according to Aristotle's
method, from the acroamaticks, going along the speculation of the nature of the heavens,
and that of the generation and corruption of sublinary things, even to the consideration
of the soul and its faculties; in sequel hereof, they had a hint at chymical extractions,
and spoke of the principles of corporeal and mixed bodies, according to the precepts of
that art.   After this, they disputed of medicine, in all its thereapeutick, pharmacopeu-
tick, and chirurgical parts; and not leaving natural magick untouched, they had exquisite disceptations concerning the secrets thereof.   From thence they proceeded to
moral philosophy, where, debating of the true enumeration of all vertues and vices,

they had most learned ratiocinations about the chief good of the life of man; and seeing the œcumenicks and politicks are parts of that philosophy, they argued learned-ly of all the several sorts of governments, with their defects and advantages; where-upon perpending, that, without an established law, all the duties of ruling and sub-jection, to the utter ruine of humane society, would he be as often violated as the irre-gularity of passion, seconded with power, should give way thereto. The Sorbonist, canonical, and civilian doctors most judiciously argued with him about the most pru-dential maximes, sentences, ordinances, acts, and statutes for ordering all manner of persones in their consciences, bodyes, fortunes, and reputation; nor was there an end put to those literate exercitations till the grammarians, rhetoricians, poets and logicians had assailed him with all the subtleties and nicest quodlibets their respective habits could afford. Now when, to the admiration of all that were there, the incomparable Crichtoun had, in all these faculties above written, and in any of the twelve languages wherein he was spoke to, whether in verse or prose, held tack to all the disputants, who were accounted the ablest scholars upon the earth in each their own profession, and publickly evidenced such an universality of knowledge, and accurate promptness in resolving of doubts, distinguishing of obscurities, expressing the members of a distinc-tion in adequate terms of art, explaining those compendious tearms with words of a more easie apprehension to the prostrating of the sublimest mysteries to any vulgar capacity, and with all excogitable variety of learning, to his own everlasting fame, en-tertained, after that kinde, the nimble witted Parisians from nine o'clock in the morn-ing till six at night; the Rector now finding it high time to give some relaxation to these worthy spirits, which, during such a long space, had been so intensively bent upon the abstrusest speculations, rose up, and saluting the divine Crichtoun, after he had made an elegant panegyrick, or encomiastick speech of half an houre's continuance, tending to nothing else but the extolling of him for the rare and most singular gifts wherewith God and nature had endowed him, he descended from his chaire, and, attend-ed by three or four of the most especial professors, presented him with a diamond ring and a purse ful of gold, wishing him to accept thereof, if not as a recompense propor-tional to his merit, yet as a badge of love, and testimony of the universitie's favour towards him. At the tender of which ceremony, there was so great a plaudite in the schoole, such a humming and clapping of hands, that all the concavities of the col-ledges there about did resound with the eccho of the noise thereof.

Notwithstanding the great honor thus purchased by him for his literary accom-plishments, and that many excellent spirits, to obteine the like, would be content to postpose all other employments to the enjoyment of their studyes, he, nevertheless, the very next day, to refresh his braines, as he said, for the toile of the former day's work, went to the Louvre in a buff-suit, more like a favourite of Mars then one of the Muses minions; where, in presence of some Princes of the court, and great ladies, that came to behold his gallantry, he carryed away the ring fifteen times on end, and broke as many lances on the Saracen.

When for a quarter of a yeer together he after this manner had disported himself, what martially, what scholastically, with the best qualified men in any faculty so ever, that so large a city, which is called the world's abridgement, was able to afford, and now and then solaced these his more serious recreations, for all was but sport to him, with the alluring imbellishments of the tendrer sexe, whose *inamorato* that he might be was their ambition; he on a sudden took resolution to leave the Court of France and return to Italy, where he had been bred for many yeers together; which designe he prosecuting within the space of a moneth, without troubling himself with long journeys, he arrived at the Court of Mantua, where immediately after his abord, as hath been told already, he fought the memorable combat whose description is above related.   Here was it that the learned and valiant Crichtoun was pleased to cast anchor and fix his abode; nor could he almost otherwise do, without disobliging the Duke, and the Prince his eldest son; by either whereof he was so dearly beloved, that none of them would permit him by any means to leave their Court, whereof he was the only privado, the object of all men's love, and subject of their discourse; the example of the great ones, and wonder of the meaner people; the paramour of the female sexe, and paragon of his own.   In the glory of which high estimation having resided at that Court above two whole yeers, the reputation of gentlemen there was hardly other-wayes valued but by the measure of his acquaintance; nor were the young unmaryed ladies, of all the most eminent places thereabouts, any thing respected of one another, that had not either a lock of his hair, or copy of verses of his composing.   Neverthe-less it happening on a Shrove-tuesday at night, at which time it is in Italy very cus-tomary for men of great sobriety, modesty, and civil behaviour all the rest of the yeer, to give themselves over on that day of carnavale, as they call it, to all manner of riot, drunkenness, and incontinency, which that they may do with the least imputation they can to their credit, they go maskt and mum'd with vizards on their faces, and in the disguise of a Zanni or Pantaloon to ventilate their fopperies, and sometimes intolerable enormities, without suspicion of being known, that this ever renowned Crichtoun, who, in the afternoon of that day, at the desire of my Lord Duke, the whole court striving which should exceed other in foolery, and devising of the best sports to excite laugh-ter; neither my Lord, the Dutchess, nor Prince, being exempted from acting their parts, as well as they could, upon a theater set up for the purpose, begun to prank it, *a la Venetiana*, with such a flourish of mimick and ethopoetick gestures, that all the courtiers of both sexes, even those that a little before that were fondest of their own conceits, at the sight of his so inimitable a garb, from ravishing actors that they were before, turned then ravished spectators.   O with how great liveliness did he represent the conditions of all manner of men! how naturally did he set before the eyes of the beholders the rogueries of all professions, from the overweening monarch to the peevish swaine, through all the intermediate degrees of the superficial courtier or proud warrior, dissembled churchman, doting old man, cozening lawyer, lying traveler, covetous merchant, rude seaman, pedantick scholar, the amourous shepheard, envious artisan, vainglorious master, and tricky servant; he did with such variety display the several humours of all these sorts of people, and with a so bewitching energy, that he seemed to be the original, they the counterfeit; and they the resemblance whereof he was the prototype.   He had all the jeers, squibs, flouts, buls, quips, taunts, whims, jests, clinches, gybes, mokes, jerks, with all the several kinds of equivocations, and other sophistical captions, that could properly be adapted to the person by whose representation he intended to inveagle the company into a fit of mirth; and would keep in that miscelany discourse of his, which was all for the splene, and nothing for the gall, such a climacterical and mercurially digested method, that when the fancy of the hearers was tickled with any rare conceit, and that the jovial blood was moved, he held it going with another new device upon the back of the first, and another, yet another, and another againe, succeeding one another for the promoval of what is a-stirring into a higher agitation; till in the closure of the luxuriant period, the decumanal wave of the oddest whimzy of all, enforced the charmed spirits of the auditory, for affording room to its apprehension, suddenly to burst forth into a laughter, which commonly lasted just so long as he had leisure to withdraw behind the skreen, shift off with the help of a page, the suite he had on, apparel himself with another, and return to the stage to act afresh; for by that time their transported, disparpled, and sublimated fancies, by the wonderfully operating engines of his solacious inventions, had from the hight to which the inward scrues, wheeles, and pullies of his wit had elevated them, descended by degrees into their wonted stations, he was ready for the personating of another carriage; whereof to the number of fourteen several kinds, during the five hours space that at the Duke's desire, the solicitation of the court, and his own recreation, he was pleased to histrionize it, he shewed himself so natural a representative, that any would have thought he had been so many several actors, differing in all things else, save the only stature of the body; with this advantage above the most of other actors, whose tongue, with its oral implements, is the onely instrument of their mind's disclosing, that, besides his mouth with its appurtenances, he lodged almost a several oratour in every member of his body; his head, his eyes, his shoulder, armes, hands, fingers, thighs, legs, feet, and breast, being able to decipher any passion, whose character he purposed to give.

First, he did present himself with a crown on his head, a scepter in his hand, being clothed in a purple robe furred with ermyne; after that, with a miter on his head, a crosier in his hand, and accoutred with a paire of lawn-sleeves; and thereafter, with a helmet on his head, the visiere up, a commanding stick in his hand, and arayed in a buff-suit, with a scarf about his middle.   Then, in a rich apparel, after the newest fashion, did he shew himself, like another Sejanus, with a periwig daubed with Cypres powder ; in sequel of that, he came out with a three corner'd cap on his head, some parchments in his hand, and writings hanging at his girdle like Chancery bills ; and next to that, with a furred gown about him, an ingot of gold in his hand, and a bag full of money by his side ; after all this, he appeares againe clad in a country-jacket, with a prong in his hand, and a Monmouth-like-cap on his head ; then very shortly after, with a palmer's coat upon him, a bourdon in his hand, and some few cockle-shels stuck to his hat, he look'd as if he had come in pilgrimage from Saint Michael ; immediately after that, he domineers it in a bare unlined gowne, with a pair of whips in the one hand, and Corderius in the other ; and in suite thereof, he honderspondered it with a pair of pannier-like breeches, a mountera-cap on his head, and a knife in a wooden sheath dagger-ways by his side ; about the latter end, he comes forth again with a square in one hand, a rule in the other, and a leather apron before him ; then very quickly after, with a scrip by his side, a sheep-hook in his hand, and a basket full of flowers to make nosegayes for his mistris ; now drawing to a closure, he rants it first *in cuerpo*, and vapouring it with gingling spurs, and his armes a kenbol like a Don Diego he strouts it, and by the loftiness of his gate, plaies the Capitan Spavento ; then in the very twinkling of an eye, you would have seen him againe issue forth with a cloak upon his arm, in a livery garment, thereby representing the serving-man ; and lastly, at one time amongst those other, he came out with a long gray beard, and bucked ruff, crouching on a staff tip't with the head of a barber's cithern, and his gloves hanging by a button at his girdle.

Those fifteen several personages he did represent with such excellency of garb, and exquisiteness of language, that condignely to perpend the subtlety of the invention, the method of the disposition, the neatness of the elocution, the gracefulness of the action, and wonderful variety in the so dextrous performance of all, you would have taken it for a comedy of five acts, consisting of three scenes, each composed by the best poet in the world, and acted by fifteen of the best players that ever lived, as was most evidently made apparent to all the spectators in the fifth and last hour of his action, which, according to our western account, was about six a clock at night, and by the calculation of that country, half an hour past three and twenty, at that time of the yeer ; for, purposing to leave of with the setting of the sun, with an endeavour nevertheless to make his conclusion the master-piece of the work, he, to that effect, summoning all his spirits together, which never failed to be ready at the cal of so worthy a commander, did by their assistance, so conglomerate, shuffle, mix, and inter-lace the gestures, inclinations, actions, and very tones of the speech of those fifteen several sorts of men, whose carriages he did personate into an inestimable ollapodrida of immaterial morsels of divers kinds, suitable to the very ambrosian relish of the Heli-conian nymphs, that, in the peripetia of this drammatical exercitation, by the inchanted transportation of the eyes and eares of its spectabundal auditorie, one would have sworne that they all had looked with multiplying glasses, and that, like that angel in the Scripture whose voice was said to be like the voice of a multitude, they heard in him alone the promiscuous speech of fifteen several actors; by the various ravishments of the excellencies whereof, in the frolickness of a jocund straine beyond expectation, the logofascinated spirits of the beholding hearers and auricularie spectators, were so on a sudden seazed upon in their risible faculties of the soul, and all their vital motions so universally affected in this extremitie of agitation, that, to avoid the inevitable charmes of his intoxicating ejaculations, and the accumulative influences of so powerfull a transportation, one of my lady Dutchess' chief maids of honour, by the vehemencie of the shock of those incomprehensible raptures, burst forth into a laughter to the rupture of a veine in her body; and another young lady, by the irresistible violence of the pleasure unawares infused, where the tender receptibilitie of her too tickled fancie was least able to hold out, so unprovidedly was surprised, that, with no less impetuositie of ridibundal passion then, as hath been told, occasioned a fracture in the other young ladie's modestie, she, not being able longer to support the well beloved burthen of so excessive delight, and intransing joys of such mercurial exhilations through the ineffable extasie of an overmastered apprehension, fell back in a swown, without the appearance of any other life into her then what, by the most refined wits of theological speculators, is conceived to be exerced by the purest parts of the separated entelechises of blessed saints in their sublimest conversations with the celestial hierarchies; this accident procured the incoming of an apothecary with restoratives, as the other did that of a surgeon with consolidative medicaments. The Admirable Crichtoun now perceiving that it was drawing somewhat late, and that our occidental rays of Phœbus were upon their turning oriental to the other hemisphere of the terrestrial globe; being withall jealous that the uninterrupted operation of the exuberant diversitie of his jovialissime entertainment, by a continuate winding up of the humours there present to a higher, yet higher, and still higher pitch, above the supremest Lydian note of the harmonie of voluptuousness, should, in such a case, through the too intensive stretching of the already super-elated strings of their imagination, with a transcendencie over-reaching Ela, and beyond the well concerted gam of rational equanimitie, involve the remainder of that illustrious companie into the sweet labyrinth and mellifluent aufractuosities of a lacinious delectation, productive of the same inconveniences which befel the two afore-named ladies; whose delicacie of constitution, though sooner overcome, did not argue, but that the same extranean causes from him proceeding of their pathetick alteration, might by a longer insisting in an efficacious agencie, and unremitted working of all the consecutively imprinted degrees that the capacity of the patient is able to containe, prevaile at last, and have the same predominancie over the dispositions of the strongest complexioned males of that splendid society, did, in his own ordinary wearing apparel, with the countenance of a Prince, and garb befitting the person of a so well bred gentleman and cavalier, καῦ ἐξοχην, full of majestie, and repleat with all excogitable civilitie, to the amazement of all that beheld his heroick gesture, present himself to epilogate this his almost extemporanean comedie, though of five hours continuance without intermission; and that with a peroration so neatly uttered, so distinctly pronounced, and in such elegancie of selected tearmes, expressed by a diction so periodically contexed with isocoly of members, that the matter thereof tending in all humility to beseech the highnesses of the Duke, Prince, and Dutchess, together with the remanent lords, ladies, knights, gentlemen, and others of both sexes of that honorable convention, to vouchsafe him the favour to excuse his that afternoon's escaped extravagancies, and to lay the blame of the indigested irregularity of his wits excursions, and the abortive issues of his disordered brain, upon the customarily dispensed with priviledges in those Cisalpinal regions, to authorize such like impertinences at Carnavalian festivals; and that, although, according to the most commonly received opinion in that country, after the nature of Load-him, a game at cards where he that wins loseth, he who, at that season of the year, playeth the fool most egregiously, is reputed the wisest man; he, nevertheless, not being ambitious of the fame of enjoying good qualities, by vertue of the antiphrasis of the fruition of bad ones, did meerly undergo that emancipatorie task of a so profuse liberty, and to no other end embraced the practising of such roaming and exorbitant diversions but to give an evident, or rather infallible demonstration of his eternally bound duty to the House of Mantua, and an inviolable testimony of his never to be altered designe, in prosecuting all the occasions possible to be laid hold on that can in any manner of way prove conducible to the advancement of, and contributing to the readiest means for improving those advantages that may best promove the faculties of making all his choice endeavours, and utmost abilities at all times, effectual to the long wished for furtherance of his most cordial and endeared service to the serenissime highnesses of my Lord Duke, Prince and Dutchess, and of consecrating with all addicted obsequiousness, and submissive devotion, his everlasting obedience to the illustrious shrine of their joynt commands. Then incontinently addressing himself to the lords, ladies, and others of that rotonda, which, for his daigning to be its inmate, though but for that day, might be accounted in nothing inferiour to the great Colisee of Rome, or Amphitheater at Neems, with a stately carriage, and port suitable to so prime a gallant, he did cast a look on all the corners thereof, so bewitchingly amiable and magically efficacious as if in his eys had bin a muster of ten thousand cupids eagerly striving who should most deeply pierce the hearts of the spectators with their golden darts. And truly so it fell out, that there not being so much as one arrow shot in vain, all of them did love him, though not after the same manner, nor for the same end; for, as the manna of the Arabian desarts is said to have had in the mouths of the Egyptian Israelites, the very same tast of the meat they loved best, so the Princes that were there did mainly cherish him for his magnanimity and knowledge; his courtliness and sweet behaviour being that for which chiefly the noblemen did most respect him; for his pregnancie of wit, and chivalrie in vindicating the honour of ladies, he was honoured by the knights, and the esquires and other gentlemen courted him for his affability and good fellowship; the rich did favour him for his judgment and ingeniosity, and for his liberality and munificence, he was blessed by the poor; the old men affected him for his constancie and wisdome, and the young for his mirth and gallantry; the scholars were enamoured of him for his learning and eloquence, and the souldiers for his integrity and valour; the merchants, for his upright dealing and honesty, praised and extolled him, and the artificers for his goodness and benignity; the chastest lady of that place would have hugged and imbraced him for his discretion and ingenuity; whilst for his beauty and comeliness of person he was, at least in the fervency of their desires, the paramour of the less continent; he was dearly beloved of the fair women, because he was handsome, and of the fairest more dearly, because he was handsomer: in a word, the affections of the beholders, like so many several diameters drawn from the circumference of their various intents, did all concenter in the point of his perfection. After a so considerable insinuation, and gaining of so much ground upon the hearts of the auditory, though in shorter space then the time of a flash of lightning, he went on, as before, in the same thred of the conclusive part of his discourse, with a resolution not to cut it, till the over abounding passions of the company, their exorbitant motions and discomposed gestures, through excess of joy and mirth, should be all of them quieted, calmed, and pacified, and every man, woman, and maid there, according to their humour, reseated in the same integrity they were at first; which when, by the articulatest elocution of the most significant words, expressive of the choisest things that fancie could suggest, and, conforme to the matter's variety, elevating or depressing, flat or sharply accinating it, with that proportion of tone that was most consonant with the purpose, he had attained unto, and by his verbal harmony and melodious utterance, setled all their distempered pleasures, and brought their disorderly raised spirits into their former capsuls, he with a tongue tip't with silver, after the various diapasons of all his other expressions, and making of a leg for the spruceness of its courtsie, of greater decorement to him then cloth of gold and purple, farewel'd the companie with a complement of one period so exquisitely delivered, and so well attended by the gracefulness of his hand and foot, with the quaint miniardise of the rest of his body, in the performance of such ceremonies as are usual at a court-like departing, that from the theater he had gone into a lobie, from thence along three spacious chambers, whence descending a back staire, he past through a low gallerie which led him to that outer gate, where a coach with six horses did attend him, before that magnificent convention of both sexes, to whom that room, wherein they all were, seemed in his absence to be as a body without a soul, had the full leisure to recollect their spirits, which, by the neatness of his so curious a close, were *quoquoversedly* scattered with admiration, to advise on the best expediency how to dispose of themselves for the future of that licentious night. During which time of their being thus in a maze, a proper young lady, if ever there was any in the world, whose dispersed spirits, by her

wonderful delight in his accomplishments, were by the power of Cupid, with the assistance of his mother, instantly gathered and replaced, did upon his retiring, without
taking notice of the intent of any other, rise up out of her boxe, issue forth at a pos-
terne door into some secret transes, from whence going down a few steps that brought
her to a parlour, she went through a large hall; by the wicket of one end whereof, as
she entered on the street, she encountered with Crichtoun, who was but even then
come to the aforesaid coach, which was hers, unto which *sans ceremony*, waving the
frivolous windings of dilatory circumstances, they both stepped up together, without
any other in their company save a waiting gentlewoman that sate in the furthest side
of the coach, a page that lifted up the boot thereof, and walked by it, and one lacky
that ran before with a kindled torch in his hand, all domestick servants of hers, as
were the coachman and postillion, who, driving apace, and having but half a mile to
go, did, with all the expedition required, set down my lady with her beloved mate at the
great gate of her own palace, through the wicket whereof, because she would not stay
till the whole were made wide open, they entered both; and injunction being given,
that forthwith after the setting up of the coach and horses, the gate should be made
fast, and none, more then was already, permitted to come within her court that night,
they joyntly went along a private passage which led them to a lanterne scalier, whose
each step was twelve foot long; thence mounting up a paire of staires, they past
through and traversed above nine several rooms on a floor before they reached her
bed-chamber; which, in the interim of the progress of their transitory walk, was with
such mutual cordialness so unanimously aimed at, that never did the passengers of a
ship in a tedious voyage long for a favourable winde with greater uniformity of desire,
then the blessed hearts of that amorous and amiable couple were, without the meanest
variety of a wish, in every jot united. Nevertheless, at last they entered in it, or
rather in an alcoranal paradise, where nothing tending to the pleasure of all the senses
was wanting; the weather being a little chil and coldish, they on a blue velvet couch
sate by one another towards a char-coale fire burning in a silver brasero, whilst in the
next room adjacent thereto a pretty little round table of cedar wood was a covering
for the supping of them two together; the cates prepared for them, and a week before
that time bespoke, were of the choisest dainties and most delicious junkets that all
the territories of Italy were able to afford, and that deservedly, for all the Romane
Empire could not produce a completer paire to taste them. In beauty she was supream, in pedigree equal with the best, in spirit not inferiour to any, and, in matter of
affection, a great admirer of Crichtoun, which was none of her least perfections : she
many times used to repaire to my lady Dutchesses court, where now and then the
Prince would cast himself, as a *l'improviste*, into her way, to catch hold the more conveniently of some one or other opportunity for receiving her employments; with the
favour whereof he very often protested, if she would vouchsafe to honour him, and be
pleased to gratifie his best endeavours with her only gracious acceptance of them,

none breathing should be able to discharge that duty with more zeal to her service, nor reap more inward satisfaction in the performance of it ; for that his obedience could not be crowned with greater glory, then by that of a permanently fixed attendance upon her commandments. His Highness complements, whereof to this noble lady he was at all times very liberal, remained never longer unexchanged then after they were delivered, and that in a coine so pretious, for language, matter, phrase, and elocution, that he was still assured of his being repayed with interest ; by means of which odds of her retaliation, she, though unknown to her self, conquered his affections, and he from thenceforth became her *inamorato ;* but with so close and secret a minde did he harbour in his heart that new love, and nourish the fire thereof in his veins, that remotely skonsing it from the knowledge of all men, he did not so much as acquaint therewith his most intimate friend Crichtoun, who, by that the sun had deprest our western horizon by one half of the quadrant of his orb, did, after supper, with his sweet lady, whom he had by the hand, returne againe to the bed-chamber wherein formerly they were ; and there, without losing of time, which by unnecessary punctilios of strained civility, and affected formalities of officious respect, is very frequently, but too much lavished away, and heedlessly regarded, by the young Adonises and faint-hearted initiants in the exercises of the Cytheræan academy, they barred all the ceremonies of Pindarising their discourse, and sprucifying it in *a la mode* salutations, their mutual carriage shewing it self, as it were, in a meane betwixt the conjugal of man and wife, and fraternal conversation of brother and sister, in the reciprocacy of their love transcending both, in the purity of their thoughts equal to this, and in fruition of pleasure nothing inferior to the other ; for when, after the waiting damsel had, by putting her beautiful mistris into her nocturnal dress, quite impoverished the ornaments of her that dayes wear, in robbing them of the inestimably rich treasure which they inclosed, and then performed the same office to the Lord of her Ladie's affections, by laying aside the impestring bulk of his journal abiliaments, and fitting him, in the singlest manner possible, with the most genuine habit *a la Cypriana* that Cupid could devise ; she, as it became an obsequious servant, and maid observant of her mistrisses directions, bidding them good night with the inarticulate voyce of an humble curtesie, locked the doors of the room behind her, and shut them both in to the reverence of one another, him to her discretion, her to his mercy, and both to the passion of each other ; who then, finding themselves not only together, but alone with other, were in an instant transported both of them with an equal kinde of rapture ; for as he looked on her, and saw the splendor of the beams of her bright eyes, and with what refulgency her alabaster-like skin did shine through the thin cawle of her Idalian garments, her appearance was like the antartick oriency of a western aurore, or acronick rising of the most radient constellation of the firmament ; and whilst she viewed him, and perceived the portliness of his garb, comeliness of his face, sweetness of his countenance, and majesty in his very chevelure, with the goodliness of his frame, proportion

of his limbs, and symmetry in all the parts and joints of his body, which through the
cobweb slenderness of his Cyllenian vestments, were represented almost in their *puris
naturalibus ;* his resemblance was like that of Æneas to Dido, when she said, that he
was in face and shoulders like a god ; or rather to her, he seemed as to the female
deities did Ganimed, when, after being carryed up to heaven, he was brought into the
presence of Jupiter.   Thus for a while their eloquence was mute, and all they spoke,
was but with the eye and hand ; yet so perswasively, by vertue of the intermutual
unlimitedness of their visotactil sensation, that each part and portion of the persons of
either was obvious to the sight and touch of the persons of both ; the visuriency of
either, by ushering the tacturiency of both, made the attrectation of both consequent to
the inspection of either ; here was it that passion was active, and action passive, they
both being overcome by other, and each the conqueror.   To speak of her hirquital-
liency at the elevation of the pole of his microcosme, or of his luxuriousness to erect a
gnomon on her horizontal dyal, will perhaps be held by some to be expressions full of
obscœness, and offensive to the purity of chaste ears ; yet seeing that she was to be his
wife, and that she could not be such without consummation of marriage, which signifieth
the same thing in effect, it may be thought, as *definitiones logicæ verificantur in rebus,*
if the exerced act be lawful, that the diction which suppones it can be of no great
transgression, unless you would call it a *solæcisme,* or that vice in grammar which im-
ports the copulating of the masculine with the feminine gender.   But as the misery of
the life of man is such, that bitterness for the most part is subsequent to pleasure, and
joy the prognostick of grief to come, so the Admirable Crichtoun, or to resume my
discourse where I broke off, I say it hapened on a Shrove-Tuesday at night, that the
ever renowned Crichtoun was warned by a great noise in the streets, to be ready for
the acting of another part ; for the Prince, who till that time from the first houre of
the night inclusively, for the space of four hours together, with all his attendants, had
done nothing else but rantit, roar, and roam from one taverne to another, with haut-
bois, flutes, and trumpets, drinking healths, breaking glasses, tossing pots, whitling
themselves with Septembral juyce, tumbling in the kennel, and acting all the deviseable feats of madness, at least so many as in their irregular judgements did seem might
contrevalue all the penance they should be able to do for them the whole Lent thereafter, being ambitious to have a kiss of his mistriss' hand, for so, in that too frolick
humour of his, he was pleased to call this young lady, before he should go to bed ;
with nine gentlemen at his back, and four pages carrying waxe tapers before him,
comes to the place where Crichtoun and the foresaid lady were, though the Prince
knew nothing of Crichton's being there, and knocks at the outer gate thereof.   No
answer is made at first, for the whole house was in a profound silence, and all of them
in the possession of Morphee, save that blessed pair of pigeon-like lovers, in whom Cupid,
for the discharge of Hymenæan rites, had inspired a joynt determination to turne that
whole night's rest to motion ; but the fates being pleased otherways to dispose of

things then as they proposed them, the clapper is up again, and they rap with a flap, till a threefold clap made the sound to rebound. With this the porter awakes, looks out at a lattice window of his lodge, and seeing them all with masks and vizards on their faces, asked them what their desire was, or what it might be that moved them to come so late in such a disguise? The Prince himself answered, that they were gentlemen desirous onely to salute my lady; which courtesie when obtained, they should forthwith be gone. The porter advertiseth the page and tells him all, who doing the same to the waiting gentlewoman, she, to receive orders from her mistris, opens the chamber doore, enters in, relates the story, and demands direction from my Lady, who immediately bids her call the page to her: she does it; he comes, and enquiring what the will of her *signoria* was with him, she enjoynes him to go down and beseech those gentlemen to be pleased to have her excused for that night, because she was abed, and not so well as she could wish to bear them company; yet if they conceived any fault in her, she should strive to make them amends for it some other time. The page accordingly acquits himself of what is recommended him; for after he had caused open the wicket of the gate, and faced the street, he first saluted them with that court-like dexterity which did bespeak him a well educated boy, and of good parentage, then told them that he was commanded by his Lady mistris to intreat them, seeing she knew not what they were, and that their wearing of vizards did in civility debar her from enquiring after their names, to take in good part her remitting of that their visit to another time, by reason of her present indisposure and great need of rest; which if they should have any pretext to except against, she would heartily make atonement for it, and give them satisfaction at any other time. The Prince's answer was, that he thought not but that he should have been admitted with less ceremony, and that though the time of the night, and his Lady mistriss her being in a posture of rest, might seem to plead somewhat for the non-disturbance of her desired solitariness, that nevertheless the uncontrolled priviledges of the season exempting them from all prescribed, and at all other times observed, boundaries, might in the carnavale-eeve, and supremest night of its law transcendent jollities, by the custome of the whole country, very well apologize for that trespass. Which words being spoken, he, without giving the page leisure to reply, pretending it was cold in the streets, rusht in at the open wicket even into the court, with all his gentlemen and torch-bearers, each one whereof was no less cup-shotten then himself. The page, astonished at such unexpected rudeness, said, with an audible voice, What do you mean, gentlemen? do you intend to break in by violence, and at such an undue time enforce my Lady to grant you admittance? Look, I pray you, to your own reputations; and if regardless of any thing else, consider what imputation and stain of credit wil lye upon you, thus to commit an enormous action because of some colour of justifying it by immunities of set times, grounded upon no reason but meer toleration, without any other warrant then a feeble inveterate prescription; therefore let me beseech you, gentlemen, if you love yourselves, and the continuation of your own good names, or tender any kind of respect to the honor of ladys, that you would be pleased of your own accords, to chuse rather to return from whence you came, or go whither elswhere you will, then to imagin any rational man wil think that your masks and vizards can be sufficient covers wherewith to hide and palliate the deformedness of this obtrusive incivility. One of the Prince's gentlemen, whose braines the fumes of Greek and Italian wines had a little intoxicated, laying hold only upon the last word, all the rest having escaped both his imagination and memory, like an empty sound which makes no impression, and most eagerly grasping at it, like a snarling curr that in his gnarring snatcheth at the taile, echoes it, incivility; then coming up closer to him, and saying, How now Jackanapes, whom do you twit with incivility? he gave him such a sound thwack over the left shoulder with his sword, scabbard and all, that the noise thereof reached to all the corners of my Ladyes bed-chamber; at which the generous page, who, besides his breeding otherwayes, was the son of a nobleman, being a little commoved and vexed at an affront so undeservedly received, and barbarously given, told the Esquire who had wronged him, that if he had but had one drop of any good blood within him, he never would have offered to strike a gentleman that wanted a weapon wherewith to defend himself; and that although he was but of fourteen yeers of age, and for strength but as a springal or stripling in regard of him, he should nevertheless, would any of those other nine gentlemen, as he called them, be pleased to favour him but with the lend of a sword, take upon him even then, and on that place, to humble his cockescomb, pull his crest a little lower down, and make him faine, for the safety of his life, to acknowledge that he is but a base and unworthy man. Whilst the gentleman was about to have shapen him an answer, the Prince, being very much taken with the discretion, wit, garb, and courage of the boy, commanded the other to silence; and forthwith taking the speech in hand himself, commended him very much for his loyalty to his mistris, and, for his better ingratiating in the page's favour, presented him with a rich saphir, to shew him but the way to my Ladyes chamber, where he vowed that, as he was a gentleman, he would make no longer stay then barely might afford him the time to kiss her hands, and take his leave. The sweet boy, being more incensed at the manner of that offer of the Prince, whom he knew not, then at the discourtesie he had sustained by his aforesaid gentleman, plainly assured him, that he might very well put up his saphir into his pocket againe, for that all the gifts in the world should never be able to gaine that of him, which had not ground enough in reason for perswading the grant thereof without them.

After that the Prince and Pomponacio, for so they called the page, had thus for a long time together debated to and againe, the reasons for and against the intended visit, with so little success on either side, that the more artifice was used in the rhetorick, the less effect it had in the perswasion; the Prince, unwilling to miss his mark, and not having in all the quivers of his reason one shaft wherewith to hit it, resolved to interpose some authority with his argumentations, and where the fox's skin could not serve, to make use of the lyon's; to the prosecuting of which intent, he with his vinomadefied retinue, resolved to press in upon the page, and maugre his will, to get up staires, and take their fortune in the quest of the chamber they aimed at; for albeit the stradling as wide as he could, of pretty Pomponacio at the door whereat they made account to force their passage, did for a while retard their designe, because of their chariness to struggle with so hopeful a youth, and tender imp of so great expectation, yet at last being loath to faile of their end, by how indirect meanes soever they might attaine thereto, they were in the very action of crowning their violence with prevalency, when the Admirable and ever-renowned Crichtoun, who at the Prince's first manning of the court taking the alarm, step'd from the shrine of Venus to the oracle of Pallas Armata; and by the help of the waiting gentlewoman, having apparelled himself with a paludamental vesture, after the antick fashion of the illustrious Romans, both for that he minded not to make himself then known, that to walk then in such like disguise was the anniversary custome of all that country, and that all, both gentlemen and others standing in that court, were in their mascaradal garments; with his sword in his hand, like a messenger from the gods, came down to relieve the page from the poste whereat he stood sentry; and when, as the light of the minor planets appeares not before the glorious rayes of Titan, he had obscured the irradiancy of Pomponacio with his more effulgent presence, and that under pretext of turning him to the page to desire him to stand behind him, as he did, he had exposed the full view of his left side, so far as the light of torches could make it perceivable to the lookers on, who being all *in cuerpo* carying swords in their hands, instead of cloaks about them, imagined really, by the badge or cognizance they saw neer his heart, that he was one of my ladie's chief domestick servants; he addressed his discourse to the Prince, and the nine gentlemen that were with him; neither of all whereof, as they were accoutred, was he able, either by the light of the tapers, or that of the moon, which was then but in the first week of its waxing, it being the Tuesday next to the first new moon that followed the purification day, to discern in any manner of way what they were; and for that he perceived by their unstedfast postures, that the influence of the grape had made them subjects to Jacchus, and that their extranean-like demeanour towards him, not without some amazement, did manifest his certainty of their not knowing him; he therefore, with another kind of intonation, that his speech might not bewray him, then that which waited upon his usual note of utterance, made a pithy panegyrick in praise of those that endeavoured, by their good fellowship and Bacchanalian compagnionry, to cheer up their hearts with precious liquour, and renew the golden age; whence descending to a more particular application, he very much applauded the ten gentlemen, for their being pleased, out of their devotion to the Lyæan god, who had with great respect been bred and elevated amongst the nymphs, not to forget, amidst the most sacred plying of their symposiasms, that duty

to ladyes which was incumbent on them, to be performed in the discharge of a visite;
then wheeling neatly about to fetch another careere, he discreetly represented to them
all the necessary circumstances at such a visit observable, and how the infringing of the
meanest title or particle of any one thereof, would quite disconcert the mutual harmony
it should produce, and bring an unspeakable disparagement to the credits and honors of
all guilty of the like delinquency. In amplifying hereof, and working upon their passions,
he let go so many secret springs, and inward resorts of eloquence, that being all perswaded
of the unseasonableness of the time, and unreasonableness of the suit, none of them, for a
thousand ducats that night, would have adventured to make any further progress in that
after which a little before they had been so eager, so profound was the character of
reverence toward that lady, which he so insinuatingly had imprinted into the hearts of
them all; wherefore they, purposing to insist no longer upon the visionary design, did
cast their minds on a sudden upon another far more haire-brained consideration; when
the Prince to one of his chief gentlemen said, We will do this good fellow no wrong;
yet before we go hence, let us try what courage is in him, that after we have made
him flee for it, we may to-morrow make one excuse for all, to the lady whom he serveth. Do not you see, sayes he, how he dandleth the sword in his hand, as if he were
about to braveer us, and how he is decked and trimm'd up in his cloaths, like another
Hector of Troy, but I doubt if he be so martial, he speaks too well to be valiant; he
is certainly more Mercurial then military, therefore let us make him turn his back,
that we may spie if, as another Mercury, he hath any wings on his heels. This fool-
ish chat no sooner was blattered out to the ears of three of his gentlemen that were
nearest to him, but the sudden drawing of their swords, though but in jest, made the
other six who heard not the Prince, as if they had bin mad to adventure the rashness
wherewith the spirit of wine had inspired them, against the prudensequal and invincible fortitude of the matchless Crichtoun; who not being accustomed to turn his back
to those that had any project against his brest, most manfully sustained their encounter; which, although furious at first, appearing nevertheless unto him, because of the
odds of ten to one, not to have been in earnest, he for twenty several bouts did but
ward their blows, and pary with the fort of his sword, till by plying the defensive part
too long, he had received one thrust in the thigh and another in the arme; the trick-
ling of his blood from the wounds whereof prompted his heroick spirit, as at a desperate stake to have at all or none, to make his tith outvy their stock, and set upon
them all. In which resolution, when from the door whereat he stood he had lanched
forth three paces in the court, having lovely Pomponacio behind him, to give him
warning in case of surprisal in the reer, and all his ten adversaries in a front before
him, who, making up above a quadrant of that periphery whereof his body was the
center, were about, from the exterior points of all their right shoulder-blades, alongst
the additional line of their armes and tucks, to lodge home to him so many truculent
semi-diameters, he retrograding their intention, and beginning his agency where they

would have made him a patient, in as short space as the most diagrammatically-skilled hand could have been able to describe lines representative of the distance 'twixt the earth and the several kardagas, or horary expeditions of the sun's diurnal motion, from his æquinoxial horizontality to the top of his meridian hight, which, with the help of a ruler, by six draughts of a pen is quickly delineated, livered out six several thrusts against them; by vertue whereof he made such speedy work upon the respective segments of that debauch'd circumference, through the red-ink-marks which his streight-drawn stroaks imprinted, that being alonged from the center-point of his own courage, and with a thunder-bolt-like-swiftness of hand radiated upon their bodies, he discussed a whole quadrant of those ten, whereof four and twenty make the circle, and laying six of the most inraged of them on their backs, left, in the other four, but a sextant of the aforesaid ring, to avenge the death of their dismal associates. Of which quaternity, the Prince being most concerned in the effects of this disaster, as being the only cause thereof, though his intentions levelled at another issue, and like to burst with shame to see himself loadned on all sides with so much dishonour by the incomparable valour of one single man, did set forward at the sword's point, to essay if in his person so much lost credit might be recovered; and to that purpose coming within distance, was upon the advancing of a thrust in quart, when the most agil Crichtoun, pareing it in the same ward, smoothly glided along the Prince's sword, and being master of its feeble, was upon the very instant of making his Highness very low, and laying his honour in the dust, when one of the three courtiers whom fortune had favoured not to fall by the hand of Crichtoun, cryed aloud, " Hold, hold! kill not the Prince." At which words the courteous Crichtoun recoyling, and putting himself out of distance, the Prince pulled off his vizard, and throwing it away, shew his face so fully that the noble-hearted Crichtoun, being sensible of his mistake, and sory so many of the Prince's servants should have enforced him, in his own defence, to become the actor of their destruction, made unto the Prince a very low obeisance, and setting his left knee to the ground, as if he had been to receive the honour of knighthood, with his right hand presented him the hilt of his own conquering sword, with the point thereof towards his own breast, wishing his highness to excuse his not knowing him in that disguise, and to be pleased to pardon what unluckily had ensued upon the necessity of his defending himself, which, at such an exigent, might have befaln to any other that were not minded to abandon their lives to the indiscretion of others. The Prince, in the throne of whose judgement the rebellious vapours of the tun had installed Nemesis, and caused the irascible faculty shake off the soveraignty of reason, being without himself, and unable to restraine the impetuosity of the will's first motion, runs Crichtoun through the heart with his own sword, and kils him. In the interim of which lamentable accident, the sweet and beautiful lady, who by this time had slipped her self into a cloth of gold petticoat, in the anterior fente whereof was an asteristick ouch, wherein were inchased fifteen several diamonds, representative of the constellation of the primest stars in the signe of Virgo, had enriched a tissue gown and wastcoat of brocado with the precious treasure of her ivory body, and put the foot-stals of those marble pillars which did support her microcosme into a paire of incarnation velvet slippers, embroydered with purple, being descended to the lower door, which jetted out to the courtwards, where Pomponacio was standing, with the curled tresses of her discheveled haire dangling over her shoulders, by the love-knots of whose naturally-guilded filaments were made fast the hearts of many gallant sparks, who from their liberty of ranging after other beauties were more forcibly curbed by those capillary fetters than by so many chaines of iron ; and in the dædalian windings of the crisped pleats whereof, did lye in ambush a whole brigade of Paphian archers, to bring the loftiest martialists to stoop to the shrine of Cupid ; and, Arachne-like, now careering, now caracoling it alongest the polygonal plainness of its twisted threds, seaze on the affections of all whose looks should be involved in her locks ; and, with a presentation exposing to the beholders all the perfections that ever yet were by the Graces conferred on the female sexe, all the excellencies of Juno, Venus, and Minerva, the other feminean deities, and semi-goddesses of former ages, seemed to be of new revived, and within her compiled, as the compactedst abridgement of all their best endowments ; stepped a pace or two into the court, with all the celerity that the intermixed passions of love and indignation was able to prompt her to. During which time, which certainly was very short, because to the motions of her angelically-composed body the quantity attending the matter of its constitution was no more obstructive, then were the various exquisite qualities flowing from the form thereof, wherein there was no blemish, the eyes of the Prince's thoughts and those were with him, for the influences of Cupid are like the actions of generation, which are said to be *in instanti*, pryed into, spyed, and surveyed from the top of that sublimely-framed head which culminated her accomplishments, down along the wonderful symmetry of her divinely-proportioned countenance ; from the glorious light of whose two luminaries, Apollo might have borrowed rayes to court his Daphne, and Diana her Endymion ; even to the rubies of those lips, where two Cupids still were kissing one another for joy of being so neer the enjoyment of her two rows of pearles inclosed within them ; and from thence through the most graceful objects of all her intermediate parts, to the heaven-like polished prominences of her mellifluent and heroinal breast, whose porphyr streaks, like arches of the ecliptick and colures, or Azimuch and Almicantar circles intersecting other, expansed in pretty veinelets, through whose sweet conduits run the delicious streams of nectar wherewith were cherished the pretty sucklings of the Cyprian goddesse, smiled on one another to see their courses regulated by the two niple-poles above them elevated, in each their own hemisphere ; whose magnetick vertue, by attracting hearts, and sympathy in their refocillation, had a more impowering ascendent over poetick lovers, for furnishing their braines with choise of fancy, then ever had the two tops of Parnassus-hill, when animated or assisted by all the wits of the Pierian

Muses; then from the snow-white galaxy betwixt those gemel-monts, whose milken paths, like to the plaines of Thessaly, do by reflexion calefie to that protuberant and convexe ivory, whose meditullian node, compared with that other, where the ecliptick cuts the æquinoxial, did far surpass it in that property whereby the night is brought in competition with the day; whence having past the line, and seeming to depress the former pole to elevate another, the inward prospect of their minde discovered a new America, or land unknown, in whose subterranean and intestine cels were secret mines of greater worth then those of either Tibar or Peru; for that besides the working in them could not but give delight unto the mineralist, their metal was so reciptible for impression, and to the mint so plyable, that alchymists profoundly versed in chymical extractions, and such as knew how to imbue it with *syndon*, and crown the *magisterum* with the *elixir*, instead of treasures merchants bring from the Indias, would have educed little worlds, more worth then gold or silver. All this from their imagination being convoyed into the penitissim corners of their souls in that short space which I have already told, she, rending her garments and tearing her haire, like one of the Graces possest with a Fury, spoke thus: " O villains! what have you done? you vipers of men, that have thus basely slaine the valiant Crichtoun, the sword of his own sexe and the buckler of ours, the glory of this age, and restorer of the lost honour of the Court of Mantua: O Crichtoun, Crichtoun!" At which last words, the Prince hearing them uttered by the lady in the world he loved best, and of the man in the world he most affected, was suddenly seazed upon by such extremity of sorrow for the unhappiness of that lamentable mischance, that not being able to sustaine the rayes of that beauty whose percing aspect made him conscious of his guilt, he fell flat upon his face, like to a dead man. But knowing *omne simile* not to be *idem*, he quickly arose, and to make his body be what it appeared, fixed the hilt of the sword wherewith he had killed Crichtoun fast betwixt two stones, at the foot of a marble statue standing in the court, after the fashion of those staves with iron pikes at both ends, commonly called Swedish feathers, when stuck into the ground to fence musketeers from the charge of horse; then, having recoyled a little from it, was fetching a race to run his brest, which for that purpose he had made open, upon the point thereof, as did Cato Vticensis, after his lost hopes of the recovery of the Commonwealth of Rome; and assuredly, according to that his intent, had made a speedy end of himself, but that his three gentlemen, one by stopping him in his course, another by laying hold on him by the middle, and the third by taking away the sword, hindred the desperate project of that autochthony. The Prince being carryed away in that mad, frantick, and distracted humour, befitting a bedlam better then a serralio, into his own palace, where all manner of edge-tools were kept from him all that sad night, for fear of executing his former designe of self-murther; as soon as to his father, my lord Duke, on the next morning by seven a clock, which by the usual computation of that country came at that season of the yeer to be neer upon fourteen hours, or fourteen a clock, the story of the former night's tragedy was related, and that he had solemnly vowed he should either have his son hanged or his head struck off, for the committing of a so ingrate, enormous, and detestable crime; one of his courtiers told him, that by all appearance his son would save his Highness' justice a labour, and give it nothing to do, for that he was like to hang himself, or after some other manner of way to turn his own Atropos. The whole Court wore mourning for him full three quarters of a yeer together. His funeral was very stately, and on his hearse were stuck more epitaphs, elegies, threnodies, and epicediums, then, if digested into one book, would have outbulk't all Homer's works; some of them being couched in such exquisite and fine Latin, that you would have thought great Virgil, and Baptista Mantuanus, for the love of their mother-city, had quit the Elysian fields to grace his obsequies ; and other of them, besides what was done in other languages, composed in so neat Italian, and so purely fancied, as if Ariosto, Dante, Petrark, and Bembo, had been purposely resuscitated, to stretch even to the utmost their poetick vein to the honour of this brave man ; whose picture till this hour is to be seen in the bed-chambers or galleries of the most of the great men of that nation, representing him on horseback, with a lance in one hand and a book in the other ; and most of the young ladies likewise, that were any thing handsome, in a memorial of his worth, had his effigies in a little oval tablet of gold hanging 'twixt their breasts, and held, for many yeers together, that metamazion, or intermammilary ornament, an as necessary outward pendicle for the better setting forth of their accoutrements, as either fan, watch, or stomacher. My lord Duke, upon the young lady that was Crichtoun's mistris and future wife, although she had good rents and revenues of her own by inheritance, was pleased to conferr a pension of five hundred ducats a yeer. The Prince also bestowed as much on her during all the days of his life, which was but short, for he did not long enjoy himself after the cross fate of so miserable an accident. The sweet lady, like a turtle bewailing the loss of her mate, spent all the rest of her time in a continual solitariness, and resolved, as none before Crichtoun had the possession of her body, that no man breathing should enjoy it after his decease.

The verity of this story I have here related concerning this incomparable Crichtoun, may be certified by above two thousand men yet living, who have known him ; and truly of his acquaintance there had been a far greater number, but that before he was full thirty two yeers of age, he was killed as you have heard. And here I put an end to the Admirable Scot.

The scene of the choicest acts of this late Heros of our time having been the country of Italy, the chief State whereof is Venice, it cannot be amiss, as I have done for Spaine, France, Holland, Denmark, Swedland, and Germany, that I make mention of these four Scotish Colonels,—Colonel Dowglas, Colonel Balantine, Colonel Lyon, and Colonel Anderson, who, within these very few yeers, have done most excellent service to the Venetian Commonwealth. Nor can I well forget that seacaptain, Captain William Scot, whose martiall atchievements in the defence of that

State against the Turks, may very well admit him to be ranked amongst the colonels; he was vice-admiral to the Venetian Fleet, and the onely renowned bane and terror of Mahometan navigators; whether they had galleys, galeoons, galiegrosses, or huge war ships, it was all one to him; he set upon all alike, saying still, The more they were, the manyer he would kill; and the stronger that the encounter should happen to be, the greater would be his honour, and his prise the richer. He oftentimes so cleared the Archipelago of the Mussulmans, that the Ottoman family at the very gates of Constantinople would quake at the report of his victories; and did so ferret them out of all the creeks of the Adriatick gulph, and so shrewdly put them to it, that sometimes they did not know in what part of the Mediterranean they might best shelter themselves from the fury of his blows. Many of their mariners turned landsouldiers for fear of him; and of their maritime officers, several took charge of caravans to escape his hand, which for many yeers together lay so heavy upon them, that he was cryed up for another Don Jean d' Austria, or Duke d' Orea, by the enemies of that Scythian generation; in spight of which, and the rancour of all their unchristian hearts, he dyed but some eighteen moneths ago in his bed, of a feaver, in the Isle of Candia.

Now, as besides those Colonels above recited, many other Scotish Colonels, since the jubilee of 1600 till the yeer 1640, have faithfully served the Venetian State against both the Christian and Turkish emperours; so, in the intervals of that time, have these following Scotish Colonels been in the service of the King of Pole, against both the Muscoviter, Turk, and Swed; to wit, Colonel Lermond, Colonel Wilson, Colonel Hunter, Colonel Robert Scot, Colonel Gordon, Colonel Wood, Colonel Spang, Colonel Gun, Colonel Robertson, Colonel Rower, and several others.

And seeing we are come so far on in the deduction of the Scotish Colonels, who for the space of thirty or fourty yeers, without reckoning the last ten, have been so famous for their valour in the continent of Europe, from whence the Isle of Britain excludes it self, that neither thick nor thin, hunger nor plenty, nor heat nor cold, was said to have been able to restraine them from giving proof thereof; and that from the hot climates of Spaine, Italy, and France, we have, in prosecuting the threed of this discourse, travelled through those of a mediocer temper, of the Low Countries, Denmark, and Hungary, even to the cold regions of Germanie, Swedland, and Pole; I hold it expedient before I shut up this enumeration of Scotish Colonels into a period, that the very Scyths and Sarmats, even to the almost subarctick incolaries, be introduced to bear record of the magnanimity of the Scotish nation; which, nevertheless, because I would not trespass upon the reader's patience in making the nomenclature too prolixe, I make account to do, by setting down only the names of those Scotish Colonels that served under the great Duke of Muscovy against the Tartar and Polonian, viz. Colonel Alexander Crawford, Colonel Alexander Gordon, Colonel William Keith, Colonel George Mathuson, Colonel Patrick Kinindmond, and Colonel Thomas Garne, who, for the height and grosseness of his person, being in his stature taller, and greater in his compass of body, then any within six kingdomes about him, was elected King of Bucharia, the inhabitants of that country being more inclined to tender their obedience to a man of a burly pitch like him, whose magnitude being every way proportionable in all its dimensions, and consisting rather in bones then flesh, was no load to the minde, nor hindrance to the activity of his body, then to a lower sized man, because they would shun equality, as near as they could, with him of whom they should make choice to be their Soveraign; they esteeming nothing more disgraceful, nor of greater disparagement to the reputation of that State, then that their King should, through disadvantage of stature, be looked down upon by any whose affaires, of concernment perhaps for the weal of the crown, might occasion a mutual conference face to face. He had ambassadors sent to him to receive the crown, scepter, sword, and all the other royal cognizances belonging to the Supreme Majesty of that nation; but I heard him say, that the only reason why he refused their splendid offers, and would not undergo the charge of that regal dignity, was because he had no stomack to be circumcised: however, this uncircumcised Garne, agnamed the Sclavonian, and upright Gentile, for that he loves good fellowship, and is of a very gentile conversation, served as a colonel, together with the forenamed five, and other unmentioned colonels of the Scotish nation in that service, against the Crim Tartar, under the command of both his and their compatriot, Sir Alexander Leslie, generalissimo of all the forces of the whole empire of Russia; which charge, the wars against the Tartarian beginning afresh, he hath re-obtained, and is in the plenary enjoyment thereof, as I believe, at this same instant time, and that with such approbation for fidelity and valour, that never any hath been more faithful in the discharge of his duty, nor of a better conduct in the infinite dangers through which he hath past.

I shall only here by the way, before I proceed any further, make bold to desire the reader to consider, seeing so short a space as thirty or four and thirty yeers time hath produced so great a number of colonels, and others above that degree of the Scotish nation, universally renowned for their valour and military atchievements in all the forraign and transmarine countries, states, and kingdoms of Christendome, what vast number of lieutenant-colonels, majors, captaines, lieutenants, ensignes, &c. besides the collateral officers of an army, such as adjutants, quartermasters, commissaries, scoutmasters, marshals, and so forth through all the other offices belonging to the milice of a nation, either by sea or land, should be found of Scotishmen to have been since the yeere one thousand and six hundred in the many several outlandish wars of Europe; which, I cannot think, if prejudicacy be laid aside, but that it will so dispose the reader that he will acknowledge the Scotish nation to have been an honorable nation, and that of late too, in their numerousness of able and gallant men totally devoted to the shrine of Mars; of which sort, as I have omitted many worthy and renowned colonels abroad, so will I not insist upon the praise of two of our countrymen, Sir John

Hume of Eatoun by name, and Francis Sinclair, natural son to the late Earl of Catnes ; the first whereof in his travels through Italy, by his overmastering, both at the blunt and sharp, the best swordsmen and fence-masters of that country, acquired the reputation of the skillfullest man in the world at the rapeer-point ; yet being killed at a battel in Denmark some few yeers agoe, to shew that there wanted not another of the same Scotish nation to supply his place, and to inherit every whit as deservedly that hight of fame conferred on him for his valour, the most couragious and magnanimous acts of the foresaid Francis Sinclair will manifest it to the full, with almost the universal testimony of all Spaine, Italy, and Germany, which for many yeers together were the theaters of his never daunted prowess. To relate all the duels wherein he hath been victorious, and but to sum them together, it would amount to a greater number then all the lessons that the most consciencious master of escrime that is, doth usually give in a whole three yeers space to him whom he intends to make a proficient in that faculty ; therefore, instead of all, as by the dimension of Hercules' foot one may judge of the stature of his body, and by the taste of a spoonful, as the saying is, to know what kinde of liquor is in a tun, I will only make mention of two actions of his, one done at the Emperour's court in Vienne, and the other at Madrid in Spaine.

The first was thus : A certain gallant nobleman of High-Germany, who by the stile of Conquerour, without any other addition, in duels, wherein he had overthrown all those of any nation that ever coped with him, having repaired to the great city of Vienne to accresce his reputation in some more degrees, by the subjection of any proud spirit there eager in that sort of contestation, whereof he heard there were many ; and notice being given to him of this Sinclair, who had a perfect sympathy with him in that kind of adventuring humour, they very quickly met with one another, and had no sooner exchanged three words, when time and place being assigned for debating the combate, they determined to take nothing in hand till first it were made known who should, to the very hazard of their lives, bear clear away the palme, and reap the credit of the bravest champion ; but the news thereof being carryed to the Emperor, who being unwilling that the victor should terminate the concertation in the blood of the vanquished, and yet desirous for his own sport, that by them somewhat might be done before him in matter of tryal which of them should prove most skilful in the handling of his armes, he enjoyned them, at a prefixed time in his own presence, to decide the controversie with foyles ; and for the better animating them thereto, assured them, that which of them soever should give the other the first three bouts, should, for his salary or *epinicion*, have a paire of spurs of beaten gold set with diamonds. The combatants very heartily embraced the condition, and were glad to turn the sharp to blunt to gaine the gold spurs ; by which means, their hope of overcoming on both sides having cheerfully brought them to the appointed place and time designed for the purpose, they had no sooner adjusted themselves in equal termes for foyles, and every thing else befitting that jeopardless monomachy, but Sinclair, at first, before he came within full distance, to try the manner of his adversarie's play, made a flourish or two of very nimble and most exquisite falsifyings ; whereat the other, conceiving them for really intended thrusts, was so disordred in his motion, that, offering to ward where he needed not, and taking the alarm too hot, Sinclair was so confident of his own sufficiency against that High-Dutchman, that when he had askt the Emperor for how many Franch bouts his Majesty would adjudge the spurs to be gained, and that the Emperor's answer was, For the first three ; Sinclair replied, If he did not give him five on end, he should be content to forfeit the spurs, and two hundred crowns besides ; whereupon immediately facing his adversary, to let him know that many ward without a cause, that cannot parry when they should, with the coinstantanean swiftness of hand and foot, gave him *de pie ferme*, a terrible slap on the breast, wherewith the German Lord did so stagger, that before he could fully recover himself the blow was doubled, and redoubled, with a sound thwack on the back of those, seconded with another bounce, not leaving him till with a push and a thump again, he had hit him seven several times, and that with the same confidence and facility that the usher of a fencing-hall useth to alonge against his master's plastron. The Emperour, by the thud of each stroak, which furthered his counting, having reckoned beyond the number of the five promised bouts, and unwilling Sinclair should lack of his due, or the other have his ribs broken, cryed aloud, " Hola ! forbear, enough." Whereupon the duellists desisting, the Emperor required them both to stand before him ; who, seeing the seven marks which the button of Sinclair's foyle, whitened with chalk, had imprinted in the other's black satin doublet, and how they lay in order after the manner of the situation of the seven stars of the little Bear, laughed heartily, for he was a peece of an astronomer, and a great favourer of mathematicians ; then addressing his speech to Sinclair, who had so much natural arithmetick as to know that seven included five, asked him, why in livering in of his thrusts he exceeded the promised number, seeing five was sufficient for gaining of the prize ; and why, being pleased to make them seven, he had fixed them in their stations after the fashion of a Charlewaine? Sinclair, to whom though astronomy might have signified somewhat to eat, for any thing he knew of the science, had nevertheless the perspicacity to make the word Charlewaine serviceable to his present purpose, very promptly answered, " Sir, I did so place them in honour of my master, CHARLES, King of Great Britain; and gave in two venees more then I was obliged to, to give your Cæsarean Majesty to understand, that, in the two kingdoms of England and Scotland, whereof that Isle consists, there are many thousands more expert then I, in matter of martial feats." At which answer the Emperor was so well pleased, that he gave him the spurs as his due for the first five, and a gold chain for the other two.

In the mean while, for the Emperor's better diversion, a certain Spanish Hidalgo of the Archduke Leopoldo's Court, made bold to relate to his Imperial Majesty how the said Francis Sinclair had in the city of Madrid performed a more notable exploit, and of far greater adventure, which was this.

Eight Spanish gentlemen being suspicious of Sinclair's too intimate familiarity with a kinswoman of theirs, whom they called Prima, that is to say, a she cozen, did all together set upon him at one time, with their swords drawn; which unexpected assault moved him to say, "Gentlemen, I doubt not but that you are valiant men, therefore, if you would have your desire of me, my intreaty is only that you would take it as becomes men of valour, and that by trying your fortune against mine, at the sword's point, one after another." The Spaniards pretending to be men of honour, not only promised to do what he required, but, the better to assure him that they would prove faithful to him in their promise, swore all of them upon a cross which they made with their swords, that they would not faile therein should it cost them all their lives. In the extremity that Sinclair was, this kind of unhoped for honest dealing did very much incourage him, especially he knowing that he and they all had but toledo-blades, whose fashion was then to be all of one length and size; in a word, conforme to paction, they fell to it, and that most cleverly, though with such fatality on the Spanish side, that in less then the space of half an hour he killed seven of them epassyterotically, that is, one after another; gratifying the eighth, to testifie he had done no wrong to the rest, with the enjoyment of his life, who, rather then to undergoe the hazard of the destiny of his fore-runners, chused to abandon his vindicative humour, and leave unrevenged the blood and honour of his male and female cosens.

Much more may be said of him, but that I will not now supererogate in magnifying the fulfilment of the reader's expectation, by the performance of more then I promised; being resolved, for brevitie's sake, to pass over with silence many hundreds of our country, such as Robert Scot, who was the deviser of leathern guns, that were in other parts much esteemed for their inventions of warlike engines.

And that since the yeer a thousand and six hundred, before which time no action hath been performed anywhere, nor from that time till this, within the Isle of Britain, by any of those colonels and others, whom I have here before recited, for which I have praised them, or otherwaies mentioned any of them, but by way of designation of their names in relation to their service abroad; nor amongst them all have I nominated above five or six that either served in, or did so much as look upon the wars of England, Scotland, and Ireland, and yet I expect not to merit blame, albeit of those general persons and colonels of the Scotish nation, whereof there is a great multitude, that have served, since the yeer 1641, in these our late wars of England, Scotland, and Ireland, I make no mention, because *multitudo* is no more *virtus* then *magnitudo*; for though there be some, and those but very some, amongst them that have been pretty well principled in reason, and had true honour before their eyes; yet seeing the great mobil of the rest, by circumvolving them into a contrary motion, hath retarded their action, and made their vertue abortive in not expressing their names, I do them favour, by such concealment obviating the imputation, which they deserve for having been in so bad company, and undersphering themselves to the bodies of those vaster orbs, whether of the State, Milice, or Church of Scotland, whose rapidity of violence might hurry them into a course quite opposite to the goodness of their own inclination. For whoever they be, whether civil or ecclesiastical, of the Scotish nation, whom the English can with any kind of reason upbraid with covetousness, the Commons of Scotland with oppression, or other states and countryes with treachery and dissimulation, it is my opinion that their names should not otherwayes be recorded but as beacons are set up where there are dangerous passages by sea, that such thrifty navigators, whether coetaneans or successors, as intend to saile with safety into the harbour of a good conscience, may thereby avoid the rocks and shelves of their greedy, tyrannous, and hypocritical dealings; nor can it be a sufficient excuse for any of those officers to say they thought they could not offend God therein, for that the kirk did warrant them in what they did; seeing they might very well know, that it becometh such as would take upon them a charge over and against the lives of others in the respective preservation and destruction of their souldier friends and foes, to have principles within themselves for the regulating of their outward actions, and not to be driven like fools for advice sake to yeeld an implicite obedience to the oracles of the Delphian presbytery, whose greatest enthusiasts, for all its cryed up infallibility, have not possibly the skill to distinguish betwixt rape-seed and musket-powder. If any say that by taking such a course, their motion seems to be the more celestial, because, in imitation of the upper orbs, it is furthered by the assistance of an external intelligence, I answer, that according to the opinion of him in whose philosophy they read those separated animations, to each of the heavens is allowed an informant as well as assisting soul; and though that were not, the intelligences are so far different, that there is hardly any similitude whereupon to fixe the comparison; for those superior ones are pure *simplicissim* acts, insusceptible of passion, and without all matter, or potentially of being affected with any alteration; but these are gross mixed patients, subject to all the disorders of the inferiour appetites, plunged in terrestrial dross, and for their profit or lucre in this world, lyable to any new impressions. That the gentry then, and nobility of Scotland, whereof for the most part did consist those fresh water officers, should by their codrawing in their presbyterian yoak, have plowed such deep and bloody furrows upon the backs of the commons of their own native soyle, is not only abominable but a thing ridiculous, and an extream scandal to the nation; for when some Laird or Lord there, whose tender conscience could embrace no religion that was not gainefull, had, for having given his voice, perhaps, to the augmentation of a minister's stipend, or done such like thing tending to the glory of the new Diana of Ephesus, obtained a commission for the levying of a regiment of horse, foot, or dragoons, under pretext of fighting for God against the malignants and sectaries, then was it that by uncessant quarterings, exacting of trencher money, and other most exorbitant pressures upon the poor tenandry of that country, such cruelty and detestable villany was used, and that oftentimes by one neighbour to another, under the notion of maintaining the Covenant, and the cause of God, that hardly have we heard in any age of such abominations done by either Turk or Infidel, and all out of a devotion to the blessed sum of money which the master of these oppressed tenants, for saving of his land from being laid wast, must needs disburse; for most of those kirk-officers of regiments, and their subordinado's, were but very seldom well pleased with the production of either man or horse, how apt soever they might seem to prove for military service, alledging some fault or other to the horse; and that the man, for lack of zeal, for any thing they knew, to the Covenant, might procure a judgement from heaven upon the whole army ; that therefore they would take but money, thereby the better to enable them to provide for such men and horses as they might put confidence into.   And if it chanced, as oftentimes it did, that a country gentleman, out-putter of foot or horse, being scarce of money, should prove so untractable as to condescend to nothing but what literally he was bound to, then by vertue of the power wherewith they were intrusted to see their souldiers well clothed, armed, and accommodated with transport money, and other such appurtenances, they had such a faculty of undervaluing whatever was not good silver and gold, that, to make up the deficiences, according to their rates, would extend to so great a sum, that hardly could any lyable to a levy, that was refractary to their desire of having money, save so much as one single sixpence by his emission of either horse or foot ; so fine a trick they had with their counterfeit religion, to make an honest poor gentleman glad to chuse the worst of two evils, for shunning a third of their own contrivance, worse then they both.

And when at any time the innocent gentlemen, in hope of commiseration, would present their grievances to the respective committees of the shires, seldom or never was there any prevention of or reparation for the aforesaid abuse, especially in the north of Scotland ; of all the parts whereof, the committees of the shires of Innernass and Ross, whether joyntly or separately sitting, proved the most barbarous and inhumane ; it being a commonly received practise amongst their Ligerheadstick wisdoms, not only to pass these and such like enormities with the foresaid officers, but to gratifie them besides for the laying of a burthen upon their neighbours, which they should have undergone themselves ; yea, to such a height did their covetousness and hypocrisie reach, that the better to ingratiate themselves in the favors of the souldiery, for the saving of their pence, when the officers, out of their laziness, would be unwilling to travel fourty or fifty miles from their quarters for the taking up of mantenance, or any arreer due of horse and foot levies, they took this savage and unchristian course, they would point at any whom they had a peck at, pretending he was no good covenanter, and that he favoured toleration ; and for that cause, being both judges and parties themselves, would ordaine him, under pain of quartering and plundering, to advance to the insatiable officers so much money as the debt pretended to be due by those remote inhabitants, though meer strangers to him, did extend to; by which means it ordinarily fell out, that the civillest men in all the country, and most plyable to good order, were the greatest sufferers; and the basest, the greedyest, and the most unworthy of the benefit of honest conversation, the onely men that were exempted, and had immunities.

Now, when many of these Laird and Lord kirk-officers had, by such unconscionable means, and so diametrically opposite to all honour and common honesty, acquired great sums of money, then was it that, like good Simeons of iniquity, they had recourse to their brother Levi for framing of protestations, their conscience not serving them to fight for a king that was like to espouse a malignant interest; under which cover, free from the tempest of war, like fruitful brood geese, they did stay at home to hatch young chickens of pecunial interest, out of those prodigious egs which the very substance of the commons had laid down to them, with a curse, to sit upon.

Yet, if for fashion sake, at the instigation of inferior officers, who were nothing so greedy as they, some shew of muster was to be made of souldiers to be sent to Sterlin-leaguer, or any where else, then were these same very men, whom, out of their pretended zeal to the good cause, they had formerly cast, either for malignancy or infencibility, and in lieu of each of them accepted of fifty or threescore dolars, more or less, inrolled in their troops or companies; when for the matter of three or four dolars, with the consent of a cup of good ale, and some promise of future plunder, they had purchased their good wils to take on with them; they approving themselves by such insinuating means good servants, in being able by the talent of their three dolars, to do the state that service for the which the poor country gentleman must pay threescore, and be forced to quit his man to boot.

Truly those are not the Scotish Colonels whom I intend to commend for valour, it being fitter to recommend them to posterity as vipers, who, to work out a livelihood to themselves, have not stuck to tear the very bowels of their mother-country, and bury its honour in the dust.

Such were not those Scotish Colonels I formerly mentioned, whose great vassalages abroad, and enterprises of most magnanimous adventures, undertaken and performed by them in other countries, might very well make a poorer climate then Scotland enter in competition with a richer soyle.

Yet seeing the intellectual faculties have their vertues as well as the moral, and that learning in some measure is no less commendable then fortitude, as those afore-named Scotish men have been famous beyond sea for the military part, so might I mention thrice as many moe of that nation as I have set down of war-like officers, who, since the yeer one thousand and six hundred, have deserved, in all those aforesaid countryes of France, Italy, Spaine, Flanders, Holland, Denmark, Germany, Pole, Hungary, and Swedland, where they lived, great renown for their exquisite abilities in all kind of literature; the greatest part of whose names I deem expedient for the present to conceal, thereby to do the more honor to some, whose magnanimity and other good parts now to commemorate, would make one appear, in the opinions of many, guilty of the like trespass with them that, in the dayes of Nero, called Rome by its proper name, after he had decreed to give it the title of Neroniana.

Nevertheless, being to speak a little of some of them before I lanch forth to cross the seas, I must salute that most learned and worthy gentleman, and most indeared minion of the Muses, Master Alexander Ross, who hath written manyer excellent books in Latine and English, what in prose, what in verse, then he hath lived yeers; and although I cannot remember all, yet to set down so many of them as on a sudden I can call to minde, will I not forget; to the end the Reader, by the perusal of the works of so universal a scholar, may reap some knowledge when he comes to read.

His *Virgilius Evangelizans*, in thirteen several books; a peece truly, which, when set forth with that decorement of plates it is to have in its next edition, will evidently shew that he hath apparelled the Evangelists in more splendid garments and royal robes, then, without prejudice be it spoken, his compatriots, Buchanan and Johnstoun, have in their paraphrastick translation of the Psalmes, done the King and prophet David. His four books of the Judaick wars, intituled, *De Rebus Judaicis libri quatuor*, couched in most excellent hexameters; his book penned against a Jesuite, in neat Latin prose, called *Rasura Tonsoris*; his *Chymera Pythagorica contra Lansbergium*; his *Additions to Wollebius and Vrsinus*; his book called *The new Planet no Planet*; his *Meditations upon Predestination*; his book intituled *The Pictures of the Conscience*; his *Questions upon Genesis*; his *Religious Apotheosis*; his *Melissomachia*; his *Virgilius Triumphans*; his four curious books of *Epigrams*, in Latin elegiacks; his *Mel Heliconium*; his *Colloquia Plautina*; his *Mystagogus-poeticus*; his *Medidus Medicatus*; his *Philosophical Touch-stone*; his *Arcana Microcosmi*; his *Observations on Sir Walter Rawley*; his *Marrow of History*, or *Epitome of Sir Walter Raleigh's Works*; his great *Chronology*, in the English tongue, set forth in folio, deducing all the most memorable things that have occurred since the Macedonian war, till within some ten or twelve yeers to this time; and his many other learned treatises, whose titles I either know not, or have forgot.

Besides all these volumes, books, and treatises here recited, he composed above three hundred exquisite sermons; which, after he had redacted them into an order and diction fit for the press, were by the merciless fury of Vulcan destroyed all in one night, to the great grief of many preachers, to whom they would have been every whit as useful as Sir Edward Cook's reports are to the lawyers. But that which I as much deplore, and am as unfainedly sorry for, is, that the fire, which on that fatal night had seazed on the house and closet where those his sermons were consumed, had totally reduced to ashes the very desks wherein were locked up several metaphysical, physical, moral, and dialectical manuscripts; whose conflagration, by philosophers is as much to be bewailed, as by theologically-affected spirits was that of his most divine elucubrations.

This loss truly was irrecoverable, therefore by him at last digested, because he could not help it; but that some losses of another nature, before and after that time by him sustained, have as yet not been repaired, lyeth as a load upon this land, whereof I wish it were disburthened, seeing it is in behalf of him who for his piety, theological endowments, philosophy, eloquence, and poesie, is so eminently qualified, that, according to the Metempsychosis of Pythagoras, one would think that the souls of Socrates, Chrysostome, Aristotle, Ciceron, and Virgil, have been transformed into the substantial faculties of that entelechy, wherewith by such a conflated transanimation he is informed and sublimely inspired. He spends the substance of his own lamp for the weal of others, should it not then be recruited with new oyle by those that have been enlightened by it? Many enjoy great benefices, and that deservedly enough, for the good they do to their coævals onely; how much more meritoriously should he then be dealt with, whose literate erogations reach to this and after ages? A lease for life of any parcel of land is of less value then the hereditary purchase thereof; so he of whom posterior generations reap a benefit, ought more to be regarded then they whose actions perish with themselves. Humane reason and common sense it self instructeth us, that dotations, mortifications, and other honorary recompences, should be most subservient to the use of those that afford literary adminicularies of the longest continuance, for the improvement of our sense and reason.

Therefore could I wish, nor can I wish a thing more just, that this reverend, worthy, and learned gentleman, Master Rosse, to whom this age is so much beholden, and for whom posterity will be little beholden to this age if it prove unthankful to him, were, as he is a favorite of Minerva, courted by the opulent men of our time, as Danae was by Jupiter, or that they had as much of Mecænas' spirit as he hath of Virgil's; for if so it were, or that this Isle of all Christendom would but begin to taste of the happiness of so wise a course, vertue would so prosper, and learning flourish, by his encouragements, and the endeavours of others in imitation of him, that the Christians needed lie no longer under the reproach of ignorance, which the Oriental nations fixe upon them in the termes of seeing but with one eye; but in the instance of Great Britain alone, to vindicate in matter of knowledge the reputation of this our Western world, make the Chineses, by very force of reason, of whose authority above them they are not ashamed, be glad to confess that the Europæans, as well as themselves, look out with both their eyes, and have no blinkard minds. Of which kind of brave men, renowned for perspicacy of sight in the ready perceiving of intellectual objects, and that *in gradu excellenti*, is this Master Rosse; the more ample expressing of whose deserved elogies, that I remit unto another time, will I hope be taken in better part that I intend to praise him againe, because *laus* ought to be *virtutis assecla*, and he is alwayes doing good.

Therefore, lest I should interrupt him, I will into France, Spain, and other countries, to take a view of some great scholars of the Scotish nation, who of late have been highly esteemed for their learning in forraign parts. Of which number he that first presents himself is one Sinclair, an excellent mathematician, Professor Regius, and possessor of the chaire of Ramus, though long after his time, in the university of Paris. He wrote, besides other books, one in folio, *De Quadratura Circuli*. Of the same profession, and of his acquaintance, there was one Anderson, who likewise lived long in Paris, and was for his abilities in the mathematical sciences, accounted the profoundlyest principled of any man of his time. In his studyes he plyed hardest the equations of algebra, the speculations of the irrational lines, the proportions of regular bodies, and sections of the cone; for though he was excellently well skilled in the theory of the planets and astronomy, the opticks, catoptricks, dioptricks, the orthographical, stereographicial, and schenographicall projections, in cosmography, geography, trigonometry, and geodesie, in the staticks, musick, and all other parts or pendicles, sciences, faculties, or arts of, or belonging to the disciplines mathematical in general, or any portion thereof, in its essence or dependances; yet taking delight to pry into the greatest difficulties, to soar where others could not reach, and, like another Archimedes, to work wonders by geometry and the secrets of numbers; and having a body too weak to sustaine the vehement intensiveness of so high a spirit, he died young, with that respect nevertheless to succeeding ages, that he left behind him a posthumary book, intituled, *Andersoni Opera*, wherein men versed in the subject of the things therein contained, will reap great delight and satisfaction.

There was another called Doctor Seaton, not a Doctor of Divinity, but one that had his degrees at Padua, and was Doctor *utriusque juris;* for whose pregnancy of wit, and vast skill in all the mysteries of the civil and canon laws, being accounted one of the ablest men that ever breathed, he was most heartily desired by Pope Vrbane the eighth to stay at Rome; and the better to encourage him thereto, made him chief Professor of the Sapience, a colledge in Rome so called; where, although he lived a pretty while with great honor and reputation, yet at last, as he was a proud man, falling at some ods with *il Collegio Romano*, the supreamest seat of the Jesuites, and that wherein the general of that numerous society hath his constant residence, he had the courage to adventure coping with them where they were strongest, and in matter of any kind of learning to give defiance to their greatest scholars; which he did do with such a hight of spirit, and in such a lofty and bravashing humour, that, although there was never yet that ecclesiastical incorporation wherein there was so great universality of literature, or multiplicity of learned men, he nevertheless misregarding what estimation they were in with others, and totally reposing on the stock or basis of his own knowledge, openly gave it out, that if those Teatinos, his choler not suffering him to give them their own name of Jesuites, would offer any longer to continue in vexing him with their frivolous chat and captious argumentations, to the impugning of his opinions, and yet in matters of religion they were both of one and the same faith, he would, like a Hercules amongst so many myrmidons, fal in within the very midst of them, so besquatter them on all sides, and, with the granads of his invincible arguments, put the braines of all and each of them in such a fire, that they should never be able, pump as they would, to finde in all the celluls thereof one drop of either reason or learning wherewith to quench it.

This unequal undertaking of one against so many, whereof some were greater courtiers with his Papal Holiness then he, shortened his abode at Rome, and thereafter did him so much prejudice in his travels through Italy and France, that when at any time he became scarce of money, to which exigent his prodigality often brought him, he could not as before expect an *ayuda de costa*, as they call it, or *viaticum*, from any Prince of the territories through which he was to pass, because the chanels of their liberality were stopped, by the rancour and hatred of his conventual adversaries.

When, nevertheless, he was at the lowest ebb of his fortune, his learning, and incomparable facility in expressing any thing with all the choicest ornaments of, and incident variety to the perfection of the Latine elocution, raised him to the dignity of being possessed with the chair of Lipsius, and professing humanity, in Italy called *buone letere*, in the famous university of Lovan ; yet, like Mercury, unapt to fix long in any one place, deserting Lovan, he repaired to Paris, where he was held in exceeding great reputation for his good parts, and so universally beloved, that both laicks and churchmen, courtiers and scholars, gentlemen and merchants, and almost all manner of people, willing to learn some new thing or other, for, as sayes Aristotle, every one is desirous of knowledge, were ambitious of the enjoyment of his company, and ravished with his conversation. For besides that the matter of his discourse was strong, sententious, and witty, he spoke Latine as if he had been another Livy or Salustius : nor, had he been a native of all the three countryes of France, Italy, and Germany, could he have exprest himself, as still he did when he had occasion, with more selected variety of words, nimbler volubility of utterance, or greater dexterity for tone, phrase, and accent, in all the languages thereto belonging.

I have seen him circled about at the Louvre with a ring of French lords and gentlemen, who hearkned to his discourse with so great attention, that none of them, so long as he was pleased to speak, would offer to interrupt him, to the end that the pearles falling from his mouth might be the more orderly congested in the several treasures of their judgements ; the ablest advocates, barristers, or counselors at law of all the Parlement of Paris, even amongst those that did usually plead *en la chambre doree*, did many times visit him at his house, to get his advice in hard debatable points. He came also to that sublime pitch of good diction even in the French tongue, that there having past, by vertue of a frequent intercourse, several missives in that idiom, betwixt him and le Sieur de Balzak, who, by the quaintest Romancealists of France, and daintiest complementers of all its lushious youth, was almost uncontrollably esteemed in eloquence to have surpassed Ciceron; the straine of Seaton's letters was so high, the fancy so pure, the words so well connexed, and the cadence so just, that Balzak, infinitely taken with its fluent yet concise oratory, to do him the honour that was truly due unto him, most lovingly presented him with a golden pen, in acknowledgement of Seaton's excelling him both in rhetorick and the art of perswasion; which gift proceeding from so great an oratour, and for a supereminency in that faculty wherein himself, without contradiction, was held the chiefest of this and all former ages that ever were born in the French nation, could not chuse but be accounted honorable. Many learned books were written by this Seaton in the Latine tongue, whose titles, to speak ingenuously, I cannot hit upon.

There was another Scotish man named Cameron, who, within these few yeers, was so renowned for learning over all the provinces of France, that, besides his being esteemed for the faculties of the minde, the ablest man of all that country, he was commonly designed, because of his universal reading, by the title of the Walking Liberary; by which, he being no less known then by his own name, he therefore took occasion to set forth an excellent book in Latine, and that in folio, intituled *Bibliotheca Movens*, which afterwards was translated into the English language.

To mention those former Scotish men, and forget their compatriot Barclay, the author of *Argenis, Icon Animorum*, and other exquisite treatises, translated out of Latine into the languages almost of every country where use is made of printing, would argue in me a great neglect: it shall suffice nevertheless for this time, that I have named him; for I hope the reader will save me a labour, and extoll his praises to as great a hight, when he shall be pleased to take the paines to peruse his works.

Yet that the learning of the travelers of the Scotish nation may not seem to be tyed to the climate of France, (although all Scots, by the privilege of the laws of that kingdome, be naturalized French, and that all the French kings, since the dayes of Charlemaine, which is about a thousand yeers since, by reason of their fidelity to that crown, have put such real confidence in the Scots, that whithersoever the king of France goeth, the Scots are nearest to him of any, and the chief guard on which he reposeth for the preservation of his royal person,) there was a Scotish man named Melvil, who, in the yeer 1627, had a pension of King Philip the fourth, of six hundred ducats a yeer, for his skilfulness in the Hebrew, Caldean, Syriack, Æthiopian, Samaritan, and Arabick tongues, beyond all the Christians that ever were born in Europe. The service he did do the Spanish King in those languages, especially the Arabick and Caldean, which, after great search made over all his ample territories, and several other kingdoms beside, for some able men to undergo the task, could not be got performed by any but him, was to translate into Latine or Spanish some few books of those six hundred great volumes, taken by Don Juan de Austria at the battel of Lepanto from the great Turk, which now lye in the great library of the magnifick palace of the Escurial, some seven leagues westward from Madrid, and otherwayes called San

Lorenço el real.   Of those and many other mental abilities of that nature, he gave after that most excellent proofs, both at Rome, Naples, and Venice.

That most learned Latine book in folio, treating of all the mathematical arts and sciences, which was written by that Scotish gentleman Sempil, resident in Madrid, sheweth that Scotish spirits can produce good fruits even in hot climates.

Another named Gordon, of the Scotish nation likewise, wrote a great Latin book in folio of chronology, which is exceeding useful for such as in a short time would attaine to the knowledge of many histories.

Another Gordon also beyond sea, penned several books of divinity in an excellent stile of Latin.   Of which kinde of books, but more profoundly couched, another Scot named Turneboll, wrote a great many.   These four eminent Scots I have put together, because they were societaries by the name of Jesus, vulgarly called Jesuits; some whereof are living as yet, and none of those that are not, dyed above fourteen years ago.

Methinks I were to blame should I in this nomenclature leave out Dempster, who for his learning was famous over all Italy, had made a learned addition to Rossinus, and written several other excellent books in Latin; amongst which, that which doth most highly recommend him to posterity, is the work which he penned of five thousand illustrious Scots, the last liver whereof, as is related in the 213. page of this book, dyed above fifty yeers since; for which, together with the other good parts wherewith he was endowed, himself was truly illustrious.

Balfour, a professor of philosophy in Bourdeaux, wrote an excellent book in Latine upon the morals; so did another of the Scotish nation, named Donaldson, upon the same very subject, and that very accurately.   Primerose, a Scotish man, who was a preacher in French at Bourdeaux, and afterwards became one of three that preached in the French church at London, wrote several good books both in Latin and French. Doctor Liddel penned an exquisite book of physick, and so did Doctor William Gordon, and both in the Latine tongue; which two Doctors were for their learning renowned over all Germany.   Pontæus, a Scotish man, though bred most of his time in France, by several writings of his obvious to the curious reader, gave no small testimony of his learning.

There was a professor of the Scotish nation within these sixteen yeers in Somure, who spoke Greek with as great ease as ever Cicero did Latine, and could have expressed himself in it as well and as promptly as in any other language; yet the most of the Scotish nation never having astricted themselves so much to the propriety of words as to the knowledge of things, where there was one preceptor of languages amongst them, there were above forty professors of philosophy; nay, to so high a pitch did the glory of the Scotish nation attaine over all the parts of France, and for so long time together continued in that obtained hight, by vertue of an ascendant the French conceived the Scots to have above all nations, in matter of their subtlety in philosophical disceptations, that there have not been till of late, for these several ages together, any Lord, gentleman, or other in all that country, who being desirous to have his son instructed in the principles of philosophy, would intrust him to the discipline of any other than a Scotish master; of whom they were no less proud then Philip was of Aristotle, or Tullius of Cratippus. And if it occurred, as very often it did, that a pretender to a place in any French university, having in his tenderer yeers been subserulary to some other kind of schooling, should enter in competition with another aiming at the same charge and dignity, whose learning flowed from a Caledonian source, commonly the first was rejected, and the other preferred; education of youth in all grounds of literature under teachers of the Scotish nation being then held by all the inhabitants of France to have been attended, *cæteris paribus*, with greater proficiency, then any other manner of breeding subordinate to the documents of those of another country. Nor are the French the only men have harboured this good opinion of the Scots in behalf of their inward abilities, but many times the Spaniards, Italians, Flemins, Dutch, Hungarians, Sweds, and Polonians, have testified their being of the same mind, by the promotions whercunto, for their learning, they in all those nations at several times have attained.

Here nevertheless it is to be understood, that neither these dispersedly preferred Scots were all of one and the same religion, nor yet any one of them a presbyterian. Some of them were, and are as yet popish prelates, such as the bishop of Vezon, and Chalmers bishop of Neems, and Signor Georgio Con, who wrote likewise some books in Latine, was by his intimacy with Pope Vrban's nephew, Don Francesco, Don Antonio, and Don Tædeo Barbarini, and for his endeavoring to advance the Catholico-pontifical interest in Great Britain, to have been dignified with a cardinal's hat, which, by all appearance, immediately after his departure from London, he would have obtained as soon as he had come to Rome, had death not prevented him by the way in the city of Genua; but had he turned to this Island with it, I doubt it would have proved ere now as fatal to him, as another such like cap in Queen Marie's time had done to his compatriot Cardinal Betoun.

By this, as it is perceivable that all Scots are not Presbyterians, nor yet all Scots Papists, so would not I have the reputation of any learned man of the Scotish nation to be buryed in oblivion, because of his being of this or this, or that, or yon, or of that other religion, no more then if we should cease to give learning and moral vertues their due, in the behalfe of pregnant and good spirits born and bred in several climates; which to withhold from them, whether Periscians, Hetroscians, or Amphiscians, would prove very absurd to the humane ingenuity or ingenuous humanity of a true cosmopolite.

For we see how the various aspect of the heavens, in their asteristick and planetary influences, according to the diversity of our sublunary situations, disposeth the inclinations of the earth's respective inhabitants differently; whence, as it is said in the

210. page of this book, the Spaniards are proud, the French inconstant, the Italians lascivious, &c. and every nation almost in their humour, not only discrepant from one another, but each having some disorderly motion which another hath not, makes the other to be possessed with some irregularity which the former wants.

We know the Hollanders are more penurious then the High-Germans, and they more intemperate then the Spaniards, who againe are more lecherous then the Hollanders. Now seeing *ex malis moribus bonæ oriuntur leges*, and that vices, like diseases of the body, must be cured with contraries, it will clearly follow, there being vices contrary to other, as well as vice to vertue, that the laws curbing those vices in the opposite extreams, must needs be very dissonant from one another.

Do not we see that in Holland to play the merchant is accounted honorable, although it be thought disgraceful in High-Germany for a gentleman to use any kind of traffick? The Spaniards hold him worse then a beast that is at any time drunk, yet the Dutchman esteems him no good fellow that sometimes is not. The Hollander deems him unworthy of the name of man that fornicates before he marry, but the Spaniard hardly doth repute him a man, who hath not exercised those male abilities whereby he is distinguished from the woman.

Thus, according to the genius of each climate, statutes, acts, and ordinances, being instituted for the regulating of men's actions, and our obedience to superior powers by custome becoming, as it were, natural, we by experience finde that the religion wherewith men are most accustomed, lyes best to their consciences.

For that it is so, we know by the vehemency of fidimplicitaries, of whom some will chuse to lose their lives before they quit their religion, although they be altogether ignorant of what they should believe till they ask the minister; whose custome, to make their consciences subservient to their choler, is to principle them with the negative faith without any great positive doctrine, for so begins the Covenant, of which kind of zealous disciples was that covenanting gentleman who burnt a great many historical and philosophical books, thinking they had been books of popery; he taking them to be such because of the red letters he saw in their titles and inscriptions.

Nor shall we need to think it strange, that in the world there are so many several religions, if we consider that the divers temperaments of our bodies alter our inclinations, from whose disparity arise repugnant laws, which long obedience makes it seem a sacriledge to violate. In my opinion, truly, there is nothing more natural then variety, yea, and that sometimes with opposition. Are not we composed of the four elements, which have their contrary as wel as symbolizing qualities? and doth not the manner of their mixture and the degrees, by more or less, of the qualities from thence flowing in the constitution of men's bodies, disagree in all the persons of the world? Hence some are melancholious, some phlegmatick, some cholerick, and some sanguinean; and every one of those more or less, according to the humour that affects him, in its quantity and quality.

Thus if men were left to themselves, every one would have a several religion; but seeing to reap good from one another, we must to one another apply our selves, and that this application without conformity would prove destructive; therefore is it that the individuals of mankinde have been still pleased to forego some natural interest they had in peculiar differences, the better to erect an uniformity in their society for that self-preservation, which is the chief end of their designes.

This making either a King or State, we come then to have laws imposed on us according to the climate or disposition of the people. And although I know there be a difference betwixt divine and humane institutions, and that it is fitting wicked thoughts be punished, as well as words or actions; yet do I appeal to the judgment of any that will, in casting his eye upon the world as it is and still hath been, consider but the various governments in the regulating of the deeds of the consciences of men, if he finde it not to be true, that over the whole universe, amongst the Christians, Jews, Paynims, and Mahumetans, both in this and former ages, religions almost have been still distinguished by secular soveraignties, each State having its own profession, and the faith of one climate being incompatible with that of another; and yet in the duties commonly observed 'twixt neighbor and neighbor in matter of buying and selling, trucking, changing, and such like sociable commutations, there is as great unanimity by the most part of the world, maintained even in the bonds of honesty, as if, as they know what pleaseth God should please them, they were of the opinion of Tamarlain, who believed that God was best pleased with diversity of religions, variety of worship, dissentaneousness of faith, and multiformity of devotion.

For this cause, prescinding from the religion of any of my compatriots, which if displeasing to God, will no doubt at last displease themselves, and hurry upon them that punishment which we ought not to aggravate before its time, by detaining from them what praise to them is due for the natural and moral accomplishments wherewith God hath endowed them for our benefit; for in praising them, we praise God, who hath made them the instruments of doing us good.

These three profound and universal scholars of the Scotish nation, Tyry of the house of Drumkilbo, Mackbrek, and Broun, deserve a rank in this list of men of literature, as well as Chisum the bishop of Vezon, and others of the Romish faith above mentioned, and for whose praises I have already apologised. Tyry wrote books of divinity in a most acurate straine; and being assistant to the General of the Jesuites, was the second person of all that vast ecclesiastical republick, which reacheth as far as to the outmost territories of all the Christian Kings and States of the whole continent of the world; a higher place then which amongst them no stranger ever attained to in Italy, which is the place of their supremest jurisdiction. Mackbrek is eminent for his literature in Pole, and Broun in Germany, and both of them authors of good books.

To hit upon the names of others such as these of the Scotish nation, renowned for learning even in remoter parts of the world, it would be a task not so proper for any, as for the great traveler Lithco, a compatriot likewayes of theirs, who in nineteen yeers space traveled three times by land over all the known parts almost of Europe, Asia, and Africk, as by a book of a pretty bulk in quarto set forth by himself, is more evidently made manifest. The said Lithco also is an author of several other books, and so was Simeon Graham, a great traveler and very good scholar, as doth appear by many books of his emission; but being otherwayes too licentious, and given over to all manner of debordings, the most of the praise I will give him, will be to excuse him in these terms of Aristotle—*Nullum magnum ingenium sine mixtura dementiæ.*

Some other eminent men for literature of the Scotish nation, besides those formerly rehearsed, have been much esteemed of abroad, although they were no Roman Catholicks; such as Doctor John Forbas, who was a professor of divinity in Leyden, and wrote an excellent book of divinity in folio, called *Irenicon.* Doctor Read likewise was an able scholar, as may appear by his book of Anatomy, and other learned writings.

Now seeing I am from beyond sea bringing the enumeration of my scholars homewards, I cannot forget the names of Doctor Balcanquel, Doctor Sibbalds, Doctor Stuart, and Doctor Michael, all able divines, and sometimes beneficed men in England.

How much the Protestant faith oweth to Doctor Robert Baron, for his learned treatises against Turnebol the Jesuite, *De objecto formali fidei,* I leave to be judged by those that have perused them. To the conversation of Doctor William Lesly, who is one of the most profound and universal scholars now living, his friends and acquaintance of any literature are very much beholding, but to any books of his emission, nothing at all; whereat every one that knoweth him wondreth exceedingly, and truly so they may; for though scripturiency be a fault in feeble pens, and that Socrates the most learned man of his time set forth no works, yet can none of these two reasons excuse his not evulging somewhat to the publike view, because he is known to have an able pen, whose draughts would grace the paper with impressions of inestimable worth; nor is the example of Socrates able to apologize for him, unless he had such disciples as Plato and Aristotle, who having deposited in their braines the scientifick treasures of their master's knowledge, did afterwards, in their own works, communicate them to the utility of future generations; yet that this Caledonian Socrates, though willing, could not of late have been able to dispose of his talent, did proceed from the merciless dealings of some wicked Anites, Lycons, and Melits of the Covenant; the cruelty of whose perverse zeal will keep the effects of his vertue still at under, till by the perswasion of some honest Lysias, the authority of the land be pleased to reseat him into his former condition, with all the encouragement that ought to attend so prime a man.

Doctor John Gordon, sometime minister of Elgin, Doctor William Hogstoun, and Doctor James Sibbet, are men who have given great proof of their learning, as well by treatises which they have divulged, as in all manner of academical exercitations. Doctor William Guild deserveth by himself to be remembered, both for that he hath committed to the press many good books tending to the edification of the soul and bettering of the minde; and that of all the divines that have lived in Scotland these hundred yeers, he hath been the most charitable, and who bestowed most of his own to publike uses. The lovingness of his heart dilates it self to many, and the center of his desires is the common weal; in matter of great edifices, where he builds not he repaires; and many churches, hospitals, colledges, and bridges, have been the objects of his beneficence. But to shew the vertue of this man beyond thousands of others richer then he, even of those that had a nearer and more immediate call to the performance of such charitable offices, when he was principal of the old Colledge of Aberdeen, and that at a time, when, by reason of the sword everywhere raging through the land, all schooles almost were laid waste; so great was his industry, so prudent his government, and so liberal his erogations, that the number of the scholars there, all the time that he ruled, did, by threescore and ten a-yeer, exceed the greatest confluence that ever was therein since the foundation of that University; to which I wish all happiness, because of him for whom this book is intended, who learned there the elements of his philosophy, under the conduct of one Master William Seaton, who was his tutor; a very able preacher truly, and good scholar, and whom I would extoll yet higher, but that being under the consistorian lash, some critick Presbyters may do him injury, by pretending his dislike of them, for being praised by him who idolizeth not their authority.

The same reason invites me not to insist upon the praises of Master William Lawder, preacher at Ava, a good divine, and excellent poet, both in Latine and English. And for the same cause must I forbear to spend encomions upon that worthy gentleman, Master David Leech, who is a most fluent poet in the Latine tongue, an exquisite philosopher and profound theolog.

Seeing I am come to speak againe of Scotish poets which have flourished of late, the foresaid Master Leech hath an elder brother named John, who hath set forth four or five most excellent books of epigrams and eclogues in the Latine tongue. One Master Andrew Ramsey, likewise, hath been the author of books of very good epigrams in Latine. Several others in that nation are and have been of late very good Latine poets; amongst which I must needs commemorate Doctor Arthur Johnstoun, a physician by profession, yet such a one as had been so sweetly imbued by the springs of Helicon, that before he was full three and twenty yeers of age, he was laureated poet at Paris, and that most deservedly, as may appear by his *Parergon*, his Paraphrastick translation of the Psalmes, wherein if he excell not, I am sure he equaleth Buchanan, and some other treatises by name to me unknown.

His brother, also, Doctor William Johnstoun, was a good poet in Latine, and a good mathematician acknowledged to be such, which was none of his meanest praises, by Master Robert Gordon of Straloch, one of the ablest men of Scotland in the mathematical faculties, and who, of all mathematicians, hath done it most honor, by having taken the paines to set down all the shires and countries thereof in most exact geographical maps ; which designe, though intended, essayed, and blocked by many others, yet was never brought to its full and compleat perfection but by this gentleman of the name of Gordon, intituled the Laird of Straloch ; who, being loath his vertue and learning should expire with himself, hath the most hopeful and best educated children of any whosoever within two hundred miles of his house.

These mathematical blades put me in mind of that Doctor Liddel, of whom, for his abilities in physick, I made mention in p. 258. which I had reason to do because of his learned books written in Latin, *De Diæta*, *De Febribus*, and *De Methodo Medicinæ*, who for his profoundness in these sciences of sensible immaterial objects, was everywhere much renowned, especially at Francfort de Maine, Francfort on the Oder, and Heidelberg, where he was almost as well known as the monstrous Bacchanalian tun that stood there in his time. He was an eminent professor of the mathematicks, a disciple of the most excellent astronomer, Tycho Brahe, and condisciple of that worthy Longomontanus ; yet, in imitation of Aristotle, whose doctrine with great proficiency he had imbued, esteeming more of truth then of either Socrates or Plato, when the new star began to appear in the constellation of Cassiopeia, there was concerning it such an intershocking of opinions betwixt Tycho Brahe and Doctor Liddel, evulged in print to the open view of the world, that the understanding reader could not but have commended both for all, and yet, in giving each his due, praised Tycho Brahe most for astronomy, and Liddel for his knowledge above him in all the other parts of philosophy.

As this Doctor Liddel was a gallant mathematician, and exquisite physician ; so being desirous to propagate learning to future ages, and to make his own kindred the more enamoured of the sweetness thereof, especially in mathematical sciences, he bequeathed fourty pounds English money a yeer, to the new Colledge of the University of Aberdeen, for the maintenance of a mathematical professor ; with this *proviso,* that the neerest of his own kinsmen, *cæteris paribus,* should be preferred before any other. This any rational man would think reasonable ; nor was it truly much controverted for the space of fourteen or fifteen yeers together after the making of the legacy ; at which time his nephew on the brother's side being a childe, and but then initiated to the rude elements of Latine, one Doctor William Johnstoun was preferred to the place, because there was none at that time of Doctor Liddel's consanguinity able to discharge it ; a reason verily relevant enough.

But by your leave, good reader, when Doctor William Johnstoun dyed, and that Doctor Liddel's nephew, Master Duncan Liddel by name, was then of that maturity of age, and provection of skil in most of the disciplines mathematical, as was sufficient for the exercise of that duty, and the meriting of his uncle's benefice, did the good men rulers at the helme there, make any conscience of the honest Doctor's latter will? No, forsooth; the oracle must be first consulted with: the ministerian philoplutaries, my tongue forks it, I have mistaken it seems one word for another, I should have said Philosophers, thought fit otherwayes to dispose thereof; for, say they, Master Duncan Liddel hath committed the hainous sin of fornication, and begot a young lass with childe, therefore his uncle's testament must be made void in what relates to his enjoyment of that dotation. O brave logick, and curious commentary upon a later will for the better explication of the mind of the defunct! Which presbyterian doctrine, had it bin in request in the daies of Socrates, what fine pass would the world have been brought to ever since that time, by that ignorance which should have over-clouded us through our being destitute of the works of Plato, Aristotle, and Euclid, with all the scholiasts that have glossed on them these two thousand yeers past; for, by all appearance, those three prime Grecians would have been forced in their younger yeers to betake themselves to some other profession then philosophy, for want of a master to instruct them in the principles thereof; for the presbytery of Athens, no doubt, would have pearched up poor Socrates upon a penitentiary pew, and outed him of his place for having two wives at once, neither whereof, whether Xantippe or Myrto, was either so handsome or good as Master Liddel's concubine, and in lieu of that trespasser, supplyed the academical chair with the breech of a more sanctified brother, whose zealous jobernolisme would never have affected the antipresbyterian spirits of Plato, Euclid, or Aristotle; nor gained to his schoole any disciples who should have been able from such a muddy fountain to derive any clear springs of learning to after ages, nor benefit posterity with any other kind of literate works then such as the pretended holy men, and accusers of Socrates, Anitus, Lycon, and Melitus by name, did set forth; which to the eyes of both body and minde, have ever since their time been of the colour of the Duke of Vandome's cloak, invisible.

But if one durst make bold to speak to those great professors of piety, I would advise them out of the Evangile, to take the beam out of their own eye before they meddle with the moat that is in their neighbor's; and to consider that the sin of theft which they committed in robbing Master Liddel of his due, is a far more hainous transgression then that single fornication; for which, besides the forfeiture of what was mortified to him, he was by them for a long time together most rigorously persecuted.

Nor do I think their fault can be better expiated, then by fulfilling the contents of the legacy, and investing Liddel in his own right; which that I may seem to avouch with the better ground of reason, I dare almost perswade my self, that there is not any within the Isle of Britain with whom, taking in all the mathematical arts and sciences together, practical and theoretick, he will not be well pleased, upon occasion, to adventure a dispute for superiority in the most, and that with a willingness to forego and renounce any claim, title, or privilege he can, or may pretend to for the chaire of mathematical professor in New Aberdeen, in case of non-prevalency.

This is more, some will say, then his outside doth promise, and that to look to him, one would not think he had such abilities. What then? do not we see in apothecaries' shops pots of the same worth and fashion containe drugs of a different value, and sometimes the most precious oyntment put in the coursest box? So may a little and plaine man in outward shape, inclose a minde high and sublime enough; a giant like spirit in a low stature, being able to overtop a Colossus with Pygmæan endowments.

But were there no other remora or obstruction to retard his intended progress in mathematical designes, the inward qualifications of his minde to the advancement of those sciences would quickly raise his person to a greater estimation; yet truly as he is in London for the present, I can no better compare him then to an automatary engine, wherein there are many several springs, resorts, and wheels, which, though when once put into a motion, would produce most admirable effects, are nevertheless forced for want of a convenient agent to give them the due brangle, to lye immobile, and without efficacy.

Such an agent is a Mecænas, a patron, a promover of learning, a favorer of the Muses, and protector of scholars; in the production of which kind of worthy men, were this land alone but a little more fertil, not only Great Britain, but the whole world besides, would be the better for it.

As for such of the Scotish nation as of late have been famous for English poesie, the first that occurs is Sir William Alexander, afterwards created Earle of Sterlin : he made an insertion to Sir Philip Sidney's Arcadia, and composed several tragedies, comedies, and other kind of poems, which are extant in a book of his in folio, intituled *Sterlin's Works*. The purity of this gentleman's vein was quite spoiled by the corruptness of his courtiership, and so much the greater pity; for by all appearance, had he been contented with that mediocrity of fortune he was born unto, and not aspired to those grandeurs of the court, which could not without pride be prosecuted, nor maintained without covetousness, he might have made a far better account of himself. It did not satisfie his ambition to have a laurel from the Muses, and be esteemed a king amongst poets, but he must be king of some new found land; and like another Alexander indeed, searching after new worlds, have the sovereignty of Nova Scotia. He was born a poet, and aimed to be a king; therefore would he have his royal title from King James, who was born a king, and aimed to be a poet. Had they stopped there, it had been well; but the flame of his honour must have some oyle wherewith to nourish it. Like another King Arthur, he must have his knights, though nothing limited to so small a number; for how many soever that could have looked out but for one day like gentlemen, and given him but one hundred and fifty pounds sterlin, without any need of a key for opening the gate to enter through the temple of vertue, which in former times was the only way to honour, they had a scale from him whereby to ascend unto the platformes of vertue, which they treading underfoot, did slight the ordinary passages, and to take the more sudden possession of the temple of honour, went upon obscure by-paths of their own, towards some secret angiports and dark postern-doors, which were so narrow, that few of them could get in till they had left all their gallantry behind them; yet such being their resolution, that in they would, and be worshipful upon any tearms, they misregarded all formerly used steps of promotion, accounting them but unnecessary; and most rudely rushing in unto the very sanctuary, they immediately hung out the orange colours to testifie their conquest of the honour of Knight-Baronet.

Their King nevertheless, not to staine his royal dignity, or to seem to merit the imputation of selling honour to his subjects, did for their money give them land, and that in so ample a measure, that every one of his Knight-Baronets had for his hundred and fifty pounds sterlin, heritably disponed unto him six thousand good and sufficient acres of Nova Scotia ground, which being but at the rate of six pence an acre, could not be thought very dear, considering how prettily in the respective parchments of disposition they were bounded and designed fruitful corne land, watered with pleasant rivers running alongst most excellent and spacious meadows; nor did there want abundance of oaken groves in the midst of very fertil plaines, for if they wanted any thing, it was the scrivener or writer's fault; for he gave order, as soon as he received the three thousand Scots marks, that there should be no defect in quantity or quality, in measure or goodness of land, and here and there most delicious gardens and orchards, with whatever else could in matter of delightful ground best content their fancies, as if they had made purchase amongst them of the Elysian Fieldes, or Mahumet's Paradise.

After this manner my Lord Sterlin for a while was very noble; and according to the rate of sterlin money, was as twelve other Lords in the matter of that frankness of disposition, which not permitting him to dodge it upon inches and ells, better and worse, made him not stand to give to each of his champions territories of the best and the most; and although there should have happened a thousand acres more to be put in the charter or writing of disposition then was agreed upon at first, he cared not; half a piece to the clerk was able to make him dispense with that. But at last, when he had inrolled some two or three hundred Knights, who, for their hundred and fifty peeces each, had purchased amongst them several millions of Neocaledonian acres, confirmed to them and theirs for ever under the great seal, the affixing whereof was to cost each of them but thirty peeces more; finding that the society was not like to become any more numerous, and that the ancient gentry of Scotland esteemed of such a whimsical dignity as of a disparagement rather then addition to their former honor, he bethought himself of a course more profitable for himself, and the future establishment of his own state; in prosecuting whereof, without the advice of his Knights, who represented both his houses of parliament, clergy, and all, like an absolute King indeed, disponed heritably to the French, for a matter of five or six thousand pounds English money, both the dominion and propriety of the whole continent of that kingdom of Nova Scotia, leaving the new Baronets to search for land amongst the Selenits in the Moon, or turn Knights of the Sun. So dearly have they bought their orange riban, which, all circumstances considered, is and will be no more honorable to them or their posterity, then it is or hath been profitable to either.

What I have said here is not by way of digression, but to very good purpose, and pertinent to the subject in hand; for as armes and arts commonly are paralelled, and that Pallas goes armed with a helmet, I held it expedient, lest the list of the scholars set down in this place should in matter of pre-eminence be too far over-peered by the roll of the souldiers above recited, that my Lord Sterlin should here represent the place of a king for the literary part, as well as there did the great uncircumcised Garne for the military, and bring Nova Scotia in competition with Bucharia.

Besides this Lord Alexander, Drummond and Wishart have published very good poems in English. Nor is Master Ogilvy to be forgot, whose translation of Virgil, and of the fables of Æsop in very excellent English verses, most evidently manifesteth that the perfection of the English tongue is not so narrowly confined, but that it may extend it self beyond the natives on this side of Barwick.

I might have named some more Scotish poets both in English and Latine, but that besides, as I often told, I intend not to make a compleat enumeration of all, there is a Latin book extant which passeth by the name of *Deliciæ Poetarum Scotorum*, where-in the Reader may finde many, even of those that have lived of late yeers, whom I have here omitted, as I have done several other able men of the Scotish nation in other faculties, such as Master David Chalmers, who in Italy penned a very good book, and that in neat Latine, treating of the antiquities of Scotland, and had it printed at Paris; as also one Simson, who wrote in Latine four exquisite books of Hieroglyphicks; and one Hart in the city of London at this present, who wrote the *Fort Royal of Scripture, &c.*

The excellency of Doctor William Davison in alchymy above all the men now living in the world, whereof by his wonderful experiments he giveth daily proof, although his learned books published in the Latine tongue did not evince it, meriteth well to have his name recorded in this place. And after him Doctor Leeth, though in time before him, designed in Paris, where he lived by the name of Letu; who, as in the practise and theory of medicine he excelled all the doctors of France, so in testimony of the approbation he had for his exquisiteness in that faculty, he left behinde him the great-est estate of any of that profession then, as the vast means possest by his sons and daughters there as yet can testifie.

Amongst those eminent doctors of physick, I ought not to forget Doctor Fraser, who was made doctor at Toulouse, with the universal approbation and applause of that famous university, and afterwards succeeded to Doctor Arthur Johnstoun's place of Physician in ordinary to the late King. There is another Scotish gentleman, likewise, of the name of Wallace, in France called Devalois, who enjoyeth, and hath so done these many yeers, the dignity of a prime counsellor of the Parlament of Grenoble, the capital city of the province of Dauphiné; and is, withal, the chief favourite and the only trustee of the grand Mareshal de Criky.

Now, as in this heterogenean miscellany we have proceeded from the body to the purse, that is, metonymically, from the physician to the lawyer, so after the same desultory manner, which may be well excused in this unpremeditated and almost extemporanean treatise, we may for the soul's sake, which in this later age, so far as metaphors may with proper significations enter in competition, hath been no less subject to poverty and diseases than any of the former two, have another hint at some of our late Scotish divines. The first whereof, and that *prioritate dignitatis*, that to my memory presenteth himself, is Doctor William Forbas, Principal once of the colledge of New Aberdeen, and afterwards made Bishop of Edenburgh; who was so able a scholar, that since the daies of *Scotus Subtilis*, there was never any that professed either divinity or philosophy in Scotland, that in either of those faculties did parallel him. He left manuscripts of great learning behind him; which, as I am informed, were bought at a good rate by Doctor Laud, late Archbishop of Canterbury and Primate of England; whose spiritual brother, Spotteswood, late Archbishop of Saint Andrews, and Chancellor of Scotland, was likewise endowed with a great deal of learning; by means whereof, although he wrote many good books, yet that wherein he bestowed most pains was a large book in folio, intituled, *The History of the Church of Scotland*, which I believe was never printed; yet the manuscript thereof, written with Spotteswod's own hand, I saw presented at Whitehall, in the lobby betwixt the little gallery and privy chamber, now called the Admiralty Court, by Maxwell late Bishop of Rosse, to the late King, who even then delivered it to his Secretary of State for Scotland, William Earl of Lanerick by name, who was the same Duke Hamiltoun of Hamiltoun that was killed at Worcester, and only brother to James Duke by the same aforesaid title, who two yeers before that lost his head at Westminster, in the Palace-yard; but what became of that manuscript afterwards I cannot tell; but this I know, that the tenderer therof, upon his knees to his late Majesty, as the gift of a deceased man, for the author dyed but the very day before, Master John Maxwel by name, was a very learned man, and author of some good books. Yet, lest the reader's humour should be inflamed with the mentioning of these three malignant prelates, I must afford him for antidote another trinity of a contrary operation, all in one dose, the ingredients whereof are Henderson, Gillespick, and Rutherford, named Alexander, George, and Samuel, all Masters truly, and have been so to my knowledge these twelve yeers past; which three have been or are, for the first two of them are dead, very able and learned men; whose books, nevertheless, for they were all authors, I will in some things no otherwayes commend then Andræas Rivetus, professor of Leyden, did the doctrine of Buchanan and Knox; whose rashness, in apologizing for them, he ascribed *præ fervido Scotorum ingenio, et ad audendum prompto.*

Truly, and without flattery be it spoken, for I believe none that knows me will twit me with that vice, the nation of Scotland hath, besides those I have here nominated, produced several excellent spirits, and that of late too, whose abilities, by the Presbyterian persecution, and the indigence it hath brought upon them, have been quite smothered, and hid as a candle under a bushel.

Many learned books written in Scotland, for want of able and skillful printers, and other necessaries requisite for works of such liberal undertaking, have perished; and sometimes after they are ready for the press, if the author in the interim happen to dy, the wife and children, for the most part, like rats and mice, that preferr the chest where the bread and cheese is kept, to the coffer wherein is the silver and gold, to save a little money, make use of the aforesaid papers, without any regard to the precious things contained in them, to fold perhaps their butter and cheese into, or to other less honourable employments. So unfortunate a thing it is, that either good spirits should be struck with penury, or that their writings should fall into the hands of ignorants.

That poverty is an enemy to the exercise of vertue, and that *non facile emergunt quorum virtutibus obstat res angusta domi,* is not unknown to any acquainted with Plutocracy, or the soveraign power of money; but if the great men of the land would be pleased to salve that sore, which possibly would not be so expensive to them as either their hawks or hounds, then peradventure would these ingenious blades sing out aloud, and cheerfully, with Martial, *Sint Mecænates non deerunt Flacce Marones;* and it might very probably be, and that in a short space, that by such gallant incitements, through a vertuous emulation who should most excell other, Scotland would produce, for philosophy, astronomy, natural magick, poesie, and other such like faculties, as able men as ever were Duns-Scotus, Sacroboscus, Reginaldus Scotus, and other compatriots of these three Scots, whose names I would not insert in the roll of the rest, because they flourished before the yeer 1600.

Now, as I have not mentioned any Scotish man to praise him for eminent actions done by him, either in the field or schoole, preceding the yeer 1600; which if I had had a minde to do, I would not have omitted the naming of the several Constables of France, Admirals, and Generals of armies, that have been of the Scotish nation in the French service; neither would I have forgot the high and honourable employments the Scots had of Charlemaine, the first occidental Emperor, nor the great exploits performed by the Scots under the conduct of Godfrey de Bullion in the conquest of Jerusalem, and afterwards under his successors in the kingdoms of Syria, Antiochia, and Egypt, against the Saracens; nor what was done by the Scots in defence of the territories of Spaine against the Moores and Æthiopians; as also I would have spoken a little of the Dukes of Chasteau le roy, and Dukes of Aubigny that were Scots;

and of Count Betun, and Count de Mongomery, who killed the King of France in tilting ; so is it that of all those I have named, whether for milice or literature, so far short I have faln in the number of the whole, that not only hath the greatest part of all been natives of the north of Scotland, but hardly have both the south and west of that country produced the fifth part of them ; such a fruitful seminary hath that other-wayes obscure climate of the world proved, in the affording of excellent spirits both for armes and arts. Whether what I have related here of the warriors and scholars of the Scotish nation that have been famous abroad, be not for uncontrollable truths received in other countries, by those that have been eye-witnesses to their actions, I appeal to Sir Oliver Fleemin, master of the ceremonies, and to Master Dury ; who, as they are both men of good judgment, and have been travelers in other states and kingdoms, so am I certainly perswaded that they cannot be altogether estranged from the report of the good reputation of those their compatriots in the places through which they passed ; which I believe the rather, for that most of them do know Sir Oliver Flee-min to be a man of excellent good parts, wise in counsel, experienced in affaires of state, true to his trust, and in six or seven of the chief languages of Christendome, the ablest, liveliest, and most pertinent spokesman of the age ; and that also they are not ignorant of the most eminent endowments wherewith Master John Dury, in Ger-many and France, where his learning is highly extolled, intituled Duræus, hath his minde qualified and imbellished ; in reason he is strongly principled, and alloweth prudence to be a directress of his actions ; he doth not subordinate his faith to the affaires of the world, although it agree not with his faith to gainestand an established authority ; he holds it more lawful to yeeld obedience to a power set up above us, then, to the hazard of the ruine of a country, to erect another ; he loveth an honest peace, and the wayes that tend to it, and with thankfulness payeth the favours of pro-tection ; he reverenceth the all-seeing Providence in the change of government, and where it commandeth, there he yeelds allegiance. But if the reader would have a more genuine character of his worth, and that which shall represent him with a greater liveliness, his best course will be to have recourse to the perusal of the several treatises composed by him, whereof he hath emitted good store.

Notwithstanding all I have written in praise of Sir Oliver Fleemin and Master John Dury, I would expatiate my pen a little more at large upon this encomiastick straine, in behalf of them both, but that I hope ere long to extoll them againe by way of duty, when they shall be pleased, out of their love and respect to Sir Thomas Vrquhart, who is the only man for whom this book is intended, for whether he be the author or some other that is but a friend or servant of his, it is not material, seeing the furtherance of his weal, and credit of his country, is the meer scope thereof, and end whereat it buts, to interpone their favour with the members of the Parliament and Councel of State, seeing they are the only two of the Scotish nation that as yet have any kind of intimacy with either of these high Courts, and second him in his just demands, to the obtaining of what in this tractate is desired in his name. And although nothing of those kinde of good offices hath by them hitherto been performed to him, lest perhaps their offering to open their mouth for any in whom there was suspicion of malignancy, might breed dislike and diminution of trust, yet must I needs desire them now to lay aside those needless fears and groundless apprehensions, and, like real friends indeed, bestir themselves to do that gentleman a courtesie, which cannot chuse, though *per impossibile* he were unthankful, but carry along with it, like all other actions of vertue, its own remuneration and reward; and if by mischance, which I hope shall not occur, their forwardness in solicitation procure a reprehensory check, then let them lay the blame upon this page, which I shall take upon my shoulder, and bear the burthen of all; there is no inchantment there. But that *Amicus certus in re incerta cernitur* was a saying of King James, of whom to make no mention amongst the literate men of the Scotish nation that have flourished since 1600, would argue in me no less debility of memory then Massala Corvinus was subject to, who forgot his own name; for besides that he was a king, history can hardly afford us amongst all the kings that ever were, Solomon and Alfonso of Aragon being laid aside, any one that was neer so learned as he; as is apparent by that book in folio, intituled, *King James his Works*, and several other learned treatises of his, which in that book are not contained.

In this list of armes and arts-men, King James obtaines a rank amongst the scholars, because the souldiery did repute him no favourer of their faculty. His Majesty is placed last, as in a Parliamentary procession, and bringeth up the reer, as General Ruven leads on the van; for as Ruven was such a meer souldier that he could neither read nor write, so King James was such a meer scholar that he could neither fight by sea nor land. He thought James the Peaceable a more royal stile then William the Conqueror, and would not have changed his motto of *Beati pacifici* for the title of *Sylla felix*, although it had been accompanyed with the victory over a thousand Mariuses; yet in his dayes were the Scots in good repute, and their gallantry over almost all countries did deserve it.

Then was it that the name of a Scot was honourable over all the world, and that the glory of their ancestors was a pass-port and safe-conduct sufficient for any traveler of that country. In confirmation whereof, I have heard it related of him who is the το ὗ ἕνεκα of this discourse, and to whose weal it is subordinated, that after his peragration of France, Spaine, and Italy, and that for speaking some of those languages with the liveliness of the country accent, they would have had him pass for a native, he plainly told them, without making bones thereof, that truly he thought he had as much honour by his own country, which did contrevalue the riches and fertility of those nations, by the valour, learning, and honesty, wherein it did parallel if not surpass them. Which assertion of his was with pregnant reasons so well backed by him, that he was not much gainesaid therein by any in all those kingdoms. But should he offer now to stand upon such high terms, and enter the lists with a spirit of competition, it fears me that in stead of laudatives and panegyricks, which formerly he used, he would be constrained to have recourse to vindications and apologies; the toyle whereof, in saying one and the same thing over and over again, with the misfortune of being the less believed the more they spoke, hath proved of late almost insupportable to the favourers of that nation, whose inhabitants, in forraign peregrinations, must now altogether in their greatest difficulties depend upon the meer stock of their own merit, with an abatement of more then the half of its value, by reason of the national imputation; whilst in former times, men of meaner endowments would in sharper extremities, at the hands of stranger-people, have carryed thorrow with more specious advantages, by the only vertue of the credit and good name of the country in general; which, by twice as many abilities as ever were in that land, both for martial prowess and favour of the muses, in the persons of private men, can never in the opinion of neighbour states and kingdoms, be raised to so great hight as publick obloquy hath deprest it. For as that city whose common treasure is well stored with money, though all its burgers severally be but poor, is better able to maintaine its reputation, then that other, all whose citizens are rich without a considerable bank; the experience whereof history gives us, in the deduction of the wars betwixt the Venetians and Genois; even so will a man of indifferent qualifications, the fame of whose country remaineth unreproached, obtaine a more amicable admittance to the societies of most men, then another of thrice more accomplished parts, that is the native of a soyle of an opprobrious name; which, although after mature examination it should seem not to deserve, yet upon the slipperiest ground that is of honor questioned, a very scandal once emitted, will both touch and stick.

This maintaining of the reputation of the Scots in these latter dayes, hath at several times, in forraign countries, occasioned adventuring of the single combat, against such inconsiderable blabs, as readily upon any small though groundless misreport are prodigal of reproaches, and cast aspersions on men of the most immaculate carriage. Many instances hereof I could produce, but to avoid prolixity, I will refer the manifestation of the truth thereof to the testimony of Captain John Mercer, whom I might have nominated for his excellency in the sword with Sir John Hume of Eatoun, and Francis Sinclair, but that in a treatise of this nature, where the subjected matter doth not all at once present it self to the memory, to place each one in order as he comes, is *methodo doctrinæ* nothing repugnant to the true series of the purpose in hand.

What ascendant he hath over others at the single rapeer, hath been many times very amply expressed by my Lord of Newcastle, and the late Earl of Essex, and, as I am informed, by this same Earl of Salisbury, besides divers others, who have been eye-witnesses to the various proofs he hath given of his exquisiteness in the art of defence; amongst whom Sir John Carnegy and Sir David Cuningham are best able to relate what with their own eyes they saw him do at Angiers, a city in France, where, after many exasperating provocations, he at last, to vindicate both his own fame and that of his native country, overthrew, in the presence of sundry gentlemen and ladies, one of the most renowned for the faculty of escrime that was in all that kingdom. Some such trials are reported to have been undergone by him here in England, with so much applause and deserved approbation, as from the mouths of men very skilful in that gladiatory profession, hath extracted, out of their sincerity of heart, an unfeigned commendation of being the best swordman of the Isle of Great Britain. Which I say not to disparage any of the English nation, for that I know there are in it as truly valourous men as any one breathing in the world, and of as good conduct for the improving of their courage, and making it effectual against their declared enemies ; but that he hath some secret puntilios in the exercise of the single sword-fight, by pursuing all manner of wards with falsifying, binding, and battering of the sword, after a fashion of his own, with all due observance of time and distance ; by providing, in case the adversary after a *finda*, going to the *parade*, discover his brest to *caveat*, and give him in a thrust in *quart*, with *ecarting* and *volting* the body ; to alonge a stoccade *coupee au ventre les deux pieds en sautant*, and other such excellent feats, which the judgment conceiving and the eye perceiving, the hand and foot, by vertue of a constant practise, execute with an incredible nimbleness and agility ; to the perfection whereof although a martially-disposed gentleman do never attaine, it can no more derogate from his eminency in military employments, then it doth eclipse the credit of a commander-in-chief of cavalry, not to make a well-managed horse to go so neatly *terre a terre*, the *incavalar*, the *ripolone*, the *passades*, the *corvetti*, the *serpegiar*, the *two steps and a leap*, the *mezere*, the *gallop galliard*, *le saut de mouton*, and other such like pleasant aires, as would a *cavallerizo*, or master of the noble art of riding. Notwithstanding the frequent hazards which many besids this Capt. Mercer, whom now I will not nominate, have run themselves upon, in defence of the good name of the Scots, the nature nevertheless of common spirits is, without any forecast of danger, to proclaim the disease of some to be a leprosie cleaving to the whole body of the nation.

Which custom, truly, as it is disapprovable for that the innocent do thereby suffer for the fault of the guilty, so do I the more dislike it, that the gentleman who in this treatise is the most concerned, when, after that to my knowledge he had received some favour, with expectation of greater ones, it no sooner happened, by his servants or some else, to be known of what country he was, but immediately the effectual courtesies formerly intended towards him were exchanged into meer superficial complements and general civilities, with this assurance, nevertheless, that out of their respects to him, they should abstaine in all times coming from doing any injury to his compatriots ; which hope of preservation of his countrymen, upon the basis of his single reputation, from the danger of future prejudice, did afford him no small contentment, although the name of his country, in matter of himself, did prove a very dismal obstruction to the prosecuting of his own good fortune ; and, to speak ingenuously, seeing it is the case of many good spirits and worthy gentlemen besides him, I could heartily wish, as no man is any where praised for his mother's being in such or such a place at the instant of his birth, that also nowhere any should receive the least detriment, either in his means or estimation, for his parents' residence when he was born.

Those productions of meer chance, and concomitances of what is totally out of the reach of our power to command, were understood by the wise and generous men of old, to deserve so little influence for procuring good or bad to the enjoyers of them, that Anacharsis, although a native of Scythia, which was then a more savage country then at this time it is, albeit now it be the seminary of a wilder people then ever Scotland did bring forth, was by Greece, the most judicious nation in the world, with great applause inrolled in the sacred septenary of the most highly-renowned men for prudence and true wisdom that ever lived there ; and Oxales, notwithstanding his being a high-lander of Genua, and born amidst the barren mountains of Liguria, was nevertheless by the mighty Emperour Tamarlain, although a stranger, and of a different religion to the boot, dignified with the charge and title of one of the prime generals of that vast Asiatick army which overthrew the Turkish Bajazet.

In imitation of which specious and remarkable examples, that the state of this Isle, without regard to Ephestian or exotick country, exterior concernments, adjuncts of fortune, or any thing beyond the sphere of our will's activity, should consider of men according to the fruits, whether good or bad, true or false, of the several acts and habits respectively, which, before the interior faculties by frequent iteration were therewith affected, did at first depend upon our own election, it is both my desire and expectation, for that the gentleman whose interest I hereby intend to promove, doth openly defie very calumny it self to be able to lay any thing to his charge, either for tergiversation, covetousness, or hypocrisie, the three foule blots wherewith his country is stained by those that, for the blemish of a few, would asperse the whole, and upon all lay the imputation of faults done but by some.

I dare swear, with a safe conscience, that he never coveted the goods of any, nor is desirous of any more in matter of worldly means, then the peceable possession of what is properly his own ; he never put his hand to any kinde of oath, nor thinks fit to tye his conscience to the implicite injunctions of any ecclesiastical tyranny. He never violated trust, alwayes kept his parole, and accounted no crime more detestable then the breach of faith. He never received money from King nor Parliament, State nor Court, but in all his employments, whether preparatory to or executional in war, was still his own paymaster, and had orders from himself. He was neither in Duke Hamilton's engagement, nor at the field of Dunbar ; nor was he ever forced, in all the several fights he hath been in, to give ground to the enemy, before the day of Worcester battel. To be masked with the vaile of hypocrisie, he reputes abominable, and gross dissimulation to contrast the ingenuity of a free-born spirit. All flattering, smoothing, and flinching for by-ends, he utterly disliketh, and thinks no better of adulatory assentations then of a gnatonick sycophantizing, or parasitical cogging; he loves to be open-hearted, and of an explicite discourse, chusing rather by such means to speak what is true to the advantage of the good, then to conceal wickedness under a counterfeit garb of devotion.

By vertue of which liberty, though reasonably assumed by him, and never exceeding the limits of prudential prescription, he in a little book lately published, of the Genealogy of his House, had, after the manner of his predecessors, who for distinction sake were usually entituled by appellative designations, his proper name affected with the agnominal addition of the word *Parresiastes*, which signifieth one that speaks honestly with freedom; not but that above all things he approveth of secrecy in the managing of affaires of the moment, and holdeth the life of all great businesses to consist in the closeness of counsel whilst they are in agitation; but as a woman should not sit with her face masked in the company of her friends at dinner, nor a man keep himself alwaies skulking behinde a buckler where there is no apearance of a foe; so should the affectedness of a servil silence utterly be exploded, when veracity of elocution is the more commendable quality.

This bound he never yet transgressed, and still purposeth to be faithful to his trust. I am not now to dispute the mutual relation of protection and obedience; and how far, to the power God hath placed above us, in imitation of Christ, we are bound to succumb. Those that are thoroughly acquainted with him know his inclinations, both that he will undertake nothing contrary to his conscience, that he will regulate his conscience by the canons of a well-grounded faith and true dictamen of reason, and that to the utmost of his power he will perform whatever he promiseth. As for those that know him not, and yet would in the censure of him as liberally criticize it as if they were his cardiognosts, and fully versed in his intentions; if they be not men in whom he is concerned, as having authority above him, he will never vex his brain, nor toyle his pen, to couch a fancy, or bestowe one drop of inke upon them for their satisfaction. It doth suffice him, that the main ground of all his proceedings is honesty; that he endeavoreth the prosecuting of just ends by upright means; and seeing the events of things are not in the power of man, he voluntarily recommendeth unto providence the over-ruling of the rest; he hath no prejudicate principles, nor will he be wedded to self-opinions.

And yet, as I conceive it, he believeth that there is no government, whether ecclesiastical or civil, upon earth that is *jure divino*, if that divine right be taken in a sense secluding all other forms of government, save it alone, from the privilege of that title; those *piæ fraudes* and political whimsies being obtruded upon tender consciences to no other end but that, without expense of war, they might be plyable in their obedience to the injunctions of the vice-gerents of the law, meerly by deterring them from acting any thing contrary to the will of the primitive legislator for fear of celestial punishment.

As for pacts and covenants, it is my opinion that he thinks they are no further obligatory, and consequently being annihilated, no more to be mentioned, much less urged, when the ground whereupon they are built, or cause for which they were taken, are not in vigour to have any more influence upon the contractors; for *idem est non esse et non operari; non entium nullæ sunt affectiones;* and *sublato fundamento tolluntur et omnia quæ illi superstruuntur.*

I am confident the Consistorian party will be so ill pleased with the freedom of this expression, that they will account him a Malignant or a sectary that hath penned it; therefore, in my conceit, to use their cavilling idiom, a Malignant and Independent will better sympathize with one another, then either of them with the Presbyter, whose principles how consistent they are with monarchy, or any other kind of temporal soveraignty, let any man judge that is versed in the story of Geneva, the civil wars of France and Bohemia, and history of Queen Mary of Scotland; although what hath been done by kirkists these last dozen of yeers had been altogether buryed in oblivion, that nothing had been known of their unanimous opposition by the Presbyterian armies at Dunslaw, Newburne, Marston-moor, and Hereford, to the late King's designes, crowned by his own imprisonment at Newcastle and Holmby; and that after proclaiming Charles the Second at the Market-cross of Edenburgh, King of the three realms of England, Scotland, and Ireland, that they had wounded him and shed his blood in the persons of the peerage of Huntely and Montrose, had been utterly forgotten.

What gallant subjects these Presbyterians have been, are for the present, and will prove in times coming, to any kinde of secular power, you may perceive by King James his ΒΑΣΙΛΙΚΟΝ ΔΩΡΟΝ, the late King's ΕΙΚΩΝ ΒΑΣΙΛΙΚΗ, and this young King's ΒΑΣΙΛΙΚΟΣ ΑΔΥΝΑΣΤΗΣ; they to basilical rule, or any other temporal soveraignty, being in all its genders, and that at all occasions, as infectious as ever was the Basilisk's sight to the eye of man.

For of a king they onely make use for their own ends, and so they will of any other supreme magistracie that is not of their own erection. Their kings are but as the Kings of Lacedemon, whom the Ephors presumed to fine for any small offence; or as the puppy Kings, which, after children have trimmed with bits of taffata, and ends of silver lace, and set them upon wainscoat cupboards besides marmalade and sugar-cakes, are oftentimes disposed of, even by those that did pretend so much respect unto them, for a two-peny custard, a pound of figs, or mess of cream.

Verily, I think they make use of kings in their Consistorian State, as we do of card kings in playing at the hundred; any one whereof, if there be appearance of a better game without him, and that the exchange of him for another incoming card is like to conduce more for drawing of the stake, is by good gamesters without any ceremony discarded: or as the French on the Epiphany-day use their *Roy de la fèbve,* or king of the bean; whom, after they have honoured with drinking of his health, and shouting, *Le Roy boit, le Roy boit,* they make pay for all the reckoning; not leaving him sometimes one peny, rather then that the exorbitancie of their debosh should not be satisfied to the full. They may be likewise said to use their king as the players at nine-pins do the middle kyle, which they call the king; at whose fall alone they aim, the sooner to obtain the gaining of their prize; or as about Christmais we do the King of Misrule, whom we invest with that title to no other end but to countenance the bacchanalian riots and preposterous disorders of the family where he is installed.

The truth of all this appears by their demeanour to Charles the Second, whom they crowned their King at Sterlin, and who, though he be, for comeliness of person, valour, affability, mercy, piety, closeness of counsel, veracity, foresight, knowledge, and other vertues both moral and intellectual, in nothing inferiour to any of his hundred and ten predecessors, had nevertheless no more rule in effect over the Presbyterian Senate of Scotland, then any of the six foresaid mock-kings had above those by whom they were dignified with the splendour of royal pomp.

That it is so, I appeal to the course taken by them for assisting him whom they called their King, against them whom I must confess they hate more then him; for, admitting of none to have any charge in State, Church, or Army, but such as had sworn to the eternity of the Covenant, and inerrability of the Presbyterian See, lest otherwise, like Achan's wedge, they should bring a judgement upon the land; some Lords, and many others so principled, after that by their King they had been intrusted with commissions to levie regiments of both horse and foot, together with other officers subordinate to them, did, under pretext of making the King a glorious king, and the Covenant to triumph at the gates of Rome, with pseudo-sanctimonial trick of zeal-legerdemaim subtilty, and performing the admirable feats of making a little weak man, unfit for military service, a tall, strong, and warlike champion, and that onely by the sweet charm of laying twenty rexdolars upon his head and shoulders; as also by the arch-angelical inchantment of fifteen double angels, had the skill to make an Irish hobbie, or Galloway nag, as sufficient for their field-fight as any Spanish genet, or Naples courser.

In prosecution of which wonderful exploits, some of them approved themselves such exquisite alchymists, that many of both the cavalry and infantry, with their arms, ammunition, and apparel, were by them converted into pure gold and silver; by means whereof, although the army shrunk into half the proposed number, in both horse, foot, and dragoons, and all the most necessary accommodations for either camp, leaguer, or march, was chymically transformed into the aforesaid wel-beloved metal, they nevertheless put such undoubted confidence into the goodness of their cause, that, by vertue thereof, no less miraculous acts were expected and promised by the prophecies of their Neo-Levites out of Scripture, to be atchieved by them against the Malignants and Sectaries, then those of Gideon with his water-lappers, and Jonathan with his armour-bearer, against the Midianites and Philistims; to so great a height did their presumption reach; and yet when it came to the push, those that had received greatest profit by the country assessments, and ruined with cruellest exactions the poor yeomanry, were the first that returned homewards, being loth to hazard their precious persons, lest they should seem to trust to the arm of flesh.

Notwithstanding this backsliding from martiall prowess of the godly officers, with the epenthesis of an *l*, in which number I inrol not all, but the greater part of those that were commissionated with the Scot-Ecclesiastical approbation, their rancour and spleen being still more and more sharpned against the English nation, they in their tedious pharisaical prayers before supper, and sesquihoral graces upon a dish of skink and leg of mutton, would so imbue the mindes of the poor swains, on whose charge they were, with vaticinations of help from heaven, against the Sennacheribs that were about to infest Hezekiah's host, and the peace of their Israel, that the most innocent sufferers having sustained more prejudice by quartering, plundering, and continual impositions of those their hypocritical countrymen, then ever their predecessors had done by all the devastations of the ancient English, Saxons, Danes, and Romans; the holier they were in outward shew, their actions proving still the more diabolical; they, in recompense of those aerial, or rather fiery ejaculations, recommended the avenging of their wrongs to God, and heartily loaded them, and that deservedly, with as many curses and execrations as they had lost of pence; the pretty effect of a good cause, and result sutable to the project of making the jure-divine presbytery a government which, besides its universality and eternity, should, in matter of dominion, be, for its sublimity, placed above all the potentates on the earth; preferring, by that account, a Scotish Moderator to a Romane Dictator; although they minded not that such as claimed most right to this generalissima-jurisdiction, were, unknown to themselves, chained in fetters of iron, as slaves to the tyrannie of two insolent masters, the concupiscible and irascible appetites.

Who doubteth, that is not blinded with the ablepsie of an implicite zeal, but that, by such contrivements, the three foresaid dominions, together with Wales, were as fully projected to be subject to the uncontrolable commands of the Kirk, as the territories of Romania, Vrbino, Ferrara, and Avignon, to the See of Rome; though with this advantage on the Pope's side, that joynt to the power wherewith he is invested by his Papality, he ruleth over those parts by the right of a secular prince, which title they cannot pretend to.

Were those kirkmen free from covetousness and ambition, whereinto that most of them are no less deeply plunged then any laick in the world, sufficient proof within these two yeers hath been given in Scotland, by their laying claim to the fifth part of all the rents of the land, under the notion of tythes; devesting noblemen of their rights of patronages, and bringing their persons to stand before them on Penitentiary pews, like so many varlets, in mendiciary and gausapinal garments; not so much for any trespass they had committed, as thereby to confirm the soveraignty of their hierarchial jurisdiction, which is neither monarchical, aristocratical, nor democratical, but a meer Plutarchy, Plutocracy, or rather Plutomanie; so madly they hale after money, and the trash of this world. If so, I say, they were not guilty of such like enormities, and that according to their talk of things above, their lives were answerable, or yet the result of their acts when all together in assemblies, synods, or presbyteries, they are congregated into one body, then to require such matters might in some measure seem excusable; because an unfeigned zeal to the furtherance of learning, piety, and good works, should be seconded with power and wealth; but that for a meer aerial discourse of those whose hearts are ingulphed in the dross of worldly affections, others should part from their own means and dignities to enrich the wives and children of hypocrites, is a crying sin before God, contrary to Saint Paul's admonition, who accounteth men infidels that do so, and the abusing of those benefits he hath vouchsafed to allow us, for the maintenance of our families, and provision for posterity.

Is there any more common saying over all Scotland in the mouthes of the laicks, then that the minister is the greediest man in the parish, most unwilling to bestow any thing in deeds of charity? and that the richer they become, without prejudice be it spoken of some honest men amongst them, the more wretched they are? grounding that assertion on this, That by their daily practice, both severally and conjunctly, it is found that for their splendour and inrichment, most of them do immire their spirits into worldly projects, not caring by what sordid means they may attain their aims; and if they make any kinde of sermocination tending in outward appearance to godliness, which seldom they do, being enjoyned by their ecclesiastical authority to preach to the times, that is, to rail against malignants and sectaries, or those whom they suppose to be their enemies, they do it but as those augurs of old, of whom Aulus Gellius speaking, saith, *Aures verbis ditant alienas, suas ut auro locupletent crumenas.*

I know I touch here a string of a harsh sound to the Kirk, of a note dissonant from their proposed harmony, and quite out of the systeme of the intended œcumenick government by them concerted; but seeing there are few will be taken with the melody of such a democratical hierarchie, that have not preallably been stung with the tarantula of a preposterous ambition, I will insist no longer on this purpose; and that so much the rather, that he, whose writings I in this tractate intermix with my own, tempers his Heliconian water with more honey then vinegar, and prefers the epigrammatical to the satyrick straine; for although, I think, there be hardly any in Scotland that proportionably hath suffered more prejudice by the Kirk then himself; his own ministers, to wit, those that preach in the churches whereof himself is patron, Master Gilbert Anderson, Master Robert Williamson, and Master Charles Pape by name, serving the cures of Cromarty, Kirkmichel, and Cullicudden, having done what lay in them, for the furtherance of their owne covetous ends, to his utter undoing: for the first of those three, for no other cause but that the said Sir Thomas would not authorize the standing of a certain pew, in that country called a desk, in the church of Cromarty, put in without his consent by a professed enemy to his House, who had plotted the ruine thereof, and one that had no land in the parish, did so rail against him and his family in the pulpit at several times, both before his face and in his absence, and with such opprobrious termes, more like a scolding tripe-seller's wife then good minister, squirting the poyson of detraction and abominable falshood, unfit for the chaire of verity, in the eares of his tenandry, who were the onely auditors, did most ingrately and despightfully so calumniate and revile their master, his own patron and benefactor, that the scandalous and reproachful words striving which of them should first discharge against him its steel-pointed dart, did, oftentimes like clusters of hemlock, or wormewood dipt in vinegar, stick in his throat; he being almost ready to choak with the aconital bitterness and venom thereof, till the razor of extream passion, by cutting them into articulate sounds, and very rage it self, in the highest degree, by procuring a vomit, had made him spue them out of his mouth into rude indigested lumps, like so many toads and vipers that had burst their gall.

As for the other two, notwithstanding that they had been borne, and their fathers before them, vassals to his house, and the predecessor of one of them had shelter in that land, by reason of slaughter committed by him, when there was no refuge for him anywhere else in Scotland ; and that the other had never been admitted to any church had it not been for the favour of his foresaid patron, who, contrary to the will of his owne friends, and great reluctancy of the ministry it self, was both the nominater and chuser of him to that function ; and that before his admission, he did faithfully protest he should all the days of his life remain contented with that competency of portion the late incumbent in that charge did enjoy before him; they nevertheless behaved themselves so peevishly and unthankfully towards their forenamed patron and master, that, by vertue of an unjust decree both procured and purchased from a promiscuous knot of men like themselves, they used all their utmost endeavours, in absence of their above recited patron, to whom and unto whose house they had been so much beholding, to out-law him, and declare him rebel, by open proclamation at the market-cross of the head town of his owne shire, in case he did not condescend to the grant of that augmentation of stipend which they demanded, conforme to the tenour of the above-mentioned decree; the injustice whereof will appeare when examined by any rational judge.

Now the best is, when by some moderate gentlemen it was expostulated, why against their master, patron, and benefactor, they should have dealt with such severity and rigour, contrary to all reason and equity ; their answer was, They were inforced and necessitated so to do by the synodal and presbyterial conventions of the Kirk, under paine of deprivation and expulsion from their benefices : I will not say, κακῦ κορακὸς κακὸν ᾠον, but may safely think that a well sanctified mother will not have a so ill instructed brat, and that *injuria humana* cannot be the lawfull daughter of a *jure divino* parent.

Yet have I heard him, notwithstanding all these wrongs, several times avouch, that from his heart he honoureth the ministerial function, and could wish that each of them had a competency of livelihood, to the end that for not lacking what is necessary for him, he might not be distracted from the seriousness of his speculative imploiments, with which above all things he would have one busied that were admitted to that charge, and to be a man of a choice integrity of life, and approved literature; he alwayes esteeming philosophy, in all its mathematical, natural, and prudential demonstrations, rules, and precepts, so convenient for imbellishing the minde of him whose vocation it is to be sequestred from the toil of worldly affaires, that the reason and will of man being thereby illuminated and directed towards the objects of truth and goodness, a church-man or pretender to divinity regardless of those sciences might be justly suspected to be ignorant of God, by caring so little for the knowledge of his creatures, and upon a sacred text oftentimes to make an unhallowed comment.

I have heard him likewise say, he would be glad, that in every parish of Scotland there were a free schoole and a standing library in the custody of the minister; with this proviso, that none of the books should be embezeled by him or any of his successors, and he impowered to perswade his parishioners in all he could to be liberal in their dotations towards the school, and magnifying of the library; to the end that besides the good would thereby redound to all good spirits, it might prove a great encouragement to the stationer and printer; that being the noblest profession amongst merchants, and this amongst artificers.

As also to intreat the civil magistrate, by the severity of the law, to curb the insolency of such notorious and scandalous sinners as should prove unpliable to the stamp of his wholesome admonitions.

As for his wife and children, if he follow the footsteps of Solomon, and ask sincerely for wisdome of God before he wed, he will undoubtedly endow him with wealth sufficient for both; for whoever marrieth, if he be wise, will either have a vertuous or a monyed woman to his marriage bed; by means of either whereof, the discretion and foresight of a judicious husband will provide a dowry for her, and education for her issue; which, in a well policied country, is better then a patrimony.

The taking of this course will advance learning, further piety, improve all moral vertues, establish true honour in the land, make trades flourish, merchandise prosper, the yeomanry industrious, gentlemen happy, and the ministers themselves richer then when their mindes were totally bent on the purchase of money; for, as patterns of godliness without morosity, and literature without affectation, being men qualified as aforesaid, by their sweetness of conversation and influence of doctrine, they would gaine so much ground upon the hearts of their acquaintance, that country-men would not onely gratifie them dayly, and load them with variety of presents, but would also after their decease rather chuse to starve themselves, then suffer the wives and children of persons so obliging to be in any want or indigence, specially if the traffick and civility of Scotland were promoved by a close union with England, not heterogeneal, as timber and stone upon ice stick sometimes together, bound by the frost of a conquering sword; but homogeneated by naturalization, and the mutual enjoyment of the same priviledges and immunities; which design being once by King James set abroach, although some of his compatriot subjects, out of ambition to be called rather profound scholars and nimble wits, then good country-men and loyal counsellors, did pertinaciously withstand the motion.

Yet seeing a wedge of wainscot is fittest and most proper for cleaving of an oaken tree, and that Sir Francis Bacon, otherwise designed by the titles of Lord Verulam and Viscount Saint Alban's, was pleased to make a speech thereupon in the Honourable House of Commons, in the fifth year of King James his raign in this dominion; it is the humble desire of the author, that the States of this Isle vouchsafe to take notice of his reasons, he being both a wise man and a good English man, after the manner as followeth.

HE BEGINS HIS DISCOURSE THUS:

" IT may please you, Master Speaker, preface will I use none, but put my self upon your good opinions, to which I have been accustomed beyond my deservings; neither will I hold you in suspense what way I will chuse, but now at the first declare my selfe, that I mean to counsel the House to naturalize the nation of Scotland; wherein nevertheless I have a request unto you, which is of more efficacy to the purpose I have in hand then all that I shall say afterwards, and it is the same request which Demosthenes did more then once, in great causes of estate, make to the people of Athens, that when they took into their hands the balls, whereby to give their voices, according as the manner of them was, they would raise their thoughts, and lay aside those considerations which their private vocations and degrees might minister and represent unto them, and would take upon them cogitations and mindes agreeable to the dignity and honour of the estate."

" For, Master Speaker, as it was aptly and sharply said by Alexander to Parmenio, when upon their recital of the great offers which Darius made, Parmenio said unto him, I would accept these offers were I as Alexander; he turned it upon him again, So would I, saith he, were I as Parmenio: so in this cause, if an honest English merchant, I do not single out that state in disgrace, for this Island ever held it honorable, but onely for an instance of private profession, if an English merchant should say, Surely I would proceed no further in the union were I as the King; it might be reasonably answered, No more would the King were he as an English merchant: and the like may be said of a gentleman in the country, be he never so worthy or suffi-

cient; or of a lawyer, be he never so wise or learned; or of any other particular condition in this kingdome : for certainly, Master Speaker, if a man shall be onely or
chiefly sensible of those respects which his particular affection and degree shall suggest
and infuse into him, and not enter into true and worthy considerations of estate, we
shall never be able aright to give counsel, or take counsel in this matter; for if this
request be granted, I account the cause obtained."

Having begun his speech after this manner, he proceeds yet further; and first, he
fully answers all the arguments concerning inconveniences that have been alledged to
ensue in case of giving way to this naturalization; next, he discloseth what greater
inconveniences would assuredly befal this land if they did not condescend to the union ;
and lastly, what gaine and benefit would redound to England by meanes thereof: all
which he displayeth in that learned speech with such exquisite reasons and impartial
judgment, that, without prejudicacie of opinion, and sense perverting passion, there is
nothing to be said against it.

He resteth not here, but in another passage thereof, after his having acknowledged
the difference or disparity betwixt the two nations in matter of external means,
giving therein the advantage to England as the richer country, he expresseth himself
in these words : " Indeed, it must be confessed, that for the goods of the mind and
body, they are *alteri nos ;* for, to do them but right, we know in their capacity and
understandings they are a people ingenious, in labour industrious, in courage valiant,
in body hard, active, and comely.   More might be said, but in commending them we
do but in effect commend ourselves, for they are of one part and continent with us ;
and, the truth is, we are participant both of their vertues and vices," &c.

He says, furthermore, in illustration of the inconveniences which England will incur in case of non-naturalizing the Scots, that "whatsoever several kingdoms or estates
have been united in soveraignty, if that union hath not been fortified and bound in with
a further union, and namely that which is now in question, of naturalization, this hath
followed, that at one time or other they have broken, being upon all occasions apt to
relapse and revolt to the former separation.   Of this assertion, the first example that I
will set before you, is of the memorable union which was between the Romans and the
Latines, which continued, from the battel at the lake of Regilla, for many yeers, until the Consulship of Caius Plautius, and Lucius Æmilius Mammercus; at which time
there began, about this very point of naturalization, that war which was called *Bel-
lum Sociale,* being the most bloody and pernicious war that ever the Roman state
endured ; wherein, after numbers of battels, and infinite sieges and surprisals of
towns, the Romans in the end prevailed, and mastered the Latines ; and as they had
the honour of the war, so, looking back into what perdition and confusion they were
neer to have been brought, they presently naturalized them all."

Immediately thereafter, setting before our eyes the example of Sparta, and the rest
of Peloponnesus their associates, he saith thus : " The state of Sparta was a nice and

jealous state of this point of imparting naturalization to their confederates ; but what was the issue of it ? After they held them in a kind of society and amity for divers yeeres, upon the first occasion given, which was no more then the surprisal of the castle of Thebes, by certain desperate conspirators in the habit of masters, there insued forthwith a general revolt and defection of their associates ; which was the ruine of their State, never after to be recovered."

In the same discourse he introduceth another example, though of latter times, which is this, that " notwithstanding the kingdome of Aragon had, in the persons of Ferdinand and Isabella, been united with the rest of Spain, and that it had so continued for many years, yet because it was severed and divided from the other kingdoms of Spaine in this point of naturalization, it fell out so, that, long after that, upon the voice of a condemned man out of the grate of a prison, towards the street, that cryed, *Libertad, Libertad,* there was raised a dangerous rebellion, which with great difficulty was supprest with an army royal ; after which victory, nevertheless, to shun further inconvenience, they were incorporated with Castile, and the remanent regions of Spaine. Pisa likewise being united unto Florence without the benefit of naturalization, upon the first sight of Charles the eighth of France, his expedition into Italy did revolt, yet afterwards it was reunited, and did obtain the foresaid benefit."

A little after, the better to perswade the Parliament to the said naturalization of the Scots, he subjoineth these words : " On the other part, Master Speaker, because it is true which the Logicians say, *Opposita juxta se posita clarius elucescunt ;* let us take a view, and we shall find that wheresoever kingdoms and states have been united, and that union incorporated by the bond of naturalization mutually, you shall never observe them afterwards, upon any occasion of trouble or otherwise, to break and sever again ; as we see most evidently before our eyes in our provinces of France ; that is to say, Guyen, Provence, Normandy, Britain, which, notwithstanding the infinite infesting troubles of that kingdome, never offered to break again. We see the like effect in all the kingdomes of Spain which are mutually naturalized ; as Castile, Leon, Valencia, Andaluzia, Granada, Murcia, Toledo, Catalonia, and the rest, except Aragon, which held the contrary course, and therefore had the contrary success. And, lastly, we see the like effect in our nation, which never rent asunder after it was united, so as we now scarce know whether the Heptarchy was a true story or a fable. And therefore, Master Speaker, when I revolve with myself these examples, and others, so lively expressing the necessity of a naturalization, I must say I do believe, and I would be sorry to be found a prophet in it, that except we proceed with this naturalization, though not perhaps in his Majestie's time, who hath such interest in both nations, yet in the mean time of his descendents, these realmes will be in continual danger to divide and break again. Now, if any man be of that careless mind, *Maneat nostros ea cura nepotes ;* or of that hard mind, to leave things to be tried by the sharpest sword, sure I am he is not of Saint Paul's opinion, who affirmeth, that whosoever useth not foresight and provision for his family, is worse then an infidel; much more if we shall not use foresight for these two kingdoms, that comprehend in them so many families, but leave things open to the peril of future division."

And so forth going on very efficaciously in confirmation of the premises, he proceeds to the benefits which arise to England by knitting the knot surer and straiter between these two realms, by communicating naturalization to Scotland. His words are these :—

" The benefits may appeare to be two ; the one surety, the other greatness. Touching surety, Master Speaker, it was well said by Titus Quintus the Romane, touching the state of Peloponnesus, that the tortoise is safe within her shell, *testudo intertegumen tuta est ;* but if there be any parts that lie open, they endanger all the rest. We know well, that although the State at this time be in a happy peace, yet for the time past, the more ancient enemy is the French, and the more late the Spaniard ; and both these had as it were their several postern-gates whereby they might have approach and entrance to annoy us ; France had Scotland, and Spaine had Ireland ; for these were but the two accesses which did comfort and encourage both these enemies to assaile and trouble us. We see that of Scotland is cut off by the union of these two kingdomes, if that it shall be made constant and permanent ; that of Ireland is cut off likewise, by the convenient situation of the west of Scotland towards the north of Ireland, where the sore was, which we see being suddenly closed by meanes of this salve ; so that as now there are no parts of the State exposed to danger to be a temptation to the ambition of forrainers, but their approaches and avenues are taken away ; for I do little doubt but these forrainers, who had so little success when they had those advantages, will have much less comfort now that they be taken from them. And so much for surety."

He goes on : " For greatness, Master Speaker, I think a man may speak it soberly, and without bravery, that this kingdom of England, having Scotland united, Ireland reduced, and shipping maintained, is one of the greatest monarchies, in forces truely esteemed, that hath been in the world ; for certainly the kingdomes here on earth have a resemblance with the kingdom of heaven, which our Saviour compareth not to any great kernel or nut, but to a very small graine, yet such a one as is apt to grow and spread ; and such do I take to be the constitution of this kingdom, if indeed our country be referred to greatness and power, and not quenched too much with the consideration of utility and wealth. For, Master Speaker, was it not, think you, a true answer that Solon of Greece made to rich King Crœsus of Lydia, when he shewed unto him a great quantity of gold that he had gathered together, in ostentation of his greatness and might ? But Solon said to him, contrary to his expectation, ' Why, Sir, if another come that hath better iron then you, he will be lord of all your gold.' Neither is the authority of Machiavel to be despised, who scorneth that proverb of

State, taken first from a speech of Mucianus, That moneys are the sinews of war, and saith, There are no true sinews of war, but the very armes of valiant men."

" Nay, more, Master Speaker, whosoever shall look into the seminary and beginning of the monarchies of the world, he shall finde them founded in poverty."

" Persia, a country barren and poor in respect of Media, which they reduced."

" Macedon, a kingdome ignoble and mercenary, untill the time of Philip the son of Amintas."

" Rome had a poor and pastoral beginning."

" The Turks, a band of Sarmachian Scyths, that in a vagabond manner made incursions upon that part of Asia which is called Turcomania, out of which, after much variety of fortune, sprung the Ottoman family, now the terrour of the world."

" So we know the Goths, Vandals, Alans, Huns, Lombards, Normans, and the rest of the northern people, in one age of the world made their descent and expedition upon the Roman Empire; and came, not as rovers to carry away prey and be gone againe, but planted themselves in a number of rich and fruitful provinces, where not only their generations, but their names, remaine to this day ; witness Lombardy, Catalonia, a word composed of Goth and Alan, Andaluzia, a name corrupted from Vandalitia, Hungaria, Normandy, and others ; nay, the fortune of the Swisses of late yeers, which are bred in a barren and mountanous country, is not to be forgotten ; who first ruined the Duke of Burgundy, the same who had almost ruined the kingdom of France, what time after the battel near Granson, the rich jewel of Burgundy, prised at many thousands, was sold for a few pence by a common Swisse, that knew no more what a jewel meant then did Æsop's cock ; and againe the same nation, in revenge of a scorn, was the ruine of the French King's affaires in Italy, Lowis the twelfth ; for that King, when he was pressed somewhat rudely by an agent of the Swissers to raise their pensions, broke into words of choler, ' What!' saith he, ' will those villains of the mountaines put a task upon me ?' which words lost him his dutchy of Milan, and chased him out of Italy."

" All which examples, Master Speaker, do well prove Solon's opinion of the authority and majesty that iron hath over gold." For confirmation hereof, a little after he says, " Seeing the nation of Spaine, which of ancient time served many ages, first under Carthage, then under Rome, after under Saracens, Goths, and others, should of late yeers take unto them that spirit as to dream of a Monarchy in the West, only because they have raised from some wild and unarmed people, mines and store of gold ; and, on the other side, that this Island of Britain, seated and named as it is, and that hath, I make no question, the best iron in the world, that is, the best souldiers of the world, shall think of nothing but accounts and audits, *meum* and *tuum*, and I cannot tell what, is truly very strange." Finally, he closeth that his speech with this period : " I have spoken, Master Speaker, out of the fountaine of my heart,

Credidi, propter quod loquutus sum, I believed, therefore I spake. So my duty is performed, the judgement is yours; God direct it for the best."

In another speech, again, used by the said Sir Francis Bacon in the lower House of Parliament, by occasion of a motion concerning the union of laws, he spoke thus:

" AND it please you, Master Speaker, were it now a time to wish as it is to advise, no man should be more forward or more earnest then my self in this wish, that his Majestie's subjects of England and Scotland were governed by one law, and that for many reasons."

" First, Because it will be an infallible assurance that there will never be any relapse in succeeding ages to a separation."

" Secondly, *Dulcis tractus pari jugo ;* if the draught lie most upon us, and the yoak lie least on them, or inverse-wise, it is not equal.

" Thirdly, The qualities, and, as I may term it, the elements of their laws and ours are such as do promise an excellent temperature in the compounded body; for if the prerogative here be too indefinite, it may be the liberty there is too unbounded; if our laws and proceedings be too prolix and formal, it may be theirs are too informal and summary."

" Fourthly, I do discern, to my understanding, there will be no great difficulty in this work ; for their laws by that I can learn, compared with ours, are like their language ; for, as their language hath the same roots that ours hath, but hath a little more mixture of Latin and French, so their laws and customs have the like grounds that ours have, with a little more mixture of the civil law and French customs."

" Lastly, The mean to this work seemeth to me no less excellent then the work it self; for if both laws shall be united, it is of necessity, for preparation and inducement thereunto, that our own laws be renewed and recompiled, then the which, I think, there cannot be a work more politick, more honorable, nor more beneficial to the subjects of the land for all ages; for this continual heaping up of laws without digesting them, maketh but a chaos and confusion, and turneth the laws many times to become but snares to the people, and therefore this work I esteem to be indeed a work, rightly to terme it, heroical, and that which if I might live to see, I would not desire to live after ; so that for this good wish of union of laws I do consent to the full." A little after he sayes, that " this union of laws should not precede the naturalization, nor yet go along with it *pari passu,* but altogether succeed it, and that not in the precedence of an instant, but in distance of time, because the union of laws will ask a great time to be perfected, both for the compiling and for the passing of them ; during all which time, if this mark of strangeness should be denied to be taken away, I fear it may induce such a habit of strangeness as will rather be an impediment then a preparation to further proceeding."

And albeit in the conclusion of his speech he saith, " that he holdeth this motion of union of laws very worthy, and arising from very good minds, but not proper for that time ;" yet do I think that, for this time, and as the juncture of affaires is for the present, it is very proper and expedient.

Therefore, although in some parcels of the foresaid discourse not here recited, many pregnant reasons to those that opposed the naturalization of the Scots, because that nation was annexed to England by inheritance, and not conquest, be exhibited, to shew that the grant of the benefit thereof should not be obstructed, for that Scotland was not a conquered country ; as also why the Scots' unwillingness to receive the English laws should be no impediment to their naturalization ; and that in Robert Calvin's case, which is extant to be seen in the seventh book of Sir Edward Cook's Reports, many excellent things are deduced in favour of the *postnati* of that realm, notwithstanding the diversity of laws, and Scotland's then unacknowledged subordination to the meer authority of this land ; yet seeing the face of affairs is quite altered from what it was then, and that the English civility and good carriage may gain so much upon the affections of the people there as to make them in a very short space to be of the same customs, manners, and language with them, I do really believe if Sir Francis Bacon and Sir Edward Cook were now living, that both of them would unanimously advise the State and Soveraity of this Island to allow unto Scotland, which neither is nor ever was a kingdom more then Wales was of old, the same priviledges and immunities, in every thing, that Wales now hath, and which the Scots have in France, a transmarine country, to enjoy everywhere in all things the emoluments and benefit competent to the free-born subjects of England ; and to this effect, to impower that nation with liberty to chuse their representatives to be sent hither to this their Soveraigne Parliament, that the publick trustees of England, Scotland, and Wales, may at Westminster jointly concur for the weal of the whole Isle, as members of one and the same incorporation.   These two Knights, one whereof was Lord High Chancellor of England, and the other Atturney General, and Lord Chief Justice of the Common Pleas, were good and wise men, full of honour, free from prevarication and by-respects, learned lawyers, excellent scholars, fluent orators, and, above all, worthy, loving, and sincere patriots of England ; for which cause I hope so many exquisite qualities meeting, as it were, in one constellation, by vertue of a powerfull influence upon the mindes of the supreme senate of the land, will incline the hearts of every one not to dissent from the judgement and approbation of these two so eminent judges and zealous English men ; and that so much the rather, that to the accomplishment of so commendable a work, we are conducted by nature it self, which, having made us *divisos orbe Britannos*, sheweth, by the antiperistatick faculty of a fountain or spring-well in the summer season, whose nature is to be the colder within it self the greater circumobresistance of heat be in the aire which surrounds it, that we should cordially close to one another, unite our forces, and the more vigorously improve the internal strength we have of our selves, the greater that the outward opposition and hostility appear against us, of the circumjacent outlandish nations which inviron us on all sides.

This was not heeded in ancient times by reason of the surquedry of the old English,

2 o

who looked on the Scots with a malignant eye; and the profound policie of the
French, in casting, for their own ends, the spirit of division betwixt the two nations to
widen the breach.   But now that the English have attained to a greater dexterity in
encompassing their *facienda's* of State, and deeper reach in considering what for the
future may prove most honourable and lucrative, will, like an expert physician to a
patient sick of a consumption in his noble parts, who applieth cordials and not corro-
sives, and lenitives rather then cauters, strive more, as I imagine, to gain the love and
affection of the Scots, thereby to save the expence of any more blood or mony, then
for overthrowing them quite in both their bodies and fortunes, to maintain the charge
of an everlasting war against the storms of the climate, the fierceness of discontented
people, inaccessibility of the hills, and sometimes universal penury, the mother of
plague and famine; all which inconveniences may be easily prevented without any
charge at all, by the sole gaining of the hearts of the country.

By which means, patching up old rents, cementing what formerly was broken, and
by making of ancient foes new friends, we will strengthen our selves, and weaken our
enemies, and raise the Isle of Britain to that height of glory that it will become formidable to all the world besides.

In the mean while, the better to incorporate the three dominions of England, Scotland, and Wales, and more firmly to consolidate their union, it were not amiss, in my
opinion, that, as little rivers, which use to lose their names when they run along into
the current of a great flood, they have their own peculiar titles laid aside, and totally
discharged into the vast gulph of that of Great Britain.

But if upon any emergent occasion, it be thought fit to make mention of Ireland,
and the several dominions of Britain, in an orderly enumeration, to place Ireland, as I
conceive it, before Scotland, is very preposterous; not but that Ireland is a far more
fertile country, and that the Irish may be as good as any men; that the Scots in these
latter yeers may be much degenerated from the magnanimity of their fore-fathers, and
that the succeeding progeny may perhaps prove little better, or as you will; for be
the soile or climate never so good or bad, with a permanence, or rather immutability
in either of those qualities, the respective natives and inhabitants thereof will nevertheless, according to the change of times, be subject to a vicissitude of vice and
vertue, as may appear by the inclinations of the Greeks and Romans now, compared
with those of their ancestors in the days of Xerxes and Hannibal; but onely that I
conceive priority to be more due to Scotland, although I should speak nothing of its
more immaculate reputation both abroad and at home, and of a longer series of Soveraigns that swayed scepter there in a continuate uninterrupted succession, and that
because of its greater conformity with and proximity to the nation of England; the
people whereof, if they would imitate the fashion of the warlike Romans, should say,
Scots and Irish, as the Romans did, Latines and Gaules, or Latins and Sicilians, by
reason of the Latins' vicinity and nearer adjacence to Rome; although Sicilie was
more fruitfull and opulent then Latium, and the Gaules more populous and every whit
as fierce in the field as the Latins.

I am afraid that I have trespassed a little upon the patience of the reader, by insisting so long in my discourse upon Scotland; yet in regard of my obligation and bound duty to the author of the above-recited lost papers, whose native soyle it is, I could hardly do less, seeing it is for the good of him that this whole tractate is compiled, and to his behalf, who expects not, as hath been said already in the 265 page, and abundantly proved by the fifteenth axiom, either recompense or punishment for his country's sake : he likewise hopeth, by vertue of the said axiom, that his being a meer prisoner of war, without any further delinquencie, will not militate much against him if the subjects of the land, by inventions of his, attain to what is conducible to them in saving of expence, as by the discovery proffered to the publick, he is able to make good when required thereto ; that either money or lands, if not both, should be due to him for the disclosure of so prime a secret, is clearly demonstrated by the sixteenth ; and that the State will be no less courteous and favourable to him then to any other prisoner of war proportionally, is plainly evidenced by the seventeenth ; that the supreme authority of the Isle, in matter of the liberty of his person, and that of his brothers and menial servants, together with the enjoyment of his own house, lands, and rents, free from sequestration, confiscation, composition, and garrisoning, should allow him the same conditions granted to any other no more deserving then himself, is manifestly proved by the eighteenth ; that therefore he should obtaine the greater, as aforesaid, is proved by the nineteenth ; and that if to no other prisoner of all his country be truly competent, but to himself alone, the ample character, in all its branches, as it is specified in the 275, 276, and 277 pages, which I have given of him, and could not conceal, being much less then his due, then, in stead of a recompence for the surplusage of wherein others are defective, which he covets not, none certainly of all the Scotish nation, whether prisoner or other, should receive from the State so great favours and courtesies as himself, because, without prejudice be it spoke to any man, he did from the beginning of these intestine broyles walk in an even, if not a more constant track of blameless carriage, free from hypocrisie, covetousness, and tergiversation, then any of his compatriots ; that notwithstanding the strictness of his allegiance to supreme authority, and the many ties of obedience that lie upon any subject whatsoever, he may by vertue of his owne merit deserve a reward from the State, is clear by the twentieth ; and that for the imparting of this invention and others to publick acceptance, which are so properly his own, that no other braine, that ever was or is, did contribute any thing to their eduction, he may lawfully claim right to a competency of retribution, is made patent by the one and twentieth.

And lastly, the author desiring no more but the grant of the foresaid demands, although by the strict rule of commutative justice, it should seem to be a reward by too many stages inferior to the discovery of so prime an invention ; yet that the State doth him neither wrong nor injustice therein, provided he be not denyed of what he requireth, is fully cleared by the two and twentieth or last axiome.

This apodictick course, by a compositive method theorematically to infer conse-

quences from infallible maximes, with all possible succinctness, I thought fit to im-
brace; because, to have analytically couched those verities, by mounting the scale of
their probation upon the prosyllogistick steps of variously-amplified confirmations,
would have been a procedure for its prolixity unsuitable to the pregnancy of the State,
whose intuitive spirits can at the first hearing discerne the strength of manifold conclusions, without the labour of subsuming, in the very bowels and chaos of their principles.

I could truly, having before my eyes some known treatises of the author, whose
muse I honour, and the straine of whose pen to imitate is my greatest ambition, have
enlarged this discourse with a choicer variety of phrase, and made it overflow the field
of the reader's understanding, with an inundation of greater eloquence; and that one
way, tropologetically, by metonymical, ironical, metaphorical, and synecdochical instruments of elocution, in all their several kinds, artificially affected, according to the
nature of the subject, with emphatical expressions in things of great concernment, with
catachrestical in matters of meaner moment; attended on each side respectively with
an epiplectick and exegetick modification; with hyperbolical, either epitatically or
hypocoristically, as the purpose required to be elated or extenuated, they qualifying
metaphors, and accompanied with apostrophes; and lastly, with allegories of all sorts,
whether apologal, affabulatory, parabolary, ænigmatick, or paræmial. And on the
other part, schematologetically adorning the proposed theam with the most especial
and chief flowers of the garden of rhetorick, and omitting no figure either of diction or
sentence, that might contribute to the ears, enchantment, or perswasion of the hearer.

I could have introduced, in case of obscurity, synonymal, exargastick, and paliloge-
tick elucidations; for sweetness of phrase, antimetathetick commutations of epithets;
for the vehement excitation of a matter, exclamation in the front, and epiphonemas
in the reer. I could have used, for the promptlyer stirring up of passion, apostrophal
and prosopopœial diversions; and, for the appeasing and settling of them, some epa-
northotick revocations, and aposiopetick restraines. I could have inserted dialogismes,
displaying their interrogatory part with communicatively pysmatick and sustentative
flourishes; or proleptically, with the refutative schemes of anticipation and subjection,
and that part which concerns the responsory, with the figures of permission and concession.

Speeches extending a matter beyond what it is auxetically, digressively, transitious-
ly, by ratiocination, ætiology, circumlocution, and other wayes I could have made
use of; as likewise with words diminishing the worth of a thing, tapinotically, peri-
phrastically, by rejection, translation, and other meanes, I could have served my self.

There is neither definition, distribution, epitrochism, increment, caracterism, hypotyposis, or any scheme figurating a speech by reason of what is in the thing to our
purpose thereby signified, that I needed to have omitted; nor, had I been so pleased,
would I have past by the figurative expressions of what is without any thing of the
matter in hand, whether paradigmatical, iconical, symbolical, by comparison, or any
other kinde of simile; or yet paradoxical, paramologetick, paradiastolary, antipopho-
retick, cromatick, or any other way of figuring a speech by opposition, being formules

of oratory, whereby we may subjoyn what is not expected; confess something that can do us no harme; yeeld to one of the members, that the other may be removed; allow an argument, to oppose a stronger; mixe praise with dispraise, and so forth, through all manner of illustration and decorement of purposes by contrarieties and repugnance.

All those figures and tropes, besides what are not here mentioned, these synecdochically standing for all, to shun the tediousness of a too prolixe enumeration, I could have adhibited to the embellishment of this tractate, had not the matter it self been more prevalent with me, then the superficial formality of a quaint discourse.

I could have firreted out of topick celluls such variety of arguments tending to my purpose, and seconded them with so many divers refutations, confirmations, and pro-syllogistick deductions, as, after the large manner of their several amplifications according to the rules of art, would, contexed together, have framed a book of a great quarto size, in an arithmetical proportion of length to its other two dimensions of bredth and thickness; that is to say, its bredth should exceed the thickness thereof by the same number of inches, and no more, that it is surpassed by the length; in which, considering the body thereof, could be contained no less then seven quires of paper at least; and yet, notwithstanding this so great a bulk, I could have disposed the contents of its whole subjected matter so appositely into partitions, for facilitating an impression in the reader's memory, and presented it to the understanding in so spruce a garb, that spirits blest with leisure, and free from the urgency of serious employments, would happily have bestowed as liberally some few houres thereon as on the perusal of a new coined romancy, or strange history of love adventures.

For, although the figures and tropes above rehearsed seem in their *actu signato*, as they signifie meer notional circumstances, affections, adjuncts, and dependencies on words, to be a little pedantical, and to the smooth touch of a delicate ear somewhat harsh and scabrous, yet in their exerced act, as they suppone for things reduplicatively as things in the first apprehension of the minde by them signified, I could, even in far abstruser purposes, have so fitly adjusted them with apt and proper termes, and with such perspicuity couched them, as would have been suitable to the capacities of courtiers and young ladies, whose tender hearing, for the most part, being more taken with the insinuating harmony of a well-concerted period, in its isocoletick and parisonal members, then with the never-so-pithy a fancy of a learned subject, destitute of the illustriousness of so pathetick ornaments, will sooner convey perswasion to the interior facultics, from thc ravishing assault of a well-disciplined diction, in a parade of curiously-mustered words in their several ranks and files, then by the vigour and fierceness of never so many powerful squadrons of a promiscuously-digested elocution into bare logical arguments; for the sweetness of their disposition is more easily gained by undermining passion then storming reason, and by the musick and symmetry of a discourse in its external appurtenances, then by all the puissance imaginary of the ditty or purpose disclosed by it.

But seeing the prime scope of this treatise is to testifie my utmost endeavours to do all the service I can to Sir Thomas Vrquhart, both for the procuring of his liberty, and intreating the State, whose prisoner he is, to allow him the enjoyment of his own, lest by his thraldome and distress, useful to no man, the publick should be deprived of those excellent inventions, whose emission totally dependeth upon the grant of his enlargement and freedom in both estate and person; and that to a State which respecteth substance more then ceremony, the body more then the shadow, and solidity more then ostentation, it would argue great indiscretion in me to become no other waies a suiter for that worthy gentleman, then by emancipating my vein upon the career of rhetoricall excursions, approving my self thereby like to those navigators, gunners, and horsemen, who use more saile then ballast, more powder then ball, and employ the spur more then the bridle.

Therefore it is, that laying aside all the considerations of those advantages and prerogatives a neat expression in fluent termes hath over the milder sexe and miniard youth, and setting before my eyes the reverence and gravity of those supereminent men to whom my expectation of their non-refusal of my request hath emboldened me to make my addresses, I hold it now expedient, without further adoe, to stop the current of my pen, and, in token of the duty I owe to him whose cause I here assert, to give way to his more literate and compleat elucubrations; which, that they may the sooner appear to the eyes of the world, for the advance of both vertue and learning, I yet once more, and that most heartily, beseech the present State, Parliament, and Supream Councel of Great Britain, to vouchsafe unto the aforesaid Sir Thomas Vrquhart of Cromarty knight, heritable Sheriff and proprietary thereof, a grant of the releasement of his person from any imprisonment whereunto, at the discretion of those that took his parole, he is ingaged; the possession likewise of his House of Cromarty, free from garisoning, and the enjoyment of his whole estate in lands, without affecting it with any other either publick or private burthen then hath been of his own contracting; and that with the dignities thereto belonging, of Hereditary Sheriffship, patronage of the three churches there, and Admiralty of the seas betwixt Catness and Innernass inclusively, with subordination, nevertheless, to the high Admiral of the land; together with all the other priviledges and immunities, which, both in his person and that of his predecessors, hath been from time to time accounted due by inheritance to the House of Cromarty, and that for the love of the whole island on which he offereth, in compensation, to bestow a benefit, under pain of forfeiture of all he hath, of ten times more worth. As this is my humble petition, so is it conform to the desires of all the best spirits of England, Scotland, Wales, and Ireland.

PITY IT WERE TO REFUSE SUCH
AS ASK BUT LITTLE, AND GIVE MUCH.

THE LIST OF THOSE SCOTS MENTIONED IN THIS BOOK WHO HAVE BEEN GENERALS ABROAD WITHIN THESE FIFTY YEERS.

Sir Patrick Ruven.
Gen. Ruderford.
Lord Spence.

S. Alexander Lesly, *Dux fœderis*.
S. Alex. Lesly, *in Moscovy*.

James King.
Marquis Lesly.
Marquis Hamilton.

THE LIST OF OTHER SCOTISH OFFICERS MENTIONED IN THIS TREATISE, WHO WERE ALL COLONELS ABROAD, AND SOME OF THEM GENERAL PERSONS.

Lieutenant-Generals.

David Lesly.
S. James Livingstoun.
William Bailie.

Major-Generals.

Lodovick Lindsay.
Robert Monro.
Thomas Ker.
S. David Drumond.
S. James Lumsden.
Robert Lumsden.
S. John Hepburn.

Lord James Dowglas.
Watchtoun Hepburn.
John Lesly.

Colonels.

Alexander Hamilton, *General of the Artillery*.
Alexander Ramsay, *Quarter-master-General*.
Col. Anderson.
Earl of Argyle.
Col. Armestrong.
Earl of Bacluch.
S. James Balantine.

S. William Balantine.
S. David Balfour.
S. Henry Balfour.
Col. Boyd.
Col. Brog.
Col. Bruce.
James Cockburne.
Col. Colon.
Lord Colvil.
Alex. Crawford.
Col. Crichtoun.
Alex. Cuningam.
George Cuningam.
Robert Cuningam.
William Cuningam.

George Dowglas.
Col. Dowglas.
Col. Dowglas.
Col. Edinton.
Col. Edmond.
Col. Erskin.
Alex. Forbas.
Alex. Forbas.
Arthur Forbas.
Fines Forbas.
John Forbas.
Lord Forbas.
S. John Fulerton.
Thomas Garne.
Alex. Gordon.
Alex. Gordon.
John Gordon.
Col. Gordon.
S. Andrew Gray.
William Gun.
Col. Gun.
S. Frederick Hamilton.
James Hamilton.
John Hamilton.
Hugh Hamilton.
S. Francis Henderson.
S. John Henderson.
Thomas Hume.

Col. Hunter.
Edward Johnston.
James Johnston.
William Johnston.
S. John Innes.
Earl of Iruin.
William Keith.
John Kinindmond.
Patrick Kinindmond.
Thomas Kinindmond.
William Kinindmond.
Walter Lecky.
Col. Lermond.
Alex. Lesly.
George Lesly.
John Lesly.
Robert Lesly.
Col. Liddel.
Andrew Lindsay.
George Lindsay.
Col. Lithco.
Col. Livingstoun.
Robert Lumsden.
Col. Lyon.
Col. Mathuson.
S. John Meldrum.
Assen Monro.
Fowles Monro.

Hector Monro.
Obstel Monro.
Col. Morison.
S. Pat. Morray.
Col. Mouat.
Col. Ramsey.
James Ramsey.
Lord Reay.
Col. Robertson.
Col. Rower.
Frances Ruven.
John Ruven.
L. Sancomb.
Col. Sandilands.
Robert Scot.
James Seaton.
James Seaton.
S. John Seaton.
William Sempil.
Francis Sinclair.
Col. Spang.
James Spence.
L. Spynay.
Robert Stuart.
Thomas Thomson.
John Urquhart.
Col. Wederburne.
Col. Wilson.

I have not mentioned here Lieutenant-General John Midletoun, Lieutenant-General Sir William Balfour, nor General Major Sir George Monro, &c. because they returned from the forraign countryes where they did officiate, though in places over both horse and foot of great concernment, before they had obtained the charge of Colonels.

As for pricking down into colums those other Scots in my book renowned for literature and personal valour, I held it not expedient; for that the sum of them doth fall so far short of the number I have omitted, that apportioned to the agregate of all who in that nation since the yeer 1650, without reckoning any intrusted in military employments, either at home or abroad, have deserved praise in armes and arts, joyntly or disjunctively, it would bear the analogy, to use a lesser definite for a greater indefinite, of a *subnovitripartient eights*; that is to say, in plain English, the whole being the dividend, and my nomenclature the divisor, the quotient would be nine, with a fraction of three-eights; or yet more clearly, as the proportion of 72 to 675.

FINIS.

For Iudgment, Learning.   witt   For Inuention. sweetness   Stile.

Logopandecteision,
OR AN
INTRODVCTION
TO THE
VNIVERSAL LANGVAGE.

Digefted into thefe Six feveral Books,

Neaudethaumata, } { *Chryseomystes,*
Chrestasebeia, } { *Neleodicastes,* &
Cleronomaporia, } { *Philoponauxesis.*

BY
Sir THOMAS URQUHART of *Cromartie*, Knight.

Now lately contrived and published
both for his own utilitie, and that of all
pregnant and ingenious Spirits.

Credere quærenti nonne hæc juſtiſſima res eſt ?
Qui non plura cupit, quam ratio ipſa jubet.

Englifhed thus,
To grant him his demands were it not juſt ?
Who craves no more, then reafon fayes he muſt.

LONDON
Printed, and are to be fold by *Giles Calvert* at the *Black-
fpread Eagle* at the Weſt-end of *Pauls;* and by *Richard
Tomlins* at the Sun and Bible near *Pye-corner.* 1653.

THE EPISTLE DEDICATORIE,
TO NO-BODY.

MOST HONOURABLE,

My non suppouent Lord, and Soveraign master of contradictions in ad-
jected terms, that unto you I have presumed to tender the dedicacie of
this introduction, will not seem strange to those that know how your concurrence did further me to the accomplishment of that new language, unto
the frontispeice whereof it is premitted.

You did assist me in the production of many special fancies, whose promulgation will perhaps exceedingly conduce to the delight of the philosophical reader; by your help, amidst the penurie of books, and want of
learned conversation, have by me been enixed several treatises, which, for
their apparent usefulnefse and curiosity, I sometime intend to consecrate to
the shrine of publique view; if none hitherto hath made choice of such a
patron, neither hath any till this hour afforded an invention of that kind.
In things whereof the proposed subject is within our reach, imitation is
imbraceable, but where the matter is transcendent, we commonly bid
patterns adiew; that porch will not befit a cottage, which is suitable to a
cathedral, nor can unusuall dedications, misbeseem tractats on an extraordinary purpose; seeing therefore skill in symmetrie bespeaks an artificer,
and gives the contexture of a work that decorum which becomes the author, I am with force of reason perswaded to this election, thereby to
glance at the proportion betwixt your favours, and my retribution; for
such were the courtesies you conferred on me, that I could not otherwayes
choose but lay hold on this expedient, to testifie my remembrance of them.

When after the fatal blow given at Worcester, on the third of September 1651, to the regal partie, I was five times plundred, pillaged, pilfred,

robbed, and rifled, and nothing almost left me, fortune could dispoil me of, save my health alone, which in the croud of so many incident difficulties, as I was forced to undergo, was most miraculously preserved; you then out of your mercie, amongst the victorious soldiers, were pleased to commiserate my condition.   When, in horses, armes, apparel, and monie, I had in that place taken from me above five hundred pounds worth English; you at that time out of pietie, amongst the Presbyterians of our army, did regret my case.   When it was told that, amidst the fury of the raging souldiery, I had above ten thousand crowns worth of papers em-

Avarus nec patientibus compatitur, nec miseris subvenit vel miseretur; sed offendit deum, offendit proximum, offendit seipsum; nam deo detinet debitum, proximo denegat necessaria, sibi subtrahit opportuna: deo ingratus, proximo impius, sibi crudelis.

bezeled, without recovery; you from your generosity of all the great men prisoners, were sorry at the lofse.   And lastly, when after my being brought to London, without either monie or goods, I had my self, and several others, both brothers and servants, whereof not any, save my self alone, had been in that city before, to provide for in every thing, that the State's allowance, which neverthelefse continued no longer then my parole was taken for their true imprisonment, did not reach unto; and that after many of my fellow prisoners, of considerable fortunes at home, had received from the Scottish factors on the exchange, in matter of borrowing monie, answers so full of churlishnefse and inhumanity, that I am ashamed the ear of any man of common honestie should hear them; then was it, whilst the charity of those bankers, and other rich Scots men at London, by little and little decayed, and became still the lefse, the greater the pitch was unto which their wealth had formerly increast; and that for six months together, from none of my kindred, alliance, nor any other of my pretended friends in Scotland, I had received so much as the mission or return of a letter, that you, such was your magnificence, were content to supply my need, and furnish me with what I lacked.

These favours I deem my self in duty the more obliged to commemorate, that they were bestowed upon me in sequel of some others of that nature, namely, when a while agoe I had a suit in law depending against

Sir James Fraser, qui hic ardet æstu avaritiæ, postea ardebit igne Gehennæ.

a gentleman neighbour of mine, for taking fifteen in the hundred, these sixteen years past and above, and refusing payment of the principall summe, that the said usurie might still continue, for the which there was given unto him by my father, securitie in land, by a present pofsefsion, worth more then thrice the monie which my father had received from him; as likewise for plundring from my tenants, in my absence, above two thou-

sand and five hundred pounds sterlin worth of goods; it was then that
your grace, in the sefsion of the land, and Committee of Estate, there
taking notice of these enormous wrongs, did doe me justice. Much about
the same time, when some ministers had maimed my rents, to strengthen
their own stipends, your reverence, sitting in the Commission of the Kirk,
were pleased to take my part against them, and patrocinate my cause. By
your highnefse also sitting then at the helm of the State of Scotland, when
a grievance for the prefsure sustained by me, was in all humility put in
before the said Committee of Estates, was I maintained against the crueltie
and indiscretion of those did overrate me in the exaction of publick dues;
and finally, when by the opprefsion of some ill affected countrey men,
under pretext of Committee acts, my vafsals and tenants had suffered extreme prejudice, streight upon the presenting of a petition thereanent,
whereof at least a hundred at severall times were tabled, your wisdome
remedied the plaintif, and did for my cause redrefse the injuries done unto
him.

O pestis maligna avaritia, semper bonis animis detestanda, quid illæsum, quid inconcussum dimittis?

That with thefe benevolences, as the most eminent effects of your inge-
nuitie, I should, as affairs then ruled, be gratified by your liberalitie, was
from day to day my constant expectation; being always perswaded to the
greater probability of my acceptance of them, that in many sound and well-
grounded opinions of mine, long before that time, you frequently jumped
with me; for when I openly said, that Presbyterie was like to turn to a
hydral Episcopacie, and that the gallantry of the English nation would
never comport with such a government, which speech was thought should
have been afserted by all the nobles and gentlemen of Scotland, you out of
your goodnefs, amongst them all, being sensible of the heavie yoke of the
democratical tyrannie of the Kirk, were pleased to justify my sayings.
Besides this, when the intending of one thing, and pretending of another,
was by me a thousand times foretold to prove destructive unto Scotland,
and that the cause of God could not produce diabolical effects, your ho-
linefs amongst the zelots of the nation, did give way to beleeve the truth
of both. And when moreover I avouched that money should never be
held in such estimation, that either to honestie, or a good name, any
summe, however so great, ought to be preferred, your discretion, amidst
many of the ecclesiastical armie, did in very deed acknowledge the veritie
of the saying, although verbally you denyed it. And at last, when to be

charitable to distreſsed men, whose misery could not with reason be imputed to their own fault, was by me represented to be an especial act of goodneſs, you, out of your love, amongst the Scotish merchants condescended to it.

Whereby most seriously perpending the manifold, or rather innumerable testimonies of your goodneſs, holineſs, grace, discretion, wisdome, liberalitie, reverence, mercie, pietie, generositie, magnificence, love, and other unexpreſsible respects, I have perceived to flow from your highneſs in behalf of me, whether I applyed my self to the nobilitie, souldierie, gentrie, clergie, or burger degree of the consistorian partie of the Scotish nation; I must needs promise, in acquital of these incomprehensible good deeds, out of your endleſs and immense bountie, so undeservedly erogated, whilst I breath, to break my parole unto you, to be to you dishonest, and prove disloyal to you in my trust, to curse you in malicious thoughts, reproach you with scandalous words, and wrong you with cruel and unconscionable deeds; to do you injustice, deceive, and cosen you; to persecute you with hatred, envie, and rancour of mind; and according to the infallible rules of the sacred evangile, dictamen of reason, and precepts of philosophie, to approve my self your faithleſs, implacable, and wicked enemie; and consequently, to your contrary opposite, every body, upright, true, and honest; and to your contradictorie foe, some body, an affectionate, trustie, stedfast, and unalterable, both friend and servant,

THOMAS VRQUHART.

THE CONTENTS OF THE FIRST BOOK,

ENTITULED

NEAUDETHAUMATA.

THE author, in this first book of his introduction, discloseth many excellent overtures, for the furtherance of literature, especially in the facility of contriving expressions for any conception the mind of man is able to afford. He plainly setteth down the analogie that ought to be betwixt things and words; and that, to make a perfect language, things semblable in nature, should be signified by words of a like pronunciation. He proveth all hitherto known tongues to be full of imperfection, both by reason of the insufficiencie of their alphabets, and for that there are many common things which cannot, without circumlocution, be expressed by them. He compareth the learned languages with one another; giveth freely his opinion of all vernacularie tongues, and demonstrateth an universal defect in all, and each of both the one and other, because of the common necessity they are driven unto, of mutual borrowing for conveniencie of elocution.

The author also, in this book, utterly rejecteth the vulgarly received opinion of the origin of languages, and very neatly twits the opposers of

those curious arts wherein there is no harm. He confuteth that dispro-
portion in matter of number twixt words and things, wherewith the smat-
trers in knowledge would cloak their inability of giving unto every thing
its proper term; and sheweth how, for the advancement of learning and
vertue, and clearing the mind of all prejudicat tenets, the brains and heart
should be purged of malice and wilful ignorance, the two plagues of a
commonwealth; the bad acquitals he hath received from some great men
of his own countrey, he but glanceth at, to incordiat other his compatriots
with more respect in times coming, to men of no lefse desert; and declareth what injury to that Deity, unto which the heavens are subservient, is
done by those lazie Sciolists, who frequently seek after supernatural causes,
where the natural is obvious to the eyes of our understanding.

The author likewise setteth forth in this book, the pofsibility of framing
a new idiome of far greater perfection, then any hitherto spoken, and that
the performance of such an undertaking will, without doubt, exceedingly
conduce to the benefit, and contentment of all ingenious schollars. By its
logopandocie, or comprehension of all utterable words and sounds articulat,
he evidenceth the universality of the proposed language, and by infallible
reason proveth whilst there is no other world but this, the impofsibility of
forming any other such.

Lastly, The author, after his delivery of a genuine and upright glofs
on three pafsages of Solomon, Terence, and Paul, in confutation of some
scholiasts, idolizers of corrupt antiquitie, who had misinterpreted those
texts concerning the nature of new inventions, most manifestly avoucheth
that exquisite inventions will never be wanting, so long as good spirits are
extant on the earth; and, in concluding this his first book, with sixtie and
six several advantages this language hath above all other, exposeth to the
view of the judicious reader many inestimable secrets, worthie the perusal
of the best wits of the time.[1]

---

[1] With the exception of the paragraphs from 38. to 49. and from 134. to 136. the first book of *Logopandecteision,* is a mere reprint of the Preface to *The Jewel.*—Ed.

THE FIRST BOOK

OF THE

INTRODVCTION

TO THE UNIVERSALL LANGUAGE, INTITULED

NEAUDETHAUMATA;

OR,

WONDERS OF THE NEW SPEECH, WHICH, AS A PREFACE
THERETO, COMPREHENDETH ITS MOST NECESSARY PRE-
NOSCENDAS, TOGETHER WITH SOME MISCELLANIE
ARTICLES CONCERNING THE AUTHOR HIMSELF.

1. WORDS are the signes of things; it being to signifie that they were instituted at first, nor can they be, as such, directed to any other end, whether they be articulate or inarticulate.

2. All things are either real or rationall; and the real, either naturall or artificial.

3. There ought to be a proportion betwixt the sign and thing signified; therefore should all things, whether real or rationall, have their proper words assigned unto them.

4. Man is called a Microcosme, because he may by his conceptions and words containe within him the representatives of what in the whole world is comprehended.

5. Seeing there is in nature such affinity 'twixt words and things, as there ought to be in whatsoever is ordained for one another; that language is to be accounted most conform to nature, which with greatest variety expresseth all manner of things.

6. As all things of a single compleat being by Aristotle into ten classes were divided, so may the words whereby those things are to be signified be set apart in their several storehouses.

7. Arts, sciences, mechanick trades, notionall faculties, and whatever is excogitable by man, have their own method, by vertue whereof the learned of these latter times have orderly digested them; yet hath none hitherto considered of a mark whereby words of the same faculty, art, trade, or science should be dignosced from those of another by the very sound of the word at the first hearing.

8. A tree will be known by its leaves, a stone by its grit, a flower by the smel, meats by the taste, musick by the ear, colours by the eye, the severall natures of things, with their properties and essentiall qualities, by the intellect; and accordingly as the things are in themselves diversified, the judicious and learned man, after he hath conceived them aright, sequestreth them in the severall cels of his understanding, each in their definite and respective places.

9. But in matter of the words whereby those things are expressed, no language ever hitherto framed hath observed any order relating to the thing signified by them: for if the words be ranked in their alphabeticall series, the things represented by them will fall to be in severall predicaments; and if the things themselves be categorically classed, the word whereby they are made known will not be tyed to any alphabetical rule.

10. This is an imperfection incident to all the languages that ever yet have been known; by reason whereof, forraign tongues are said to be hard to learn, and when obtained, easily forgot.

11. The effigies of Jupiter in the likenesse of a bull, should be liker to that of Io metamorphosed into a cow, then to the statue of Bucephalus, which was a horse; and the picture of Alcibiades ought to have more resemblance with that of Coriolanus, being both handsome men, then with the image of Thersites, who was of a deformed feature; just so should things semblable in nature be represented by words of a like composure; and as the true intelligible species do present unto our minds the similitude of things as they are in the object, even so ought the words expressive of our conceptions so to agree or vary in their contexture, as the things themselves which are conceived by them do in their natures.

12. Besides this imperfection in all languages, there is yet another, that no language upon the face of the earth hath a perfect alphabet, one lacking those letters which another hath, none having all, and all of them *in cumulo* lacking some. But that which makes the defect so much the greater, is, that these same few consonants and vowels commonly made use of are never by two nations pronounced after the same fashion; the French A with the English being the Greek Hτa, and the Italian B with the Spanish, the Hebrew *vau*.

13. This is that which maketh those of one dominion so unskilful in the idiome of

another, and after many yeers abode in a strange land, despair from attaining at any time to the perfect accent of the language thereof, because, as the waters of that stream cannot be wholesome whose source is corrupted, nor the superstructure sure whereof the ground-work is ruinous, so doth the various manner of pronouncing one and the same alphabet in severall nations, produce this great and lamentable obstruction in the discipline of languages.

14. The *g* of the Latin word *legit,* is after four several manners pronounced by the English, French, Spanish, and Dutch ; the *ch* likewise is differently pronounced by divers nations ; some uttering it after the fashion of the Hebrew *shin,* as the French do in the word *chasteau, chascun, chastier, chatel ;* or like the Greek *kappa,* as in the Italian words *chiedere, chiazzare, chinatura ;* or as in Italy are sounded the words *ciascheduno, ciarlatano ;* for so do the Spanish and English pronounce it, as in the words *achaque, leche, chamber, chance :* other nations of a gutteral flexibility, pronounce it after the fashion of the Greek *χ.* Nor need we to labor for examples in other letters, for there is scarce any hitherto received, either consonant or vowel, which in some one and other, taking in all nations, is not pronounced after three or four several fashions.

15. As the alphabets are imperfect, some having but 19 letters, others 22, and some 24, few exceeding that number, so do the words composed of those letters in the several languages come far short of the number of things, which, to have the reputation of a perfect tongue, ought to be expressed by them.

16. For supply of this deficiencie, each language borrows from another ; nor is the perfectest amongst them, without being beholden to another, in all things enunciable, bastant to afford instruction. Many astronomical and medicinal terms have the Greeks borrowed from the Arabians, for which they by exchange have from the Grecians received payment of many words naturalized in their physical, logical, and metaphysical treatises. As for the Latin, it oweth all its scientifick dictions to the Greek and Arabick, yet did the Roman Conquest give adoption to many Latin words in both these languages, especially in matters of military discipline and prudential law.

17. And as for all other languages as yet spoke, though to some of them be ascribed the title of original tongues, I may safely avouch there is none of them which, of it self alone, is able to afford the smattring of an elocution fit for indoctrinating of us in the precepts and maximes of moral and intellectual vertues.

18. But, which is more, and that which most of all evinceth the sterility of all the languages that since the deluge have been spoke, though all of them quintesenced in one capable of the perfections of each, yet that one so befitted and accommodated for compendiousness and variety of phrase, should not be able, amidst so great wealth, to afford without circumlocution the proper and convenient representation of a thing, yea of many thousands of things, whereof each should be expressed with one single word alone.

19. Some languages have copiousness of discourse, which are barren in composition; such is the Latine. Others are compendious in expression, which hardly have any flexion at all; of this kind are the Dutch, the English, and Irish.

20. Greek hath the agglutinative faculty of incorporating words, yet runneth not so glib in poesie as doth the Latine, though far more abundant. The Hebrew likewise, with its auxiliary dialects of Arabick, Caldean, Syriack, Æthiopian, and Samaritan, compoundeth prettily, and hath some store of words, yet falleth short by many stages of the Greek.

21. The French, Spanish, and Italian, are but dialects of the Latine, as the English is of the Saxon tongue, though with this difference, that the mixture of Latine with the Gaulish, Moresco, and Gotish tongues, make up the three first languages; but the meer qualification of the Saxon with the old British, frameth not the English to the full, for that, by its promiscuous and ubiquitary borrowing, it consisteth almost of all languages; which I speak not in dispraise thereof, although I may with confidence aver, that were all the four aforesaid languages stript of what is not originally their own, we should not be able with them all, in any part of the world, to purchase so much as our breakfast in a market.

22. Now, to return from these to the learned languages, we must acknowledge it to be very strange, why, after thousands of yeers continual practice in the polishing of them by men of approved faculties, there is neither in them, nor any other tongue hitherto found out, one single word expressive of the vice opposite either to temperance or chastity in the defect, though many rigid monks, even now a-days, be guilty of the one, as Diogenes of old was of the other.

23. But that which makes this disease the more incurable, is, that when an exuberant spirit would to any high researched conceit adapt a peculiar word of his own coyning, he is branded with incivility, if he apologize not for his boldness, with a *Quod ita dixerim parcant Ciceronianæ manes, Ignoscat Demosthenis genius,* and other such phrases, acknowledging his fault of making use of words never uttered by others, or at least by such as were most renowned for eloquence.

24. Though learning sustain great prejudice by this restraint of liberty to endenizon new citizens in the commonwealth of languages, yet do I conceive the reason thereof to proceed from this, that it is thought a less incongruity to express a thing by circumlocution, then by appropriating a single word thereto, to transgress the bounds of the language; as in architecture it is esteemed an error of less consequence to make a circuitory passage from one room to another, then by the extravagancie of an irregular sallie, to frame projectures disproportionable to the found of the house.

25. Thus is it, that, as according to the largeness of the plat of a building, and compactedness of its walls, the work-master contriveth his roofs, platforms, outjettings, and other such like parts and portion of the whole, just so, conform to the extent and reach which a language in its flexions and compositions hath obtained at first,

have the sprucest linguists hitherto been pleased to make use of the words thereto belonging.

26. The bonification and virtuification of Lully Scotus's hexeity, and albedineity of Suarez, are words exploded by those that affect the purity of the Latine diction; yet if such were demanded, what other no less concise expression would comport with the neatness of that language, their answer would be, *altum silentium;* so easie a matter it is for many to find fault with what they are not able to amend.

27. Nevertheless, why for representing to our understandings the essence of accidents, the fluency of the form as it is *in fieri,* the faculty of the agent and habit that facilitates it, with many thousands of other such expressions, the tearms are not so genuine as of the members of a man's body, or utensils of his house; the reason is, because the first inventers of languages, who contrived them for necessity, were not so profoundly versed in philosophical quiddities as those that succeeded after them; whose literature increasing, procured their excursion beyond the representatives of the common objects imagined by their forefathers.

28. I have known some to have built houses for necessity, having no other aime before their eyes but barely to dwell in them, who nevertheless in a very short space were so enriched, that after they had taken pleasure to polish and adorn what formerly they had but rudely squared, their moveables so multiplyed upon them, that they would have wished they had made them of a larger extent.

29. Even so, though these languages may be refined by some quaint derivatives and witty compositions, like the striking forth of new lights and doors, outjetting of crenels, erecting of prickets, barbicans, and such like various structures upon one and the same foundation, yet being limited to a certain basis, beyond which the versed in them must not pass, they cannot roam at such random as otherwise they might, had their language been of a larger scope at first.

30. Thus, albeit Latine be far better polished now then it was in the days of Ennius and Livius Andronicus, yet had the Latinists at first been such philosophers as afterward they were, it would have attained to a great deal of more perfection then it is at for the present.

31. What I have delivered in freedome of the learned languages, I would not have wrested to a sinister sense, as if I meant any thing to their disparagement, for truly I think the time well bestowed which boyes in their tender yeers employ towards the learning of them, in a subordination to the excellent things that in them are couched.

32. But ingenuously I must acknowledge my averseness of opinion from those who are so superstitiously addicted to these languages, that they account it learning enough to speak them, although they knew nothing else; which is an errour worthy rebuke, seeing *Philosophia sunt res, non verba;* and that whatever the signes be, the things by them signified ought still to be of greater worth.

33. For it boots not so much by what kind of tokens any matter be brought into

our minde, as that the things made known unto us by such representatives be of some considerable value; not much unlike the Innes-a-court-gentlemen at London, who, usually repairing to their commons at the blowing of a horn, are better pleased with such a signe, so the fare be good, then if they were warned to courser cates, by the sound of a bell or trumpet.

34. Another reason prompteth me thereto, which is this, that in this frozen climate of ours, there is hardly any that is not possessed with the opinion, that not only the three fore-named languages, but a great many other, whom they call originals—whereof they reckon ten or eleven in Europe, and some fifty-eight more, or thereabouts in other nations—were at the confusion of Babel, immediately from God by a miracle infused into men; being induced to believe this, not so much for that they had not perused the interpretation of the Rabbies on that text, declaring the misunderstanding whereunto the builders were involved by diversity of speech, to have proceeded from nothing else but their various and discrepant pronunciation of one and the same language, as that they deemed languages to be of an invention so sublime, that naturally the wit of man was not able to reach their composure.

35. Some believe this so pertinaciously, that they esteem all men infidels that are of another faith; whilst in the mean while I may confidently assever, that the assertors of such a tenet doe thereby extremely dishonour God, who doing whatever is done by nature, as the actions of an ambassador, as an ambassador, are reputed to be those of the soveraign that sent him, would not have the power he hath given to nature to be disclaimed by any, or any thing said by us in derogation thereof.

36. Should we deny our obedience to the just decree of an inferiour judge, because he from whom his authority is derived did not pronounce the sentence? Subordinate magistrates have their power, even in great maters, which to decline, by saying they have no authority, should make the averrer fall within the compass of a breach of the statute called *scandalum magnatum.*

37. There are of those with us that wear gowns and beards longer then ever did Aristotle and Æsculapius; who when they see an eclipse of the sun or moon, or a comet in the aire, straight would delude the commons with an opinion that those things are immediately from God, for the sins of the people, as if no naturall cause could be produced for such like apparitions.

38. I saw once a young man, who, for his cunning conveyance in the feats of Leger Demaine, was branded by some of that fry for sorcery; and another, for being able, by vertue of the masson word, to make a masson whom he had never seene before, without speaking, or any other apparent signe, come and salute him, reputed by many of the same litter to have had a familiar; their grosse ignorance moving them to call that supernaturall, or above the naturall reach of meere man, whereof they knew not the cause.

39. By which meanes, mathematicall thaumaturgies, opticall magick, secrets of

nature, and other philosophicall mysteries, being esteemed to be rancke witchcraft, they ruine the best part of learning, and make their owne unskillfullnes supreame judge, to passe an irrevocable sentence upon the condemnation of knowledge.

40. The matter, notwithstanding, would be of lesse danger were this the worst; but to this ignorance of theirs is concomitant so much wickednes, that when an action of any extraordinary performance is done, although by a man of a most approvable conversation, and to a very good end, such as the curing of the diseased, or releeving men out of apparent peril, yet if the cause thereof be unknowne to them, they will not be so charitable as to attribute the effect to a good angel, albeit their faith obliege them to beleeve that the spirits belonging to any of the nine celestiall orders, are, for the atchievement of such masteries, in nothing inferior to the infernall demons; but instead of Gabriell, Raphaell, Michaell, and such good spirits, by whom, I think, it is more probable an honest man would be assisted in works of a strange and hidden operation then by the bad ones, they ascribe the wonderfullnes of the exploit to the inspiration of Beelzebub, Abadon, Lucifer, or some other of the fiends of hell; so malevolently they asperse the reputation of gallant men, whose deeds surpass their capacity.

41. Truly, those two qualities of ignorance and wickedness conjoyned, are of such pernicious consequence, that no nation or commonwealth wherein they get footing, is able long to subsist; for rapine, covetousnes, and extortion flowing from the one, as from the other doth all manner of basenes, pusillanimity, and cowardize, ignorance affecteth the braine and wickednes the heart; yet both the braine and heart of a common weale, by the mischeivously vnskillfull, and illiterately malicious, are equally depraved.

42. For remedy of so generall a calamity, seeing universality hath its existence in individualls, would each amend but one, the totall would be quickly rid of this lamentable infection.

43. Therefore, since ever I understood any thing, knowing that the welfare of the body of a government consisteth in the intirenes of its noble parts, I always endeavoured to employ the best of my brain and heart, towards the furtherance of the honour of that country unto which I did owe my birth.

44. In prosecuting whereof, as the heart is *primum vivens,* so was it my heart, which, in my younger years, before my braines were ripened for eminent undertakings, gave me the courage for adventuring in a forrain climat, thrice to enter the lists against men of three severall nations, to vindicate my native country from the calumnies wherewith they had aspersed it; wherein it pleased God so to conduct my fortune, that after I had disarmed them, they in such sort acknowledged their error, and the obligation they did owe me for sparing their lives, which justly by the law of arms I might have taken, that in lieu of three enemies that formerly they were, I acquired three constant friends, both to my selfe and my compatriots, whereof by severall gal-

lant testimonies they gave evident proofe, to the improvement of my country's credit, in many occasions.

45. As my heart hath been thus devoted to the love of my native soile, so have my braines to the honour thereof discharged so much duty, that betwixt what is printed and what ready for the presse, I have set forth above a hundred severall bookes, on subjects never hitherto thought upon by any.

S. d. B. 2. art. 53, 54, 56, 57, 58.
46. Let no man think that I have spoke this in hope of future benefit, or by way of regret I should have faild therof in times past; vertue, in my estimation, whether morall or intellectuall, carrying alwayes along with it a recompence sufficient; nor yet out of pride, or vaine glory in extolling of my own praises, which, as willingly as to live, I would have smothered, but that the continuall receiving of bad offices for my good intentions, hath wrought this excursion out of my pen.

47. Could any man imagine I should have been singled out amongst all those of Scotland to suffer most prejudice without a cause; that the wickedest of all the land should be permitted to possesse the best part of my inheritance, vnder colour of a law, by meer iniquity; and other, little better then he, to gape after the remainder, without any fault of mine?

48. Who would think that some of my tenants, whilst I was from home, being killed, and neer upon three thousand pound sterlin worth of goods taken from them by a pack of villaines, who could pretend for their robery no other excuse but that they had been plundered by others, no reparation or justice should be granted, although oftentimes demanded; that I should be extorsed, in matter of publique dues, beyond any of my neighbours; that a garrison should be placed within my house, and kept there ten months together, to my almost utter undoing, upon no other pretence but that the stance thereof is stately, and the house it selfe of a notable good fabrick and contrivance; and, in the mean while, a party both of horse and foot remain nevertheles quartered upon my lands till the remotest Highlands should pay their sessemony; that neighbor garrisons, besides my own, should by parties inforce me, upon their governours' bare tickets, to furnish them with what provisions they pleased, and yet nothing thereof be allowed unto me, although I presented a bill to that purpose to the Scots Committee of Estates, as I did for the quartering of severall troops of horse, for many months together, without any allowance.

49. These grievous pressures, with many other, and as many more I have sustained by the ministry of the land, whereof I make account in the large treatise of my Aporrexises to give notice more at length, have occasioned this digression in a part; which likewise having proceeded from a serious consideration of the two aforesaid scurvie qualities, that move the inhabitants of this Ile to run every foot to supernatural causes, engageth me to say, that as it is a maxim in philosophy that *entia non sunt multiplicanda sine necessitate,* so that it is no lesse incongruity to avouch, that a thing hath miraculously been done by God, or that for atchievement thereof the help

of an evill spirit, because of his being reputed of more experience then man, hath been required thereto, when in the mean while, perhaps, the performance of it by secondary means of an ordinary working, is obvious to any that have the dexterity to open his eyes to see the truth.

50. For which cause they are much to blame, that think it impossible for any man naturally to frame a language of greater perfection then Greek, Hebrew, or Latine.

51. For who, instead of affording the true cause of a thing, unnecessarily runs to miracles, tacitely acknowledgeth that God naturally cannot do it; wherein he committeth blasphemie, as that souldier may be accounted guilty of contumacie and disobedience, who, rejecting the orders wherewith an inferiour officer is authorized to command him, absolutely refuseth compearance, unless the General himself come in person to require it of him.

52. As there is a possibility such a language may be, so doe I think it very requisite such a language were, both for affording conciseness and abundance of expression.

53. Such as extoll those languages most, are enforced sometimes to say, that *Laborant penuria verborum ;* and thereunto immediately subjoyn this reason, *Quia plures sunt res quam verba.*

54. That is soon said, and, *ad pauca respicientes facile enuntiant.* But here I ask them how they come to know that there are more things then words, taking things, as in this sense they ought to be taken, for things universal; because there is no word spoken, which to the conceit of man is not able to represent more individuals then one, be it sun, moon, Phœnix, or what you will, even amongst verbs, and syncategorematical signes, which do onely suppone for the modalities of things; therefore is each word the sign of an universal thing, Peter signifying either this Peter, or that Peter, and any whatever name, surname, or title, being communicable to one and many.

55. Thus though both words and thoughts, as they are signs, be universal, yet do I believe that those who did attribute less universality to words then things, knew not definitely the full number of words, taking words for any articulate pronunciation.

56. Nay, I will go further : there is no alphabet in the world, be the calculator never so well skill'd in arithmetick, by vertue whereof the exact number of words may be known, because that number must comprehend all the combinations that letters can have with one another, and this cannot be done if any letter be wanting ; and consequently, by no alphabet as yet framed, wherein, as I have already said in the twelfth article, there is a deficiency of many letters.

57. The universal alphabet therefore must be first conceived, before the exactness of that computation can be attained unto.

58. Then is it, when, having couched an alphabet materiative of all the words the mouth of man, with its whole implements, is able to pronounce, and bringing all these words within the systeme of a language, which, by reason of its logopandochie, may deservedly be intituled The Universal Tongue, that nothing will better merit the

labour of a grammatical arithmetician then, after due enumeration, *hinc inde*, to appa-riate the words of the universal language with the things of the universe.

59. The analogie therein 'twixt the signe and thing signified holding the more exactly, that as, according to Aristotle, there can be no more worlds but one, because all the matter whereof worlds can be composed is in this ; so can there be no universal language but this I am about to divulge unto the world, because all the words enunci-able are in it contained.

60. If any officious critick will run to the omnipotency of God for framing more worlds, according to the common saying, Nothing is impossible to God, that implies not a contradiction, so must he have recourse to the same omnipotent power for fur-nishing of man with other speech-tools then his tongue, throat, roof of the mouth, lips, and teeth, before the contexture of another universal language can be warped.

61. That I should hit upon the invention of that, for the furtherance of philosophy, and other disciplines and arts, which never hitherto hath been so much as thought upon by any, and that in a matter of so great extent, as the expressing of all the things in the world, both in themselves, actions, ways of doing, situation, pendicles, relations, connexions, pathetick interpositions, and all other appurtenances to a perfect elocution, without being beholding to any language in the world ; insomuch as one word will hardly be believed by our fidimplicitary gown-men, who, satisfied with their predecessors' contrivances, and taking all things litterally, without examination, blate-rate, to the nauseating even of vulgar ears, those exotick proverbs, There is no new thing under the sun, *Nihil dictum quod non dictum prius*, and, Beware of philosophers ; authorizating this on Paul, the first on Solomon, and the other on Terence.

62. But, poor souls, they understand not that in the passage of Solomon is meant, that there is no innovation in the essence of natural things ; all transmutations on the same matter, being into forms, which, as they differ from some, so have an essential uniformity with others pre-existent in the same kind.

63. And when it was said by Paul, Beware of philosophers, he meant such sophis-ters as themselves, who, under the vizzard of I know not what, corrupt the channels of the truth, and pervert all philosophy and learning.

64. As for the sayings of Terence, whether Scipio couched them or himself, they ought to be inferred rather as testimonies of neat Latine, then for asserting of infallible verities.

65. If there hath been no new thing under the sun, according to the adulterate sense of those pristinary lobcocks, how comes the invention of syllogisms to be attri-buted to Aristotle, that of the sphere to Archimedes, and logarithms to Neper? It was not Swart, then, and Gertudenburg, that found out gunpowder and the art of printing, for these two men lived after the decease of Solomon.

66. Had there been canon in Solomon's dayes, Rehoboam, by all appearance,

would have made use of them for the recovery of his inheritance; nor had some mention of artillery been omitted in the books of the Macchabees.

67. Pancerola's Treatise *De novis adimpertis*, although Polydor Virgil were totally forgot, would be, had there been no new thing since Solomon penn'd Ecclesiastes, but as a discourse of platonick reminiscences, and calling to minde some formerly lost fancies.

68. Truly, I am so far from being of the opinion of those archæomanetick coxcombs, that I really think there will alwayes be new inventions where there are excellent spirits.

69. For, as I ascribe unto my self the invention of the trissotetrall trigonometry, for facility of calculation by representatives of letters and syllables, the proving of the equipollencie and opposition both of plaine and modal enunciations by rules of geometry, the unfolding of the chiefest part of philosophy by a continued geographical allegory, and above a hundred other severall books on different subjects, the conceit of so much as one whereof never entered into the brains of any before my self, although many of them have been lost at Worcester fight, so am I confident that others after me may fall upon some strain of another kind, never, before that, dreamed upon by those of foregoing ages.

70. Now to the end the reader may be more enamored of the language, wherein I am to publish a grammer and lexicon, I will here set down some few qualities and advantages peculiar to it self, and which no language else, although all other concurred with it, is able to reach unto.

71. First, There is not a word utterable by the mouth of man, which, in this language, hath not a peculiar signification by it self, so that the allegation of Bliteri by the Summulists will be of small validity.

72. Secondly, Such as will harken to my instructions, if some strange word be proposed to them, whereof there are many thousands of millions, deviseable by the wit of man, which never hitherto by any breathing have been uttered, shall be able, although he know not the ultimate signification thereof, to declare what part of speech it is; or if a noun, unto what predicament or class it is to be reduced, whether it be the sign of a real or notional thing, or somewhat concerning mechanick trades in their tooles or tearmes; or if real, whether natural or artificial, complete or incomplete; for words here do suppone for the things which they signifie, as when we see my Lord General's picture, we say, there is my Lord General.

73. Thirdly, This world of words hath but two hundred and fifty prime radices, upon which all the rest are branched; for better understanding whereof, with all its dependant boughs, sprigs, and ramelets, I have before my Lexicon set down the division thereof, making use of another allegory, into so many cities, which are subdivided into streets, they againe into lanes, those into houses, these into stories, whereof each room standeth for a word; and all these so methodically, that who observeth my pre-

cepts therein, shall, at the first hearing of a word, know to, what city it belongeth, and consequently not be ignorant of some general signification thereof, till, after a most exact prying into all its letters, finding the street, lane, house, story, and room thereby denotated, he punctually hit upon the very proper thing it represents in its most specifical signification.

74. Fourthly, By vertue of adjectitious syllabicals annexible to nouns and verbs, there will arise of several words, what compound, what derivative, belonging in this language to one noune or to one verb alone, a greater number then doth pertaine to all the parts of speech in the most copious language in the world besides.

75. Fifthly, So great energy to every meanest constitutive part of a word in this language is appropriated, that one word thereof, though but of seven syllables at most, shall comprehend that which no language else in the world is able to express in fewer then fourscore and fifteen several words; and that not only a word here and there for masteries sake, but severall millions of such, which, to any initiated in the rudiments of my grammar, shall be easie to frame.

76. Sixthly, In the cases of all the declinable parts of speech, it surpasseth all other languages whatsoever, for whilst others have but five or six at most, it hath ten, besides the nominative.

77. Seventhly, There is none of the learned languages but hath store of nouns defective of some case or other; but in this language there is no heteroclite in any declinable word, nor redundancie or deficiencie of cases.

78. Eighthly, Every word capable of number, is better provided therewith in this language then by any other; for in stead of two or three numbers, which others have, this affordeth you four; to wit, the singular, dual, plural, and redual.

79. Ninthly, It is not in this as other languages, wherein some words lack one number, and some another, for here each casitive or personal part of speech is endued with all the numbers.

80. Tenthly, In this tongue there are eleven genders; wherein likewise it exceedeth all other languages.

81. Eleventhly, Verbs, mongrels, participles, and hybrids, have all of them ten tenses besides the present; which number no language else is able to attain to.

82. Twelfthly, Though there be many conjugable words in other languages defective of tenses, yet doth this tongue allow of no such anomaly, but granteth all to each.

83. Thirteenthly, In lieu of six moods which other languages have at most, this one enjoyeth seven in its conjugable words.

84. Fourteenthly, Verbs here, or other conjugable parts of speech, admit of no want of moodes, as do other languages.

85. Fifteenthly, In this language the verbs and participles have four voices, although it was never heard that ever any other language had above three.

86. Sixteenthly, No other tongue hath above eight or nine parts of speech, but this hath twelve.

87. Seventeenthly, For variety of diction in each part of speech, it surmounteth all the languages in the world.

88. Eighteenthly, Each noun thereof, or verb, may begin or end with a vowel or consonant, as to the peruser shall seem most expedient.

89. Nineteenthly, Every word of this language, declinable or indeclinable, hath at least ten several synomymas.

90. Twentiethly, Each of these synomymas, in some circumstance of the signification, differeth from the rest.

91. One and twentiethly, Every faculty, science, art, trade, or discipline, requiring many words for expression of the knowledge thereof, hath each its respective root from whence all the words thereto belonging are derived.

92. Two and twentiethly, In this language the opposite members of a division have usually the same letters in the words which signifie them; the initial and final letter being all one, with a transmutation only in the middle ones.

93. Three and twentiethly, Every word in this language signifieth as well backward as forward, and however you invert the letters, still shall you fall upon significant words, whereby a wonderful facility is obtained in making of anagrams.

94. Four and twentiethly, There is no language in the world, but for every word thereof it will afford you another of the same signification, of equal syllables with it, and beginning or ending, or both, with vowels or consonants as it doth.

95. Five and twentiethly, By vertue hereof there is no hexameter, elegiack, saphick, asclepaid, iambick, or any other kind of Latine or Greek verse, but I will afford you another in this language of the same sort, without a syllable more or less in the one then the other, spondæ answering to spondæ, dactil to dactil, cæsure to cæsure, and each foot to other, with all uniformity imaginable.

96. Six and twentiethly, As it trotteth easily with metrical feet, so at the end of the career of each line hath it the dexterity, after the manner of our English and other vernaculary tongues, to stop with the closure of a rime; in the framing whereof, the well-versed in that language shall have so little labour, that for every word therein he shall be able to furnish at least five hundred several monosyllables of the same termination with it.

97. Seven and twentiethly, In translating verses of any vernaculary tongue, such as Italian, French, Spanish, Slavonian, Dutch, Irish, English, or whatever it be, it affords you words of the same signification, syllable for syllable, and in the closure of each line a rime, as in the original.

98. Eight and twentiethly, By this language, and the letters thereof, we may doe such admirable feats in numbers, that no cyphering can reach its compendiousness; for whereas the ordinary way of numbring by thousands of thousands of thousands of

thousands, doth but confuse the hearer's understanding, to remedy which I devised, even by cyphering it self, a farre more exact manner of numeration, as in the treatise of arithmetick which I have ready for the press is evidently apparent. This language affordeth so concise words for numbering, that the number for setting down, whereof would require in vulgar arithmetick more figures in a row then there might be grains of sand containable from the center of the earth to the highest heavens, is in it expressed by two letters.

99. Nine and twentiethly, What rational logarithms doe by writing, this language doth by heart, and by adding of letters, shall multiply numbers, which is a most exquisite secret.

100. Thirtiethly, The digits are expressed by vowels, and the consonants stand for all the results of the Cephalism, from ten to eighty-one inclusively, whereby many pretty arithmetical tricks are performed.

101. One and thirtiethly, In the denomination of the fixed stars, it affordeth the most significant way imaginary; for by the single word alone which represents the star, you shall know the magnitude, together with the longitude and latitude, both in degrees and minutes of the star that is expressed by it.

102. Two and thirtiethly, By one word in this language we shall understand what degree, or what minute of the degree of a sign in the zodiack, the sun, or moon, or any other planet is in.

103. Three and thirtiethly, As for the year of God, the moneth of that yeer, week of the moneth, day of that week, partition of the day, hour of that partition, quarter and half quarter of the hour, a word of one or two syllables at most in this language will express it all to the full.

104. Four and thirtiethly, In this language also, words expressive of herbs represent unto us with what degree of cold, moisture, heat, or driness they are qualified, together with some other property distinguishing them from other herbs.

105. Five and thirtiethly, In matter of colours, we shall learn by words in this language the proportion of light, shadow, or darkness commixed in them.

106. Six and thirtiethly, In the composition of syllables by vowels and consonants, it affordeth the aptest words that can be imagined for expressing how many vowels and consonants any syllable is compounded of, and how placed in priority and situation to one another. Which secret in this language is exceeding necessary for understanding the vigour of derivatives in their variety of signification.

107. Seven and thirtiethly, For attaining to that dexterity which Mithridates, king of Pontus, was said to have, in calling all his soldiers, of an army of threescore thousand men, by their names and surnames, this language will be so convenient, that if a general, according to the rules thereof, will give new names to his souldiers, whether horse, foot, or dragoons, as the French use to do to their infantry by their *noms de guerre,* he shall be able, at the first hearing of the word that represents the name of a

souldier, to know of what brigade, regiment, troop, company, squadron, or division he is, and whether he be of the cavalry or of the foot, a single souldier or an officer, or belonging to the artillery or baggage. Which device, in my opinion, is not unuseful for those great captains that would endear themselves in the favour of the souldiery.

108. Eight and thirtiethly, In the contexture of nouns, pronouns, and preposital articles united together, it administreth many wonderful varieties of laconick expressions, as in the grammar thereof shall more at large be made known unto you.

109. Nine and thirtiethly, Every word in this language is significative of a number, because, as words may be increased by addition of letters and syllables, so of numbers is there a progress *in infinitum*.

110. Fourtiethly, In this language every number, how great soever, may be expressed by one single word.

111. One and fourtiethly, As every number essentially differeth from another, so shall the words expressive of severall numbers be from one another distinguished.

112. Two and fourtiethly, No language but this hath in its words the whole number of letters, that is, ten vowels, and six and twenty consonants, by which means there is no word escapes the latitude thereof.

113. Three and fourtiethly, As its interjections are more numerous, so are they more emphatical in their respective expression of passions, then that part of speech is in any other language whatsoever.

114. Four and fourtiethly, The more syllables there be in any one word of this language, the manyer several significations it hath; with which propriety no other language is endowed.

115. Five and fourtiethly, All the several genders in this language are as well competent to verbs as nouns; by vertue whereof, at the first uttering of a verb in the active voice, you shall know whether it be a god, a goddess, a man, a woman, a beast, or any thing inanimate, and so thorow the other five genders, that doth the action, which excellencie is altogether peculiar unto this language.

116. Six and fourtiethly, In this language there is an art, out of every word, of what kind of speech soever it be, to frame a verb; whereby, for expressing all manner of actions, a great facility is attained unto.

117. Seven and fourtiethly, To all manner of verbs, and many syncategorematical words, is allowed in this language a flexion by cases, unknown to other tongues, thereby to represent unto our understandings more compendious expressions then is possible to afford by any other means.

118. Eight and fourtiethly, Of all languages, this is the most compendious in complement, and consequently fittest for courtiers and ladies.

119. Nine and fourtiethly, For writing of missives, letters of state, and all other manner of epistles, whether serious or otherways, it affordeth the compactest stile of

any language in the world; and therefore, of all other, the most requisite to be learned by statesmen and merchants.

120. Fiftiethly, No language in matter of prayer and ejaculations to Almighty God is able, for conciseness of expression, to compare with it; and therefore, of all other, the most fit for the use of church-men, and spirits inclined to devotion.

121. One and fiftiethly, This language hath a modification of the tense, whether present, preterite, or future, of so curious invention for couching much matter in few words, that no other language ever had the like.

122. Two and fiftiethly, There is not a proper name in any country of the world, for which this language affords not a peculiar word, without being beholding to any other.

123. Three and fiftiethly, In many thousands of words belonging to this language, there is not a letter which hath not a peculiar signification by it self.

124. Four and fiftiethly, The polysyllables of this language do all of them signifie by their monosyllables, which no word in any other language doth, *ex instituto*, but the compound ones; for, though the syllabical parts of *exlex* separately signifie as in the compound, yet those of *homo* doe it not, nor yet those of *dote* or *domus*, as in the whole; and so it is in all other languages, except the same; for there are in the Italian and Latine tongues words of ten, eleven, or twelve syllables, whereof not one syllable by it self doth signifie any thing at all in that language, of what it doth in the whole; as *adolescenturiatissimamente, honorificicabilitudinitatibus, &c.*

125. Five and fiftiethly, All the languages in the world will be beholding to this, and this to none.

126. Six and fiftiethly, There is yet another wonder in this language, which, although a little touched by the by in the fifty eighth article of this preface, I will mention yet once more; and it is this, That though this language have advantage of all other, it is impossible any other in time coming surpass it, because, as I have already said, it comprehendeth, first, all words expressible; and then, in matter of the obliquity of the cases and tenses, the contrivance of indeclinable parts, and right disposure of vowels and consonants, for distinguishing of various significations within the latitude of letters, cannot be afforded a way so expedient.

127. Seven and fiftiethly, The greatest wonder of all is, that of all the languages in the world, it is easiest to learn; a boy of ten years old, being able to attain to the knowledge thereof, in three moneths space; because there are in it many facilitations for the memory, which no other language hath but it self.

128. Eight and fiftiethly, Sooner shall one reach the understanding of things to be signified by the words of this language, then by those of any other, for that as logarithms in comparison of absolute numbers, so do the words thereof in their initials respectively vary according to the nature of the things which they signifie.

129. Nine and fiftiethly, For pithiness of proverbs, oracles, and sentences, no language can paralel with it.

130. Sixtiethly, In axioms, maximes, and aphorisms, it is excellent above all other languages.

131. One and sixtiethly, For definitions, divisions, and distinctions, no language is so apt.

132. Two and sixtiethly, For the affirmation, negation, and infinitation of propositions, it hath proprieties unknown to any other language, most necessary for knowledge.

133. Three and sixtiethly, In matters of Enthymems, Syllogisms, and all manner of illative ratiocination, it is the most compendious in the world.

134. Sixtie fourthly, Negative expressions are more compendiously uttred in this language then in any other in the world.

135. Sixtie fifthly, The infinitant terms by this tongue are in one single word expressed, which succinctness is by no other language afforded.

136. Lastly, There is not any phrase whatsoever, which, for being peculiar to one speech, and consequently in all other to be improperly taken, wherewith each known tongue in the world is most variously stored, hath, when translated from its original idiome, the denomination of Græcism, Latinism, Scotism, Anglicism, and so forth; but in this universal language is so well admitted, that, in losing nothing of its genuine liveliness, it beareth along with it, without any diminution either of sense or expression, the same very emphasis in the stream which it had at the spring, the like whereof is in no other language to be found.

137. Besides these sixty and six advantages above all other languages, I might have couched thrice as many more, of no less consideration then the aforesaid, but that these same will suffice to sharpen the longing of the generous Reader, after the intrinsecal and most researched secrets of the new grammar and lexicon which I am to evulge.

THE PREFACE TO THE SECOND BOOK,

ENTITULED

CHRESTASEBEIA.

THE scope of the Author, in this his second book, is to plead for the removal of some impediments which stand in the way of emitting those his works of a curious invention, wherewith he intends to gratifie this Isle; in doing whereof, he observeth a very compendious and most commendable method, for prosecuting of the noble designe proposed in the general title of the introduction. Natural philosophie teacheth us, that one form is to be expelled before another can be introduced upon the subjected matter; for which cause Aristotle very wisely constituted privation for one of the three principles of nature. No judicious architect will begin to erect a fabrick, till the ground be first cleansed of the rubbish which hindreth the laying of the foundation. Arts, disciplines, and sciences, for being qualities, as are the faculties whence they emane, though of another species, are predioamentally claſsible under accidents, that have their eſsential dependance on that substance which, without derogating any thing from the soul of man, may properly be said to be the body, whose livelihood consisting in a maintenance by external means, the Author very rationally

thence inferreth a necefsity of being established in the estate of his predecefsors, for the production of his brain-ifsues in many elaboured secrets.
Those the Author metaphorically termeth moveables, thereby to claim the
benefit of an act of Parliament for his redintegration into his progenitors'
land ; and yet that he should make so disproportionate a parallel, he layeth
the weight upon the iniquity of the times, and rigour of flagitators, whose
lamentable wrongs done unto him he most egregiously amplifyeth by three
notable examples ; and in sequel thereof describeth usurie to the life, together with the brutishnefs of the churlish exactors of it. Why to the promised language is premised this introduction, and that the promulgation
thereof is retarded, the Author, besides what is said, inserteth this other
reason, least its inconsiderate prostitution should make it be undervalued ; to confirm this, he sheweth by three or four pregnant examples
how enjoyment abates affection, and by ten instances more, how in the
estimation of ill-poised judgements, very precious things have been post-
posed to quisquiliary trash : for witnefsing the transcendencie of the effects
of mental faculties, beyond those of either body or fortune, he points at
Scotus and Sacrobosco ; but in collatiotioning learning with warfare, he
leaves the odds undecided. What large donatives have been bestowed on
learned men for their encouragement to literature, he specifyeth by eight
several examples ; and by seven more, the indefatigable pains taken by
eminent schollars of former ages in the prosecuting of their studies ; all
which the author is pleased to display before us, the better thereby to extoll the gifts of the intellectual part ; and where he transiently lets fall a
word in praise of his own elucubrations, he excuseth it by the necefsity of
avoiding a greater evil, subjoyning therto for better illustration three specious presidents of a king, a prophet, and a saint, all divinely inspired ;
and finally closeth all with a certainty, upon the removal of obstructions,
of performing whatever he hath promised, the contexture of all which
being maturely perpended, cannot choose but be pleasing to the industrious
reader.

THE SECOND BOOK

INTRODVCTION

INTITULED

CHRESTASEBEIA ;

OR,

IMPIOUS DEALING OF CREDITORS.

WHEREIN THE SEVERITY OF THE CREDITORS OF THE AU-THOR'S FAMILY IS DESIRED TO BE REMOVED, AS A MAIN IMPEDIMENT TO THE PRODUCTION OF THIS UNIVER-SAL LANGUAGE, AND PUBLICATION OF OTHER NO LESS CONSIDERABLE TREATISES.

Avarus prius sac-cum implet quam ani-mum.

1. WHY it pleased me to set forth this preamble apart, without annexing thereto the rudiments of the language, by the faith I owe to truth, it was against my will, and the cause thereof did meerly proceed from without.   First, for that all the papers concerning that subject were lost at the spoil after Worcester fight; and next, there being in Scotland of those that would despoyl me of my whole land, who care as little for learning as a sow doth for a pearl; should I have publiquely exposed these treasures,

Interea,ple-no cum tur-get saculus ore, crescit amor num-mi quantum ipsa pecunia crescit.

like Æsop's cock, they would have preferred a barley corn before them.
2. And although I expect no applause from them, whose Arcadian ears by the warbling of no nightingale are to be demulceated, yet by reason of the power they have in the land, I thought fit to stop my pen for a while, least otherwise I should fail of my designe in the preservation of my predecessor's inheritance.

3. For albeit it might be thought unreasonable, that I should be denuded of those possessions my ancestors have enjoyed these one and twenty hundred years and upwards, and that by them to whom I was never beholding insomuch as a pennie, nor any of my predecessors, save my father alone, whose facility in making of unprofitable bargains they abused for inriching of themselves, and at whose hands they have gained so much, although they never get a penny from mee, they can be no losers.

Avari animus nullo satiatur lucro.

4. Yet as if I were their debtor, of which title the civilest nations in the world will acquit me, I demand of the state, and authority established, this favour amongst others, that they would allow me the benefit of the six and thirtieth statute of the fifth Parliament of King James the Third, which never yet was repealed, in so far as it provideth, that the debtor's moveable goods be first valued and discussed, before his lands be apprised, much less possessed.

Suos hospites male remunerat avarus; serpens est in sinu, ignis in gremio, mus in pera.

5. And if, conform to the aforesaid act, this be granted, I doe promise shortly to display before the world, ware of greater value then ever from the East Indias was brought in ships to Europe.

6. And though there be many, even of my father's creditors, that will postpose it to a little money, yet are not diamonds and gold of the less worth, because the Americans make more account of iron and beads.

Qui studet nummis, hic præfert infima summis: condita factori præponit, et ejus amori.

7. I have seen of those that choosed sugar before ambergrece, because they deemed it sweeter to the tast; and preferred black Tours velvet to pure Segovia scarlet, for that it seemed softer to the touch; yet is not such a simple and unskilful misprising of things to passe for a rule amongst the better sort, for inhansing or imparing of their prices.

8. For truth being *in indivisibili*, as is the essence of what ever is, who is most versed in the nature and properties of a thing is alwayes best able to dignosce of its value.

9. A shooe-maker cannot judge so uprightly of an elabourate picture, as a cunning artist in the trade of painting; nor an illiterate soldier pry so profoundly in a metaphysical argument, as a learned philosopher brought up with quiddities.

10. A ploughman is better acquainted with tilling then bills of exchange; and a merchant banker with the rate of what in the hundred is to be taken from Amsterdam to Venice, then what fair he should go to for buying of the cheapest and best cattel.

11. Seamen will prove as ridiculous in making on foot their approaches to a fort, as land warriors in the conding of a ship; and it will become a clown as ill to complement with a lady, as a courtier to carry burthens; each trade or vocation having its own genius, and no man being skill'd in all alike.

12. I have heard an Italian of good report say, That, with the money got from a lapidarie for a box of precious stones, he bought a signiorie of land, which the owner, ignorant in such, would not have disponed for a hundred times as many jewels.

13. And have likewise known a citizen in Paris that would not have let out one

single chamber of his, though but for a moneth, for six times more cochenile, then at the hands of others, well seen in the like chaffer, afforded the money for which he was glad to set a nineteen yeares lease of his whole house together, consisting of ten rooms as good, which is the proportion of thirteen thousand six hundred and eighty to one.

14. Out of which instances is to be collected, that seeing men of all professions trade for money, who usually are unexpert in the commodities of one another's vocation; if it occurre that the debtor and creditors be of several faculties, the debtor must otherwayes then with the chevisance of his imployment, labour for the contentment of his creditor of another calling, and consequently, money being the common measure of all merchandize, must needs sell to some other for the payment of him.

15. The case in some measure is my own, considering the condition wherein, for the present, I am made to stand with my father's creditors, whose lack of insight in the ware I would make sale of, together with their earnest pressing me for money, enforce me, for the better obtaining of the last, to have recourse to those that are more skilful in the first to dispone it to.

Vid. art. 69. Hic bona pars hominum decepta cupidine falsa, Nil satis est, inquit.

16. Yet if I were not netled by such a sect of bawling and obstreperous seekers, in a time so unfertil of good shifts, and wherein I have already essayed the uneffectualness of all other manner of means, this vendacity should never have appeared in me of a commodity, which to appreciate at the rate of any coyn, I would have accounted a kind of simonie, and a course which had my land been as cleer of merchants as my minde is of mercinariness, I had not daigned to stoop to for a kingdom.

Ergo sollicitæ tu causa pecunia vitæ es. Tu vitiis hominum crudelia pabula præbes; semina curarum de capite orta tuo.

17. But for want of other expedients, making bold to pitch on this, I heartily supplicate the subsidiarie courtesie of the State aforesaid, towards the emancipation and infranchising of my mind from the drudgery and servile ploddings wherewith it hath been captivated, how to perform duty to those fæneratorie masters.

Fænus est onus etiam divitibus intollerabile, *says Plutarch.* Magnum malum est hominibus avaritia, idcirco quod homines magnis et multis in-

18. Who always sticking close about me, like a cluster of stinging wasps, and thundring upon me charges, as unwelcom to any generous spirit, as is the touch of an Ibis' penne to a crocodile, have so fretted, galled, and pricked me to the very soul, that all the faculties thereof, have by them been this great while most pitilesly and atrociously inslaved, and incarcerated in the comfortless dump of searching for wherewith to close their yawning mouths, and stop their gaping.

19. For truly I may say, that above ten thousand severall times, I have by those flagitators been interrupted for money, which never came to my use, directly or indirectly one way or other, at home or abroad, any one time whereof I was busied about speculations of greater consequence then all that they were worth in the world; from which, had not I been violently pluck'd away by their importunity, I would have emitted to publick view above five hundred several treatises on inventions never hitherto thought upon by any.

commodis conflictantur propter immensam pecuniæ cupiditatem.

Vid. lib. 5. Ar. 43.   Avarus omnia devorans vellet nullum hominem esse, ut omnia solus possideret.

20. But as a certain shepheard on a time, according to the Epimythist, would have perswaded the fox not to destroy his flock, till he had got their fleeces, the wool whereof was to be employed in cloth for the royal robes of the Soveraign of the land; unto whom the fox replied, That his main interest being to fatten himself and his cubbs, he did not find himself so much concerned in either Soveraign or subject, that upon any such pretext, how specious soever, he would leave his terrier unmagazined of all manner of provision competent for his vulpecularie family. Excusatio avaritiæ est cumulare pro filiis.

21. Even so may I avouch, that the nature of the most part of this strange kind of flagitators, being without any consideration or regard to the condition of a gentleman, or whether the improvement or impairing of his fortunes should further or retard the progress of the countrie's fame, totally to employ themselves in a coin-accumulating way towards the multiplying of their trash, and heedful accrescing of the Mammon drosse, wherein their lucre-hailing minds and consopiated spirits lie intombed and im-buryed. Nullum est justitiæ in cordibus illorum vestigium, in quibus avaritia sibi fecit habitaculum.

22. For again, as the old Hyena of Quinzie, as it is reported in some outlandish stories, after he had seized upon the sublimest witted Gymnosophist of that age, on purpose to feed upon him, being a hungred, did vilifie and misregard the tears and sorrow, justly shed and conceived by the inhabitants of that populous and magnificent city, for the apparent loss of such unparallelled wisdom and exquisite learning, as through the death of so prime a philosopher was like for ever to redound to the whole Empire of China; and altogether postposing them to the satisfying of his base appetite with one poor meal of meat, and that only in a sorry breakfast he was to take out of his bowels, killed him, tore him in pieces, and greedily snatched up that repast, the better to dispose his stomach within three houres thereafter for another of the like nature. Omnium scelerum gravissima est avaritia, cum omnia humana et divina jura, cultumque vel ipsius dei pessundare consuevit, cum nihil sit tam sanctum quod avaritia violare non soleat.

23. Just so, amongst many of my father's creditors, hath there bin a generation of such tenacious publicans, that cared so little what the countrey in general might be concerned in any man's private interest, though much by some singular good friends of mine hath been spoke to them in my own particular, that through their cruelty and extreme hard usage, I have beene often necessitated to supply out of my brains what was deficient in my purse, and provide from a far what should have been afforded at home, one half tearm's interest, although but of a pettie and trivial summe, being in their eyes of more esteem then the quintessence of all the liberal arts, together with that of the moral vertues, epitomized in the person of any, though imbellished to the boot, with all other accomplishments whatsoever; for discategorically, in despight of all order, by marshalling *quality* after *habere*, they have still preferred the possession of a little lumber and baggagely pelf to all the choicest perfections of both body and mind. Quid non mortalia pectora cogis, auri sacra fames. Qui malunt locupletari crumenas quam Camænas consulere. Ab ipsis etiam statu isexigerent, ut aiunt, farinas.

24. And indeed, to speak ingenuously, as the sparrow, whom a late Archbishop of Canterbury weeped to see as often forced to fall back, as it strove to flye upwards, by reason of a little peeble stone, fast at the end of a string, that was tyed to her foot; the contemplatively devout prelate thereby considering that the sincerest minds, even

of the most faithfull, are oftentimes impeded from soaring to their intended height, because of the clog of worldly incumbrances which depresseth them.

Nunquam expletur cupiditatis sitis, nam cupiditati nihil est satis.
25. Even so may it be said of my self, that when I was most seriously imbusied about the raising of my own and countrie's reputation to the supremest reach of my endeavours, then did my father's creditors, like so many millstones hanging at my heels, pull down the vigour of my fancie, and violently hold at under what other wayes would have ascended above the sublimest regions of vulgar conception.

Nil avaro molestius, nullum est hominum genus quod tam auri habendi cupiditate intabescat.
26. Thus I being, as another Andromeda, chained to the rock of hard usage, and in the view of all my compatriots, exposed to the merciless dragon usurie, I most humbly beseech the soveraign authority of the countrey, like another Perseus mounted on the winged Pegasus of respect to the weal and honour thereof, to releeve me, by their power, from the eminent danger of the jaws of so wild a monster.

Vid. B. 3. Art. 8. Inflammatur lucro avaritia et non extinguitur, quasi gradus quosdam cupiditatis habet, et quo plures ascenderit eo ad altiora festinat, unde fit gravior ruina lapsuro.
27. Which maketh the very meanest and most frivolous summe of any, like the giant Ephialtes, who grew nine inches every moneth, immensely to spread forth its exuberant members, without any other sustenance or nourishment then the meer invisible flux of time, that starveth all things else, until it extend it self at last to a mighty huge Colossus of debt, able, like that of the Rhodes, to take fastning upon two territories at once.

28. And in recompence of a so illustrious and magnificent action, unto the State of this land, as fittest patron for such a present, will I tender some of the aforesaid moveables, whose value I doe warrantably make account to be of no less extent then in the estimation of all the universities of both nations, and other pregnant spirits of approved literature, shall centuplate the worth of the whole money, that for debt can be asked by those creditors, out of the profoundest exorbitancy of their covetousness.

29. By my appealing thus to a judicatorie, conflated of the prime lights of the Isle, and who, as all wise men else, do more magnifie and extoll the endowments of the mind, then those of either body or fortune, it is very perceptible unto which of these three branches of good this offer of mine is to be reduced.

30. No man will deny, that is not destitute of common sense, but that Scotus and Sacrobosco brought more reputation to Scotland by their learned writings, then if they had enriched it with gallioons loaded full of gold, and that it had been better for that nation to have lost many millions of angels then that, through penurie or any other accident, the workes of those gallant men had been buried in oblivion.

31. For as in both body and mind, the instruments of the nobler faculties are esteemed of the greater value, so in a politick incorporation so much the more should be respected and dignified the advancers of the reputation thereof, then the accrescers of its wealth, that of the three degrees of goodness, the qualifications of the mind have the precedency.

Cum avaritia alicui dominatur
32. And although there be legions in Scotland of those Gadarenal swine that will prefer the taste of a skyball to the fragrancy of the most odiferous jasmin, who also

like so many dunghil fowles, to a grain of wheat will postpose the most precious pearl that is ; and haling only after sensual things, reduplicatively as sensual, give no repast at all to the better part, which preposterously dancing attendance after the inferiour appetites hath its eyes in a veternatorie somnolency shut up from the prospect of all mental speculations.

(margin) subjectus malis omnibus demonstratur; quia de a-varitia omnia ma-la oriuntur, et peccato-rum om-nium spinæ producun-tur.

33. Yet the essence of man consisting in reasonability, he may be said to have little of man in him that regards not another the more for having his reason imbellished with the addition of litterature.

34. Which hath been held in such grandissim account by the prudentest of pristin ages, that making it come in competition with Souldiery it self, they did not stick to aver that Greece, which of all nations was most renowned, and most worthy to be most renowned, both for wit and valour, did owe more cordial praise and commendation to the philosophers thereof, then to all its most military and warlike champions ; preferring in this case knowledge in sciences to fortitude in the fields, and the habits of the intellectual faculties to those of the moral.

35. But unfeignedly, seeing to the soundest judgments of any, and most consentaneous to one another in their adherence to apodictick conclusions, is oftentimes incident a repugnancy of opinion in matter of dialectical ratiocination ; and that some of them, in a veri-similitudinary probability of prevalency on both sides of the argument doe ferret, out of topick celluls, mediums prompting them to have in greater estimation magnanimity of courage then vivacity of spirit.

36. I will in so far as concerns my self, for that I hope ere long to breath in such auspicious dayes as will give way to my good destinie, to present me with those favorable opportunities may make my deservings appear equally recommendable in both, rather choose to suspend the pronouncing of my verdict, then by any sentiment of mine positively to determine of the pre-eminence of either.

37. However, to discend more particularly to the purpose, seeing it is every where uncontroversibly acknowledged that the goods of the mind are of more worth then those of fortune ; and by consequence, the pregnantly conceived, and maturely ennixed offspring of my own brain, which, least I should seem to philotize it, I in all humility submit to the unpartial censure of the choicest spirits, of farre greater value then any peece of money due to my father's creditors.

38. I do ardently desire and supplicat the State not to suffer the majesty and sacred name of soveraign authority, under colour of a law, any more to be abused in favours of those men who have made use thereof in several charges against me, formerly in the name of both the King Charleses, and now in that of the keepers of the liberties of England, to no other end but to rob me of my predecessor's inheritance without any procurement of mine.

39. Withall, I heartily intreat them to vouchsafe the patronizing of the present I am to make unto them ; and in testimony of their acceptance of it, exoner me of the

(margin) O Avare sordidius nihil est,

nihil est te spurcius uno, qui potes insidias dona vocare tua. Sic avidis fallax indulget piscibus hamus, Callida sic stultas decipit esca feras.

burthen of these flagitators, by taking such a course as to their discretions shall seem most expedient, which, if they consider aright, were it for the defrayment of greater sums, will be of small difficulty.

40. And here I promise, by the faith I owe to God, that this courtesie so conferred, shall, if I live, as seed sown in a fertil soyl, yeeld a hundred fold, to the promoving of the reputation of the land.

41. Which, in an age so full of calumnies, and wherein the most zealous thoughts do not escape mis-interpretation, is not to be rejected, nor any thing in that kind which may conduce to the undeceiving of forraigners of any prejudicate opinion of late conceived by them against the integrity of our countreymen.

42. Some will say that I demand much, and things unusuall to be granted; others again, that I promise far more, and am too prodigal in my own praises. But my self will avouch, that as my demand is reasonable, so would I have ere now performed what I promised, and not spoke so much as one syllable in my own favours, but that by one and the same occasion I was necessitated to doe the one, and forbear the other.

43. It is ordinary amongst seamen to say, the tempest so increas'd, that, for safety of my life, I was glad to throw my goods over board. I have heard soldiers likewise affirm, and have seen that they have heartily abandoned their purse to the prevailing enemy, for obtaining the better quarter; yet to examine either of these actions aright, they were but mixt ones tending to the lesser evil; voluntarie, *secundum quid*, but *simpliciter*, unwilling.

44. Just so is it, that for shunning of the greater harm, to wit, the inconveniency might ensue upon the vilifying of my brain-works, I choosed both to restrain their emission, and commend what was to be promulgated; either of which, had it not been for the aforesaid necessities, would have been as unwelcome to me as to the merchant was the casting out of his goods into the sea, or to the soldier, the delivery up of his purse unto his foe.

45. Enjoyment commonly abates estimation, but longing doth increase it; and as there are of those who, for one night of a lady, have bestowed double the means would have sufficed for a joyncture to the mother of their lawful children, although a better and more handsome woman to the boot; so are vulgar spirits, for the most part, highly mistaken in their sense of the true value of things of any importance.

46. Judas valued at three hundred pence the box of ointment which Mary poured on the feet of Christ, whom himself sold for thirty.

47. I have seen of them that accounted no more of ambergrece then of fuller's earth, though in some parts a handfull of the one will be worth a thousand cart loads of the other.

48. I have likewise heard of a hundred crowns given for a fresh salmon, where the Scots pint of wine did cost but three half pence; and of a salmon every whit as good got for six pence, where so much wine of no better kind would have stood you in half-a-

crown, which is the proportion of twenty thousand to one. For who at Toledo, with the hundred crowns got for a salmon, supposed fresh, which at Aberdeen he bought for a sixpence, did purchase four thousand pints of wine which at his return to Aberdeen yeelded him two thousand crowns, hath clearly obtained twenty thousand sixpences for one ; or who at Aberdeen, with the two crowns got for four pints of wine which at Toledo he bought for a sixpence, did purchase twenty fresh salmons which at his return to Toledo yeelded him two thousand crowns, hath in the same manner for one six pence obtained twenty thousand, which is a hundred to one two hundred times told.

49 Of these examples there are many, which to summe up in one of a more dis-proportioned mistake then any of the rest, I will tell you, that there happening a gentleman of very good worth to stay awhile at my house, who, one day amongst many other, was pleased, in the deadst time of all the winter, with a gun upon his shoulder, to search for a shot of some wild fowl ; and after he had waded through many waters, taken excessive pains in quest of his game, and by means thereof had killed some five or six moor fowls and partridges, which he brought along with him to my house, he was by some other gentlemen, who chanced to alight at my gate, as he entred in, very much commended for his love to sport ; and, as the fashion of most of our countrymen is, not to praise one without dispraising another, I was highly blamed for not giving my self in that kind to the same exercise, having before my eys so com-mendable a pattern to imitate ; I answered, though the gentleman deserved praise for the evident proof he had given that day of his inclination to thrift and laboriousness, that nevertheless I was not to blame, seeing whilst he was busied about that sport, I was imployed in a diversion of another nature, such as optical secrets, mysteries of natural philosophie, reasons for the variety of colours, the finding out of the longitude, the squaring of a circle, and wayes to accomplish all trigonometrical calculations by sines, without tangents, with the same compendiousness of computation, which, in the estimation of learned men, would be accounted worth six hundred thousand par-tridges, and as many moor-fowles.

50. But notwithstanding this relation, either for that the gentlemen understood it not, or that they deemed the exercise of the body to be of greater concernment then that of the minde, they continued firme in their former opinion, whereof I laboured not to convince them, because I intended, according to their capacities, to bear them company.

51. In the mean while that worthy gentleman, who was nothing of their mind, for being wet and weary after travel, was not able to eat of what he had so much toyled for, whilst my braine recreations so sharpened my appetite, that I supped to very good purpose. That night past, the next morning I gave six pence to a footman of mine, to try his fortune with the gun, during the time I should disport my self in the break-ing of a young horse ; and it so fell out, that by I had given my selfe a good heat by riding, the boy returned with a dozen of wild fouls, half moor foule, half partridge,

whereat being exceeding well pleased, I alighted, gave him my horse to care for, and forthwith entred in to see my gentlemen, the most especiall whereof was unable to rise out of his bed, by reason of the Gout and Sciatick, wherewith he was seized for his former daye's toyle.

Vide Art. 6, 7, 9, 10, 11, 13, 46, 47, 48, 49, B. 6. Art. 51, 52, 53, 54, 55.
Vide Art. 46. of the first Book, and 54, 56. of this same.

52. Thus seeing matters of the greatest worth may be undervalued by such as are destitute of understanding, who would reap any benefit by what is good, till it be appreciated, should be charie of its prestitution ; let this therefore suffice, why to this preface or introduction, I have not as yet subjoyned the Grammar and Lexicon.

53. But why it is I should extoll the worth thereof, without the jeopardy of vaine glory, the reason is clear and evident, being necessitated, as I have told in the fifth and twenty eight articles of the same book, to merchandise it for the redintegrating of an ancient family, it needeth not be thought strange, that in some measure I descend to the fashion of the shop-keepers, who to scrue up the buyer to the higher price, will tell them no better can be had for mony, 'tis the choicest ware in England, and if any can match it, he shall have it for nought.

54. So in matter of this literatorie chaffer, I determined not to be too rash in the prestitution thereof, least it should be villified ; yet went on in my laudatives, to procure the greater longing, that an ardent desire might stir up an emacity, to the furtherance of my proposed end.

Hi admiratores auri oderunt virtutis indolem et omnes honestas artes.

55. Thus the first step of this scale being to avoid the dispreciative censure of plebeculary criticks, who, as children preferr an apple to an inheritance, or, Esau like, postposing their birth-right to a dish of pottage, have no regard of intellectual perfections, where they come in competition with any sensual goodnesse ; or if they doe consider of them, in so far as concerneth new inventions, they slightingly use to vent themselves thus, the matter is not great, another could have done it, what serveth it for edification, philosophy is dangerous, the apostle himself avoucheth it, and other such quisquiliary diblaterations, to the opprobrie of good spirits, and cloak of their own ignorance, they cast in the face of learning, that there is more humanity in the voice of a bull, or that of the wildest bear that ever was, then in the speech of those monsters.

56. The second step thereof is my elogiarie interthets, in extolling the proposed matter, without any philotary presumption, whereof, in the most authentick writings, there wanteth not store of presidents.

57. Moses, in a book commonly said to be of his own writing, intituled himself, the meekest man upon the face of the earth ; and Paul, in the 11 of the 2 to the Corinthians, which was an epistle of his own, ascribed to himself the stile of one of the chiefest of the apostles, magnifying likewise his own learning therein, and other qualifications wherewith he was endowed.

58. Nor was David, for all his heinous transgressions, free from this manner of exalting himselfe ; for in severall of his psalmes, he wished to be judged according to

his righteousnesse : all which, though proceeding from the pen of man, had the Spirit of God for the Dictator.

59. Truths related to a good end, carry not along with them any blemish of ostentation, and the intention being that which specifieth the action, such self commendatives are not to be dispraised, seeing they bring us to the third step of the scale, which is seriously to long after learning.

60. Men of the greatest renown among the ancients have been so taken with the love thereof, that some divested themselves of large patrimonies and vast possessions, the better to attend their studies ; such was Anaxagoras. Others pulled out their own eyes, that they might be subject to the lesse distraction from philosophical speculations, as did Democritus. Others again, like Carneades, with metaphysical raptures were so taken up, that when set downe to table to eat, they forgot to put their hands to their mouthes.

61. Nor was this at starts, but so indefatigably studious were the most of those prime men in times of old, that Simonides writ his poesies, Chrysippus his logick, and Isocrates his Panathenaicon, when each of them was full fourscore yeares of age ; it being likewise reported by Cicero, that Sophocles in his hundreth yeare write the tragedie of Oedipus.

62. From this earnest desire of literature wee ascend another step, which is, to hold him in great estimation that is well qualified therewith, and not permit the offspring of his brain to perish, through the defect of worldly goods wherewith to support it.

63. Of that most noble kind of favorers of learning was Alexander the Great, who allowed several thousands of men to attend upon Aristotle in the writing of his Natural History, for which, when done, he gave him in a donative two hundred and fifty thousand pounds sterlin. Lorgius Licinius to Plinie the younger would have given four hundred thousand crowns for his Annals ; and Marcus Popilius Andronicus for a little treatise of that sort got sixteen thousand ducates.

64. Isocrates, for one oration which he pend, had given unto him six thousand two hundred and forty pounds sterlin ; and Antonius, the Son of Severus, to Oppianus the poet gave a crowne for every verse of a great poesie, which he had written of the nature of fishes.

65. Ptolomie on Cleombrotus the phisitian bestowed a hundred talents ; and at how dear a rate Aristotle bought the books of Speusippus, and Plato those of Philolaus the Pythagorian, is clearly set down in Aulus Gellius and Valerius Maximus.

66. Notwithstanding what hath been said, I would not have it to be thought that these largesses were so much competent prices for the learning approved of, as manifest testimonies of the giver's unfeigned affection to the learned man.

67. For, as there is no known proportion betwixt a crooked line and a streight, and that the angle of contingence is lesse then the least acute angle that is, so cannot all the transitory goods in the world be paralleled with those of the mind, if either we

The reader may be pleased to have recourse to the 22 axioms mentioned in a Book of mine entituled, *The vindication of the reputation of Scotland.*

beleeve Ovid, whilst he saith, *Nil non mortale tenemus, pectoris, exceptis, ingeniique bonis ;* or the Dutch poet Buschius in this his epigram :

> Ingenium, virtus, sapientia, cedere fato
> Non norunt tristi, nec didicere mori :
> Nec cole (si cordis quid habes) sunt cætera mortis,
> Divitiæ, robur, gloria, fama, genus.

Or yet Julius Scaliger, who in his sixt book *De Re Poëtica,* intituled Hypercriticus, professeth, that he had rather have been the author of Pindar's Pythionick and Ne-meonick lines, then King of Aragon, although he accounted them far short in value to the third Ode of Horace's fourth book, or ninth of his third, which nevertheless he esteemed to be by many stages inferiour to Virgil's verses, at so high a rate he valued the mind's endowments.

Vid. 8. 3. Art. 12.   68. Seeing thus it is then, that, being put into one ballance, the scale of learning depresseth the other, I would not expose any such talent of mine for external means, were it possible for any else to buy, with all the moneys in the world, that which I would preserve therewith, to wit, that antiquitie of race, by a continuat discent from many predecessors, in one and the same land, which would be altogether buryed in oblivion by dispossessing me of my ancient inheritance.

Vide Art. 16. Perpe-tuo lignis crescit cre-scentibus ignis; orco sive mari mens æquipara-tur avari.   69. Yet were I free from the slavery of flagitators, though most of the Island should disapplaud my writings, I would nevertheless emit them, without hope of any further recompence; for a deed of vertue, whose reward is in the action it self, makes the very doing thereof to passe for a competent remuneration.

70. But the exigence of my estate and fortune requiring another course to be taken, I will on this fourth step of the scale, as on its landing-place, expatiat my self upon the equity of my demand, and assurance of the performance of what I promise ; for the better doing whereof, I make account to speak somewhat of our family, other some of the rigour of the flagitator, a little of what the Law in justice may provide for either of us, and, lastly, to mount the highest degree of all, by closing with a perswasion to have my ancestors' inheritance made free to me and mine.

IN FLAGITORES. Ep. 1.

> Scotorum è templis nunc exulat omnis imago,
> Sculpta nec in saxo sed nec in ære manet.
> Causa patet nimirum, unum est venerabile numen,
> Nec colimus, quanquam novimus efse deum.
> Aurea nam postquam Scotis affulsit imago,
> Numina sola colunt quæ gravis arca tenet.

THE DESIGNE OF THE THIRD BOOK,

ENTITULED

CLERONOMAPORIA.

As in the book immediately foregoing, the Author very plainly hath pointed at the main block which lyeth in the way as a hindrance to the progreſs of his brain-itineraries ; so in this, the third of his Introduction, doth he, with great perspicacity, educe most peremptory reasons out of the clearest springs of both modern and ancient, divine and humane law, why it should be removed. In the mean while, the better to prepare the Reader towards a matter of so prime concernment, he begins the purpose with a peculiar and domestick narrative of the manner how those impediments were cast in, to the end that the more unjustly he was dealt with by the persons who did inject them, the greater justice may appear in his relief from their oppreſsions. To have mentioned such particulars, and unfolded them to the view of the publick, did very much damp the genius of the Author, who, could he have otherwayes done, would undoubtedly have manifested a most cordial dislike of any motion tending to approve the offring unto Pan the sacrifice of the houshold gods, or disclosing to all the mysteries of penatal rites ; but the threed of the discourse hanging thereupon, without a gap in its contexture, it could not be avoyded. Especially that generous and worthy knight, the Author's father, having been un-paralleledly wronged by false, wicked, and covetous men, himself being of all men living the justest, equallest, and most honest in his dealings, his humor was, rather than to break his word, to lose all he had, and stand to his most undeliberate promises, what ever they might cost; which too strict adherence to the austerest principles of veracity, proved often-times dammageable to him in his negotiations with many cunning sharks, who knew with what profitable odds they could scrue themselves in upon the windings of so good a nature. He, in all the (neer upon) sixtie years that he lived, never injured any man voluntarily, though by protecting and seconding of some unthankfull men he did much prejudge himself; he never refused to be surety for any, so cordial he was towards his ac-quaintance, yet, contrary to all expectations, his kindnefse therein was attended by so much good luck, that he never payed above two hundred pounds English for all his vadimonial favors. By the unfaithfulnes, on the one side, of some of his menial servants, in filching from him much of his personal estate, and falsehood of several chamberlains and bayliffs to whom he had intrusted the managing of his rents, in the unconscionable discharge of their receits, by giving up one account thrice, and of such accounts many; and, on the other part, by the frequency of disadvan-tagious bargains, which the slienefs of the subtil merchant did involve him in, his lofs came unawares upon him, and irresistibly, like an armed man; too great trust to the one, and facility in behalf of the other, occasioning so grievous a misfortune, which neverthelefs did not proceed from want of knowledge or abilitie in natural parts, for in the businefs of other men he would have given a very sound advice, and was surpafsing dextrous in arbitrements, upon any reference submitted to him, but that hee thought it did derogate from the nobility of his house and reputation of his person, to look to petty things in matter of his own affairs. Whereupon, after forty years custom, being habituated thereunto, he found himself at last, to his great regret, insensibly plunged into inextricable difficulties; in the large field whereof, the insatiable Creditor, to mak his harvest by the ruine of that family, struck in with his sickle, and by masking himselfe with a vizard composed of the rags of the Scotish law, in its severest sense, claims the same right to the whole inheritance that Robinhood did to

Frankindal's money, for being master of the purse wherein it was. Those wretched and unequitable courses, indefatigably prosecuted by mercilefs men to the utter undoing of the Author and exterminion of his name, have induced him, out of his respect to antiquity, his piety to succefsion, and that intim regard of himself which by divine injunction ought to be the rule and measure of his love towards his neighbour, to set down in this parcel of his Introduction, the cruel usage wherewith he hath been served these many years past by that inexorable race, the lamentable preparatives which, by granting their desires, would ensue to the extirpation of worthie pedigrees, and the unexemplifyable injustice thereby redounding to him who never was in any thing obliged to them. The premifses he enlargeth with divers quaint and pertinent similies, and after a neat apparelling of usury in its holiday garments, he deduceth, from the laws and customs of all nations, the tender care that ought to be had in the preservation of ancient families; the particulars whereof, in matter of ordonance, he evidenceth by the acts of Solon, the decrees of the Decemvirs, and statutes of the Twelve Tables; and for its executional part, in the persons of Q. Fabius, Tiberius the Emperor, and the Israelitish observers of the sacred institution of Jubilees. By which enarration nothing is more clearly inferred, then that, seeing both Jews and Gentiles, Painims and Christians, in their both monarchical and polyarchical governments, have been so zealous in their obsequiousnefs to so pious a mandate, that the present age being no lefs concerned in the happy fruits thereof then the good dayes of old, the splendid authority of this Isle should be pleased not to eclipse their commendation by innovating any thing in the Author's case. Who, decyphering the implacability of flagitators, by showing how they throw in obstacles retarding their own payment, thereby tacitly to hasten his destruction, and hinting at the unnatural breach of some of his fiduciaries, he particularizeth the candor of his own endeavours, and nixuriencie to give all men contentment; the discourse whereof, in all its periods, very well deserveth the serious animadversion of the ingenious Reader.

2 u

AD ILLUSTRISSIMOS DOMINOS COMITIORUM SERE-
NISSIMI STATUS ANGLICANI.

Carmen Προϲφϵνητικον.

SCOTIA quam vidit sublimi sede superbam,
　Præque aliis unam sæpe tulifse caput ;
Eheu prisca domus generoso stemmate felix
　Urcharti diro fœnore prefsa jacet.
Commodat æra viris usuræ subdolus author,
　(Æra sed in turpem conduplicanda sinum)
Hinc erosus ager vastus, victique penates,
　Et lex conspicuos turbat iniqua lares.
At vos o patres, legum queis summa potestas,
　Quique datis populis jura benigna tribus,
Ne sinite indigno ruat ut domus optima lapsu,
　Terraque ut immeritum rapta relinquat herum :
Ille sacer Musis lotus Parnafside lympha,
　Vivat, et Aonii gloria prima chori :
Primus Hyperboreum musas qui duxit ad axem,
　Cum stupuit dominum barbara terra suum.
Pone lyram Pataræe tuam, tu barbiton Orpheu,
　Sint licet et carmen saxa secuta tuum :
Ille rudem populum primus feritate remota,
　Jufserat Aonios edidicifse modos.
Nunc querulæ lugent sylvæ, collesque nivosæ,
　Gens viduata dolet, monticolæque gemunt.
Nec Pan Arcadiæ sylvis tam sæpè vocatur,
　Quam nunc Urchartum terra relicta sonat.
Patres bellorum primi, pacisque columnæ,
　Ferte o, nam meritam ferre potestis opem.
Creditor heu totas sylvas est, flumina potat,
　Et centena avido jugera ventre premit.
Ut Scylla in medio fertur latrare profundo,
　Sorbet et æquoreas dira Charibdis aquas :
Utque rates avidis claudit Godwinus arenis,
　Gazaque cum domino non reditura suo.
Sed neque pulsa fames, det tandem Jupiter ut sit
　Carne vorax propria, visceribusque satur.

THE THIRD BOOK

OF THE

INTRODVCTION,

INTITULED

CLERONOMAPORIA ;

OR,

THE INTRICACY OF A DISTRESSED SUCCESSOR, OR APPARENT HEIR.

WHEREIN, FOR THE BETTER EVULGING OF THIS UNIVERSAL
TONGUE, AND OTHER WORKS, THE PRESERVATION OF
THE AUTHOR'S ANCIENT INHERITANCE IS BY THE
LAWES OF ALL NATIONS PLEADED FOR.

1. MAY it therefore be considered, in the first place, that a competent estate, which these many yeares past hath yeelded a thousand pounds sterling of rent, although hardly the fifth part of that, either in extent of bounds or revenue, which some 900 yeares agoe, from the dayes of my forefather Zeron upwards, till those of Nomostor, who was the first of my progenitors that stayed to inhabit the land of Cromartie, being consecutively, through a direct uninterrupted series for the most part, and lineall discent of threescore and twelve severall ancestors, from father to sonne, for the space of neer upon fourscore two Iubiles at 25 yeares each, served and retoured heires, almost alwayes, to their immediately foregoing predecessors in the same family, continued, devolved, and transmitted, with many especial royalties, privileges, and immunities from one another, and in all integrity preserved untill the time of the ma-

jority and perfect age of my father; who, according to the prescript form of the country, received it then from his guardian or tutor, as they called him, without any burthen of debt, how little soever, or provision of brother, sister, or any other of his kindred or allyance wherewith to affect it; he having nothing else, being void of all manner of incumbrances, to care for out of so considerable means, blest with so much freedome, but himself and lady alone, my mother, it pleased his father-in-law, my Lord Elphingston, then high treasurer of Scotland, at the time of the marriage to require of him so to manage the foresaid patrimony, with such ease and plenty, through a various change of neighbours, and so carefully conveyed unto him, that in compensation of the courtesie received from his predecessors, and to retaliate so great a favour, he should be oblieged and tyed to leave unto her eldest son, to be begotten of her, who some 5 yeares afterwards happened to be I, the said estate, in the same freedome and entirenesse every way that it was left unto himself, which before many noble men and others he solemnly promised to doe to the utmost of his power.

Fœnus extremæ impudentiæ signum. Lucri promissio est quasi esca in muscipula.
2. Neverthelesse, by incogitancy one way, or what else I know not, and on the other side, by the extortion and rapine of some usurious cormorants, whose money then was constantly laid out as a bait for improvident men of great revenues to be hooked by; the fortune of his affairs turned so far otherwayes from the byass they had been put in, to the regret and heavy dislike of all his friends and his own likewise at last, when he knew not how to help it, that all he bequeathed unto me his eldest Son, in matter of worldly means, was twelve or thirteen thousand pounds sterling of debt, five brethren all men, and two sisters almost mariageable, to provide for, and lesse to defray all this burden with by six hundred pounds sterling a year, although the warres had not prejudiced me in a farthing, then what for the maintaining of himself alone in a peaceable age he inherited for nothing.

Avarus animus nullo lucro satiatur, Auri namque fames parto fit major ab auro.
3. But that which did make my case the more to be commiserated, was that all these huge and exorbitant summes were charged on me by those to whom I was never obliged in a penny, nor whose money ever came to that fine that it might be known to what good end it was borrowed; there being nothing more certain then that the education of his whole children, comprehending my self, and all together with what he expended on his daughters' portions, and other wayes disbursed for suretyship, did not in all amount to above two yeares rent and a half of that estate which he totally enjoyed for six and thirty years together; and that in such halcyonian dayes, without any compulsory occasion of bestowing his means otherwayes then might best please himself, that till two yeares before his decease it was not known by the commons of the land what the words of musqueteer and pikeman did signifie.

Lucrum facit homines deteriores, et nisi lucrum es-
4. Notwithstanding all this, and that neither directly nor indirectly I had a hand in the contracting of so much as one two-pence of the aforesaid burden, those creditors (all Scots) dealt so rigorously with me, that by their uncharitable severity, even in my father's time, it was done what lay in them to shake me loose of my progenitor's

inheritance, and denude me of what I was born unto, by investing themselves in the right of those lands that through the continuat race of six dozen of predecessours, as aforesaid, were after the expiring of many ages, by their valour, vertue, and industry, most heedfully transmitted to these late yeares, free from all intanglements, claims, and intricate pretences whatsoever. set, nemo fere esset improbus, *saith* Volateranus.

5. Yet did I thereby attain to the greater portion of my father's blessing; who, conscious of the prejudice I sustained, by leaving me, contrary to the promise made to his father-in-law and ancient custome of the countrey, so much inthralled, had of me that respect and remembrance, although in another dominion for the time, that, besides his constant bewailing the hard condition whereunto he had redacted his house in my person, during all the time of that long and lingring disease whereof at last he died, he so generously and lovingly, as truly he was one of the best men in the world, acquit himself two dayes before his decease, that he had all my six brothers strongly bound and obliged before famous witnesses, himself being one, and the prime of all, especially my nearest brother intituled the Laird of Dun Lugas, for whose occasion, to sharpen his thankfullnesse the bond was conceived, because of that portion in land he received from him worth above 3000 pounds English money, under pain of his everlasting curse and execration, to assist, concur with, follow, and serve me, (for those are the words,) to the utmost of their power, industry, and means, and to spare neither charge, nor travel, though it should cost them all they had, to release me from the undeserved bondage of the domineering creditor, and extricate my lands from the impestrements wherein they were involved; yea, to bestow nothing of their owne upon no other use, till that should be done; and all this under their own hand writing, secured with the clause of registration to make the opprobrie the more notorious in case of failing, as the paper itself, which I have *in retentis*, together with another signed to the same sense, by my mother, and also my brothers and sisters, Dunbugar only excepted, will more evidently testifie. This was done in August in the year 1642, some 4 yeares after the hatching of the Covenant.

6. Thus lacking nothing I could have desired of him, but what by my grand-father he was ingaged to leave me in matter of temporal means, I must in all humility make bold to beg the permission to proceed a little further in this purpose, seeing it doth not diamerally militate against the reverence I owe to the established authority, and municipall laws of the land.

7. In competition with which, though by the laws and statuts of many of the most civilized parts of Europe, the punishment or correction inflicted for faults of undertaking excessive burthens upon ancient estates, be meerly personal, and not, like Gehazie's leprosie, derived to posterity; there being more regard had to the memory of worthy and renowned gentlemen, whose reputation they would not have laid in the dust by the supine remissness of any one of their successors, then to the raising up of the fortunes of those who have no other vertue to recommend them by, but the stupid neglect, forgetfulness, and improvident cariage of those that borrowed their money. Qui in magnis opibus sunt avidiores, et sitibundi in medio oceani gurgite.

Vid. B. 2.
Art. 27.
Avaritia est
porta mortis
et radix om-
nium malo-
rum. Ar-
gentum et
aurum non
extinguit
argenti et
auri cupidi-
tatem; neque
si plura pos-
sideas, coer-
cetur plura
possidendi
cupiditas.

Avarus,
saith St.
Austin, est
inferno simi-
lis, nam
quantum-
cumque de-
voraverit
nunquam
dicet satis.
Sic quan-
quam om-
nes thesauri
confluxerint
in avarum,
non satiabi-
tur.
Heu crescit
scelerata si-
tis, prædæ-
que recentis
incestus jam
flagrat amor,
nullusve pe-
tendi cres-
cendique
pudor.

Contemnen-
da est cupi-
ditas quæ
quidem ve-
luti ignis
quanto plus
accipit tanto
plus requi-
rit.

Vide B. 2.
Art. 68.

8. Whereby, like the indwellers of Guinea, they may be said to purchase their gold sleeping; for in whose hand soever any little heap thereof is sequestred upon obligation, the smallest time of any engendreth interest thereon, which is no sooner bred, then apt to propagate another progenie of the same pregnancie with the first to beget a third, and so forth from term to term, by the incestuous copulation of the parent with the whole children together, and with each a part, and every child conjunctly and severaly with all the rest; one brood springing forth of another, and another again out of that, producing still, in that progressive way of procreation, a new increase of the like nature with the former.

9. And all by vertue of a bond dormant, lying passibly in the greasie cobweb of a musty chest, whose master, perhaps, being lulled all this while in a dull lethargy of ease, awaketh not, like the angell Apollyon, in the eleventh of the Apocalypse intituled Abadon, but to the destruction of some one or other of his paper-fettered slaves, proving such a bad one indeed to whom he hath concredited his goods, that he never abandoneth them till his covetousness, making that the fertilest thing of any which of it self is most unfruitful, have, in the unconscionable multiplying of such a graceless generation, reared up that unhallowed result from a spark, as it were, in a corner of their houses, to the hight of a most prodigious flame, to consume them, their wives and children, with their whole estates and fortunes for ever.

10. Yet seeing the rigour of the law of Scotland seems rather, as the times have been this while past, to favour and abett the unmercifull creditor then the debtor's innocent successor, I have till this hour, although not without some inward reluctancy, chosen rather to undergoe the sternness and austerity thereof, then legislatively to supplicate the eversion of an established custom.

11. Albeit, what ever lawyers say, I be sure, that law, as it is conform to equity and justice, requireth as well, if not more, that there be antidots and preservative remedies for men's estates in lands, as for the fortunes of them whose stock is onely in money.

12. Especially, in the behalf of those, whom to deprive of their old possessions, as is glanced at a little in the sixtie eight article of the second book, would ingulph and bury in forgetfulness that antiquity of line which all the riches on earth is not able to purchase, and consequently, making nobility stoop to coyn, and vertue to gain, bring the only support and props of honour to serve as fewel to the unquenchable fire of avaritious hearts.

13. And I may very well say, seeing it cohæres with the purpose in hand, that I sustain a greater prejudice in being debarred from my lands, which were more then two and twenty hundred years agoe acquired by the valour and prudence of my predecessors, then the sons of the aforesaid creditors can doe, by the want of the money

O avare jungantur solium Cræsi Cyrique tiaræ, Nunquam dives eris nunquam satiabere quæstu.

pretended to be due to them for my father's debt, the overthrow of a worthy family *Lucrum justitiæ præferunt impii.* being more deplorable then the missing of what a thiefe may filch out of a clout; and have reaped as little benefit of the summes so lent, as the brats they are as yet to beget have done of the revenues which should be mine.

14. What forcible statutes have been published in former ages, for obviating the decay of honorable houses, is not unknown to those that are any thing versed in the historie of prudential law.

15. In this, the ablest and most judicious men on earth have imployed the best of their wits; and Solon, that famous legislator amongst the Athenians, and wisest man then living, made acts so favourable for the preservation of antient families, and so strictly to be observed, that the controveners of them, so long as the splendor of that republick lasted, were by the Areopagits most exemplarily and condignly punished, as the reliques of the Attick laws, till this day, will sufficiently bear record.

16. Nor was this so conscientious an ordonance so totally proper to the commonweal of the Greeks, but that the remanent of the world, in those happy times of old, did tast of the wholesome influence and goodness of it.

17. The Decemvirs, amongst the Romans, instituted and ordained, that those who were apt, by their mis-government and reckless conduct, to endanger the undoing and subversion of their predecessor's house, to the apparent detriment and damage for ever of such as by nature were designed to succeed after them in that family, should be disabled from disponing lands, alienating any whatsoever goods, and contracting debts, in such sort, that whosoever should meddle or deal with them in either of those kinds, should do it at their owne hazard and perill, without hope of restitution of any loss or hinderance they might sustain thereby, as manifestly may be seen by the law Julianus, in the paragraph *de cura furiosorum,* and in the law *is cui bonis* in the paragraph *de verbis obligatoriis.*

18. Which being conform to that other law of the twelve tables, whereby such like inconsiderate persons were appointed to have surveyers and controulers set over them, and wholy prohibited and interdicted from all manner of managing their own affairs, as the words of the text it self more succinctly declares, *Quando bona tua paterna avitaque negligentia tua disperdis, liberosque tuos ad egestatem perducis, ob eam rem tibi, ea re, commercioque interdico.*

19. It is apparent how hainous, horrid, and sacrilegious an offence it seemed to be in those happy dayes, to have a hand in pulling down the monuments of their forefather's vertue, and demantling the honour of their house by dilapidating their estate.

20. And least these premised acts should be thought to have been but good laws ill obeyed and worse executed, such rigorous punishment was inflicted upon the delinquents in them, that no person guilty, of what age or condition soever, was spared.

21. As may be instructed by Quintus Fabius, son to Quintus Fabius the great,

surnamed Allobrogicus, who, by an edict of Quintus Pompeius Prætor, was curbed and inhibited from doing, by his misguiding and unadvised cariage, any harm or prejudice to the house of his progenitors.

22. And by that prodigal senator of threescore yeares of age, otherways wise enough, over whom the Emperour Tiberius did constitute and impose a tutor or governour, that, to the impoverishing of his issue, he might not have power to lavish away the estate he never acquired.

23. The causes which moved them to inact and publish those statutes, being no lesse urgent now then they were then, should, as I conceive it, astrict and oblige us to be every whit as zealously fervent as they in the observing of them.

24. Chiefly being warranted thereto by the sacred Scripture it self, in the Old Testament, whereof the people of Israel is said to have been enjoyned to marry in their own tribes, jubilees appointed, and all debts whatsoever, after the revolution and expired date of so many years, ordained to be discharged, annulled, freely acquit, all bonds and bills rescinded and cancelled, and all this only for the preservation of antient houses.

25. Of which the countrie of Scotland also, till within these fourscore ten yeares, was so exactly carefull, that Signior David, one of Queen Marie's prime courtiers, could not, for all the money he was master of, obtain in that whole dominion the purchase of one hundred pounds sterlin of rent in land, whereby to acquire the benefit of a Scottish title, the more to ingratiat himself, being an Italian, in the favour of the nation ; so unwilling, in those good days, was every one to break upon any parcel of their predecessors' inheritance.

26. Seeing thus it is then, that all nations, and almost all religions, both Jews and Gentiles, have had the benefit of so commendable and pious a custome, shall Scotland alone be deprived and destitute of it, and that only since it is said by themselves to have received the puritie of the gospel, and about the year of the jubilee, no man will think it that hath any good opinion of the nation ?

27. But although it were so, as God forbid it ever come to that pass, and that like to the most rigid levellers, who would inchaos the structure of ancient greatness into the very rubbish of a neophytick parity, it were inacted there be no more regard had thereafter of pristin honour then of old garments ; and that none be thereby dignifyed, but in so far as the number, weight, and measure of modern coyn shall serve to inhanse him.

28. Yet with some probability doe many harbour in their breasts the opinion, that with a never so little auxiliary suffrage of publick order, there should be found amongst them and the successors of those that in divers good offices, not to speak of my self, have been obliged to the proprietaries of our house, severals who would of their own accord, in what they could, without any great incitement thereto, supply the deficiency

of the law in that point, and further of themselves the redintegration of my predecessor's family in my person.

29. Notwithstanding all this, the embracing of the foresaid subsidiarie expedient, being too far below my inclination, I doe really imagine that, without the conscriptitious adjutancie of the state, I shall enterprise but impossibilities, and never enjoy the proposed end; which nevertheless, my bashfullness and naturall aversness from craving what might put me to a blush if denyed, would never have permitted me to prosecute by such means, if by the iniquitie of the times, disloyalty of some I did put trust into, and rough harshness of the unplacable creditors, I had not been frustrated of my other designs.

Nullum est officium tam sanctum atque solenne quod non avaritia comminuere atque violare soleat.

30. For albeit, to the most frugall, it might seem a task very difficult to make the payment of my father's debt consist with the preservation of my forefathers' estate, when, by the malignant influences of concredited summes, the land rents do usually shrink in, to the accrescing of the burthen; there being nothing more certain, then that the apprising of lands, serving of inhibitions, arresting of farms in the hands of tenants, purchasing of letters for delivering up of the manor house, and other such like most rigorous proceedings whereby one is made illegal, would have disabled any, though never so well affected, from putting his means to the best avail, and taking that safe course for himself and creditors together, which otherways, with lesse disadvantage to either, might be performed by one that were free of these lets and disturbances.

Avaritia crudeles efficit eos qui ei serviunt, et animus avari sepulchrum est.

31. Whereupon ensue such dismal inconveniences, that commonly, when a gentleman's estate begins to be clogged with such like impestrements, little or no use at first is made of the rents thereof; either for that the tenants, for fear of creditors, attachings, and arrestments, pay not their due, least they be forced to repay it, and so, through the uncertainty of masters' spending all on themselves, become some times insufficient debtors; or for that merchants, being afraid to fall into the reverence of creditors, because of inhibitions and arrestments, dare not bargain for victuall or any such like annual commoditie; both or either being like to drive on the decadence of a house to its utter desolation at last.

Avaritia omnis injustitiæ fomes est, et avarus communis omnium hostis, cujus arculæ sunt sepulchra in quibus sepeliuntur vitæ pauperum.

32. So that instead of a double benefit that ought to accrew to both the debtor and creditor, by the timely payment of both lands and money rent, a twofold prejudice for the most part, through the strictness of the creditors, is incurred, to wit, the one by delaying their own pay, and the other by hastning the ruine of the house of their debtor; as if men should be tyed to defray great summes of money, and yet not get leave to make use of their own means wherewith to do it, there being hardly any shift remaining for a man so used but to have recourse to his wits.

33. Nor is it any thing less lamentable, that the law of Scotland, in matter of Horning, should be a main furtherance of this inconvenience, by debarring any one lying under the lash thereof, from getting payment at the hands of others of never so

just debts due to them ; whereby a greater load being laid on him that is already over-burthened, Machiavel's policie of breaking the bruised reed, and thrusting him over head and eares in the water that was in it to the chin, is very punctually observed.

Similis est pecunia u-surarii mor-sui aspidis, percussus enim ab as-pide quasi delectatus vadit in som-num, et per suavitatem soporis mo-ritur.

34. Which rugged, crosse, and thwarting procedures so incensed, damped, and exasperated my father, that a charge from a creditor being as the hissing of a basilisk, the disorderly troubles of the land being then far advanced, though otherways he disliked them, were a kind of refreshment to him and intermitting relaxation from a more stinging disquietnesse.

35. For that our intestin troubles and distempers, by silencing the laws for a while, gave some repose to those that longed for a breathing time, and by hudling up the terms of Whitsuntide and Martimass, which in Scotland are the destinated times for payment of debts, promiscuously with the other seasons of the year, were as an oxymel julip wherewith to indormiat them in a bitter sweet security.

36. Yet for all this, and notwithstanding the grievousness of such solicitudinary and luctiferous discouragements, able to appall the most undaunted spirits, and kill a very Paphlagonian partridge that is said to have two hearts, I did nevertheless, without attristing my self a jot, undergoe the defrayment of the debt, although not as a debtor,

Usuræ libe-ros servos faciunt.

with as much alacrity and cheerfulnesse as if it had been of my own undertaking ; and took such speedy course therein, that immediately after my father's decease, for my better expedition in the discharge of those burthens, having repaired homewards I did sequestrate the whole rent, my mother's joynture excepted, to that use only, and, as I had done many times before, betook my self to my hazards abroad, that by vertue of the industry and diligence of those, whom, by the advise and deliberation of my nearest friends I was induced to intrust with my affairs, the debt might be the sooner defrayed, and the ancient house releeved out of the thraldome it was so unluckily faln into.

37. But it fell out so far otherwayes, that after some few years residence abroad, without any considerable expence from home, when I thought, because of my having mortified and set apart all the rent to no other end then the cutting off and defalking of my father's debt, that accordingly a great part of my father's debt had been discharged, I was so far disappointed of my expectation therin, that whilst, conform to the confidence reposed in him whom I had intrusted with my affairs, I hoped to have been exonered and relieved of many creditors, the debt was only past over and transferred from one in favours of another, or rather of many in the favours of one, who, though he formerly had gained much at my father's hands, was notwithstanding at the time of his decease, none of his creditors, nor at any time mine ; my Egyptian bondage by such means remaining still the same, under task masters different only in name, and the rents neverthelesse taken up to the full, to my no small detriment and prejudice of the house standing in my person.

38. The aime of some of those I concredited my weightest adoes unto, being, as is

most conspicuously apparent, that I should never reap the fruition nor enjoyment of any portion, parcell, or pendicle of the estate of my predecessors, unlesse by my fortune and endeavours in forrain countries, I should be able to acquire as much as might suffice to buy it, as we say, out of the ground.

39. And verily, though not in relation to these ignoble and unworthy by-ends, it was my purpose and resolution to have done so, which assuredly, had not the turbulent divisions of the time been such as to have crossed and thwarted the atchievements of more faisible projects, I would have accomplished two or three severall ways ere now.

40. And yet, for all the stops and inconveniences that flowed from the late unhappy stirrs and garboyls in both nations, I had, by all probability, got a great many thousand pounds thereof, had not a wretched, poor, and trivial summe, scarce worth the naming, been more prevalent with the aforesaid party.

41. By reason of whose injurious and unequitable dealing, in appropriating to themselves and converting, by all appearance to their own use, my rents, and neither purging the land, nor exonerating me of any considerable part of the burthen wherewith either it or I stood affected, I was moved to face about and return homewards, to take that solid and deliberate course with the crazed estate left unto me, as might make the subsistence of my house compatible with the satisfaction of my father's creditors.

42. To which effect, with might and main to the uttermost of my abilitie, I strove with pecunial charms and holy water out of Pluto's cellar, to exorcise and lay the spirit lately raised and raging abroad, without the besprinkling of a chrysopast hyssop not to be conjured ; my successfulness therein amounting, *non obstans* all interveening impediments, to the final discussing of some of these creditors, and, in a plausible way, according to the exigence of the persons and circumstances of the nature, condition, and quality of their security, to dispatch the residue of them epassyterotically, that is, one after another. *Quæstum facile negligit generosus animus, inquit Hieronymus.*

43. And to this end applyed all my aforesaid rents, save so much as for publick dues and augmentation of ministers' stipends were exacted of me; in the latter whereof, because of the hereditarie loss which I thereby am like to sustain, I will make bold to insist a little, with that reverence nevertheless which becomes me to the church, and to the established ecclesiastical order of the land.

44. Here neverthelesse, let the good reader be pleased to take along with him for his better conceiving of the unmercifulness and indiscretion of my father's creditors, how, when to some of them I had offered present possession of land til they should be found paid, and unto others who formerly had been victual merchants, had made tender of my rents of that kind, at very easie rates, to be delivered by my deputies without their running of any hazzard at the hands of a distressed tenandrie : the answer of the former was, that they would have no land, but money, and of the other, that though they had often before that traffiqued in such like commodities, yet *Nulla ditari ratione potestis avari, vos faciunt inopes quas cumulatis opes. Hujusmodi lucra hominem comparare decet*

propter quæ nunquam in posterum doliturus sit.

that then, for being taken up with other more publick businesses they could not accept of my proffer, but wishing I might have the fortune to deal with those would give the greatest prices, expected I should not fail to let them have the money for defalcation of some of their accounts.

De damno alterius nemo lucrum spectet. Qui lucra lenta fugit damna repente subit. Non habet eventus sordida præda bonos. Nam quæ male parta domi accumulantur nihil salutis habent.

45. By which their subdolous and crafty tergiversation from what in a time of peace they would have so eagerly embraced, they have made it too evidently apparent, that in prosecuting of their own ease, they have aimed at my utter destruction, both their resolutions concentring in this, that they thought it more expedient, by a little forbearance, to suffer their unhallowed sums to increase for the better obtaining afterwards of my whole estate to themselves, then by any ways medling with my rents in a tumultuous time, to bring me the sooner in a capacity of enjoying my own, through the diminution of my father's debts by their receivings. This pit they digged for me, which that they should fall into themselves were both just and equitable.

IN FLAGITATORES. Ep. 1.

Tros quondam Æneas Harpyias, virginis ora,
  Atque ungues volucrum vidit habere truces.
Namque fame rabidus dum littore prandia sumit,
  Omnia fœdarunt vel rapuere viro.
Creditor his similis, perturbans omnia, pacem
  Nullam vicini qui sinit efse sui.
Harpyiæ proprios certant defendere fines,
  Ille tamen pejor, namque aliena rapit.

ALTERUM.

Non satis apparet cur nomina creditor omnis
  Accipit à credo ; res ratione vacat.
Debuerat potius vocitari incredulus, et sic
  Sortiri merito nomina digna suo :
Efse avidus nullum nam credit in æthere numen,
  Nec quenquam fidum Creditor efse virum.

THE SCOPE OF THE FOURTH BOOK,

ENTITULED

CHRYSEOMYSTES.

THE Author having, in the two preceding books, very orderly proceeded from the manifestation of the huge log of flagitators lying in his way, to the displaying of pregnant reasons why the said impediment should be removed, for the weal of the whole Isle whose literature by his endeavours he is to improve; in this fourth book of his Introduction he maketh mention of another block, which, though not of so immense a bulk, ought neverthelefs, for its repugnancie with the proposed end, be as well laid aside as the former, and that is, the unjust decrees wherewith the Presbyterian Commifsion hath robbed him of a great deal of his rents. He, for compendiousnefs sake, begins with the figure of Apophasis, to say he intends not to expostulate for the injurie sustained by that Kirkomanetick tyrannie which despoyled him of his right of patronage to his churches, and from thence descendeth to a plain narration, how, contrary to an established Union by Act of Parliament, and in opposition to seven relevant reasons, to any one whereof they would not daigne to make answer, the Commifsion of the Kirke, without giving any hearing to the Author's advocats, decerned one of his good priests to have an augmentation out of his patron's rents, though equivalent to as much more as was pofsefsed by his predecefsor in that church; and the churches of the other parish, in spite of both law and reason, to be disunited, and to each of the ministers thereof more stipend mortifyed, then to them both formerly was thought to be sufficient.   This is one of the chips of the block of Presbyterial government, which, because the violent afsertors thereof would, by a pretended *jure divino* authority, pertinaciously obtrude upon our consciences, and co-efsentiat it in the object of our faith with the most orthodox ecclesiastical doctrine, the Author very civilly, without falling upon the common school-controversies, twists out a discourse concerning fables, sorcerers, and distracted people, wherein they will be found as erroneous in their opinions as in their rule opprefsive.   The Author desires to have the prolixity of the digrefsion for this cause excused, that who would encounter with such an adversary must step a little aside to cope with him aright. He walks in no known tract, his actions are arbitrary, and pafsion directs his motions; and where he finds evasions suitable to his hypocrisie, Proteus never transformed himself into so many shapes as he will doe for his own ends.   What the Author speaks of the devotion of his ancestors before the nativitie of our Saviour, and when afterwards the only Romish faith was embraced by them; of the antiquitie of his tenandrie, and their skilfulnefs in the ceremonies of pristine sacrifice; of vindicating old customs from the aspersions of Neoterick Sciolists, and maintaining the ingeniositie of fables; of the consistence of poetical fictions with true divinity, and sympathie twixt old and new Rome in their rites and mysteries of religion; and, lastly, of hypocondriack and fanatical braines, and the great perpetrations of horrible unjustice in Scotland, by the too frequent mistakes of their diseases, is to no other purpose, but in view of the courteous Reader to career his spirits along the bounds the rigid presbyter would not have to be trod upon, and to make that judicatory perceive, to whom he makes his appeale, how unfit it were that any consistorian vaile should darken the light of his elucubrations.   After all, he closeth with the covetousnefs and inflexibility of the selfish Kirkist, which, as it is connexed with foregoing pafsages, to the discretion of the gentle peruser cannot come unseasonably.

THE FOURTH BOOK

OF THE

INTRODVCTION,

INTITULED

CHRYSEOMYSTES ;

OR,

THE COVETOUS PREACHER.

WHEREIN THE RIGOUR OF THE SCOTISH KIRK, BEYOND
THAT OF THE CHURCHES IN FORMER AGES, IS SHEWN
TO HAVE VERY MUCH OBSTRUCTED THE AUTHOR'S
DESIGN IN THE EMISSION OF THIS NEW IDIOME,
AND OTHER TRACTATES OF THAT NATURE.

1. HERE I omit the Kirk's denuding me of my heritable right of patronage to the churches of the Shire, whereof my predecessors have above these two decades of ages been both hereditary Sheriffs and sole proprietaries; as likewise to make mention of the five chalders rent of additionall stipend, any year worth 500 l. Scotch, which the minister of Cromartie hath now, more then his foregoing incumbent in that charge did enjoy.

2. I will only speak a word or two of my two other churches, which when seperated in former times, and those of late too, had but 300 l. Scotch of allowance betwixt them both, which neverthelesse was a great matter then in proportion to the little stock whence it was to be educed, and therefore, together with other more relevant causes, were by a commission to that effect by the Parliament then sitting in the

year 1617, united into one, and ordained after the decease of either of the two that then preached in them, to have the cure of them served singly by the survivor, and so consecutively from one another, by one alone.

Presbyter
in mundo
non est qui
dicit abun-
do.
Clericus an-
nosus licet
imber sit
furiosus,
non poscit
prunam
dum
drachmam
suscipit
unam.

3. But when the stipauctionarie tide, immediately after the Duke of Hamiltoun's unluckie ingagement, begun to overflow the land, and that I thought with sufficient bulwarks of good argument to have stayed the inundation thereof, from the two fore-said half churches I was violently driven, like a feather before a whirlewind, notwith-standing all my defences, to the sanctuary of an inforced patience.

4. For though I did put in these subsequent reasons against the disuniting and ad-jectitious provision of the aforesaid two churches,

First, that both parishes togither are but three miles long, and one of the churches therof, called the kirk of Cullicudden, seated in the middle or near by, so that the dwelling house of the remotest parishioner of either of the parishes will not be above a mile and a half distant from that church, and yet within 40 miles of that place, and that in a plain country, there are of those whose dwelling house in the parish is six-teen miles distant from the parish kirk.

5. Secondly, that there are not thirty-six ploughs labouring in both, and when acknowledged to be united they shall be found the least parish in the country, both for rent, people, and bounds.

6. Thirdly, That these two have been but one parish, by all appearance, from the beginning; for Cullicudden is built after the fashion of a church, but that other, now called Kirkmichael, is in its edifice like but to a chappell.

7. And forsooth, it was nothing else but a chappel which one of my predecessors, in the time that the Romish religion was universally professed in Scotland, caused to be built for his own ease of devotion.

8. For having a pretty summer dwelling adjacent thereto, within the precinct of the parish of Cromartie, and three miles distant from the church thereof, he chused rather then weekly to go so far to hear mass and other such liturgies as, on the Sundays and many festivall days, are amongst the Catholick Romans till this hour in use, to be at the charge of that petty fabrick, and the maintenance of a chaplain, whereby, with the lesse labour, to exercise his devotion at his own doores.

9. And in testimony thereof, my father not thinking it should have been at any time destinated for a parish church, but a place only for preaching with the more ease to the auditorie, caused make it as much longer as it was before, which evidently sheweth, it being the shortest church as yet in all the country, that it could not at first have been but a chapel.

10. Nor is it to be thought strange why my ancestors of late have been pleased to expend so much on structures to a religious end, seeing as my father, who was the first protestant that ever was of our house, bestowed the charge of the additional length of the half of the whole of that chappel which now they call a kirk; and as some of

my progenitors bestowed all those lands in the parochin of Rose Marknie, which now are in the possession of Robert Leslie of Finrasie, upon the Bishop, Dean, and Chapter of Ross, and that others of them were at the cost of building the churches of Cromartie and Cullicudden, and many other monuments, betokening their zeal to the Romish faith then professed : so amongst their forefathers were there severals of our familie, who, before the days of Christ, in the same foresaid parishes, founded many temples, delubres, and fanes, for sacrificing in the groves and high places to Jupiter, Juno, Mars, Pallas, Mercurie, Venus, and Diana, the reliques whereof are as yet in my land obvious to the eye of any curious antiquarie, and so much extant till this day as by the circularie, oval, triangulary, or square figure, together with the various manner in situation of the stones, will, to an intelligible Mythologist and well versed in rites of old, make it easily discernible to which of the heathenish deities the respective dedication was made.

11. That in my bounds should be seen remainders of so great antiquity is much, yet is it more to have them in a country so remote from the territories of the Theonomothets, and legislators of the divinity of the ancient poets ; but most strange of all it is, that in my lands should be found of those who, though they can neither read nor write, will neverthelesse be able to exchange discourse with any concerning the nature of the heathenish deities, and afford pertinent reasons for the variety of sacrifices and other circumstantial points usual to be performed in the days of old.

12. I asked them how they came by this knowledge ; they told me that their fathers taught them it, who had it from their progenitors, unto whom, say they, it was derived from their first fore-fathers that accompanyed my predecessors Alypos, Beltistos, Nomostor, Astioremon, and Lutork, in their aboriginarie acquest of the land of their ancestors' residence, and in this their relation they were so punctually exact, that some of them by nomenclature, in a lineall pedigree from father to son of above threescore severall persons, instructed their dependence upon our family in one and the same land three hundred years before the days of our Saviour.

13. That this is very probable, and that none hath a more ancient tenandrie then my self, I doe the rather beleeve it, that both historie and the most authentick tradition we have, avoucheth the first labourers and manurers of the land to have come along with my ancestors Beltistos, Nomostor, and Lutork, and for their good service done, especially to the last of those three, received leases thereupon in the quality of yeomans, who were so well pleased with what they got, that after they had most contentedly spent the best of their age, when decrepit years did summon them to pay their last due to nature, they bequeathed unto their children the hereditarie obedience they did owe their master, to whom they left their blessing and best wishes.

14. Which proved so effectual in advancing obsequiousness on the one side, and protection on the other, that in his posterity they were most fortunate from generation to generation, and so deeply ingaged to each in the long continuate succession of our

house, that the children of their children, in a subsecutive progress of dad to brat, and sire to suckling, have, til this houre, through so vast a flux of time, remained tenanciarie enjoyers for pay of those their respective rooms, without any interruption of assedation, or breach of lease, which, at the expiring of any 5 years end, might, unwronged the late possessor, have been bestowed on any other.

15. I have farmers, who, albeit neither they, their fathers, nor fore-fathers, ever payed to me or any of my predecessors, above fifteen pounds sterlin a year, dwell neverthelesse in the self same house which hath been inhabited by their ancestors from parent to child, above nine hundred years together, though none of them ever yet had a lease for above five years.

16. But of such as have removed a furlong or two from the place of their progenitors' abode, there are that can reckon, in their own familiar pedigree, a row of antecessors who have dwelt in that country above a thousand years beyond that time.

17. Although this constancy of residence be commendable, yet doth it carry along with it this disadvantage, that the progenie of these firm abiders is always of a small extent, for the most part, as may appear by seven or eight several surnames in two parishes of my land, whereof scarce one was ever heard of in any other place of the world.

18. The reason hereof proceedeth from that, when at first, after the manner of the plantation of the Israelites in the Palestine each tribe by it self, my predecessor had assigned to every family apart, its own allotted parcel of ground, they very suddenly took such deep root therein, that to their successors they left an irremovable ascriptitiarinesse to the soyl in which they had been ingraffed.

19. Each hamlet by that means, decenarie or wapentake, to use the Saxon word, having its peculiar Clan, as we call it, or name of a kinred, none whereof will from that portion of land bouge with his will to any other, upon never so great advantages offered unto him, the interflitting from one parish to another, though conterminal, being of such a mutual displeasingness, that all and each of them esteem of it as of an extrusive proscription to the Barbadoes, or depulsorie exile to Malagask.

20. It is amongst such of both sexes that are found some philarchæan zealots, whose pristin and breborian customs, savouring of superstition, manifest great antiquity; many of them endeavour the prosecuting of good ends with an upright intention, by exolet and palephasian means utterly exploded; which secessive course of sanctimonial dutie hath successively been followed by many with such inveterate proneness, that some of our neoterick sacricolaries have been much scandalised at the hereditariness thereof.

21. We, for being Christians, ought to avow that those ways, although such as were trod upon with great observancie by the antient gentils, should nevertheless, for deviating from the streight paths of the present profession of the country, be nothing at all relyed upon, because they were excogitated by the only wit of man : so for the

same reason and faith we owe to him who is the truth as well as the way, should all of us endeavour to be upright in our judgement, and not to determine rashly of a fault, but to consider thereof according to the nature of its delinquencie, without aspersing it with the guilt of another crime.

22. To punish a fornicator for murther, or a theef for fornication, is an act of injustice, because the first begetteth rather then kills, and the other rather takes then gives; and to chastise one for an offence which he hath not committed, is a meer oppressing of the innocent, for that whatever secret sin he have that may deserve it from above, it is without any cause knowne to him that inflicts the correction.

23. So is it, that we may esteem that censure unreasonable and injurious, which imputes to sorcerie what meerly proceeds from the frivolous practise of poetical divinity; and that scholar a bad proficient, that is mistaken in the exercise of that whereof in the schools he was taught the speculation.

24. I have heard of a sillie old wife, who, for doing some prettie feats wherein she had been instructed by her mother, according to a prescript manner set down in some of the verses of Homer, whom neither of them had the skill to peruse, but had learned the contents from their progenitrices upwards through many ages, was branded with the imputation of having the concomitancie of a demon, and accused of witchcraft by him, who being a professor of the Greek, whipt a boy for not getting these verses by heart, it being the task that was enjoyned him for a day's lesson, as if the devil had been more assistant to the operation then the theorie, and that it had been lawfull for them to studie what was felonie for others to enact.

25. Amongst this meaner sort of people, there are some who tenaciously cleaving to their frets of old, doe very often repair at set times to fountains, oak-trees, little round hillocks, and great stone heaps, where, with pre-conceived words and motions befitting the service, they doe things truly not approvable, because unwarranted by the best religionaries of the time; yet that there is charm, fascination, inchantment, infernal assistance, or any thing else more then meer custom in them, may safely be denied, for that in the choicest of the ancient of the both Greek and Latin poets, are couched in set terms, words expressive of all the points of that poeticall liturgie.

26. Who doubteth hereof, let him read Homer, Virgil, Theocrit, Hesiod, Pindar, Aristophanes, Ovid, Claudian, Horace, Martial, and others, which if he doe not, his laziness to peruse these books should not be of such prevalencie over our credulitie, as to make us beleeve that others doe devilishly, because he knoweth not what it is they doe; otherwise, as is said in the 30th article of this first book, the Lesbian rule of the various degrees of ignorance would be the sole directory to the overthrow of knowledge.

27. According to the unstreightness of which canon square, or pattern, in what countrey soever it shall happen men of eminent condition for place and fortune, (whose example usually is the only line and level whereby the multitude and body of

the people is ordered, both in their lives and opinions), to be so regulated as implicit-ly to follow such leaders, and without any further examination, to ply as they bow, jog as they wag, redandruate as they ampirvat, and every way bestirre themselves after their motions, more constantly in that their inconstancie then the rising of the billows of the sea, at the boysterous and impetuous thuds of a raging Boreas : there is nothing more infallible then that a countrey, kingdome, or common-weal sick of the ablepsie of such an epidemical sectatorship, of which disease, incivility, malice, usurie, ignorance, and hypocrisie are the ordinary symptoms, must needs by the frequencie of its convulsions against reason, equity, and conscience, though under pretext of a law, perish, and be ruined at last, either by the violence and furie of a forraine enemy, or by intestin broyles and commotions within itself, or by both togither ; so dangerous a thing it is willfully to hudwink the mind, and blind-man-buf't, in the propatularie view of a meridian sun, as if we were quoquoversedly mufled in the sable mantle of Cimmerian darknesse.

28. It is a bad acquital we give the ancients of great literature for their pains taking to civilize our manners, and instruct our minds in all the choicest and most researched mysteries of learning and true philosophie, by the lovely, sweet, and curi-ous allurements of poeticall devises, to twit them with the name of devils, fiends, and infernal spirits.

29. Whether it be so or no, I appeal to all the judicious mythologists of this age, whereof some being most eminent in their knowledge of theologie and of choise litera-ture in other commendable faculties, have in their learned writings made most evident-ly appear what sacred rayes of true divinity lie hid in those excellent fables of old.

30. Such as say that fables are lies, and therefore, not unlike to have proceeded from the deceiver and father of lies, understand not well what belongs to truth, and derogat much from the most authentick writings of any, wherein allegories, parables, and apologues are almost every where obvious to the reader's perusal.

31. Complexed truth is in affirmation and negation, which in matter of signes enunced of one another, hath its plenarie signification in the things by them signified, as when we say, *man is reasonable*, we mean not that the word *man* is the word *rea-sonable*, but that the thing for which the word man suppones hath reason in it.

32. Even so is it in a fable, where the epimythie or morality thereof is supposed to be signified by the words, and not the litteral sense, which by them is expressed but *in actu signato*, as it were, and not *exercito*.

33. As the fables in Æsop of the Wolf and the Lamb, the Lyon and Mouse, the Frog and the Oxe, the Grashoper and the Pismire, the Bull and the Goat, the Dove and the Magpie, the Eagle and the Raven, the Cuckow and the Hawk, the Bee and the Bear, the Dog and the Sheep, the Stork and the Fox, are verified in their epimy-thetical sense, by some great men's oppressing of the innocent ; by the thankful retri-bution of a received favour ; by the ruine that pride brings upon the arrogant man ;

by the advantage of careful industrie beyond wanton idleness; by kicking against those their betters whom misfortune suppresseth; by the hazard that many good men run to be deceived; by undertaking things foolishly beyond their power; by keeping themselves wisely within bounds; by the patience rather to endure somewhat, then in being revenged to suffer more; by the huge prejudice which false witnessing bringeth upon many; and by the great delight we oftentimes conceive in clinching and retorting jeers, jests, and pranks; all which to avow not to be as truly expressed by that affabulatory manner of speech as by a plain historical enarration of the purpose decyphered by it, is to ascribe lesse vigour to the rayes of the sun at noon in an estival solstice, then when in Capricorn he is meerly horizontal.

34. As in copious languages there are severall words made use of for setting forth one and the same thing to our understandings, whereof neverthelesse each apart is a sufficient signe for its representation, though not with such imbellishment, so, should we dissever truths from elocutions framed in this kind of way, we would open a door to the destruction of eloquence, by banishing from our discourse all figurative utterance in the delicious varietie of tropes and schemes.

35. There are moe ways to the wood then one, as the common saying is, and from the circumference to the center may be drawn infinite sines, whereof nevertheless not any can fall perpendicularly on the basis save one; yet is the obliquitie of any of those radial lines the lesse the nearer it approach the perpendicular, and so much the greater, the less that the angle be which with the basis it comprehendeth.

36. Just so, there being one sole God omnipotent upon whom the conservation of the whole world dependeth, which is the ground-work and basis whence is erected that perpendicular of perfection and true knowledge attained unto by the only saints in heaven and celestial hierarchies, there proceedeth from the circumference of the duty of man an innumerable diversitie of religious sects and faiths, tending all and each of them very cordially to the aforesaid basis of incomprehensible goodness, whereof there is not one that, by reason of humane frailty commixed with it, declineth not a little from that orthogonal streightnesse which in the Theocathetos is required.

37. However, there is nothing more sure then that as the more amply, by learning and integritie of heart, the acute angle, to call it so, of a profession be dilated, it will prove the more orthodoxical; so the greater deflexion that by wickednesse and ignorance it be brought to from the proposed uprightnesse, it will be the lesse warrantable.

38. By which account, although all be directed to one end, yet because of the imperfections which anavulsibly adhere to the soul whilst it remains invested with mortality, there being none of them without some blemish, the difference onely is in more and lesse, better and worse.

39. Neverthelesse, albeit in every State almost, there be a discrepance in the manner of regulating the consciences of the people, yet without any danger of heresie may

the mysteries of one and the same devotion be displayed unto us after several fashions, as the variety of the signes taketh not away the unity of the thing that is represented by them.

40. The trumpet incourageth troops of horse, the same is done by kettle-drums; the foot is animated by the tambour, and with our Highlanders the bag-pipe effectuates every whit as much. The Mahumetans repair no faster to their *moschees*, at the voyce of *La ilha, illa alha*, which calleth them thereto, then we doe to our churches at the knell of the bell, though of an inarticulat sound.

41. If the thing be the same which is signified, as likewise the conception we have of that thing, although the signes be various, which to that our conception doe represent it, whereat is it, I pray you, that we startle? Is not the sacred Word interpreted as well anagogically as literally, and allegorically as well as after any of the other ways, yet are all the said expositions accounted authentick, and the same authority attributed to each.

42. It is evident to such as will look out with their own eyes, that the first instituters of fables which admit of a physical as well as moral sense, did, in their pluralitie of gods, aim at the knowledge and worship of one onely divinity, in whose perfection they conceived all other deities to concenter as substantial qualities flowing from his vertue, power, and goodnesse.

43. Do not our selves affirm, that all that truly can be said of God is God himself, because of his simplicissime abstractednesse, pure act, and substance, void of all matter and composition : and yet what is more commonly said amongst our theologs, then that many are the attributes of God, which kind of speech they maintain to be necessary for our better understanding; hence the word Anthropopathie, a descending to the capacity of man.

44. God is just, he is loving, powerful he is, and wise; yet all and each of those qualities in the abstract belonging to him, are God himself. Astræa, Cupid, Mars, and Apollo, by the pristin poets have been made, by a metonymical trope, to stand concretively for the divulsives of the justice, love, power, and wisdom of God; not much unlike to the second notions to which we grant an objective existence in the mind.

45. That the heathen did beleeve in the unity of the Godhead, is also apparent by this, that all their deities of both sexes were in consanguinity and affinity with Jupiter, which is as much to say as that all power, vertue, goodness, and efficacy, proceeds from God.

46. Neptune was esteemed the power of God in the seas; Minerva the power of God in learning; Pluto the power of God in subterranean concavities; Bacchus, in wine; Ceres, in corn; Nemesis, in revenge; and so through all whatever may concern God's efficacious working, in relation either to the qualitie whence it floweth, the

subject that receives it, or place wherein it operateth by emanation, or any other kind of production.

47. To make use therefore, either in our discourse or writings, of the words Bellona, Hebe, Æolus, Mercurie, Aphrodite, Hercules, Pan, Saturn, Hymen, and so forth through the whole list of poetical terms, for warfare, youth, wind, eloquence, lust, vertue, the universe, time, virginity, and almost all that is of any importance, either for subsisting by its self or qualifying of us, doth so little derogate from the puritie of our religion, that, in my opinion, our manners are improved by it, our language inriched, and by vertue of rethorical tropes suggesting to our minds two several things at once, the spirits of such as are studious of learning filled with a most wonderful delight.

48. And why should not Greek and Latin words of so sublime expression obtain acceptance in this our English tongue, when many ultramarine termes of very low consideration, and vernacularie in our neighbour nations, receive admittance in it?

49. *Ruitmaster, ruit, plunder,* and *proveant* are Dutch, yet have we made them English; the French words of *parole, cavalleer, van, rear,* are now by us spoke usually; we have likewise made perfect English of the Spanish words *junto, begotero, balcone, montera;* as also of those Italian ones, *piazza, montebanco, curvetti, ciarlatano,* with many moe both of these and other languages, which luxurious wits of forrain education for the greater emphasis have obtruded upon their maternal idiome.

50. Nay, I will goe further; by those excellent fancies is so curiously imbellished the doctrine of both the Law and Gospel, that in a book entituled *Mystagogus Poeticus* written by Mr Alexander Rosse, you may find how prettily God is represented by Apollo, by Atlas, by Jupiter, by Neptune, by Prometheus; his Spirit by Boreas, and his Word by Ariadne; how Christ is the true Æsculapius, and how vively he is evidenced by Amphion, by Apollo, by Aristæus, by Aurora, by Bacchus, by Bellerophon, by Cadmus, by Ganymed, by the Genii, by Hercules, by Mercurie, by Minerva, by Neptune, by Orpheus, by Perseus, by Prometheus, and by Theseus; how Christians are expressed by Hercules, by Jason, by Sphinx, and by Ulysses; and how, lastly, the church is signified and set forth by Atlas, by Ceres, by Diana, and by Jason's Ship.

51. And all this by the elucubrations of that worthie gentleman Master Alexander Rosse, whose praise, in that late book set forth by me in vindication of the honor of Scotland, I thought expedient not to omit.

52. That the Catholick Romans have constantly, and as yet doe, after the manner of the learned Paynims of old, most heartily relish variety of consecrations, plurality of invocations, and adoring one and the same thing under a great diversitie of titles, is apparent by the several names of churches, huge legend of saints, and different dedications to one dietie: as of one edifice to Christ the Redeemer, and of another to Christ the Mediator, of one to our Lady of Help, and of another to our Lady of

Mercie; even as the warlike Romans devoted their temples to Iupiter Feretrius, and Iupiter Stator, to Diana Lucina, and Diana Fluena.

54. In this likewise they agree, that amongst the heathnish Philosophers there were many sects, such as Stoicks, Academicks, Peripateticks, Pythagoreans, and Cynicks, and amongst those we call Papists there are divers orders of Monks, Friars, Thomists, and Scotists; subdivided again into ecclesiasticall incorporations, such as Cordeliers, Recollects, Succolants, Capuchins, Fueillans, Iacobins, Dominicans, Augustins, Iesuits, Teatins, Oratorians, Benedictins, Cartusians, Carmelists, and many other of that nature, discrepant more in name then opinion, in habit then profession.

55. That there is great uniformity in both doctrine and discipline betwixt the churches of the ancient and modern Romans, will never be denied by any that, having applied his mind to the philosophical poesie of the one and scholastick divinitie of the other, is well versed in the rites of both.

56. And truly there is so great knowledge wrapt under the vail of that affabulatorie divinity of old, that not to beleeve in the truth of many points thereof will argue as much senslesnesse and stupiditrie in him that is so incredulous, as it can of miscreance and infidelitie in the person of any that would question the infallible events of the most authentick revelations of the other.

57. It is said by them that Saturn was the son of Coelus and Thetis, that he devoured all his children, save Iupiter, Iuno, Neptune, and Pluto, that he disgorged them again, and after he devirilised Coelus, was expelled his kingdome by Jupiter.

58. And say not we the same, though in other words, whilst we avouch that time is measured by the motion of the heavens, and ebbing and flowing of the sea; that the elementarie and mixed bodies are corruptible, whilst the elements themselves, in their purest natures, are not so; that the corruption of one thing is the generation of another; that there can be no more worlds but one; and that it lieth not in the power of time to limit the duration of the celestial influences, in all which it seems that the ancients did philosophate pretty handsomely.

59. Had they remained there, it had been well, but when they begun to adulterate that knowledge with superstition, and out of conscience to immolate the bloodie sacrifices of young infants upon the altars of Saturn, then was it that their profession became detestable to all the civill men in the world, and what was commendable therein, even abhorred, because of its intermixture with so much wickednesse.

60. Yet is it the part of wise men to sever the good from the bad, and without any relation to times, to adhere to what of it self is rightest, and to account that religion damnable, what ever it be, that destroyeth mutuall duties and authorizeth cruelty.

61. The poets say that Vulcan was the son of Jupiter and Juno; that he was lame, that he was thrust out of heaven, that he was fostred by Thetis and the sea nymphs, that he had Venus and Aglaia to his wives, that the semence wherewith he

thought to have imbued Minerva had its diffluence on the earth, and that he was the smith who made the armour of the gods.

62. And doe not wee, though in other termes, affirm the same, whilst we say that fiery meteors are begot in the air, by the motion, heat, and influence of heaven; that the flame of our fire ascends not in a straight line, but crookedly; that lightning and thunderbolts fall out of the air upon the earth; that naturall heat is intertained by radicall moisture, and the ignean mixtures in the second region by marine exhalations; that beautie, light, and splendor are concomitant with the heat of fire; that heaven for being pure from the commistion of elementarie qualities, remaineth still a virgin, in spight of that naturall heat, which diffused on terrestriall things, maketh them fruitfull in generation; and that naturall heat is the armour and defence of our life, by which we are preserved from our destruction, our life and motion ceasing when it is gone : now what can be said against this, but that their way of expression is somewhat more figurative and eloquent ?

63. The ancient heathens did assever that Bacchus was the son of Jupiter and Semele, saved out of her ashes, when Jupiter in his coit had burnt her with thunder; that he was cherished in his father's thigh, nourished by the Hyades, bred in Egypt, and afterwards conquered the Indians; that he had both a virgin and a bull's face; was sometimes male, sometimes female; now with a beard, anon without one; that he was worshipped on the same altar with Minerva, and accompanied by the Muses; that whilst he was a child Mercurie carried him to Macris, the daughter of Aristæus, to have his lips anointed with honey; that he slew the serpent Amphisbena; that virgins were his priests, himself painted naked, and the mag-pie consecrated to him; that he was turned into a lyon, was called Liber and Dionysius, and the first that made bargains; that he was three years with Proserpina, and that he was torn by the Titans, buried, and revived again.

64. Though this relation seem a little fabulous, yet doe we maintain the truth thereof, whilst we affirm that the vine tree by the influence of a warm air produceth grapes; that ashes are excellent dung for vines; that the best wine is where the soyl is hot, subject to thunder, and where the trees are parched with the rays of the sun; that Egypt is a fit climate for that liquor; that moisture maketh it prosper very much; and that the Indians were very temulencious symposiasts; that there is a hudge difference and almost incredible, betwixt the effects of wine moderately and immoderately taken ; that wine drunk with mediocrity conduceth much to wisdome and learning, and refineth our wits with eloquence, which bringeth us to a felicity of expressing our selves most sweetly in the best things that are ; that wine killeth sorrow, utterly banisheth it from all joviall congregations, in pulling from it the sting at both ends of melancholie, wherewith both the beginning and closure of all commensall meetings are for the most part stung without this Lyæan liquor; that sometimes wine makes men effeminate, prompts them to reveal secrets, and oftentimes occasioneth much prating;

that many times it inrageth those that drink it; that it maketh men to talk freely, and stirreth up the mind to high attempts; that commonly it is in taverns that men are aptest to bargain-making, when they are well whitled with Septembral juyce; that it will be three years before the vine tree can come to its full perfection, and that its twigs cut off and set in the earth will afterwards bring forth good and sufficient grapes.

65. Doe not both these ways tend to the signifying of the self same conception of one and the same thing? truly they doe: yet is it with this discrepance, that our conceit thereof is naked and bare, and theirs apparelled with an expression of more pomp and statelinesse.

66. To run after this manner, albeit in never so percursorie a way, through the remainder of what is extant of this kind of inveloped philosophie, would require a treatise of a greater bulk then these few miscellanie schedules are able to inclose.

67. Yet is it a thousand pities that the knowledge of all arts and sciences, both practical and theoretick, having been very ingeniously shrowded, by the learned men of old, under the most gorgeous cover of poetical fancies, there should not of that pretious mantle now be seen so much as the ten thousandth part; too severe innova- tors, by an ubiquitarie conflagration, having devored the rest.

68. Truly I lament it, and could wish from my heart that the diverse exquisite books written on that subject, by Orphee, Musæus, Linus, Phurnutus, Palæphat the Stoick, Dorothee, Evanthes, Heraclit of Pontus, Silen of Chio, Anticlides, Evartes, Zenon, Cleanthes, Chrysippus, and several thousands compiled by other authors, which have been lost these many hundred yeares agoe, whereof I beleeve some were amongst those of curious arts mentioned in the nineteenth of the Acts, were at this time obvious to our perusal.

69. I say not this to undervalue other books, for the Spirit of God hath taught us that the two Testaments of the law and gospel doe far excel them; but only to give you to understand that diamonds are not the worse, they be inchassed in gold, nor a patacoon to be rejected, because a Portugal ducat is better.

70. Yet may the Oro de Tibar, and Plata de Peru, which are the best gold and silver that are any where, that being of 24 carats, or quilates as they call them there, and this full twelve-pennie fine, abate much of their proper value, by being allayed with baser metal; there being nothing admits of mixture, which is not capable of being adulterated.

71. And likewise the unskilfulnesse of the receiver may contribute much to the un- dervaluing of very good coin, as I have seen by some the cross dolar of a Hanse town, because of its circular shape, preferred to a Spanish ryal of eight of a polygo- nal form; the insufficiency, by the touchstone of the eye, consisting in the figure.

72. Even so have these melliffluently relishing devises sustained great detriment in the estimation of many, partly by reason of the blind superstition of some pusilla- nimous zelots addicted to that kind of devotion; and on the other part, because of the

uncharitable mistakes therein of some supercilious coxcombs, who, avoiding to be instructed aright, are every jot as peremptory in their doom as they are certain in their unskilfulness.

73. Both which, the one for depraving a thing by the intermixture of some badness with it, and the other for condemning that as ill whereof he knows not the goodnesse, are like the Syrtes and Symplegades, or rocks and quicksands of errour, to be shun'd by those that would sail into the haven of truth.

74. As for my self, I never yet had such prejudicate aversnesse from old tenets, nor implicit adherence to new positions, whither at home or abroad, but that I always thought it most beseeming one of a liberal education, to keep the middle course that tends to truthwards, without regard to either pristin or modern opinion, ephestian or exotick.

75. Which resolution of mine, to hold on in an even path to what is rightest without straying to either side, begot such opposition in others to whose conduct I was loath to deliver up my judgement, that because of fascination, incubation, succubation, peragration with fairies, and other such communication with foul spirits, I had openly purged many of both sexes whom they esteemed guilty, I was forthwith reputed an obstinate assertor of erronious doctrine, and that with the greater vehemency of bitternesse, that I who was but raw, young, and lately come from my travels, would not without examination give trust to aged men of long experience, albeit in matters contrary to both common sense and reason.

76. Yet as a child, though but of ten years old, is not obliged to believe it is dark when the sun shines, although a man of threescore should swear it to him, so, such weak arguments *à testimonio* having never been of great prevalency with me, I caused send for one of either sex that were supposed rivals in diabolical venerie, the male with the succub, and the female with the incub. And after I had spoken kindly to them in generals, I intreated them with all gentlenesse possible, to tell me freely whether it was so or no, as it was reported of them, (the Reader must understand that these two knew not other, and that it was not at one time nor in one place that I thus examined them) their answer was, for they were not suspicious of any harm from me, that it was true enough, yet wisht because of their so ingenuous confession, that I would be pleased never to bear testimonie against them ; I promised to do so, but withall considering how, in all other incident purposes, they were alwayes every whit as pertinent as any what ever man or woman else of their condition, I streight conceived there might be a crack in their imagination.

77. The young man was two-and-twenty years old, very bashfull, yet prone to lasciviousness, and a handsome youth ; she was some five-and-twentie, nothing so pleasant as he, and had it not been for a little modesty that restrained her, a very sink of lust. All this I perceived at the first view, and therefore, the better to try an experiment thereon, I commanded, at the time they were in my father's house, an

insomniatorie and exoniretick potion, for stirring up of a libidinous fancie, to be given unto each of them; I also directed one of my footboys to attend the woman with all possible respect and outward shew of affection; the like I required of one of my mother's chambermaids to be done in behalf of the young man. Which injunctions of mine were by these two servants with such dexterity prosecuted, that the day after each their night's repose of those two hypochondriacks, which happened to be within a moneth of one another, when I had called for them and after I had fairly insinuated my self into their minds by a smooth discourse, asked, whether that night as formerly they had in their bodies felt any carnal application of the fowl spirit, or if they did, in what likeness they received him? To this both of them made answer, that of all the nights which ever they had enjoyed, it was that night respectively wherein unto them both the spirit was most intirely communicative in feats of dalliance, and that in the representation of the boy and chambermaid whom I had appointed to wait on them as they went to bed.

78. This ingenuous declaration of theirs confirmed me in my former opinion, which with more degrees of certainty increased, when I heard that within a short while after, the imagination of two had turned to a fornication of four; for which though I caused to punish them all, the fantasiasts were thereby totally cured, who, becoming afterwards yoke-mates in wedlock to the two servants of our house, were in all times comming sound enough in fancie, and never any more disquieted with such like apprehensions.

79. In these the cure proved easie, but in many that kind of disease taketh such deep root that no remedie can prevail. I saw at Madrid a bald-pated fellow who beleeved he was Iulius Cæsar, and therefore went constantly on the streets with a laurel crown on his head; and another at Toledo, who would not adventure to goe abroad unlesse it were in a coach, chariot, or sedane, for fear the heavens should fall down upon him.

80. I likewise saw one in Saragosa, who, imagining himself to be the lawfull King of Aragon, went no where without a scepter in his hand; and another in the kingdome of Granada, who beleeved he was the valiant Cid that conquered the Mores.

81. At Messina in Sicilie, I also saw a man that conceived himself to be the great Alexander of Macedone, and that in a ten years space he should be master of all the territories which he subdued; but the best is, that the better to resemble him he always held his neck awry, which naturally was streight and upright enough; and another at Venice, who imagined he was Soveraign of the whole Adriatick Sea, and sole owner of all the ships that came from the Levante.

82. Of men that fancied themselves to be women, beasts, trees, stones, pitchers, glasse, angels, and of women whose strained imaginations have falne upon the like extravagancies, even in the midst of fire and the extremest pains fortune could inflict upon them, there is such variety of examples, amongst which I have seen some at

Rome, Naples, Florence, Genua, Paris, and other eminent cities, that to multiply any moe words therein, were to load your ears with old wives' tales, and the trivial tattle of idly imployed and shallow braind humorists.

83. Thus am I forced to deliver my opinion in opposition to some of our Kirkists, who would burden my conscience with manyer tenets then are fit for it, and lighten my estate of more mony then is due to them; for proof of the latter whereof, as I have already in refutation of their covetous disjoyning of what was legally united, and splitting one parish into two, deduced three pregnant reasons why the two forementioned churches should remain as one church belonging to one parish, I will in sequel of the sixth article of the same book say,

84. Fourthly, That in the uplifting of all taxes and impositions in former times, these two pretended churches have been still rated as one parsonage, as the rolls of the stint can sufficiently bear record.

85. Fifthly, There are in both these pretended parishes not above three hundred communicants, so that the great charge of soules needeth not much obstruct the union, seeing there is to be found in a shire not far from thence eight thousand parishioners resorting to one parish kirk.

86. Sixthly, That the whole parishioners of both, *nemine contradicente,* did, and doe as yet most unanimously accord to the union.

87. Seventhly, That to have the union ratified by the General Assembly of the land, as it was past in the days of King Iames the sixth, I offered, if another place might be pitched upon more expedient, for the ease of these two half parishes, to cause build a church therein upon my own charges.

88. Yet for answer to these aforesaid reasons, in my opinion relevant enough, a decreet by the Commission of the Kirk was pronounced against me, in favours of the two men serving at the cure of that Kirk and chappel, providing yearly to each of them 4 chalders victual, and 400 marks Scotch in monie, besides their glebe, as they call it, and vicarage; although before that time, by reason of the smalnesse of the tiths of the parish, their expectation did never reach to above five chalders rent for both, without any monie at all, and that they would have been exceedingly well pleased to have accepted of less had they been free of a brotherly suggestion to my prejudice, which for fear of deprivation they were forced to lay hold on.

89. With this ecclesiastical pressure whereby my rents are diminished, another from the same fountain, though of a higher nature, was inflicted on me by a kirkman, whose covetousnesse reaching the procurement of an unjust decree through non-defence in my absence, at an inferiour court, against four of my especial tenants, for some farmes pretended to be due to his mother as the wife of an ecclesiastical dignary; he prosecuted the action with such indignation, violence, avarice, and extortion, so prevaricatly and contrarily to both divine and humane laws, that I purposely conceal his name, least the divulging thereof should prove scandalous to his fellow-labourers in

the spirituall vineyard, for tollerating a man of such oppressive courses to domineer in the pulpit, by vertue of a supposed call from God for the preaching of his word.

90. Many things may be spoken of the unstreight carriage of this man, who, as I am informed, is about as yet to vex my tenants in Farnesse, as formerly he hath done those of my townes of Davistone and Pettistone; which if he doe, let him assure himself that I will lay open the wickednesse of his disposition to the view of the whole Isle, as perspicuously as his face is weekly apparent to his parish at Rosmarkney.

91. But for the time I will forbear, in hope of his repentance, which no sooner can appear then I shall be apt to forgive, my humour leading me never to insist in twitting any that is not of an obdur'd spirit; nor had these three ministers against whom I writ in that book of mine entituled Exscibalauron, or Exskybalochrysos, sustained the lash of my pen, had they then been sensible of the wrong done me, or acknowledged their faults, as afterwards they did, for although I hate dissimulation, I can upon a cordial remorse for any injurie committed pardon my cruellest and most inveterate enemie.

92. Why men that should make profession of learning, doe goe about to vex and disquiet me, is most wonderfull, seeing it is not unknown to all that are acquainted with me, that there is none breathing doth more respect and reverence it then I, and that by all appearance I am like, by God's assistance, to give greater proofs thereof to posterity, then any whosoever that hath been, is, or will be ready to display open banner against me.

93. Bavius and Mævius were both envious of the worth of Virgil, and covetous of his means; but although the ruine of Virgil had acquired them an empire, yet had not so vast a purchase been able to contrevalue the infamie which by that one hexameter, *Qui Bavium non odit amet tua carmina Mævi*, did redound to them both.

94. I will apply nothing, it being the Reader's part some times to infer consequences where the modesty of the writer will not permit it; but setting forward in the proposed method, doe make account to glance a little at the other branch of the dichotomie, mentioned in the forty-second article of the third book as very obstructive to the defrayment of private debts, to wit, publique dues.

Epig. Primum.

Ardochæ duri fodiebant arva Coloni,
     Laſsabatque graves terra profunda boves.
Finrasus invasit: tunc longæ rastra quieti
     Tradidit, et non est quo fodiatur ager.
Scire libet quænam sit tristis causa rapinæ,
     Quid poterant terræ, quid meruiſse solum;

Iphigenia domi nimirum nubilis illi
 Dotanda est, proprio non tamen illa solo.
Debita fallaci socero nam Burgius heros
 Detulit, injusta qui rapit arva manu.
Sponsam ambit juvenis : pater agros ambit, et illi
 Inde Ligone carent : illa Ligone suo.
Protinus armatas trahit in sua vota cohortes,
 Authores culpæ substituitque suæ.
Arva novo tibi sunt Cromarti danda colono ;
 Sic fodietur amans : sic fodietur ager.

Epig. Secundum.

Etheiam quondam Patrio Cromartius heros
 Iure habuit, raptam nunc tamen alter habet :
Ruraque fallaces aluerunt devia vulpes,
 Semper et hos laqueo ducere moris erat ;
Sed postquam has sedes cepisti Finrase, pejor
 Incipis his cunctis vulpibus efse lupus.

Epig. Tertium.

Ut succum toto morbus de corpore ducit,
 Evacuata trahens ofsa liquore suo,
Torrida dum totis concrescant viscera fibris,
 Et subito in rugas cedat adusta cutis ;
Divitias populi totas sic Creditor haurit,
 Seque unum nummis Hydrope pejor alit.
Argenti venas rimatur, et undique quærit
 Abdita siqua auri gutta vel una fluit ;
Vos estis medici, Patres, si dicere fas est,
 Vos soli huic morbo ferre potestis opem.

Epig. Quartum.

Socratici fertur patientia longa mariti,
 Xantippe lingua clara fuifse tua,

Ille tuo pulsus clamore obduruit, etsi
    Lingua lacefsito est ære sonora magis.
Huc ades, o venerande senex, tentamina linque
    Talia virtuti non satis æqua tuæ.
Voce sua turbet solum te creditor unus,
    (Sufficiuntque tamen non duo tresve mihi)
Xantippen querulam vere laudabis, et ipse
    Judice te posthac (crede) beatus eris.

Epig. Quintum.

The Scripture says that three things always crave,
The raging sea, the barren womb, and grave;
I dare not adde to Scripture, but I say,
That creditors do crave far worse then they.
When I have render'd by mortalitie
To the grave her due, she craves no more of me;
No strong desire can make me satisfy't,
Nor yawning womb command my appetite:
Besides, there's pleasure here, in debt there's none,
And when once laid in grave all grief is gone.
No sea constrains you to entrust your frayl
Plank to the waves, or forceth to hoise sayl;
Or yet, suppose it could against your will,
There's hopes of calm, or of a harbour still;
There's storm on storm when creditors do crave,
And every interest a rolling wave.
O let me debtor be to th' other three,
Free me from Farcher, Fraser, Fendrasie!

Epig. Sextum.

That he might in opprefsion be free,
Fendrasie took the kirk upon his side,
Who were of avarice as full as he,
And for the goods of all men gap'd as wide.

Those that beheld him saint-like veyl'd did wonder,
And marvelled that he was chang'd so much,
When Satan's claws were suddenly seen under,
And all were startled at his hellish clutch;
'Twas like his father, who's the root of evil,
Who, taking angel shapes, is still a devil.

EPIG. SEPTIMUM.

SINCE your selves are unto the devil as due,
You usurers, as debtors' cash to you,
To trust you so the devil does us wrong,
For you'l not trust your debtor half so long;
But it's confefs'd, indeed, there may be lets,
And creditors by chance may lose their debts;
But though the devil gets no use at all,
Yet is he sure t' obtain the principall.

EPIG. OCTAVUM.

LIKE as the tyrant plunder'd mightie Jove
Out of his golden vesture, and him told,
A woollen one might now far fitter prove,
Because the season waxed somewhat cold;
And from the god of physick, Phœbus' son,
The golden beard in bitter scorn he took,
And said it was not fit he should have on,
Since his own sire a beard could never brook:
Even so, my creditors, with charitie
And fellow-feeling piety pofsest,
In our estates would make a paritie,
For conscience, say they, not lands, is best.
Pox take your gryping conscience! let me
Enjoy m' estate, and keep your charitie.

3 A

O CREDITORUM dira et immitis cohors,
    Furiisque cunctis sævior,
Quorum sonorus clamor exanimat meum
    Uritque pectus tædio!
Namque ira nunquam numinis vestras sinet
    Impune fraudes pergere,
Cum vos hiatu capiet immenso niger
    Sinuque claudet Tartarus.
Tum scire, si fas ista mortali, libet
    Quas Æacus pœnas paret.
Megæra properat, properat Alecto ferox
    Incincta tortis anguibus ;
Caliginosam sæva Tisiphone facem
    Intrantibus vobis quatit.
Nec non catenas certat extensas triceps
    Averni custos rumpere,
Et linquit ales Titij exosum jecur,
    Ad vos opimos advolans.
Saxumque dirum Sisyphi vobis datur,
    Sitisque vobis Tantali ;
Istisque cunctis pejus interea manet,
    Majusque tormentis erit.
Absumet hæres omnia, et exosos lares
    Divendet insignis nepos ;
Ibitque tremula, et pene procumbens fame
    Proles parentis perfidi ;
Virique conjux tenera in abjecti sinu
    Alga jacebit vilior ;
Et cuncta vobis ista Mercurius feret,
    Ibitque certus nuncius.

THE INTENT OF THE FIFTH BOOK,

ENTITULED

NELEODICASTES.

WHAT is to be last in the execution being commonly first in the intention, the Author, conform to that order, begun this isagogical treatise, as is apparent by the first book thereof, intituled, *The Wonders of the New Language ;* but in the continuation of the matter thorow all the books following, he quits that analytical method, and betakes him to the compositive, wherein priority in cause hath its citeriority in description. Thus, therefore, as in the third book were deduced reasons why the impediment mentioned in the second should be removed, so to the fifth hath the Author reserved the exprefsion of his regret for want of remedy against such injuries as under which, in the fourth, he had discovered a prefsure. In a word, the third block which doth lie in the way of the Author's excellent undertakings, is the lack of redrefs, after petition put in, for the wrongs he had sustained : yet doth he not insist so long thereupon as on the former, because the court before which he did addrefs himself was somewhat more homogeneal, and that to decline the Kirk's authority *in civilibus,* he conceived it to be no heteroclitism. Both judicatories were constituted the epitomes and abridgements of greater ones, the Parliament and Afsembly ; that passing under the name of a Committee, and this of a Commifsion.   But, truly, such was the influence the ecclesiastical party in this, had over the secular in that, in imitation of the larger bodies which they represented, who had the same ascendent and subordinacy in rule and dependencie, that he was thereby plunged into the more lamentable sufferings, the higher the exclamations against the consistorian clergie on all sides soared to this Picrologie, that no good aspect was to be expected from a conjunction of so malevolent luminaries.   After the enumeration of many grievous lofses from souldiers and others, which the Author, contrary to the laws of the nation and equity it self, was enforced to undergo without reparation, he falls in the next place to discufs the flagitator, whose poyson, by reason of its universality of diffluence on all his best endeavours, requireth a careful administration of antidotes to be set down in each of all the six books of this Introduction.   To this purpose, in several particulars he instanceth their implacability, their unnaturality, and unconscionablenefs ; he discloseth three plausible overtures most untowardly rejected by them, and in amplification of their cunning and rigour, hath a learned disceptation concerning prodigality and covetousnefs ; he bringeth against them arguments both from conscience and law, in its supremest legislation, and with sentences of a vigorous and strong impression, most accurately illustrates them.   The tender care should be had of ancient houses he again inculcates ; and, lastly, to perswade the publike to exoner him of the forementioned burdens, he ratiocinates *a minori ad majus* of monopolies, in ampler benefits granted to men of no desert, wherein he needeth not doubt to have furnished matter abundant for the satisfaction of the impartial Reader.

THE FIFTH BOOK

OF THE

INTRODVCTION,

INTITULED

NELEODICASTES;

OR,

THE PITILESS JUDGE.

WHEREIN THE AUSTERITY OF THE LAW OF SCOTLAND, TO-
GETHER WITH THE PARTIALITY OF THOSE THAT PRO-
FESSED IT A WHILE AGO, IS MADE APPEAR TO BE
A GREAT HINDERANCE TO THE PRESENT PRO-
MULGATION OF THE UNIVERSAL SPEECH,
AND FUTURE EVULGEMENT OF OTHER
EXCELLENT INVENTIONS.

1. THE publike pressures which in Scotland I was inforc'd to undergo, (in matter of tax and loan, monthly maintenance, additional sess-money, transient quarters, constant and assistant quartering horse, foot, and dragoon-levies, besides neer £ 3000 sterling worth of goods, as it stands upon record under the hands of those gentlemen authorized for commissioners to take upon oath and probation the just account of their losses, most basely and unworthily, whilst I was absent from the country, robbed and plundered from my tenants, against whom no pretext of quarrel could be had but the love of their means, they being never sufferers but for their innocencie and too conscionable neighbourhood,) did extend to so vast a proportion, that my lands

thereby were more sadly dealt with then those of any subject within the dominion; and my self, from time to time, brought under the sufferance of such exorbitant impositions as would have been almost insupportable to any of the country, though of a free estate.

2. But that which made my condition the more bewailable, was, that in spight of that distributive justice, according to which the then Estates of the nation enjoyned each one ratably to lend his shoulder to the common burden, I was, by over-prizing of my lands, emitting too great a proportion of horse and foot, and extraordinary quartering at all occasions, singled out apart to sustain the calamity alone, without that wretched comfort, called *Solatium miseris*, of any other to share with me therein.

3. Which, had it been inflicted on me as a punishment for an offence, albeit pretended, were somewhat tolerable; but all the doers could say, was, that what they did then, they had warrant for; under the mask and vizard whereof, the sordid and corrupt commissaries, with the ravenous Neoptoleman presidiaries, did grinde the faces of my poor men, and suck the very blood out of my estate.

4. This disorder of order-monging multitudes, without prejudice be it spoke of a well-disciplined souldiery, together with the specious pretences that some have grasped at to do iniquity by a law, hath truly run in such an over-flowing speat and inundation of violence against me, that what by the cruelty and high hand of neighbouring flagitators and others, and continual current of unavoidable taxes, my poor tenants were so incompassionately plucked, mangled, torn in pieces, and shuffled, that they and I both, for all our endeavours, (the publike burden alone, besides other pressures, having in some yeers, over and above the whole rent of the land, put me to a hundred pounds English money on the score,) have not been able to give, in matter of the principal, a full repast to the rest of those craving a hungred creditors, who, by reason of the foresaid obstacles barring my determination, remain as yet unsatisfied.

Nihil est profecto molestius quam vicinus avarus, says Joh. Decollo.

5. Of whom nevertheless not any almost, notwithstanding all these difficulties which yet procreate this one and the greatest stop of all, that no merchant is to be had for land, without huge loss to the disponer, men of flourishing estates having sold their lands of late at easie rates, to shun the pressures of so frequent impositions and assesments, will abate a mite of the due the law in its rigour doth allow, nor out of a fellow-feeling of my sufferings, relent never so little of the extremity.

Stolidus est qui propter spem majoris, rem præsentem et certam, licet parvam, non amplectitur.

6. For whether land hath been undone and impoverished by unseasonable years, or begger'd and exhausted by the rapine of unruly soldiers, they will alwayes have their money to yeeld a super-abundant and fruitful crop, and the rent thereof, in despite of the fortune of the nation, to hold out most plenteously to the full.

Turpia lucra fœnoris, et velox usura inopes trucidat.

Sed male parta male dilabuntur.

7. However, though to any judicious and well-poysed brain, it would seem strange that by such men, what is naturally barren shall be still made fruitful, even when, by the hardness of the times, what is naturally fruitful is still made barren.

Hæc prima est scelerum mater, quæ semper ha-

8. I could nevertheless, in so far as concerns my own particular, be well pleased not

to decline the fertilizing of that sterility, if the state think such kind of men worthy of being so nearly taken notice of, provided the judicatory of the land debar me not from the benefit of that justice which, without too palpable a partiality, cannot be denyed to a very stranger, though but passing by never to return again. bendo plus sitiens pa-
tulis rima-
tur faucibus
aurum.

9. For the most of all that I demand springeth from these two branches; first, that to have restitution of all that wrongously hath been taken from me and my tenants, I be permitted to take my course against the meanes of the robber, who, by having disabled them, through so great a spoil, from paying their farmes ever since and these seven years to come, so well as formerly they did, will prejudge me in thrice as great a summe as all they were pillaged of did amount to; and next, that King James his act, concerning the most important clause in decreets of apprising, may be conceived as it ought to be, in favours of them that offer moveables of more worth then the debt that is required. Sir James
Fraser of
Darkhouse,
of whom no
good can be
truly spoken
but that he
is dead.

Avarus, nisi
cum moritur,
nihil recte
facit, *says*
Publius

10. Now, lest I should seem to protract time, and involve the reader into a labyrinth of discourse upon this so exuberant a purpose, the amplification whereof, should I give way thereto, would with little difficulty draw from my pen more volumes, time not failing me, then ever Origen wrote, as is manifest by those aporrectical interthetes I have already couched; whereof nevertheless I have not the twentieth part, nor any considerable portion of other more worthy manuscripts of mine, which I having left behind me at Cromartie, were in the time of my imprisonment at London by the sequestrator Dundasse's rifling of my library, most wretchedly embezled, and unluckily scattered amongst those that prefer'd clean paper to any writing that is, I will, after having mentioned somewhat of the matter climacotially proposed in the seventieth article of the second book, make bold to conduct the reader to the reposing-room of a closure, there to remain, if it please him, till it be high time to require his progress towards the ten excogitable cities mentioned in the 73 article of the first book. *Mimus*,
avaro quid
mali optes
nisi ut diu
vivat? Non
sibi non
aliis prodest
dum vivit
avarus, et
prodest aliis
et sibi dum
moritur.

11. Seeing the matter already spoke of concerneth me and my father's creditors, both of us ayming at one and the same thing, to wit, the enjoyment of the estate of my progenitors, I shall desire the reader, by what I am to say, to take notice which of us hath best right thereto, first in conscience, then according to law.

12. Conscionably therefore to talk thereof, in some of the most civil parts of the world it is thought unjust that the infection of debt, like a hereditary disease, should be derived to posterity, but onely transmitted to those that from the indebted receive a benefit equivalent to the debt; conscience requiring that each one be a faithful administrator to his posterity of the means which from his predecessors he hath received; nothing being made lyable to his own debt but his own conquest; his personal deservings, and nothing else, being that which ought to expiate his personal faults. Vid. Art.
63.

13. Hence it followeth by the same equity as aforesaid, seeing neither any of my fore-fathers, nor yet my self, were obliged in so much as one farthing to any of those creditors, that consequently neither their estate nor mine should be affected with the

burthen which concerned us not, but onely the means of him that was the party contractor; whereby the whole shire of Cromartie, and baronries of Bray and Fishery in Scotland, ought clearly to be mine, for having belonged to my progenitors five hundred and twenty yeers before the incarnation; it being enough that I lose two hundred pounds sterling a yeer of old rent, which my father put away, together with all his own conquest and moveables belonging either to him or any other of my ancestors.

Hydropico similis, nunquam satiatur avarus, infelix requie nocte dieque caret.

14. But the lucripetary poscinummios lending a deaf adder's ear to these kinde of motions, because the rigour of the Scotish law against the heirs of ancient families alloweth not the admittance of such a desire to soften the hardness of their hearts, it was told them,

Non solum liberalitatis est, sed etiam commoditatis plerumque aliquid de suo jure relaxare.

15. First, That seeing I had nothing answerable to the annual rents of those creditors but the yeerly rent of the land, and that estates in land should be as well weighed in the balance of justice as stocks in money, it could not be but reasonable that as much were defalked from creditors' interests, as by publike dues have been exhausted out of my land-rents.

·Vtilia non omnia quæ profutura videntur. Effugere cupiditatem, regnum est vincere.

16. Secondly, That for the payment of what sums of debt the creditor could with reason claim right to, he might be pleased to take penny-worths, not according to his own cutting and carving, but as judicious men employed therein, should discern of their value; there being nothing more common amongst burgers, whom the law certainly cannot with reason favour more then landed men, then that if a merchant fall into any decadence in his means, although by his own procurement, his creditors must take of his moveables, as by the prime magistrats of the town they shall be appreciated, and at no under-rate.

In lucrando modus sectandus. Sed illis crescentem sequitur cura pecuniam.

17. Thirdly, For further trial of their discretion, it was propounded, seeing it was their resolution to have my lands to go to the payment of another's debt, that they would therefore vouchsafe to give some voluntary courtesie for lightning of the burthen; which favour, considering the smallness of the sums at the first borrowing, and yet the smaller use they were put to, there being none living but the creditors themselves that had any benefit thereby, and yet how vastly and exsuperantly they have accresced since, may very well be granted.

Avari rectas cogitationes non admittunt, et lucri gratia corpus et animum diabolo prostituunt.

18. These most reasonable overtures prevailing as little as the former, with those cunning creditors, who, when my father needed no money, knowing his disposition to borrow and ability to pay, did for their own ends lend unto him whatever he pleased, that thus, by laying out a worm, as it were, to catch a salmon, taking occasion of his profuseness they might make their own covetousness the main groundwork of their enrichment.

19. For which prodigality, I have already dispensed with all that ever he acquired, and a hundred thousand pounds Scotish more, besides seven or eight yeers' rents of my lands which I gave them totally, save so much thereof as for publike dues I could not get avoided to abalienate from their acceptance.

20. Yet as if this their covetousness were such an illustrious and heroick vertue as could not be recompensed, (all that ever they got from my father, or yet from my self, taking no more bulk in the immense gulph thereof, then would a grain of millet-seed in the throat of an ass,) they refused to take land in part of payment of the superplus of the debt; not but that in their own thoughts they esteem the land much more worth then the money to be discharged for it, themselves having given greater sums of money for worse land, and less of it; but that by this their seeming refusal, to be free of their cruelty otherways, I might be necessitated, out of desperation, to cast it into their laps half for nought.

21. Which, that I might the sooner be enforced to do, they demanded, besides their principal sums, which oftentimes were but failies of bargains, their interests, reer-interests, expences in seeking after them, and the interest of those expences, without having any regard to the difficulties of the times, which eat up the rents in publike disbursements; and had laid such politick courses for insnaring me in the trap of an unthrifty bargain, that by their forestalling the bank, there was no money to be had in borrowing for my behove, but onely from themselves.

22. Had this been the worst, it should never by me have been mentioned; but to conceal it I were to blame, after that I was ascertained of what inward joy was conceived amongst them, when they had fondly assured themselves of the truth of my being killed at Worcester-battel, and for the gladness of the tidings, had madified their nolls to some purpose with the liquor of the grape.

23. And how, when afterwards they understood the contrary to be verified by letters under my own hand, and that by being, no thanks to them, in as good health as any of themselves, they were like to be disappointed of their abominable and unchristian hopes, they then threw in the way of my credit all the impediments that they could, to debar me from money, that the withholding of necessary helps might, if possible, snatch away what the sword had spared.

24. As also, what underhand-dealing there was for arresting of my person at London, by men with whom neither my father nor I had ever any dealing, notwithstanding of my being a prisoner upon parole to the Councel of State, and likewise what plotting was in Scotland by that fry of men against me, after I was allowed by the State the favour of five months time to go thither and return again, is well known by those that were employed by them in those unconscionable negotiations.

25. What congeeing, cringing, doffing of hats, making of legs, and petitioning there was of the Judges of Scotland, the Commissioners for the sequestrations at Leith, and others, by many of those men, that they, good souls, who have always been found true and trusty to their own profits, should not, for my lawless and unwarrantable joyning with Charles, for so some called him, in the invasion of England, be debarred from their legal rights to the enjoyment of my father's lands, apprised by them for

In illis neque pecuniæ modus est, neque cupiditatum, quas nulla præda unquam improbe parta minuit, sed auget potius, atque inflammat. Vltroneæ vilescunt merces et pretia facilitate decrescunt. Retia ubique tendunt ad nummos.

Lucrum in arca, damnum in conscientia.

Voluntas fingendi et mentiendi est eorum qui lucrum desiderant.

their most precious and inestimable money, is not unknown to any that for business did frequent the courts of justice in that country.

26. Furthermore, to shew the craftiness and subdolous pranks of some of those creditors, of whose discharges I was content some two yeers ago to accept, for sums of money I had given them towards the defrayment of certain debts due upon bonds, which they, perceiving my forwardness to relieve them, and having a further project in their own mindes, pretended they were so mislayd, that they could not come at them so soon as the urgencie and pressing haste of my then-incident occasions might require, did, very subtilly, or rather knavishly, at my last going down to Edinburgh from London, demand payment from me by vertue of those bonds, which then they had to shew readily enough, thinking the discharges they had given me had been utterly lost at Worcester; and although some of them, by means of the clauses of

Divitias per falsitates acquirere, opprobrium est. registration which they contained, might have been put upon record, that nevertheless that should help me nothing, because the Scotish registers were removed to the Tower of London, and therefore, in their conceit, never to be exposed hereafter to the inspection of any of the Scotish nation. So cunning this generation of usurers is of late become in Scotland.

27. But when they saw that those their acquittances, which by the discretion of one Captain Goodwin, in Colonel Pride's regiment, had been recovered out of the spoil at Worcester, were produced before them, they then looking as if their noses had been a bleeding, could not any longer for shame retard my cancelling of the aforesaid bonds.

28. Who doth not account such a trick a deep piece of iniquity, doth not positively know what belongs to sin; but who thinketh any more of it, and of all the formerly-mentioned abominations, then of a flea-bite to the sting of a scorpion, in regard of Robert Lesly of Finrasie's far more wicked contrivances against me, hath no skill in comparatives.

29. For albeit of all the friends he ever had, the most deserving was my father, by whose intercession alone he obtained, for the space of one and twenty yeers together,

Maxima cupiditas rationem pervertit, ac mentem a suo statu removet. fourscore pounds sterling a yeer; yet for exchange, as it seemed then, of so great a favour, he having lent him eight hundred pounds English money, when my father neither needed nor required it; and having by mischance on the one side, and subtilty on the other, got his bond thereupon, he was the first that led apprisings against his lands; and not content with that, to the end he might obtain the marrow of his estate to himself, procured the most of all his other creditors to take the same violent course against him.

30. And though when in the time of my Lord Montross's over-running of the north of Scotland, he knew not what course to take for the securing of his gold, silver, evi-

Cupiebam tuam ingratitudinem silentio dissimulare, dences, and other things of value, from the hands of the Irish, it pleased my mother, out of courtesie, to take into her own custody the trunks wherein those things were, and place them within my house of Cromartie; of all which, although she made such a good account unto him, that now he hath them at his own disposure, yet, like that snake mentioned in the fable, which, in stead of thanks for the warmth of a good fire bestowed on his almost-starv'd-for-cold joynts, without which he had assuredly died, did leap up in the face of his host, to destroy him, with his whole family, he hath ever since applied the utmost of his wit to the undoing both of her and me, and the utter subversion of all the remnant of our house. *sed meam modestiam tua vicit improbitas.*

31. That such bad acquitals should have by him been rendred to my father and mother, for those of so considerable favors of theirs conferred on him who was born a gentleman, for he is the third in descent from Norman Leslie that, for killing his master Cardinal Betoun, was justly forfeited of his estate, is truely very strange. *Tu omnium ingratissime pro summis officiis, quantum potes maleficorum reponis.*

32. Strange likewise it is, that by the continuance of his miscarriages towards me, I should be necessitated in my own defence against him, who, as if there were a cannibal-like leprosie over his heart, impeditive of the susceptibility of thanks, hath never any way been sensible, in the least measure, of the several good offices done unto him, to afford yet another evidence of the height of his ingratitude, which is this. *Tu pro officiis ea reponis ingratissimum monstrum, quæ hostis non faceret hosti.*

33. When some four yeers ago, with all the horse and foot he was able to command, he came in a hostile manner to take possession of a farm of mine called Ardoch; unto which, as Sir Robert Farquhair can testifie, he had no more just title, then to the town of Jericho mentioned in the Scriptures; and that at the offer of such an indignity to our house, some of the hot-spirited gentlemen of our name would even then have taken him, with his three sons, bound them hand and foot, and thrown them within the flood-mark, into a place called the Yares of Vdol, there to expect the coming of the sea in a full tide, to carry him along to be seized in a soil of a greater depth, and abler to restrain the insatiableness of his immense desires, then any of my lands within the shire of Cromartie. *Improbi cum maxime beneficia acceperint, tunc maxime ad maleficia animantur.*

34. Then, when in hopes he would behave himself more legally in times coming, prove a better neighbour, and more conscionable man, I had restrained their fury, curbed their sudden attempt, and allowing him, together with those were with him, a pass and safe-conduct to their own houses, I did not permit so much as a hair of any of their heads to be touched; his retribution of thanks to me for my then so publikely-manifested affection to him in the preservation of his life, under God, appeared in nothing else, (he like another Mithridates, feeding his gall on no other nutriment but on the poyson of that rancour he had most maliciously conceived against me and my family,) but in the present setting of himself to work for laying the platform of a most mischievous plot, to my total and unavoidable destruction.

35. In pursuance whereof, having adjoyned to himself Colonel Archibald Strachan, then designed Lieutenant-colonel, good John Forbas of Innernass, Lieutenant Huchison, and others who may be named hereafter, that under pretext of saving my tenants from being quartered upon, with which punishment they were threatned even out of the pulpit of Cromartie, by an intimation made to that effect from the minister's own

mouth, who nevertheless, as I believe, knew nothing of the plot, unless I should go to Innernass my self, to conduce with the officers for some ease of an extraordinary sess was then to be imposed on me; hoping by such means, when I should be in that town, that by vertue of a caption stollen out against me by James Sutherland, tutor of Duffus, I should be deprived of my liberty, and kept in durance there till Finrasie should be fully satisfied in all his demands.

Avarus etiam diis molitur fallacias.

36. This wicked device proved so universally odious to all the ingenuous spirits that heard of it, that his own wife having it in a perfect abomination, because of the bad sequeles she was certain could not chuse but ensue upon such pernicious machinations, did not enjoy her self long after, but died very discontented at the wilfulness of her husband; for truely she was a very discreet and judicious woman, and so was his mother, who, though she loved him as well as any mother could do her son, was still in all differences betwixt him and me more for me then him, because she studied always to have reason on her side.

Eo productus est furor, ut sit res periculosissima magna beneficia in aliquem conferre : nam quia turpe putat non reddere, non vult esse cui reddat.

37. The above-written Robert, finding that this his subtil contrivance had failed of its aimed-at effect, and that there appeared as much baseness in the one as rashness in the other attempt, did forecast another way how to bring about his covetous designes; which, that he might the better do, after that he had most glibly insinuated himself into the favour of the aforenamed Archibald Strachan, and that he had a pretty while before that moved a young gentleman in Morray, (who afterwards married one of his daughters, and who, had he been free from the infection of his father-in-law's untoward suggestions, would have assuredly dealt very courteously with me, he being the heir of one of my father's creditors,) to make over his rights to him, to be consolidated with his other pretended claims, for the which he was to give him a good round sum of money, and his daughter to the boot.

Ingratitudo est ventus urens, siccans fontes pietatis, et fluenta gratiæ.

38. Now, to the end he might bestow his daughter with the least charge he could to himself, he procured an order for Colonel Strachan to quarter a whole troop of horse upon my tenandry, till I should transact for a sum to be paid to his son-in-law; which verily was the greatest part of his portion, he chusing rather my land should lie waste, then that his daughter were not well laboured.

Ingratum dixeris, et omnia dixeris.

O tempora! O mores!

39. The injustice of this action, against which Strachan even at first had some inward reluctancie, stamped within a little thereafter into the Colonel's minde those deep impressions of regret for the perpetration thereof, from whence sprung forth so many various prickles of soul-disturbing thoughts for it, and some other of his more notorious actings upon the advice of a so oppressive counseller, as that, his conscience being exceedingly stung with remorse, he was not able a while before he died to refrain from these abrupt exclamations, " Wo to thee, Finrasie! accursed be thy consultations, shame fall on them!" and so forth; after this manner fretting and vexing himself several times in private at the very single memory of that one man, as some of those that heard him in his soliloquies a little before his decease can bear record.

40. And truly thus much I can testifie myself, that to my own hearing he did acknowledge his hearty sorrow for the indefatigable pains he took for neer upon twelve months together, at the request of the said Finrasie, in procuring a garison to be setled within my house at Cromartie, whereof the governour, being a Leslie, was, though otherways a passing civil young gentleman, imbued in a very short space with such corrupt documents from his cousen Robert, that before the disbanding of that garison, for which courtesie I owe the thanks to Lieutenant-General David Leslie, who I perswade my self did never approve of Finrasie's proceedings against me, begun to keep such a high hand in my absence over all that had in me any interest, that in the most unreasonable of his demands, as his written orders as yet can bear witness, his loftiness was such, that he kept a strain like that of Solyman the Magnificent to the petty Princes of Christendom.

41. Not without a design, as is supposed, to indear himself the more intrinsecally in the favours of the young gentlewomen Finrasie's daughters, whose father, like another Charles of Burgundie, keeps them by all appearance the longer unhusbanded that they may serve him for so many stalking-horses, whereby to intangle some neighbouring woodcocks, through an expectation of wiving them, in a confederacy with him and opposition to my family, against which he hath so injustly denounced war.

42. The garison being removed from Cromartie, and honest Robert thereby disappointed of any further assistance from governor Leslie in the driving on of his projects, he betakes himself to another course, and laying hold on the occasion of a meeting amongst the gentlemen of the name of Mackenzie, put in this humble suit unto them, that they would be pleased to move the Earl of Seaforth, their chief and his superior, to allow him the favour of protection, and to further him to the possession of those my lands he had apprized for moneyes due by my father to him; which discourse, as he amplified after the best manner he could for his own advantage, so had he an especial care to make no mention of his ungrateful miscarriage within a year before that unto my Lord's own self; whose lawful commands, though both his father and he had formerly unto that honourable family sworn unfeigned obedience, he not onely sleighted in not undergoing those duties which as a vassal it became him to discharge, and which the primest gentlemen thereabouts, out of the meer tye of neighbourhood, did unanimously perform, but contrary to the homage he did owe unto my Lord, and personal good offices he had received from him, adjoyned himself with might and main, in both counsel and action, to those that had vowed the ruine of both him and his name, had plundred his and their lands, dipt their hands in the blood of his servants, and burnt some of the best houses of his kinsmen.

43. All which things being very well known to the worthy juncto of the aforesaid gentlemen, his petition was justly rejected; not so much for that in both consanguinity and allyance I had unto his lordship a very near relation, or that the predecessors of us both had for these many hundreds of years kept a most entire and amicable corres-

pondence, as that his demands were totally of themselves unreasonable, and that, although they had been better grounded, my Lord was not conceived to be in honour bound to protect him, who had infringed his faith and forfeited his loyaltie to him whose vassal he was.

Lucri spes omnia diffi-cilia facit jucunda.

44. Whereas these rubs in the way of a plain-meaning man would have quickly made him to desist from such violent undertakings, he on the contrary was by such repulses the more eager on his game; what would have proved discouragements to others did animate him, and the greatest spur to his action was the iniquity of the cause; he left no winde unsailed by, nor oar unplyed he could make use of; he importuned the Kirk, solicited the State, courted the souldierie, feasted the lawyers, cajoled, smoothed, and flattered gentlemen, merchants, and men of all degrees, to gain friends both in heaven and hell for my destruction, and that with such vigilance and circumspection, cunning and reservedness, without sparing either cost or travel, that had the time I was forced

Vid. lib. 2. Art. 19.

to bestow in my own defence on avoyding his grins, shunning his traps, and with no small charge and trouble preserving my self from his various and manifold snares, been spent after the manner I intended, I would, by God's assistance, in that space of leisure have emitted those things which to the Isle of Britain would have been of greater emolument, then all the estate he is worth in the world twenty times told.

45. But he misregarding these things, which did no more relish with him then a French galliard in the ears of a Spanish mule, and setting at nought my enjoyment of any spare hours upon what occasion soever, did even at my last being in Cromartie, where I was not to stay above two months, by reason of my being engaged to the State upon parole to return to London at a prefixed day, plod and forecast how without offending authority, I being a prisoner of war, he might so secure my person in Scotland as not to be released till he were contented in all his demands.

46. In the prosecuting of this plot by his two elder sons and brother George, many of the English officers both of horse and foot, together with the deputy-governour of that English garison in my house, being most earnestly spoke to, he found them of such another temper then the Presbyterian commanders he had formerly employed against me, that neither the beauty of his daughters nor glistering of his gold being able to tempt them to a condescendment to his unjust desires, in spight of his way-laying of me, and conducing with English messengers at Elguin in Morray to apprehend me, I securely traveled thorow all the best towns of Scotland, and thereby making a safe retreat to London, wisht him for the future to employ his motto of *Gripe fast*, with the griffin pounces of his arms, upon some other prey then me, who knows him already so well, that he being of Norman extraction, there can no proverb be more fitly applied to him, then that of *Qualis corvus, tale ovum*.

47. Several gentlemen of good account, and others of his familiar acquaintance, having many times very seriously expostulated with him why he did so implacably demean himself towards me, and with such irreconciliability of rancor, that nothing could

seem to please him that was consistent with my weal, his answers most readily were these: " I have (see ye ?) many daughters (see ye ?) to provide portions for, (see ye ?) and that (see ye now ?) cannot be done, (see ye ?) without money; the interest (see ye ?) of what I lent, (see ye ?) had it been termely payed, (see ye ?) would have afforded me (see ye now ?) several stocks for new interests; I have (see ye ?) apprized lands (see ye ?) for these summes (see ye ?) borrowed from me, (see ye now?) and (see ye ?) the legal being expired, (see ye now ?) is it not just (see ye ?) and equitable (see ye ?) that I have possession (see ye ?) of those my lands, (see ye ?) according to my undoubted right, (see ye now ?)"

48. With these over-words of " see ye" and " see ye now," as if they had been no less material then the Psalmist's *Selah,* and *Higgaion Selah,* did he usually nauseate the ears of his hearers when his tongue was in the career of uttering any thing concerning me; who always thought that he had very good reason to make use of such-like expressions, " do you see," and " do you see now," because there being but little candour in his meaning, whatever he did or spoke was under some colour.

49. For under colour of religion he did sow the seeds of division betwixt me and the Kirk, and devised such abominable lyes of me as the lyke were never hatcht in hell: under colour of being against tyranny, he sent his sons along with Colonel Strachan to the overthrow of Montross, whom he called James Graham, the, &c. as now he doth his Master by the name of Charles Stuart: under colour of being for monarchy, he hyed away his eldest son to Dunbar, where being taken prisoner, he was kept fast for a twelvemonth at New-castle; and under what colour soever he can shew himself with the least detriment in publick, doth he alwayes with the greatest security drive on his private benefit.

50. So that such as talk and discourse with him, who goes alwayes masked and vizarded with colours and pretences to what he intends not, ought not onely to see, to see well, and better see; to see well now, and see well then, but with all the perspicacy of sight and prying inspection that may be, to look upon his concealed objects, pore into them, and cast an eye on what from open view he purposely withholdeth, to the end that in discovering by such opticks the fallacies of the sight of our mind, we be not deluded by finding under the cloak of righteousness nothing else but the Babylonish garment and accursed thing.

51. Let the reader, I beseech him, excuse my having so long detained him upon the wretched subject of this man, who like a fox in his den, living in my progenitors' lands of Ethie, hides or shews his pawes as he sees the prey in a conveniencie to let go or lay hold upon; and in compensation, seeing *contrariorum eadem est ratio,* I will set before him another of my father's creditors, who in the commendative deserveth as much to be insisted upon, as the other in the vituperatory part.

52. As of the ten lepers whom Christ healed, one believed in him, and of the two crucified theeves, one was saved; so were it a pity if amongst so many creditors, there

could not be found one honest man ; but far more pitty it were, that he being a man of such approved integrity, I should be silent in his praises, and not extol his worth.

Quæstus magnus conscientiæ puritas. Bona est substantia, cui non est peccatum in conscientia.

53. Vertue was the foundation of his wealth, and he never loved to gain any thing by the loss of another ; of the many debtors that have been beholden to him, he never offered to put the bonds of any in the register ; yet hath God in his goodness towards him, blessed him with prosperity, whilst others that had blamed him for his lenity, and had themselves extended the rigour of the Scotish law to the extreamest cruelty imaginary, till they had obtained to the outmost farthing, all that out of the depth of their covetousness they could have required from my father, and afterward had in their jollity vaunted of the immense profit that thereby accrued unto them, are now, although it be not long since the time of their ostentive rigour, in a despicable condition, and fit objects of divine wrath, to be punished with that poverty, which most unmercifully for their own inrichment they would have inflicted upon their betters.

Nemo injustum habet lucrum sine justo damno, tamen non sic sapit lucrum quam dolet damnum.

54. But may William Robertson of Kindeasse, or rather *Kindnesse,* for so they call this worthy man, for his going contrary to that stream of wickedness which carryeth headlong his fellow-creditors to the black sea of unchristian-like dealing, enjoy a long life in this world, attended with health, wealth, a hopeful posterity, and all the happiness conducible to eternal salvation ; and may his children after him, as heires both of his vertues and means, derive his lands and riches to their sons, to continue successively in that line from generation to generation, so long as there is a hill in Scotland, or that the sea doth ebbe and flow.

Honestum est lucrum quo nemo læditur ; juste acquiritur, et nulli præjudicatur.

55. This hearty wish of mine, as chief of my kinred, I bequeath to all that do and are to carry the name of Vrquhart, and adjure them, by the respect they owe to the stock whence they are descended, for my father's love and mine to this man, to do all manner of good offices to each one that bears the name of Robertson, both for the personal deservings of the gentleman I have now mentioned, as for that, as it is a common saying that the Skeens ought to be Robertsons, there is nothing more certain then that the Robertsons should be Vrquharts ; for besides that their own coat-armour doth in some measure manifest it, the first of that name was a son of Robert, the second brother of Endymion Vrquhart ; which Robert, a little after the decease of Charlemain, in emulation of his uncle Carolo, was so renowned for his chivalrie and valiant atchievements in Italy, and other forrain countries, that his offspring hath ever after been designed by his name, as the Forbasses were by that of Φόρβας, the second brother of Vocompos.

56. O that I might continue longer upon this subject ! But the scope of this treatise not permitting it, I must of necessity have a fling at the creditors of another temper.

Avaritia (inquit Chrysost.)

57. For whose preying like wolves upon the innocent flock, whom by captions, arrestments, inhibitions, apprisings, and other base weapons of the rigour of the Scot-

est canis rabidus, et insatiabilis ebrietas.

ish law, they endeavour to devour without reason or conscience, I may safely avouch, (conform to that ancient saying, *Arma tenenti, omnia dat qui justa negat,*) that, *Expedit, ut jus tenenti qui justa negat, aliquid saltem de suo amittat.*

58. Thus it is clear, in regard of their stubbornness and refractary carriage against all conscience, equity, and reason, as said is, that they get neither wrong nor injustice done them, although they be made to forgo their principal, as well as their annual; it being more conducible to the publike good, that the innocent enjoy the means of their forefathers, then that the monuments of vertue become the inheritance of the vicious. *Tantum est malum non se continere intra proprios penates majoribus inhiando, ut propria sæpe pereant.*

59. I know now they will exclaim, that they are scandalized, in being called vicious for doing what the law allows them; but truely I must answer them that fornication is accounted to be a sin, even by those from whom a permission floweth to commit it, as at Rome and Avignon; and that likewise for the hardness of the people's hearts, Moses did tolerate adultery; and what else can be said of fœnory more then venery, but that as too much illicite kindness occasioneth the one, the meer lack of charity admits the other to be connived at for the less prejudice of the poor, in behalf of whom the law suffereth rather that they should pay a little usury, then to be altogether undone for want of trust? *Pejor existimatur civis fœnerator, quam fur, says Cato De re rustica. Vsurarius super omnes mercatores est maledictus, says Chrysost. in his 38 Hom. upon Matthew.*

60. Yet not to call it a sin, were to bely both divine and humane law; under pretext of either whereof, that they should go about to undermine ancient and worthy families, doth make their sin to be so much the more prodigious.

61. Those that are any thing versed in the morals, will acknowledge prodigality not to be a vice half so dangerous as covetousness, because it swerveth less from justice, which is the common measure of all vertues; for as it is *nobilius dare quam accipere,* so may it be truely said, that he doth rather *tribuere cuique suum* that giveth too much of his own, then who exceeds in taking from his neighbour. *Avaritia omnis improbitatis est metropolis. Nullum est vitium tetrius avaritia; nam inopiæ pauca desunt, avaritiæ multa.*

62. Now the properest effects of justice being to reward and punish, according to the receiver's demerit, there is no doubt but that both prodigality and covetousness should fall under the compass of the penal statutes; and this more then that, because, as the apostle says, it is the root of all evil.

63. It is a tenet, that faults being personal, the punishment of them ought not to be transferred to after-ages, as is said in the twelfth article of this book, unless they did militate treasonably against a prince or commonweal; in which case, for the publike good, *ut amor filiorum terrorem parentibus incutiat incurrendi crimen læsæ Majestatis, necesse est, ideoque justum, aliquantillum deflectere ab ea justitia, quæ privatis accommodari solet negotiis;* even as we finde, contrary to the ordinary course of nature, for the weal of the universe *ad evitandum vacuum,* air to descend, and water to amount. *Avaritia animam et corpus effeminat, nec ullus tam firmum præsidium habet, quod avaritia infringere et debilitare non poterit.*

64. Of this nature of punishment, I have been participant with all my predecessors of the paternal line, since the reign of Eugenius Octavus, in the days of my fore-

3 c

father Zeron, who had the greatest part of his estate taken from him, for no other trespass then his too great hospitality to a Prince of his own kinred, as in the Παντο-χρονόχανον, or Genealogie of our House lately published, is more fully deduced.

In nullum avarus bonus, in se pessimus. Omnia des cupido, sua non perit inde cupido.

65. But this other kinde of transgression, being in a matter onely twixt subject and subject, it follows that the successor of neither the prodigal, nor covetous man, should *eo nomine* be punished; much less should any, for his predecessor's covetousness be rewarded; nothing more shocking against common sense it self, then to make the recompence for vertue be the reward of vice, whereby the very pillars of equity would be quite subverted and overthrown.

Æstimat esse parum sibi quicquid habet cor avarum, ac quoque semper hiat major pars ut sibi fiat.

66. How can it then be called justice, that the successor of the prodigal, for no other reason but his predecessor's prodigality, shall have his whole inheritance discerned to be the inheritance of the son of a covetous man, and that meerly for his covetousness; the onely recommendable quality for which he obtains it being a constant purpose and resolution to hook his neighbour's means unto him, by eights and tens in the hundred, and other such baits, whereby improvident and inconsiderate men of great revenues are oftentimes entangled?

Avaro tam deest quod habet quam quod non habet, quia aut non habita concupiscit ut habeat, aut habita metuit ne amittat; et dum in adversis sperat prospera, in prosperis formidat adversa.

67. Were it not less prejudicial to the publike, and more equitable in it self, that a covetous man should forgo both of his principal and interest, then that he who is neither prodigal nor covetous, should be denuded of the estate of his forefathers, which never was acquired by him that contracted the debt?

68. Although the Lords of the Session, or any other inferiour judicature, were never invested with power to judge otherways then according to the customs of the country positively written, and municipal laws of the land of Scotland, yet the high Court of the Parliament of the Commonwealth, by vertue of their legislative authority, may for the weal of the publike transcend the bounds of any written law, much more that unto which they were never tied, and of a stranger-country now under their command.

69. And as it is a common saying, *Interest Reipublicæ nequis re sua male utatur,* so doth it very much concern the reputation of a Commonwealth that ancient considerable families be preserved from ruine, if possible.

Nulla est res quæ ad maleficium magis impellat quam avaritia, nec justitiæ sit infestior.

70. If creditors say they get injustice done to them by it, I answer with Tacitus, *(Dato sed non concesso) Quod habet iniqui contra singulos utilitate publica rependitur;* or with Plutarch, *A justitia in parvis negotiis deflectendum est, si ea uti volemus in magnis.*

71. For if it be lawful to cut off an arm for the preservation of the body, how much more lawful is it to defalk somewhat from the exorbitant sums of merciless creditors, for the preservation of an ancient family, in favour of him that never was the debtor; seeing the commonweal, for his appearance of good service thereto, may be highly concerned in his fortune?

72. These few points I have premitted, to make those creditors pliable to reason, in undergoing any such course as it shall please the State to command or perswade

them to; who, as I make account, will take them from off my hand, and settle me with freedom in the inheritance of my predecessors, and that for the reasons formerly mentioned.

73. Although the State pay them not to the full, or perhaps pay them, for so much as concerns me, with a pardon; yet ought they to be thankful to the State for what is left them, and not grumble at the publike severity, that others no less faulty then they, have sustained a milder lash; seeing, as in the edecimation of criminal souldiers, the nine associates have no reason to complain of partiality, because the tenth escapes unpunished, it becometh these aforesaid creditors to remain contented with that mercy to others, which proceeds from those who are just to them, although they suffer by it; *nam plurimis damnum infligitur, quibus nulla fit injuria.* And such of them as are most clamorous in seeking, considering what benefit by usurious bargains they had from my father, though they neither from the State nor me get any thing at all, can be no losers.

74. However it go, I should not be deprived of my fore-fathers' lands, because of many reasons which I have already deduced. Nor is this unwillingness in me to part from my land a vice, as is their tenaciousness in keeping of money; for, *si parva licet componere magnis,* as the king of Spain spent in the defence of Flanders more ryals of eight then would cover the face of the whole country, as is commonly reported, so to preserve my inheritance, whatever it cost, it defends the honour and reputation of the house which I represent.

75. And ingenuously, as when I collationed in the sixty second article of this same book, prodigality with covetousness, viz. that prodigality whereby one lavishly expendeth his rents, and unnecessarily involveth himself into a labyrinth of debt; and not that other, which by alienating his predecessors' ancient inheritance, destroyeth the whole stock in so far as lies in him, I did prefer prodigality to covetousness as the lesser vice; so should I now compare with the covetousness of an usurer, the profuseness of him that maketh no conscience to dispone unto strangers the land of his ancestors, I would find his fault a great deal more unpardonable then that of the usurer.

76. For who turnes his land into money, devirilizeth and emasculates what is naturally procreative, and by consequence, bending his course to what is more imperfect, deserveth greater blame then who to the eunuch and spadonian money, allowes a constant pregnancy, by imagining every peny to be both father and mother, still begetting, and still bearing, and the child still growing *per juxta positionem;* whom, if the debtor finde not beside the parent at the semestral period, he must educe another of the pre-supposed bulk, or lye by it, as one that hath not faith enough; because although both be unnatural, yet for that the latter aymeth at what is of choicer worth, it merits less imputation; the intention of making what is barren fruitful, albeit impossible to do, being more commendable then of exchanging what is by nature fertile, for that which produceth and bringeth forth nothing but rust and dross.

Suum cuique pulchrum.

Est amor et rerum cunctis tutela suarum.

Avarus est insatiabilis cui nec totus mundus obolus est.

Avaritia latentium indagatrix lucrorum, manifestæ prædæ avidissima vorago, neque habendo fructu felix, quamvis cupiditate quærendi miserrima.

LOGOPANDECTEISION.

388

*Omnis ava-
rus ex potu
sitim mul-
tiplicat,
quia cnm
ea quæ ap-
petit adep-
tus fuerit,
ad appeten-
da alia am-
plius anhe-
lat.*

77. However, although by what is already said, my declining to pay those men needed not be imputed to me, for want of equity towards them in my proceedings, they having received much from me, and often, and I from them never any thing at all; my obligations to them being so prescinded from all specialities and particular restrictions, that they never could shew neither what, nor when, nor time, nor place, nor any other circumstance whatsoever, denotating the existence of any thing on earth, wherewith to upbraid my acceptance; yet I shall wish, if so it please the publike, that they be satisfied and reimbursed of what they can with any kinde of reason demand.

78. For as Julius Cæsar, after he had repudiated his wife, being desired to call her home, because the judges had absolved her from that adultery whereof with Clodius she was accused, did very gallantly reply, That the wife of Cæsar must be free of suspicion, as well as guilt; so, though I may vindicate my self and the land of my progenitors from the stain of that debt wherewith some peevish and malicious men would adulterate the hitherto-immaculate purity of our family; yet would I rather chuse some little coin should be bestowed on them, therewith to stop their bawling mouthes, then have any the meanest distrust or jealousie remaining, though without a cause.

79. I expect that the publike will be pleased to undergo, after what manner to them shall seem most fit, the performance thereof; which that they do, even in the most expensive way, is no new thing, and in matters of far less concernment.

80. Many have had their estates made up by monopolies, and other such publike exactions, who afterwards employed the utmost of their power for subverting the State, to which they had been so much beholding, although before that time they had never made apparent their deservings for so great a favour.

81. How many have there been about the courts of kings, who having no higher qualification, then to sweep the privie rooms, or at most to make the king's bed, were short while after so bedaubed with honours, that although their endowments continued still in the same degree of baseness, they disdained the touching of a missive directed to them, whereof the superscription spoke not, *To the most noble, high, and potent Earl*, with other signorial titles, attended by an *et cætera* in the reer?

82. Cheating at cards, dice, bowling, tennis, or any other game, where confederacie or betraying of trust hath at any time proved advantagious, and all those other sneaking means that are commonly at corrupt courts practised, for cramming their bags full of money upon any terms, have been in many places this long time the usual scale of promotion, and very often the most infallible way for attaining to most sublime and splendid dignities; which sort of nobility, without valour, wit, or learning, may be fitly termed a kinde of metaphysical wonder, or relation *sine fundamento et fundandi ratione.*

83. I have seen beyond sea a Marquess of twenty thousand crowns a yeer, who,

albeit he obtained both his title and rents, for having served his prince in the quality of a pander, would nevertheless have sworn with as much grandeur, and pretended conscience upon his honour, as if he had been a conqueror of several mighty nations. I have likewise known of those that have been lorded above their fellow-courtiers, for their greater dexterity in the winding of a hunting-horn; in which faculty, nevertheless, the education of a shepherd or postilion was sufficient to make one in a very short space by far to excel them.

84. This evidenceth many to have been enriched by the publike, whose service thereto, or merit otherways, deserveth scarcely the retribution of private thanks. As for my self, because I have promised to do for the publike that which shall be better then ten times my estate, I cannot think it will be imputed for boldness to me, to require it be made free for my proposed service; and for doing thereof, such debt as shall be thought fit to defray, be forthwith made a publike burthen, with the publike expence to be discharged, if so to them it seem expedient, and no otherways.

85. But seeing it hath been said by some who not long since did sit at the helm of the Scotish State, when by one of the most eminent persons in the army, an exemption but from some few months maintenance, now called the sess, of my own lands was demanded, in compensation of thrice as much which I had disbursed upon warrants from the publike, for which by an Act of Parliament there was allowed retention in future dues of that nature, with assurance that my endeavours to the honour of my country should quickly appear for deserving worth a greater courtesie—That when such endeavours should be made effectual, it would be then time enough to appoint a recompense; the illess noble Lord not considering that the refusal was unjust, though I had not been endowed with faculties for any such designe, the like not having been denied to any well-affected gentleman but myself; nor taking notice that by those and such-like enormous pressures, I have been these twelve yeers past disabled from prosecuting so powerfully my intended purpose, as otherwise I would have done had I been clear of those impediments.

86. I will therefore halt a little in the divulgement of this my great undertaking, lest I should participate in such kind of men's precipitancy, by showing no less rashness in my exposing of precious things to their acceptance, then they have done of incogitancie by their sudden rejecting the grant of my most equitable requests.

THE PROJECT OF THE SIXTH BOOK,

ENTITULED

PHILOPONAUXESIS.

THE Author in the first five books having very posedly digested the
causes promptive to the removal of all obstacles impediting the exposal of
his brain-endeavours, doth, in this sixth and last of his Introduction, prove
that the concefsion of these his just demands will prove conducible to all
industrious negotiations and employments whatsoever. And whereas by
the usurer the contrary was upbraided, he retorts back the dart of that
obloquie on whence it came, and sheweth what innumerable prejudices
have redounded to merchandizing, scholarship, husbandry, mechanism, nobility, gentry, disport, exercise, and, in sum, to all the persons, profefsions,
and diversions of honest men, of what degree or quality soever, by the
gangrene wherewith usury and avarice hath seized upon the land, since
the domination of hypocrisie over its inhabitants. He declareth, likewise,
much of these calamities in behalf of all those forenamed vocations, arts,
disciplines, recreations, and those that plied all or either of them, to have
occurred by reason of his own particular prefsures under the fœnoratory
yoak. And therefore, to extricate him out of those impesterments, and

disintangle his estate from the intricacies wherein the flagitator keepeth it involved, he sues the supreme authority and begs the favour of a judge, whose qualifications he delineates. He solveth all the scruples that oppose his suit, and evidently demonstrateth the grant thereof to endanger the preparative of no incidence for the like in any time to come. Finally, he knowing that any man in a chamber desirous to enjoy the light of the sun, would be offended at him who by holding the windows shut should detain him in darkneſs, as also be displeased with such a one as would keep fast the door against that person did intend to present him with a rich diamant ; seeing the expansion of a door and window-leaf is able to admit the brightneſs of the one and wealth of the other, he expects that the State, considering how easily he may be disburdened of the aforesaid letts, and how upon their removal dependeth an illumination and enrichment of the minde in the knowledge of divers exquisite things, will not wittingly lose a matter of so great concernment for the not-performance of so mean a task ; for when utility may be obtained with ease, and the steps to profit trod upon with facility, it needeth not to be imagined, where wisdom superiorizeth most, that such conveniences will be set at nought and omitted. In hopes therefore of a gracious retribution, and with a strenuous aſsurance of a plenary discharge of his promise, the Author very daintily closing this sixth book, puts a catastrophe to the whole Introduction ; the publishing of the book it relates to, depending totally upon the removal of the often-aforementioned impediments, then which the Author asks no more for helps ; for, *Qui impedimenta tollit, præstat adminicula.*

THE SIXTH BOOK

OF THE

INTRODVCTION,

INTITULED

PHILOPONAUXESIS;

OR,

FURTHERANCE OF INDUSTRY.

WHEREIN IS EVIDENCED THAT THE GRANT OF THE AU-
THOR'S DEMANDS WILL PROVE, BESIDES THAT OF THE
UNIVERSAL LANGUAGE AND OTHER KINDES OF LI-
TERATURE, CONDUCIBLE TO ALL MANNER OF
OTHER VERTUOUS UNDERTAKINGS
WHATSOEVER.

1. If there happen to be any who, for the better repelling of my demands, would alleadge, all other reasons failing them, that the grant thereof might prove very damageable to traders in merchandise, whose fortune wholly consists in the frugal managing of their money, it may very fitly be answered, if they be Scotish merchants who move the doubt, that by casting in such a scruple they most unjustly impute that fault to others whereof themselves are very hainously guilty, seeing under the title of merchant, and mask of the honesty thereof, they do that which of any thing is to merchandizing most destructive.

Quis metus
aut pudor
est usquam
properantis
avari.

2. They lend money upon usury to none but such as have estates in land, without any regard to traffique; for whether the intention of the lender be considered, or use that the borrower commonly puts it to, all mercantil negotiation is exceedingly eclipsed by it.

3. There being nothing surer, then that for the most part such-like borrowers, in hawks, hounds, wenching, gaming, tipling, swaggering, fidling, rioting, revelling, and other such-like profligate courses of a most effusive and vast expence, squander away the money so lent, without casting an eye to any thing tending to the furtherance of the exchange of ware, towards the necessary use of man.

4. And that likewise the lenders of money unto such men, minding chiefly their own ingreatning, when they think a competent time hath expired, for engendering upon the emitted coin a progenie numerous enough for their enrichment, require from their respective debtors the sum at first so lent, with its usurious attendants; which, if obtained, they, possibly at the hands of some other no less debosh'd then the former debtors, make purchase of some land; if not, then are they sure, by decrees of apprising, according to the harsh law of Scotland, to take possession of the land of the debtor. *Hiincubant et excubant ut auro insidientur. Diu tamen vivant avari, nam se diutius torquebunt.*

5. So that however the matter go, being certainly assured of land, which was the thing they aimed at, as soon as they finde themselves invested therewith, they cast off the vizard of merchant, wherewith they cheated the world, and turning once landed men, they altogether scorn to traffique any longer.

6. But the best is, that the sons of those, because of their fathers having acquired land, (though the said fathers, by vertue of their long-accustomed parsimony, snudge out their own time, without any danger of thraldome by debt,) strive usually to be renowned, the better to appear gentleman-like, for such extravagant actions, as carrying along with them profuseness of charge, occasioned the sale of those lands which by their fathers were purchased. *Quanta dementia est sui hæredis res procurare, et sibi negare omnia! O egregiam phrenesin, egenus vivere, ut dives moriare!*

7. And as from the same causes, with all their concomitances, proceed always the same effects; so doth such a course of life as was kept by those that did dilapidate the foresaid lands at first, produce an inevitable necessity of redisponing them, and that oftentimes to the first abalienators' sons, who, bitten with penury, for the lavishness of their fathers, become miserable scrape-goods for their children's subsistence. *Prodigus est natus de parco patre creatus. Pecunia avaro supplicium est.*

8. After which manner, the generation of one livelihood being the corruption of another, the son of the covetous spending what the father of the prodigal had gained, and the son of the prodigal re-acquiring what the father of the covetous had put away; prodigality and covetousness, in this alternative vicissitude, were the two master-wheels that hurried Scotland into confusion; and hypocrisie the Jehu that drove the chariot with such velocity, that since the national subscribing of the first covenant, one and the same estate in lands hath been observed, according to the manner of the fore-mentioned circulation of covetous men and prodigals, succeeding in the veece of one another, to have interchangeably been possest by four several owners, *hinc inde ;* the seller being still as it were the buyer's predecessor in a diametral line, as in a direct one the prodigal was to the covetous, or inversedly, the covetous to the prodigal; and this not onely in one or two, but in above five hundred several parts of *Non sibi, sed aliis aries sua vellera portat; sic aliis cumulat dives avarus opes. Est furor haud dubius, quin est manifesta phrenesis, ut locuples moriaris,*

egeno vivere
fato.
Quod parcus quæres,
effundet prodigus hæres.
Dives es ut
Crœsus, sed
vivis pauper
ut Irus.
Cui plus licet quam
par est, plus
vult quam
licet.

Ea cupiditas habendi
istos invasit
homines, ut
possideri
magis quam
possidere
videantur.

the country; wherein what the covetous father of one family had bought from the prodigal father of another, the covetous son of that other did recover from the prodigal son of the first, and that with so little vertue in either, that oftentimes the purchase flowed from the greater vice.

9. By such a vicious flux and reflux, within these ninety yeers, upon the channel of land-rents, so great prejudice hath redounded, and daily redoundeth to the worthy profession of merchandizing, the disponer not being accustomed with traffique, and the purchaser disdaining any longer to exercise it; that all manual trades in that nation are now almost totally failed, and have fallen of late into such a palpable decadence, that hardly shall a man be found, where these men have being, that can make a pair of boots aright, or taylor skilful enough to apparel one in the fashion, although he see the patern before him.

10. Other trades of weaving silver lace, knitting silk stockins, sowing of cut-work, with five hundred more depending on the hammer, needle, or pencil, in other countries as commonly practised as cookery with us, may in Scotland now, wherever the usurer lives, be as well put amongst the *antiqua deperdita*, as the malleability of glass, liquability of stone, or incombustibility of linen.

11. And the reason is, Though they had the dexterity to make the ware, there is no merchant to buy it; all such being turned by usury to mongrel-gentlemen, and all gentlemen thought unthrifty, that turn not usurers; whose both inclinations being to convert all into money, save so much victual and clothes as barely may preserve their bodies from starving, which a corner of their own country-farm will sufficiently afford, all gallantry of invention is ruined, exquisite artificers discouraged, and civility it self trod under foot for want of commerce.

Locum virtutis deseruit et obruitur, qui
semper in
augenda
festinat re.

12. Thus it being clear, that promiscuous usury, the gentleman being no more ashamed of it then the burger, hath been the overthrow of merchandise in Scotland, which is so commendable a profession, and so agreeable to learning and true wisdom, that as by literature we are justly called microcosms, for being able to comprehend all manner of things under specieses in the predicament of quality; so may we be as well termed the same, for our ability by merchandising, were we so inclined, to bring within the compass of our possession whatever is in the category of *habere*.

Nec a mortuo sermonem, nec ab
avaro gratiam expectes.

13. There is no doubt, but to have antipathy against such opposers of honest negotiation, is to sympathize with good men; and not to abhor them with a perfect hatred, in so far as Christian charity will allow us, is to be enemies to both civility and discretion.

Avaritia ad
injuriam usque grassatur.

In omne
nefas præci-

14. What great harm they have done to the whole isle of Britain, by their violence against me, not mentioning their obstructing my intellectual faculties, which, to the opprobry of mankinde it self, they oftentimes have most inhumanely laboured to suppress, I will instruct how, in my person, these men have hindered navigation, commerce by the export, import, and transport of commodities, manufactures, fodinary

employments for coal and minerals, agriculture for tillage, pasturage, and planting, *pites hos adigunt nummi.* and many other such feasible projects of industry, tending altogether to the promoval of both wealth and civility in a land.

15. I have, or at least had, before I was sequestred, a certain harbour or bay, in goodness equal to the best in the world, adjacent to a place, which is the head town of the Shire; whereby I am intituled both sherif and proprietary, the shire and town being of one and the same name with the harbour or bay; whose promontaries on each side, vulgarly called Souters, from the Greek word σωτηρες, that is to say, *Salvatores* or *Savers*, from the safety that ships have when once they are entred within them, had that name imposed on them by Nicobulus the Druyd, who came along with my predecessor Alypos in the dayes of Eborak, that founded York some 698 years before Ferguse the First; at which time that whole country, never before discovered by the Greeks, was named Olbion by the said Alypos, whose description in the Παντοχρονό-χανον doth specifie it more at large.

16. This harbour, in all the Latine maps of Scotland, is called *Portus Salutis;* by reason that ten thousand ships together may within it ride in the greatest tempest that is as in a calm; by vertue of which conveniency, some exceeding rich men, of five or six several nations, masters of ships, and merchant adventurers, promised to bring their best vessels and stocks for trading along with them, and dwell in that my little town with me, who should have been a sharer with them in their hazard, and, by subordinating factors to accompany them in their negotiation, admitted likewise for a partner in their profit and advantages.

17. By which means, the foresaid town of Cromarty, for so it is called, in a very short space, would have easily become the richest of any within threescore miles thereof; in the prosecuting of which designe, I needed not to question the hearty concurrence of Aberdeen, which, for honesty, good fashions, and learning, surpasseth as far all other cities and towns in Scotland, as London doth for greatness, wealth, and magnificence, the smallest hamlet or village in England.

18. Nor was I suspicious of any considerable opposition in that my project from any town, save Innernasse alone, whose magistrates, to the great dishonour of our whole nation, did most foully evidence their own baseness in going about to rob my town of its liberties and privileges.

19. Yet was that plague of flagitators, wherewith my House was infected, so pernicious to that purpose of mine, that some of them lying in wait, as a thief in the night, both for my person and means, cannibal-like to swallow me up at a breakfast; they did, by impeding the safety of my travelling abroad, arresting whatever they imagined I had right unto, and inhibiting others from bargaining, most barbarously and maliciously cut off all the directory preparatives I had orderly digested, for the advantage of a business of such main concernment, and so conducible to the weal of the whole Island, to the great discouragement of those gallant forreners, of which that ever-re- *Avari, says Chrysostom, sunt fures et latrones, ubique inutiles et pejores ipsis meretricibus: maxima pars horum in morbo jactatur eodem.*

nowned gentleman for wit and excellencie in many good parts, Sir Philbert Vernati by name, was one; who being of Italian parents, by birth a Dutchman, and by education expert in all the good languages of the Christian world, besides the Arabick and Sclavonian tongues, wherein he surpass'd, had a great ascendant in counsel over all the adventrous merchants of what nation soever; whereof, without the foresaid lets of those barbarous obstructers, some by all appearance had so concurred with me, that by their assistance I would ere now have banished all idleness from the commons, maintained several thousands of persons of both sexes, from the infant to the decrepit age, found employments proportionable to their abilities, bastant to afford them both entertainment and apparel in a competent measure; by various multitudes of squameary flocks of several sizes, colours, and natures, educed out of the bowels of the ocean both far and neer, and current of fresh water streams, more abundance of wealth then that whole country had obtained by such a commodity these many yeers past; erected ergastularies for keeping at work many hundreds of persons in divers kindes of manufactures; brought from beyond sea the skillfull'st artificers could be hired for money, to instruct the natives in all manner of honest trades; perswaded the most ingenious hammermen to stay with me, assuring them of ready coin for whatever they should be able to put forth to sale; addicted the abjectest of the people to the servitritiary duty of digging for coals and metals, of both which in my ground there is great appearance, and of the hitting of which I doubt as little, as of the lime and free-stone quarries hard at my house of late found out, which have not been these two hundred yeers remarked; induced masters of husbandry to reside amongst my tenants, for teaching them the most profitable way, both for the manner and season, of tilling, digging, ditching, hedging, dunging, sowing, harrowing, grubbing, reaping, threshing, killing, milling, baking, brewing, batling of pasture ground, mowing, feeding of herds, flocks, horse, and cattel; making good use of the excrescence of all these; improving their herbages, dayries, mellificiaries, fruitages; setting up the most expedient agricolary instruments of wains, carts, slades, with their several devices of wheels and axle-trees, plows and harrows of divers sorts, feezes, winders, pullies, and all other manner of engines fit for easing the toyl and furthering the work; whereby one weak man, with skill, may effectuate more then fourty strong ones without it; and leaving nothing undone that, by either sex of all ages, might tend to the benefit of the labourer, or rather in applying most industriously the outmost of their vertue to all the emoluments of a country farm, or manual trade.

20. I would have encouraged likewise men of literature, and exquisite spirits for invention, to converse with us for the better civilizing of the country, and accommodating it with a variety of goods, whether honest, pleasant, or profitable; by vertue whereof, the professors of all sciences, liberal disciplines, arts active and factive, mechanick trades, and whatever concernes either vertue or learning, practical or theoretick, had been cherished for fixing their abode in it.

21. I had also procured the residence of men of prime faculties for bodily exercises, such as riding, fencing, dancing, military feats of mustering, imbattleing, handling the pike and musket, the art of gunnery, fortification, or any thing that in the wars belongeth either to defence or assault, volting, swimming, running, leaping, throwing the bar, playing at tennis, singing, and fingring of all manner of musical instruments, hawking, hunting, fowling, angling, shooting, and what else might any way conduce to the accomplishment of either body or minde, enriching of men in their fortunes, or promoving them to deserved honours.

22. All these things, and many more, for export of the commodities of this Island to the remotest regions of the earth, import from thence of other goods, or transport from one forraign nation to another, and all for the conveniency of our British inhabitants, whether for their integrity and uprightness of conversation, gain and utility in their meanes, or delight and recreation in their disports, I would undoubtedly have ere now provided to the full, in being, as by a friend of mine was written of me in an epistle of his premised to a book intituled The Genealogie of the Family of the Urquharts, a Mecænas to the scholar, a pattern to the souldier, a favorer of the merchant, a protector of the trades-man, and up-holder of the yeoman, had not the impetuosity of the usurer overthrown my resolutions, and blasted my aims in the bud.

23. Now, if you would know what it is that the usurer bestoweth on the country in compensation of so large a benefit whereof he hath deprived it, I will tell you; it is laziness, greed, obstinacy, pride, beggarliness, hatred, envy, treachery, contempt of betters, oppression, hypocrisie, cruelty, contention, cowardliness, continual heart-burning, disquietness, and miscontentment of minde, misregard of true honour, vilifying of vertue, and disdain of learning, with other many such like perturbations of a most odiously wicked and grievously troubled spirit.

24. Amongst such, he is accounted a thrifty gentleman who bestirreth himself the space of two daies in the whole year about the ingetting of his interests, although all the rest of the time he be more lither then a dormouse; and when he hath got this money, covetousness will not permit him, howbeit to the debtor it prove destructive, to make any other use thereof, then by joyning it to the parent which did procreate it, to beget thereon an incestuous brat of the same kinde, enixible at another term.

25. They will not be perswaded to forgo this fashion of living, because it is easie, although it be often told, that goods so acquired can never prosper, for that their gaine is grounded on the visible loss of another.

26. The trades-man gets no imployment; for though he make some curious work fit for sale, the merchant will not buy it, because his money beforehand is designed to beget interest; nor yet the gentleman, because the monster of the merchant's interest hath devoured his land-rents; thus the merchant is idle, the gentleman begger'd, and

Ad quid prodest multa quidem possidere, et nihil agere ? Nulli potest secura contingere vita, qui de re producenda nimium cogitat.

Modum non habet avaritia, nec capiendo expletur sed incitatur; hoc egentior, quo plura quæsivit. Avaritia desideratis rebus non extinguitur, sed augetur; nam more ignis, cum

ligna quæ consumit acceperit excrescit, et unde videtur ad momentum flamma comprimi, paulo post cernitur dilatari. Spes mali lucri initium est jacturæ.

Avaros Diogenes Hydropicis comparat; quia illi argento pleni, hi aqua referti amplius desiderant, idque utrique in sui perniciem.

the artificer starved for want, and all by the gallant vertue of usury, so much cryed up in Scotland.

27. Fear of piracy and shipwreck will not permit those men to adventure the launching forth in the depth; and uncertainty how the prices may rule, deters them from the hazard of bargains by land; thus the seas are not sailed, nor the ground half tilled, nor doth that parcel thereof which is laboured, for lack of apt materials wherewith to manure it, 'yeeld half the increase which otherwise it would, and yet they would be rich; whereby it is manifest, that their ignorance is great, their laziness far greater, but their covetousness and avarice is far the greatest of all.

28. Their chief felicity consists in wealth; that wealth is money; which money, when they have obtained, they know not how to use it; yet rather then not have it, they will do whatever is not good, although what is good they will not do, for the purchasing thereof; they will not labour for riches by prosecuting of industrious exercises, yet would prove treacherous for it; they will take no frugal course to attain to means, yet will they rob, pillage, filch, pilfer, and purloyn, ere they want money.

29. They will not with us metallurgize it, or dig one fathom deep into the ground to search for a mine or mineral, although the surface give apparent signes thereof, being like the Prostapheresicians of late times, who could not see the invention of logarithms, which they had lying before their eyes, and yet their thoughts are so immersed in the earth, that the sublimest of them do seldome reach a fathom above it; nor would they for the most part reach that hight, but to derogate from their superiors, whom in duty they are bound to bear respect to, and to denude them in all they can of their rights, whereby the better to grasp at somewhat for the fatning of themselves.

30. Another way they have no less detestable then this, whereupon they very ordinarily walk to get themselves approved men of high spirit, and that is biviated into two paths, one whereof they tread in for oppressing of the poor, and men of meaner chevisance then themselves, and in the other for contemning the worth, valour, learning, or whatever else is most commendable in him whose means they aim at.

31. Nay, they go so far on in this their sordid and abominable humour, that slighting all manner of learning and inrichment of the minde, they account sciences and liberal arts but conceits and toys compared to money, which by these clusterfists is held in so great estimation, that though they will chuse to be hanged, before they trouble themselves with taking any kinde of vertuous course for the obtaining of it, they do nevertheless repute honesty it self to consist therein, and will commonly say, that such a one is honester then another, by so many hundred pounds a year.

32. Notwithstanding all these unworthy and base endeavours of theirs, I have constantly observed them to remain still poor and needy; the reason whereof is, that their

Fidelis terra, infidele mare, insatiabile lucrum.

Hæc vera est causa ne cives quidquam honestum, bonumve curent; cum insatiabili auri et argenti cupiditate, honesta pariter et inhonesta officia complectantur; et quicquid agunt, sive fas sive nefas, id habeatur, ut pecuniascumulent,quibus subministrantibus, veluti pecora, ventri et veneri serviunt. Plat. 8. de Legibus.

Aurum omnes victa jam pietate colunt.

Cum illorum affluentia crescit simul inopia: insanus medio flumine quærit aquas. Divitem esse non est honestum, sed ex honestis divitem esse. Avarorum doctrina est tanti teipsum putato, quantum habueris. Damnum potius quam turpe lucrum eligendum.

laziness and pusillanimity not permitting them to search for wealth in the azure bosom of Thetis, or secessive regions of the earth, where the title *primi occupantis* would prove right sufficient enough for the possessor, they aim only at what belongeth to their neighbour, one or other.

33. Who possibly being of the same disposition of avarice towards them, if the tenaciousness of the one interchangeably encounter with the covetous humour of the other, with an equal number of degrees of intensive greed, darted and received to and from each on either side, both parties, because of the parity of reaction, will remain in the same condition as before, without bettering or impairing their fortune. *Semper avarus eget congesto pauper in auro, inter opes mendicus opum.*

34. But if there be any difference in the aforesaid qualities, betwixt the two contesters for each others means, he in whom the degrees thereof are most remiss, will, as by a cannibal, be devoured by the other; which other, perhaps, being so served by a third, and he againe by another, there will follow a perpetual consecutive course of intergulping one another, till the devil, by snatching up the last in him, have quite swallowed them all, and so rid the world of those ignominious rakehels, by whom it had been so long impestred. *Avarus dum colligit, colligitur: et dum vult esse præda, fit præda. Gula primo parenti abstulit paradisum, avaritia diviti aperuit infernum.*

35. Such men, as is said already in the 27 article of this same book, will not apply themselves to navigation, because it is hazardous; nor to trading by land, because it is painful; nor yet to the ripping up of the bowels of the earth for wealth, because it is uncertain; and yet they would be rich and have store of money, which to attain unto, they take this course for the most part. Such as have land make use of some ascriptitiary varlets for the manuring of it, who in their agricolary work, follow not the prescript rules of husbandry as they are most approvable by reason, but as they were most in use in the daies of their fore-fathers; for whensoever the land-lords are desired, for improving of the lands, to do other wayes, their answer is, That they will not alter the fashion of their grandfathers who were honest men, and the times then were good. *Illi morbo qui permanet in venis, et inhærit in visceribus, nec inveteratus evelli potest, nomen est avaritia.*

36. Nevertheless, when the wife or children gape for new provisions, then it is that the peevish shifts are set abroach, of incroaching upon their neighbour's pasture-ground or corn-land by removing of the march-stones, or as aforesaid; or if they have a little money, they pack it up in a clout, then upon good security concredit it to some one or other, who after the expiring of a prefixed time mutually condescended on, shall be bound to restore the said clout-birth, with an additional increase; which when obtained, by its coalescencie with the former heap is produced a new parent, with parturiencie for more store.

37. This is called vertue, and hath been of all other the commonest way of thrift, since usury in Scotland hath been in any request; yet by the means thereof, the whole country is impoverished, and no man rich; for those that, in the estimation of the vulgar, are accounted most wealthy, have nothing else but money, which not being wealth, but the measure of appreciating it, they can no more, to speak the truth of *Pecunia non satiat avaritiam, sed irritat. Cui nihil est quod habet, nihil illum constat habere.*

them, be reputed rich, then Strafford's, my Lord-lieutenant of Ireland's ape, which had a thousand pound sterling hid in a hole.

Avarus est tanquam balneatoris asinus, qui cum ligna sarmenta-que depor-tet, tamen semper fumo ac fa-villis opple-tus est: nec unquam fit particeps, neque bal-nei, neque teporis, nec munditiei. Toto mun-do eget, cu-jus non ca-pit mundus cupidita-tem.

38. I'll not deny, but that a vertuous man with less money, would quickly become rich; because with it he would purchase those commodities which are the true riches that fortune bestoweth on us; but that mony maketh these men such, I utterly disavow it, for in their cloaths they are poor, in their attendance mean, their fare course, and in their houses so bare and naked, that unless it be the wife or the daughter, and that peradventure not much worth neither, you shall not perceive a moveable that merits the looking on; and why? there is no trades-man in the country to make it, nor merchant to bring it home; and though both these were, whom, as in the 26 article of this same book I said already, they banished from the land, they have not the heart to buy it.

39. Whereby it is evident, that either the usurer storeth up nought but money, or if he exchange it for ware, the chaffer that he buyeth with it, is that which in many civil countries, to appreciate at the rate of any coin, hath been accounted sacriledge, to wit, the inheritance of land, the proportion whereof with money is more irrational then that of the diagonal to the side, or diameter to the circumference.

Nonne mor-bus insaniæ similis ac miserandus videtur, si-quis ob id non utatur veste quod algeat, ne-que pane quod esuri-at, neque di-vitiis quod divitiarum sit avidus.

40. The poor from the rich, of this kinde of men, differ but little in their meat, drink, cloathes, and lodging; and all these a fox hath in and about his terrier; so that, truely who purveyeth but what is meerly necessary for the life of man, may be said to have but the providence of a beast: doth not the pismire and the bee every whit as much, and almost every fowl of the air?

41. To what end our knowledge, if it make not all things vendible conduce to our behalf, and wealth suppeditative of whatever exceedeth not that extent? I would have cloth from the draper, silks from the mercer, lace from the millener, hangings from the upholster, trinkets from the trigler, jewels from the lapidary, books from the sta-tioner, marmalads from the confectioner, course dulciaries from the grocer, essences from the perfumer, and any thing else either of merchant or artificer belonging to that microcosme, whereof I am the little world.

Peccatum avaritiæ mentem, quod affece-rit, ita gra-vem reddit, ut ad ap-petenda sublimia tolli non possit. Pauperio-rem se judi-cat omnis abundans, quod sibi deesse arbitratur quicquid ab aliis possidetur.

42. Do those men I have been speaking of so? I doubt if they understand the names of the trades I have related; nor are such professions to subsist by them, whose thoughts being fixed on money, as the load-stone on the pole-star, consider not of what is convenient either for their minde or body.

43. I have heard of one with us of the cattel aforesaid, worth a thousand pound sterling a year, who had no other book in his house but the Bible, and that onely to have a chapter in readiness after meat, when the minister should come to see him; all the paper he had was full of sneesing-powder, nor had he other pen but that where-with he took it; so careful he was of materials for the exercise of the mind.

44. As for the preservation of the health of the body, prevention of diseases, or

remedies against them, they are so well versed in the terms of art concerning them, that the word Apothecary may signifie somewhat to eat for any thing they know; Surgeons and Physicians coming along like the burgers of some towns to their land-meers but once in the five years.

45. Thus hath the usurer in less then fourscore and ten years space that he hath domineered in the land, made some of us no less savage and barbarous then the wildest beast that is; and if he roam at such random but for twenty years more, the Satyr and the Centaure will in their lower parts have more humanity then many of us shall in our brains.

46. For he resteth not in the destruction of the merchant and artificer, but likewise layeth his heavy hand upon the scholar, who, by reason of not allowing him compe-tencie of maintenance at the schools, doth not, one amongst fourty bred amidst them, even when they have past their whole course of learning, know how to spell the En-glish tongue aright.

47. By means of which gross imperfection, I now and then have sustained my self no small prejudice in the expence of time; for although I compose no treatises, whe-ther in prose or verse, without some considerable deliberation, yet for the most part, for couching them in a hand not very legible, for truly I am no good scribe, and not being able to finde, neither in my own family, nor within a great many miles about me, one skilful enough in vernacular orthography, I have oftentimes been at a great deal of more paines in enditing of them to the writers, and amending their erratas, then at first I was in the framing and writing of them both.

48. Nor is there any hope in haste of amending this fault; for the most of the parents of that country, ever since the dayes of our grandfathers, have by the trium-phancie of usury, had the inclinations of their mindes so mechanically protruded upon the contempt of letters, that their children have with their very mother's milk, im-bued an aversness from learning, and all the *utendas* conducible thereto, fearing they should hinder the advancement of their private fortunes, according to the trivial say-ing, *Vbi multum de intellectu, ibi parum de fortuna*; whereof, to speak nothing of the manifold great discouragements which, in the progress of literature, I have from my infancy had through the whole tract of my time till this very present minute, the late course taken for sequestrating whatever belonged to me, gave no small experiment.

49. For I have found at home, even in those that love me better then they did any body else, and in the eyes of the world most entirely, a very heavy and deplorable omission in taking a course, like Martha who was onely busied about external things, for the preservation of corn, cattel, plate, with other goods and utensils, whilst they were altogether neglective of securing what they themselves knew I preferred to all these moveables, as appeared even when they so slighted my library, that not a book thereof escaped the touch of Dundasse's fingers; although there were not three there-in which were not of mine own purchase, and all of them together, in the order where-

Quæ est aviditas concupis-centiæ, cum et ipsæ bel-luæ habeant modum; tunc enim rapiunt quando esu-riunt; vero prædæ cum senserint satietatem [desistunt]; sed insatia-bilis est avaritia divitum.

in I had ranked them, compiled like to a compleat nosegay of flowers, which in my
travels I had gathered out of the gardens of above sixteen several kingdoms, by having their thoughts plunged and totally immersed in an extraordinary care for these
things, which with little expence and less labour, were obtainable about our owne
doors; all which books, had not that worthy and most consciencious gentleman Col.
Tho. Fitch, to whom I was then unknown, contremanded the sequestrator's purpose
of sending them to Leith in a ship, then ready to launch forth from Cromarty, had
assuredly been thrown into the bottom of the sea, for the vessel within two days thereafter was taken by the Hollander, or tossed amongst the Flemish stationers in their
shops at Amsterdam, never any more to be thumb'd in this Isle.

50. But Providence, which doth not always go along in its dispensation of events
according to the expectation of the forecasters, permitted not what they would have
most concealed to slip out of the reach of Dundasse's hands; unwilling, as it were for
their preposterous election, that any thing should be saved, though the loss of both
was mine; with this difference, nevertheless, that upon giving of bonds and good security, they were repossessed with the other moveables; but as for my books, although
I obtained an order from the Commissioners for the sequestration at Leith to Captain
Dundass, requiring him to let me have the refusal of them; yet he not pleasing to
come to Cromartie, where they were fast locked into trunks, whereof himself had the
keys, I was not able, for all the favour I could make till this hour, to obtain either the
getting or buying of any of them, save a few of those which under pretext of the sequestrator's having medled with them, being stollen, and afterwards dispersed thorow
the country, were through good intelligence by me happily recovered.

51. The little care had of my papers and books by those to whom they were intrusted, being a branch springing from the epidemical tree of ignorance, which, together with hypocrisie, usury, oppression, and iniquity, took root in these parts, when
uprightness, plain-dealing, and charity, with Astræa, took their flight with Queen
Mary of Scotland into England, where, not without the incitement of those her subjects, who from her own dominions had expelled her, she lost her life; since which
time, what devastation hath by usury been made amongst the most ancient families of
that country, he that runs may read it upon all the prime castles of the land.

Avari om-
nem ordi-
nem tur-
bant, estque
avaritia arx
omnium
malorum.

52. The usurer thus, as is obvious to the eyes of any, being the chiefest occasion of
the ignorance of Scotland, and of a huge deal of wickedness besides, as in my own
particular may be instanced; for as of any knowledge that, by the favour of God, is
in me, he would rob the whole world; so goeth he about to despoil me of all my
means and inheritance against all reason, therefore could I say no less; but who would
have more, I remit him to my aporrectical intervals in the Mennippæan satyrs, whereof he may see five hundred times as much, when the order obtained for recovering
those my manuscripts, which Dundass the sequestrator medled with at Cromartie,
shall prove more effectual.

53. What I have spoke of this sort of untoward men is in some measure to incite the State, to whom in all humility I make my address, to consider of the many wrongs I have most unjustly sustained by them ; for reparation whereof, I heartily desire my inheritance may be made free unto me, and the priviledges of my ancient House kept entire, after the above written proposed way ; which engaging me to the exposing of some moveables in exchange, of a sufficient stamp and currant pass, I must acknowledge my self obliged, in the strictest manner can be conceived, towards the discharge of that duty.

54. However, in stead of too hastie publishing my intent therein, which for some reasons mentioned in the four and fiftieth of the second book, and other articles to that sense, is most expedient for the time to forbear ; I humbly propose to take this course for the satisfaction of the publike, that in case I perform not, at a competent time to be prefixed for the purpose, whatever I have promised, I shall be willing to forfeit both life and lands ; the later whereof will, even in the estimation of those craving men, double the worth of all the money that they can, with any kinde of pretext of reason, demand from me. This is *adhibere cautionem Mutianam*, and to prescribe the readiest way how to avoid deluding.

55. Onely thus far, I would have the judges of my offer to be learned and judicious men, and not such as will prefer a fishe's eye to a diamant, a bable to a scepter, and tilling, harrowing, sowing, reaping, mowing, planting, and feeding of the flocks and cattel, to all the seven liberal arts, their encyclopedia being agriculture ; for men of that nature, being meerly led by the sense, will never discern of things aright. Vide Book 2, Art. 6, 7, 9, 10, 11, 12, 13, 46, 47, 48, 49, 52.

56. It was by such amongst the Turks that Famagusta in the Isle of Cyprus, none of them at that time carrying any respect to the inward worth of a Christian, that the Earl of Paphos, though the compleatest courtier and gallantest man of that age, was made to carry on his shoulders a packet full of mortar for the repairing of a breach.

57. A horse fit for the wars is oftentimes, by the indiscretion of his master, appointed to go round in a mill, and perhaps esteemed less worth then a blind jade, that in the discharge of that circumambulatory office shall be found to surpass him.

58. A country hoydon, in carrying loads, will excel a gentleman of fashion ; and I have known a young handsom woman prefer a man, for building of a peat-stack in a comely proportion, to be her husband, before a gentleman who, for his valour, very shortly after became a colonel of both horse and foot.

59. Silly mindes have abject thoughts, and though eagles catch not flyes, cameleons do. With such therefore whose spirits soar not a grasshopper's leap above the ground, we are not to meddle, lest, as Midas twixt Pan and Apollo, and the ass between the cuckow and the nightingale, they pronounce an erroneous sentence, to the disgrace of themselves and opprobrie of learning.

60. It is only the generous spirit indued with knowledge, to whose judicious arbi-

trement I do heartily submit my self and all my endeavours, because such a one will not deny but that a private gentleman may enter in paction with the potentest State that is, for matters touching the furtherance of the good fame thereof; that though, as Protestants avouch, in our service towards Almighty God we merit nothing, yet if in the performance of good offices to the publike, we transcend the bounds of the ordinary duty of a subject, we may justly be said to supererogate at the hands of any sovereign authority in the world; and that learning, even in time of war, is to be held in estimation, for that he who is the God of glory and peace, is likewise the Lord of hosts.

61. Nor is there any doubt but that he will acknowledge the profound literature of a native, to bring great reputation to his country; that such a reputation is there far more worth then riches, and consequently riches to be amply disposed on for the promoval of that learning, whether it be by donatives and largesses, positively to give encouragements to him that is so qualified; or by a negative assistance, to remove, whatever it cost, the obstructions of those, whether creditors or others, that meschantly stand in the gap to hinder the progress of the effects thereof.

62. He will also avouch, that in all well-policed commonweals, there are remedies appointed for helping of the debtor, much more the *Aquopet*, who is in case to do his country service, as well as, if not rather then, the creditor, that doth nought but for his own ends, without regard of the publike; and likewise, that such creditors as are but flagitators, craving money from those to whom they never lent any, should, will they, nill they, be enforced to confer courtesies, in abating of their sums, upon them that never were their debtors, but onely enthralled to them for the debts of others.

The Aquopet is he from whom debts are sought, although he owe them not.

Quæ sint aliena volunt adjicere.

Hi sæpius victi sua spe frustrantur. De male partis non gaudebit tertius hæres. Neque enim divitiæ injustæ unquam constantes sunt.

63. Nor will such a gallant man fail to assever, but that it is more honourable for Britain, that my family, which hath stood therein for a space of ninety and four generations, be established for my doing unto that my foresaid country service, then permitted, through the rigour of a dangerous law, by the covetousness of those, whose money neither I nor any of my progenitors ever saw, to be ruined and overthrown, for setting up of I know not what, which shall not, nor ever yet hath been seen in the like occasion, to stand till the third heir, or a full age; and that the fall of an ancient House, which mutilates the country, is more deplorable then the defalking of some interests, which doth but as it were shave off the hair of some greedy wretch.

64. I am also confident, that in the opinion of such a man, antiquity of race, *cæteris paribus*, is to be preferred; and that to rescind private covetousness for a publike good, is to do no wrong at all.

65. The verity of all these things being asserted, as in reason it ought, I offer to the publike to make good my parole, provided they liberate my estate from the bondage of the flagitator.

Voraciores purpura et

66. By disinthralling me thus from the slavery of the importunate riposcones, I accomplishing my part, the publike will gain the reputation of re-establishing into its

pristine integrity a family of great antiquity, of furthering the course of learning and good letters, of relieving the innocent from unjust oppressions; and to do this, will obtain the unanimous consent and approbation of all the souldiers, gentlemen, commons, and people of either sex, within the whole land, the flagitators onely excepted. *dolia inexplebilia.*

67. For which cause, seeing I am drawing to a closure, if any happen to imagine this my suit to be the more unobtainable, that the preparative thereof may endanger the disquieting of the state with showers of petitions, to have publike charges allocated for the payment of private debts;

68. My answer is, That my case in this particular being quite different from that of any other within the dominion of Scotland, whether regard be had to me, to my father's creditors, or the land in debate betwixt us, there is none who by vertue of any favour by me demanded from the supream power of the land, can for his interest in the like suit, pretend a right to the same courtesie to be performed on his behalf.

69. For if we consider the land which I claim title to, as the undoubted inheritance of my predecessors, it is a land which never was bought nor sold, nor otherways derived to my progenitors from any soveraign power then by bare confirmations of their former rights; the like whereof cannot with truth be avouched of any land in the isle of Britain, and therefore the more heedfully to be preserved from being a prey to the unclean harpyes of usury.

70. If again I be looked upon as one who for any personal courtesie done to my self, was never obliged to any one of them who call themselves creditors; how I have obliged every one of them by having given to each a hundred times more then ever I had received from them all together; how withal I am willing to renounce my right to any thing that ever was acquired by my father; and how lastly I am content not onely to pass by the laying of any title to those many several lands of my progenitors within the shires of Cromartie and Aberdeen, which in his own time he heritably disponed away and abalienated; but also to discharge them of the vast sums of money many of them unmercifully pilled out of my rents ever since my father's decease; I am certainly perswaded no compatriot of mine by such reasons will pretend to the like; or if it happen he should, which I believe he cannot, that offer which I make to the publike, beyond the reach of common imitation, will quell the ambition of that suit, the obtaining whereof totally dependeth upon examples he is not able I suppose to follow.

71. To these I furthermore adjoyn this other circumstance, That in all the isle of Britain there shall not be found a crew of such rigorous and merciless creditors, William Robertson onely excepted, who without respect to any thing else then their own meer enrichment, care not what misery their debtor and his posterity be brought into by their procurement; which procedure, considering how of eight or nine times I was surety for country-men of mine, I was always forced to pay the debt; how likewise, of a hundred times at least, that money by others of them had been borrowed from

me, I would ever have been well pleased to forgo all interests for the bare sum which I lent; and how nevertheless I do not plead immunity or exemption from any debt due by my self, my condition, I thank God for it, being such, with all manner of people I have had to deal with, of what country soever, that upon three hours warning, I shall pay all I owe in the world, and to the utmost farthing give satisfaction to all those that properly can be called my creditors, may very well be thought to furnish ground sufficient for what I have deduced, by way of grievance against the aforesaid flagitators.

72. Wherefore I likewise answer, if ever there fall forth a contingencie of the like occasion, in all its specialties and circumstances, the lack of any one whereof will undoubtedly alter the case; that is to say, if, besides what I have already said, a good deal of contiguous rent, priviledged with the title of a shire within it self, and worthily possessed for the space of two thousand thirty and nine years, by threscore and twelve several generations of heritable sheriffs, and sole owners of the whole shire, descended, for the most part, of one another in a direct consecutive and uninterrupted line from father to son, accordingly served and retoured heirs to their immediately-foregoing predecessors in the same family, happen to undergo the lamentable disaster of being legally threatned to be taken away by creditors, for vast sums of money, from the righteous heir, who never was bound, nor any of his ancestors, save his father alone, to them or any of theirs, in so much as the value of one bare groat, and himself nevertheless able, out of the nimble reach and perspicacity of his wit, to afford stuff equivalent to both land and money joyned in one.

Vide Art. 42, 44, 53, 54, 59, &c. of the Second Book, and others, for vindicating the Author from Philotisme. 73. If ever, I say, it chance that all these prenotated restrictions, and limited designations, occur in any country-man of mine, which I trust will first cost the revolution of the great platonick year, the State should have my advice, were there twenty of them, to instal them, other means failing, upon the publick charge, in the place of their fore-fathers, with all emoluments and profits thereupon depending; that like so many radiant stars in one constellation, they might dart an influence propitious to the furtherance of the glory of this Island.

74. And in truth, for my owne part, before that in the person of such a one, should be seen the overthrow of the house of his progenitors, I would allow him the adminiculary succour of half my meanes, when at best, for his aid of support, and think in so doing to gaine by the bargain; being certaine, besides that it is a deed of vertue, whose recompence, for being held by all moralists to be in the action it self, makes the very doing thereof to pass for a sufficient reward, that for a gratuity of that importance, so seasonably administered, from a spark of such a nature, would never be wanting a most thankful acquital to the utmost of his power.

75. After which manner, without striving for examples, the publick may be throughly and fully assured of me, and of the infallibility of my grateful return, which

shall be alwaies ready; for that my inclination leadeth me, not to receive any thing in that kind, unless it be as willingly erogated as it shall be accepted of.

76. Therefore to conclude, seeing there is not any Scotish man breathing, who is not as much, if not rather more beholding to me, then I am to him; and that my humour serves me rather to apply my self to the good of many in general, then to be wedded to any particular interest; I humbly desire, for that neither my self, nor any of my predecessors, have at any time been subject to any other then the supream authority, that by the sacred influence therof, I may be freed from the bondage of the supposed creditor, whose discretion being as the broken rod of Egypt to repose upon, let me adjure the publick, by all their sacred and most endeared tyes to patriotisme, antiquity, honour, vertue, learning, and what else may be reputed most laudable in the behalf of one totally addicted to their command, seriously to consider of the premisses, to homologate what I demand, vouchsafe the patrociny of my offer, and Mecenatize the request of him, who in rearing up monuments of his engagement to them for so splendid a favour, and for memory thereof erecting trophies of thankfulness to their fame, shall withall research all other occasions, wherein he may most deservingly approve himself their eternally-devoted servant,

THOMAS VRQUHART.

THE EPILOGUE.

THAT I whilst a prisoner was able to digest and write this Treatise, is an effect meerly proceeding from the courtesie of my Lord General Cromwel, by whose recommendation to the Councel of State my parole being taken for my true imprisonment, I was by their favour enlarged to the extent of the lines of London's communication ; for had I continued as before, coopt up within walls, or yet been attended still by a guard, as for a while I was, should the house of my confinement have never been so pleasant, or my keepers a very paragon of discretion, and that the conversation of the best wits in the world, with affluence of all manner of books, should have been allowed me for the diversion of my minde, yet such an antipathie I have to any kinde of restraint wherein my self is not entrusted, that notwithstanding these advantages, which to some spirits would make a jayl seem more delicious then freedom without them, it could not in that eclipse of liberty lie in my power to frame myself to the couching of one sillable, or contriving of a fancie worthy the labour of putting pen to paper, no more then a nightingale can warble it in a cage, or linet in a dungeon.

Here must I not forget the obligation I owe to that most generous gentleman Captain Gladmon, for speaking in my favour to my Lord General ; which gallantry in him, upon so small acquaintance, shall afsuredly be remembered by me with a stedfast resolution to embrace all the opportunities wherewith fortune shall present me, for performance of the best offices I can in testimony of my thankfulnefs.

The kindly usage of the Marshal-General, Captain Alsop, whilst I was in his custody, I am bound in duty so to acknowledge, that I may without difsimulation avouch, for courtesies conferred on such as were within the verge of his authority, and fidelity to those by whom he was intrusted with their tuition in that restraint, that never any could by his faithfulnefs to the one and loving carriage to the other bespeak himself more a gentle-man, nor in the discharge of that military place acquit himself with a more universally-deserved applause and commendation.

The enumeration of these aforesaid courtesies, will not permit me to for-get my thankfulnefs to that reverend preacher, Mr Roger Williams of Providence in New England, for the manifold favours wherein I stood ob-liged to him above a whole month before either of us had so much as seen other, and that by his frequent and earnest solicitation in my behalf of the most especial members both of the Parliament and Councel of State; in doing whereof he appeared so truely generous, that when it was told him how I, having got notice of his so undeserved respect towards me, was desirous to embrace some sudden opportunity whereby to testifie the af-fection I did owe him, he purposely delayed the occasion of meeting with me till he had, as he said, performed some acceptable office worthy of my acquaintance; in all which, both before and after we had conversed with one another, and by those many worthy books set forth by him, to the advancement of piety and good order, with some whereof he was pleased to present me, he did approve himself a man of such discretion and inimit-ably-sanctified parts, that an Archangel from heaven could not have shewn more goodnefs with lefs ostentation.

3 F

TO THE READER.

Sweet and judicious Reader,

Although you have been detained all along this little Tractate upon the particulars of a private family, and that the Author at the first sight doth thereby seem to minde rather his owne profit then your instruction, yet so much confidence is reposed in your ingenuity, that it is credibly thought you will not expect great apologies from him whose best endeavours you know already have been much devoted to your service ; especially for that your interest in the future establishment of his fortune, all things being well considered, appeareth every whit as great as his owne ; for, albeit in the eyes of the vulgar most of the benefit of an estate seemeth to accrue to him that enjoyeth it, yet if the fruition thereof in his person be but a mean to a further end, communicable by many thousands, unto each of whom is of it exposed as plenary a possession as to himself, his share must needs, by that account, in regard of theirs of so great a number, be but very little : herein therefore it is evident, that the Reader in the Author's settlement is as much concerned as himself ; for who desireth any thing, is also desirous of the means whereby it is to be attained unto. Thus, there being no pofsibility of the Author's publication of excellent treatises unlefs he be reseated in the estate of his predecefsors, the Reader, of whatever condition, with whom literature is in any estimation, should concur with, afsist, and help him forwards to the prosecution of those his just demands, if not for any love to the Author, yet [for] his owne sake at least, and that for the knowledge which thereby may redound to himself, which, to value things aright, must needs be of more importance then any interest the

Author can have in the means of his progenitors; for what can the Author and his posterity suffer of damage by the want of his estate comparable to the prejudice sustainable by the many readers and their succefsors through lack of his writings? unlefs one would think that the goods of fortune are more highly to be prized then those of the minde; the contrary whereof hath been very clearly evidenced in many several pafsages of the foregoing Tractate.

Vade Liber, totumque refer mea damna per orbem,
 Hostibus affigens stigmata nigra meis;
Contingatque mihi Siculi fortuna Poetæ,
 Cui fatale metrum non minus ense fuit;
Nec posthac demptum dices mihi creditor ensem,
 Si calamo pofsim te jugulare meo.

PROQUIRITATIONS.

Seeing the scope and chief end of this foregoing Tractate is to perswade the State out of their wisdom to condescend to the just demands of the Author, there can no number like that of *two and thirty*, which by the Rabbies of old was ascribed to *Wisdom*, and by Pythagoras to *Justice*, be pitched upon so apposite for comprehending and terminating the sum of these subsequent *Proquiritations,* according to the tenour of this algebraical hexastick :

> Of Postulatas a sursolid, whose
> Content doth twice that square of squares inclose,
> Which is the double of the cube of two,
> Is here display'd for th' Author's sake, to shew
> > How that square dealing will him best become,
> > Whereby he gets his own *in solidum.*

1. Seeing, from the creation of the world it hath pleased the Author to deduce his extraction, without baulking since the days of Adam so much as one of his progenitors on the paternal side—that the said Author may be put in a consistence of protracting his posterity through as many hereditary successors in a lineal descent, according to the contents of the preceding Tractate, is the desire of   K. F.

2. Seeing the grant of what is demanded in this Treatise can no way introduce a preparative of any dangerous consequence, as hath been evidently shewn in the above written introduction—that it may be thought expedient, without any suspicion of being troubled upon the like grounds by any other of this Island, to condescend to his desires therein, is the hearty wish of   P. O.

3. Seeing the covenanters, who are at this time accounted the State's adversaries, kept, some three yeers ago, a garison in the Author's house for the space of a twelve-month ; and that, for these many yeers past, by several exactions, tolerated plunder-ings, and other such like unmerciful dealings, without any just occasion given, his rents have been made almost totally unserviceable—that he may now, for his greater peace in the future, be exonered of the English garison which is in his house, and, after its removal, have himself fully setled in his own, with all maner of ease and tranquility, is the humble desire of   N. Wa.

4. That to the overthrow of equity in the person of the Author, the rigour of a wrested law be not permitted to become the executioner of the spleen and covetous-ness of his implacable adversaries, is the earnest desire of   B. H.

5. That the Shire of Cromartie, which ever from the beginning hath been the re-ceptacle of the most harmless inhabitants, be not bestowed on any other then the Author, whose predecessors, for uprightness and integrity of carriage, were not, if equalled, inferiour to the best of any nation, is the longing desire of   Yo. Bn.

6. That the Author being as a clear spark from whence gleameth the greatest part of the pure light that is to be seen of any learned invention in that country of Scot-land, it be not quenched and quite extinguished by the foul and black water of an usurious puddle, drunk up there by too many of the natives almost of all sorts, is the humble request of   Bu. Ts.

7. That they who look meerly to the present time, without any regard of the future, be not permitted to deprive him of his means, who for the good of after-ages employs his spare hours most vertuously, is the true desire of   D. J.

8. That those who, long before the distractions of Scotland, had enslaved them-selves to the abominable vice of oppressing others, be not permitted, now that by their means that country is brought lowe, to meddle with the estate of him who never in-jured any, is the earnest suit of   E. G.

9. Seeing he is born to the profit of few, who thinketh onely on the people of his age ; and to that of fewer, whose thoughts exceed not the reach of his own proper interest—that due consideration may be had of the difference betwixt the Author's competitors of dark and narrow projects, and his own splendid and ample endeavours, comprehensive by appearance of the whole latitude of time, is the strong desire of
                                          X. Ya.

10. That outlandish nations, where the Author's fame dwells advantagiously with an expansed reputation, will most highly extol the restorers of him to his own, for an act of perfect and well-principled generosity, is the confident opinion of   Ai. Bs.

11. Seeing there is none, considering the relations and tyes whereunto the Author by nature and duty was bound, can with any shew of reason be accounted more blame-less then he—that he have his sequestration taken off, his person no longer detained as a prisoner of war, and some competent acknowledgement allowed him for the great

loss he hath sustained by the rigour of the unmerciful, not to say knavish, subsequestrator, is the real desire of V. Fs.

12. Seeing the Author's treatises are conducible to posterity, for the benefit whereof the most splendid states and potentates do usually undergo great hazards and difficulties—that out of respect to succeeding ages, and hope of their due retribution in praises, he may be better rewarded then if he were a present time-server, without consideration of the future, is the humble suit of Ei. Z.

13. That he whose good name is like to be eternized to following ages, after that unto nature he hath paid the due which mortality will require of him, shall not in his life-time have his just demands denied by that authority whose representators upon equity promise to lay the foundation of an immortal fame, is the hope of A. S.

14. That the Author's family being one of the greatest antiquity in Scotland, and by an especial providence until this time preserved from that utter subversion intended by the iniquity of his covetous and dissembled enemies, should obtain, *cæteris paribus*, as large a measure of protection as any other race in the whole Isle of Britain, and himself favoured with the grant of all that in his foregoing Treatise is demanded by him, is the real wish of Gh. En.

15. Seeing the Author hath been still faithful to his trust, never culpable of parolbreaking, but always true in every word and action—that the discretion of the present authority will not suffer him to be exposed to the inhumane dealing of those countrymen of his who for their own ends make no bones of being guilty of greater breaches, is the hearty wish of Wh. Y.

16. That the power now in being will not permit that to be exposed to sale which never hitherto was made vendible in any preceding age, and that the lands and Shire of Cromartie, which by none that ever breathed were either bought or sold, should, by a peculiar grant paramount, be in the heritable possession of the Author, as neerest in line and by descent to the aborigenary owner, is the earnest request of T. Wi.

17. The Author having been very often, with an applause *hinc inde*, conversant both abroad and within the four seas, and sometimes for several months together, without the variety of any other company, with many choice English gentlemen—that by any supreme authority of that nation he should be singled out to suffer as much as the most inveterate disaffecters, out of a national antipathy, of both their rule and countrymen, is not the expectation of Wo. Kn.

18. That the reasons deduced by the Author in the above written Treatise, why he should not be made liable to any other debt then that of his own contracting, may be so relished by [those] in whose power it is to make them effectual, as that thereby he may be forthwith exonered of any other burthen, is the earnest wish of C. W.

19. Seeing the Author's unwillingness to pin his faith implicitly to the sleeve of the ministery, or to the single backless tenets *in Ecclesiasticis* of any church-man whatsoever, did exclude him from military charges in their covenanting armies; and

that therefore, having at no time been under their banner, he by all appearance should be looked upon with the more amicable eye by those who did reduce their unlimited power, is the humble opinion of M. Gs.

20. There being none in Scotland less covetous then he, nor more averse from the excessive love of money—that it may please those, in whom the power of protection is, so to protect him, as that he be not made a prey to the most avaritious men of any, and such as respect silver and gold beyond whatever else is most precious in the world, is the request of L. Ch.

21. That the Author's aversness from acknowledging an ecclesiastical soveraignty above the lawful supreme authority *in civilibus,* be not a motive to deal more rigorously with him then with those time-servers who turn tail to every government, without bearing affection to any, is the suit of V. Ye.

22. There being very few gentlemen in his condition, who to the press so freely adventure their names on subjects of any elaboured strain—that the Author's thus favouring this Island with elucubrations beyond the reach of his competitors, be not met for that his publike service with such a permissive attolerance or connivence from the State, as might hurry upon him most grievous detriments by his own country-men in his private fortunes, is the cordial desire of Q. O.

23. That the exemplary civility of the Author, for being apt to have influence on the mindes of the rudest of his kindred and neighbours, even unto the remotest hills of Scotland, may be of efficacy to perswade such amicable spirits at the helm of publike affairs, as would heartily endeavour the bringing of the two nations into as strict an union and neer conformity in laws, liberties, priviledges, customs, maners, and language, as is possible and expedient, to settle and stablish him in the inheritance of his predecessors, is the opinion of Du. Th.

24. That sublime, natural, and moral philosophy, mathematicks, poesie, and many other kindes of good literature, should not be any longer supprest by the injustice of devouring and insatiable seekers, ignorant of every thing that is not lucrative for the bag, is the cordial request of Au. Ps.

25. Seeing many in all the corners almost of this Island live at ease, who enjoy more of their neighbour's unlawfully-acquired goods, then formerly they had of their own—that the Author, who never yet could, for the importunity of waspish seekers, and terrour of a rigorous law, most often in the mouthes, or at the disposure of partial men, get applied in the most fertile yeer that was, for his own use, the tenth part of his rents, should now by a paramount magnificence, reap the fruits of his own meanes, without the hazard of such terrible soakers, is the vehement desire of
Gu. Du.

26. Seeing the Author's designes have been for these many yeers, the same, in matter of furthering manufactures and commerce, together with all maner of trading and negotiation, with the most industrious of England and other nations—that the

present authority will not, in favour of those that have obstructed the performance of so worthy enterprises, denude him of his just inheritance, is the real hope of

Yi. Pn.

27. As the overthrow of vice should be the establishment of vertue—that the reducing of his opposers into a more narrow sphere of action then that wherein formerly they were wont to bestir themselves, should make the Author to be reseated in the inheritance of his ancestors, by those who hitherto have professed the subdument of irregular spirits, is the confident expectation of

Tm. Ou.

28. That the vexation uncessantly for these ten yeers past, sustained by the author from men of unsatisfiable appetites, in matter of worldly means, may not, as formerly, to the great hinderance of divulging treatises conducible to posterity, be any longer an impediment unto him, is the cordial wish of

R. Yu.

29. As the love of goodness more then money, deserveth a larger influence of grace—so, that the Author's affection to the equitable customs and innate civility of the English nation, being of a more generous temper then that sullen and selfish disposition in many others, which doth no longer relish their conversation then it is found apt to shore up the advantage of some pecuniary interest, may be regarded with an eye of greater favour, is the hearty request of

Gn. We.

30. Seeing there are many gentlemen of considerable estates, who, though actually in charge against the English, as pretended opposers of Presbytery, did either enrich themselves, or by their levies and quarterings in the Kirk's service, received great profits, to the no small damage of the country, do nevertheless, and that justly too, enjoy their means at this time, which good fortune notwithstanding in them I wish no man to envie, with as much tranquillity as before—that the Author, who never yet had any benefit to the prejudice of another, be placed, if not in a better, at least, according to the rules of distributive justice, in an equal condition with any of those, is the real expectation of

Tu. J.

31. That a plenary grant of the Author's demands, after the manner above specified in this noble Tractate of his Introduction, will prove a great encouragement to good spirits, and hinderance to none in the prosecuting of vertuous endeavours, is the stedfast and firm opinion of

Wu. Fn.

32. That this is the unanimous desire, wish, request, suit, opinion, hope, and expectation of all the good persons of either sexe, with whom of any nation, in whatever country, whether at home or abroad, the Author hath been formerly acquainted, is duely testified and affirmed by

Tn. Vs.

THE CYPHRAL DISTICH.

5.3.27.38.32.14.21.8.66.8.70.39.5.9.12.18.2.3.56.
5.1.7.3.2.13.19.3.25.9.3.16.6.
25.15.13.6.11.20.5.1.2.12.1.20.20.49.20.20.35.33.
4.6.8.35.5.38.5.5.18.10.3.11.32.42.

Of carping Zoil and despightful Momus,
Let th' innate baseness be exiled from us,
Who worthily would hear or read this book ;
For if upon this Cyphral Distich look
An honest skilful man, he'll therein finde
His own heart's wishes, and the Author's minde.

———————

PARVA PETO, DEBENS MINUS, ET PLUS SPONDEO ; AT ISTIS
PLURA DABIT GENIO SPERO CAMŒNA MEO.

Englished thus ;

LITTLE I ASK, I OWE LESS ON THE SCORE,
I PROMISE MUCH, YET HOPE TO PERFORM MORE.

FINIS.

418

POSTSCRIPT.

THE supplemental or interstitiary verses in Latine and English, at the end almost of every book inserted and subjoyned to fill up blanks, being composed in the Author's absence, by a friend of his who at the printing of this book had the charge for the time of the Corrector of the presses, the Reader is hereby desired to pass by them, as little or nothing material to the scope of the Treatise: especially the word *creditor*, which hath always very deservedly signified a correlative of great trust and honesty, being taken in some places there, in a harsher sense then was fitting; the Author's intention in this Tractate being onely to lash the insatiable flagitators, who to themselves most injuriously usurp the title of creditors, and not those others, who may justly pass by the name of true creditors indeed; which kinde of good people he doth not onely love and respect, but holds it in a maner an unpardonable sin wilfully to delay or defraud them of their due, as any whose debtor he was can sufficiently bear record.

LONDON, FEBRUARY $\left\{ \begin{array}{l} \text{5. 1652. STILO VETER. QUOAD MENSEM;} \\ \qquad \text{ET NOVO, QUOAD ANNUM.} \\ \text{15. 1653. STILO NOVO. QUOAD MENSEM;} \\ \qquad \text{ET VETER, QUOAD ANNUM.} \end{array} \right.$

THOUGH in this almost extemporary Treatise, composed amidst most of the disturbances that are incident to one totally destitute of encouragements from without for undertaking enterprises of the like nature, and by the Author himself, in scribled sheets and half sheets, before the ink oftentimes was well dry, given out to two several printers, one alone not being fully able to hold his quill a going, there should have occurred manyer escapes of the press then there are pages in the book, considering how the animadversion of the revises was altogether recommended to the compositors at the case, who were, through the odnefs of the hand wherein the copie was written, very frequently apt to mistake the sense of both single words and full members of periods, it needeth not to be thought strange. May the Reader therefore be pleased to excuse all, and with his pen to correct these ensuing *Errata*, as it is hereafter shewn how they should be amended.

———————

[The list of *Errata* is omitted, as they have been corrected in the text, with the exception of the word *credere* in the motto on the title-page, for which read *cedere*.]

TABLE OF CONTENTS.

PRINTED BY H. AND J. PILLANS,
EDINBURGH.

3 5282 00290 7106